CLYMER™

HARLEY-DAVIDSON

SPORTSTER EVOLUTION • 1991-1994

The world's finest publisher of mechanical how-to manuals

INTERTEC® PUBLISHING CORPORATION

P.O. Box 12901, Overland Park, Kansas 66282-2901

FIRST EDITION
First Printing August, 1994

Printed in U.S.A.

ISBN: 0-89287-619-0

Library of Congress: 94-75187

Technical photography by Ron Wright and Randy Stephens.

Technical illustrations by Steve Amos and Robert Caldwell.

COVER: Photographed by Mark Clifford, Mark Clifford Photography, Los Angeles, California. Harley-Davidson Sportster courtesy of Bartels' Harley-Davidson, Marina Del Rey, California.

INTERTEC® PUBLISHING CORP.

President and CEO Raymond E. Maloney

Group Vice President Dan Fink

EDITORIAL

Editorial Director
Randy Stephens

Editors
Mike Hall
Mark Jacobs

Technical Writers
Robert Mills
Ron Wright
Ed Scott
Michael Morlan

Inventory/Production Manager
Terry Distin

Lead Editorial Assistant
Shirley Renicker

Editorial Assistants
Veronica Bollin
Elizabeth Couzens

Technical Illustrators
Steve Amos
Robert Caldwell
Mitzi McCarthy
Diana Kirkland

MARKETING

Director of Marketing
Chris Charlton

Advertising and Promotions Manager
Katherine Hughes

Advertising Assistant
Hilary Lindsey

Art Director
Anita Blattner

SALES AND ADMINISTRATION

Director of Sales
Dutch Sadler

Accounts Manager
Ted Metzger

Sales Coordinator
Lynn Reynolds

Customer Service and Administration Manager
Joan Dickey

The following books and guides are published by Intertec Publishing Corp.

CLYMER™ SHOP MANUALS
- Boat Motors and Drives
- Motorcycles and ATVs
- Snowmobiles
- Personal Watercraft

ABOS®/INTERTEC BLUE BOOKS® AND TRADE-IN GUIDES
- Recreational Vehicles
- Outdoor Power Equipment
- Agricultural Tractors
- Lawn and Garden Tractors
- Motorcycles and ATVs
- Snowmobiles
- Boats and Motors
- Personal Watercraft

AIRCRAFT BLUEBOOK-PRICE DIGEST®
- Airplanes
- Helicopters

I&T SHOP SERVICE™ MANUALS
- Tractors

INTERTEC SERVICE MANUALS
- Snowmobiles
- Outdoor Power Equipment
- Personal Watercraft
- Gasoline and Diesel Engines
- Recreational Vehicles
- Boat Motors and Drives
- Motorcycles
- Lawn and Garden Tractor

CONTENTS

QUICK REFERENCE DATA

TIRE PRESSURE

	psi	kg/cm²
Up to 300 lb. load*		
Front	30	2.1
Rear	36	2.5
Up to GVWR maximum load**		
Front	30	2.1
Rear	40	2.8

* 300 lb. load includes rider, passenger and cargo.
** The gross vehicle weight rating (GVWR) is listed on a decal mounted on the frame.

ENGINE OIL

Type	HD rating	Viscosity	Lowest ambient operating temperature
HD Multigrade	HD 240	SAE 10W/40	Below 40° F
HD Multigrade	HD 240	SAE 20W/50	Above 40° F
HD Regular Heavy*	HD 240	SAE 50	Above 60° F
HD Extra Heavy*	HD 240	SAE 60	Above 80° F

* Not recommended for use when ambient temperature is below 50° F.

ENGINE AND PRIMARY DRIVE/TRANSMISSION OIL CAPACITIES

Oil tank*	3 U.S. qts. (2.8 L, 2.5 imp. qts.)
Primary drive/transmission	
1991-1992	40 U.S. oz. (1,183 ml, 41.7 imp. oz.)
1993-1994	32 U.S. oz. (946 ml, 33.3 imp. oz.)

* With filter.

RECOMMENDED LUBRICANTS AND FLUIDS

Brake fluid	DOT 5 silicone-based
Front fork oil	HD Type E or equivalent
Battery top up	Distilled water
Transmission	HD Sport Trans Fluid or equivalent
Fuel	87 pump octane or higher leaded or unleaded

TIGHTENING TORQUES

	ft.-lb.	N•m
Air filter		
Backplate-to-carburetor screws	3-5	4.1-6.8
Backplate-to-cylinder head bolts		
1991-1992	35	47.5
1993-on	10-20	13.6-27.1
Cover screws	3-5	4.1-6.8
Primary cover drain plug	14-21	19-28
Primary chain adjuster locknut	20-25	27-34
Rear axle nut	60-65	81-88
Left-hand footpeg locknut	16-28	22-38
Spark plugs	11-18	15-24
Oil pressure switch	5-7	6.8-9.5

FRONT FORK OIL CAPACITY

	Wet		Dry	
	U.S. oz.	ml	U.S. oz.	ml
1991	9.0	266	10.2	302
1992-on				
83 Hugger	10.7	316	12.1	358
All other models	9.0	266	10.2	302

TUNE-UP SPECIFICATIONS

Engine compression	120 psi (8.3 kg/cm^2)
Spark plugs	
Type	HD No. 6R12
Gap	0.038-0.043 in. (0.97-1.09 mm)

IGNITION TIMING SPECIFICATIONS

Idle speed	V.O.E.S Connected	V.O.E.S. Disconnected
Fast: 1,750*	40° BTDC	Approximately 16° BTDC
Normal: 950-1,050	30° BTDC	Approximately 7.5° BTDC

* Set ignition timing @ 1,650-1,950 rpm with V.O.E.S. connected.

CARBURETOR IDLE SPEED SPECIFICATIONS

Slow idle speed setting	950-1,050 rpm
Idle speed when setting ignition timing	1,650-1,950 rpm

ELECTRICAL SPECIFICATIONS

Battery capacity	12 volt, 19 amp hr.
Ignition coil	
Primary resistance	2.5-3.1 ohms
Secondary resistance	
1991-1992	11,250-13,750 ohms
1993-on	10,000-12,500 ohms
Alternator	
Stator coil resistance	0.2-0.4 ohms
AC voltage output	19-26 VAC per 1,000 rpm
Voltage regulator	
AC voltage output	13.8-15 volts @ 75° F
Amperes @ 3,600 rpm	22 amps

BRAKE SPECIFICATIONS

Disc pad thickness (minimum)	0.062 in. (1.57 mm)
Brake disc	
Diameter	
Front and rear	11.5 in. (292.1 mm)
Thickness (minimum)	
Front	0.180 in. (4.57 mm)
Rear	0.205 in. (5.21 mm)

CHAPTER ONE

GENERAL INFORMATION

This Clymer shop manual covers all Harley-Davidson Sportster models from 1991-1994.

Troubleshooting, tune-up, maintenance and repair are not difficult, if you know what tools and equipment to use and what to do. Step-by-step instructions guide you through jobs ranging from simple maintenance to complete engine and suspension overhaul.

This manual can be used by anyone from a first time do-it-yourselfer to a professional mechanic. Detailed drawings and clear photographs give you all the information you need to do the work right.

Some of the procedures in this manual require the use of special tools. The resourceful mechanic can, in many cases, think of acceptable substitutes for special tools—there is always another way. This can be as simple as using a few pieces of threaded rod, washers and nuts to remove or install a bearing or fabricating a tool from scrap material. However, using a substitute for a special tool is not recommended as it can be dangerous to you and may damage the part. If you find that a tool can be designed and safely made, but will require some type of machine work, you may want to search out a local community college or high school that has a machine shop curriculum. Shop teachers sometimes welcome outside work that can be used as practical shop applications for advanced students.

Table 1 lists model coverage.

Table 2 lists general specifications.

Table 3 lists dry and curb weight specifications.

Table 4 lists gross vehicle weight ratings.

Table 5 lists fuel tank capacity.

Table 6 lists U.S. to metric conversion. Metric and U.S. standards are used throughout this manual.

Table 7 lists general torque specifications. Critical torque specifications are found in table form at the end of each chapter (as required). The general torque specifications in **Table 7** should be used when a critical torque specification is not listed in the appropriate end of chapter table.

Table 8 lists conversion tables.

Table 9 lists American tap drill sizes.

Table 10 lists a wind chill chart that can be used to better prepare yourself when riding your Harley in cold weather.

Tables 1-10 are at the end of the chapter.

MANUAL ORGANIZATION

This chapter provides general information useful to Harley vehicle owners and mechanics. In addition, information in this chapter discusses the tools and techniques for preventive maintenance, troubleshooting and repair.

Chapter Two provides methods and suggestions for quick and accurate diagnosis and repair of problems. Troubleshooting procedures discuss typical symptoms and logical methods to pinpoint the trouble.

Chapter Three explains all periodic lubrication and routine maintenance necessary to keep your Harley operating well. Chapter Three also includes recommended tune-up procedures, eliminating the need to consult other chapters constantly on the various assemblies.

Subsequent chapters describe specific systems, providing disassembly, repair, assembly and adjustment procedures in simple step-by-step form. If a repair is impractical for a home mechanic, it is so indicated. It is usually faster and less expensive to take such repairs to a dealer or competent repair shop. Specifications concerning a specific system are included at the end of the appropriate chapter.

NOTES, CAUTIONS AND WARNINGS

The terms NOTE, CAUTION and WARNING have specific meanings in this manual. A NOTE provides additional information to make a step or procedure easier or clearer. Disregarding a NOTE could cause inconvenience, but would not cause damage or personal injury.

A CAUTION emphasizes areas where equipment damage could occur. Disregarding a CAUTION could cause permanent mechanical damage; however, personal injury is unlikely.

A WARNING emphasizes areas where personal injury or even death could result from negligence. Mechanical damage may also occur. WARNINGS *are to be taken seriously*. In some cases, serious injury and death have resulted from disregarding similar warnings.

SAFETY FIRST

Professional mechanics can work for years and never sustain a serious injury. If you observe a few rules of common sense and safety, you can enjoy many safe hours servicing your own machine. If you ignore these rules you can hurt yourself or damage the equipment.

1. Never use gasoline as a cleaning solvent.

WARNING

Gasoline should only be stored in an approved safety gasoline storage container, properly labeled. Spilled gasoline should be wiped up immediately.

2. Never smoke or use a torch in the vicinity of flammable liquids, such as cleaning solvent, in open containers.
3. If welding or brazing is required on the machine, remove the fuel tanks to a safe distance, at least 50 feet away.
4. Use the proper sized wrenches to avoid damage to fasteners and injury to yourself.
5. When loosening a tight or stuck nut, be guided by what would happen if the wrench should slip. Be careful; protect yourself accordingly.
6. When replacing a fastener, make sure to use one with the same measurements and strength as the old one. Incorrect or mismatched fasteners can result in damage to your Harley and possible personal injury. Beware of fastener kits that are filled with cheap and poorly made nuts, bolts, washers and cotter pins. Refer to *Fasteners* in this chapter for additional information.
7. Keep all hand and power tools in good condition. Wipe greasy and oily tools after using them. They are difficult to hold and can cause injury. Replace or repair worn or damaged tools.
8. Keep your work area clean and uncluttered.
9. Wear safety goggles during all operations involving drilling, grinding, the use of a cold chisel or *any* time you feel unsure about the safety of your eyes. Safety goggles (**Figure 1**) should also be worn when solvent and compressed air are used to clean parts.

WARNING

The improper use of compressed air is very dangerous. Using compressed air to dust off your clothes, bike or workbench can cause flying particles to be blown into your eyes or skin. ***Never*** *direct or blow compressed air into your skin or through any body opening (including cuts) as this can cause severe injury or death. Compressed air should be used carefully; never allow children to use or play with compressed air.*

10. Keep an approved fire extinguisher nearby (**Figure 2**). Be sure it is rated for gasoline (Class B) and electrical (Class C) fires.

11. When drying bearings or other rotating parts with compressed air, never allow the air jet to rotate the bearing or part. The air jet is capable of rotating them at speeds far in excess of those for which they were designed. The bearing or rotating part is very likely to disintegrate and cause serious injury and damage. To prevent bearing damage when using compressed air, hold the inner bearing race (**Figure 3**) by hand.

12. Never work on the upper part of the bike while someone is working underneath it.

13. Never carry sharp tools in your pockets.

14. There is always a right way and wrong way to use tools. Learn to use them the right way.

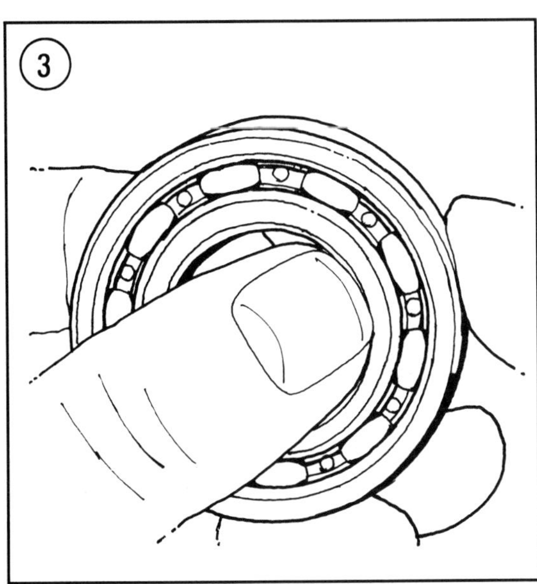

SERVICE HINTS

Most of the service procedures covered are straightforward and can be performed by anyone reasonably handy with tools. It is suggested, however, that you consider your own capabilities carefully before attempting any operation involving major disassembly.

1. "Front," as used in this manual, refers to the front of the motorcycle; the front of any component is the end closest to the front of the motorcycle. The "left-" and "right-hand" side refer to the position of the parts as viewed by a rider sitting on the seat and facing forward. For example, the throttle control is on the right-hand side. These rules are simple, but confusion can cause a major inconvenience during service.

2. Whenever servicing the engine or transmission, or when removing a suspension component, the bike should be secured in a safe manner. If the bike is to be parked on its jiffy stand, check the stand to make sure it is secure and not damaged. Block the front and rear wheels if they remain on the ground. A small hydraulic jack and a block of wood can be used to raise the chassis or you can use a commercial bike stand. If the transmission is not going to be worked on and the drive chain or drive belt is connected to the rear wheel, shift the transmission into first gear.

3. Repairs go much faster and easier if the bike is clean before you begin work. There are special cleaners for washing the engine and related parts. Spray or brush on the cleaning solution, following the manufacturer's directions. Rinse parts with a garden hose. Clean all oily or greasy parts with cleaning solvent as you remove them.

WARNING
***Never** use gasoline as a cleaning agent. It presents an extreme fire hazard. Be sure to work in a well-ventilated area when using cleaning solvent. Keep a fire extinguisher, rated for gasoline fires, handy in any case.*

CAUTION
Never allow cleaning solvents to contact an O-ring drive chain. These chemicals will cause the O-rings to swell, damaging the drive chain.

4. Much of the labor charged for by mechanics is to remove and disassemble other parts to reach the defective unit. It is usually possible to perform the preliminary operations yourself and then take the defective unit to the dealer for repair.

5. Once you have decided to tackle the job yourself, read the entire section *completely* while looking at the actual parts before starting the job. Make sure you have identified the proper procedure. Study the illustrations and text until you have a good idea of what is involved in completing the job satisfactorily. If special tools or replacement parts are required, make arrangements to get them before you start. It is frustrating and time-consuming to get partly into a job and then be unable to complete it.

NOTE
Some of the procedures or service specifications listed in this manual may not be applicable if your Harley has been modified or if it has been equipped with non-stock equipment. When modifying or installing non-stock equipment, file all printed instruction or technical information regarding the new equipment in a folder or notebook for future reference. If your Harley was purchased second hand, the previous owner may have installed non-stock parts. If necessary, consult with your dealer or the accessory manufacturer on components that may change tuning or repair procedures.

6. Simple wiring checks can be easily made at home, but knowledge of electronics is almost a necessity for performing tests with complicated test gear.

CAUTION
Improper testing can sometimes damage an electrical component.

7. Disconnect the negative battery cable (**Figure 4**) when working on or near the electrical, clutch or starter systems and before disconnecting any wires. On all models covered in this manual, the negative terminal will be marked with a minus (–) sign and the positive terminal with a plus (+) sign.

WARNING
Never disconnect the positive battery cable unless the negative cable has been disconnected. Disconnecting the positive cable while the negative cable is still connected may cause a spark. This could ignite the hydrogen gas given off by the battery, causing an explosion.

8. During disassembly, keep a few general cautions in mind. Force is rarely needed to get things apart. If parts are a tight fit, such as a bearing in a case, there is usually a tool designed to separate them. Never use a screwdriver to pry parts with machined surfaces such as crankcase halves. You will mar the surfaces and end up with leaks.

9. Make diagrams (or take a Polaroid picture) wherever similar-appearing parts are found. For instance, crankcase bolts are often not the same length. You may think you can remember where everything came from—but mistakes are costly. There is also the possibility that you may be sidetracked and not return to work for days or even weeks—in which time carefully laid out parts may have become disturbed.

10. Tag all similar internal parts for location and mark (A, **Figure 5**) all mating parts for position. Record number and thickness of any shims as they

are removed; measure with a vernier caliper or micrometer. Small parts such as bolts can be identified by placing them in plastic sandwich bags (B, **Figure 5**). Seal and label them with masking tape.

11. Place parts from a specific area of the engine (e.g. cylinder head, cylinder, clutch, primary drive, etc.) into plastic boxes (C, **Figure 5**) to keep them separated.

12. When disassembling transmission shaft assemblies, use an egg flat (the type that restaurants get their eggs in) (D, **Figure 5**) and set the parts from the shaft in one of the depressions in the same order in which they were removed.

13. Wiring should be tagged with masking tape and marked as each wire is removed. Again, do not rely on memory alone, especially if the wiring was changed by a previous owner.

14. Finished surfaces should be protected from physical damage or corrosion. Keep gasoline off painted surfaces.

15. Use penetrating oil on frozen or tight bolts, then strike the bolt head a few times with a hammer and punch (use a screwdriver on screws). Avoid the use of heat where possible, as it can warp, melt or affect the temper of parts. Heat also ruins finishes, especially paint and plastics.

16. No parts removed or installed (other than bushings and bearings) in the procedures given in this manual should require unusual force during disassembly or assembly. If a part is difficult to remove or install, find out why before proceeding.

17. Cover all openings after removing parts or components to prevent dirt, small tools, etc. from falling in.

18. Recommendations are occasionally made to refer service or maintenance to a Harley-Davidson dealer or independent Harley-Davidson repair shop. In these cases, the work will be done more quickly and economically than if you performed the job yourself.

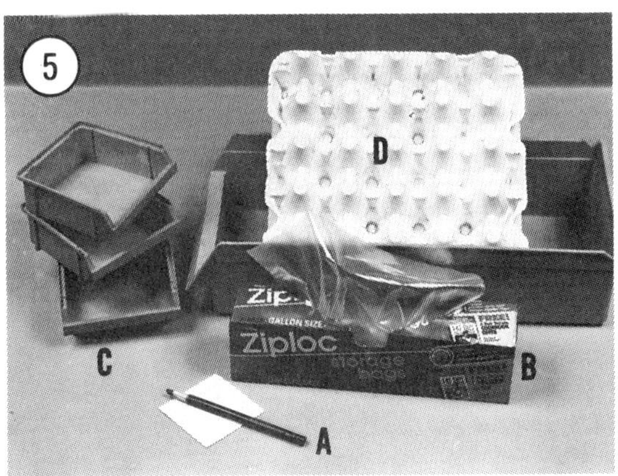

19. In procedural steps, the term "replace" means to discard a defective part and replace it with a new or exchange unit. "Overhaul" means to remove, disassemble, inspect, measure, repair or replace defective parts, reassemble and install major systems or parts.

20. Some operations require the use of a hydraulic press. It would be wiser to have these operations performed by a shop equipped for such work, rather than to try to do the job yourself with makeshift equipment that may damage your machine.

21. When assembling parts, be sure all shims and washers are replaced exactly as they came out.

22. Whenever a rotating part butts against a stationary part, look for a shim or washer.

23. Use new gaskets if there is any doubt about the condition of the old ones.

24. If it becomes necessary to purchase gasket material to make a gasket, measure the thickness of the old gasket (at an uncompressed point) and purchase gasket material with the same approximate thickness.

25. Heavy grease can be used to hold small parts in place if they tend to fall out during assembly. However, keep grease and oil away from electrical and brake components.

26. Never use wire to clean out jets and air passages. They are easily damaged. Use compressed air to blow out the carburetor only if the diaphragm has been removed first.

27. A baby bottle makes a good measuring device. Get one that is graduated in fluid ounces and milliliters. After it has been used for this purpose, do *not* let a child drink out of it as there will always be an oil residue in it.

28. Take your time and do the job right. Do not forget that a newly rebuilt engine must be broken in just like a new one.

SERIAL NUMBERS

Harley-Davidson makes frequent changes during a model year, some minor, some relatively major. All Harley models in this manual can be identified by their individual 17 digit Vehicle Identification Number (VIN); for example, 1HD4CAM13RY200010 as it would appear on the steering head. See **Figure 6**.

This number is stamped into the steering head (**Figure 7**). It is also recorded on a label fixed onto the steering head. The engine is identified with an abbreviated VIN number stamped onto the left-hand crankcase at the base of the rear cylinder block (**Figure 8**); for example, CAMR200010.

NOTE
When Harley-Davidson makes a running change during a production year, the bikes, depending on where they are produced during production, are identified as an early or late model for that year. For example, if a production change was made during the 1991 production run, the bikes, depending on where they were manufactured during the actual run, would be referred to as an Early 1991 or Late 1991 model. If you run across this type of designation in this manual that pertains to your

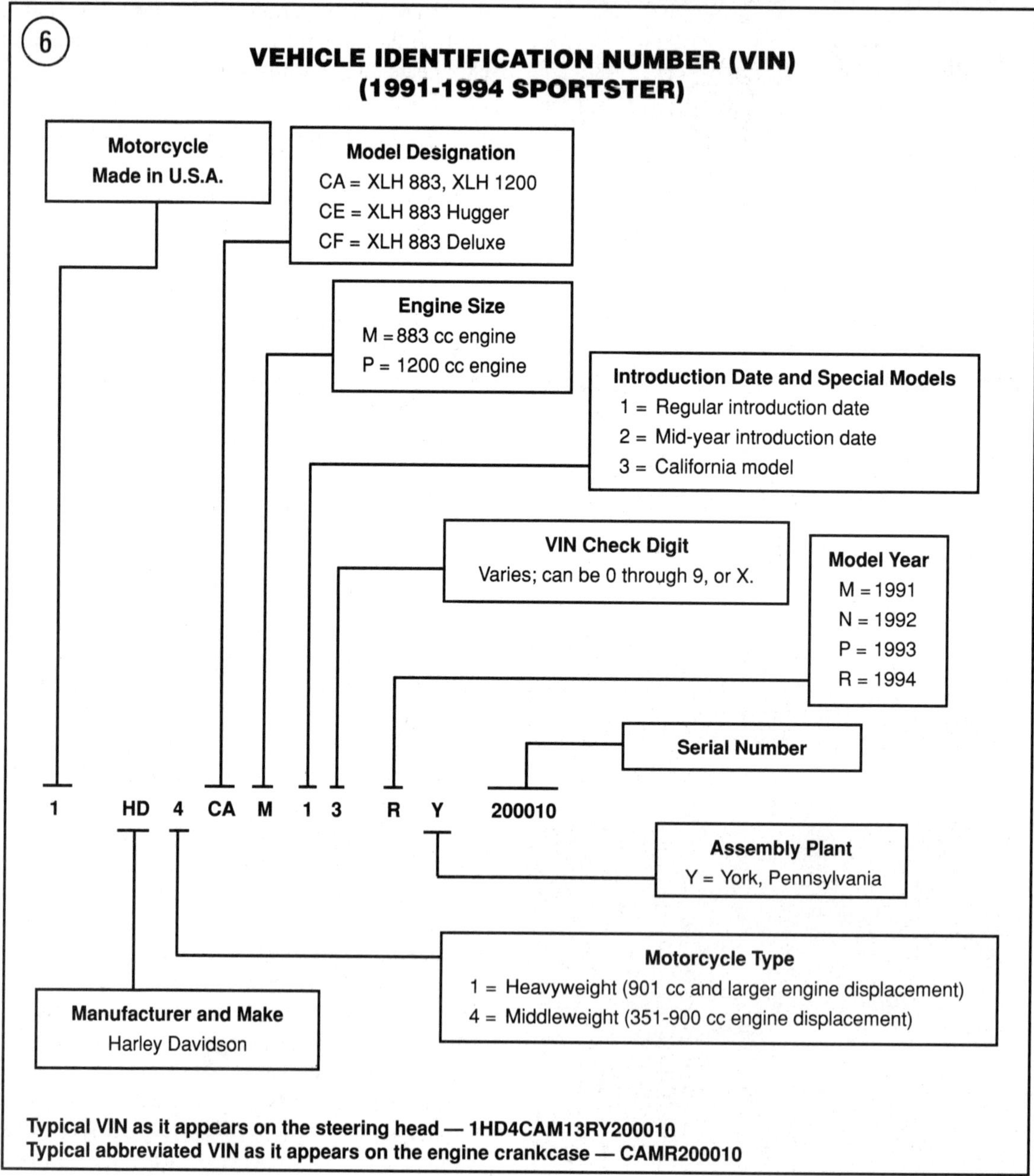

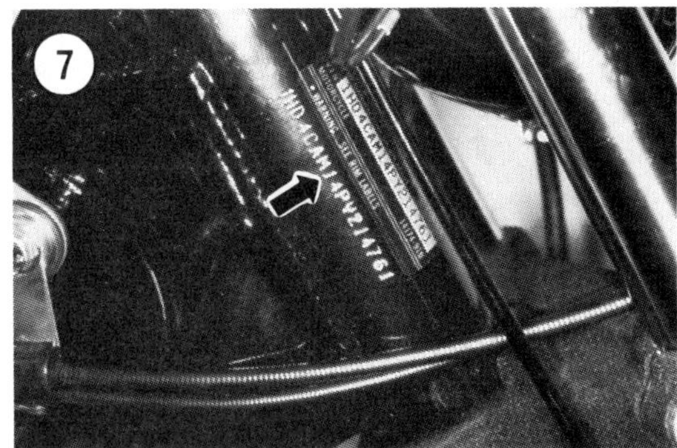

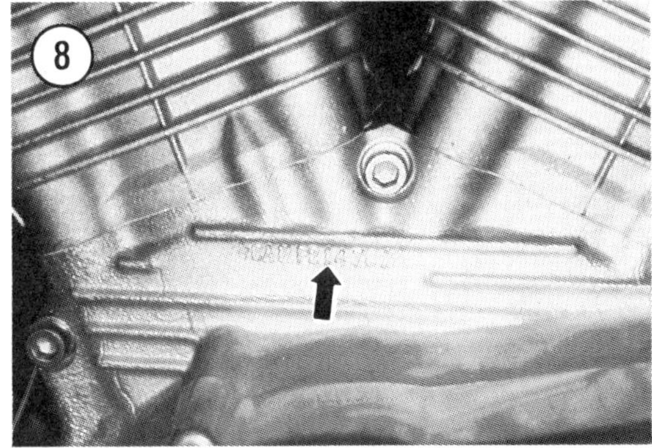

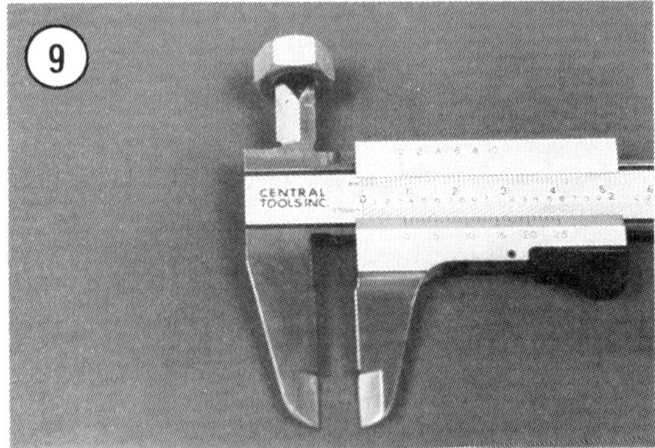

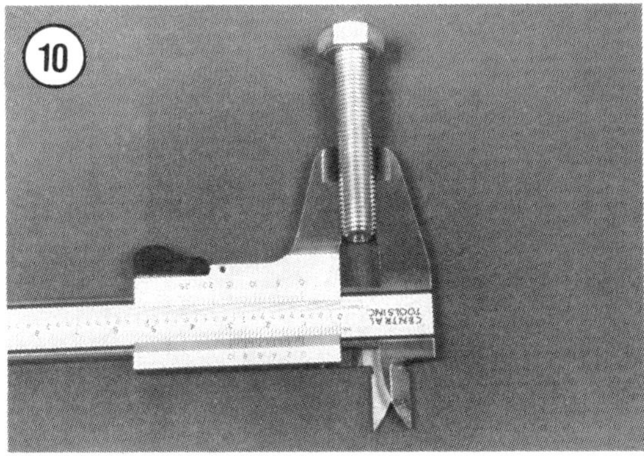

model, use your vehicle's VIN number and the information listed under "Introduction Date and Special Models" in ***Figure 6*** *to identify your model as an early or late model.*

PARTS REPLACEMENT

When you order parts from the dealer or other parts distributor, always order by the full 17 digit VIN number.

Compare new parts to old before purchasing them. If they are not alike, have the parts manager explain the difference to you.

TORQUE SPECIFICATIONS

Torque specifications throughout this manual are given in foot-pounds (ft.-lb.) and newton-meters (N•m).

Table 7 lists general torque specifications for nuts and bolts that are not listed in the respective chapters. To use the table, first determine the size of the bolt or nut. Use a vernier caliper and measure the inside dimensions of the threads of the nut (**Figure 9**) and across the threads for a bolt (**Figure 10**).

FASTENERS

The materials and designs of the various fasteners used on your Harley are not arrived at by chance or accident. Fastener design determines the type of tool required to work the fastener. Fastener material is carefully selected to decrease the possibility of physical failure.

Nuts, bolts and screws are manufactured in a wide range of thread patterns. To join a nut and bolt, the diameter of the bolt and the diameter of the hole in the nut must be the same. It is just as important that the threads on both be properly matched.

The best way to tell if the threads on 2 fasteners are matched is to turn the nut on the bolt (or the bolt into the threaded hole in a piece of equipment) with fingers only. Be sure both pieces are clean. If much force is required, check the thread condition on each fastener. If the thread condition is good but the fasteners jam, the threads are not compatible. A thread pitch gauge (**Figure 11**) can also be used to determine pitch. Harley-Davidson motorcycles are manufactured with American standard fasteners.

The threads are cut differently than those of metric fasteners (**Figure 12**).

Most threads are cut so that the fastener must be turned clockwise to tighten it. These are called right-hand threads. Some fasteners have left-hand threads; they must be turned counterclockwise to be tightened. Left-hand threads are used in locations where normal rotation of the equipment would tend to loosen a right-hand threaded fastener.

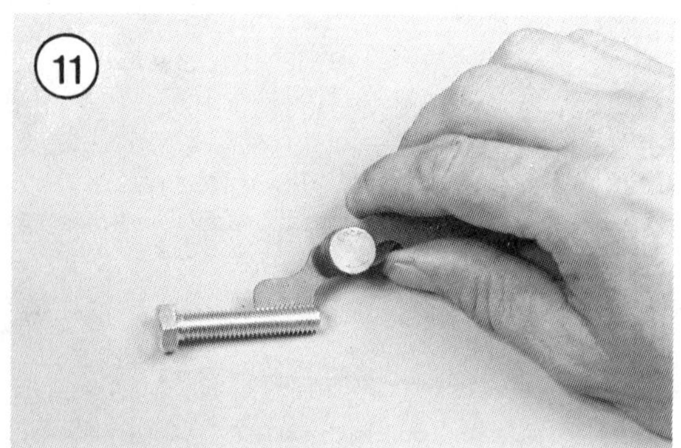

American Threads

American threads come in a coarse or fine thread. Because both coarse and fine threads are used for general use, it is important to match the threads correctly so you do not strip the threads and damage one or both fasteners.

American fasteners are normally described by diameter, threads per inch (TPI) and length; **Figure 13** shows the first 2 specifications. For example, 3/8 × 2 indicates a bolt 3/8 in. in diameter with 16 threads per inch, 2 in. long. The measurement across 2 flats on the head of the bolt or screw (**Figure 14**) indicates the proper wrench size to be used. **Figure 10** shows how to determine bolt diameter.

Markings found on American bolt heads indicate tensile strength. For example, a bolt with no head marking is usually made of mild steel, while a bolt with 2 or more markings indicates a higher grade material. **Figure 15** indicates the various head markings with SAE grade identification. When torquing SAE bolts not listed in a torque specification table, refer to the head marking (**Figure 15**) and then to **Table 7** for the torque specification.

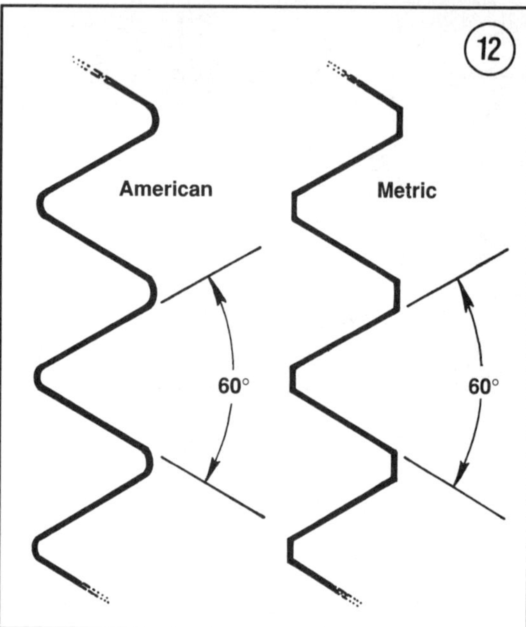

Determining Bolt Length

When purchasing a bolt from a dealer or parts store, it is important to know how to specify bolt length. The correct way to measure bolt length is to measure the length starting from underneath the bolt head to the end of the bolt (**Figure 16**). Always measure bolt length in this manner to avoid purchasing bolts that are too long.

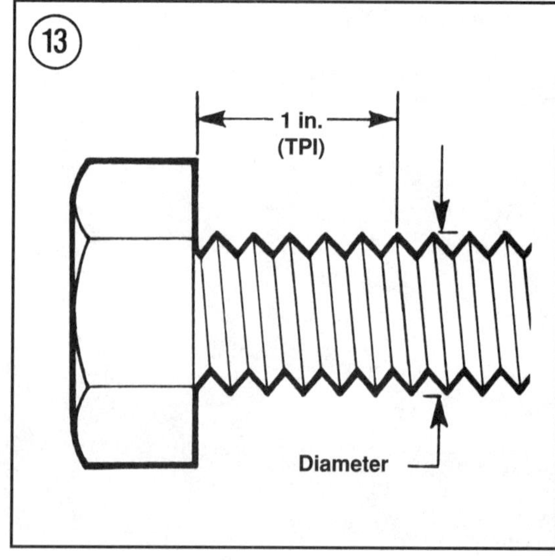

Machine Screws

Machine screw refers to a numbering system used to identify screws smaller than 1/4 in. Machine screws are identified by gage size (diameter) and threads per inch. For example, 12-28 indicates a 12 gage screw with 28 threads per inch.

There are many different types of machine screws. **Figure 17** shows a number of screw heads requiring different types of turning tools. Heads are also designed to protrude above the metal (round) or to be slightly recessed in the metal (flat). See **Figure 18**.

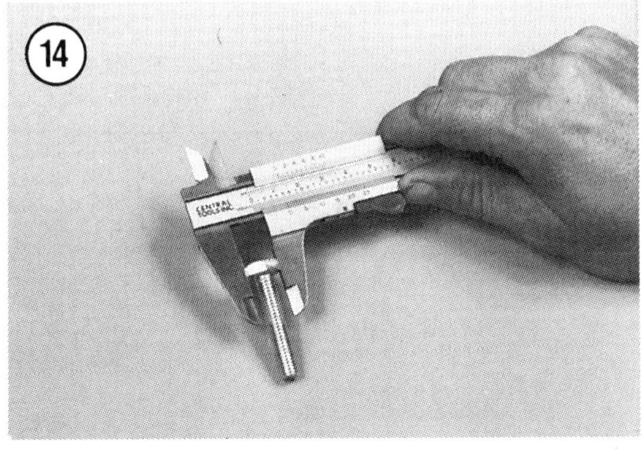

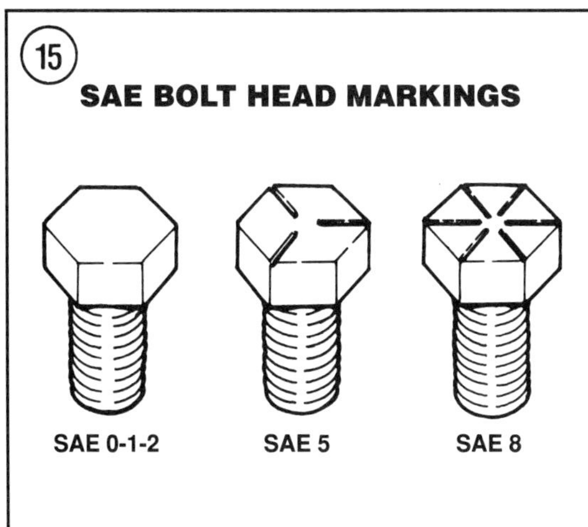

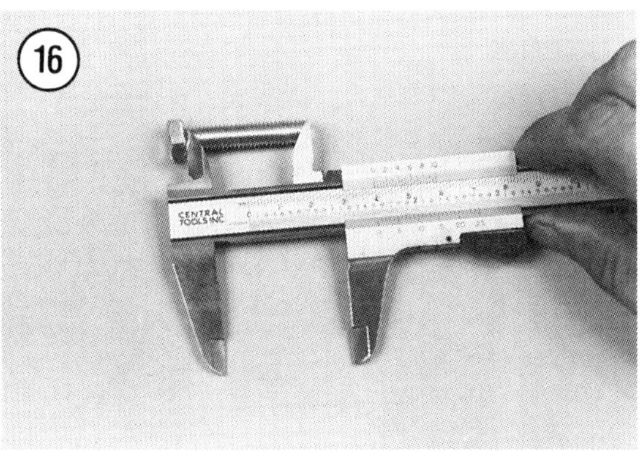

Bolts

Commonly called bolts, the technical name for these fasteners is cap screw. Refer to *American Threads* in this section for additional information.

Nuts

Nuts are manufactured in a variety of types and sizes. Most are hexagonal (6-sided) and fit on bolts, screws and studs with the same diameter and pitch.

Figure 19 shows several types of nuts. The common nut is generally used with a lockwasher. Self-locking nuts have a nylon insert which prevents the nut from loosening; no lockwasher is required. Wing nuts are designed for fast removal by hand. Wing nuts are used for convenience in non-critical locations.

To indicate the size of a nut, manufacturers specify the diameter of the opening and the thread pitch. This is similar to bolt specifications, but without the length dimension. The measurement across 2 flats on the nut (**Figure 20**) indicates the proper wrench size to be used.

Self-locking Fasteners

Several types of bolts, screws and nuts incorporate a system that develops an interference between the bolt, screw, nut or tapped hole threads. Interference is achieved in various ways: by distorting threads, coating threads with dry adhesive or nylon, distorting the top of an all-metal nut, using a nylon insert in the center or at the top of a nut, etc.

Self-locking fasteners offer greater holding strength and better vibration resistance. Some self-locking fasteners can be reused if in good condition. Others, like the nylon insert nut, form an initial locking condition when the nut is first installed; the nylon forms closely to the bolt thread pattern, thus reducing any tendency for the nut to loosen. When the nut is removed, the locking efficiency is greatly reduced. For greatest safety, it is recommended that you install new self-locking fasteners whenever they are removed.

Washers

There are 2 basic types of washers: flat washers and lockwashers. Flat washers are simple discs with a hole to fit a screw or bolt. Lockwashers are designed to prevent a fastener from working loose due to vibration, expansion and contraction. Lockwashers should be installed between the bolt head or nut and a flat washer. **Figure 21** shows several types of washers. Washers are also used in the following functions:

a. As spacers.
b. To prevent galling or damage of the equipment by the fastener.
c. To help distribute fastener load during torquing.
d. As fluid seals (copper or laminated washers).

Note that flat washers are often used between a lockwasher and a fastener to provide a smooth bearing surface. This allows the fastener to be turned easily with a tool.

NOTE
As much care should be given to the selection and purchase of washers as that given to bolts, nuts and other fasteners. Beware of washers that are made of thin and weak materials. These will deform and crush the first time they are used in a high torque application.

Cotter Pins

Cotter pins (**Figure 22**) are used to secure fasteners in a special location. The threaded stud, bolt or axle must have a hole in it. Its nut or nut lock piece has castellations around its upper edge into which the cotter pin fits to keep it from loosening. When *properly* installed, a cotter pin is a positive locking device.

The first step in properly installing a cotter pin is to purchase one that will fit snugly when inserted through the nut and the mating thread part. This should not be a problem when purchasing cotter pins through a Harley-Davidson dealer; you can order them by their respective part numbers. However, when you stop off at your local hardware or automotive store, keep this in mind. The cotter pin should not be so tight that you have to drive it in and out, but you do not want it so loose that it can move or float after it is installed.

Before installing a cotter pin, tighten the nut to the recommended torque specification. If the castellations in the nut do not line up with the hole in the bolt or axle, tighten the nut until alignment is

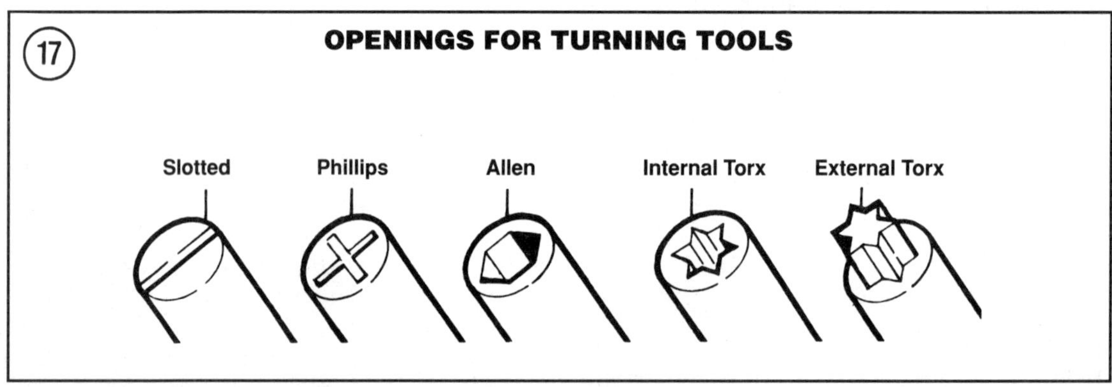

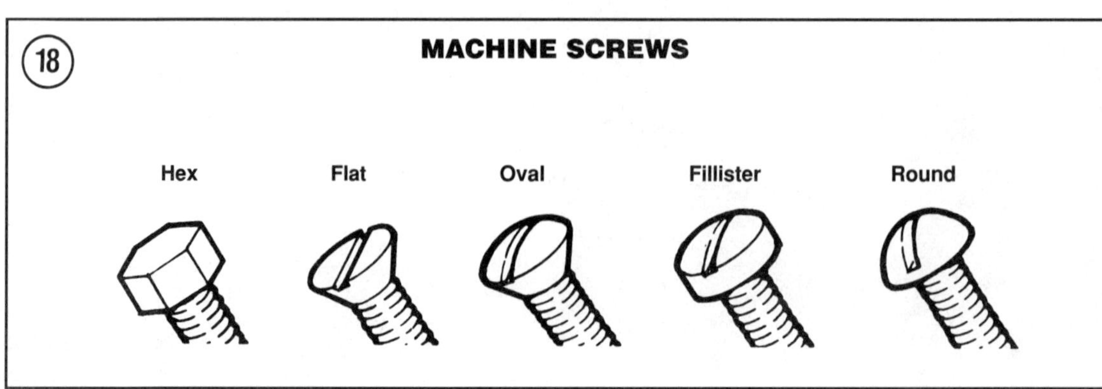

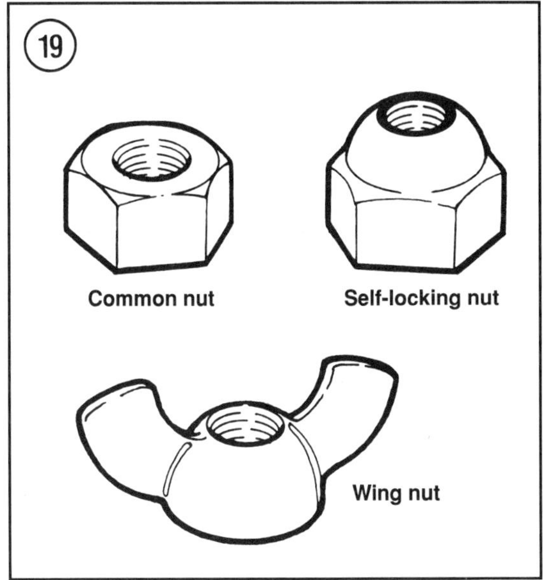

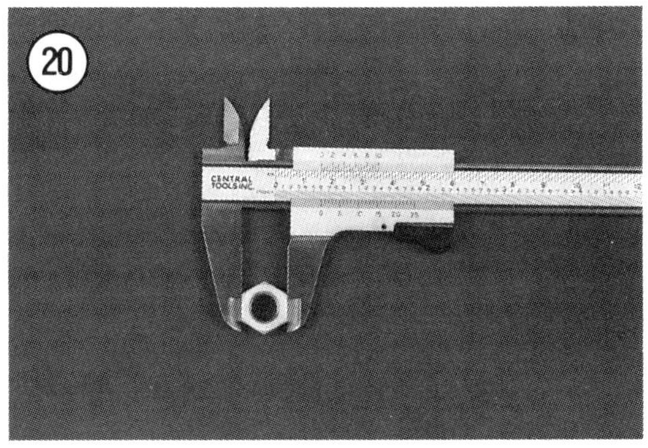

achieved. Do not loosen the nut to make alignment. Insert a *new* cotter pin through the nut and hole, then tap the head lightly to seat it. Bend one arm over the flat on the nut and the other against the top of the axle or bolt (**Figure 22**). Cut the arms to a suitable length to prevent them from snagging on clothing, or worse, your hands, arms or legs; the exposed arms will cut flesh easily. When the cotter pin is bent and its arms cut to length, it should be tight. If you can wiggle the cotter pin, it is improperly installed.

Cotter pins should not be reused as their ends may break and allow the cotter pin to fall out and perhaps the fastener to unscrew itself.

Circlips

Circlips can be of internal or external design. They are used to retain items on shafts (external type) or within tubes (internal type). In some applications, circlips of varying thicknesses are used to control the end play of parts assemblies. These are often called selective circlips. Circlips should be replaced during installation, as removal weakens and deforms them.

Two basic styles of circlips are available: machined and stamped circlips. Machined circlips (**Figure 23**) can be installed in either direction (shaft or housing) because both faces are machined, thus creating two sharp edges. Stamped circlips (**Figure 24**) are manufactured with one sharp edge and one

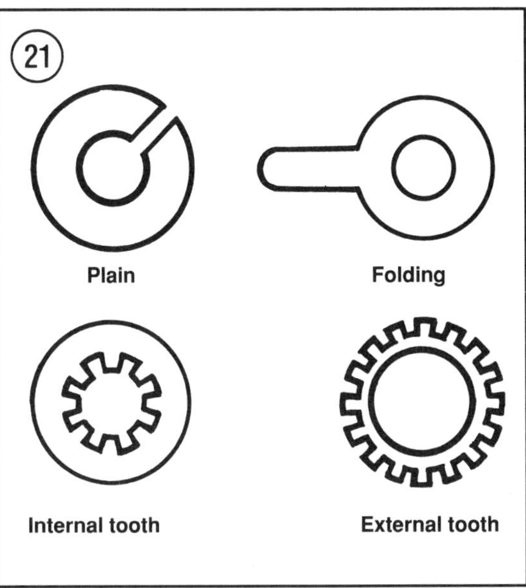

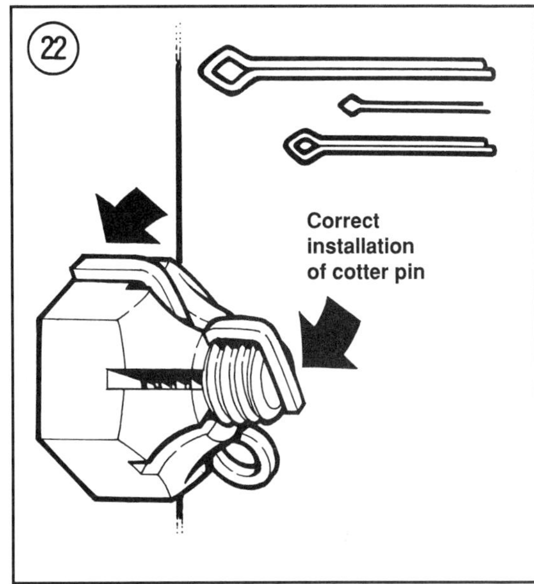

rounded edge. When installing stamped circlips in a thrust situation, the sharp edge must face away from the part producing the thrust. When installing circlips, observe the following:

a. Circlips should be removed and installed with circlip pliers. See *Circlip Pliers* in this chapter.
b. Compress or expand circlips only enough to install them.
c. After the circlip is installed, make sure it is completely seated in its groove.

Transmission circlips become worn with use and increase side play. For this reason, always use new circlips whenever a transmission is to be reassembled.

LUBRICANTS

Periodic lubrication assures long life for any type of equipment. The *type* of lubricant used is just as important as the lubrication service itself, although in an emergency the wrong type of lubricant is better than none at all. The following paragraphs describe the types of lubricants most often used on motorcycle equipment. Be sure to follow the manufacturer's recommendations for lubricant types.

If any unique lubricant is recommended by Harley-Davidson it is specified in the service procedure.

Generally, all liquid lubricants are called "oil." They may be mineral-based (including petroleum bases), natural-based (vegetable and animal bases), synthetic-based or emulsions (mixtures). "Grease" is an oil to which a thickening base has been added so that the end product is semi-solid. Grease is often classified by the type of thickener added; lithium soap is commonly used.

Engine Oil

Four-cycle oil for motorcycle and automotive engines is graded by the American Petroleum Institute (API) and the Society of Automotive Engineers (SAE) in several categories. Oil containers display these ratings on the top or label (**Figure 25**).

API oil grade is indicated by letters; oils for gasoline engines are identified by an "S."

Viscosity is an indication of the oil's thickness. The SAE uses numbers to indicate viscosity; thin oils have low numbers while thick oils have high numbers. A "W" after the number indicates that the viscosity testing was done at low temperature to simulate cold-weather operation. Engine oils fall into the 5W-30 and 20W-50 range.

Multi-grade oils (for example 10W-40) are less viscous (thinner) at low temperatures and more viscous (thicker) at high temperatures. This allows the oil to perform efficiently across a wide range of engine operating conditions. The lower the number, the better the engine will start in cold climates. Higher numbers are usually recommended for engine running in hot weather conditions.

Grease

Greases are graded by the National Lubricating Grease Institute (NLGI). Greases are graded by number according to the consistency of the grease; these range from No. 000 to No. 6, with No. 6 being the most solid. A typical multipurpose grease is NLGI No. 2. For specific applications, equipment manufacturers may require grease with an additive such as molybdenum disulfide (MOS2).

Also recommended for axle and swing arm pivot shafts is an anti-seize lubricant (**Figure 26**). This is

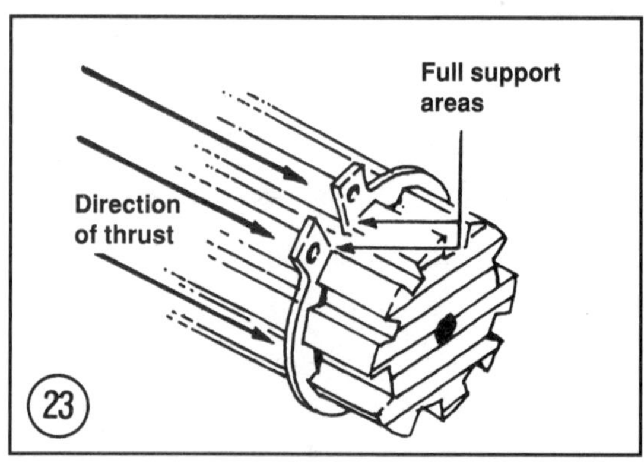

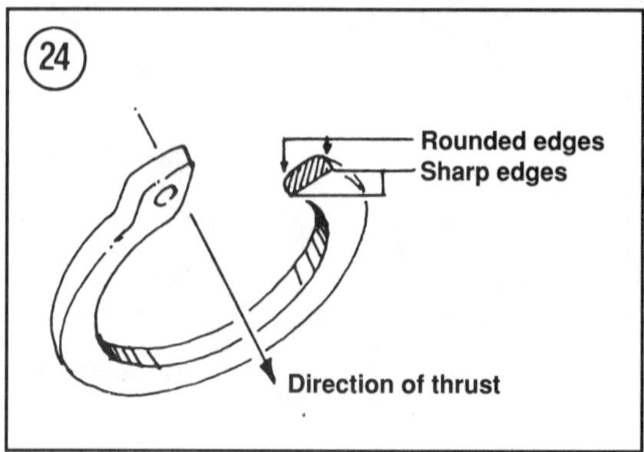

necessary to prevent the pivot points from corroding and locking up.

RTV GASKET SEALANT

Room temperature vulcanizing (RTV) sealant is used on some pre-formed gaskets and to seal some components. RTV is a silicone gel supplied in tubes and can be purchased in a number of different colors.

25

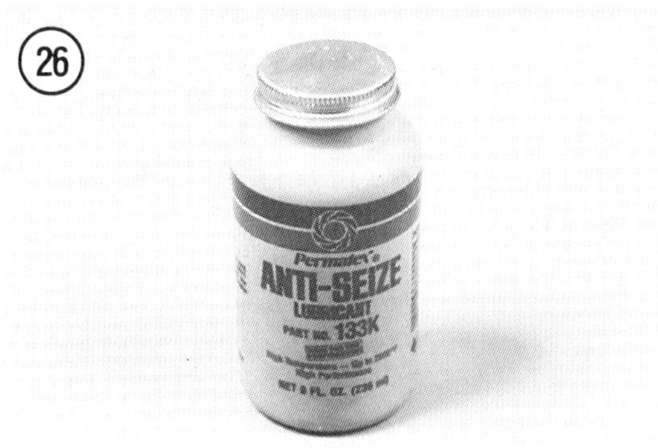

26

27

Moisture in the air causes RTV to cure. Always place the cap on the tube as soon as possible when using RTV. RTV has a shelf life of one year and will not cure properly when the shelf life has expired. Check the expiration date on RTV tubes before using and keep partially used tubes tightly sealed.

Applying RTV Sealant

Clean all gasket residue from mating surfaces. Surfaces should be clean and free of oil and dirt. Remove all RTV gasket material from blind attaching holes, as it can cause a "hydraulic" effect and affect bolt torque.

Apply RTV sealant in a continuous bead. Circle all mounting holes unless otherwise specified. Torque mating parts within 10 minutes after application.

THREADLOCK

A chemical locking compound should be used on all bolts and nuts, even if they are secured with lockwashers. A locking compound will lock fasteners against vibration loosening and seal against leaks. Loctite 242 (blue) and 271 (red) are recommended for many threadlock requirements described in this manual (**Figure 27**).

Loctite 242 (blue) is a medium strength threadlock and component disassembly can be performed with normal hand tools. Loctite 271 (red) is a high strength threadlock and heat or special tools, such as a press or puller, may be required for component disassembly.

Applying Threadlock

Surfaces should be clean and free of oil, grease, dirt and other residue; clean threads with an aerosol electrical contact cleaner before applying the Loctite. When applying Loctite, use a small amount. If too much is used, it can work its way down the threads and stick parts together not meant to be stuck.

GASKET REMOVER

Stubborn gaskets can present a problem during engine service as they can take a long time to remove. Consequently, there is the added problem of secondary damage occurring to the gasket mating surfaces from the incorrect use of gasket scraping tools. To quickly and safely remove stubborn gaskets, use a spray gasket remover. Spray gasket remover can be purchased through automotive parts houses. Follow the manufacturer's directions for use.

EXPENDABLE SUPPLIES

Certain expendable supplies are required during maintenance and repair work. These include grease, oil, gasket cement, wiping rags and cleaning solvent. Ask your dealer for the silicone lubricants, contact cleaner and other products which make maintenance simpler and easier. Cleaning solvent or kerosene is available at some service stations or hardware stores.

BASIC HAND TOOLS

Many of the procedures in this manual can be carried out with simple hand tools and test equipment familiar to the average home mechanic. Keep your tools clean and in a tool box. Keep them organized with the sockets and related drives together, the open-end combination wrenches together, etc. After using a tool, wipe off dirt and grease with a clean cloth and return the tool to its correct place.

Top quality tools are essential; they are also more economical in the long run. If you are now starting to build your tool collection, stay away from the "advertised specials" featured at some parts houses, discount stores and chain drug stores. These are usually a poor grade tool that can be sold cheaply and that is exactly what they are—*cheap*. They are usually made of inferior material, and are thick, heavy and clumsy. Their rough finish makes them difficult to clean and they usually don't last very long. If it is ever your misfortune to use such tools, you will probably find out that the wrenches do not fit the heads of bolts and nuts correctly and damage the fastener.

Quality tools are made of alloy steel and are heat treated for greater strength. They are lighter and better balanced than cheap ones. Their surface is smooth, making them a pleasure to work with and easy to clean. The initial cost of good quality tools may be more but they are cheaper in the long run. Don't try to buy everything in all sizes in the beginning; do it a little at a time until you have the necessary tools.

The following tools are required to perform virtually any repair job. Each tool is described and the recommended size given for starting a tool collection. Additional tools and some duplicates may be added as you become familiar with your Harley. Harley-Davidson motorcycles are built with American standard fasteners. If you are starting your collection now, buy American sizes.

Screwdrivers

The screwdriver is a very basic tool, but if used improperly it will do more damage than good. The slot on a screw has a definite dimension and shape. Through improper use or selection, a screwdriver can damage the screw head, making removal of the screw difficult. A screwdriver must be selected to conform to the shape of the screw head used. Two basic types of screwdrivers are required: standard (flat- or slot-blade) screwdrivers (**Figure 28**) and Phillips screwdrivers (**Figure 29**).

Note the following when selecting and using screwdrivers:

a. The screwdriver must always fit the screw head. If the screwdriver blade is too small for the screw slot, damage may occur to the screw slot and screwdriver. If the blade is too large, it cannot engage the slot properly and will result in damage to the screw head.
b. Standard screwdrivers are identified by the length of their blade. A 6 in. screwdriver has a blade six inches long. The width of the screwdriver blade will vary, so make sure that the blade engages the screw slot the complete width of the screw.

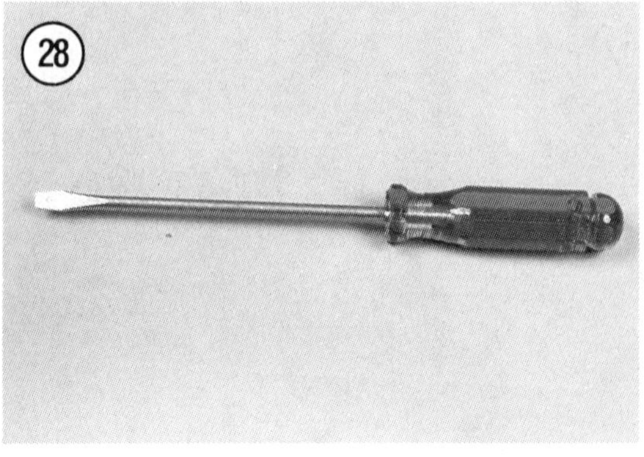

c. Phillips screwdrivers are sized according to their point size. They are numbered one, two, three and four. The degree of taper determines the point size; the No. 1 Phillips screwdriver will be the most pointed. The points become more blunt as their number increases.

NOTE
You should also be aware of another screwdriver similar to the Phillips, and that is the Reed and Prince tip. Like the Phillips, the Reed and Prince screwdriver tip forms an "X" but with one major exception, the Reed and Prince tip has a much more pointed tip. The Reed and Prince screwdriver should never be used on Phillips screws and vice versa. Intermixing these screwdrivers will cause damage to the screw and screwdriver. If you have both types in your tool box and they are similar in appearance, you may want to identify them by painting the screwdriver shank underneath the handle.

d. When selecting screwdrivers, note that you can apply more power with less effort with a longer screwdriver than with a short one. Of course, there will be situations where only a short handle screwdriver can be used. Keep this in mind though, when having to remove tight screws.
e. Because the working end of a screwdriver receives quite a bit of abuse, you should purchase screwdrivers with hardened tips. The extra money will be well spent.

Screwdrivers are available in sets which often include an assortment of common and Phillips blades. If you buy them individually, buy at least the following:

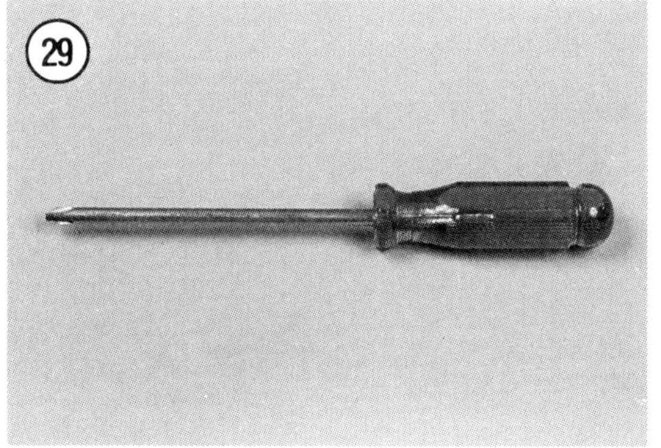

a. Common screwdriver—5/16 × 6 in. blade.
b. Common screwdriver—3/8 × 12 in. blade.
c. Phillips screwdriver—size 2 tip, 6 in. blade.
d. Phillips screwdriver—size 3 tip, 6 and 8 in. blade.

Use screwdrivers only for driving screws. Never use a screwdriver for prying or chiseling metal. Do not try to remove a Phillips, Torx or Allen head screw with a standard screwdriver (unless the screw has a combination head that will accept either type); you can damage the head so that the proper tool will be unable to remove it.

Keep screwdrivers in the proper condition and they will last longer and perform better. Always keep the tip of a standard screwdriver in good condition. **Figure 30** shows how to grind the tip to the proper shape if it becomes damaged. Note the symmetrical sides of the tip.

Pliers

Pliers come in a wide range of types and sizes. Pliers are useful for cutting, bending and crimping. They should never be used to cut hardened objects or to turn bolts or nuts. **Figure 31** shows several pliers useful in repairing your Harley.

Each type of pliers has a specialized function. Slip-joint pliers are general purpose pliers and are used mainly for holding things and for bending. Needlenose pliers are used to hold or bend small objects. Water pump pliers can be adjusted to hold various sizes of objects; the jaws remain parallel to grip around objects such as pipe or tubing. There are many more types of pliers.

CAUTION
Pliers should not be used for loosening or tightening nuts or bolts. The pliers' sharp teeth will grind off the nut or bolt corners and damage it.

CAUTION
If slip-joint or water pump pliers are going to be used to hold an object with a finished surface, wrap the object with tape or cardboard for protection.

Vise-Grip Pliers

Vise-grip pliers (**Figure 32**) are used to hold objects very tightly while another task is performed on the object. While vise-grip pliers work well, caution should be followed with their use. Because vise-grip pliers exert more force than regular pliers, their sharp jaws can permanently scar the object. In addition, when vise-grip pliers are locked into position, they can crush or deform thin wall material.

Vise-grip pliers are available in many types for more specific tasks.

Circlip Pliers

Circlip pliers (**Figure 33**) are special in that they are only used to remove or install circlips. When purchasing circlip pliers, there are two kinds to distinguish from. External pliers (spreading) are used to remove circlips that fit on the outside of a shaft. Internal pliers (squeezing) are used to remove circlips which fit inside a housing.

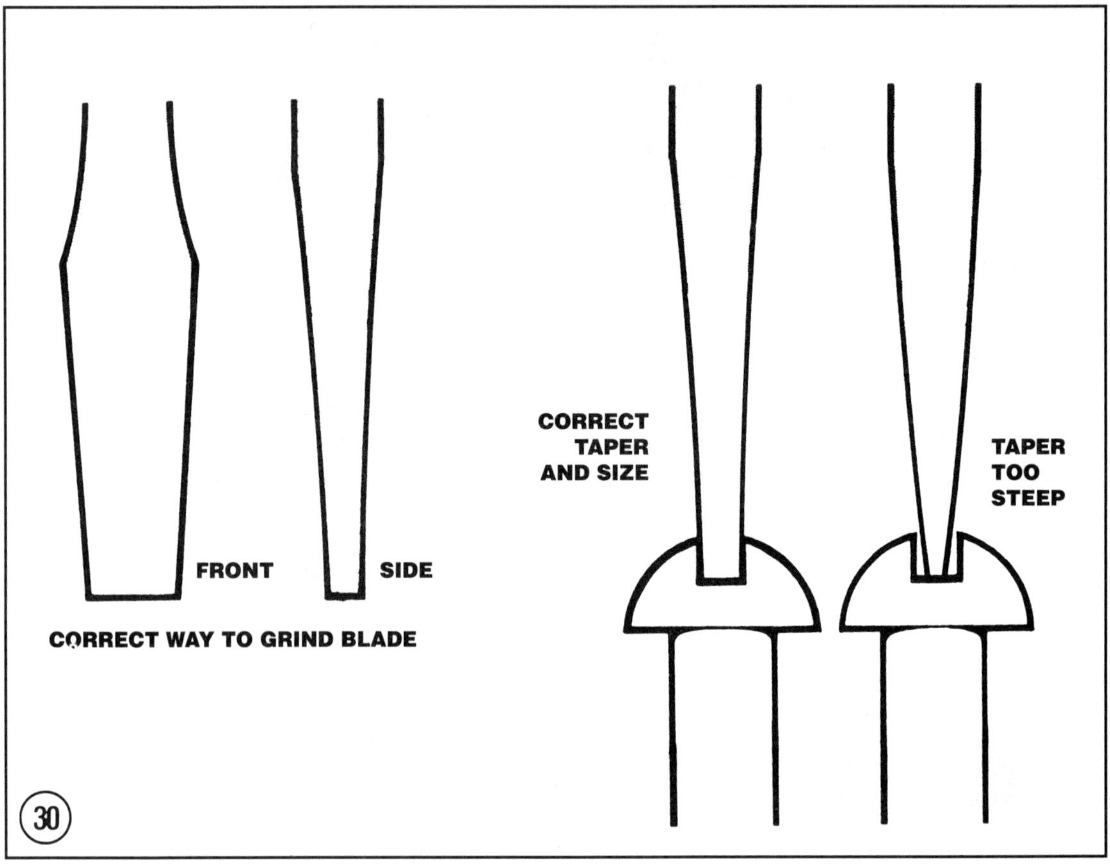

FRONT

SIDE

CORRECT WAY TO GRIND BLADE

CORRECT TAPER AND SIZE

TAPER TOO STEEP

30

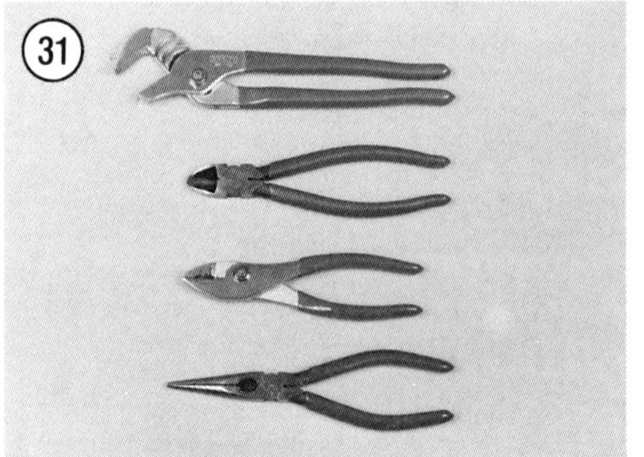

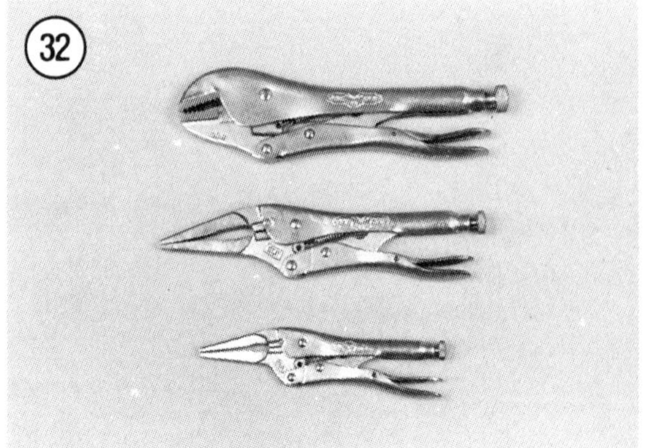

WARNING
Because circlips can sometimes slip and "fly off" during removal and installation, always wear safety glasses when servicing them.

Box-end, Open-end and Combination Wrenches

Box-end and open-end wrenches are available in sets or separately in a variety of sizes. The size number stamped near the end refers to the distance between 2 parallel flats on the hex head bolt or nut.

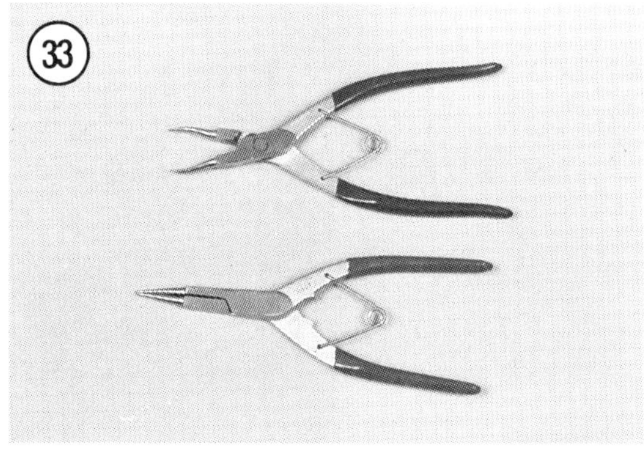
33

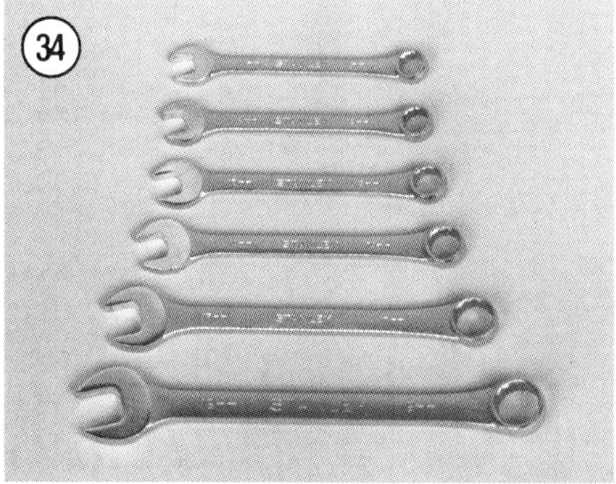
34

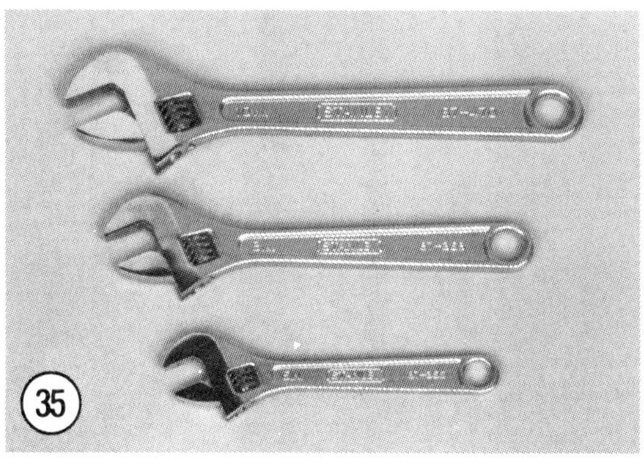
35

Box-end wrenches are usually superior to open-end wrenches. Open-end wrenches grip the nut on only 2 flats. Unless a wrench fits well, it may slip and round off the points on the nut. The box-end wrench grips on all 6 flats. Both 6-point and 12-point openings on box-end wrenches are available. The 6-point gives superior holding power; the 12-point allows a shorter swing.

Combination wrenches (**Figure 34**) which are open-end on one side and box-end on the other are also available. Both ends are the same size.

No matter what style of wrench you choose, proper use is important to prevent personal injury. When using a wrench, get into the habit of pulling the wrench toward you. This technique will reduce the risk of injuring your hand if the wrench should slip. If you have to push the wrench away from you to loosen or tighten a fastener, open and push with the palm of your hand; your fingers and knuckles will be out of the way if the wrench slips. Before using a wrench, always think ahead as to what could happen if the wrench should slip or if the fastener strips or breaks.

Adjustable Wrenches

An adjustable wrench can be adjusted to fit nearly any nut or bolt head which has clear access around its entire perimeter. Adjustable wrenches are best used as a backup wrench to keep a large nut or bolt from turning while the other end is being loosened or tightened with a proper wrench. See **Figure 35**.

Adjustable wrenches have only two gripping surfaces which makes them more subject to slipping off the fastener and damaging the part and possibly your hand. See *Box-end, Open-end and Combination Wrenches* in this chapter.

These wrenches are directional; the solid jaw must be the one transmitting the force. If you use the adjustable jaw to transmit the force, it will loosen and possibly slip off.

Adjustable wrenches come in all sizes but something in the 6 to 8 in. range is recommended as an all-purpose wrench.

Socket Wrenches

This type is undoubtedly the fastest, safest and most convenient to use. Sockets which attach to a ratchet handle (**Figure 36**) are available with 6-point or 12-point openings and 1/4, 3/8, 1/2 and 3/4 in. drives. The drive size indicates the size of the square hole which mates with the ratchet handle.

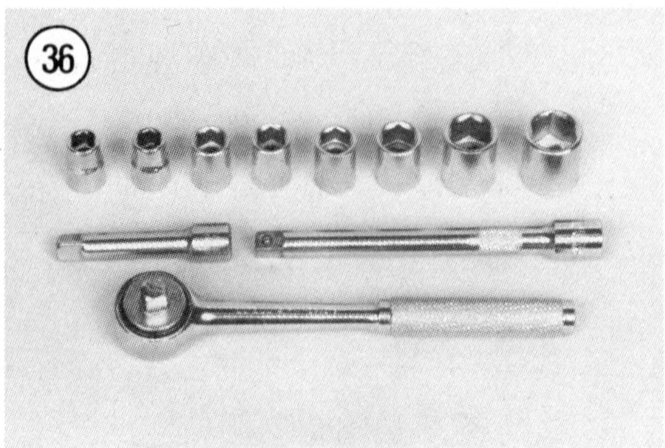
36

Torque Wrench

A torque wrench (**Figure 37**) is used with a socket to measure how tightly a nut or bolt is installed. They come in a wide price range and with either 3/8 or 1/2 in. square drive. The drive size indicates the size of the square drive which mates with the socket.

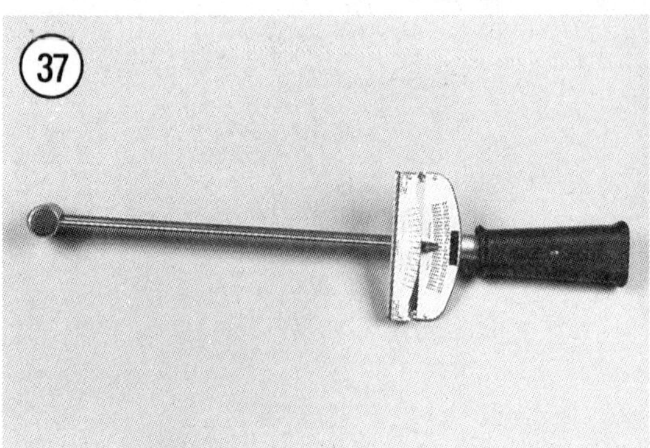
37

Impact Driver

This tool makes removal of tight fasteners easy and eliminates damage to bolts and screw slots. Impact drivers and interchangeable bits (**Figure 38**) are available at most large hardware and motorcycle dealers. Don't purchase a cheap one as it won't work as well and will require more force than a moderately priced one. Sockets can also be used with a hand impact driver. However, make sure the socket is designed for use with an impact driver or air tool. Do not use regular hand type sockets, as they may shatter during use.

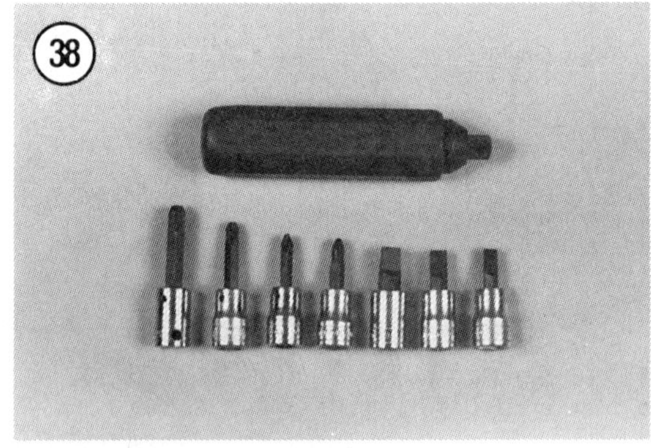
38

Hammers

The correct hammer (**Figure 39**) is necessary for repairs. Use only a hammer with a face (or head) of rubber or plastic or the soft-faced type that is filled with buckshot. These are sometimes necessary in engine teardowns. *Never* use a metal-faced hammer on engine or suspension parts, as severe damage will result in most cases. Ball-peen or machinist's hammers will be required when striking another tool, such as a punch or impact driver. When striking a hammer against a punch, cold chisel or similar tool, the face of the hammer should be at least 1/2 in. larger than the head of the tool. When it is necessary to strike hard against a steel part without damaging it, a brass hammer should be used. A brass hammer can be used because brass will give when striking a harder object. Brass hammers are used when truing crankshafts.

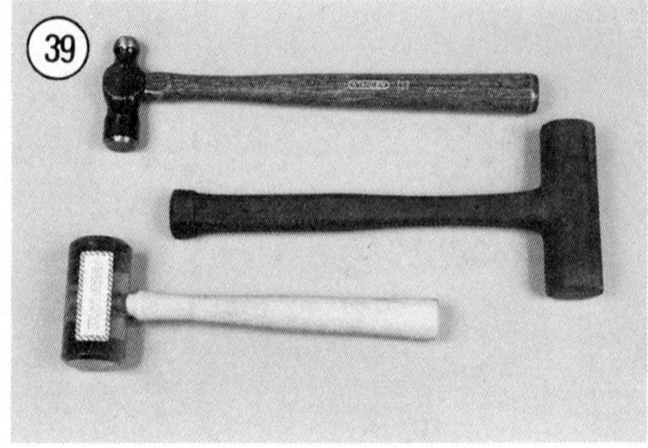
39

When using hammers, note the following:

a. *Always* wear safety glasses when using a hammer.

b. Inspect hammers for damaged or broken parts. Repair or replace the hammer as required. Do *not* use a hammer with a taped handle.

c. Always wipe oil or grease off of the hammer *before* using it.

d. The head of the hammer should always strike the object squarely. Do not use the side of the hammer or the handle to strike an object.

e. Always use the correct hammer for the job.

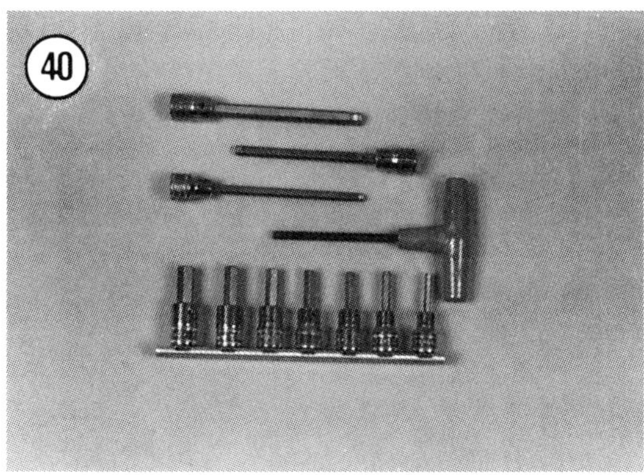

40

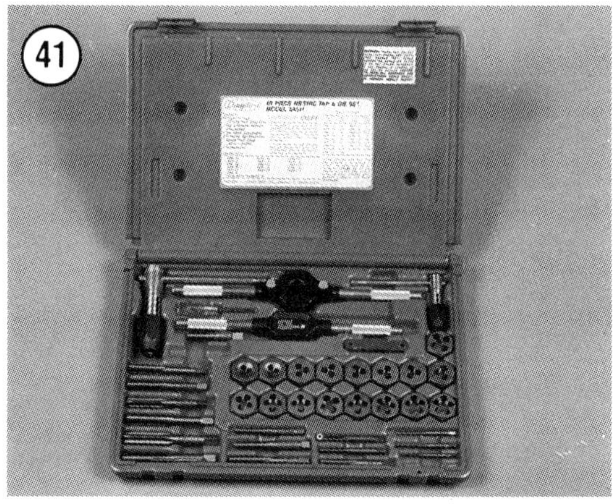

41

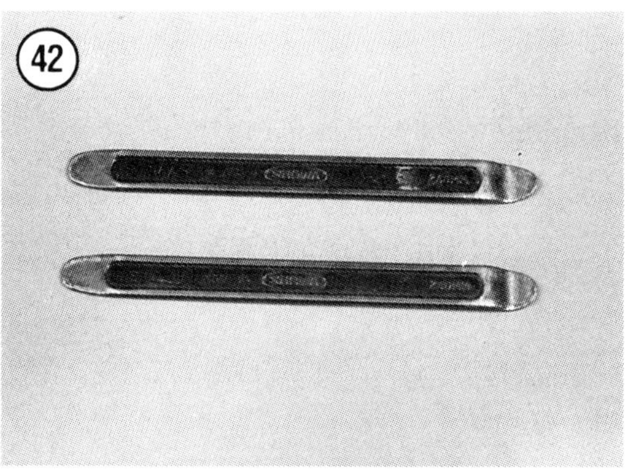

42

Allen Wrenches

Allen wrenches (**Figure 40**) are available in sets or separately in a variety of sizes. These sets come in SAE and metric sizes, so be sure to buy a SAE set. Allen bolts are sometimes called socket bolts.

Harley-Davidson uses Allen bolts throughout the bike. Sometimes the bolts are difficult to reach and it is suggested that a variety of Allen wrenches be purchased (e.g. socket driven, T-handle and extension type) as shown in **Figure 40**.

Tap and Die Set

A complete tap and die set (**Figure 41**) is a relatively expensive tool. But when you need a tap or die to clean up a damaged thread, there is really no substitute. Be sure to purchase one for American Standard (SAE) threads when working on your Harley.

Tire Levers

When changing tires, use a good set of tire levers (**Figure 42**). Never use a screwdriver in place of a tire lever; refer to Chapter Ten for tire changing procedures using these tools. Before using the tire levers, check the working ends of the tool and remove any burrs. Don't use a tire lever for prying anything but tires. **Figure 42** shows a regular pair of 10 in. long tire levers. However, for better leverage when changing tires on your Harley, you may want to invest in a set of 16 in. long tire irons. These can be ordered through your dealer.

Bike Stand

Because Sportsters are not equipped with centerstands, you will need some safe means of raising your Harley's wheels off of the ground during many of the service procedures described in this manual. And when raising your Harley, you do not want to improvise a bike stand with available materials to just get you by. Consider the physical damage that can occur if your bike falls onto a cement floor.

There are a number of accessory bike stands that can be used to raise and support your Harley safely during service. Most are designed for shop use only. The bike stand shown in **Figure 43** was made out of heavy duty pipe. There is a stand available that is both useful and innovative. Along with using it in your shop or garage, it can be folded into a compact size so that it can be packed with your other travel gear and taken along for emergency use on the road. When selecting a bike stand, make sure that it can be used on Harley-Davidson motorcyclcs. Always check the stability of the bike stand before walking away from the bike or when working it.

Drivers and Pullers

These tools are used to remove and install oil seals, bushings, bearings and gears. These will be called out during service procedures in later chapters as required.

TEST EQUIPMENT

Multimeter or Volt-ohm Meter

This instrument (**Figure 44**) is invaluable for electrical system troubleshooting and service. A few of its functions may be duplicated by homemade test equipment, but for the serious mechanic it is a must. Its uses are described in the applicable section of the book.

Compression Gauge

An engine with low compression cannot be properly tuned and will not develop full power. A compression gauge measures engine compression. The one shown in **Figure 45** has a flexible stem with an extension that can allow you to hold it while turning the engine over. Press-in rubber tipped types (**Figure 46**) are also available. Open the throttle all the way when checking engine compression. See Chapter Three.

Cylinder Leak Down Tester

By positioning a cylinder on its compression stroke so that both valves are closed and then pressurizing the cylinder, you can isolate engine problem areas (e.g. leaking valve, damaged head gasket, broke, worn or stuck piston rings) by listening for escaping air through the carburetor, exhaust pipe, cylinder head mating surface, etc. To perform this procedure, a leak down tester and an air compressor

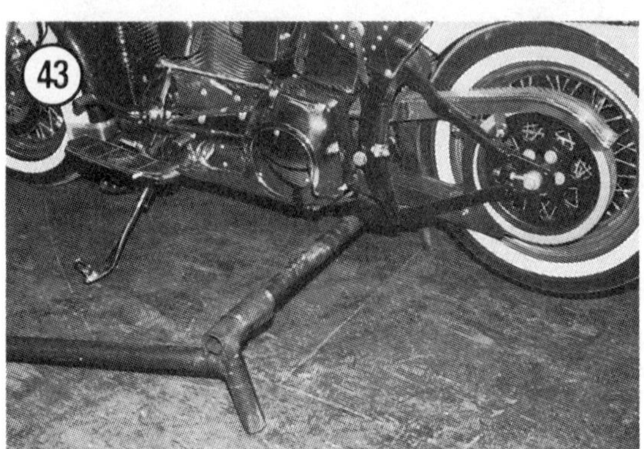

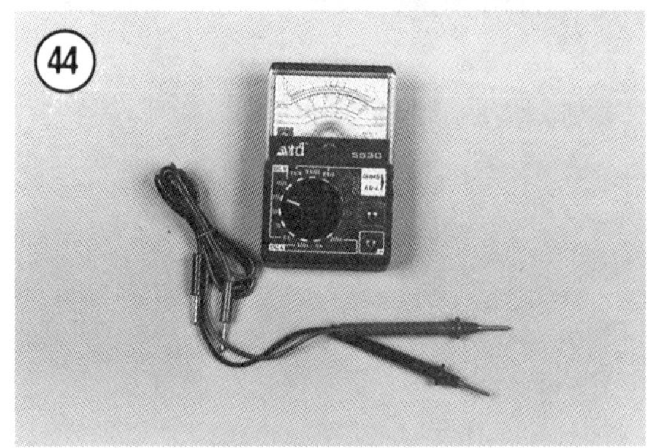

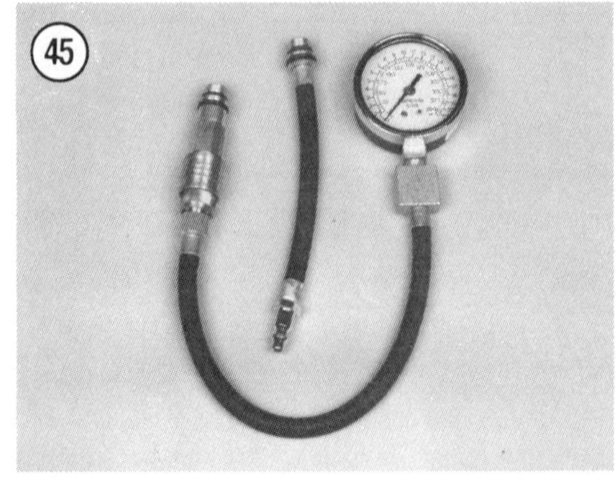

are required. This procedure is described in Chapter Three as it pertains to the Harley-Davidson Evolution engines. Cylinder leak down testers can be purchased through Harley-Davidson dealers, accessory tool manufacturers and automotive tool suppliers.

46

Battery Hydrometer

A hydrometer (**Figure 47**) is the best way to check a battery's state of charge. A hydrometer measures the weight or density of the sulfuric acid in the battery's electrolyte in specific gravity.

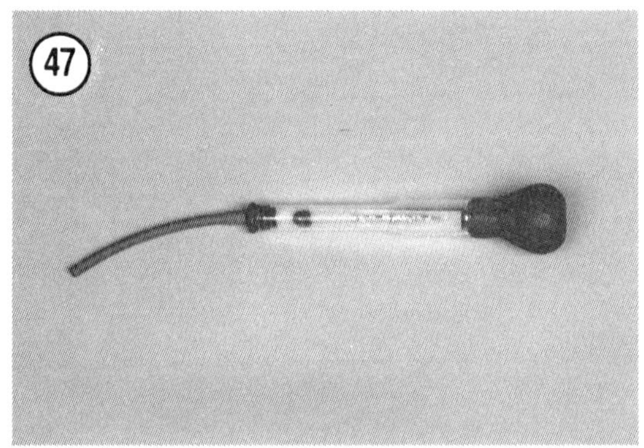

47

Portable Tachometer

A portable tachometer (**Figure 48**) is necessary for tuning. Ignition timing and carburetor adjustments must be performed at specified engine speeds. The best instrument for this purpose is one with a low range of 0-1,000 or 0-2,000 rpm and a high range of 0-4,000 rpm. Extended range (0-6,000 or 0-8,000 rpm) instruments lack accuracy at lower speeds. The instrument should be capable of detecting 25 rpm on the low range.

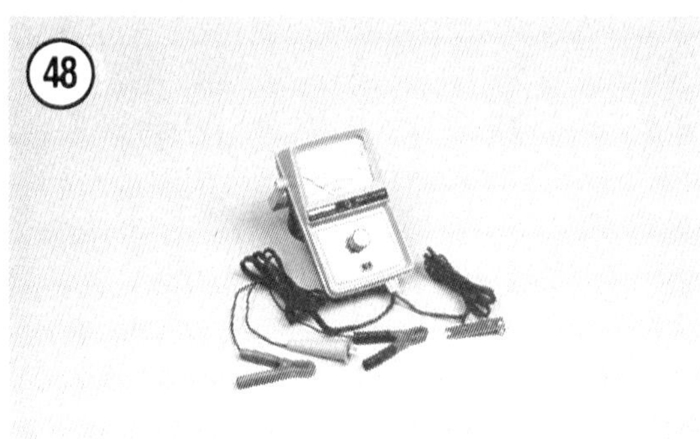

48

Timing Light

Suitable timing lights range from inexpensive neon bulb types to powerful xenon strobe lights (**Figure 49**). A light with an inductive pickup is recommended to prevent any possible damage to ignition wiring.

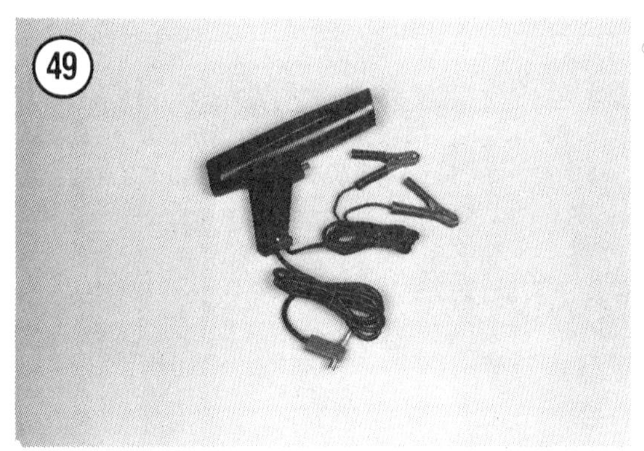

49

PRECISION MEASURING TOOLS

Measurement is an important part of servicing your Harley. When performing many of the service procedures in this manual, you will be required to make a number of measurements. These include basic checks such as engine compression and spark plug gap. As you become more involved with engine disassembly and service, measurements will be required to determine the condition of the piston and cylinder bore, crankshaft runout and so on. When making these measurements, the degree of accuracy will dictate which tool is required. Precision measuring tools are expensive. If this is your first experience at engine service, it may be more worthwhile to have the checks made at a dealer. However, as your skills and enthusiasm increase for doing your own service work, you may want to begin purchasing some of these specialized tools. The following is a description of the measuring tools required during engine overhaul.

Feeler Gauge

The feeler gauge (**Figure 50**) is made of either a piece of a flat or round hardened steel of a specified thickness. Wire gauges are used to measure spark plug gap. Flat gauges are used for all other measurements.

Vernier Caliper

This tool (**Figure 51**) is invaluable when it is necessary to measure inside, outside and depth measurements with close precision. It can be used to measure the thickness of shims and thrust washers. It is perhaps the most often used measuring tool in the motorcycle service shop. Vernier calipers are available in a wide assortment of styles and price ranges.

Outside Micrometers

The outside micrometer (**Figure 52**) is used for very exact measurements of close-tolerance components. It can be used to measure the outside diameter of a piston as well as for shims and thrust washers. Outside micrometers will be required to transfer measurements from bore, snap and small hole gauges. Micrometers can be purchased individually or in a set.

Dial Indicator

Dial indicators (**Figure 53**) are precision tools used to check crankshaft and drive shaft runout limits. For motorcycle repair, select a dial indicator with a continuous dial (**Figure 54**).

Cylinder Bore Gauge

The cylinder bore gauge is a very specialized precision tool. The gauge set shown in **Figure 55** is comprised of a dial indicator, handle and a number of length adapters to adapt the gauge to different

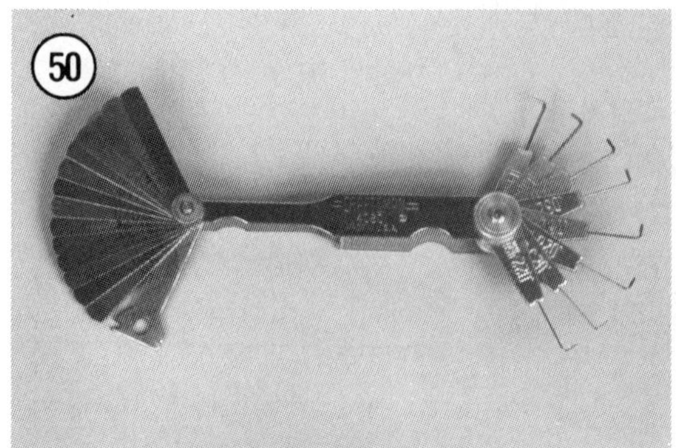

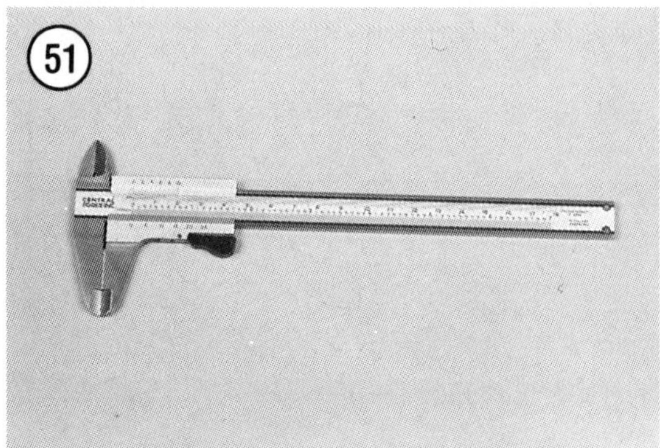

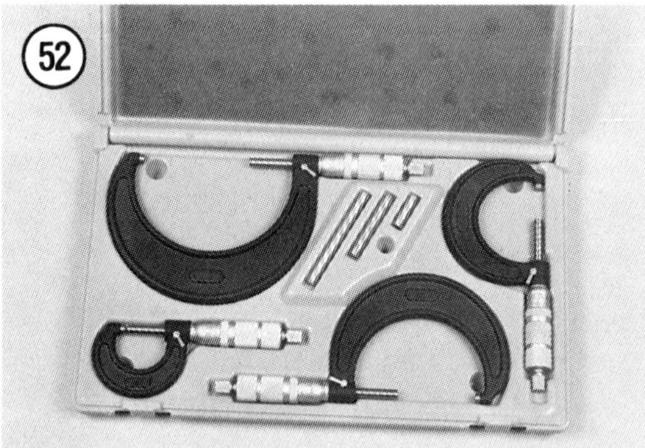

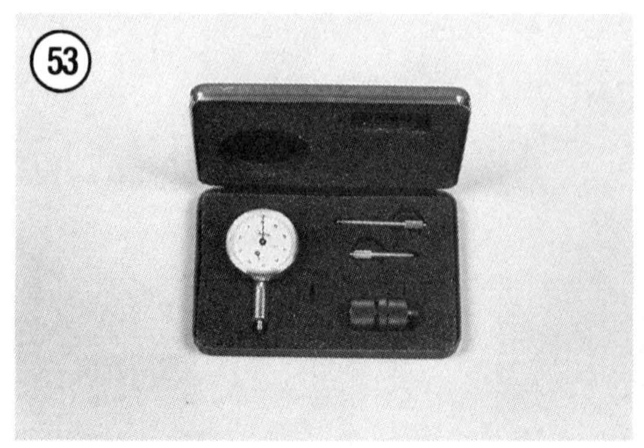

bore sizes. The bore gauge can be used to make cylinder bore measurements such as bore size, taper and out-of-round. An outside micrometer must be used together with the bore gauge to determine bore dimensions.

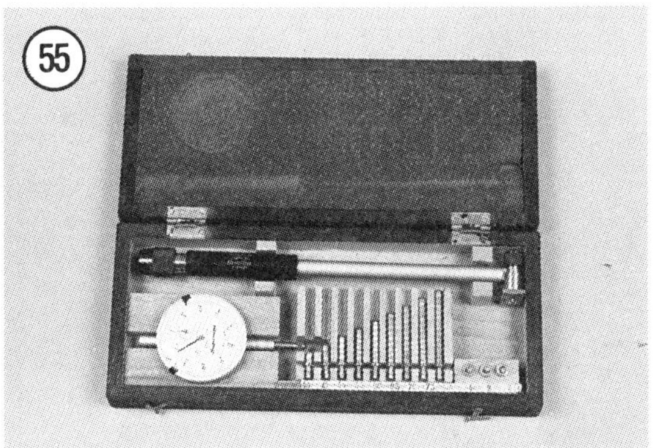

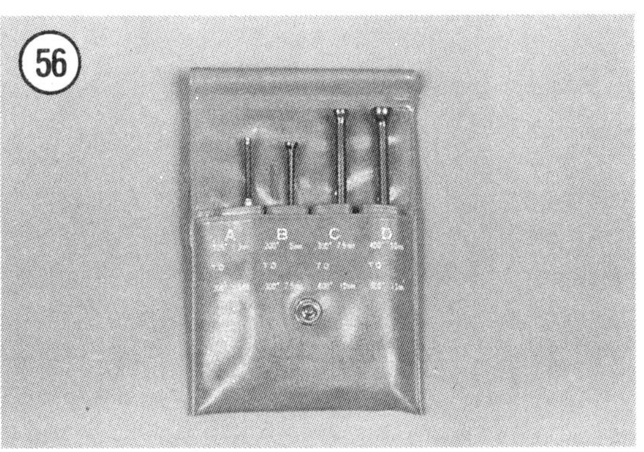

Small Hole Gauges

A set of small hole gauges (**Figure 56**) allows you to measure a hole, groove or slot ranging in size up to 1/2 in. (12.7 mm). An outside micrometer must be used together with the small hole gauge to determine bore dimensions.

Telescoping Gauges

Telescoping gauges (**Figure 57**) can be used to measure hole diameters from approximately 5/16-6 in. (8-150 mm). Like the small hole gauge, the telescoping gauge does not have a scale gauge for direct readings. Thus, an outside micrometer is required to determine bore dimensions.

Screw Pitch Gauge

A screw pitch gauge (**Figure 58**) determines the thread pitch of bolts, screws, studs, etc. The gauge

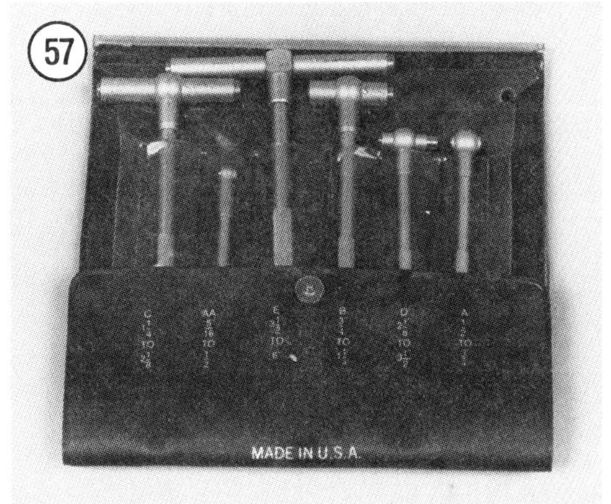

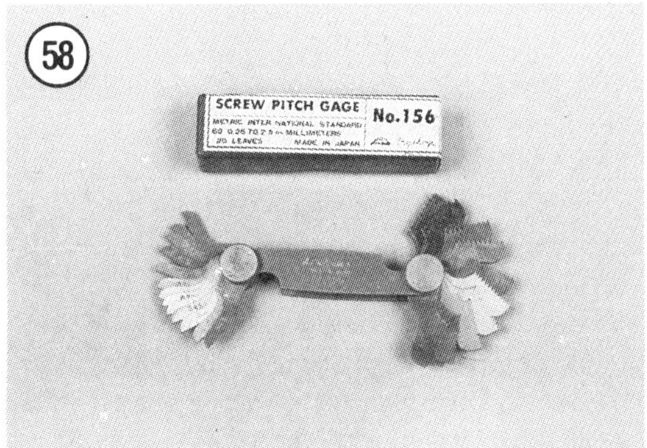

is made up of a number of thin plates. Each plate has a thread shape cut on one edge to match one thread pitch. When using a screw pitch gauge to determine a thread pitch size, try to fit different blade sizes onto the bolt thread until both threads match.

Surface Plate

A surface plate can be used to check the flatness of parts or to provide a perfectly flat surface for minor resurfacing of cylinder head or other critical gasket surfaces. While industrial quality surface plates are quite expensive, the home mechanic can improvise. A thick metal plate can be put to use as a surface plate. The metal surface plate shown in **Figure 59** has a piece of sandpaper glued to its surface that is used for cleaning and smoothing cylinder head and crankcase mating surfaces.

NOTE
Check with a local machine shop on the availability and cost of having a metal plate resurfaced for use as a surface plate.

CLEANING SOLVENT

With the environmental concern that is prevalent today concerning the disposal of hazardous solvents, the home mechanic should select a water soluble, biodegradable solvent. These solvents can be purchased through dealers, automotive parts houses and large hardware stores.

Selecting a solvent is only one of the problems facing the home mechanic when it comes to cleaning parts. You need some type of tank to clean parts as well as to store the solvent. There are a number of manufacturers offering different types and sizes of parts cleaning tanks. While a tank may seem a luxury to the home mechanic, you will find that it will quickly pay for itself through its efficiency and convenience. When selecting a parts washer, look for one that can recycle and store the solvent, as well as separate the sludge and contamination from the clean solvent. Most important, check the warranty, if any, as it pertains to the tank's pump. Like most tools, when purchasing a parts washer, you get what you pay for.

WARNING
Having a stack of clean shop rags on hand is important when performing engine work. However, to prevent the possibility of fire damage from spontaneous combustion from a pile of solvent soaked rags, store them in a lid sealed metal container until they can be washed or discarded.

NOTE
To avoid absorbing solvent and other chemicals into your skin while cleaning parts, wear a pair of petroleum-resistant rubber gloves. These can be purchased through industrial supply houses or well-equipped hardware stores.

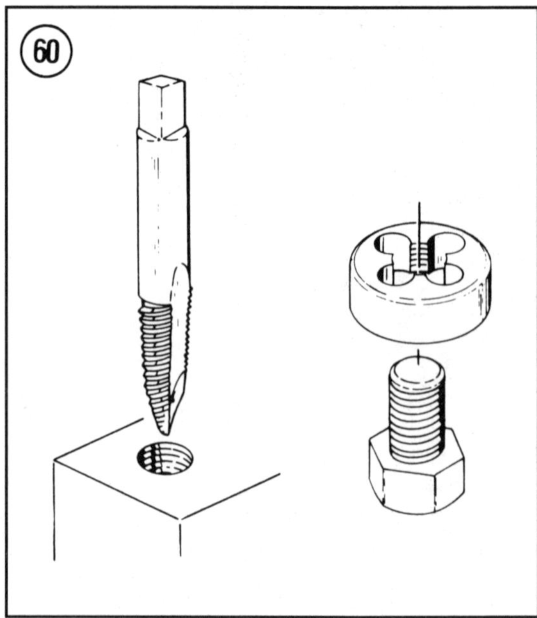

OTHER SPECIAL TOOLS

A few other special tools may be required for major service. These are described in the appropriate chapters and are available from Harley-Davidson dealers or other manufacturers as indicated.

MECHANIC'S TIPS

Removing Frozen Nuts and Screws

When a fastener rusts and cannot be removed, several methods may be used to loosen it. First, apply penetrating oil such as Liquid Wrench or WD-40 (available at hardware or auto supply stores). Apply it liberally and let it penetrate for 10-15 minutes. Rap the fastener several times with a small hammer; do not hit it hard enough to cause damage. Reapply the penetrating oil if necessary.

For frozen screws, apply penetrating oil as described, then insert a screwdriver in the slot and rap the top of the screwdriver with a hammer. This loosens the rust so the screw can be removed in the normal way. If the screw head is too chewed up to use this method, grip the head with vise-grip pliers and twist the screw out.

Avoid applying heat unless specifically instructed, as it may melt, warp or remove the temper from parts.

61

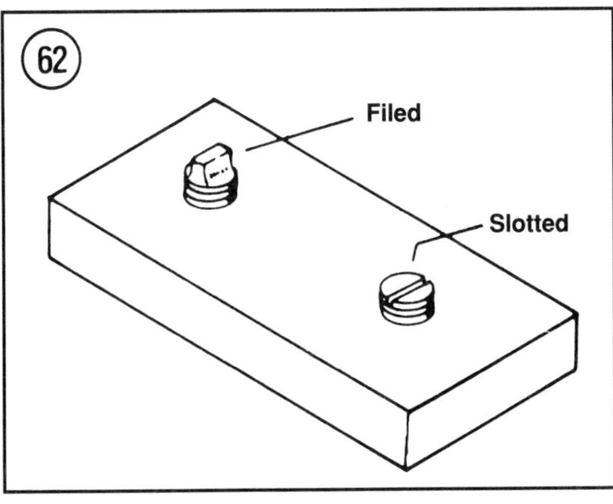

62

Remedying Stripped Threads

Occasionally, threads are stripped through carelessness or impact damage. Often the threads can be cleaned up by running a tap (for internal threads on nuts) or die (for external threads on bolts) through the threads. See **Figure 60**. To clean or repair spark plug threads, a spark plug tap can be used.

If an internal thread is damaged, it may be necessary to install a Helicoil (**Figure 61**) or some other type of thread insert. These kits have all of the necessary parts to repair a damaged internal thread.

If it is necessary to drill and tap a hole, refer to **Table 9** for SAE tap drill sizes.

Removing Broken Screws or Bolts

When the head breaks off a screw or bolt, several methods are available for removing the remaining portion.

If a large portion of the remainder projects out, try gripping it with vise-grip pliers. If the projecting portion is too small, file it to fit a wrench or cut a slot in it to fit a screwdriver. See **Figure 62**.

If the head breaks off flush, use a screw extractor. To do this, centerpunch the exact center of the remaining portion of the screw or bolt. Drill a small hole in the screw and tap the extractor into the hole. Back the screw out with a wrench on the extractor. See **Figure 63**.

Removing Broken or Damaged Studs

If a stud is broken or the threads severely damaged, perform the following. A tube of Loctite 271 (red), 2 nuts, 2 wrenches and a new stud will be required during this procedure (**Figure 64**).

NOTE
The following steps describe general procedures for replacing a typical stud. However, if you are replacing cylinder studs, refer to ***Cylinder Stud Replace-***

ment in Chapter Four. Do ***not*** *use the following steps to replace cylinder studs. The improper installation of cylinder studs can cause cylinder head leakage.*

1. Thread two nuts onto the damaged stud. Then tighten the 2 nuts against each other so that they are locked.

NOTE

If the threads on the damaged stud do not allow installation of the 2 nuts, you will have to remove the stud with a stud remover.

2. Turn the bottom nut counterclockwise and unscrew the stud.

3. Threaded holes with a bottom surface should be blown out with compressed air as dirt buildup in the bottom of the hole may prevent the stud from being torqued properly. If necessary, use a bottoming tap to true up the threads and to remove any deposits.

4. Install 2 nuts on the top half of the new stud as in Step 1. Make sure they are locked securely.

5. Coat the bottom half of a new stud with Loctite 271 (red).

6. Turn the top nut clockwise and thread the new stud securely.

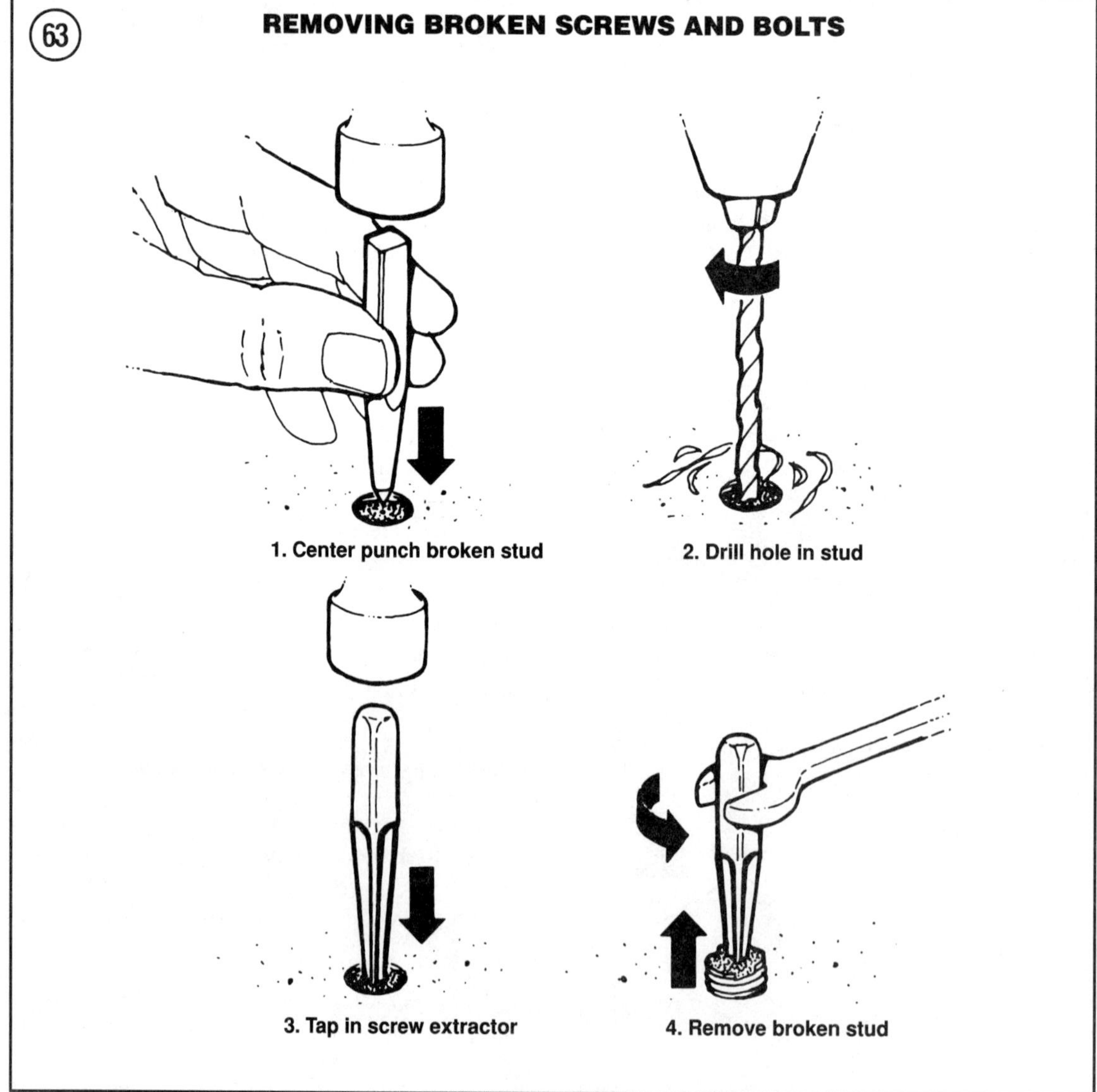

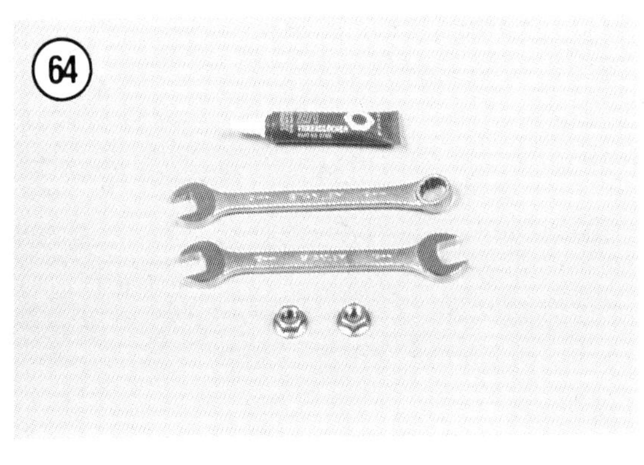
64

65

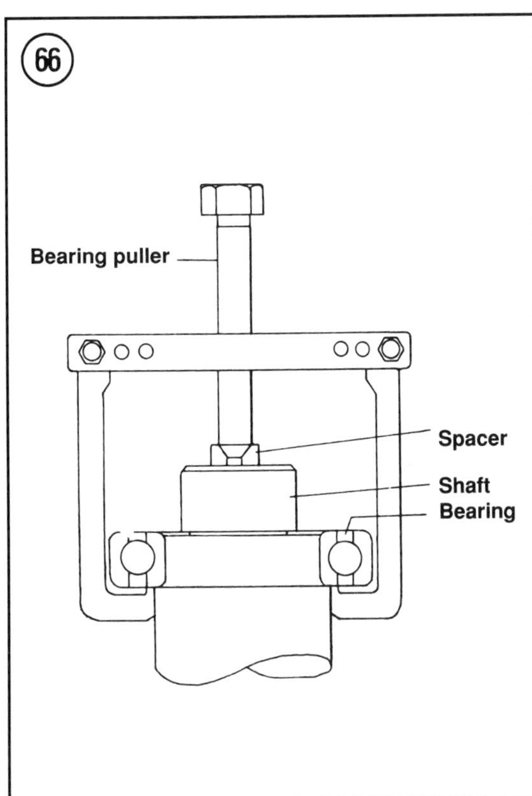

66

7. Remove the nuts and repeat for each stud as required.

8. Follow Loctite's directions on cure time before assembling the component.

BALL BEARING REPLACEMENT

Ball bearings (**Figure 65**) are used throughout your Harley's engine and chassis to reduce power loss, heat and noise resulting from friction. Because ball bearings are precision made parts, they must be maintained by proper lubrication and maintenance. When a bearing is found to be damaged, it should be replaced immediately. However, when installing a new bearing, care should be taken to prevent damage to the new bearing. While bearing replacement is described in the individual chapters where applicable, the following can be used as a guideline.

NOTE

Unless otherwise specified, install bearings with the manufacturer's mark or number on the bearing facing outward.

Bearing Removal

While bearings are normally removed only when damaged, there may be times when it is necessary to remove a bearing that is in good condition. Depending on the situation, you may be able to remove the bearing without damaging it. However, bearing removal in some situations, no matter how careful you are, will cause bearing damage. Care should always be given to bearings during their removal to prevent secondary damage to the shaft or housing. Note the following when removing bearings.

1. When using a puller to remove a bearing on a shaft, care must be taken so that shaft damage does not occur. Always place a piece of metal between the end of the shaft and the puller screw. In addition, place the puller arms next to the inner bearing race. See **Figure 66**.

2. When using a hammer to remove a bearing on a shaft, do not strike the hammer directly against the shaft. Instead, use a brass or aluminum spacer between the hammer and shaft (**Figure 67**). In addition, make sure to support *both* bearing races with wood blocks as shown in **Figure 67**.

3. The most ideal method of bearing removal is with a hydraulic press. However, certain procedures must be followed or damage may occur to the bearing, shaft or case half. Note the following when using a press:

   a. Always support the inner and outer bearing races with a suitable size wood or aluminum spacer ring (**Figure 68**). If only the outer race is supported, the balls and/or the inner race will be damaged.
   b. Always make sure the press ram (**Figure 68**) aligns with the center of the shaft. If the ram is not centered, it may damage the bearing and/or shaft.
   c. The moment the shaft is free of the bearing, it will drop to the floor. Secure or hold the shaft to prevent it from falling.

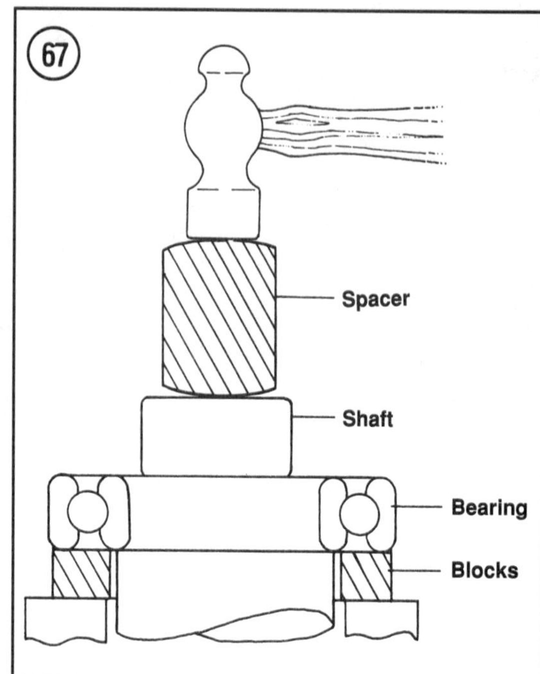

Bearing Installation

1. When installing a bearing in a housing, pressure must be applied to the *outer* bearing race (**Figure 69**). When installing a bearing on a shaft, pressure must be applied to the *inner* bearing race (**Figure 70**).
2. When installing a bearing as described in Step 1, some type of driver will be required. Never strike the bearing directly with a hammer or the bearing will be damaged. When installing a bearing, a piece of pipe or a socket with an outer diameter that matches the bearing race will be required. **Figure 71** shows the correct way to use a socket and hammer when installing a bearing over a shaft.
3. Step 1 describes how to install a bearing in a case half and over a shaft. However, when installing a bearing over a shaft and into a housing at the same time, a snug fit will be required for both outer and inner bearing races. In this situation, a spacer must be installed underneath the driver tool so that pressure is applied evenly across *both* races. See **Figure 72**. If the outer race is not supported as shown in **Figure 72**, the balls will push against the outer bearing track and damage it.

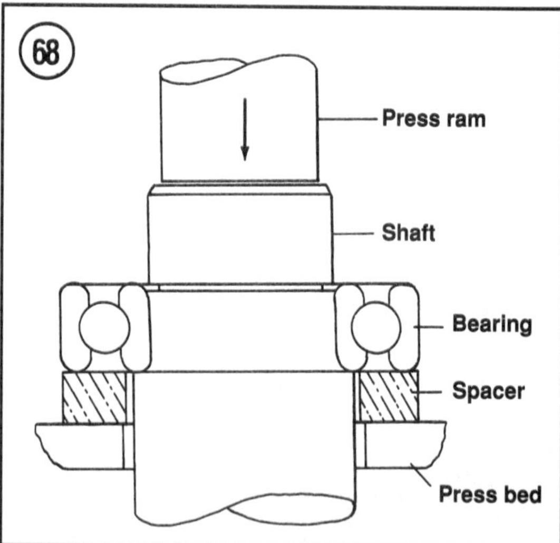

Shrink Fit

1. *Installing a bearing over a shaft*: When a tight fit is required, the bearing inside diameter will be smaller than the shaft. In this case, driving the bearing on the shaft using normal methods may cause

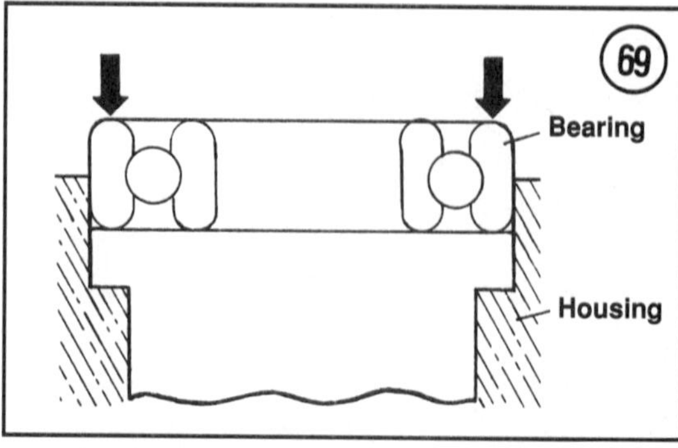

bearing damage. Instead, the bearing should be heated before installation. Note the following:

a. Secure the shaft so that it can be ready for bearing installation.

b. Clean the bearing surface on the shaft of all residue. Remove burrs with a file or sandpaper.

c. Fill a suitable pot or beaker with clean mineral oil. Place a thermometer (rated higher than 248° F) in the oil. Support the thermometer so that it does not rest on the bottom or side of the pot.

d. Remove the bearing from its wrapper and secure it with a piece of heavy wire bent to hold it in the pot. Hang the bearing in the pot so that it does not touch the bottom or sides of the pot.

e. Turn the heat on and monitor the thermometer. When the oil temperature rises to approximately 248° F, remove the bearing from the pot and quickly install it. If necessary, place a socket on the inner bearing race and tap the bearing into place. As the bearing chills, it will tighten on the shaft so you must work quickly when installing it. Make sure the bearing is installed all the way.

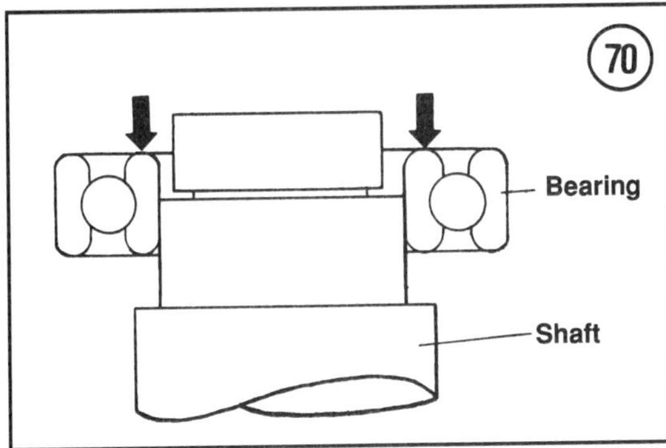

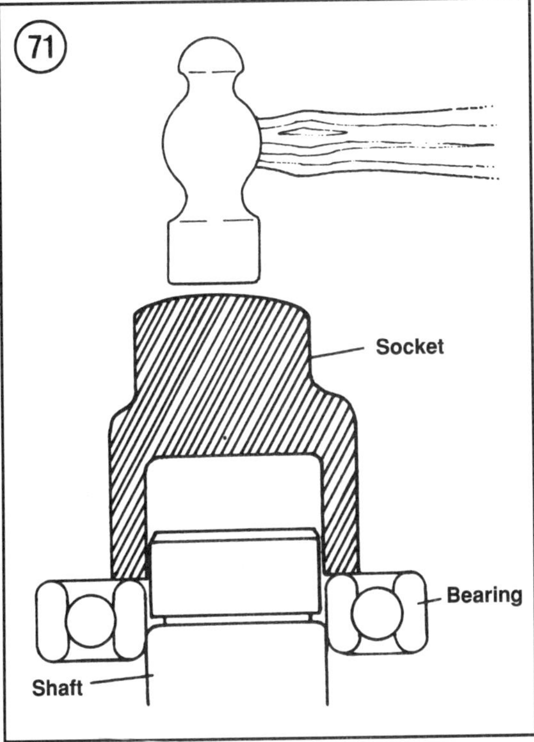

2. *Installing a bearing in a housing*: Bearings are generally installed in a housing with a slight interference fit. Driving the bearing into the housing using normal methods may damage the housing or cause bearing damage. Instead, the housing should be heated before the bearing is installed. Note the following:

CAUTION

Before heating the crankcases in this procedure to remove the bearings, wash the cases thoroughly with detergent and water. Rinse and rewash the cases as

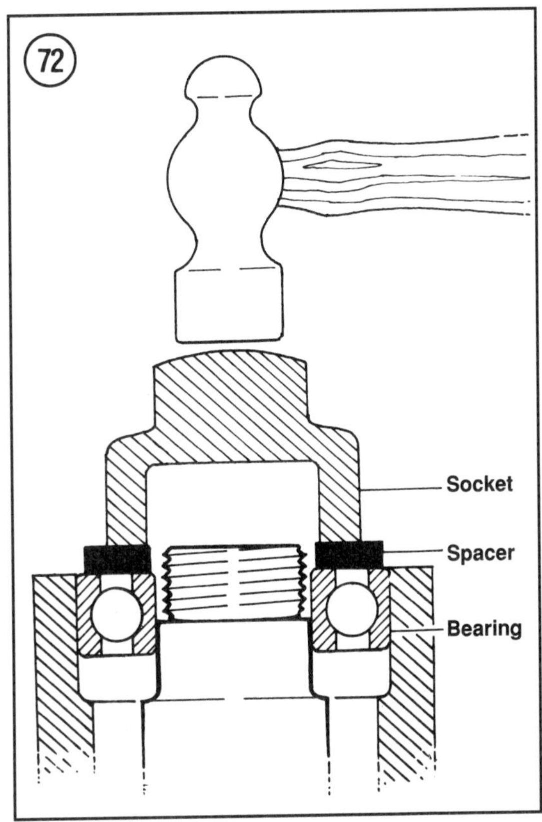

required to remove all traces of oil and other chemical deposits.

a. The housing must be heated to a temperature of about 212° F in an oven or on a hot plate. An easy way to check to see that it is at the proper temperature is to drop tiny drops of water on the case as it heats up; if they sizzle and evaporate immediately, the temperature is correct. Heat only one housing at a time.

CAUTION
Do not heat the housing with a torch (propane or acetylene)—never bring a flame into contact with the bearing or housing. The direct heat will destroy the case hardening of the bearing and will likely warp the housing.

b. Remove the housing from the oven or hot plate and hold onto the housing with a kitchen pot holder, heavy gloves, or heavy shop cloths—*it is hot.*

NOTE
A suitable size socket and extension works well for removing and installing bearings.

c. Hold the housing with the bearing side down and tap the bearing out. Repeat for all bearings in the housing.
d. While heating up the housing halves, place the new bearings in a freezer if possible. Chilling them will slightly reduce their overall diameter while the hot housing assembly is slightly larger due to heat expansion. This will make installation much easier.

NOTE
Always install bearings with the manufacturer's mark or number facing outward.

e. While the housing is still hot, install the new bearing(s) into the housing. Install the bearings by hand, if possible. If necessary, lightly tap the bearing(s) into the housing with a socket placed on the outer bearing race. *Do not* install new bearings by driving on the inner bearing race. Install the bearing(s) until it seats completely.

OIL SEALS

Oil seals (**Figure 73**) are used to contain oil, water, grease or combustion gasses in a housing or shaft. Improper removal of a seal can damage the housing or shaft. Improper installation of the seal can damage the seal. Note the following:

a. Prying is generally the easiest and most effective method of removing a seal from a housing. However, always place a rag underneath the pry tool to prevent damage to the housing.
b. Grease should be packed in the seal lips before the seal is installed.
c. Oil seals should always be installed so that the manufacturer's numbers or marks face out.
d. Oil seals should be installed with a socket placed on the outside of the seal as shown in **Figure 74**. Make sure the seal is driven squarely into the housing. Never install a seal by hitting against the top of the seal with a hammer.

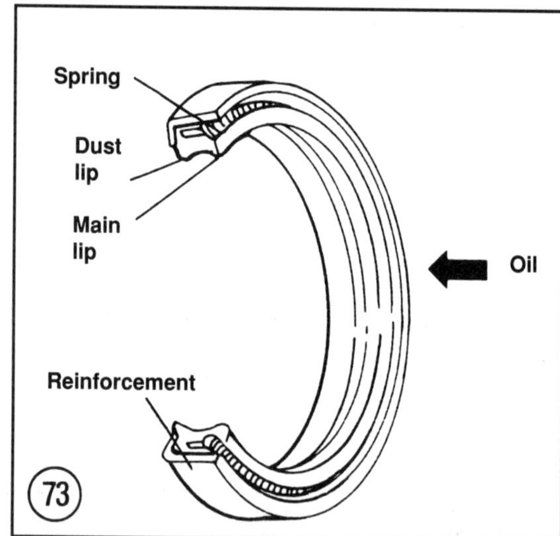

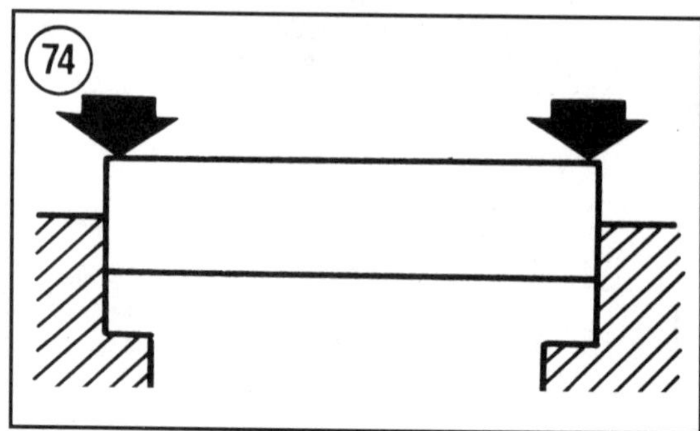

Table 1 MODEL DESIGNATION

1991-on
XLH 883
XLH 883 Hugger
XLH 883 Deluxe
XLH 1200

Table 2 GENERAL SPECIFICATIONS

	in.	mm
Wheelbase		
883 cc Hugger		
1991-1992	60.5	1,537
1993-on	59	1,499
All other models	60.2	1,529
Overall length		
883 cc Hugger		
1991	87.6	2,225
1992-on	87.25	2,216
All other models	87.6	2,225
Overall height		
883 cc*	47.5	1,207
883 cc Deluxe		
1994	47.5	1,207
All other models	49.75	1,264
Overall width		
883 cc*	32	813
All other models	33	838.2
Ground clearance		
883 cc Hugger		
1991	5.90	149.9
1992-on	4.50	114.3
All other models	6.75	171.5

* Standard model.

Table 3 OVERALL VEHICLE WEIGHT*

Model	lbs.	kg
1991-1993		
883 cc** and 883 cc Hugger	472	214.1
883 cc Deluxe	484	219.5
1200 cc	470	213.2
1994		
883 cc**	488	221
883 cc Hugger	485	220
883 cc Deluxe	494	224
1200 cc	490	222

* Vehicle weight as shipped from factory.
** Standard model.

Table 4 GROSS VEHICLE WEIGHT RATINGS

	lbs.	kg
Gross vehicle weight rating (GVWR)	900	408.2
Gross axle weight ratings (GAWR)		
Front	320	145.1
Rear	580	263.1

* GVWR is the maximum allowable vehicle weight. This weight will include combined vehicle, rider(s) and accessory weight.

Table 5 FUEL TANK CAPACITY

	U.S. gal.	Liters	Imp. gal.
Total	2.25	8.5	1.87
Reserve	0.25	0.94	0.21

Table 6 DECIMAL AND METRIC EQUIVALENTS

Fractions	Decimal in.	Metric mm	Fractions	Decimal in.	Metric mm
1/64	0.015625	0.39688	33/64	0.515625	13.09687
1/32	0.03125	0.79375	17/32	0.53125	13.49375
3/64	0.046875	1.19062	35/64	0.546875	13.89062
1/16	0.0625	1.58750	9/16	0.5625	14.28750
5/64	0.078125	1.98437	37/64	0.578125	14.68437
3/32	0.09375	2.38125	19/32	0.59375	15.08125
7/64	0.109375	2.77812	39/64	0.609375	15.47812
1/8	0.125	3.1750	5/8	0.625	15.87500
9/64	0.140625	3.57187	41/64	0.640625	16.27187
5/32	0.15625	3.96875	21/32	0.65625	16.66875
11/64	0.171875	4.36562	43/64	0.671875	17.06562
3/16	0.1875	4.76250	11/16	0.6875	17.46250
13/64	0.203125	5.15937	45/64	0.703125	17.85937
7/32	0.21875	5.55625	23/32	0.71875	18.25625
15/64	0.234375	5.95312	47/64	0.734375	18.65312
1/4	0.250	6.35000	3/4	0.750	19.05000
17/64	0.265625	6.74687	49/64	0.765625	19.44687
9/32	0.28125	7.14375	25/32	0.78125	19.84375
19/64	0.296875	7.54062	51/64	0.796875	20.24062
5/16	0.3125	7.93750	13/16	0.8125	20.63750
21/64	0.328125	8.33437	53/64	0.828125	21.03437
11/32	0.34375	8.73125	27/32	0.84375	21.43125
23/64	0.359375	9.12812	55/64	0.859375	22.82812
3/8	0.375	9.52500	7/8	0.875	22.22500
25/64	0.390625	9.92187	57/64	0.890625	22.62187
13/32	0.40625	10.31875	29/32	0.90625	23.01875
27/64	0.421875	10.71562	59/64	0.921875	23.41562
7/16	0.4375	11.11250	15/16	0.9375	23.81250
29/64	0.453125	11.50937	61/64	0.953125	24.20937
15/32	0.46875	11.90625	31/32	0.96875	24.60625
31/64	0.484375	12.30312	63/64	0.984375	25.00312
1/2	0.500	12.70000	1	1.00	25.40000

Table 7 GENERAL TORQUE SPECIFICATIONS (FT.-LB.)*

	Body Size or Outside Diameter									
Type**	**1/4**	**5/16**	**3/8**	**7/16**	**1/2**	**9/16**	**5/8**	**3/4**	**7/8**	**1**
SAE 2	6	12	20	32	47	69	96	155	206	310
SAE 5	10	19	33	54	78	114	154	257	382	587
SAE 7	13	25	44	71	110	154	215	360	570	840
SAE 8	14	29	47	78	119	169	230	380	600	700

* Convert ft.-lb. specification to N•m by multiplying by 1.38.
** Fastener strength of SAE bolts can be determined by the bolt head "grade markings." Unmarked bolt heads and cap screws are usually to be mild steel. More "grade markings" indicate higher fastener quality.

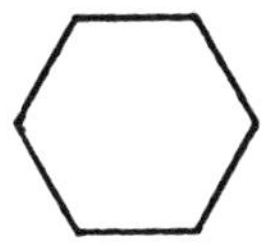
SAE 2

SAE 5

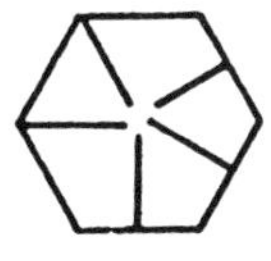
SAE 7

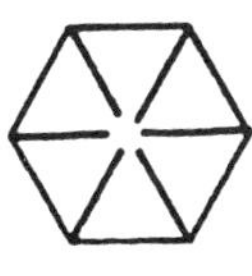
SAE 8

Table 8 CONVERSION TABLES

Multiply	By	To get equivalent of
Length		
Inches	25.4	Millimeter
Inches	2.54	Centimeter
Miles	1.609	Kilometer
Feet	0.3048	Meter
Millimeter	0.03937	Inches
Centimeter	0.3937	Inches
Kilometer	0.6214	Mile
Meter	3.281	Mile
Fluid volume		
U.S. quarts	0.9463	Liters
U.S. gallons	3.785	Liters
U.S. ounces	29.573529	Milliliters
Imperial gallons	4.54609	Liters
Imperial quarts	1.1365	Liters
Liters	0.2641721	U.S. gallons
Liters	1.0566882	U.S. quarts
Liters	33.814023	U.S. ounces
Liters	0.22	Imperial gallons
Liters	0.8799	Imperial quarts
Milliliters	0.033814	U.S. ounces
Milliliters	1.0	Cubic centimeters
Milliliters	0.001	Liters
Torque		
Foot-pounds	1.3556	Newton-meters
Foot-pounds	0.138255	Meters-kilograms
Inch-pounds	0.1130	Newton-meters
Newton-meters	0.7375622	Foot-pounds
Newton-meters	8.8507	Inch-pounds
Meters-kilograms	7.2330139	Foot-pounds
Volume		
Cubic inches	16.387064	Cubic centimeters
Cubic centimeters	0.0610237	Cubic inches

(continued)

Table 8 CONVERSION TABLES (continued)

Multiply	By	To get equivalent of
Temperature		
Fahrenheit	(F – 32) 0.556	Centigrade
Centigrade	(C × 1.8) + 32	Fahrenheit
Weight		
Ounces	28.3495	Grams
Pounds	0.4535924	Kilograms
Grams	0.035274	Ounces
Kilograms	2.2046224	Pounds
Pressure		
Pounds per square inch	0.070307	Kilograms per square centimeter
Kilograms per square centimeter	14.223343	Pounds per square inch
Speed		
Miles per hour	1.609344	Kilometers per hour
Kilometers per hour	0.6213712	Miles per hour

TABLE 9 AMERICAN TAP DRILL SIZES

Tap thread	Drill size	Tap thread	Drill size
#0-80	3/64	1/4-28	No. 3
#1-64	No. 53	5/16-18	F
#1-72	No. 53	5/16-24	I
#2-56	No. 51	3/8-16	5/16
#2-64	No. 50	3/8-24	Q
#3-48	5/64	7/16-14	U
#3-56	No. 46	7/16-20	W
#4-40	No. 43	1/2-13	27/64
#4-48	No. 42	1/2-20	29/64
#5-40	No. 39	9/16-12	31/64
#5-44	No. 37	9/16-18	33/64
#6-32	No. 36	5/8-11	17/32
#6-40	No. 33	5/18-18	37/64
#8-32	No. 29	3/4-10	21/32
#8-36	No. 29	3/4-16	11/16
#10-24	No. 25	7/8-9	49-64
#10.32	No. 21	7/8-14	13/16
#12-24	No. 17	1-8	7/8
#12-28	No. 15	1-14	15/16
1/4-20	No. 8		

Table 10 WINDCHILL FACTOR

Estimated Wind Speed in MPH	Actual Thermometer Reading (° F)*											
	50	40	30	20	10	0	–10	–20	–30	–40	–50	–60
	Equivalent Temperature (° F)*											
Calm	50	40	30	20	10	0	–10	–20	–30	–40	–50	–60
5	48	37	27	16	6	–5	–15	–26	–36	–47	–57	–68
10	40	28	16	4	–9	–21	–33	–46	–58	–70	–83	–95
15	36	22	9	–5	–18	–36	–45	–58	–72	–85	–99	–112
20	32	18	4	–10	–25	–39	–53	–67	–82	–96	–110	–124
25	30	16	0	–15	–29	–44	–59	–74	–88	–104	–118	–133
30	28	13	–2	–18	–33	–48	–63	–79	–94	–109	–125	–140
35	27	11	–4	–20	–35	–49	–67	–82	–98	–113	–129	–145
40	26	10	–6	–21	–37	–53	–69	–85	–100	–116	–132	–148
**	**Little Danger** (for properly clothed person)				**Increasing Danger**			**Great Danger**				
					• Danger from freezing of exposed flesh •							

* To convert Fahrenheit (°F) to Celsius (°C), use the following formula: $°C = 5/9 \times (°F - 32)$.

** Wind speeds greater than 40 mph have little additional effect.

CHAPTER TWO

TROUBLESHOOTING

Every motorcycle engine requires an uninterrupted supply of fuel and air, proper ignition and adequate compression. If any of these are lacking, the engine will not run.

Diagnosing mechanical problems is relatively simple if you use orderly procedures and keep a few basic principles in mind.

The troubleshooting procedures in this chapter analyze typical symptoms and show logical methods of isolating causes. These are not the only methods. There may be several ways to solve a problem, but only a systematic approach can guarantee success.

Never assume anything. Do not overlook the obvious. If you are riding along and the bike suddenly quits, check the easiest, most accessible problem spots first. Is there gasoline in the tank? Has a spark plug wire fallen off?

If nothing obvious turns up in a quick check, look a little further. Learning to recognize and describe symptoms will make repairs easier for you or a mechanic at the shop. Describe problems accurately and fully. Saying that "it won't run" isn't the same thing as saying "it quit at high speed and won't start," or that "it sat in my garage for 3 months and then wouldn't start."

Gather as many symptoms as possible to aid in diagnosis. Note whether the engine lost power gradually or all at once. Remember that the more complicated a machine is, the easier it is to troubleshoot because symptoms point to specific problems.

After the symptoms are defined, areas which could cause problems are tested and analyzed. Guessing at the cause of a problem may provide the solution, but it can easily lead to frustration, wasted time and a series of expensive, unnecessary parts replacements.

You do not need fancy equipment or complicated test gear to determine whether repairs can be attempted at home. A few simple checks could save a large repair bill and lost time while the bike sits in a dealer's service department. On the other hand, be realistic and do not attempt repairs beyond your abilities. Service departments tend to charge heavily for putting together a disassembled engine that may have been abused. Some won't even take on such a job—so use common sense, don't get in over your head.

Electrical specifications are listed in **Table 1** and **Table 2** at the end of the chapter.

OPERATING REQUIREMENTS

An engine needs 3 basics to run properly: correct fuel/air mixture, compression and a spark at the correct time (**Figure 1**). If one or more are missing, the engine will not run. If all three engine basics are present, but one or more is not working properly, the engine may start, but it will not run properly.

The electrical system is the weakest link of the 3 basics. More problems result from electrical breakdowns than from any other source. Keep that in mind before you begin tampering with carburetor adjustments and the like.

If the machine has been sitting for any length of time and refuses to start, check and clean the spark plugs and then look to the gasoline delivery system.

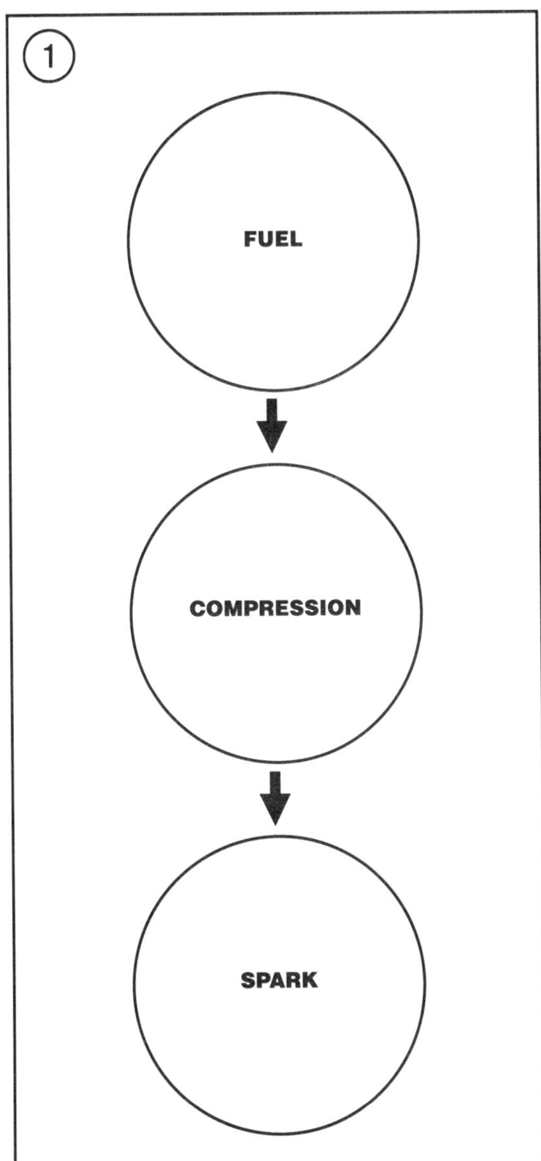

This includes the fuel tank, fuel shutoff valve and fuel line to the carburetor. Gasoline deposits may have formed and gummed up the carburetor jets and air passages. Gasoline tends to lose its potency after standing for long periods. Condensation may contaminate the fuel with water. Drain the old fuel (fuel tank, fuel line and carburetor) and try starting with a fresh tankful.

TROUBLESHOOTING INSTRUMENTS

Chapter One lists the instruments needed and gives instruction on their use.

TESTING ELECTRICAL COMPONENTS

Many dealers and parts houses will not accept returns on electrical parts purchased from them. When testing electrical components, make sure that you perform the test procedures as described in this chapter and that your test equipment is working properly. If a test result shows that the component is defective but the reading is close to the service limit, have the component tested by a Harley-Davidson dealer to verify the test result before purchasing a new electrical component.

EMERGENCY TROUBLESHOOTING

When the bike is difficult to start, or won't start at all, it doesn't help to wear down the battery. Check for obvious problems even before getting out your tools. Go down the following list step by step. If the bike still will not start, refer to the appropriate troubleshooting procedures which follows in this chapter. As described under *Operating Requirements*, the engine requires 3 basics before it will start and run properly. The following procedure will illustrate steps for checking each of the 3 basic engine principles.

1. Visually inspect the bike for gas or oil leakage, loose wires or other abnormal conditions. If you did not find anything that could cause a starting problem, proceed with the following.

2. Make sure the engine STOP switch is not in the OFF position (**Figure 2**).

WARNING
*Do **not** use an open flame to check for fuel in the tank. A serious explosion is certain to result.*

3. Is there fuel in the tank? Open the filler cap and rock the bike. Listen for fuel sloshing around.

NOTE
If the engine has not been run for some time, gasoline deposits may have gummed up carburetor jets and air passages. In addition, gasoline tends to lose its potency after standing for long periods or you may find water in the tank. Drain the old gas and try starting with a fresh tankful.

4. Is the fuel supply valve (**Figure 3**) in the ON position? If the fuel level in the tank is low, turn the valve to RESERVE to make sure you get the last remaining gas.
5. Is the enrichener knob (**Figure 4**) in the correct position? The enrichener knob should be pulled out when starting a cold engine and pushed in when restarting a warm or hot engine. If the enrichener system does not seem to be operating correctly, adjust it as described in Chapter Three.

NOTE
Unlike a choke, the enrichener system does not use detent positions on the enrichener shaft. When attempting to start the engine, and depending on whether the engine is cold, warm or hot, the enrichener can be operated in any position from closed to fully out. It is important to remember that engine speed increases as the enrichener knob is pulled out.

NOTE
The condition of your engine's spark plugs is a deciding factor in its performance and an important reference point during troubleshooting and general maintenance. To avoid mixups when removing the spark plugs in Step 6, make sure to identify each plug so that you know from which cylinder it came from.

6. After attempting to start the engine, immediately remove the spark plugs (**Figure 5**) and check their firing tips. Refer to Chapter Three for information on reading spark plugs. Fuel should be present on both plugs' firing tips; this indicates that fuel is flowing from the fuel tank to the engine. If there is no sign of fuel on the plugs, suspect a fuel delivery problem; refer to *Fuel System* in this chapter. If it appears that there is water on the plugs, water has probably entered the engine from contaminated fuel or there is water in the crankcase.
7. Perform a spark test as described under *Engine Fails to Start (Spark Test)* in this chapter. If there is a strong spark, perform Step 8.
8. Check cylinder compression as follows:

2

3

4

a. Turn the fuel valve OFF.

b. Remove and ground the spark plugs against the cylinder head. The spark plugs must be grounded when performing the following steps or the ignition system will be permanently damaged.

WARNING
When grounding the spark plugs, make sure the plugs are placed away from the spark plug holes in the cylinder head. You will be placing your fingers over the cylinder head spark plug holes, and you could be shocked if you accidentally touch a plug while cranking the engine.

c. Put your finger over one of the spark plug holes.

d. Crank the engine with the starter button. Rising pressure in the cylinder should force your finger off of the spark plug hole. This indicates that the cylinder probably has sufficient cylinder compression to start the engine.

e. Repeat for the opposite cylinder.

f. Lack of cylinder compression indicates a problem with that cylinder. This could be worn or damaged piston rings or a holed piston. Refer to *Engine* in this chapter.

NOTE
Engine compression can be checked more accurately with a compression gauge as described in Chapter Three.

g. Reinstall the spark plugs.

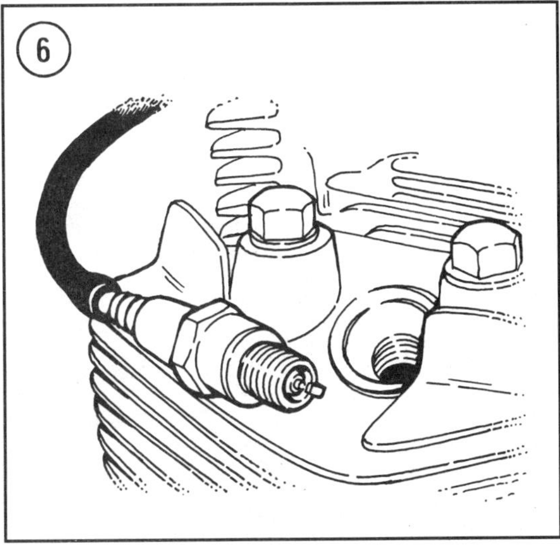

Engine Fails to Start (Spark Test)

Perform the following spark test to determine if the ignition system is operating properly.

1. Remove the spark plugs.
2. Connect the spark plug wire and connector to the spark plug and touch the spark plug base to a good ground like the engine cylinder head. Position the spark plug so you can see the electrodes. See **Figure 6**. Repeat for the other spark plug.
3. Crank the engine over with the starter. A fat blue spark should be evident across the spark plug electrodes.

WARNING
Do not hold the spark plug, wire or connector or a serious electrical shock may result. If necessary, use a pair of insulated pliers to hold the spark plug or wire. The high voltage generated by the ignition system could produce serious or fatal shocks.

4. If the spark is good, check for one or more of the following possible malfunctions:
   a. Obstructed fuel line or fuel filter.
   b. Leaking head gasket(s).
   c. Low compression.
5. If the spark is weak or if there is no spark, check for one or more of the following:
   a. Loose electrical connections.
   b. Dirty electrical connections.
   c. Loose or broken ignition coil ground wire.
   d. Broken or shorted high tension lead to the spark plug.
   e. Discharged battery.

f. Damaged battery connection.
g. Damaged ignition system component.

Engine is Difficult to Start

Check for one or more of the following possible malfunctions:

a. Fouled spark plug(s).
b. Improperly adjusted enrichener valve.
c. Intake manifold air leak (**Figure 7**).
d. Plugged fuel tank filler cap or vent hose.
e. Clogged carburetor fuel line.
f. Contaminated fuel system.
g. Improperly adjusted carburetor.
h. Faulty ignition unit.
i. Faulty ignition coil.
j. Damaged ignition coil wires.
k. Incorrect ignition timing.
l. Low engine compression.
m. Engine oil too heavy (winter temperatures).
n. Discharged battery.
o. Faulty starter motor.
p. Loose or corroded starter and/or battery cables.
q. Loose wire or connector between the ignition sensor and module.
r. Air filter backplate EVAP butterfly valve stuck closed or damaged.

Engine Will Not Turn Over

Check for one or more of the following possible malfunctions:

a. Ignition switch turned OFF.
b. Faulty ignition switch.
c. Engine run switch in OFF position.
d. Faulty engine run switch.
e. Loose or corroded starter and/or battery cables (solenoid chatters).
f. Discharged or defective battery.
g. Defective starter motor.
h. Faulty starter solenoid.
i. Faulty starter shaft pinion gear.
j. Slipping overrunning clutch assembly.
k. Seized piston(s).
l. Seized crankshaft bearings.
m. Broken connecting rod(s).

ENGINE PERFORMANCE

In the following check list, it is assumed that the engine runs, but is not operating at peak performance. This will serve as a starting point from which to isolate a performance malfunction.

Fouled Spark Plugs

If the spark plugs continually foul, note the following:

a. Air filter element severely contaminated.
b. Incorrect heat range spark plug; see Chapter Three for correct heat range spark plugs to use in your model.
c. Fuel mixture too rich.
d. Worn or damaged piston rings.
e. Worn or damaged valve guide oil seals.
f. Excessive valve stem-to-guide clearance.
g. Incorrect carburetor float level.

Engine is Difficult to Start

a. Fouled spark plug(s).
b. Improperly adjusted enrichener valve.
c. Intake manifold air leak (**Figure 7**).
d. Plugged fuel tank filler cap or vent hose.
e. Clogged carburetor fuel line.
f. Contaminated fuel system.
g. Improperly adjusted carburetor.
h. Faulty ignition unit.
i. Faulty ignition coil.
j. Damaged ignition coil wires.
k. Incorrect ignition timing.
l. Low engine compression.
m. Engine oil too heavy (winter temperatures).
n. Discharged battery.

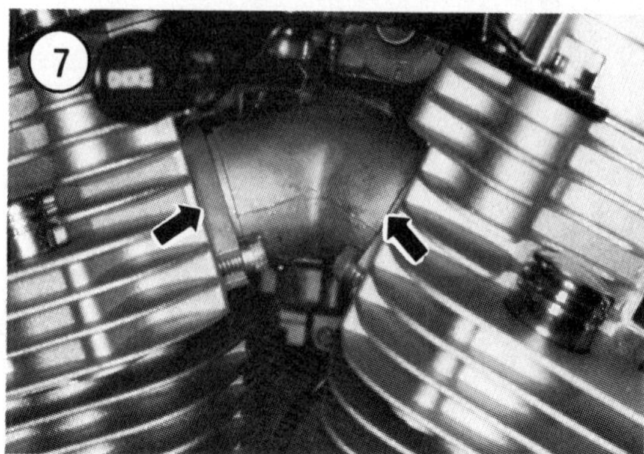

o. Faulty starter motor.
p. Loose or corroded starter and/or battery cables.
q. Loose wire or connector between the ignition sensor and module.
r. Air filter backplate EVAP butterfly valve stuck closed or damaged.

Engine Runs but Misses

a. Fouled or improperly gapped spark plugs.
b. Damaged spark plug cables.
c. Incorrect ignition timing.
d. Faulty ignition components.
e. Obstructed fuel line or fuel shutoff valve.
f. Obstructed fuel filter.
g. Clogged carburetor jets.
h. Battery nearly discharged.
i. Loose battery connection.
j. Short circuit due to damaged wiring or insulation.
k. Water in fuel.
l. Weak or damaged valve springs.
m. Incorrect valve timing.
n. Damaged valve(s).
o. Dirty electrical connections.
p. Air filter backplate EVAP butterfly valve stuck closed or damaged.
q. Intake manifold or air filter air leak (**Figure 7**).

Engine Overheating

a. Incorrect carburetor adjustment or jet selection.
b. Ignition timing retarded. This could be due to improper adjustment or defective ignition component(s).
c. Improper spark plug heat range.
d. Damaged or blocked cooling fins.
e. Oil level low.
f. Oil not circulating properly.
g. Leaking valves.
h. Heavy engine carbon deposit.

Smoky Exhaust and Engine Runs Roughly

a. Clogged air filter element.
b. Carburetor adjustment incorrect—mixture too rich.
c. Enrichener not operating correctly.
d. Water or other contaminants in fuel.
e. Clogged fuel line.
f. Spark plugs fouled.
g. Ignition coil defective.
h. Ignition module or sensor defective.
i. Loose or defective ignition circuit wire.
j. Short circuit from damaged wire insulation.
k. Loose battery cable connection.
l. Incorrect cam timing.
m. Intake manifold or air filter air leak (**Figure 7**).

Engine Loses Power

a. Carburetor incorrectly adjusted.
b. Engine overheating.
c. Ignition timing incorrect due to faulty ignition component(s).
d. Incorrectly gapped spark plugs.
e. Obstructed muffler.
f. Dragging brake(s).

Engine Lacks Acceleration

a. Carburetor mixture too lean.
b. Clogged fuel line.
c. Ignition timing incorrect due to faulty ignition component(s).
d. Dragging brake(s).

Valve Train Noise

a. Bent pushrod(s).
b. Faulty hydraulic lifter(s).
c. Bent valve.
d. Rocker arm seizure or damage (binding on shaft).
e. Worn or damaged cam gear bushing(s).
f. Worn or damaged cam gear(s).

ELECTRIC STARTING SYSTEM

The starting system consists of the battery, starter motor, starter relay, solenoid, start switch, starter mechanism and related wiring.

When the ignition switch is turned on and the start button pushed in, current is transmitted from the battery to the starter relay. When the relay is activated, it in turn activates the starter solenoid which mechanically engages the starter with the engine.

Starting system problems are relatively easy to find. In most cases, the trouble is a loose or corroded electrical connection.

Troubleshooting Preparation

Before troubleshooting the starting system, make sure that:

a. The battery is fully charged.
b. Battery cables are of the proper size and length. Replace cables that are damaged, severely corroded or undersize.
c. All electrical connections are clean and tight.
d. The wiring harness is in good condition, with no worn or frayed insulation or loose harness sockets.
e. The fuel tank is filled with an adequate supply of fresh gasoline.
f. The spark plugs are in good condition and properly gapped.
g. The ignition system is correctly timed and adjusted.

Troubleshooting is intended only to isolate a malfunction to a certain component. If further bench testing is required, remove the suspect component and test it further.

Troubleshooting

The basic starter-related troubles are:

a. Engine cranks very slowly or not at all.
b. Starter spins but does not crank engine.
c. Starter will not disengage when start button is released.
d. Loud grinding noises when starter runs.

Perform the steps listed under *Troubleshooting Preparation*. When making the following voltage checks, test results must be within 1/2 volt of battery voltage.

CAUTION

Never attempt to operate the starter by pushing the starter button for more than 5 seconds at a time. If the engine fails to start, wait a minimum of 10 seconds to allow the starter to cool. The starter can be damaged by failing to observe this caution.

Engine cranks very slowly or not at all

1. If the starter does not work, check the intensity of the headlight with the ignition switch turned on. If the headlight dims or does not come on at all, the battery or connecting wires are most likely at fault. Check the battery with a hydrometer as described in Chapter Eight. Check wiring for breaks, shorts and dirty connections. If the battery is okay, check the starter connections at the battery, solenoid and start

switch. Check continuity between the battery and ignition switch with an ohmmeter.

2. If the headlight is bright but dims or goes out when the start button is pressed, check for a corroded or loose connection at the battery. Wiggle the battery terminals and recheck. If the starter turns over, you've found the problem. Clean and/or replace corroded or damaged cables as required.

3. If the headlight remains bright or dims only slightly when cranking, the trouble may be in the starter, solenoid or wiring. Check the start switch, engine stop switch, starter relay and the solenoid. Check each switch by bypassing it with a jumper wire. If the starter spins, check the solenoid and wiring to the ignition switch.

4. If the headlight dims severely when the start button is pressed, the battery is nearly dead or the starter is shorted to ground.

Starter spins but does not crank engine

1. Remove the primary cover as described in Chapter Five.

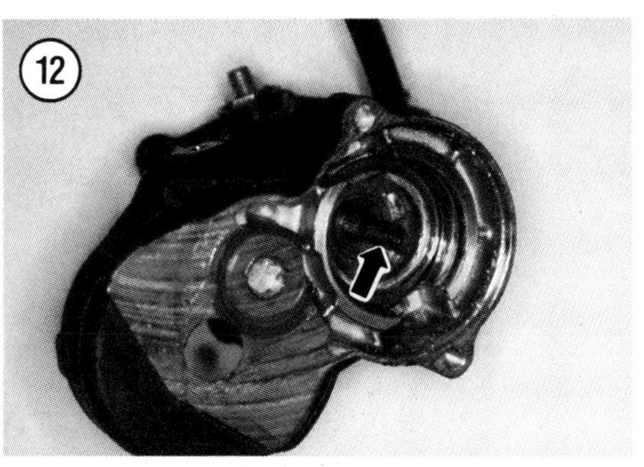

2. Check the starter pinion gear (A, **Figure 8**). If the teeth are chipped or worn, inspect the clutch flywheel ring gear (B, **Figure 8**) for the same problems.

3. If the pinion gear and flywheel ring gear are in good condition, disassemble the starter and check the armature shaft (**Figure 9**) for corrosion or damage. See Chapter Eight.

4. If there is no corrosion, suspect a damaged overrunning clutch assembly (**Figure 10**):

   a. The idler gear rollers (**Figure 11**) and/or compression spring (**Figure 12**) are damaged.

   b. The overrunning clutch (**Figure 10**), idler gear (**Figure 11**) and solenoid gear teeth are damaged.

   c. Pinion gear shaft does not slide smoothly during engagement.

   d. The overrunning clutch assembly fails to operate after the engine has started.

Starter will not disengage when start button is released

1. A sticking solenoid can cause this problem, which may be due to a worn solenoid compression spring or other internal damage. If the solenoid is damaged, it must be replaced as a unit.

2. On high-mileage models, the pinion gear (A, **Figure 8**) can jam on a worn clutch ring gear (B, **Figure 8**). Unable to return, the starter will continue to run. This condition usually requires ring gear replacement.

3. Check the start switch and starter relay for internal damage. Test the start switch as described in Chapter Eight. Test the starter relay as described in this chapter.

NOTE

The starter relay is mounted underneath the seat.

Loud grinding noises when starter runs

This can be caused by improper meshing of the starter pinion and clutch ring gear (A and B, **Figure 8**) or by a broken overrunning clutch mechanism (**Figure 10**). Remove and inspect the starter as described in Chapter Eight.

Component Testing

This section describes testing of individual starting system components. Refer to Chapter Eight for starter service.

Starter Relay Testing

You can check starter relay operation with an ohmmeter, jumper wires and a fully charged 12-volt battery.

The starter relay is mounted underneath the seat. See **Figure 13A** (1991-1993) or **Figure 13B** (1994).

1. Disconnect and remove the starter relay from the starting circuit on the bike.
2. Connect an ohmmeter and 12-volt battery between the relay terminals as shown in **Figure 14**. This setup will energize the relay for testing.
3. Check for continuity through the relay contacts with the ohmmeter while the relay coil is energized. The ohmmeter should read 0 ohms (continuity). If there is no continuity, replace the starter relay.

Starter Current Draw Test

This test will determine whether current is flowing in the starter circuit, and whether the current flow is excessive because of a short in the circuit or from a mechanical problem in the starter drive mechanism. An induction ammeter will be required for this

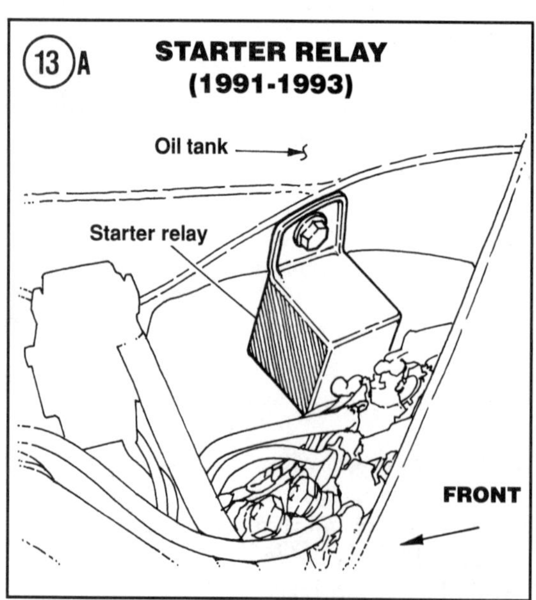

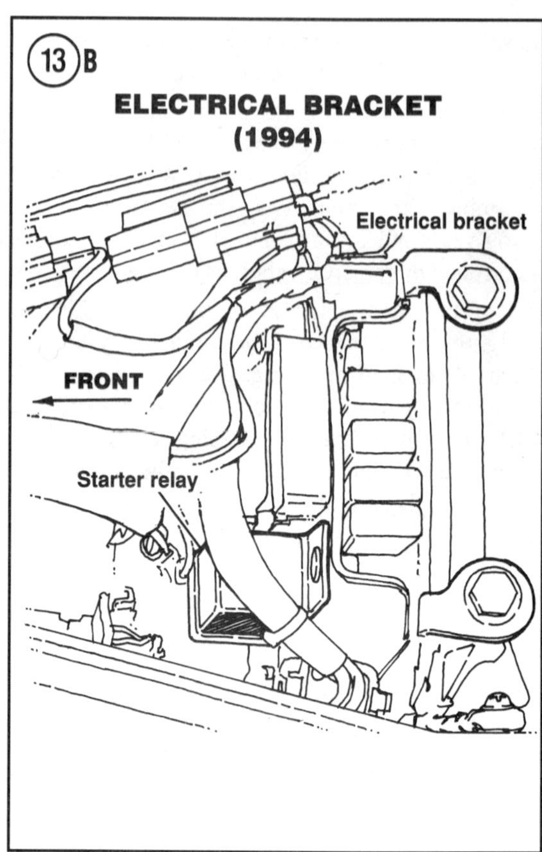

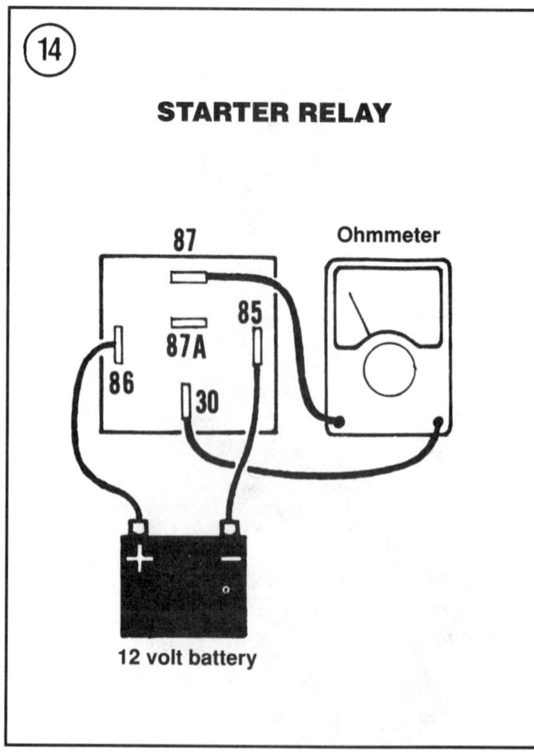

test. Current draw specifications are listed in **Table 1**.

NOTE
The battery should be fully charged when performing the following test.

1. Shift the transmission into NEUTRAL.

2. Disconnect the 2 spark plug caps at the spark plugs. Then ground the plug caps with 2 extra spark plugs. Do not remove the spark plugs in the cylinder heads.

3. Connect a jumper cable to the battery terminal and then to the ammeter lead. Connect a second jumper cable to the short heavy solenoid stud, then connect the cable to the ammeter. See **Figure 15**.

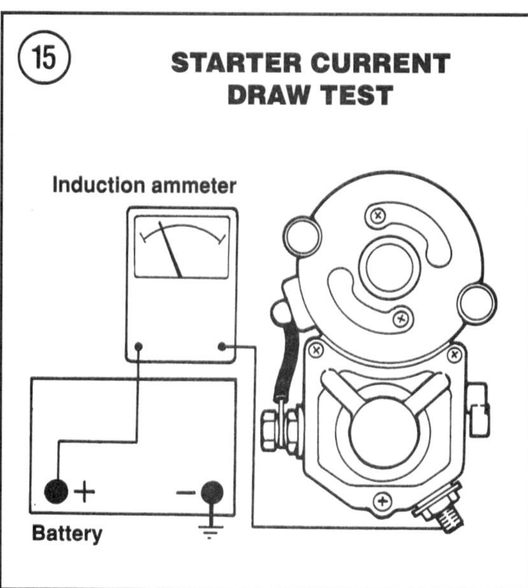

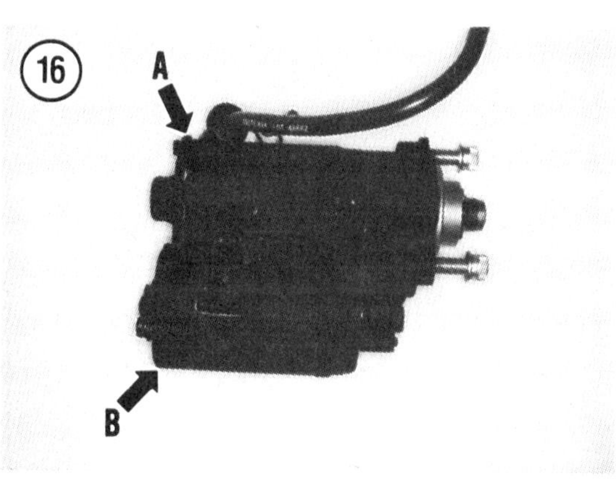

4. Turn the ignition switch ON and press the start button for approximately 10 seconds. Note the ammeter reading.

NOTE
Initially, the current draw will be very high when the start button is first pressed, then it will drop and hold at a lower level. This second level or reading is the one you should refer to during this test.

5. If the current draw exceeds the specified current draw rating listed in **Table 1**, suspect a faulty starter or starter drive mechanism. Remove and service these components as described in Chapter Eight.

6. Disconnect the ammeter and the 2 jumper cables.

Solenoid Testing (Bench Tests)

A fully charged 12-volt battery and 3 jumper wires will be required for the following tests.

1. Remove the starter motor (A, **Figure 16**) as described in Chapter Eight. The solenoid (B, **Figure 16**) must be installed on the starter motor during the following tests. Do not remove it.

2. Disconnect the "C" field wire terminal at the starter motor (**Figure 17**) before performing the following tests.

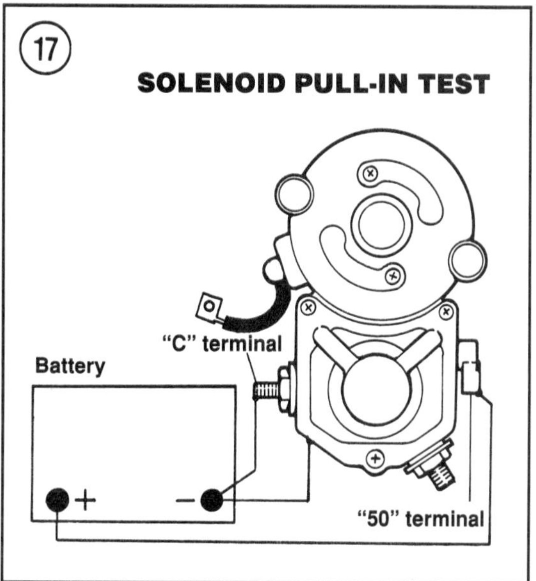

CAUTION

Because battery voltage will be applied directly to the solenoid and starter in the following tests, do not leave the jumper cables connected to the solenoid for more than 3-5 seconds. Failure to observe this caution can cause solenoid damage. Read the following procedure through to acquaint yourself with the procedures and test connections, then make the tests in order and without interruption.

3. Make the following tests in order:
   a. Using 3 jumper wires, connect a battery to the starter motor as shown in **Figure 17**. The pinion shaft should *pull* into the housing.
   b. Disconnect the "C" terminal jumper wire at the negative battery terminal and connect it to the positive battery terminal; see **Figure 18**. The pinion shaft should *remain* in the housing.
   c. Disconnect the jumper wire at the "50" starter terminal (**Figure 19**); the pinion shaft should *return* to its original position. Disconnect all of the jumper wires from the solenoid and battery.
4. Replace the solenoid if the starter shaft failed to operate properly as described in Step 3. See *Solenoid Replacement* in Chapter Eight.

CHARGING SYSTEM

The charging system consists of the battery, alternator and a solid state rectifier/voltage regulator.

The alternator generates an alternating current (AC) which the rectifier converts to direct current (DC). The regulator maintains the voltage to the battery and load (lights, ignition, etc.) at a constant voltage regardless of variations in engine speed and load.

A malfunction in the charging system generally causes the battery to remain undercharged.

Service Precautions

Before servicing the charging system, observe the following precautions to prevent damage to any charging system component.

1. Never reverse battery connections. Instantaneous damage may occur.
2. Do not short across any connection.
3. Never attempt to polarize an alternator.
4. Never start the engine with the alternator disconnected from the voltage regulator/rectifier, unless instructed to do so in testing.
5. Never start or run the engine with the battery disconnected.
6. Never attempt to use a high-output battery charger to assist in engine starting.
7. Before charging battery, disconnect the negative battery lead.
8. Never disconnect the voltage regulator/rectifier connector with the engine running. The voltage regulator/rectifier is mounted on the front frame down tubes (**Figure 20**).

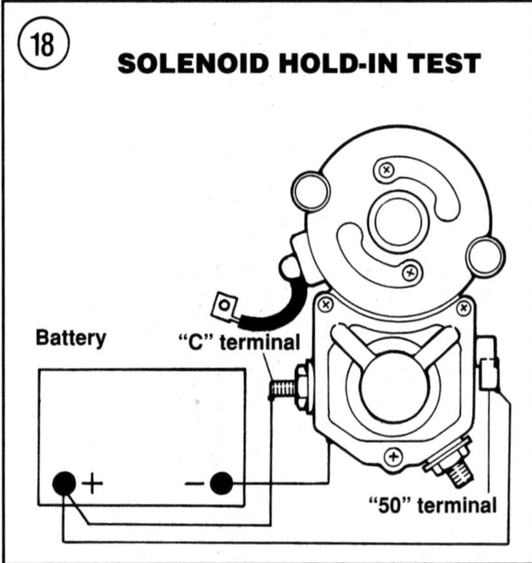

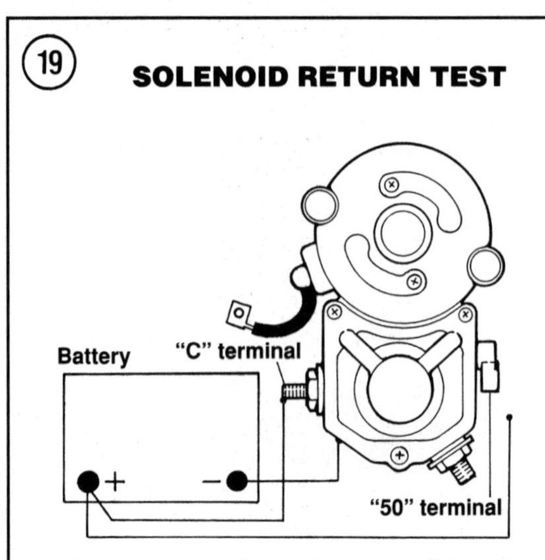

9. Do not mount the voltage regulator/rectifier unit at another location.
10. Make sure the battery negative terminal is connected to both engine and frame.

Testing

Whenever the charging system is suspected of trouble, make sure the battery is fully charged before going any further. Clean and test the battery as described in Chapter Eight. If the battery is in good condition, test the charging system as follows.

If your battery runs down when riding the motorcycle, perform the *Current Draw Test*. If the battery runs down when the motorcycle is not being used, perform the *Voltage Regulator/Rectifier Test* in this chapter.

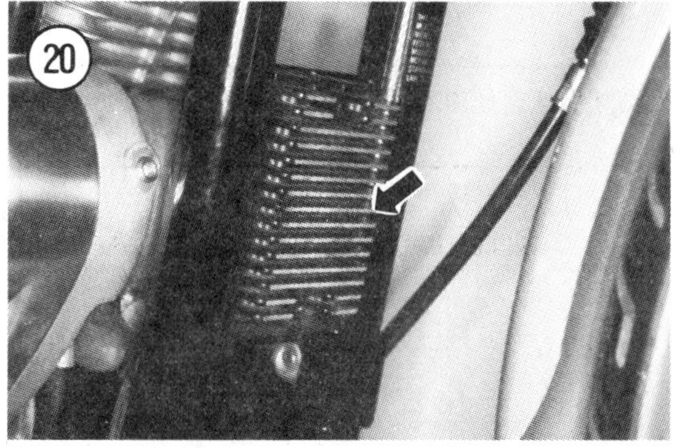

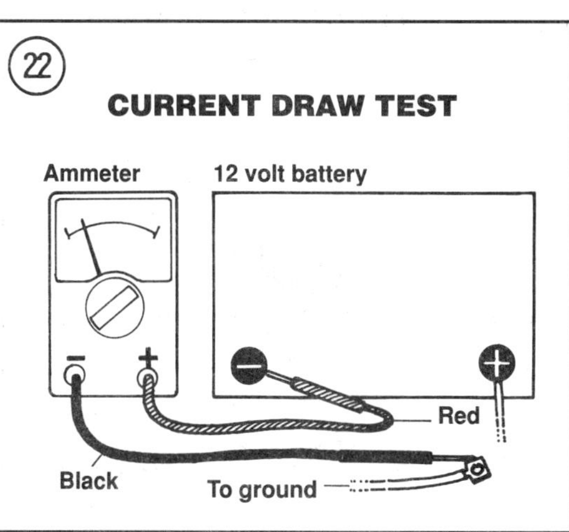

Current Draw Test

If the battery keeps going dead, especially when the bike is not being used, the problem may be caused by excessive current draw on the bike's electrical system.

The following is a 2-part test to measure the current draw on the electrical system. The first part (Step 2) measures current draw with the ignition switch turned off. Perform this test if the battery goes dead when the bike is not being used. The second part (Step 3) measures current draw with all of the bike's accessories turned on. Perform this test when you know the charging system is working correctly but the battery is still going dead.

An ammeter and induction load tester will be required for this test; see **Figure 21**, typical. If you do not have the proper test equipment, have the test performed by a Harley-Davidson dealer or an independent service shop familiar with Harley-Davidson service.

1. To perform the following tests, the battery must be fully charged. Use a hydrometer to check the specific gravity as described in Chapter Eight, and bring the battery up to full charge, if required.
2. Test 1: Perform the following:
   a. Turn the ignition switch off.
   b. Disconnect the negative battery terminal at the battery. Connect an ammeter between the negative battery terminal and the negative battery cable as shown in **Figure 22**.
   c. With the ignition switch OFF, read the amount of current indicated on the ammeter. It should be 3 milliamperes (mA) or less. While this is not a lot of current, a higher reading indicates an excessive current draw that can drain the battery.
3. Test 2: Perform the following:

NOTE
When using an induction load tester, read and follow the manufacturer's instructions. As a rule, you do not want to leave the load switch ON for more than 20 seconds at a time, or tester damage may occur from overheating.

a. Connect an induction load tester into your bike's electrical circuit following the manufacturer's instructions.
b. Turn the ignition switch on (but do not start the engine). Then turn on all electrical accessories and switch the headlight beam to HIGH.
c. Read the amp reading (current draw) on the induction load tester. The recorded current draw reading should be 18.50 amps or less.

4. Owner-installed accessories can increase the current draw and drain the battery. The combined current draw of both stock and aftermarket electrical components may be too much for the bike's charging system. You can check this by disconnecting all of the aftermarket equipment and repeating this test; if the current draw is now within specifications (Step 2 or Step 3), you have found the problem. However, if you have not added any electrical aftermarket accessories to your bike, the excessive current draw may be due to a short circuit.

NOTE
If the charging system on your bike is working correctly but your bike is experiencing excessive current draw from added-on electrical accessories, consider adding a power reducer to your bike's electrical system. Contact Kriss Mfg. & Machine Inc., P.O. Box 35331, Tucson, AZ, 85740.

Charging System Output Test

An induction load tester will be required for this test procedure.

1. To perform this test, the battery must be fully charged. Use a hydrometer to check the battery specific gravity as described in Chapter Eight, and bring the battery up to full charge, if required.

NOTE
When using an induction load tester, read and follow the manufacturer's instructions. As a rule, you do not want to leave the load switch ON for more than 20 seconds at a time, or tester damage may occur from overheating.

2. Connect the induction load tester negative and positive leads to the battery terminals. Then place the tester's load test induction pickup between the wire connecting the 30 amp circuit breaker to the voltage regulator. See **Figure 23**.

3. Start the engine and slowly bring its speed up to 2,000 rpm while reading the load tester scale. With

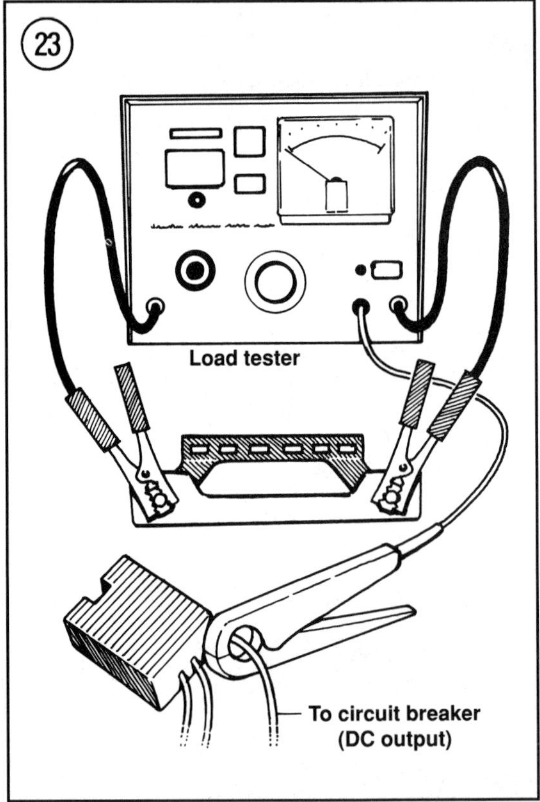

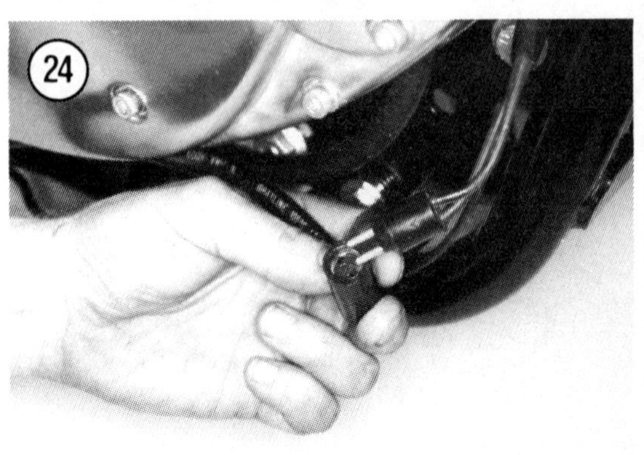

the engine idling at 2,000 rpm, operate the load tester switch until the voltage scale reads 13.0 volts. The tester should show an alternator current output reading of 19-23 amps.

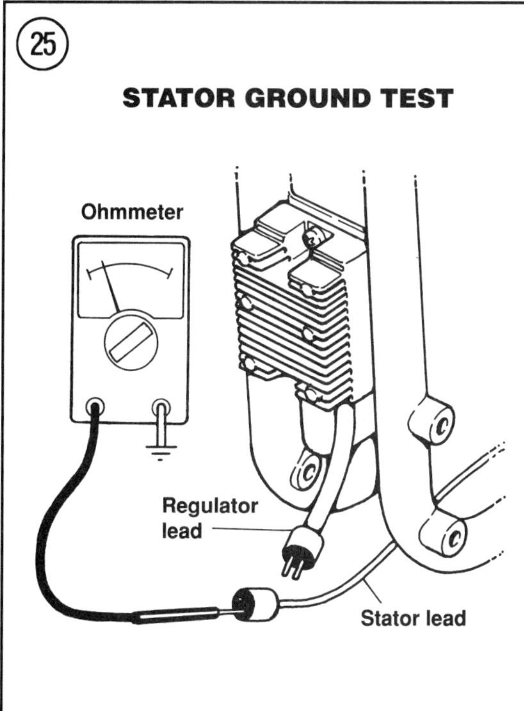

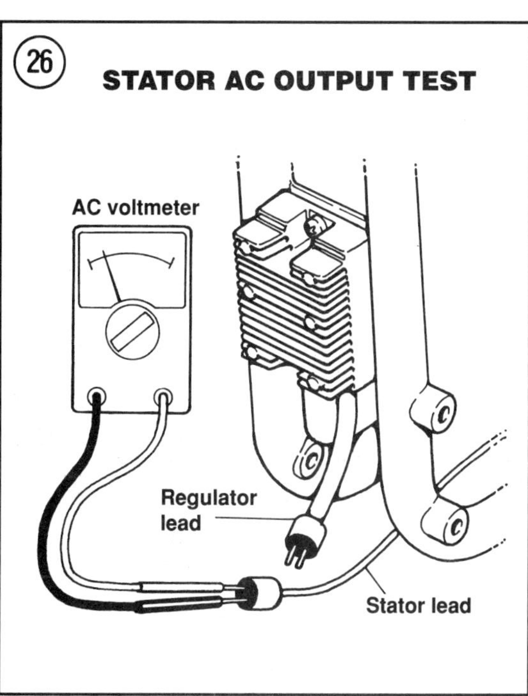

4. With the engine still running at 2,000 rpm, turn the load switch off and read the load tester voltage scale. Battery voltage must not exceed 15 volts. Turn the engine off and then disconnect the load tester from the bike.
5. An incorrect reading in Steps 3 and 4 indicates that:
   a. The voltage regulator/rectifier unit (**Figure 20**) is damaged.
   b. There is a short circuit in the bike's wiring system.

Stator Check

1. With the ignition turned off, disconnect the regulator/rectifier connector that is located below the crankcase (**Figure 24**).
2. Connect an ohmmeter between either stator socket and ground (**Figure 25**). Set the ohmmeter to the R × 1 scale. The ohmmeter should read infinity (no continuity). If the reading is incorrect, the stator is grounded and must be replaced. Repeat this test for the other stator socket.
3. Connect an ohmmeter between both stator sockets. Set the ohmmeter to the R × 1 scale. The ohmmeter should read 0.2-0.4 ohms. If no needle movement was noticed, or if the resistance is higher than specified, the stator must be replaced.
4. Check stator AC output as follows:
   a. Connect an AC voltmeter across the stator pins as shown in **Figure 26**.
   b. Start the engine and slowly increase idle speed. Voltmeter should show a reading of 19-26 volts AC per each 1,000 rpm.
   c. If the AC voltage output reading is below the prescribed range, the trouble is probably a faulty stator (**Figure 27**) or rotor. If these parts

are not damaged, check for a faulty regulator/rectifier (**Figure 20**).

NOTE
*When the above checks show a faulty stator, check the stator wires where they are held in place by the flat metal clamp plate shown in **Figure 28**. The clamp plate may have rubbed through the wire's insulation. This is a common source of stator plate damage.*

5. Reconnect the regulator/rectifier connector (**Figure 24**).

IGNITION SYSTEM

All Sportster models in this manual are equipped with a solid state transistorized ignition system. This system provides a longer life for the components and delivers a more efficient spark throughout the entire speed range of the engine than breaker point systems. See **Figure 29**.

Most problems involving failure to start, poor driveability or rough running are caused by trouble in the ignition system.

Note the following symptoms:

a. Engine misses.
b. Stumbles on acceleration (misfiring).
c. Loss of power at high speed (misfiring).
d. Hard starting or failure to start.
e. Rough idle.

Most of the symptoms can also be caused by a carburetor that is dirty, worn or improperly adjusted.

Precautions

Several precautions should be strictly observed to avoid damage to the ignition system.

1. Do not reverse the battery connections. This reverses polarity and can damage the ignition components.
2. When checking spark, or whenever the engine is cranked with the spark plugs removed from the cylinder heads, the spark plugs must be grounded to the engine (**Figure 30**).
3. Do not "spark" the battery terminals with the battery cable connections to check polarity.
4. Do not disconnect the battery cables with the engine running. A voltage surge will occur which will damage the ignition components and possibly burn out the lights. A spark may occur which can cause the battery to exploded and spray acid.
5. Do not operate the start switch if the ignition module (**Figure 31**) is not grounded to the frame. The black wire leading out of the ignition module wiring harness is the ground wire. Check the end of the wire for corrosion or damage.
6. Whenever working on any part of the ignition system, first turn the ignition switch OFF or disconnect the battery negative (–) lead (**Figure 32**). This is done to prevent damage to the ignition system components from an accidental short circuit.
7. Keep all connections between the various units clean and tight. Be sure that the wiring connections are pushed together firmly to help keep out moisture.
8. Make sure all ground wires are properly attached and free of oil and corrosion.

Troubleshooting Preparation

If you suspect a problem with the ignition system, perform the following procedures in order.

1. Check the wiring harness and all plug-in connections to make sure that all terminals are free of corrosion, all connectors are tight and the wiring insulation is in good condition.
2. Check all electrical components that are grounded to the engine for a good ground. For ground connections, see **Figure 29** and the wiring diagram at the end of this book for your model. These will include the ignition module, battery-to-frame and engine-to-frame ground wires and straps.
3. Make sure that all ground wires are properly connected and that the connections are clean and tight. Clean connectors with electrical contact cleaner.

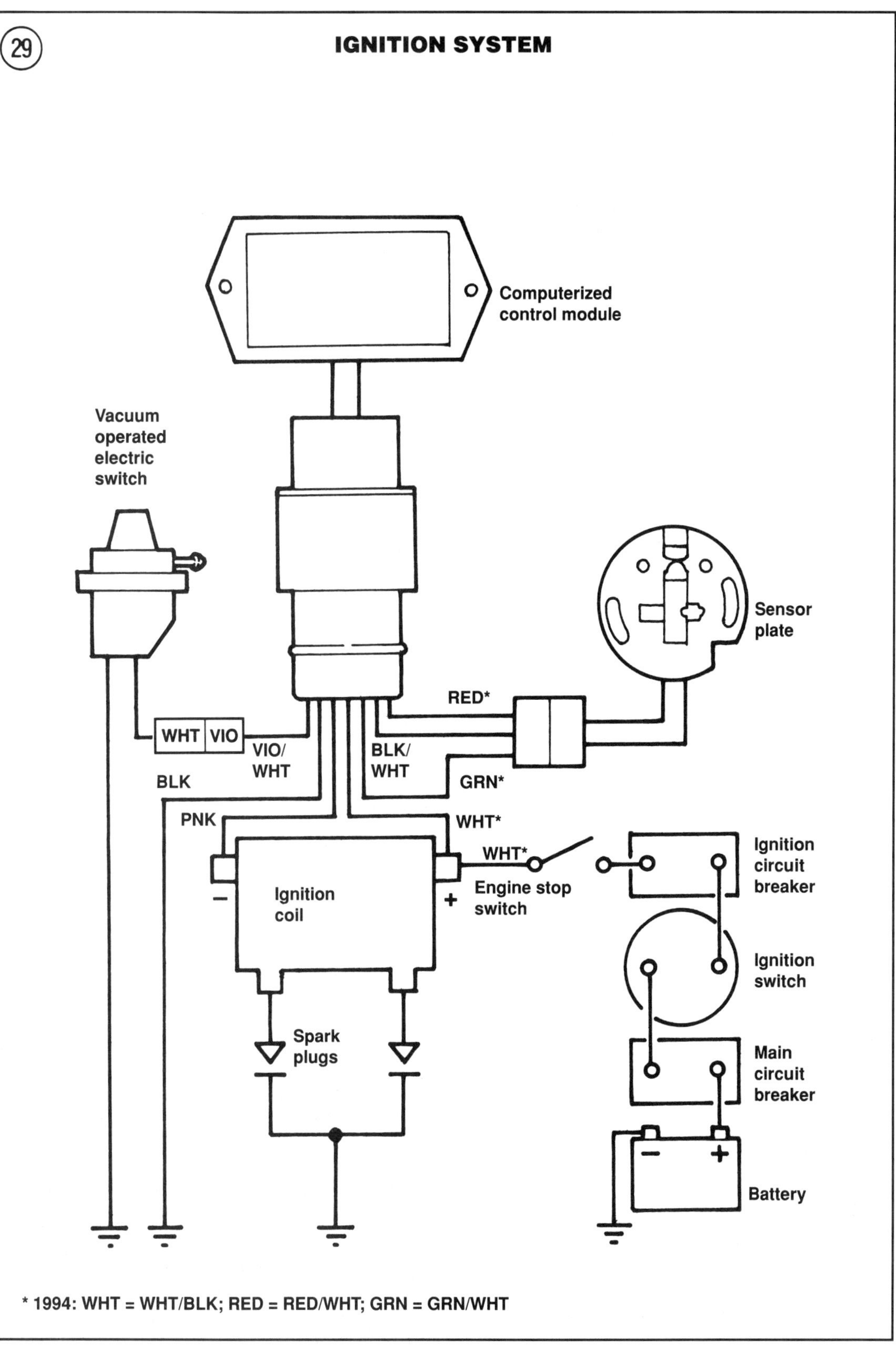
29
IGNITION SYSTEM
Computerized control module
Vacuum operated electric switch
Sensor plate
RED*
WHT
VIO
VIO/ WHT
BLK/ WHT
GRN*
BLK
PNK
WHT*
WHT*
Ignition circuit breaker
Engine stop switch
Ignition coil
Ignition switch
Spark plugs
Main circuit breaker
Battery
* 1994: WHT = WHT/BLK; RED = RED/WHT; GRN = GRN/WHT

4. Check remainder of the wiring for disconnected wires and short or open circuits.
5. Check the ignition circuit breaker to make sure it is not defective.

NOTE
The ignition circuit breaker is mounted underneath the seat.

6. Make sure the fuel tank has an adequate supply of fuel and that the fuel is reaching the carburetors.
7. The battery must be fully charged. Use a hydrometer to check the specific gravity as described in Chapter Eight, and bring the battery up to full charge, if required.
8. Check spark plug cable routing. Make sure the cables are properly connected to their respective spark plugs. If cable routing is correct, perform the *Engine Fails to Start (Spark Test)* in this chapter. If there is no spark or only a weak one, recheck with a new spark plug(s). If the condition remains the same with new spark plugs and if all external wiring connections are good, the problem is most likely in the ignition system; perform the following tests. If a spark is obtained, the problem is not in the ignition or coil. Check the fuel system.

Ignition Test (No Spark at Spark Plug)

Refer to **Figure 29** when performing these procedures.

1. To perform this test, the battery must be fully charged (11-13 volts DC). Use a hydrometer to check the specific gravity as described in Chapter Eight, and bring the battery up to full charge, if required.
2. Check that the black ignition module ground lead is fastened securely. Check also that the battery ground lead is fastened and in good condition.

NOTE
*When performing the following test procedures, it will be necessary to fabricate a test jumper from 2 lengths of 16 ga. wire, 3 clips and a 0.33 MFD capacitor; see **Figure 33**. The test jumper should be long enough to reach from the ignition coil to a good engine ground.*

NOTE
A voltmeter is required to perform the following tests.

3. Perform the following:
   a. On 1991-1993 models, connect the red voltmeter lead to the white ignition coil wire terminal

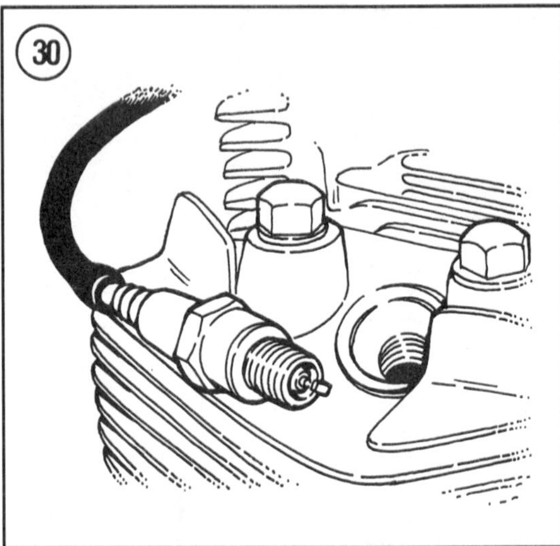

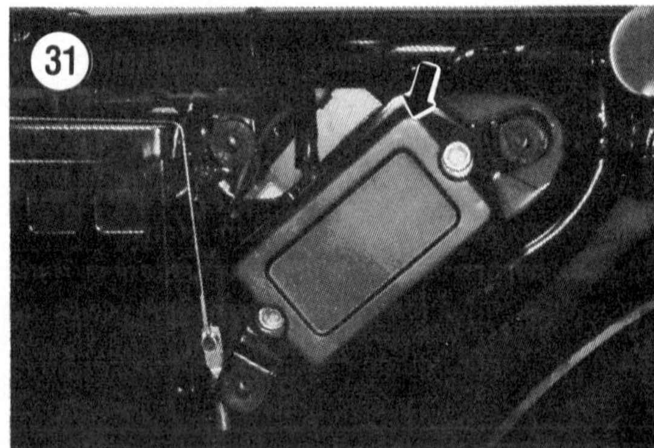

and the black voltmeter lead to ground (**Figure 34**). On 1994 models, connect the red voltmeter lead to the white/black ignition coil wire terminal and the black voltmeter lead to ground (**Figure 34**).

b. Turn the ignition switch ON. The voltmeter should read 11-13 volts. Turn the ignition switch OFF. Note the following.

c. Voltage correct: Proceed to Step 4.

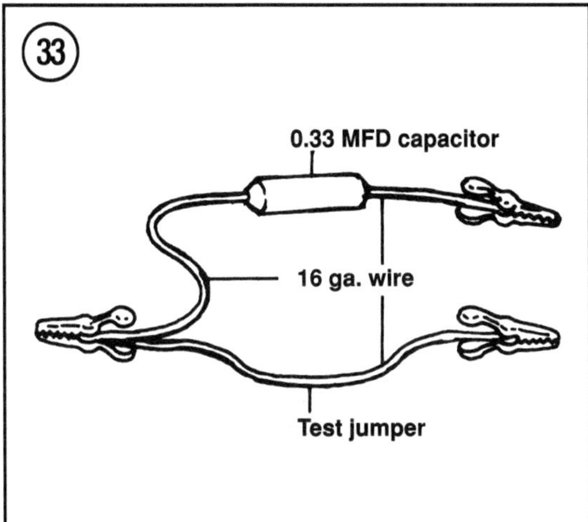

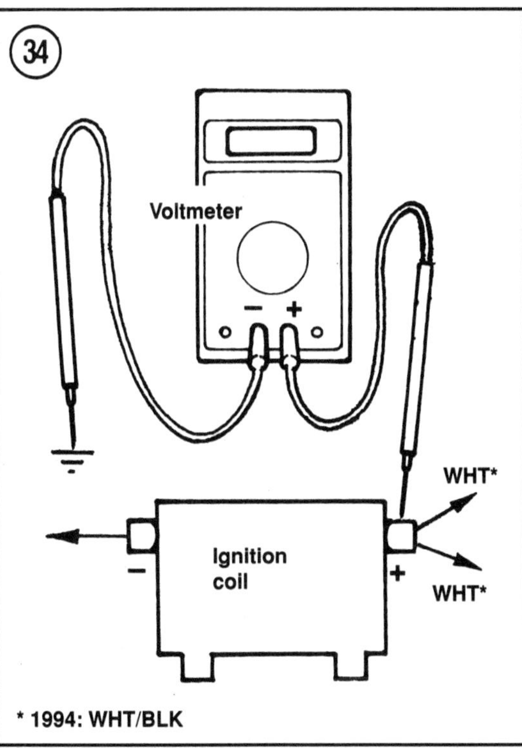

d. Voltage incorrect: Check the main and ignition circuit breakers; refer to Chapter Eight. Also check for loose or damaged ignition system wiring.

4. Perform the following:
   a. Disconnect the pink wire from the ignition coil terminal (**Figure 35**).
   b. Turn the ignition switch ON.
   c. Connect the black voltmeter lead to ground. On 1991-1993 models, connect the red voltmeter lead to the white and pink ignition coil terminals separately (**Figure 35**). On 1994 models, connect the red voltmeter lead to the white/black and pink ignition coil terminals separately (**Figure 35**). The voltmeter should read 12 volts at both terminals. Turn the ignition switch OFF. Note the following.
   d. Voltage correct: Proceed to Step 5.
   e. Voltage incorrect: Check the ignition coil resistance as described in this chapter. If the resistance is within the prescribed range, proceed to Step 5.
5. Perform the following:

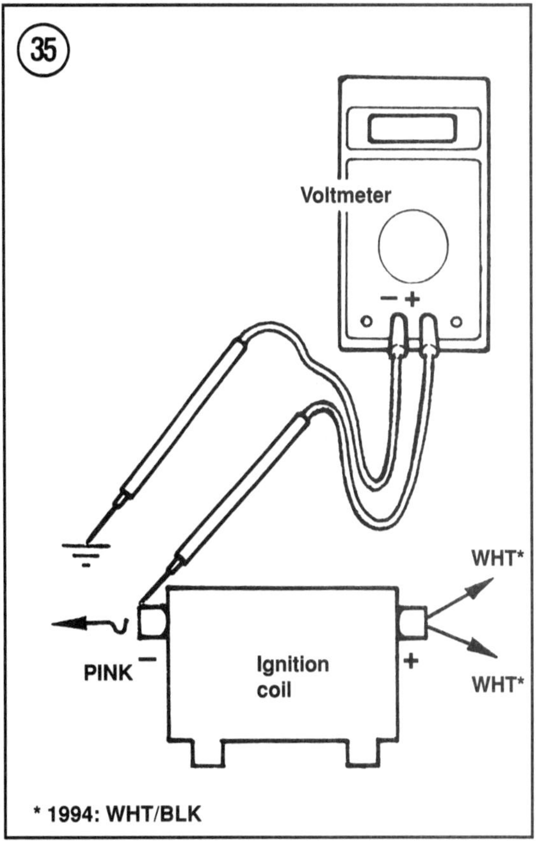

2

a. Disconnect the pink wire from the ignition coil terminal (**Figure 36**) if you have not already done so.
b. Remove one of the spark plugs. Then connect the spark plug wire and connector to the spark plug and touch the spark plug base to a good ground like the engine cylinder head (**Figure 37**). Position the spark plug so you can see the electrodes.
c. Turn the ignition switch ON.
d. Connect the jumper wire (without the capacitor) between a good engine ground and the ignition coil pink terminal as shown in **Figure 36**. Then momentarily touch the jumper wire with the capacitor to the ignition coil pink terminal (**Figure 36**) while observing the spark plug firing tip. The spark plug should spark. Turn the ignition switch OFF and remove the jumper wire assembly. Note the following.
e. Spark: Proceed to Step 6.
f. No spark: Replace the ignition coil.
g. Do not reinstall the spark plug at this time.

6. Perform the following:
a. Reconnect the ignition coil pink wire to its terminal on the ignition coil.
b. Turn the ignition switch ON.
c. Disconnect the sensor plate electrical connector (**Figure 40**).
d. On 1991-1993 models, connect the red voltmeter lead to the ignition module red wire socket and the black voltmeter lead to the ignition module black/white pin as shown in **Figure 38**. On 1994 models, connect the red voltmeter lead to the ignition module red/white wire socket and the black voltmeter lead to the ignition module black/white pin as shown in **Figure 38**. The voltmeter should read 12 ±0.5 volts. Disconnect the voltmeter and turn the ignition switch OFF. Note the following.
e. Voltage correct: Proceed to Step 7.
f. Voltage incorrect: Check the ignition module ground wire (**Figure 31**) and the module for dirty or loose-fitting terminals. If okay, proceed to Step 7.

7A. On 1991-1993 models, turn the ignition switch ON. Then momentarily ground a screwdriver across the ignition module green and black/white connector pins (**Figure 39**) while observing the spark plug firing tip. There should be a strong spark at the spark plug firing tip as the screwdriver is *removed*. Note the following:

a. Spark: Check the sensor resistance as described in this chapter.
b. No spark: Check the ignition module resistance as described in this chapter.

7B. On 1994 models, turn the ignition switch ON. Then momentarily ground a screwdriver across the ignition module green/white and black/white connector pins (**Figure 39**) while observing the spark plug firing tip. There should be strong spark at the

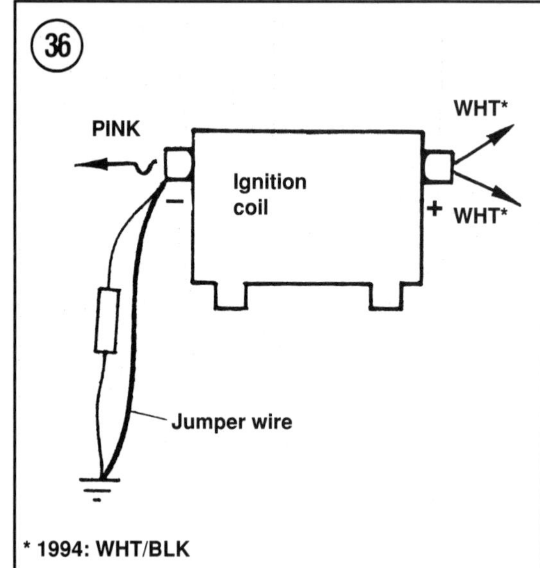

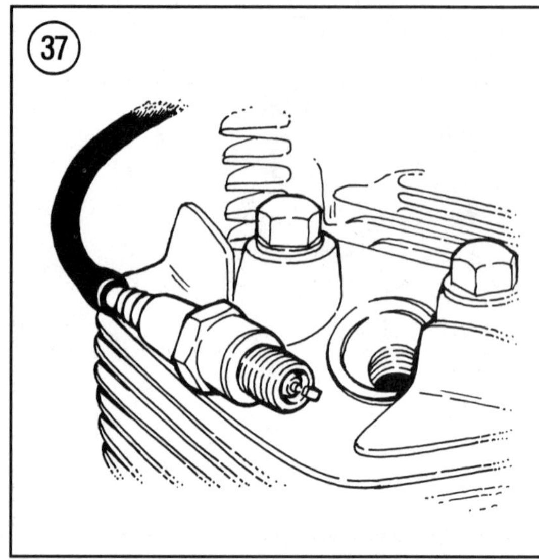

spark plug firing tip as the screwdriver is *removed*. Note the following:

a. Spark: Check the sensor resistance as described in this chapter.

b. No spark: Check the ignition module resistance as described in this chapter.

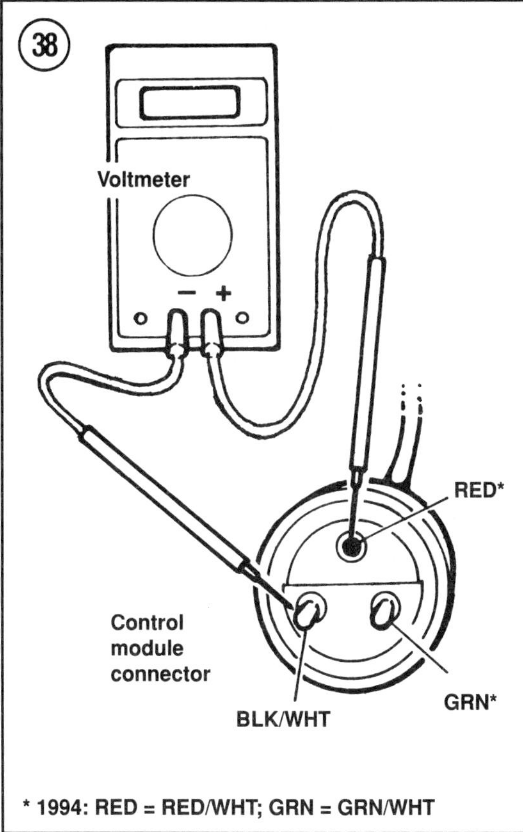

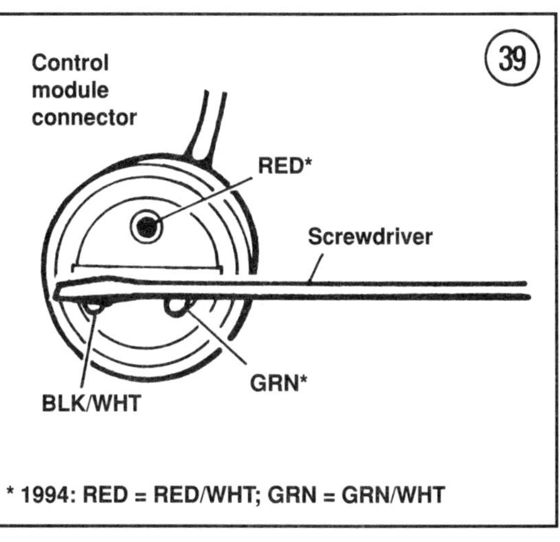

8. Install and reconnect all parts removed for this procedure. If there is still no spark, either retest or have a Harley-Davidson dealer test the ignition system.

Ignition Test (Intermittent Ignition Problems)

Intermittent problems are usually caused by temperature or vibration variances. Perform the following.

Temperature test

NOTE
Steps 1-4 must be performed with the engine cold.

1. Remove the outer timing cover, inner timing cover and gasket as described in Chapter Eight.
2. Start the engine.
3. Spray the sensor (**Figure 40**) with a Freon coolant (available at electronic supply stores). If the engine dies, replace the sensor as described in Chapter Eight.
4. Allow the engine to warm to normal operating temperature. Then apply heat to the sensor with a blow dryer. If the engine dies, replace the sensor as described in Chapter Eight.
5. Remove the left-hand side cover. With the engine running, apply heat to the ignition module (**Figure 31**) with a blow dryer or heat gun. If the engine dies, replace the module as described in Chapter Eight.
6. Install the inner timing cover, gasket and outer timing cover as described in Chapter Eight.

Vibration test

Read this procedure completely through before starting. Refer to **Figure 41**.

1. Check the battery connections (**Figure 32**). Retighten or repair as required.

2. On 1991-1993 models, check the module ground wire connection. If necessary, remove the ground wire at the frame and scrape all paint at the mounting point. Using a star washer, reinstall the ground wire.

3. Start the engine and retest. If there is still an intermittent problem, proceed to Step 4.

4. On 1991-1993 models, disconnect the white *ignition stop switch* wire terminal (**Figure 29**) at the ignition coil. On 1994 models, leave the white/black wire connected.

NOTE
*On 1991-1993 models, do not disconnect the white module wire at the ignition coil. See the wiring diagram at the end of this book and **Figure 41**.*

5A. On 1991-1993 models, connect a 16 ga. jumper wire from the positive battery terminal to the white ignition coil terminal.

5B. On 1994 models, connect a 16 ga. jumper wire from the positive battery terminal to the white/black wire ignition coil terminal.

WARNING
Steps 4 and 5 have by-passed the ignition stop switch. When performing Step 6, the engine can only be stopped by removing the jumper wire. Test by removing the jumper wire before riding the bike. It is suggested to test ride the bike on a paved surface in a secluded area away from all traffic. If you do not feel that you can perform this test safely, or if you do not have access to a safe riding area, refer testing to a Harley-Davidson dealer.

6. Test ride the bike. If the intermittent problem has stopped, there is a problem with the ignition kill switch. If the problem continues, vibration may have

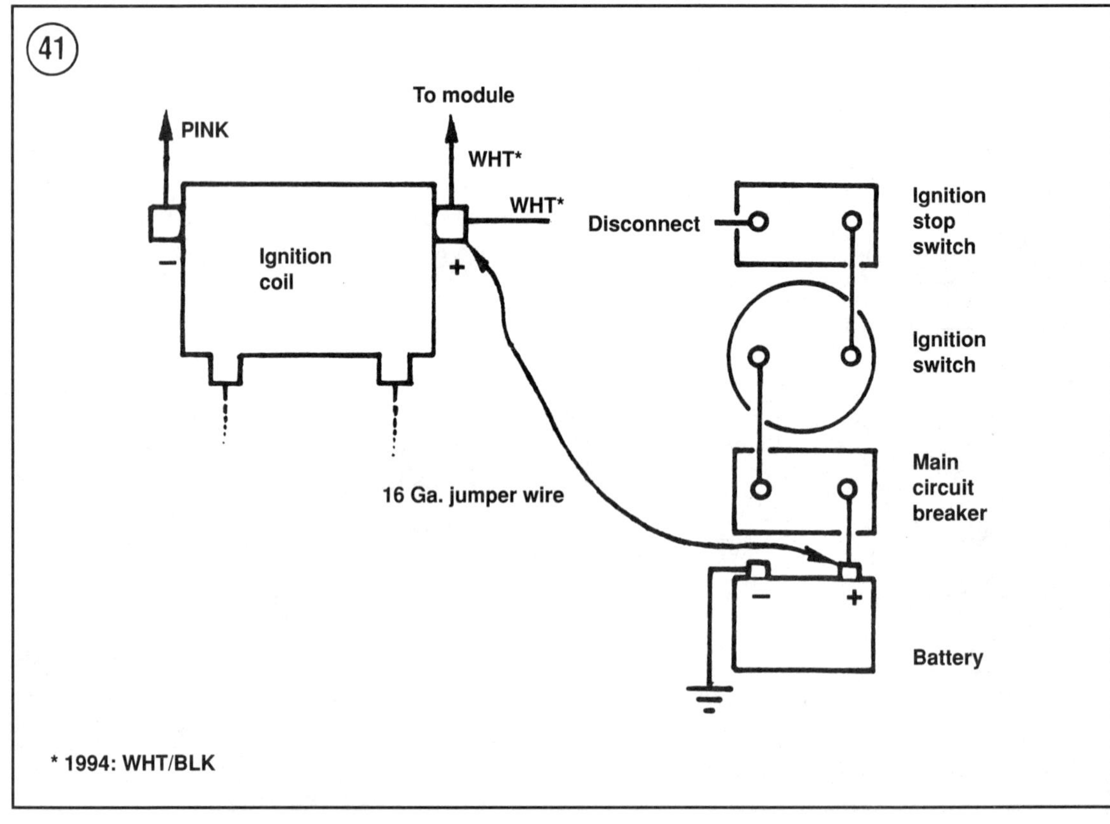

caused loose connections in the starter circuit safety switches.

7. Stop the bike and then shift it into NEUTRAL. Disconnect the jumper wire and reconnect the white wire (1991-1993) at the ignition coil terminal.

Ignition Coil Testing

If the coil condition is doubtful, there are several checks which can be made. Disconnect the coil secondary and primary wires before testing.

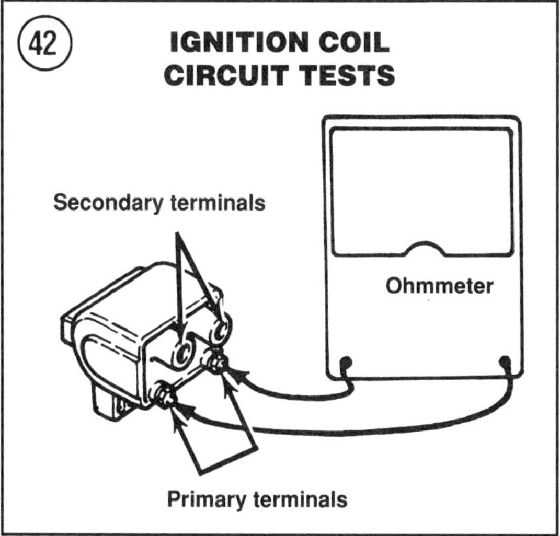

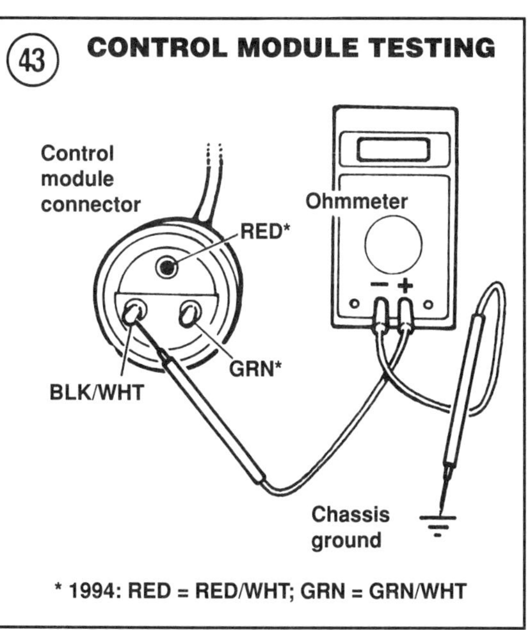

NOTE
When switching between ohmmeter scales in the following tests, always cross the test leads and zero the needle to assure a correct reading.

1. Set an ohmmeter on R × 1. Measure the coil primary resistance between both coil primary terminals (**Figure 42**). Compare reading to specification listed in **Table 2**.
2. Set the ohmmeter on R × 100. Measure the coil secondary resistance between both secondary terminals (**Figure 42**). Compare reading with **Table 2**.
3. Replace the ignition coil if it does not test within specifications in Step 1 or Step 2.

Ignition Module and Sensor Resistance Testing

The following tests should be performed with the Harley-Davidson KMT multimeter (part no. HD-35500). If any other meter is used, the results may be different than the specified values listed in these tests. If you do not have the Harley-Davidson KMT multimeter, it is suggested that you do not purchase replacement parts based upon your meter's test results, as electrical components normally cannot be returned.

NOTE
In the following tests, the red ohmmeter lead is always considered to be the positive lead and the black ohmmeter lead is the negative lead. Refer to the instructions provided with the KMT multimeter for proper operation.

Refer to **Figure 43** when performing this procedure.

1. Disconnect the battery negative terminal.
2. Disconnect the module (**Figure 31**) to sensor (**Figure 40**) connector.
3. Connect the red ohmmeter lead to the black/white module pin and the black ohmmeter lead to ground.
4. The correct resistance reading should be 0-1 ohm. If the reading exceeds 1 ohm, replace the module.
5. Reconnect the module to sensor connector.

Ignition Module Harness Resistance Test

1. Turn the ignition stop switch (**Figure 44**) to the OFF position.
2. Disconnect the 7-prong ignition module electrical connector (**Figure 45**).
3. Disconnect the sensor plate 3-prong electrical connector (**Figure 45**).

NOTE
When making the following resistance tests, cross the ohmmeter's test leads and zero the needle to assure a correct reading.

4. Set the ohmmeter to the R × 1 scale.
5. See **Figure 45**. On 1991-1993 models, connect the red ohmmeter lead to the No. 4 ignition module connector socket (on the wiring harness side, not on the module side). On 1994 models, connect the red ohmmeter lead to pin No. 7 (black wire) on the ignition module connector (on the wiring harness side, not on the module side). Connect the black ohmmeter lead to a good engine ground. Wiggle the wiring harness and read the resistance indicated on the ohmmeter. It should be 0-1 ohm. Note the following:
   a. If the resistance reading is correct, perform Step 6.
   b. If a high resistance reading is obtained, check for dirty or loose-fitting terminals or a bare or damaged wire; clean and repair as required.
6. Connect the red ohmmeter lead to the No. 1 ignition module connector socket (on the wiring harness side, not on the module side). Connect the black ohmmeter lead to a good engine ground. Wiggle the wiring harness and read the ohmmeter scale. It should be infinity (high resistance). Note the following:
   a. If the reading is infinity, perform Step 7.
   b. If the meter shows a resistance reading, the wire is shorting out to ground. Repair the wire and retest.
   c. On 1991-1993 models, repeat this test for the following ignition module connector sockets (**Figure 45**): No. 2, 3, 5, 6 and 7.
   d. On 1994 models, repeat this test for the following ignition module connector sockets (**Figure 45**): No. 2, 3, 4, 5 and 6.
7. Check each of the ignition module socket wires (except No. 4 on 1991-1993 or No. 7 on 1994) for continuity with an ohmmeter set on the R × 1 scale. The reading for each wire should be 0-1 ohm. An infinite reading indicates that there is an open in the wire; check for a dirty, loose-fitting or a damaged connector or wire.

FUEL SYSTEM

The fuel system consists of the fuel tank, fuel valve, fuel line and carburetor. The throttle and enrichener cables and the throttle grip should also be included in the operation of the fuel system.

During engine operation, fuel will flow from the fuel tank, through the fuel valve and into the carburetor where it is mixed with air before entering the engine. If fuel flow is entering the carburetor incorrectly (too much or too little), the engine will not run properly.

Many owners automatically assume that the carburetor is at fault when the engine does not run properly. While fuel system problems are not uncommon, carburetor adjustment is seldom the answer. In many cases, adjusting the carburetor only compounds the problem by making the engine run worse.

Fuel system troubleshooting should start at the fuel tank and work through the system, reserving the carburetor as the final point. Most fuel system problems result from an empty fuel tank, sour fuel, a dirty air filter or clogged carburetor jets.

Identifying Carburetor Conditions

The following list can be used as a guide when distinguishing between rich and lean carburetor conditions.

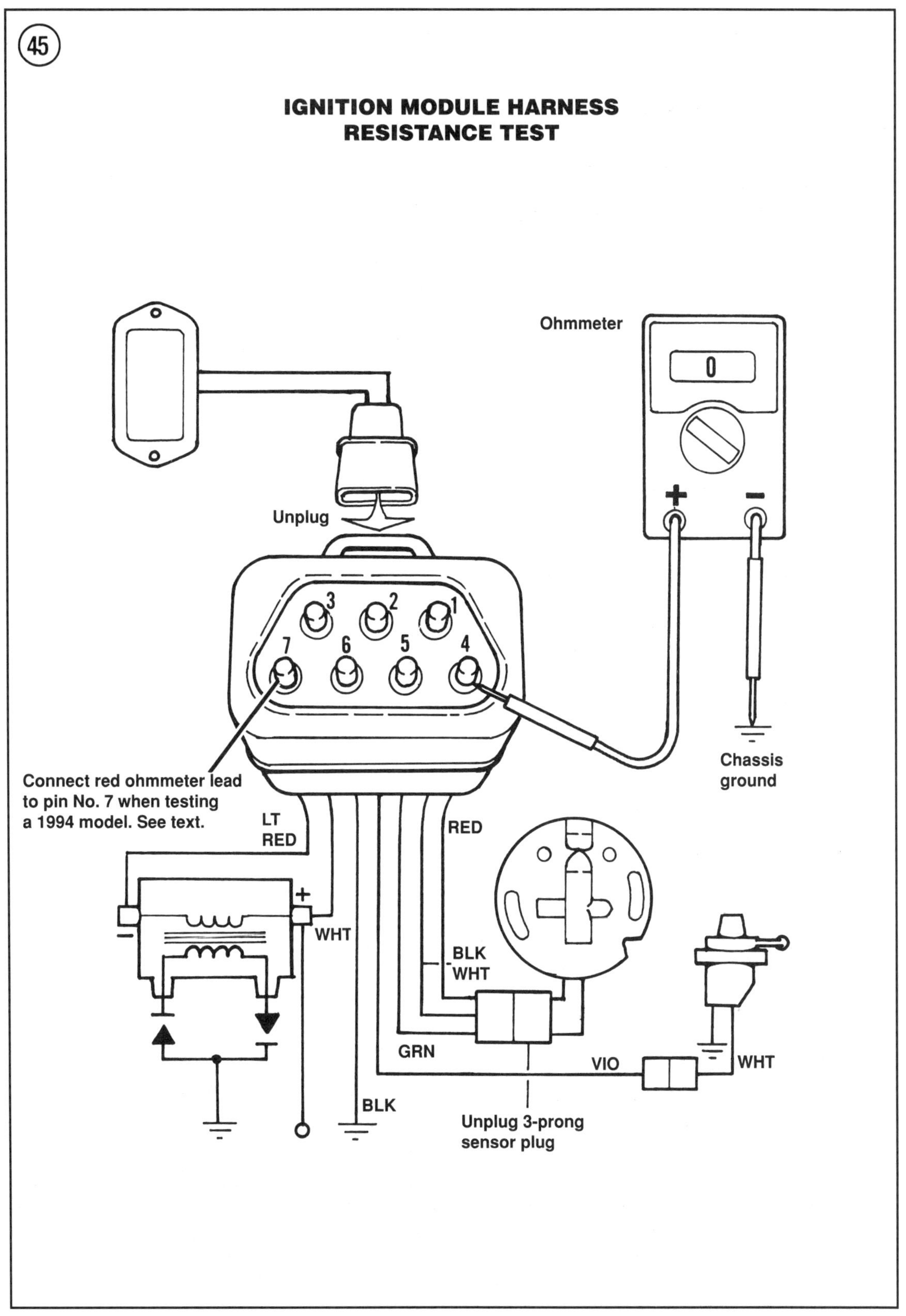
45
IGNITION MODULE HARNESS
RESISTANCE TEST
Ohmmeter
0
+
−
Unplug
3
2
1
7
6
5
4
Chassis
ground
Connect red ohmmeter lead
to pin No. 7 when testing
a 1994 model. See text.
LT
RED
RED
+
−
WHT
BLK
WHT
GRN
VIO
WHT
BLK
Unplug 3-prong
sensor plug

When the engine is running rich, one or more of the following conditions may be present:

a. The spark plug(s) will foul.
b. The engine will miss and run rough when it is running under a load.
c. As the throttle is increased, the exhaust smoke becomes more excessive.
d. With the throttle open, the exhaust will sound choked or dull. Bringing the motorcycle to a dead stop and trying to clear the exhaust with the throttle held wide open does not clear up the sound.

When the engine is running lean, one or more of the following conditions may be present:

a. The spark plug firing end will become very white or blistered in appearance.
b. The engine overheats.
c. Acceleration is slower.
d. Flat spots are felt during operation that feel much like the engine is trying to run out of gas.
e. Engine power is reduced.
f. At full throttle, engine rpm will not be steady.

Troubleshooting

Fuel system problems should be isolated to the fuel tank, fuel valve and filter, fuel hoses, external fuel filter (if used) or carburetor. The following procedures assume that the ignition system is working properly and is correctly adjusted.

Fuel delivery system

As a first step, check the fuel flow. Remove the fuel tank cap and look into each tank. If there is fuel present, disconnect the battery ground cable as a safety precaution. Then check that the fuel valve is turned OFF (**Figure 46**). Disconnect the fuel hose at the carburetor and put the hose into a container to catch any discharged fuel.

NOTE
Make sure there is a sufficient supply of fuel in each tank to allow the fuel valve to work in its normal operating position.

WARNING
Make sure there are no open flames in the area when performing the following.

The fuel valve controls fuel flow from the fuel tank to the carburetor. The fuel valve on all models is a 3-position valve (**Figure 46**). Because a gravity-feed type fuel delivery system is used, fuel should always be present at the fuel valve. Turn the fuel valve so that the end of the handle faces down (valve is in normal operating position). Fuel should flow into the container. Turn the fuel valve so that the end of the handle faces up (valve is in RESERVE). Fuel should flow into the container. If there is no fuel from the hose:

a. The fuel valve may be shut off or blocked by rust or foreign matter. If fuel flows in the RE-

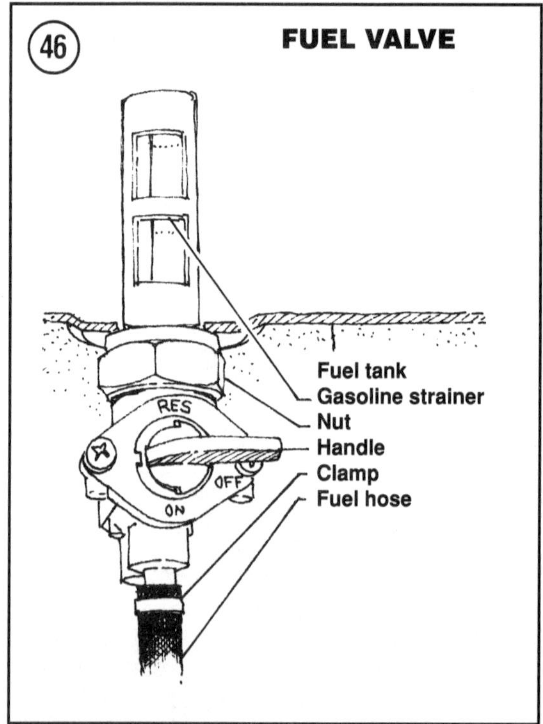

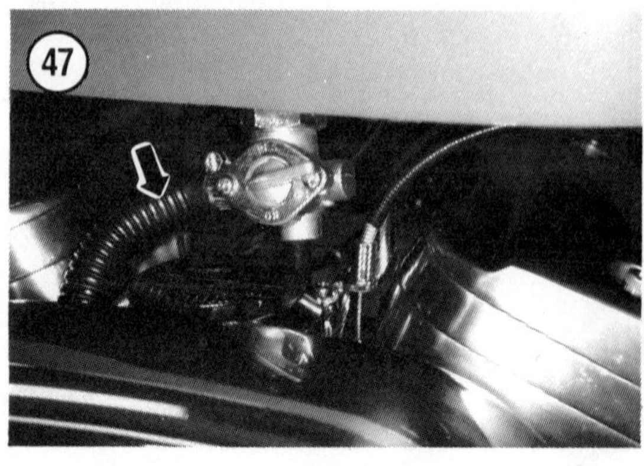

SERVE but not in the ON position, the fuel level in the tank may be too low. If the fuel level is high enough to flow in the ON position, the ON side of the valve is clogged. This would also hold true if the RESERVE side failed to work properly.

b. The fuel hose may be stopped up or kinked. Remove the fuel hose and then clear the hose with compressed air. If the hose is plugged, replace it.

WARNING

*When reconnecting the fuel hose, make sure the hose is inserted through the nylon hose insulator (**Figure 47**). Do not operate the engine without the insulator properly installed.*

c. The fuel tank is not properly vented. Check by opening the fuel tank cap. If fuel flows with the cap open, check for a plugged vent. On other models, check for a plugged fuel tank vent hose.

If a good fuel flow is present, fuel is reaching the carburetor. Examine the fuel in the container for rust or dirt that could clog or restrict the fuel valve filter and the carburetor jets. If there is evidence of contamination, it will be necessary to clean and flush the fuel tank, fuel valve assembly, hoses and carburetor. Refer to Chapter Seven for fuel system service.

If you are getting a good fuel flow from the fuel tank to the carburetor and the fuel is not contaminated with dirt or rust, refer to the troubleshooting chart in **Figure 48** for additional information.

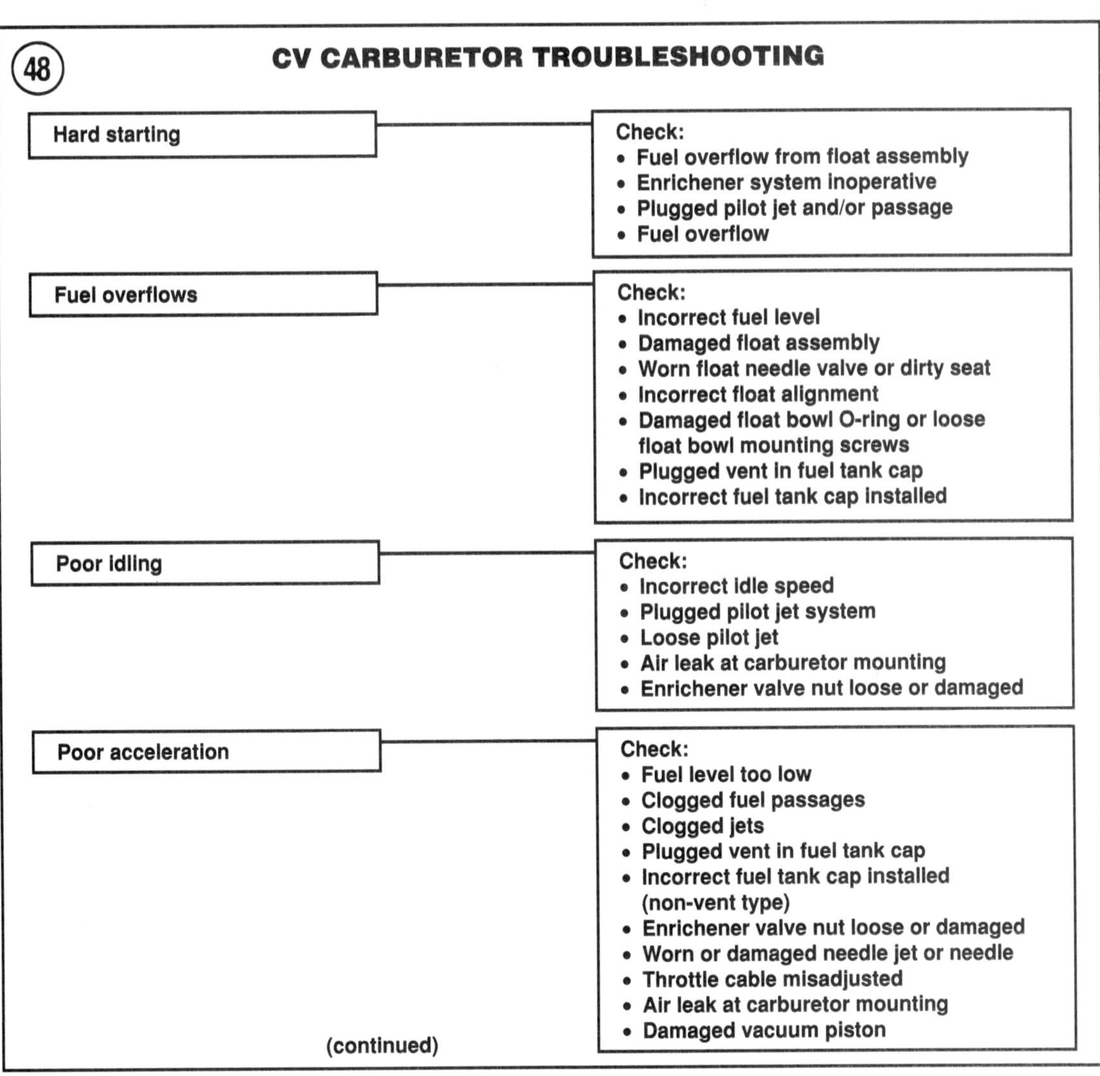

(continued)

(48) (continued)

Symptom	Check
Poor power at low engine speeds	Check: • Incorrect idle speed adjustment • Contaminated air filter element • Damaged vacuum piston • Worn or damaged needle jet or needle • Clogged pilot jet system • Plugged vent in fuel tank cap • Enrichener valve nut loose or damaged • Plugged vent in fuel tank cap • Clogged fuel supply • Air leak at carburetor mounting
Poor power at high engine speeds	Check: • Incorrect fuel level • Loose or plugged main jet • Contaminated air filter element • Damaged vacuum piston • Worn or damaged needle jet or needle • Plugged float bowl vent or overflow • Enrichener valve nut loose or damaged • Plugged vent in fuel tank cap • Clogged fuel supply • Air leak at carburetor mounting
Poor fuel economy	Check: • Incorrect enrichment use • Damaged vacuum piston • Contaminated air filter element • Loose jets • Fuel level too high • Worn or damaged needle jet or needle • Plugged float bowl vent • Enrichener valve nut loose or damaged • Incorrect carburetor adjustment
Vacuum piston doesn't rise in bore correctly	Check: • Vacuum piston binds in bore • Diaphragm torn or damaged • Vacuum piston spring binding • Diaphragm cap loose or damaged • Piston vent clogged • Diaphragm incorrectly installed (pinched at lip)
Vacuum piston doesn't close	Check: • Broken spring • Diaphragm torn or damaged • Vacuum piston binds in bore

Fuel level system

The fuel supply system is shown in **Figure 49**. Proper carburetor operation is dependent on a constant and correct carburetor fuel level. As fuel is drawn from the float bowl during engine operation, the float level in the bowl drops. As the float drops, the float needle moves away from its seat and allows fuel to flow through the seat into the float bowl. Fuel entering the float bowl will cause the float to rise and push against the float needle. When the fuel level reaches a predetermined level, the needle is pushed against the float seat to prevent the float bowl from overfilling.

If the float needle doesn't close, the engine will run rich or flood with fuel. Symptoms of this problem are rough running, excessive black smoke and poor acceleration. This condition will sometimes clear up when the engine is run at wide open throttle, as the fuel is being used up before the float bowl can overfill. As the engine speed is reduced, however, the rich running condition repeats itself.

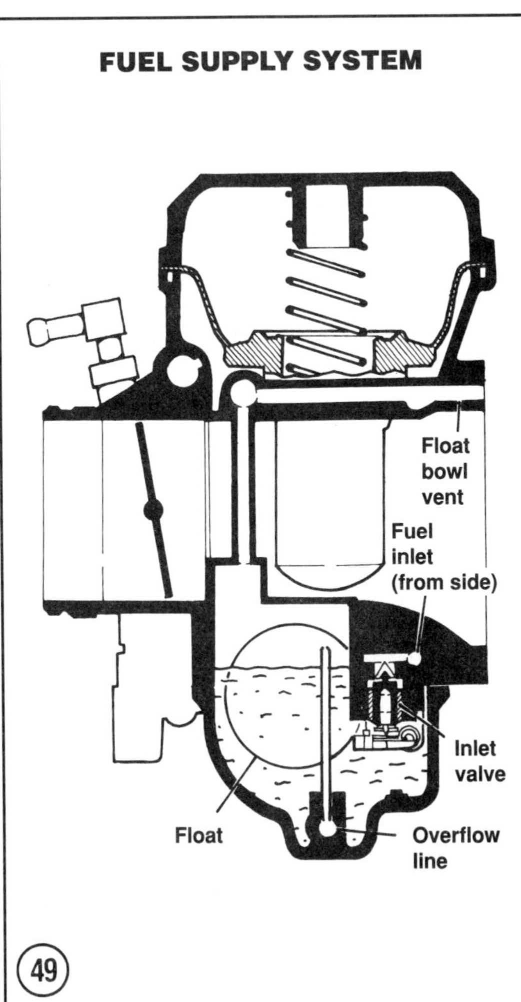

Figure 48 lists several things that can cause fuel overflow. In most instances, it can be as simple as a small piece of dirt trapped between the needle and seat or an incorrect float level. If you see fuel flowing out of the overflow tube connected at the bottom of the float bowl, the float valve is being held open. First check the position of the fuel valve. Turn the fuel lever OFF if it was left in the ON or RESERVE position. Then tap on the carburetor (not too hard) and turn the fuel valve back on. If the fuel flow stopped running out of the overflow tube, you may have dislodged whatever it was holding the needle off of its seat. If fuel continues to flow from the overflow tube, it will be necessary to remove and service the carburetor. See Chapter Seven.

Starter or enrichener system

A cold engine requires a very rich mixture. On all models, a cable actuated enrichener valve is used for cold-starting. The enrichener system can cause difficult cold starting. If your engine has become difficult to start when cold, first check the enrichener cable adjustment as described in Chapter Three. If the adjustment is correct, refer to the possible causes listed under "Hard Starting" in **Figure 48**.

Accelerator pump system

Because the carburetor cannot supply enough fuel during sudden throttle openings (quick acceleration), a lean air/fuel mixture will cause hesitation and poor acceleration. To prevent this condition, all of the factory Harley-Davidson carburetors are equipped with a diaphragm type accelerator pump system. See **Figure 50**. A spring-loaded neoprene diaphragm is installed in a pump chamber at the bottom of the float bowl. During sudden acceleration, the diaphragm is compressed by the pump lever, forcing fuel out of the pump chamber through a check valve and into the carburetor venturi. This additional fuel richens the existing air/fuel mixture to prevent engine hesitation. The diaphragm spring returns the diaphragm to its uncompressed position, allowing the chamber to refill with fuel for its next use. The check valve prevents fuel from back flowing into the chamber during pump operation.

If your bike hesitates during sudden acceleration or if it suffers from overall poor acceleration, perform the checks listed under "Poor Acceleration" in **Figure 48**. If the accelerator pump system is faulty, it will necessary to service the carburetor as described in Chapter Seven.

ENGINE NOISES

Often the first evidence of an internal engine problem is a strange noise. That knocking, clicking or tapping sound which you never heard before may be warning you of impending trouble.

While engine noises can indicate problems, they are difficult to interpret correctly; inexperienced mechanics can be seriously misled by them.

Professional mechanics often use a special stethoscope (which looks like a doctor's stethoscope) for isolating engine noises; see **Figure 51**. You can do nearly as well with a "sounding stick" which can be an ordinary piece of doweling or a section of small hose. By placing one end in contact with the area to which you want to listen and the other end near your ear, you can hear sounds emanating from that area. The first time you do this, you may be horrified at the strange sounds coming from even a normal engine. If you can, have an experienced friend or mechanic help you sort out the noises.

Consider the following when troubleshooting engine noises:

1. *Knocking or pinging during acceleration*— Caused by using a lower octane fuel than recommended. May also be caused by poor fuel. Pinging can also be caused by a spark plug of the wrong heat range. Refer to *Correct Spark Plug Heat Range* in Chapter Three.
2. *Slapping or rattling noises at low speed or during acceleration*— May be caused by piston slap, i.e., excessive piston-cylinder wall clearance.
3. *Knocking or rapping while decelerating*— Usually caused by excessive rod bearing clearance.
4. *Persistent knocking and vibration*— Usually caused by worn main bearing(s).
5. *Rapid on-off squeal*— Compression leak around cylinder head gasket(s) or spark plugs.
6. *Valve train noise*— Check for the following:
   a. Bent push rod(s).
   b. Defective tappets.
   c. Valve sticking in guide.
   d. Worn cam gears and/or cam.
   e. Damaged rocker arm or shaft. Rocker arm may be binding on shaft.

ENGINE LUBRICATION

An improperly operating engine lubrication system will quickly lead to engine damage. The engine

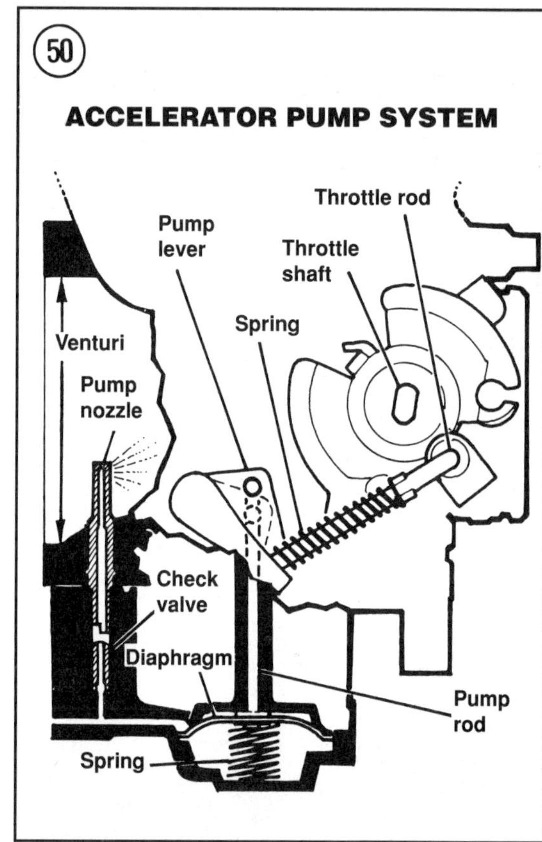

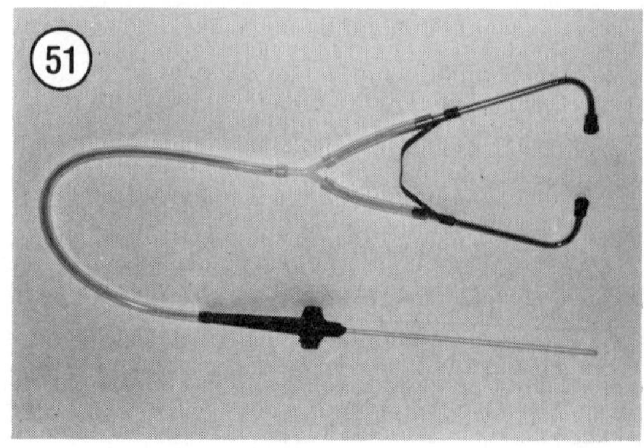

oil tank should be checked weekly and the tank refilled, as described in Chapter Three. Oil pump service is covered in Chapter Four.

Oil Light

The oil light, mounted on the indicator light panel (**Figure 52**), will come on when the ignition switch is turned to ON before starting the engine. After the engine is started, the oil light should go off when the engine speed is above idle.

If the oil light does not come on when the ignition switch is turned to ON and the engine is not running, check for a burned out oil light bulb. If the bulb is okay, check the oil pressure switch (**Figure 53**) as described in Chapter Eight.

If the oil light remains on when the engine speed is above idle, turn the engine off and check the oil level in the oil tank (**Figure 54**) as described in Chapter Three. If the oil level is satisfactory, check the following:

a. Oil may not be returning to the tank from the return line. Check for a clogged or damaged return line or a damaged oil pump.
b. If you are operating your Harley in conditions where the ambient temperature is below freezing, ice and sludge may be blocking the oil feed pipe. This condition will prevent the oil from circulating properly.

NOTE

Because water is formed during combustion, it can collect in the engine if the engine is run at moderate speeds for short periods of time, especially during winter months. If you ride your bike for short trips and then turn the engine off and allow it to cool before it has reached maximum operating temperature, water that is formed each time the engine is started will begin to accumulate in the engine's lubrication system. This buildup of water, as it mixes with the oil, will form sludge deposits. Sludge is a thick, creamy substance that will clog oil feed and return systems (oil filter, lines, etc.). This can accelerate engine wear and result in engine failure. In addition, when the ambient temperature falls below freezing, water in the tank and oil lines will freeze, thus preventing proper oil circulation and lubrication. To prevent sludge buildup in your engine, note the following:

1. When operating your Harley in cold/freezing weather, be aware of how long you actually run the engine—the engine is colder in winter months and will take longer to warm up. Run the engine for longer periods so that it can reach maximum operating temperature. This will allow water that has formed in the engine to vaporize and to be blown out through the engine breather.

2. Change the engine oil more frequently. This step can prevent sludge from accumulating in sufficient quantities which can cause engine damage.
3. Flush the oil tank at each oil change. Refer to Chapter Three for oil change and tank flush procedures.

Oil Consumption High or Engine Smokes Excessively

Check engine compression and perform a cylinder leakage test as described in Chapter Three. Causes can be one or more of the following:

a. Worn valve guides.
b. Worn valve guide seals.
c. Worn or damaged piston rings.
d. Restricted oil tank return line.
e. Oil tank overfilled.
f. Oil filter restricted.
g. Leaking cylinder head surfaces.

Oil Fails to Return to Oil Tank

a. Oil lines or fittings restricted or damaged.
b. Oil pump damaged or operating incorrectly.
c. Oil tank empty.
d. Oil filter restricted.

Excessive Engine Oil Leaks

a. Clogged air filter breather hose.
b. Restricted or damaged oil return line to oil tank.
c. Loose engine parts.
d. Damaged gasket sealing surfaces.
e. Oil tank overfilled.

CLUTCH

All clutch troubles, except adjustments, require partial clutch disassembly to identify and cure the problem. Refer to Chapter Five for clutch service procedures.

Clutch Chatter or Noise

This problem is generally caused by worn or warped friction and steel plates. Also check for worn or damaged bearings.

Clutch Slippage

a. Incorrect clutch adjustment.
b. Worn friction plates.
c. Weak or damaged diaphragm spring.
d. Damaged pressure plate.

Clutch Dragging

a. Incorrect clutch adjustment.
b. Warped clutch plates.
c. Worn or damaged clutch shell or clutch hub.

TRANSMISSION

Transmission symptoms are sometimes hard to distinguish from clutch symptoms. Refer to Chapter Six for transmission service procedures. Be sure that the clutch is not causing the trouble before working on the transmission.

Jumping Out of Gear

a. Incorrect shifter pawl adjuster.
b. Worn or damaged shifter parts.
c. Bent shift forks.
d. Severely worn or damaged gears.

Difficult Shifting

a. Worn or damaged shift forks.
b. Loose or damaged detent plate.
c. Worn or damaged shifter shaft assembly.
d. Worn or damaged detent arm.
e. Worn shift fork drum groove(s).
f. Loose, worn or damaged shifter fork pin(s).
g. Damaged shifter shaft splines.

Excessive Gear Noise

a. Worn or damaged bearings.
b. Worn or damaged gears.
c. Excessive gear backlash.

ELECTRICAL PROBLEMS

If bulbs burn out frequently, the cause may be excessive vibration, loose connections that permit sudden current surges, or the installation of the wrong type of bulb.

Most light and ignition problems are caused by loose or corroded ground connections. Check these prior to replacing a bulb or electrical component.

EXCESSIVE VIBRATION

Excessive vibration is usually caused by loose engine mounting hardware. High speed vibration may be due to a bent axle shaft or loose or faulty suspension components. Vibration can also be caused by the following conditions:

a. Broken frame.
b. Severely worn primary chain.
c. Tight primary chain links.
d. Loose or damaged upper engine mounting bracket.
e. Improperly spaced upper engine mounting bracket.
f. Improperly balanced wheel(s).
g. Defective or damaged wheel(s).
h. Defective or damaged tire(s).
i. Internal engine wear or damage.

FRONT SUSPENSION AND STEERING

Poor handling may be caused by improper pressure, a damaged or bent frame or front steering components, worn wheel bearings or dragging brakes. Possible causes for suspension and steering malfunctions are listed below.

Irregular or Wobbly Steering

a. Loose wheel axle nut(s).
b. Loose or worn steering head bearings.
c. Excessive wheel hub bearing play.
d. Damaged cast wheel.
e. Spoke wheel out of alignment.
f. Unbalanced wheel assembly.
g. Worn hub bearings.
h. Incorrect wheel alignment.
i. Bent or damaged steering stem or frame (at steering neck).
j. Tire incorrectly seated on rim.
k. Excessive front end loading from non-standard equipment.

Stiff Steering

a. Low front tire air pressure.
b. Bent or damaged steering stem or frame (at steering neck).
c. Loose or worn steering head bearings.

Stiff or Heavy Fork Operation

a. Incorrect fork springs.
b. Incorrect fork oil viscosity.
c. Excessive amount of fork oil.
d. Bent fork tubes.

Poor Fork Operation

a. Worn or damaged fork tubes.
b. Fork oil capacity low due to leaking fork seals.
c. Bent or damaged fork tubes.
d. Contaminated fork oil.
e. Incorrect fork springs.
f. Heavy front end loading from non-standard equipment.

Poor Rear Shock Absorber Operation

a. Weak or worn springs.
b. Damper unit leaking.
c. Shock shaft worn or bent.
d. Incorrect rear shock springs.
e. Rear shocks adjusted incorrectly.
f. Heavy rear end loading from non-standard equipment.
g. Incorrect loading.

BRAKE PROBLEMS

All models are equipped with front and rear disc brakes. Good brakes are vital to the safe operation of any vehicle. Perform the maintenance specified in Chapter Three to minimize brake system problems. Brake system service is covered in Chapter Fourteen. When refilling the front and rear master cylinders, use only DOT 5 silicone-based brake fluid.

Insufficient Braking Power

Worn brake pads or disc, air in the hydraulic system, glazed or contaminated pads, low brake fluid level, or a leaking brake line or hose can cause this problem. Visually check for leaks. Check for worn brake pads. Check also for a leaking or damaged primary cup seal in the master cylinder. Bleed and adjust the brakes. Rebuild a leaking master cylinder or brake caliper. Brake drag will result in excessive heat and brake fade. See *Brake Drag* in this section.

Spongy Brake Feel

This problem is generally caused by air in the hydraulic system. Bleed and adjust the brakes.

Brake Drag

Check brake adjustment, looking for insufficient brake pedal and/or hand lever free play. Also check for worn, loose or missing parts in the brake calipers. Check the brake disc for warpage or excessive runout.

Brakes Squeal or Chatter

Check brake pad thickness and disc condition. Make sure that the pads are not loose; check that the anti-rattle springs are properly installed and in good condition. Clean off any dirt on the pads. Loose components can also cause this. Check for:

a. Warped brake disc.
b. Loose brake disc.
c. Loose caliper mounting bolts.
d. Loose front axle nut.
e. Worn wheel bearings.
f. Damaged hub.

Table 1 STARTER MOTOR TEST SPECIFICATIONS

Current draw	
1991-1992	150 amps max.
1993-on	
Range	140-180 amps
Maximum	180 amps

Table 2 ELECTRICAL SPECIFICATIONS

Battery capacity	12 volt, 19 amp hr.
Ignition coil	
Primary resistance	2.5-3.1 ohms
Secondary resistance	
1991-1992	11,250-13,750 ohms
1993-on	10,000-12,500 ohms
Alternator	
Stator coil resistance	0.2-0.4 ohms
AC voltage output	19-26 VAC per 1,000 rpm
Voltage regulator	
AC voltage output	13.8-15 volts @ 75° F
Amperes @ 3,600 rpm	22 amps

CHAPTER THREE

PERIODIC LUBRICATION, MAINTENANCE AND TUNE-UP

The service life and operation of your Harley-Davidson will depend on the maintenance it receives. This is easy to understand, once you realize that a motorcycle, even in normal use, is subjected to tremendous heat, stress and vibration. When neglected, any bike becomes unreliable and actually dangerous to ride.

All motorcycles require attention before and after riding them. The time spent on basic maintenance and lubrication will provide you with the utmost in safety and performance as well as maintaining and actually increasing your Harley's monetary investment. Minor problems are often found during these inspections that are simple and inexpensive to correct at the time. If they are not found and corrected at this time they could lead to major and more expensive problems later on. Letting things go is a bad and costly habit to get into. Harley-Davidson motorcycles are some of the most well designed and manufactured motorcycles sold today. Maintain the image by maintaining your bike.

Regular cleaning of the bike is also very important. It makes routine maintenance a lot easier by not having to work your way through a build-up of road dirt to get to a component for adjustment or replacement. Routine cleaning also allows you to see a damaged component or leak that can be repaired or replaced as soon as the damage occurs. If a damaged part is allowed to deteriorate it may create an unsafe riding condition that could lead to a possible accident.

If this is your first bike, start out by doing simple tune-up, lubrication and maintenance. Tackle more involved jobs as you become more acquainted with the bike.

Certain maintenance tasks and checks should be performed weekly. Others should be performed at certain time or mileage intervals. Still others should be done whenever certain symptoms appear. Some maintenance procedures are included under *Tune-up* at the end of this chapter. Detailed instructions will be found there. Other steps are described in the following chapters. Chapter references are included with these steps.

The service procedures and intervals shown in **Table 1** are recommended by Harley-Davidson. **Tables 1-10** are located at the end of the chapter.

ROUTINE SAFETY CHECKS

The following safety checks should be performed prior to the first ride of the day.

General Inspection

1. Inspect the engine for signs of oil or fuel leakage.
2. Check the tires for embedded stones. Pry them out with a suitable tool.
3. Make sure all lights work.

NOTE
At least check the brake light. It can burn out anytime. Motorists can't stop as quickly as you and need all the warning you can give.

4. Inspect the fuel lines and fittings for wetness.
5. Make sure the fuel tank is full of fresh gasoline.
6. Check the operation of the front and rear brakes. Add DOT 5 silicone-based brake fluid to the front and rear master cylinders as required.
7. Check the operation of the clutch. If necessary, adjust the clutch free-play as described in this chapter.
8. Check the throttle operation. The hand throttle should move smoothly with no sign of roughness, sticking or tightness. The throttle should snap back when released. Adjust throttle free play, if necessary, as described in this chapter.
9. Check the rear brake pedal. It should move smoothly. If necessary, adjust free play as described in this chapter.
10. Inspect the front and rear suspension. Make sure they have a good solid feel with no looseness.
11. Check the exhaust system for damage.
12. Check drive chain or rear drive belt adjustment.

CAUTION
*When checking the tightness of the exposed fasteners on your Harley, do **not** include the cylinder head bolts in this process. Harley-Davidson lists a specific bolt tightening sequence to prevent cylinder head and cylinder distortion, head leakage and stud failure. When tightening the cylinder head bolts, follow the procedure for your model described in Chapter Four.*

Engine Oil Tank Level

Refer to *Periodic Lubrication* in this chapter.

Tire Pressure

Tire pressure must be checked with the tires cold. Correct tire pressure, listed in **Table 2**, varies with the load you are carrying. Refer to *Tire Pressure* under *Tires and Wheels* in this chapter.

Battery

Check the battery electrolyte level. The level must be maintained within the MIN and MAX battery markings (**Figure 1**).

For complete details, see *Battery* in Chapter Eight.

Lights and Horn

With the engine running, check the following:

1. Pull the front brake lever and check that the brake light comes on.
2. Push the rear brake pedal down and check that the brake light comes on soon after you have begun depressing the pedal.
3. Check to see that the headlight and taillight are on.
4. Move the dimmer switch up and down between the high and low positions, and check to see that both headlight elements are working.
5. Push the turn signal switch to the left position and right position and check that all 4 turn signal lights are working.
6. Push the horn button and make sure that the horn blows loudly.
7. If the horn or any light failed to work properly, refer to Chapter Eight.

MAINTENANCE INTERVALS

The services and intervals shown in **Table 1** are recommended by the factory. Strict adherence to these recommendations will go a long way toward insuring long service from your Sportster. If the bike is run in an area of high humidity, the lubrication service must be done more frequently to prevent possible rust damage.

For convenient maintenance of your motorcycle, most of the services shown in **Table 1** are described in this chapter. Those procedures which require more than minor disassembly or adjustment are covered elsewhere in the appropriate chapter. The *Table of Contents* and *Index* can help you to locate a particular service procedure.

CLEANING YOUR HARLEY

Regular cleaning of your Harley is important. It makes routine maintenance a lot easier by not having to work your way through built-up dirt to get to a component for adjustment or replacement. It also makes the bike look like new even though it may have many thousands of miles on it.

If you ride in a farming area or where there is a lot of rain or road salt residue in the winter, clean the bike off more often in order to maintain the painted, plated and polished surfaces in good condition. Keep a good coat of wax on the bike during the winter to prevent premature weathering of all finishes.

Washing the bike should be done in a gentle way to avoid damage to the painted and plated finishes and to components that are not designed to withstand high-pressure water. Try to avoid using the coin-operated car wash systems as the cleaning agents may be harmful to the plastic parts on the bike. Also the rinse cycle is usually fairly high pressure and will force water into areas that should be kept dry.

Use a mild detergent (mild liquid dish washing detergent) or a commercial car washing detergent available at most auto parts outlets. Be warned, these detergents will remove some of the wax that you have applied to the finish. Follow the manufacturer's instructions for the correct detergent-to-water mixture.

If the lower end of the engine and frame are covered with oil, grease or road dirt, spray this dirt with a commercial cleaner like Gunk Cycle Cleaner, or equivalent. However, keep this cleaner off of the plastic components, O-ring drive chains and drive belts as it may damage the component. Follow the manufacturer's instructions and rinse with *plenty of cold water*. Do not allow any of this cleaner residue to settle in any pockets as it will stain or destroy the finish of most painted parts.

Use a commercial tar-stain remover to remove any severe road dirt and tar stains. Be sure to rinse all areas thoroughly with plenty of clean water to make sure all of the tar-stain remover is rinsed off of all surfaces.

Prior to washing the plastic and painted surfaces of the bike, make sure the surfaces are cool. Do not wash a hot bike as you will probably end up with streaks since the soap suds will start to dry prior to being rinsed off.

CAUTION

Do not allow water (especially under pressure) to enter the air intake, brake assemblies, electrical switches and connectors, instrument cluster, wheel bearing areas, swing arm bearings or any other moisture sensitive areas of the bike.

After all of the heavily soiled areas are cleaned off, use the previously described detergent, warm water and a soft natural sponge and carefully wash down the entire bike, including the wheels and tires. Always wet the bike down *before* washing with your detergent soaked sponge or rag. This will remove dirt from sensitive areas and prevent scratching. Don't use too much detergent as it will be difficult to rinse off all of the soap suds thoroughly. After all areas have been washed, rinse off the soap suds with *low-pressure cold water*. Make sure all of the detergent residue is thoroughly rinsed off.

NOTE

Before washing the fuel tank, check for small pebbles, metal shavings or dirt stuck to or partially hidden in your sponge and rags. These objects may scratch and mar the tank's finish. As you wash your bike, rinse the sponge or rag frequently to remove accumulated dirt.

Straddle the bike and kick up the jiffy stand. Then lean it to both sides to allow all water to drain off the top of the cylinder block and other horizontal surfaces. If you have access to compressed air, *gently* blow excess water from areas where the water may have collected. Do not force the water into any of the sensitive areas mentioned in the previous *CAUTION*. Gently dry off the bike with a chamois, a clean soft turkish towel or an old plain T-shirt (no transfers or hand-painted designs, these may scratch the tank).

If you have mounted a windshield on your Harley, be careful when cleaning it; windshields can be easily scratched or damaged. Do not use a cleaner with an abrasive or a combination cleaner and wax. Never use gasoline or cleaning solvent. These products will either scratch or totally destroy the surface finish of the windshield.

Clean the windshield with a soft cloth or natural sponge and plenty of water. Dry thoroughly with a soft cloth or chamois—do not press hard.

WARNING

The brake components may have gotten wet. If they are damp or wet they will not be operating at their optimum effectiveness. Be prepared to take a longer distance to stop the bike right after washing the bike. Ride slowly and lightly apply the brakes to dry off the pads.

Start the engine and let it reach normal operating temperature. Take the bike out for a *slow and careful* ride around the block to blow off any residual water. Bring the bike back to the wash area and dry off any residual water streaks from the painted and plated surfaces.

Once the bike is thoroughly dry, get out the polish, wax and Armour All and give the bike a good polish and wax job to protect the painted, plated and polished surfaces.

TIRES AND WHEELS

Tire Pressure

Tire pressure should be checked and adjusted to maintain the tire profile, good traction and handling and to get the maximum life out of the tire. A simple, accurate gauge (**Figure 2**) can be purchased for a few dollars and should be carried in your motorcycle tool kit. The appropriate tire pressures are shown in **Table 2**.

NOTE

*After checking and adjusting the air pressure, make sure to reinstall the air valve cap (**Figure 3**). The cap prevents small pebbles and dirt from collecting in the valve stem; these could allow air leakage or result in incorrect tire pressure readings.*

Tire Inspection

The tires take a lot of punishment, so inspect them periodically for excessive wear, deep cuts, imbedded objects such as stones, nails, etc. If you find a nail or other object in a tire, mark its location with a light crayon prior to removing it. This will help to locate the hole for repair. Refer to Chapter Nine for tire changing and repair information.

Check local traffic regulations concerning minimum tread depth. Measure with a tread depth gauge (**Figure 4**) or small ruler. As a guideline, replace tires when the tread depth is 5/16 in. (8.0 mm) or less.

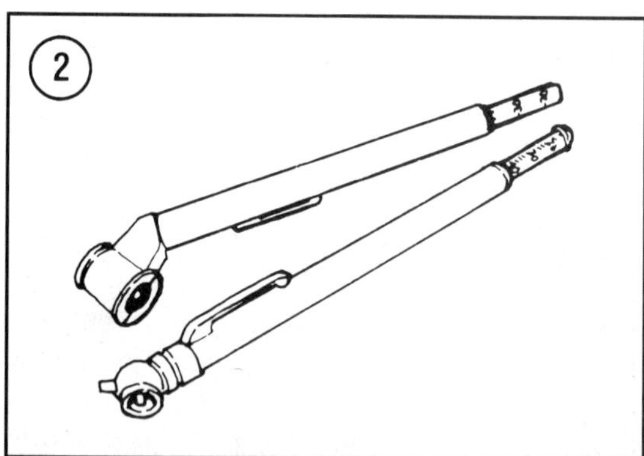

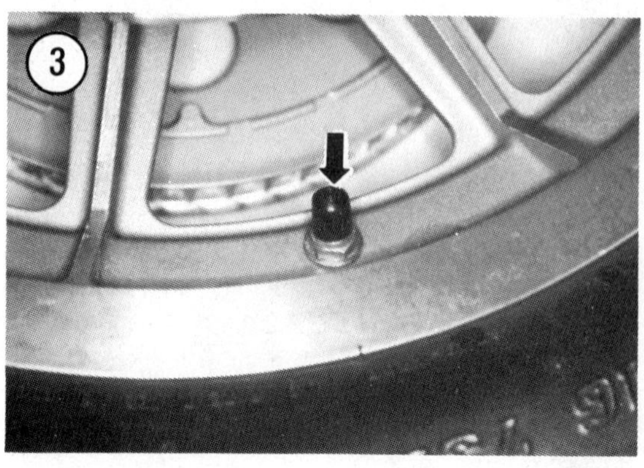

Wheel Spoke Tension

On spoke wheels, the spokes should be checked frequently for loosening or breakage. Loose spokes can cause spoke, rim and hub breakage. Refer to Chapter Nine for spoke service.

Rim Inspection

Frequently inspect the wheel rims. If a rim has been damaged it might have been knocked out of alignment. Improper wheel alignment can cause severe vibration and result in an unsafe riding condition. If the rim portion of an alloy wheel is damaged the wheel must be replaced, as it cannot be repaired. Refer to Chapter Nine for rim service.

PERIODIC LUBRICATION

Oil

Oil is graded according to its viscosity, which is an indication of how thick it is. The Society of Automotive Engineers (SAE) system distinguishes oil viscosity by numbers. Thick oils have higher viscosity numbers than thin oils. For example, an SAE 5 oil is a thin oil while an SAE 90 oil is relatively thick.

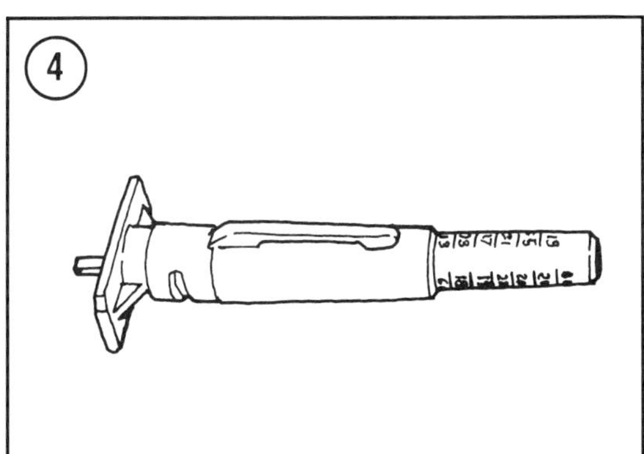

Grease

A good quality grease (preferably waterproof) should be used (**Figure 5**). Water does not wash grease off parts as easily as it washes oil off. In addition, grease maintains its lubricating qualities better than oil on long and strenuous rides.

Oil Tank Inspection

Before checking the oil level, inspect the oil tank for cracks or other damage. If oil seepage is noted on or near the tank, find and repair the problem. Check all of the oil tank mounting bolts for loose or missing fasteners; replace or tighten fasteners as required. Check the hose connections on the tank. See **Figure 6** (1991-1993) or **Figure 7** (1994). Each hose should be secured with a hose clamp. Check each hose for swelling, cracks or damage; otherwise, oil leakage may occur and cause engine damage.

Oil Tank Level Check

A remote oil tank (A, **Figure 8**) is mounted on the right-hand side of the bike. The oil level in the tank should be checked prior to each ride as oil consumption is relative to engine speed and engine tune. In addition, the engine will consume less oil and run cooler when the oil level in the tank is kept relatively high.

Engine oil level is checked with the dipstick mounted in the tank filler cap (B, **Figure 8**).

1. Start and run the engine for approximately 10 minutes or until the engine has reached normal operating temperature. Then turn the engine off and allow the oil to settle in the tank.
2. Have an assistant support the bike so that it stands straight up. If the bike is supported on the jiffy stand when checking the oil level, an incorrect reading will be obtained.
3. Wipe off the oil tank filler cap and the area around the cap with a clean rag, then remove the filler cap and dipstick (**Figure 9**). Wipe the dipstick off with a clean rag and reinsert the cap all the way into the

oil tank. Withdraw filler cap once again and check oil level on dipstick. Dipstick has 2 marks (**Figure 10**). If oil level is at or below lower mark, add 1 quart (0.946 mm) of engine oil to the oil tank. Do not overfill beyond the specified point as the oil will overflow and an air space is required in the tank. Add the recommended weight engine oil indicated in **Table 3** to correct the oil level.

4. Wipe off and then reinstall the filler cap.

5. As a safety precaution, check the oil tank drain plug or hose for tightness.

Engine Oil and Filter Change

The factory-recommended oil and filter change interval is specified in **Table 1**. This assumes that the motorcycle is operated in moderate climates. In extreme climates, oil should be changed more often. The time interval is more important than the mileage interval because combustion acids, formed by gasoline and water vapor, will contaminate the oil even if the motorcycle is not run for several months. If a motorcycle is operated under dusty conditions, the oil will get dirty more quickly and should be changed more frequently than recommended.

Oil for motorcycle and automotive engines is graded by the American Petroleum Institute (API) and the Society of Automotive Engineers (SAE) in several categories. Oil containers display these ratings on the top of the oil can or on the bottle label (**Figure 11**).

Use only a detergent oil with an API rating of SF or SG. Try to use the same brand of oil at each change. Refer to **Table 3** for correct oil viscosity to

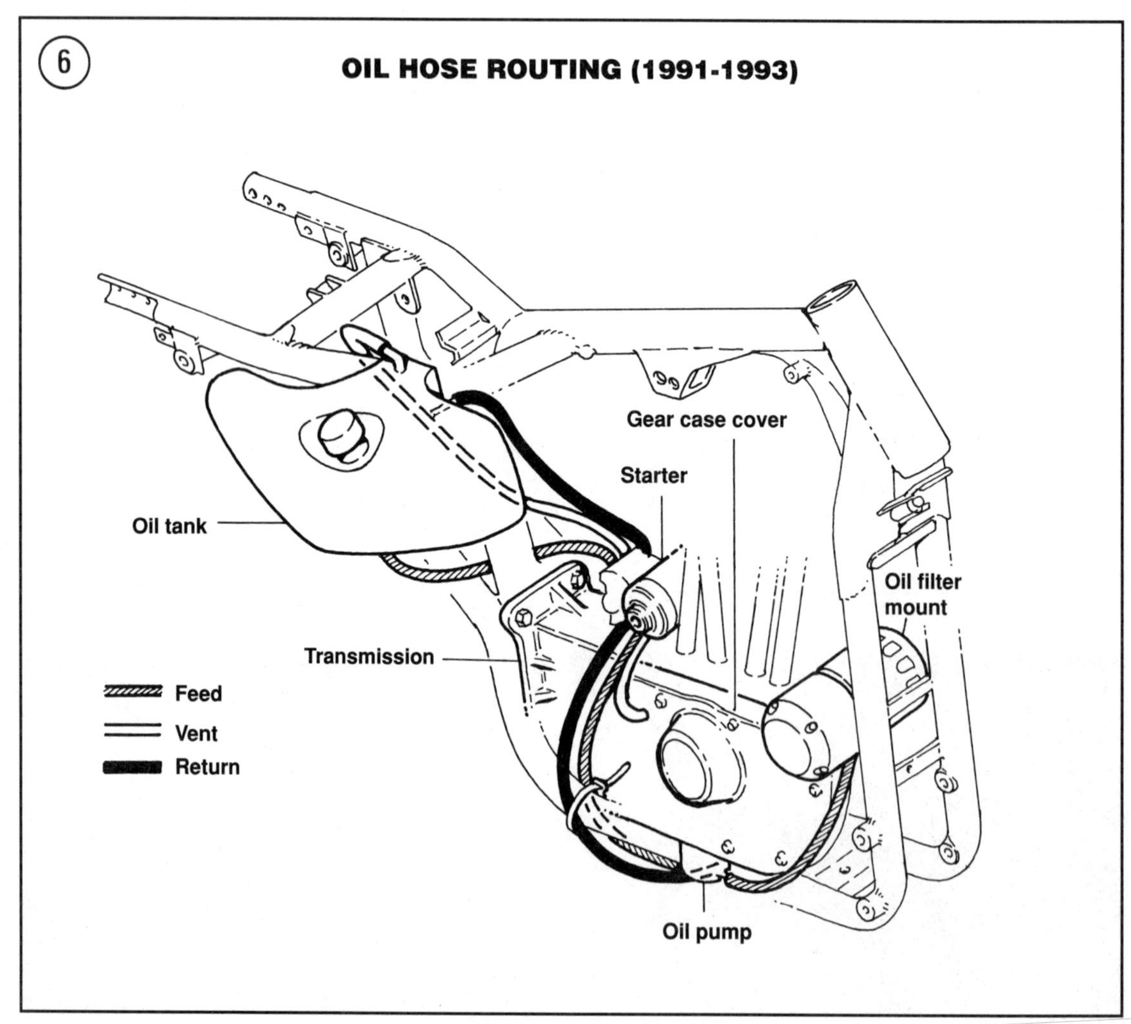

use under anticipated ambient temperatures (not engine oil temperature).

To change the engine oil and filter you will need the following:

a. Drain pan.

b. Funnel.

c. Wrench (for drain plug models).

d. 3 quarts of oil.

e. Oil filter element.

There are a number of ways to discard the used oil safely. The easiest way is to pour it from the drain pan into a gallon plastic bleach, juice or milk container for disposal. Some service stations and oil retailers will accept your used oil for recycling.

7

OIL HOSE ROUTING (1994)

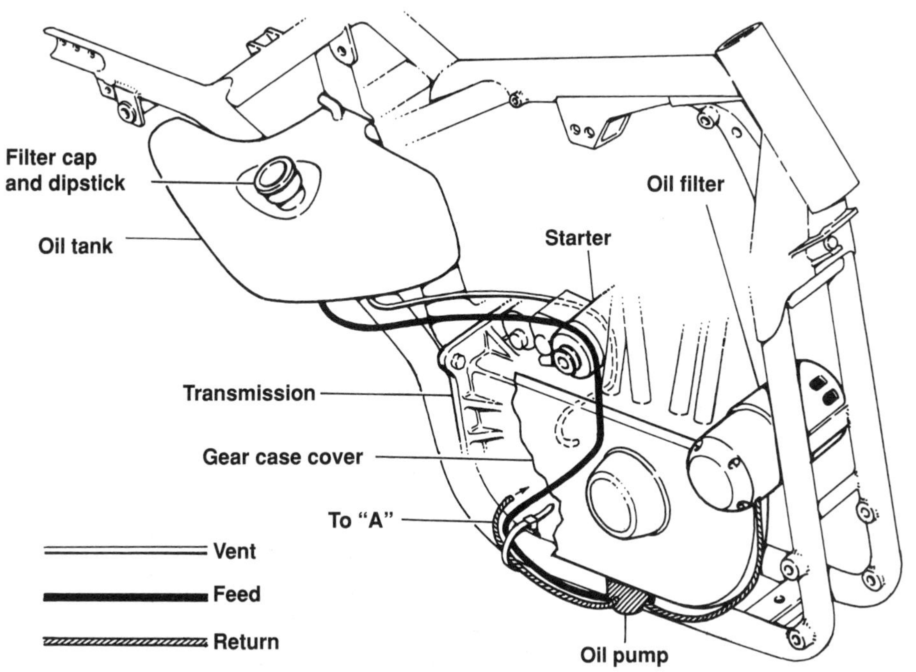

Filter cap and dipstick
Oil tank
Oil filter
Starter
Transmission
Gear case cover
To "A"
Vent
Feed
Return
Oil pump

There may be a recycling center in your area that accepts oil. Do not discard the oil in your household trash or pour it onto the ground.

1. Start and run the engine for approximately 10 minutes or until the engine has reached normal operating temperature. Then turn the engine off and allow the oil to settle in the tank. Support the bike so that the oil can drain completely.

NOTE
Before removing the oil tank cap, thoroughly clean off all dirt and oil around it.

2. Place a drain pan beside the bike.
3. Locate the oil drain hose mounted on the bottom of the oil tank. Note the following:
   a. On 1991-1993 models, the drain hose is secured to the battery tray lug on the left-hand side of the bike (**Figure 12**).
   b. On 1994 models, the drain hose is secured to a lug on the rear muffler mount on the left-hand side of the bike (**Figure 13**).
4. Remove the clamp securing the oil hose in place and insert the open end of the hose over the drain pan and allow the oil tank to drain completely. To speed up the oil flow, remove the oil filler cap (B, **Figure 8**) from the oil tank.
5. Service the oil filter as follows:
   a. Place an oil drain pan underneath the oil filter.
   b. Remove the filter with a filter wrench (**Figure 14**). Turn the oil filter counterclockwise to remove it.
   c. Discard the oil filter.
   d. Wipe the crankcase gasket surface with a clean, lint-free cloth.
   e. Pour approximately 4 fl. oz. (120 ml) of new engine oil into the new oil filter (**Figure 15**). Allow the oil to soak into the filter element.
   f. Coat the neoprene gasket on the new filter with clean oil (**Figure 16**).
   g. Screw the filter onto the crankcase *by hand* until the filter gasket just touches the base, i.e., until you feel the slightest resistance when turning the filter. Then tighten the filter *by hand* 1/2-3/4 turn more.

CAUTION
Do not overtighten and do not use a filter wrench or the filter may leak.

6A. On 1991-1993 models, secure the oil tank drain hose to the lug on the base of the battery tray with the original clamp (**Figure 12**).

6B. On 1994 models, secure the oil tank drain hose to the lug on the muffler mount with the original clamp (**Figure 13**).

7. Fill the oil tank with the correct viscosity (**Table 3**) and quantity (**Table 4**) of oil—minus the 4 fl. oz. (120 ml) previously added to the oil filter.

8. On 1994 models, remove air from the oil tank drain hose as follows:

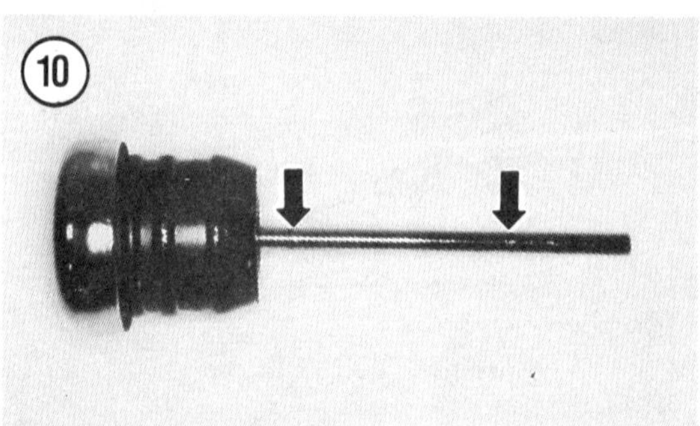
10

11

12

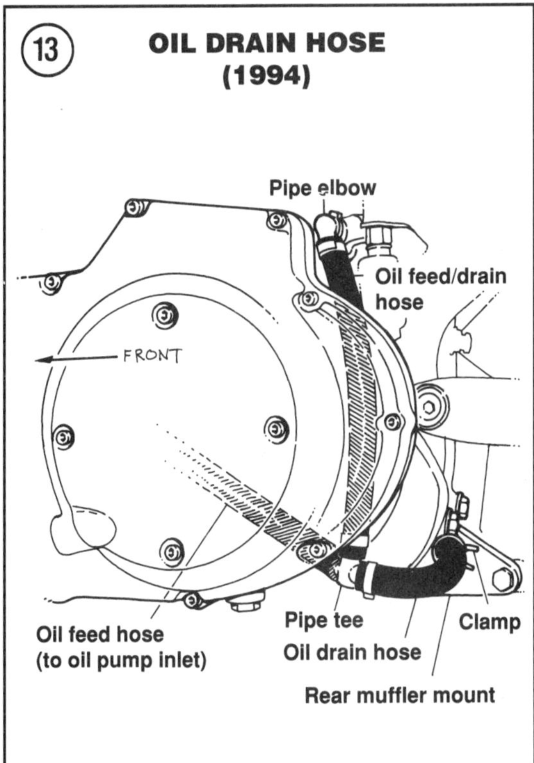

a. Move the drain pan so that it is underneath the drain hose.

b. Disconnect the oil drain hose (**Figure 13**) from the rear muffler mount lug and allow a small amount of oil to drain from the open end of the hose, then reconnect the hose and secure it with its clamp.

CAUTION

On 1994 models, Step 8 must be performed to prevent oil pump cavitation.

9. Wipe off and insert the filler cap (**Figure 9**) into the oil tank.

10. Start the engine and allow it to idle. Check that the oil pressure signal light turns off when the engine speed is 1,000 rpm or higher.

11. Check for oil leaks at the oil tank drain hose and oil filter.

12. Turn the engine off.

Oil Pressure Check

1. Disconnect the oil pressure switch electrical connector at the switch (**Figure 17**).

NOTE

***Figure 17** shows the oil pressure switch with the oil filter removed for clarity. The oil filter must be installed on the bike when checking oil pressure.*

2. Remove the oil pressure switch (**Figure 17**) from the 45° elbow on the engine.

3. Install the oil pressure gauge adapter (part No. HD-96940-52A) and the oil pressure gauge (part No. HD-96921-52A) onto the oil pressure switch fitting.

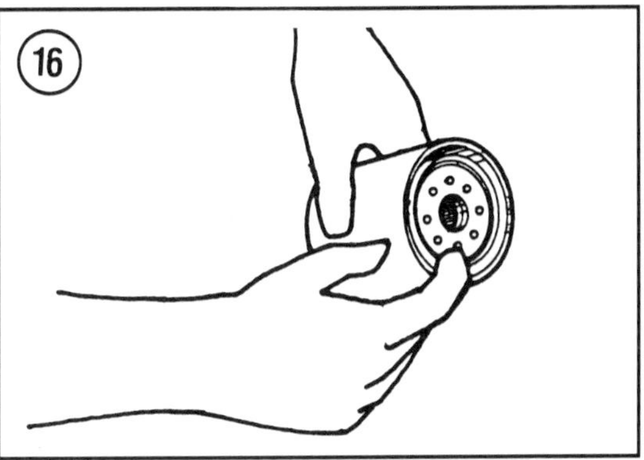

4. Start and run the engine until it reaches normal operating temperature—driven at least 20 miles (32 km) at above 50 mph (80 km/h).
5. At 2,500 rpm, oil pressure should read 10-17 psi (69-117 kPa). At idle, oil pressure should read 7-12 psi (48-83 kPa).
6. Turn the engine off. If the oil pressure reading is incorrect, refer to *Engine Lubrication* in Chapter Two.

WARNING
The engine and exhaust pipes will be hot when performing the following steps. Work carefully to avoid burning yourself.

7. Remove the oil pressure gauge adapter and the oil pressure gauge.
8. Apply Hylomar or Teflon Pipe Sealant to the oil pressure switch threads prior to installation. Install the switch and tighten to the torque specification in **Table 6**.

Transmission Oil Level Check

Inspect the transmission oil level at the interval listed in **Table 1**. If the bike has just been run, allow it to cool down (approximately 10 minutes), then check the oil level. When checking the transmission oil level, do not allow any dirt or foreign matter to enter the case opening.
1. Park the bike on a level surface and support it so that it is standing straight up. Do not support it with the jiffy stand.
2A. On 1991-1993 models, perform the following:
  a. Remove the oil level plug mounted at the rear of the primary cover, on the crankcase; see **Figure 18**.
  b. The transmission oil level should be level with the plug opening.
  c. If the oil level seems low, remove the primary chain inspection cover (**Figure 19**).
  d. Add transmission oil (**Table 5**) through the inspection cover opening until it begins to flow through the oil level hole (**Figure 18**). Continue to allow the oil to flow through the hole until it stops. At this point, the oil level is correct.
  e. Reinstall the inspection cover and its O-ring (**Figure 19**), if removed.
  f. Reinstall the oil level plug and its gasket (**Figure 18**).

2B. On 1994 models, perform the following:
  a. Remove the left-hand footpeg assembly.
  b. Remove the clutch inspection cover (2, **Figure 20**).
  c. Check that the oil level is even with the bottom of the clutch diaphragm spring.
  d. If the oil level is low, add transmission oil (**Table 5**) through the inspection cover opening.
  e. Reinstall the inspection cover and its O-ring.
  f. Reinstall the left-hand footpeg. Tighten its locknut to the torque specification in **Table 6**.

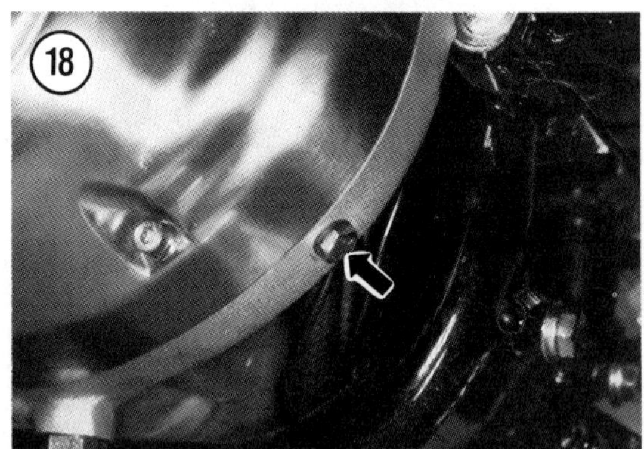

CAUTION
Do not overfill the primary housing. Overfilling may cause clutch drag or hard clutch engagement.

3. Wipe off any spilled oil from the primary cover.

Transmission Oil Change

Change the transmission oil at the intervals specified in **Table 1**.

To change the transmission oil, you will need the following:

a. Drain pan.

b. Funnel.

c. Box-end wrench for drain plug.

d. Transmission oil (**Table 5**).

1. Ride the bike until the transmission oil reaches normal operating temperature. Usually 10-15 minutes of stop and go riding is sufficient. Shut the engine off.

NOTE
There are 2 important reasons for draining the transmission oil while it is hot. First, hot oil will drain more quickly. Second, contaminants in the oil will drain with it, instead of settling in the bottom of the transmission case, ready to mix with the new oil.

2. Park the bike on a level surface and support it so that it is standing straight up. Do not support it with the jiffy stand.

3. Place a drain pan underneath the primary cover drain plug.

(20) **CLUTCH RELEASE MECHANISM (1994)**

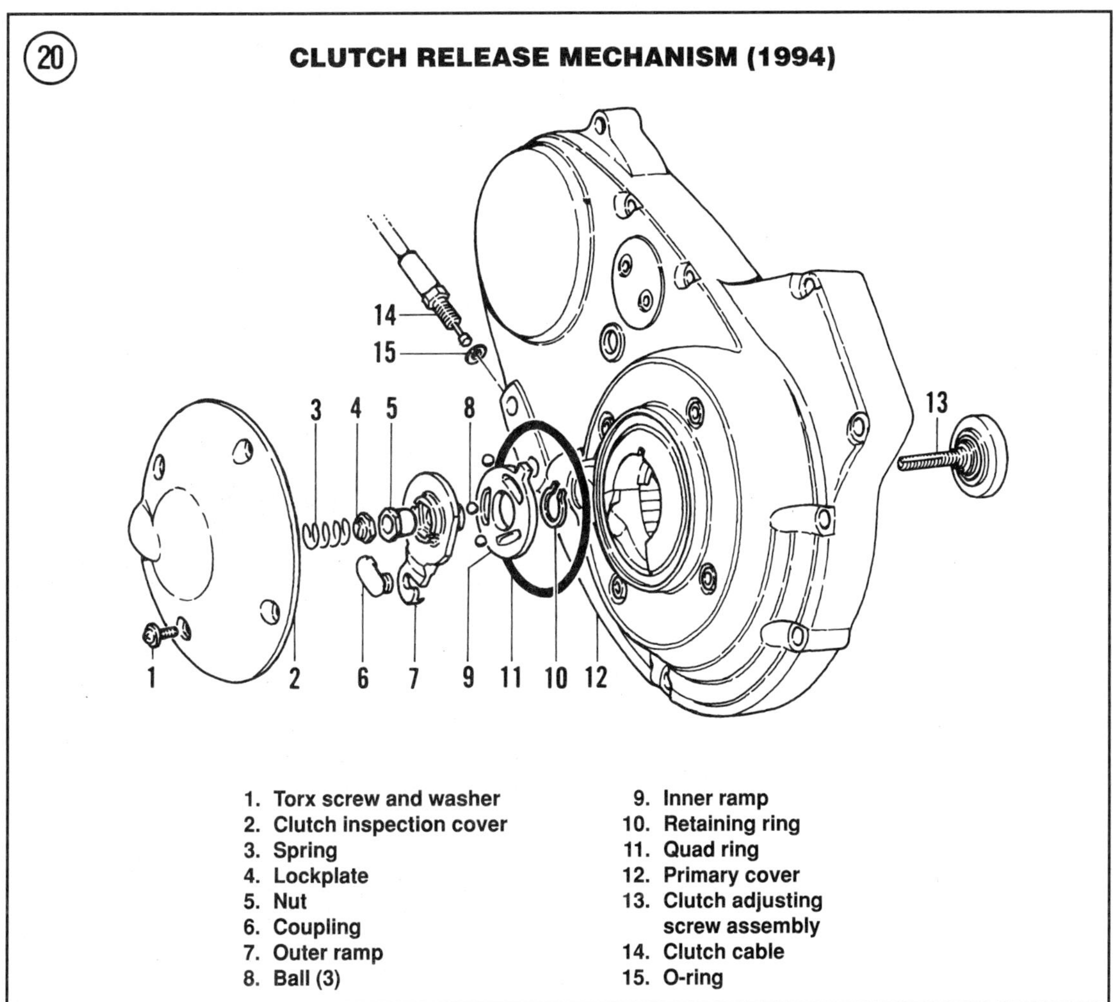

1. Torx screw and washer
2. Clutch inspection cover
3. Spring
4. Lockplate
5. Nut
6. Coupling
7. Outer ramp
8. Ball (3)
9. Inner ramp
10. Retaining ring
11. Quad ring
12. Primary cover
13. Clutch adjusting screw assembly
14. Clutch cable
15. O-ring

4. Remove the drain plug and gasket (**Figure 21**). Allow the oil to drain.

WARNING
Do not allow the oil to spill onto the ground where the rear tire may contact it later. Wipe up all oil spills immediately.

5. Check the drain plug gasket for damage and replace if necessary.
6. The drain plug is magnetic. Check the plug for metal debris that may indicate transmission wear, then wipe the plug off. Replace the plug if the head and/or threads are damaged.
7. Install the drain plug and its gasket into the bottom of the primary cover and tighten to the torque specification in **Table 6**.
8. Refill the primary cover through the inspection cover (**Figure 19** or **Figure 20**) with the recommended quantity (**Table 4**) and type (**Table 5**) transmission oil.
9. Reinstall the inspection cover and its O-ring.

Front Fork Oil Change

The fork oil should be changed at the intervals specified in **Table 1**.

1. Place a drain pan beside one fork tube and remove the drain screw and washer (**Figure 22**). Apply the front brake lever and push down on the forks and release. Repeat this procedure until all of the fork oil is drained.
2. Inspect the sealing washer on the drain screw; replace if necessary.
3. Reinstall the drain screw and washer. Tighten securely.
4. Repeat Steps 1-3 for the opposite fork tube.

CAUTION
Do not allow the fork oil to come in contact with any of the brake components.

5. Raise and secure the front end so that the front tire clears the ground. Both fork tubes should be fully extended.

CAUTION
Make sure the vehicle is supported securely.

6. Remove the fork cap from one fork tube (**Figure 23**).
7. Insert a small funnel into the opening in the fork tube.

NOTE
*If fork has been disassembled, refill with "dry" quantity; otherwise refill with "wet" quantity. See **Table** 7.*

NOTE
*In order to measure the correct amount of fluid, use a **discarded** baby bottle. These bottles have measurements in milliliters (ml) and fluid ounces (oz) imprinted on the side. Mark the bottle with "Shop Use Only" after using it.*

8. Fill the fork tube with the correct viscosity and quantity of fork oil. Refer to **Table 7**. Remove the small funnel.
9. Check the condition of the fork cap O-ring and replace if damaged.
10. Reinstall the fork cap and O-ring (**Figure 23**).
11. Repeat Steps 6-10 for the opposite side.

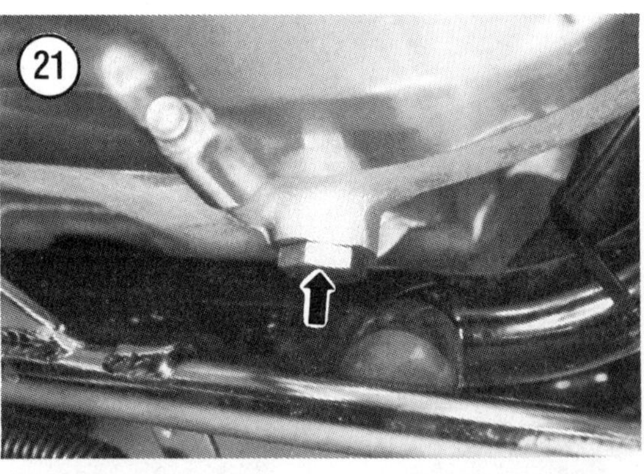
21

22

12. Lower the front wheel so that it rests on the ground.

13. Road test the bike and check for leaks.

Control Cables

The control cables should be lubricated at the intervals specified in **Table 1**. At this time, they should also be inspected for fraying, and the cable sheath should be checked for chafing; **Figure 24** shows a cable damaged from improper routing. Damaged cables should be replaced immediately.

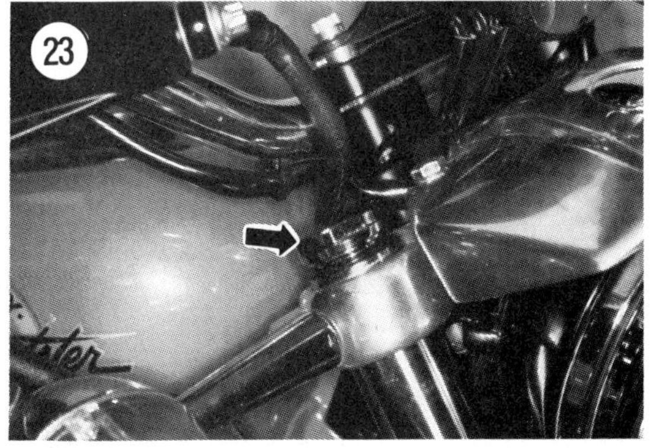

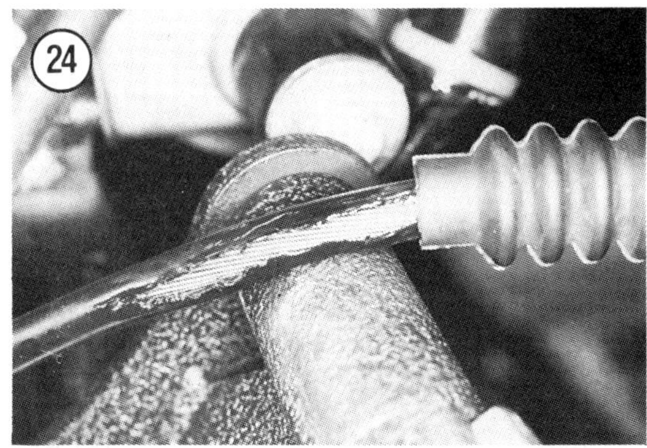

They can be lubricated with any of the popular cable lubricants and a cable lubricator.

NOTE
The main cause of cable breakage or cable stiffness is improper lubrication. Maintaining the cables as described in this section will assure long cable service life.

NOTE
*The enrichener cable (***Figure 25***) must have sufficient cable resistance to work properly. Do not lubricate the enrichener cable or its conduit.*

1. Disconnect the clutch cable from both ends as described under *Clutch Cable* in Chapter Five.
2. Disconnect the throttle cables at both ends as described under *Throttle Cables* in Chapter Seven.
3. Attach a lubricator to the cable following the manufacturer's instructions (**Figure 26**).

NOTE
Place a shop cloth at the end of the cable(s) to catch all excess lubricant that will flow out.

4. Insert the nozzle of the lubricant can into the lubricator, press the button on the can and hold it down until the lubricant begins to flow out of the other end of the cable. If lubricant squirts out around the lubricator, it is not clamped to the cable properly. Loosen and reposition the cable lubricator.

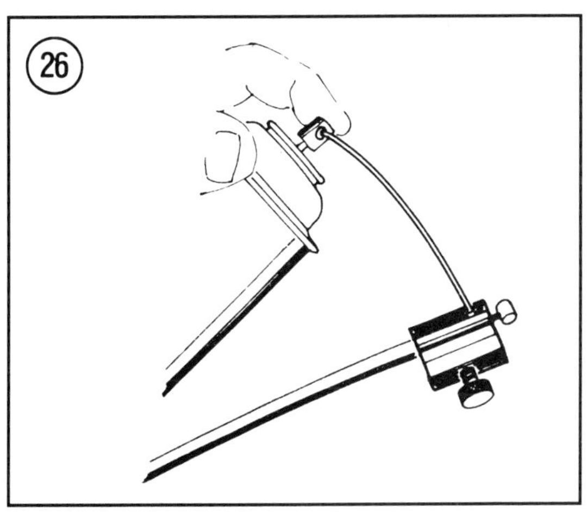

NOTE
If the lubricant does not flow out of the other end of the cable, check the entire length of the cable for fraying, bending or other damage. Replace the cable if damaged.

5. Remove the cable lubricator. Wipe off all excess lubricant from the cable end.
6. Reconnect the clutch cable as described in Chapter Five. Adjust the cable as described in this chapter.
7. Reconnect the throttle cables as described in Chapter Seven. Adjust the throttle cables as described in this chapter.

Speedometer Cable Lubrication

Lubricate the cable every year or whenever needle operation is erratic.

1. Disconnect the speedometer cable from underneath the speedometer (**Figure 27**).
2. Pull the cable from the sheath.
3. If the grease is contaminated, thoroughly clean off all old grease.
4. Thoroughly coat the cable with a good grade of multi-purpose grease and reinstall into the sheath.
5. Reinstall the cable into its sheath. Turn the cable to engage it with the speedometer drive unit. When the cable stops turning, it is properly engaged.

Drive Chain Lubrication

Harley-Davidson recommends the following chain lubes for their standard and O-ring drive chains:

a. *Standard drive chain:* Harley-Davidson Chain Spray or Harley-Davidson High-Performance Chain Lube.
b. *O-ring drive chains:* Harley-Davidson High-Performance Chain Lube or an automotive lubricant rated API GL-5 with a viscosity index of SAE 80 or 90.

1. Support the bike so that the rear wheel clears the ground.
2. Shift the transmission to NEUTRAL.
3. Oil the bottom chain run (**Figure 28**) with a suitable chain lubricant. Concentrate on getting the lubricant down between the side plates, pins, bushings and rollers of each chain link. Rotate the wheel and oil the entire chain.
4. Wipe off excess lubricant from the chain.

Miscellaneous Lubrication Points

Lubricate the clutch lever; front brake lever; rear brake lever; jiffystand pivot; and footrest pivot points. Use SAE 10W/30 motor oil.

PERIODIC MAINTENANCE

Maintenance intervals are listed in **Table 1**.

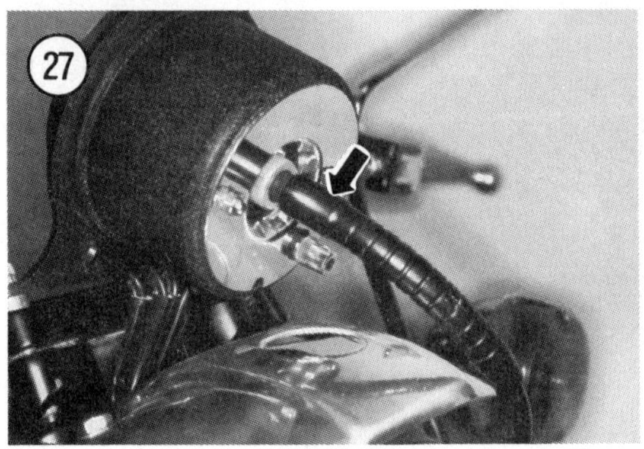

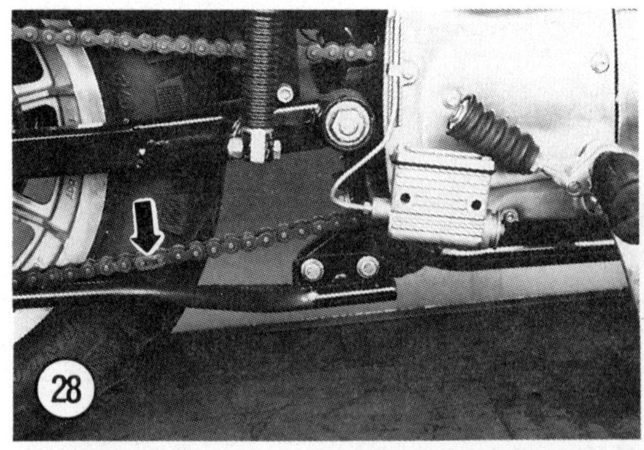

Primary Chain Adjustment

1. Disconnect the negative battery cable.
2. Remove the gearshift lever, if necessary.
3. Remove the primary chain inspection cover. See **Figure 29**, typical.
4. Turn the primary chain to find the tightest point on the chain. Measure chain free play at this point.
5. Measure the primary chain free play through the inspection cover hole (**Figure 30**). The primary chain free play measurements are:
   a. *Cold engine:* 3/8-1/2 in. (9.5-12.7 mm).
   b. *Hot engine:* 1/4-3/8 in. (6.3-9.5 mm).

NOTE

If the free play measurements are incorrect, perform Step 6.

6. Loosen the chain adjuster locknut (A, **Figure 31**) and turn the adjuster (B, **Figure 31**) clockwise to reduce free play or counterclockwise to increase free play. Tighten the primary chain adjuster locknut to the torque specification in **Table 6**.

NOTE

If you cannot set the primary chain free play within the specifications listed in Step 5, the chain adjuster and/or the primary chain are worn and require replacement. Refer to Chapter Five.

7. Reinstall the primary chain inspection cover (**Figure 29**) and its O-ring.

3

Drive Chain Adjustment

NOTE

As drive chains stretch and wear in use, the chain will become tighter at one point. The chain must be checked and adjusted at this point.

1. Turn the rear wheel and check the chain for its tightest point. Mark this spot and turn the wheel so that the mark is located on the chain's lower run, midway between both drive sprockets. Check and adjust the drive chain as follows.
2. Have a rider mounted on the seat.
3. Push the chain up midway between the sprockets on the lower chain run and check the free play (**Figure 32**). The free play should be 1/4 in. (6.3 mm).

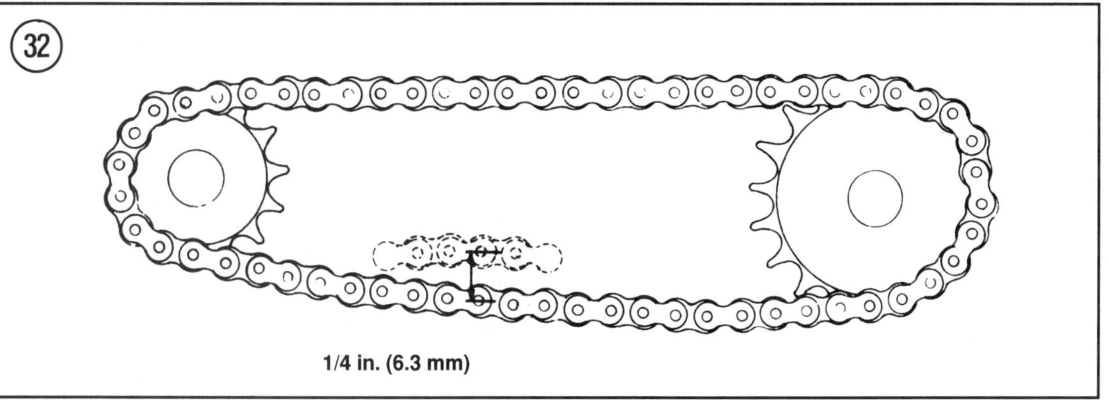

4. If chain adjustment is incorrect, adjust it as follows.
   a. Remove and discard the rear axle cotter pin (A, **Figure 33**).
   b. Loosen the rear axle nut (B, **Figure 33**).
   c. Loosen the axle adjuster locknuts (C, **Figure 33**).
   d. Turn each axle adjuster in or out as required, in equal amounts to maintain rear wheel alignment. The correct amount of chain free play is listed in Step 3.
   e. When the chain free play is correct, check chain alignment with the tool shown in **Figure 34**; you can make the tool out of 1/8 in. aluminum or brass rod. Insert the end of the tool into the index hole in the swing arm as shown in A, **Figure 35**. Slide the rubber grommet along the tool until it aligns with the center of the axle (B, **Figure 35**). Now check alignment on the opposite side, comparing the rubber grommet position with the center of the axle. The alignment on both sides of the axle must be the same. If necessary, adjust the axle with the axle adjusters, while at the same time maintaining correct chain free play.
   f. Tighten the axle nut to the torque specification in **Table 6**. Secure the axle nut and axle with a new cotter pin. Tighten the chain adjuster locknuts securely.

5. If you cannot adjust the drive chain within the limits of the chain adjusters, the chain and sprockets are properly worn and require replacement. Inspect and measure the chain as described in the following section.

WARNING
Excessive free play or a worn chain can result in chain breakage; this could cause a serious accident.

Drive Chain/Sprocket Wear Inspection

A quick check will give you an indication of when to actually measure chain wear. At the rear sprocket, pull one of the links away from the sprocket. If the link pulls away more than 1/2 the height of a sprocket tooth (**Figure 36**), measure chain wear as follows:

1. Remove and discard the rear axle cotter pin.
2. Loosen the axle nut and tighten the chain adjusters to move the wheel rearward until the chain is tight (no slack).
3. Lay a scale along the top chain run (**Figure 37**), and measure the length of any 20 links in the chain, from the center of the first pin you select to the 21st pin. If the link length is longer than 12 7/8 in. (327 mm), install a new drive chain.

CAUTION
Do not cut a worn drive chain in order to continue to use it.

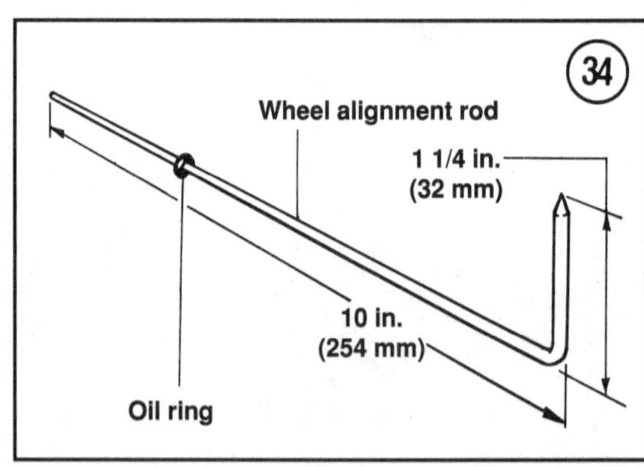

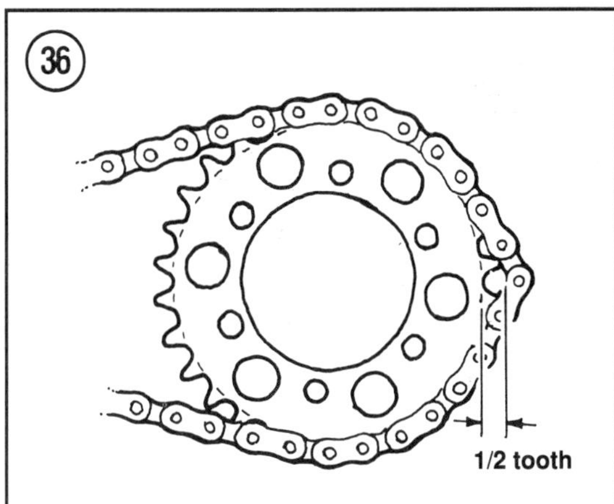

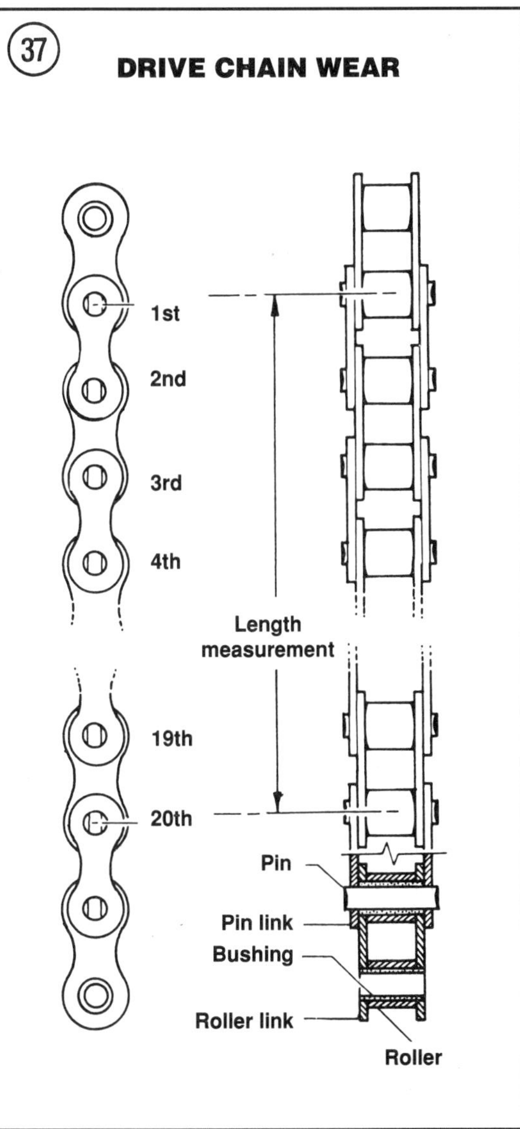

4. Check the inner plate chain faces (**Figure 38**). They should be lightly polished on both sides. If they show considerable uneven wear on one side, the sprockets are not aligned. Severe wear requires chain and sprocket replacement.
5. If the drive chain is worn, inspect the rear wheel and engine sprockets for the following defects:
   a. Undercutting or sharp teeth.
   b. Broken teeth.
6. If wear is evident, replace the chain and sprockets as a set, or you'll soon wear out a new drive chain.
7. Adjust chain play as described in this chapter.

3

Drive Chain Cleaning

1. Remove the drive chain.
2. Immerse the chain in a pan of kerosene and allow it to soak for about a half hour. Move it around and flex it during this period so that dirt between the pins and rollers may work its way out.

CAUTION
Only kerosene should be used to clean O-ring drive chains. Do not use gasoline, solvent, or paint thinner. Steam cleaning should also be avoided as it will damage the O-ring material.

3. Scrub the rollers and side plates with a stiff brush and rinse away loosened grit. Rinse it a couple of times to make sure all dirt is washed out. Hang up the chain and allow it to dry thoroughly.
4. Lubricate the drive chain as described in this chapter.

CAUTION
Always check both sprockets every time the drive chain is removed. If any wear is visible on the teeth, replace the sprocket. Never install a new chain over worn sprockets or a worn chain over new sprockets.

Final Drive Belt Inspection/Adjustment

The final drive belt (**Figure 39**) stretches very little after the first 500 miles of operation, but it should be inspected for tension and alignment according to the maintenance schedule (**Table 1**).

1. Turn the rear wheel and check the drive belt for its tightest point on its lower strand (**Figure 40**). This is the point along the belt that free play should be measured.
2. Park the bike so that it is supported on its jiffy stand and with the transmission in NEUTRAL.

NOTE
The drive belt should be cold when measuring free play.

3. With a force of 10 lb. applied to the middle of the lower belt strand, the lower belt strand should deflect 9/16-11/16 in. (14.3-17.5 mm). See **Figure 40** and **Figure 41**.
4. If the belt tension is out of specification, adjust as follows:
   a. Remove and discard the rear axle cotter pin (A, **Figure 33**).
   b. Loosen the rear axle nut (B, **Figure 33**).
   c. Loosen the axle adjuster locknuts (**Figure 42**).
   d. Turn each axle adjuster in or out as required, in equal amounts to maintain rear wheel alignment. The correct amount of drive belt free play is listed in Step 3.
   e. When the chain free play is correct, check chain alignment with the tool shown in **Figure 34**; you can make the tool out of 1/8 in. aluminum or brass rod. Insert the end of the tool into the index hole in the swing arm as shown in A, **Figure 35**. Slide the rubber grommet along the tool until it aligns with the center of the axle (B, **Figure 35**). Now check alignment on the opposite side, comparing the rubber grommet position with the center of the axle. The alignment on both sides of the axle must be the same. If necessary, adjust the axle with the axle adjusters, while at the same time maintaining correct chain free play.

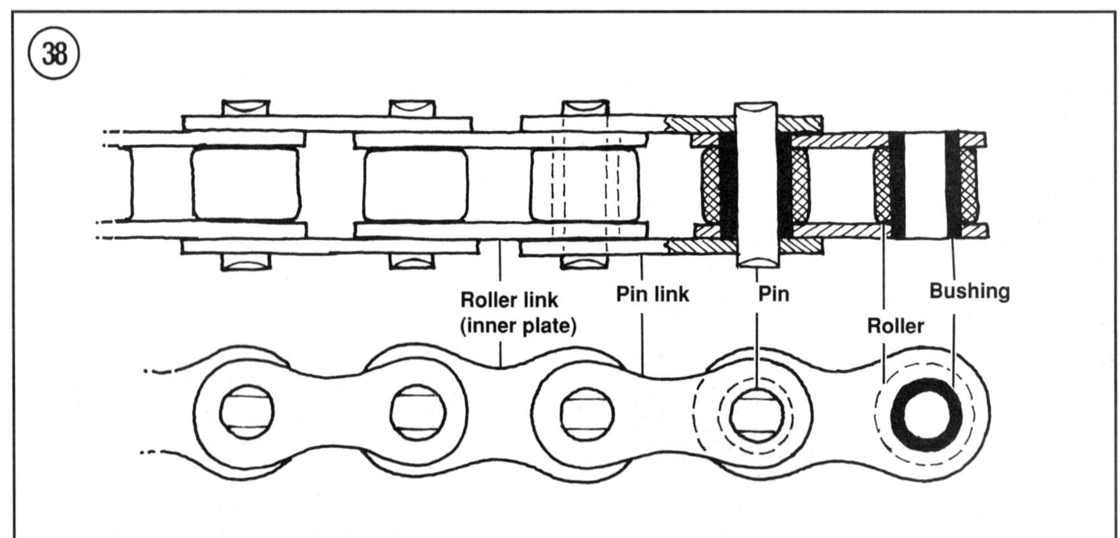

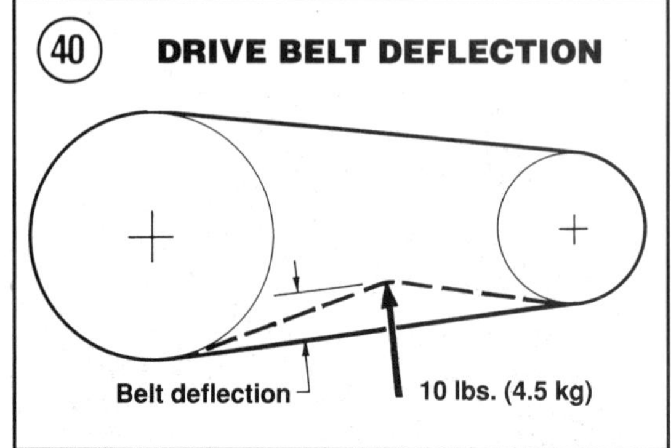

f. Tighten the rear axle nut to the torque specification in **Table 6**. Secure the axle nut and axle with a new cotter pin. Tighten the drive belt adjuster locknuts securely.

Disc Brake Inspection

The hydraulic brake fluid in the disc brake master cylinder should be checked every month. The disc brake pads should be checked at the intervals specified in **Table 1**. Using a flashlight, check the brake pad friction material on each pad; see **Figure 43**, typical. If the thickness of the friction material is 1/16 in. (1.6 mm) or less, replace the brake pads as described in Chapter Twelve.

Disc Brake Fluid Level

1A. *Front brake:* Level the master cylinder assembly by turning the handlebar assembly. Brake fluid should be visible through the inspection window on the master cylinder reservoir (**Figure 44**).

1B. *Rear brake:* Support the bike so that the rear master cylinder is level. Brake fluid should be visible through the inspection window on the master cylinder reservoir (**Figure 45**).

2. If the level is low, perform the following.
3. Wipe the master cylinder cover with a clean shop cloth.
4. Remove the cover screws and cover and lift the diaphragm out of the housing. Correct the level by adding fresh DOT 5 silicone-based brake fluid.

WARNING
Use silicone-based brake fluid clearly marked DOT 5 only and specified for

3

disc brakes. Others may vaporize and cause brake failure.

5. Reinstall all parts.

NOTE

If the brake fluid was so low as to allow air in the hydraulic system, the brakes will have to be bled. Refer to Chapter Twelve.

Disc Brake Lines and Seals

Check brake lines between the master cylinder and the brake caliper. If there is any leakage, tighten the connections and bleed the brakes as described in Chapter Twelve. If this does not stop the leak or if a line is obviously damaged, cracked, or chafed, replace the line and seals and bleed the brake.

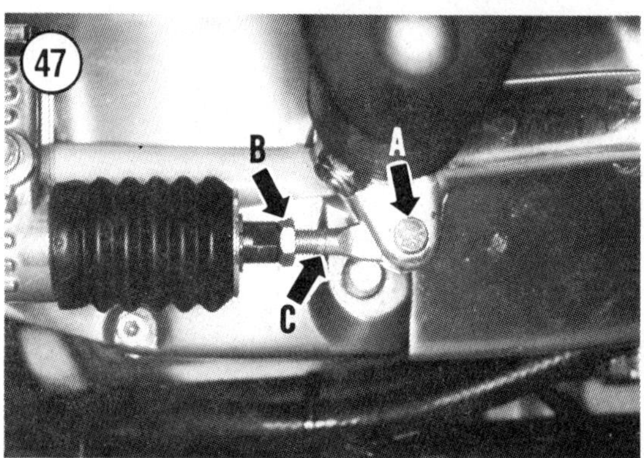

Disc Brake Fluid Change

Every time you remove the reservoir cap a small amount of dirt and moisture enters the brake fluid. The same thing happens if a leak occurs or when any part of the hydraulic system is loosened or disconnected. Dirt can clog the system and cause unnecessary wear. Water in the fluid vaporizes at high temperatures, impairing the hydraulic action and reducing brake performance.

To change brake fluid, follow the brake bleeding procedure in Chapter Twelve. Continue adding new fluid to the master cylinder and bleeding at the calipers until the fluid leaving the calipers is clean and free of contaminants and air bubbles.

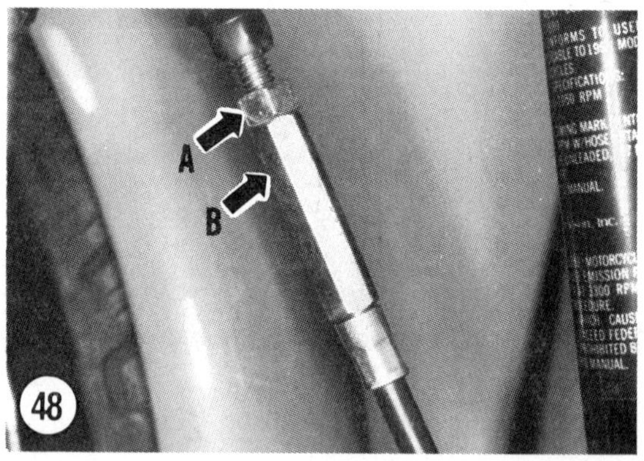

WARNING

Use silicone-based brake fluid clearly marked DOT 5 only. Others may vaporize and cause brake failure.

Front Disc Brake Adjustment

The front disc brake does not require periodic adjustment.

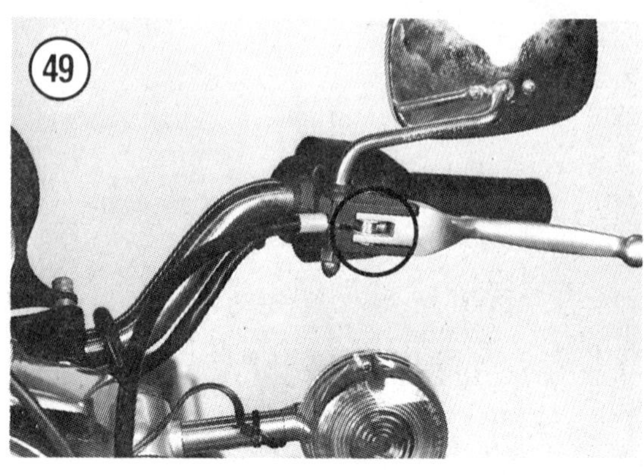

Rear Brake Pedal Linkage Inspection

Check the rear brake pedal linkage assembly for loose, damaged or missing parts.

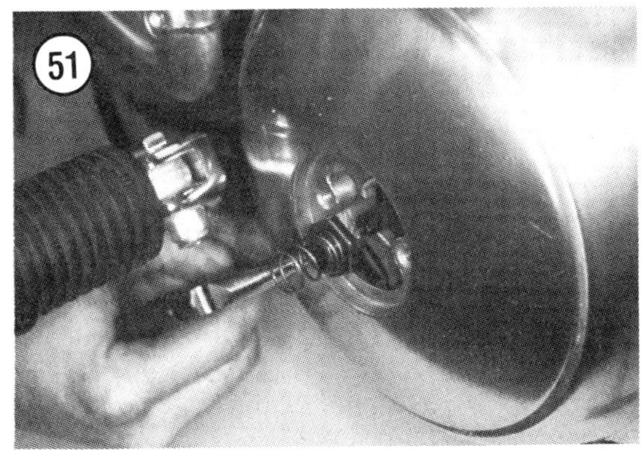

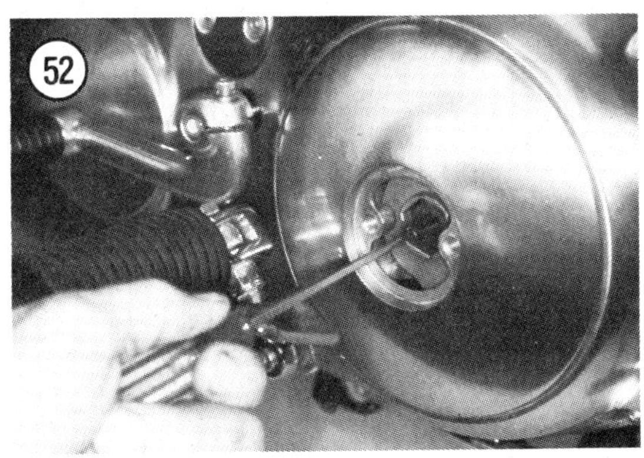

Rear Brake Pedal Adjustment

1. Position the bike so that it is resting straight up on a level surface.
2. Check the brake pedal position in relation to the floor. The brake pedal should be parallel with the floor (**Figure 46**). If adjustment is necessary, perform Step 3.
3. To adjust the rear brake pedal:
   a. Remove the cotter pin securing the clevis pin (A, **Figure 47**) to the rear brake pedal and remove the clevis pin.
   b. Disconnect the brake rod end from the brake pedal.
   c. Loosen the locknut (B, **Figure 47**) and turn the brake rod end (C, **Figure 47**) as required to reposition the brake pedal.
   d. When the adjustment is correct, reinstall the clevis pin through the brake rod end and brake pedal. Secure the clevis pin with a new cotter pin.

Brake Caliper Mounting Bolts

Check the rear brake caliper mounting bolts for tightness. Refer to Chapter Twelve for tightening torques.

Clutch Adjustment (1991-1993)

1. Slide the rubber boot away from the clutch cable adjuster (**Figure 48**).
2. Loosen the cable locknut (A, **Figure 48**) and turn the adjuster (B, **Figure 48**) to provide as much cable slack at the clutch lever (**Figure 49**) as possible.
3. Support the bike so that it sits straight up.
4. Remove the clutch inspection cover (**Figure 50**).
5. Slide the spring with the attached lockplate off of the adjusting screw flats; see **Figure 51**.
6. Turn the clutch adjusting screw counterclockwise until the screw stops. Then turn the clutch adjusting screw 1/4 turn clockwise. See **Figure 52**.
7. Install the lockplate and spring (**Figure 51**) onto the adjusting screw flats. See **Figure 53**.

NOTE

If the lockplate hex will not align with the recess in the outer ramp, slightly

3

rotate the adjusting screw clockwise until alignment is met.

8. Install the clutch inspection cover along with its O-ring. Install and tighten the cover screws securely.
9. Turn the clutch cable adjuster (B, **Figure 48**) to remove all slack in the cable. Then pull the clutch cable ferrule away from the clutch lever bracket and measure the free play; see **Figure 54**. Turn the clutch cable adjuster (B, **Figure 48**) until the free play between the cable ferrule and the clutch lever bracket is 1/16-1/8 in. (1.6-3.2 mm).
10. Hold the clutch cable adjuster and tighten its locknut (A, **Figure 48**) securely.
11. Slide the rubber boot over the clutch cable adjuster.

Clutch Adjustment (1994)

1. Slide the rubber boot away from the clutch cable adjuster (**Figure 48**).
2. Loosen the cable locknut (A, **Figure 48**) and turn the adjuster (B, **Figure 48**) to provide as much cable slack at the clutch lever (**Figure 49**) as possible.
3. Support the bike so that it sits straight up.
4. Remove the left-hand footpeg.
5. Remove the clutch inspection cover (**Figure 55**).

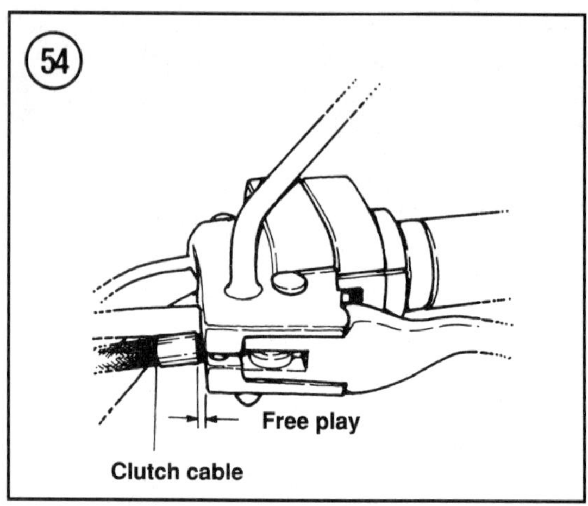

55

CLUTCH RELEASE MECHANISM (1994)

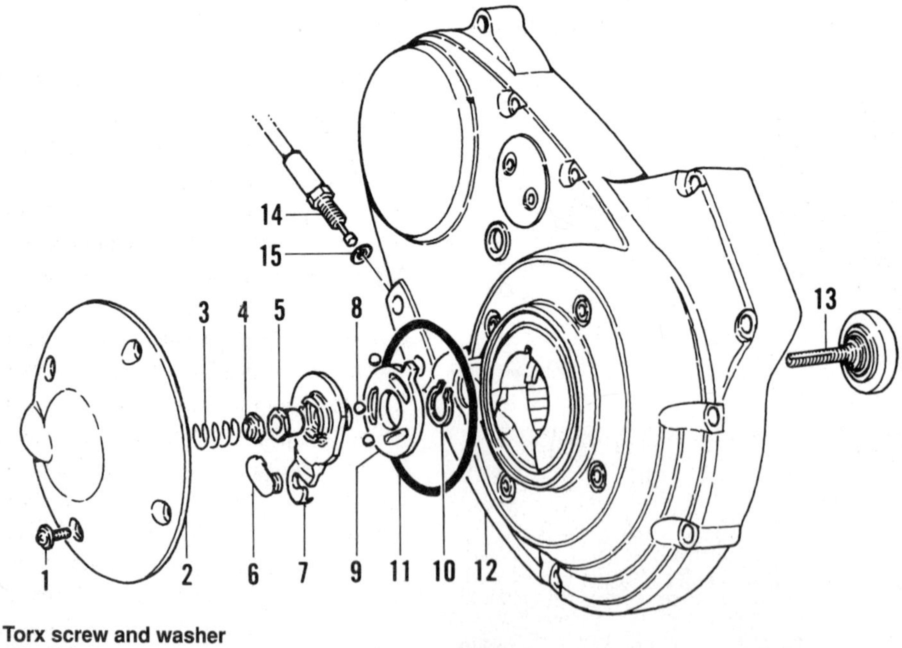

1. Torx screw and washer
2. Clutch inspection cover
3. Spring
4. Lockplate
5. Nut
6. Coupling
7. Outer ramp
8. Ball (3)
9. Inner ramp
10. Retaining ring
11. Quad ring
12. Primary cover
13. Clutch adjusting screw assembly
14. Clutch cable
15. O-ring

NOTE
*Do not damage or lose the quad ring installed in the primary cover; see **Figure 55**.*

6. Slide the spring with the attached lockplate off of the adjusting screw flats; see **Figure 55**.
7. Turn the clutch adjusting screw counterclockwise until the screw stops. Then turn the clutch adjusting screw 1/4 turn clockwise. See **Figure 55**.
8. Install the lockplate and spring (**Figure 55**) onto the adjusting screw flats. See **Figure 55**.

NOTE
If the lockplate hex will not align with the recess in the outer ramp, slightly rotate the adjusting screw clockwise until alignment is met.

9. Install the quad ring if removed. Then install the clutch inspection cover. Install and tighten the cover screws securely.
10. Turn the clutch cable adjuster (B, **Figure 48**) to remove all slack in the cable. Then pull the clutch cable ferrule away from the clutch lever bracket and measure the free play; see **Figure 54**. Turn the clutch cable adjuster (B, **Figure 48**) until the free play between the cable ferrule and the clutch lever bracket is 1/16-1/8 in. (1.6-3.2 mm).
11. Hold the clutch cable adjuster and tighten its locknut (A, **Figure 48**) securely.
12. Slide the rubber boot over the clutch cable adjuster.
13. Tighten the left-hand footpeg locknut to the torque specification in **Table 6**.

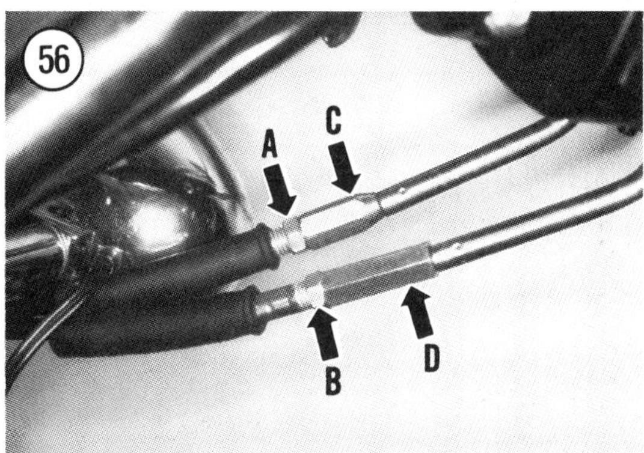

Throttle Cable(s)

Check the throttle cable(s) from grip to carburetors. Make sure it is not kinked or chafed. Replace it if necessary.

Make sure that the throttle grip rotates smoothly from fully closed to fully open. Check at center, full left and full right position of steering.

Throttle Cable Adjustment

1. Loosen the friction screw on the throttle housing.
2. Slide the rubber boots away from the throttle cable adjusters.
3. Loosen both cable adjuster locknuts (A and B, **Figure 56**), then turn the cable adjusters (C and D) clockwise as far as possible.
4. With the motorcycle's front wheel pointing straight ahead, open the throttle fully with the throttle grip and hold it in this position. Then turn the throttle cable adjuster (C, **Figure 56**) counterclockwise until the throttle cam stop (A, **Figure 57**) just touches the carburetor stop plate (B, **Figure 57**). If you are not sure if the throttle valve is fully open, turn the pulley by hand to see if there is more movement. Tighten the throttle cable adjuster locknut (A, **Figure 56**). Release the throttle grip.
5. With the motorcycle's front wheel turned all the way to the right, lengthen the idle cable adjuster (D, **Figure 56**) until the lower end of the idle cable just contacts the spring in the carburetor cable guide (C, **Figure 57**). Tighten the locknut (B, **Figure 56**).
6. Start the engine and rev it several times to be sure the engine returns fully to idle. If the engine does not return to idle, loosen the idle cable adjuster locknut (B, **Figure 56**) and turn the idle cable adjuster (D, **Figure 56**) clockwise as required. Tighten the cable adjuster (B, **Figure 56**).
7. Support the bike so that the front wheel is off the ground. Start the engine and allow it to idle, then turn

the handlebar from side to side. The engine idle speed must not rise above idle throughout the handlebar movement. If the idle speed rises, readjust the throttle cables. If this does not fix the problem, check the throttle cables for proper routing or possible damage.

WARNING
Do not ride the motorcycle until the throttle cable adjustment is correct. A sticking or improperly adjusted throttle cable can cause you to crash.

Enrichener (Choke) Cable Adjustment

The enrichener knob (**Figure 58**) should move from fully open to fully closed without any sign of binding. The knob should also stay in its fully closed or fully open position without creeping. If the knob does not stay in position, adjust tension on the cable by turning the knurled plastic nut behind the enrichener knob (**Figure 58**) as follows.

NOTE
The enrichener cable must have sufficient cable resistance to work properly. Do not lubricate the enrichener cable or its conduit.

1. Loosen the hex nut behind the mounting bracket. Then move the cable to free it from the mounting bracket slot.
2. Hold the cable across its flats with a wrench and turn the knurled plastic nut counterclockwise to reduce cable resistance (**Figure 59**) so that the knob can slide inward freely.
3. Turn the knurled plastic nut clockwise so that sufficient cable resistance (**Figure 59**) is maintained on the cable. Continue adjustment until the knob remains stationary when pulled all the way out while at the same time the knob movement is smooth.
4. Reinstall the cable into the slot in the mounting bracket. Tighten the hex nut to secure the cable to the mounting bracket.

Fuel Shutoff Valve/Filter

Refer to Chapter Seven for complete details on removal, cleaning, and installation of the fuel shutoff valve.

Fuel Line Inspection

Inspect the fuel lines from the fuel tank to the carburetor. If any are cracked or starting to deteriorate, they must be replaced. Make sure the small hose clamps are in place and holding securely.

WARNING
A damaged or deteriorated fuel line presents a very dangerous fire hazard to both the rider and the bike if fuel should spill onto a hot engine or exhaust pipe.

Exhaust System

Check all fittings for exhaust leakage. Tighten all bolts and nuts; replace any gaskets as necessary. Removal and installation procedures are described in Chapter Seven.

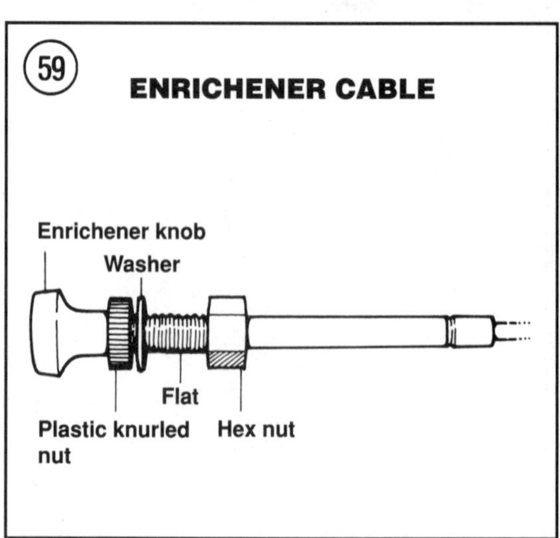

Air Filter Removal/Installation

A clogged air filter can decrease the efficiency and life of the engine. Never run the bike without the air filter installed; even minute particles of dust can cause severe internal engine wear.

The service intervals specified in **Table 1** should be followed with general use. However, the air filter should be serviced more often if the bike is ridden in dusty areas.

The air filter on all models is installed on the right-hand side of the bike. See **Figure 60**.

1. Remove the air filter cover (**Figure 61**).
2. Remove the air filter (**Figure 62**).
3. Clean the filter as described in this chapter.
4. If necessary, remove the air filter housing as follows:

a. Remove the cylinder head backplate bolts (A, **Figure 63**).

CAUTION

When removing the screws in substep b, do not allow the screws to engage the backplate insert sleeve threads. Doing so will damage the screw threads.

b. Loosen the screws (B, **Figure 63**) 1-2 turns in a crisscross pattern. Continue until the screws disengage from the carburetor holes. Remove the backplate along with the screws.

NOTE

Do not remove the screws from the backplate unless the backplate is going to be replaced.

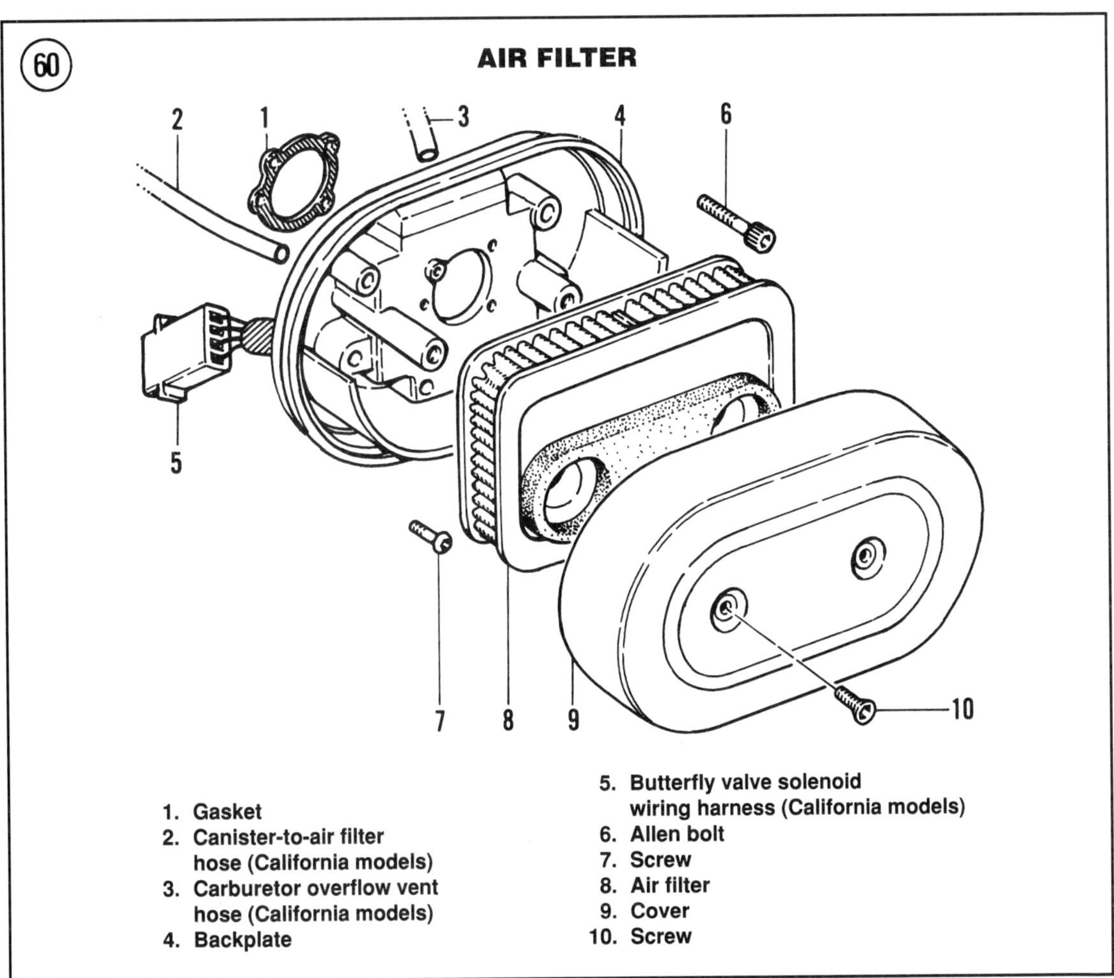

1. Gasket
2. Canister-to-air filter hose (California models)
3. Carburetor overflow vent hose (California models)
4. Backplate
5. Butterfly valve solenoid wiring harness (California models)
6. Allen bolt
7. Screw
8. Air filter
9. Cover
10. Screw

3

c. On California models, label and then disconnect the hoses at the backplate; see **Figure 60**. Disconnect the butterfly valve solenoid wiring 4-pin connector.
d. Remove the backplate and gasket from the carburetor.

5. Installation is the reverse of these steps. If the backplate assembly was removed, install a new carburetor gasket. Tighten the backplate screws and bolts to the torque specification in **Table 5**.

Air Filter Cleaning

Refer to **Figure 60** for this procedure.

NOTE
When servicing an aftermarket air filter, follow the manufacturer's instructions.

1. Inspect the element and make sure it is in good condition. If the element does not fit its frame properly, replace it.
2. Clean the air filter in warm, soapy water.

WARNING
Do not use solvents or gasoline to clean the air filter. These chemicals may cause an intake system fire. This can result in injury and loss of the vehicle.

3. Dry the air filter with low pressure compressed air—32 psi (221 kPa maximum).
4. View the air filter with a strong light source. If you can see light evenly passing through the element, it is sufficiently clean.
5. Clean out the inside of the air box with a shop rag and cleaning solvent. Remove any foreign matter that may have passed through a broken filter element.
6. Do not install the air filter until it is completely dry.

Wheel Bearings

The wheel bearings should be cleaned and repacked at the intervals specified in **Table 1**.

Refer to Chapter Nine for complete service procedures.

Steering Play

The steering head should be checked for looseness at the intervals specified in **Table 1**. Adjustment procedures are given in Chapter Ten.

Steering Head Bearings

The steering head bearings should be repacked at the intervals specified in **Table 1**; see Chapter Ten for service procedures.

Rear Swing Arm Bearings

Lubricate the rear swing arm bearings at the intervals specified in **Table 1**; see Chapter Eleven for service procedures.

Rear Swing Arm Pivot Shaft Bolt

Check the rear swing arm pivot shaft bolt tightness at the intervals listed in **Table 1**. Refer to Chapter Eleven for tightening torques.

Rear Shock Absorbers

At the specified intervals (**Table 1**), check the rear shock absorbers for leaking seals or other damage.

Engine Mount Bolts

At the specified intervals (**Table 1**), check the engine mount bolts for looseness or missing parts. Refer to Chapter Four for tightening torques.

Front Forks

Periodically check the front fork mounting bolts for tightness. Refer to Chapter Ten for torque specifications.

Nuts, Bolts, and Other Fasteners

Constant vibration can loosen many fasteners on a motorcycle. Check the tightness of all fasteners, especially those on:

a. Engine mounting hardware.
b. Engine crankcase covers.
c. Handlebar and front forks.
d. Gearshift lever.
e. Sprocket bolts and nuts.
f. Brake pedal and lever.
g. Exhaust system.
h. Lighting equipment.

TUNE-UP

A complete tune-up restores performance and power that is lost due to normal wear and deterioration of engine parts. Because engine wear occurs over a combined period of time and mileage, the engine tune-up should be performed at the intervals specified in **Table 1**. More frequent tune-ups may be required if the bike is ridden primarily in stop-and-go traffic.

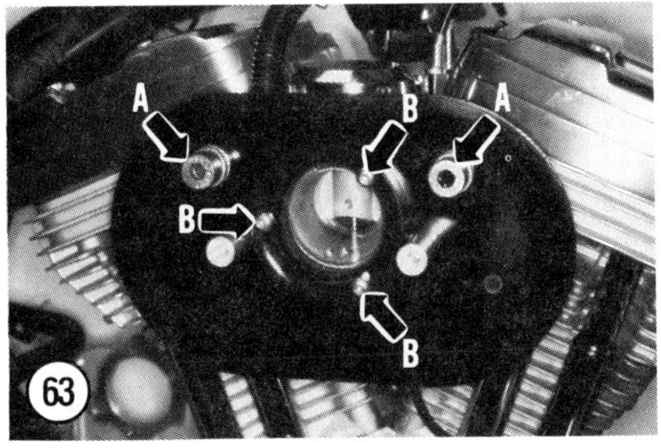

Table 8 summarizes tune-up specifications.

Before starting a tune-up procedure, make sure to first have all new parts on hand.

Because different systems in an engine interact, the procedures should be done in the following order:

a. Clean or replace the air filter element.
b. Check engine compression.
c. Check or replace the spark plugs.
d. Check the ignition timing.
e. Adjust carburetor idle speed.

To perform a tune-up on your Harley-Davidson, you will need the following tools:

a. Spark plug wrench.
b. Socket wrench and assorted sockets.
c. Compression gauge.
d. Spark plug wire feeler gauge and gapper tool.
e. Ignition timing light.

Air Filter

The air filter element should be cleaned or replaced prior to doing other tune-up procedures, as described in this chapter.

Compression Test

At every tune-up, check cylinder compression. Record the results and compare them at the next check. A running record will show trends in deterioration so that corrective action can be taken before complete failure.

The results, when properly interpreted can indicate general cylinder, piston ring and valve condition.

1. Warm the engine to normal operating temperature. Set the choke and throttle valves so that they are completely open.
2. Remove the spark plugs (**Figure 64**) and properly ground the spark plugs with the spark plug wires to the cylinder heads.
3. Connect the compression tester to one cylinder following manufacturer's instructions (**Figure 65**).
4. Have an assistant crank the engine over until there is no further rise in pressure.
5. Remove the tester and record the reading.
6. Repeat Steps 3-5 for the other cylinder.

When interpreting the results, actual readings are not as important as the difference between the readings. Standard compression pressure is shown in **Table 8**. Pressure should not vary from cylinder to cylinder by more than 10 percent. Greater differences indicate worn or broken rings, leaky or sticky valves, blown head gasket or a combination of all.

If compression readings do not differ between cylinders by more than 10 percent, the rings and valves are in good condition. If a low reading (10 percent or more) is obtained on one of the cylinders, it indicates valve or ring trouble. To determine which, pour about a teaspoon of engine oil through the spark plug hole onto the top of the piston. Turn the engine over once to clear some of the excess oil, then take another compression test and record the reading. If the compression returns to normal, the valves are good but the rings are defective on that cylinder. If compression does not increase, the valves require servicing. A valve could be hanging open but not burned or a piece of carbon could be on a valve seat.

NOTE

If the compression is low, the engine cannot be tuned to maximum performance. The worn parts must be replaced and the engine rebuilt.

Cylinder Leakage Test

A cylinder leakage test can determine engine problems from leaking valves, blown head gaskets or broken, worn or stuck piston rings. A cylinder leakage test is performed by applying compressed air to the cylinder and then measuring the percent of leakage. A cylinder leakage tester and an air compressor are required to perform this test (**Figure 66**).

Follow the manufacturer's directions along with the following information when performing a cylinder leakage test.

1. Start and run the engine until it reaches normal operating temperature.
2. Remove the air filter assembly. Then set the throttle and choke valves in their wide open position.
3. Remove the ignition timing inspection plug from the crankcase (**Figure 67**).
4. Set the piston for the cylinder being tested to TDC on its compression stroke.
5. Remove the spark plugs (**Figure 64**).

NOTE

The engine may want to turn over when air pressure is applied to the cylinder. To prevent this from happening, shift the transmission into fifth gear and lock the rear brake pedal so that the rear brake is applied.

6. Make a cylinder leakage test following the manufacturer's instructions. Listen for air leaking while noting the following:
   a. Air leaking through the exhaust pipe points to a leaking exhaust valve.
   b. Air leaking through the carburetor points to a leaking intake valve.

NOTE

Air leaking through the valves can also be caused by pushrods that are too long.

   c. Air leaking through the ignition timing inspection hole points to worn or broken piston rings, a leaking cylinder head gasket or a worn piston.
7. Repeat for the other cylinder.
8. Any cylinder with 12 percent cylinder leakdown requires further service.

Correct Spark Plug Heat Range

Spark plugs are available in various heat ranges that are hotter or colder than the spark plugs originally installed at the factory.

Select plugs in a heat range designed for the loads and temperature conditions under which the engine will operate. Using incorrect heat ranges can cause piston seizure, scored cylinder walls or damaged piston crowns.

In general, use a hotter plug for low speeds, low loads and low temperatures. Use a colder plug for high speeds, high engine loads and high temperatures.

NOTE
In areas where seasonal temperature variations are great, a "two-plug system" — a cold plug for hard summer riding and a hot plug for slower winter operation may prevent spark plug and engine problems.

The reach (length) of a plug is also important. A longer than normal plug could interfere with the valves and pistons causing permanent and severe damage. Refer to **Figure 68**. The standard heat range spark plugs are listed in **Table 8**.

3

Spark Plug Cleaning/Replacement

1. Grasp the spark plug leads as near to the plug as possible and pull them off the plugs.

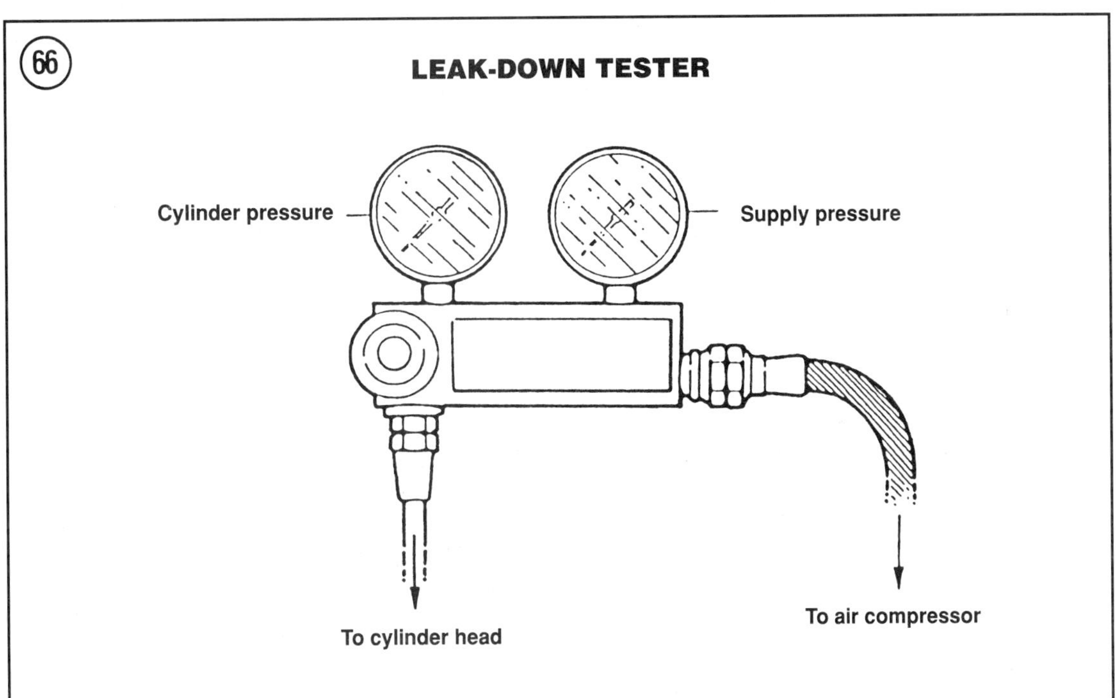

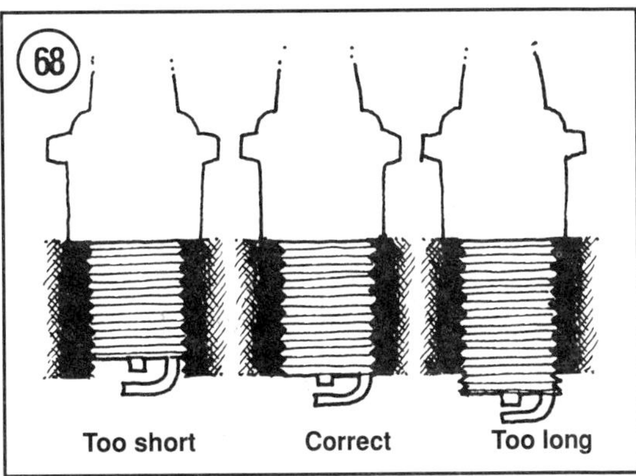

SPARK PLUG CONDITION

NORMAL

- Identified by light tan or gray deposits on the firing tip.
- Can be cleaned.

GAP BRIDGED

- Identified by deposit buildup closing gap between electrodes.
- Caused by oil or carbon fouling. If deposits are not excessive, the plug can be cleaned.

OIL FOULED

- Identified by wet black deposits on the Insulator shell bore and electrodes.
- Caused by excessive oil entering combustion chamber through worn rings and pistons, excessive clearance between valve guides and stems or worn or loose bearings. Can be cleaned. If engine is not repaired, use a hotter plug.

CARBON FOULED

- Identified by black, dry fluffy carbon deposits on insulator tips, exposed shell surfaces and electrodes.
- Caused by too cold a plug, weak ignition, dirty air cleaner, too rich a fuel mixture or excessive idling. Can be cleaned.

LEAD FOULED

- Identified by dark gray, black, yellow or tan deposits or a fused glazed coating on the insulator tip.
- Caused by highly leaded gasoline. Can be cleaned.

WORN

- Identified by severely eroded or worn electrodes.
- Caused by normal wear. Should be replaced.

FUSED SPOT DEPOSIT

- Identified by melted or spotty deposits resembling bubbles or blisters.
- Caused by sudden acceleration. Can be cleaned.

OVERHEATING

- Identified by a white or light gray insulator with small black or gray brown spots and with bluish-burnt appearance of electrodes.
- Caused by engine overheating, wrong type of fuel, loose spark plugs, too hot a plug or incorrect ignition timing. Replace the plug.

PREIGNITION

- Identified by melted electrodes and possibly blistered insulator. Metallic deposits on insulator indicate engine damage.
- Caused by wrong type of fuel, incorrect ignition timing or advance, too hot a plug, burned valves or engine overheating. Replace the plug.

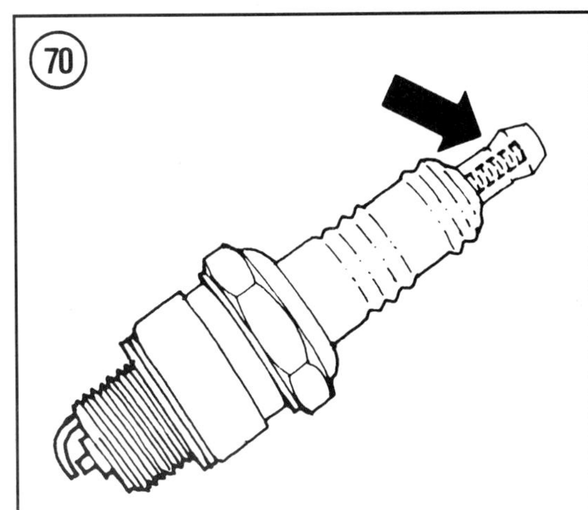

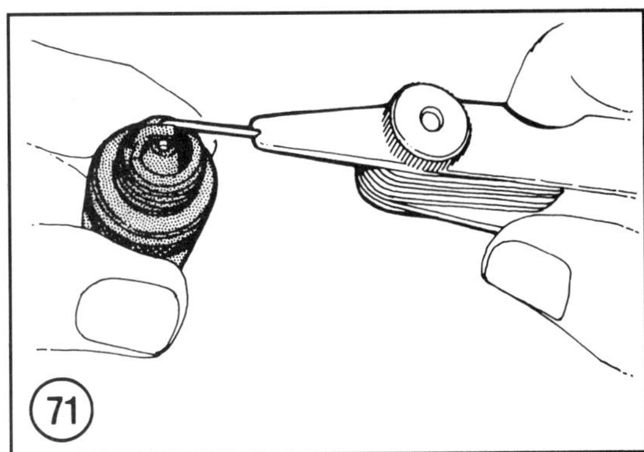

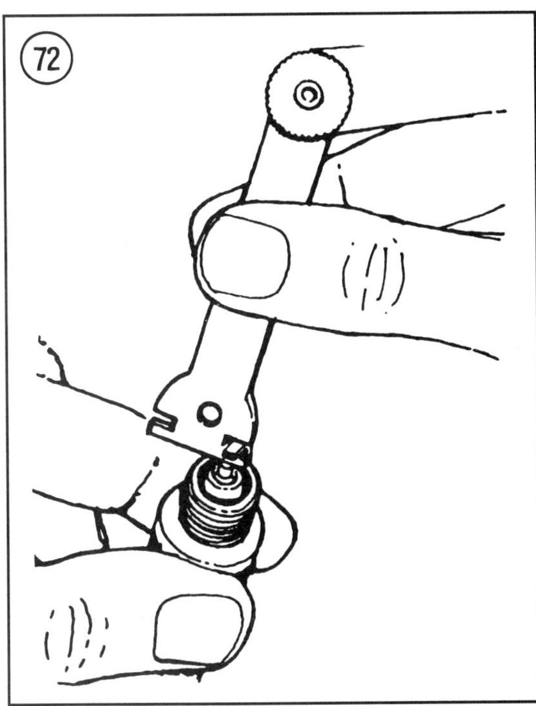

2. Blow away any dirt that has accumulated in the spark plug wells.

CAUTION
The dirt could fall into the cylinders when the plugs are removed, causing serious engine damage.

3. Remove the spark plugs with a spark plug wrench.

NOTE
If plugs are difficult to remove, apply penetrating oil such as WD-40 or Liquid Wrench around base of plugs and let it soak in about 10-20 minutes.

4. Inspect spark plug carefully. Look for plugs with broken center porcelain, excessively eroded electrodes and excessive carbon or oil fouling (**Figure 69**). Replace such plugs.

NOTE
Spark plug cleaning with the use of a sand-blast type device is not recommended. While this type of cleaning is thorough, the plug must be perfectly free of all abrasive cleaning material when done. If not, it is possible for the cleaning material to fall into the engine during operation and cause damage.

Spark Plug Gapping and Installation

New plugs should be carefully gapped to ensure a reliable, consistent spark. You must use a special spark plug gapping tool.

1. Remove the new plugs from the box. Screw in the small pieces that may be loose in each box (**Figure 70**).
2. Insert a wire gauge between the center and the side electrode of each plug (**Figure 71**). The correct gap is listed in **Table 8**. If the gap is correct, you will feel a slight drag as you pull the wire through. If there is no drag, or the gauge won't pass through, bend the side electrode *with the gapping tool* (**Figure 72**) to set the proper gap (**Table 8**).
3. Put a small drop of oil or anti-seize compound on the threads of each spark plug.
4. Screw each spark plug in by hand until it seats. Very little effort is required. If force is necessary, you have the plug cross-threaded or the spark plug threads in the cylinder head are damaged or contami-

nated with carbon or other debris; unscrew it and try again.

5. Tighten the spark plugs to the torque specification in **Table 6**. If you don't have a torque wrench, an additional 1/4 to 1/2 turn is sufficient after the gasket has made contact with the head. If you are reinstalling old, regapped plugs and are reusing the old gasket, only tighten an additional 1/4 turn.

NOTE

Do not overtighten. Besides making the plug difficult to remove, the excessive torque will squash the gasket and destroy its sealing ability.

6. Install each spark plug wire. Make sure it goes to the correct spark plug.

Reading Spark Plugs

Much information about engine and spark plug performance can be determined by careful examination of the spark plugs. This information is only valid after performing the following steps.

1. Ride bike a short distance at full throttle.
2. Turn off kill switch before closing throttle and simultaneously pull in clutch. Coast and brake to a stop. *Do not* downshift transmission while stopping.
3. Remove spark plugs and examine them. Compare them to **Figure 69**.

If the insulator is white or burned, the plug is too hot and should be replaced with a colder one.

A too-cold plug will have sooty deposits ranging in color from dark brown to black. Replacing with a hotter plug and check for too-rich carburetion or evidence of oil blow-by at the piston rings.

If any one plug is found unsatisfactory, discard both.

Ignition Timing Adjustment

Ignition timing specifications are listed in **Table 9**.

1. Remove the plug from the timing hole on the right side of the engine (**Figure 67**). A clear plastic viewing plug is available from Harley-Davidson dealers to minimize oil spray. Make sure the plug doesn't contact the flywheel after screwing it in.
2. On 883 cc models, attach a tachometer to the engine following the manufacturer's instructions.
3. Connect an inductive clamp-on timing light to the front cylinder spark plug wire following the manufacturer's instructions.
4. Start the engine and allow it to warm to normal operating temperature. Then set idle speed at 1,650-1,950 rpm.
5. Aim the timing light at the timing inspection hole. At 1,650-1,950 rpm, the front cylinder's advance mark should appear in the center of the inspection window as shown in **Figure 73**.

NOTE

If the mark does not align, adjust the ignition timing, starting with Step 6. If the ignition timing is correct, proceed to Step 9.

6. Remove the sensor plate outer cover, inner cover and gasket as described under *Ignition Component Replacement* in Chapter Eight.
7. Loosen the timing plate sensor plate screws (**Figure 74**) just enough to allow the plate to rotate. Start the engine and turn the plate as required so that the advanced mark is aligned as described in Step 5. To adjust the plate, use a screwdriver in the plate's slot. Make sure idle speed specified in Step 5 is maintained when checking timing. Tighten the screws (**Figure 74**) and recheck ignition timing.
8. Install the sensor plate gasket, inner cover and outer cover as described in Chapter Eight.
9. As part of the tune-up, check the vacuum operated electric switch (VOES) as follows:

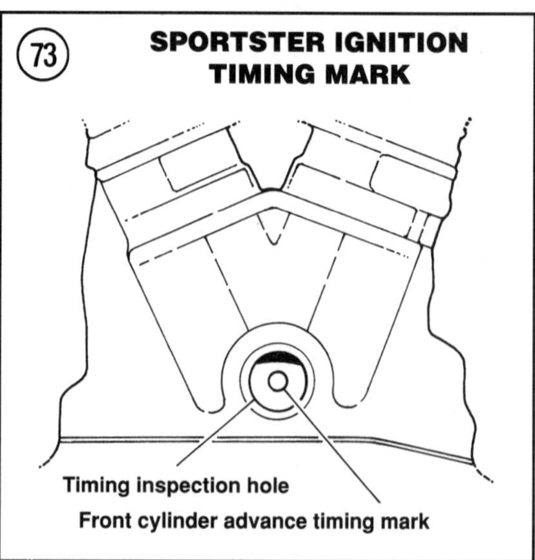

CAUTION

The Vacuum Operated Electric Switch (VOES) must be tested at each tune-up and replaced if malfunctioning. A damaged VOES switch will allow too high a spark advance and result with severe engine knock and damage.

a. Start the engine and allow to idle.

b. On 1991-1992 models, disconnect the VOES vacuum hose at the carburetor (**Figure 75**) with the engine idling at 950-1,050 rpm. Maintain this engine rpm when performing the following.

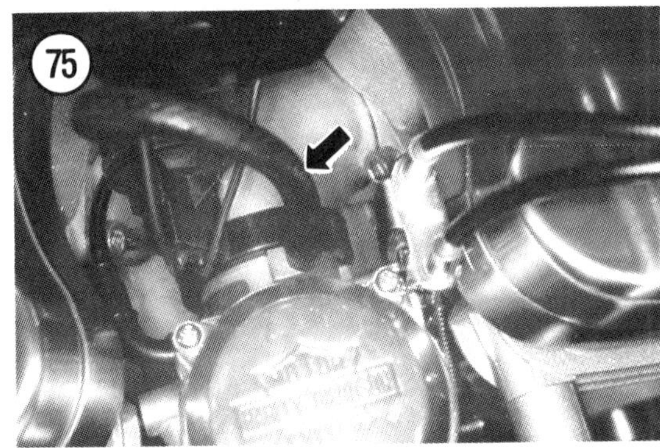

c. On 1993-on models, disconnect the VOES vacuum hose at the carburetor (**Figure 75**) with the engine idling at 1,650-1,950 rpm. Maintain this engine rpm when performing the following.

d. Plug the carburetor VOES port. With the port blocked, the engine speed should decrease and the ignition timing should retard—check with the timing light. When the vacuum hose is reconnected to the VOES port, the engine speed should increase.

e. If the engine failed to operate as described in substep c, check the VOES wire connection at the ignition module. Also check the VOES ground wire for looseness or damage. If the wire connections are okay, test the VOES switch as described in Chapter Eight.

10. Reinstall the timing hole plug (**Figure 67**).

11. Remove the timing light and tachometer (if used).

12. Reset the engine idle speed as described in the following procedure.

Carburetor Idle Speed Adjustment

1. On 883 cc models, attach a tachometer to the engine following the manufacturer's instructions.
2. Start the engine and warm it to normal operating temperature. Check that the enrichener knob is closed (**Figure 76**).
3. Set the idle speed with the idle adjust screw (**Figure 77**). See **Table 10** for specifications.
4. The idle mixture is set and sealed at the factory. It is not intended to be adjustable.
5. Rev the engine a couple of times and see if the idle speed is constant. If necessary, readjust the idle speed by turning the idle adjust screw (**Figure 77**).
6. On 883 cc models, disconnect and remove the tachometer.

Table 1 PERIODIC MAINTENANCE (1985-ON)*

Interval	Service
Initial 500 miles (800 km); thereafter 2,500 miles (4,000 km)	Check brake pad wear Check brake disc wear Inspect fuel valve, fuel line and all fittings for leaks Check engine idle speed Check battery fluid level; refill with distilled water Check electrical equipment and switches for proper operation Check throttle operation Operate and check enrichener cable operation Check tire pressure and tread wear
Initial 500 miles (800 km); thereafter every 5,000 miles (8,000 km)	Change engine oil and replace oil filter Inspect and clean air filter Check rear drive chain or belt tension; adjust if necessary Inspect primary chain Check primary chain tension; adjust if necessary Change primary drive/transmission oil Check clutch adjustment; adjust if necessary Check brake fluid level; refill with DOT 5 brake fluid Check rear brake pedal adjustment; adjust if necessary Perform general lubrication to equipment specified in this chapter Check ignition timing Check vacuum operated electric switch (VOES) Check rear swing arm pivot shaft tightness Check engine mount bolt tightness Inspect rear shock absorber Check all exposed fasteners for tightness** Lubricate rear swing arm bearing
Initial 500 miles (800 km) and first 5,000 miles (8,000 km); thereafter every 10,000 miles (16,000 km)	Check steering bearing adjustment
Every 2,500 miles (4,000 km)	Check engine oil level Check primary drive/transmission oil level
Every 5,000 miles (8,000 km)	Inspect rear brake caliper mounting pins and boots; lubricate pins and boots during reassembly Inspect and lubricate rear brake and shifter linkage assembly Lubricate throttle control sleeve Lubricate speedometer cable
Initial 5,000 miles (8,000 km); thereafter every 10,000 miles (16,000 km)	Inspect spark plug gap and condition
Every 10,000 miles (16,000 km)	Replace spark plugs Replace front fork oil Lubricate steering bearings Clean and lubricate wheel bearings

* This maintenance schedule should be considered a guide to general maintenance and lubrication intervals. Harder than normal use and exposure to mud, water, high humidity, etc., will naturally dictate more frequent attention to most maintenance items.

** Except cylinder head bolts. Cylinder head bolts should be tightened by following the procedure listed in Chapter Four. Improper tightening of the cylinder head bolts may cause head leakage.

Table 2 TIRE PRESSURE

	psi	kg/cm²
Up to 300 lb. load*		
Front	30	2.1
Rear	36	2.5
Up to GVWR maximum load**		
Front	30	2.1
Rear	40	2.8

* 300 lb. load includes rider, passenger and cargo.
** The gross vehicle weight rating (GVWR) is listed on a decal mounted on the frame.

Table 3 ENGINE OIL

Type	HD rating	Viscosity	Lowest ambient operating temperature
HD Multigrade	HD 240	SAE 10W/40	Below 40° F
HD Multigrade	HD 240	SAE 20W/50	Above 40° F
HD Regular Heavy*	HD 240	SAE 50	Above 60° F
HD Extra Heavy*	HD 240	SAE 60	Above 80° F

* Not recommended for use when ambient temperature is below 50° F.

Table 4 ENGINE AND PRIMARY DRIVE/TRANSMISSION OIL CAPACITIES

Oil tank*	3 U.S. qts. (2.8 L, 2.5 imp. qts.)
Primary drive/transmission	
1991-1992	40 U.S. oz. (1,183 ml, 41.7 imp. oz.)
1993-1994	32 U.S. oz. (946 ml, 33.3 imp. oz.)

* With filter.

Table 5 RECOMMENDED LUBRICANTS AND FLUIDS

Brake fluid	DOT 5 silicone-based
Front fork oil	HD Type E or equivalent
Battery top up	Distilled water
Transmission	HD Sport Trans Fluid or equivalent
Fuel	87 pump octane or higher leaded or unleaded

Table 6 TIGHTENING TORQUES

	ft.-lb.	N·m
Air filter		
Backplate-to-carburetor screws	3-5	4.1-6.8
Backplate-to-cylinder head bolts		
1991-1992	35	47.5
1993-on	10-20	13.6-27.1
Cover screws	3-5	4.1-6.8
Primary cover drain plug	14-21	19-28
Primary chain adjuster locknut	20-25	27-34
Rear axle nut	60-65	81-88
Left-hand footpeg locknut	16-28	22-38
Spark plugs	11-18	15-24
Oil pressure switch	5-7	6.8-9.5

Table 7 FRONT FORK OIL CAPACITY

	Wet		Dry	
	U.S. oz.	ml	U.S. oz.	ml
1991	9.0	266	10.2	302
1992-on				
883 Hugger	10.7	316	12.1	358
All other models	9.0	266	10.2	302

Table 8 TUNE-UP SPECIFICATIONS

Engine compression	120 psi (8.3 kg/cm^2)
Spark plugs	
Type	HD No. 6R12
Gap	0.038-0.043 in. (0.97-1.09 mm)

Table 9 IGNITION TIMING SPECIFICATIONS

Idle speed	V.O.E.S Connected	V.O.E.S. Disconnected
Fast: 1,750*	40° BTDC	Approximately 16° BTDC
Normal: 950-1,050	30° BTDC	Approximately 7.5° BTDC

* Set ignition timing @ 1,650-1,950 rpm with V.O.E.S. connected.

Table 10 CARBURETOR IDLE SPEED SPECIFICATIONS

Slow idle speed setting	950-1,050 rpm
Idle speed when setting ignition timing	1,650-1,950 rpm

CHAPTER FOUR

ENGINE

All models are equipped with the V2 evolution engine, an air-cooled 4-cycle, overhead-valve V-twin engine. The engine has three major assemblies: engine, crankcase and gearcase. Viewed from the engine's right side, engine rotation is clockwise.

This chapter provides complete service and overhaul procedures, including information for disassembly, removal, inspection, service and reassembly of the engine. **Tables 1-3** at the end of this chapter provide complete engine service specifications.

Work on the engine requires considerable mechanical ability. You should carefully consider your own capabilities before attempting any operation involving major disassembly of the engine.

Much of the labor charge for dealer repairs involves the removal and disassembly of other parts to reach the defective component. Even if you decide not to tackle the entire engine overhaul after studying the text and illustrations in this chapter, it can be cheaper to perform the preliminary operations yourself and then take the engine to your dealer. Since dealers have lengthy waiting lists for service (especially during the spring and summer season), this practice can reduce the time your unit is in the shop. If you have done much of the preliminary work, your repairs can be scheduled and performed much quicker.

General engine specifications are listed in **Table 1**. **Tables 1-7** are found at the end of the chapter.

SERVICE PRECAUTIONS

Whenever you work on your Harley, there are several precautions that should be followed to help with disassembly, inspection, and reassembly.

1. Before beginning the job, re-read Chapter One of this manual. You will do a better job with this information fresh in your mind.
2. In the text there is frequent mention of the left-hand and right-hand side of the engine. This refers to the engine as it is mounted in the frame, not as it sits on your workbench.
3. Always replace a worn or damaged fastener with one of the same size, type and torque requirements. Make sure to identify each bolt before replacing it with another. Bolt threads should be lubricated with engine oil, unless otherwise specified, before torque is applied. If a tightening torque is not listed in **Table 4** (end of this chapter), refer to the torque and fastener information in Chapter One.

NOTE

All of the washers and fasteners used in the engine are hardened. Make sure to use exact replacement fasteners as described in Step 3.

4. Use special tools where noted. In some cases, it may be possible to perform the procedure with makeshift tools, but this procedure is not recommended. The use of makeshift tools can damage the components and may cause serious personal injury. Where special tools are required, these may be purchased through any Harley-Davidson dealer. Other tools can be purchased through your dealer, or from a motorcycle or automotive accessory store.
5. Before removing the first bolt and to prevent frustration during installation, get a number of boxes, plastic bags and containers and store the parts as they are removed (**Figure 1**). Also have on hand a roll of masking tape and a permanent, waterproof marking pen to label each part or assembly as required. If your Harley was purchased second hand and it appears that some of the wiring may have been changed or replaced, it will be helpful to label each electrical connection before disconnecting it.
6. Use a vise with protective jaws to hold parts. If protective jaws are not available, insert wooden blocks on either side of the part(s) before clamping them in the vise.
7. Remove and installed pressed-on parts with an appropriate mandrel, support and hydraulic press. **Do not** try to pry, hammer or otherwise force them on or off.
8. Refer to the **Table 4** at the end of the chapter for torque specifications. Proper torque is essential to assure long life and satisfactory service from components.
9. Discard all O-rings and oil seals during disassembly. Apply a small amount of grease to the inner lips of each oil seal to prevent damage when the engine is first started.
10. Keep a record of all shims and where they came from. As soon as the shims are removed, inspect them for damage and write down their thickness and location.
11. Work in an area where there is sufficient lighting and room for component storage.

SPECIAL TOOLS

Where special tools are required or recommended for engine overhaul, the tool part numbers are provided. Harley-Davidson tool numbers have a "HD" prefix. These tools can be purchased through Harley-Davidson dealers. Tools unique to Harley-Davidson service can also be purchased through any number of accessory manufacturers.

SERVICING ENGINE IN FRAME

Many components can be serviced while the engine is mounted in the frame:

a. Rocker arm cover.
b. Cylinder head.
c. Cylinder and pistons.
d. Camshaft.
e. Gearshift mechanism.
f. Clutch.
g. Transmission.
h. Carburetor.
i. Starter motor and gears.
j. Alternator and electrical systems.

ENGINE REMOVAL

WARNING
Because of the explosive and flammable conditions that exist around gasoline, always observe the following precautions:

a. Disconnect the negative battery cable. See **Figure 2**, typical.
b. Gasoline dripping onto a hot engine component may cause a fire. Always allow the engine to cool completely before working on any fuel system component.
c. Spilled gasoline should be wiped up immediately with dry rags. Then store the rags in a

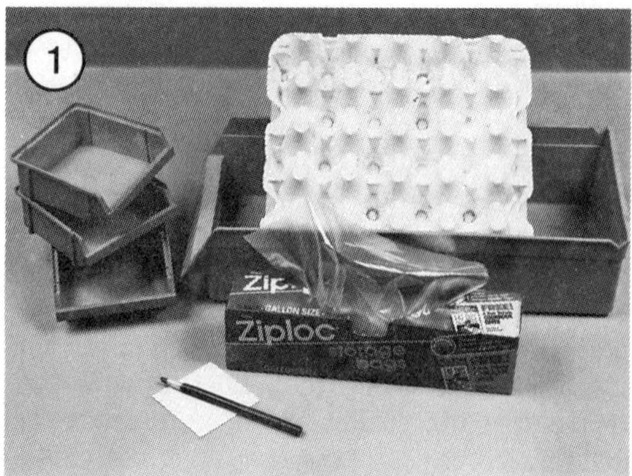

suitable metal container until they can be cleaned or disposed of. Do not store gas or solvent soaked rags in an open container in your shop.

d. Do not service any fuel system component while in the vicinity of open flames, sparks or while anyone is smoking.
e. Always have a fire extinguisher close at hand when working on the engine.

1. Thoroughly clean the engine exterior of dirt, oil and foreign material, using one of the cleaners designed for this purpose.
2. If the engine is going to be disassembled, check engine compression and perform a leak down test as described in Chapter Three. Record the measurements so that you can refer to them later.
3. Support the bike with a bike stand.
4. Remove the seat bolt and remove the seat.
5. Disconnect the negative battery cable (**Figure 2**).
6. Remove the battery and battery tray as described in Chapter Eight.
7. Remove the horn as described in Chapter Eight.
8. Remove the fuel tank as described in Chapter Seven.

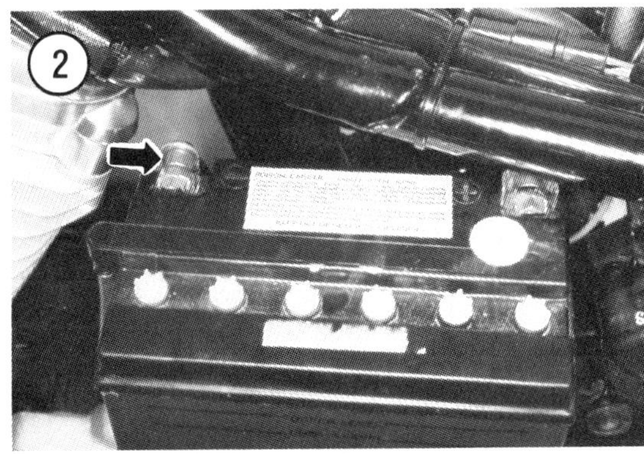
2

3

9. Remove the exhaust system as described in Chapter Seven.
10. Remove the air filter assembly and backplate as described in Chapter Three.
11. Disconnect the spark plug wires and set them out of the way.
12. Remove the ignition coil as described in Chapter Eight.
13. Remove the enrichener knob bracket mounting screw and set the enrichener knob aside.
14. Disconnect the VOES (**Figure 3**) hose at the carburetor.
15. Disconnect the VOES electrical connector at the ignition module.
16. Remove the carburetor as described in Chapter Seven.
17. Remove the intake manifold, if necessary, as described in Chapter Seven.
18. Remove the top center engine mount (**Figure 4**) as follows:
    a. Remove the bolts, washers and lockplate securing the top center engine mount to the frame. Check for a shim (9, **Figure 4**) mounted between the top center engine mount and frame; this shim is not used on all models.
    b. Remove the enrichener knob (**Figure 5**) if it was not removed with the carburetor.
    c. Using an Allen wrench, loosen the Allen bolts securing the top center engine mount to the cylinder heads.
    d. Remove the Allen bolts (A, **Figure 6**), flat washers and lockwashers.
    e. On 1991-1993 models, remove the VOES ground wire (**Figure 7**) when removing the rear cylinder head bolt and set the wire aside.
    f. Remove the top center engine mount (B, **Figure 6**) and shim (if used).

NOTE
Check the VOES wire for damage. Repair the wire or connector, if necessary, before reinstalling the engine.

19. Remove the top front engine mount (**Figure 8**) as follows:
    a. Pry off the side reflectors (**Figure 9**) from the front frame tubes. See **Figure 10**.
    b. Loosen then remove the bolts (A, **Figure 11**) and washers securing the top front engine mount to the frame mounting bracket. Remove

4

(4) TOP CENTER ENGINE MOUNT

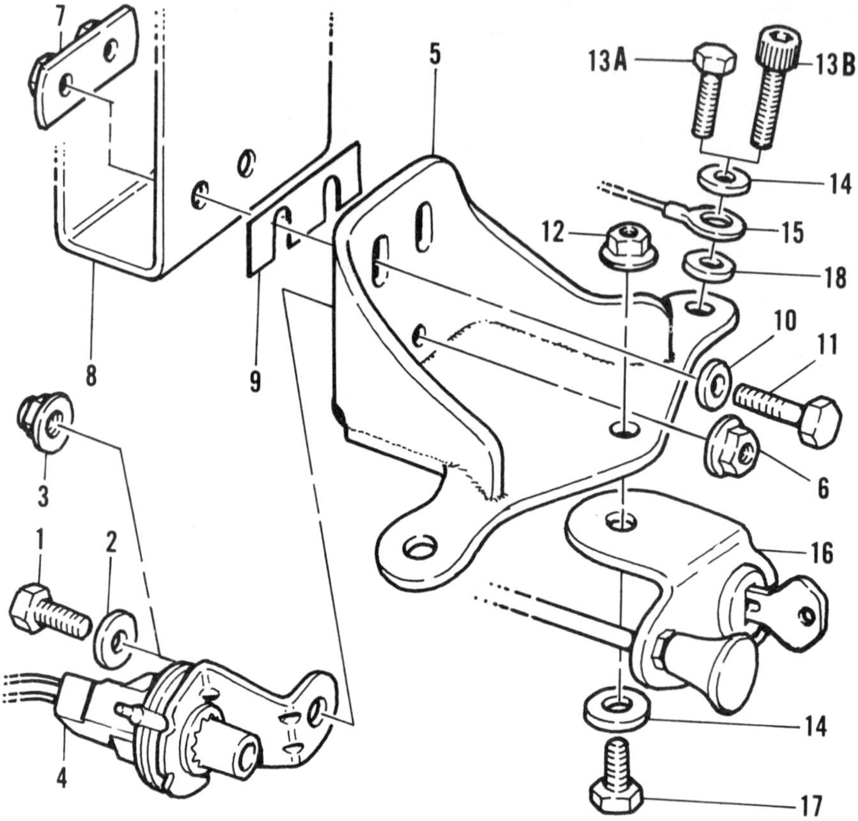

1. Bolt (1991)
2. Washer (1991)
3. Locknut (1992-on)
4. Vacuum-operated electric switch (VOES)
5. Top center engine bracket
6. Locknut
7. Nut plate
8. Frame
9. Shim
10. Washer
11. Bolt
12. Locknut
13A. Bolt (1991)
13B. Bolt (1992-on)
14. Washer
15. VOES ground wire (1991-1993)
16. Ignition bracket
17. Bolt
18. Flat washer (1991-1992)/ external tooth lockwasher (1993-on)

the nut plate (5, **Figure 8**) from the frame mounting bracket.

c. Loosen the bolt (B, **Figure 11**) and nut securing the top front engine mount to the front cylinder block.

d. Remove the bolt, nut, lockwashers and flat washers.

e. Remove the top front engine mount (C, **Figure 11**).

NOTE
The engine top end can be serviced at this point.

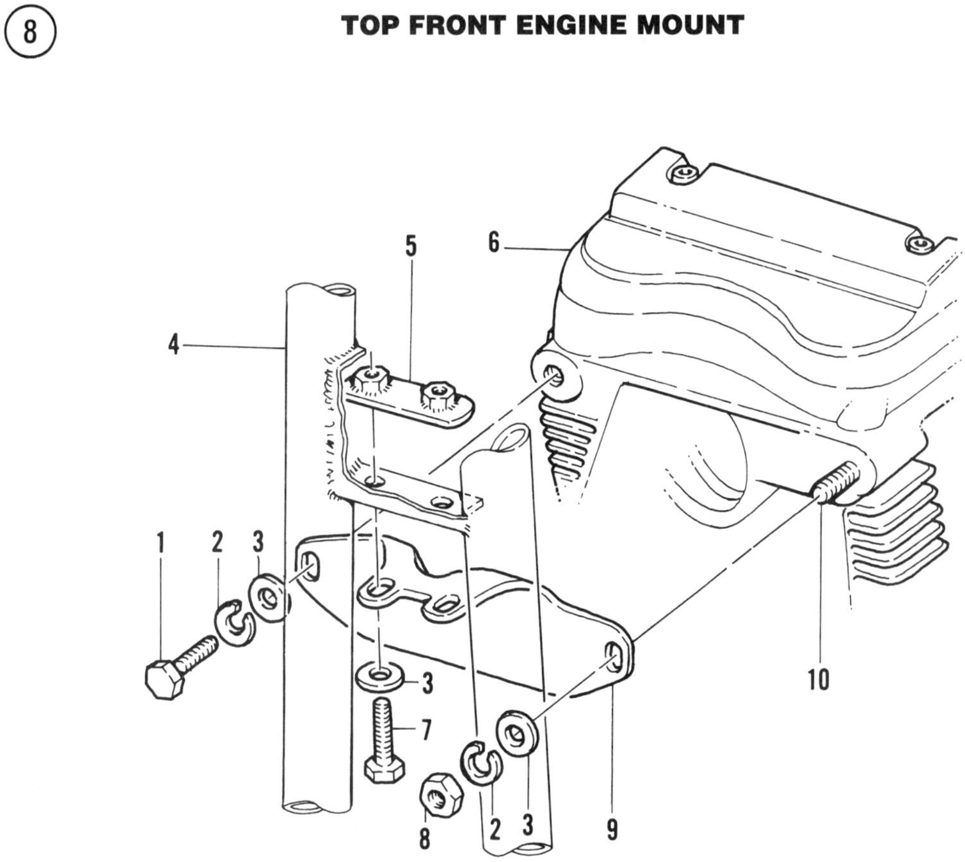

8

TOP FRONT ENGINE MOUNT

1. Bolt
2. Lockwasher
3. Washer
4. Frame downtube
5. Nut plate
6. Engine
7. Bolt
8. Nut
9. Top front engine bracket
10. Stud

NOTE
If you are going to disassemble the engine top end, perform Step 20. If you are going to remove the engine as a complete assembly, proceed to Step 21.

20. Remove the cylinder heads and cylinders as described in this chapter.

CAUTION
*Install a piece of 1/2 in. (13 mm) I.D. hose over each cylinder stud (**Figure 12**) to prevent stud damage when handling the engine in the following steps.*

21. Remove the rear sprocket cover (A, **Figure 13**) as follows:

a. Using an Allen wrench, loosen then remove the rear brake master cylinder mounting bolts (B, **Figure 13**) and washers.

NOTE
It is not necessary to disconnect the brake line at the master cylinder.

b. Remove the clevis pin cotter pin at the rear brake pedal. Then remove the clevis pin (**Figure 14**) and disconnect the brake pedal from the brake rod end.
c. Remove the screw and clip (C, **Figure 13**) securing the brake line to the sprocket cover.
d. Loosen then remove the Allen bolts and washers securing the sprocket cover to the engine. Remove the sprocket cover (A, **Figure 13**) together with rear brake pedal and linkage assembly.

22. Loosen the rear axle nut and the rear drive chain or drive belt adjusters. Then slip the drive chain or drive belt (**Figure 15**) off of the drive sprocket.

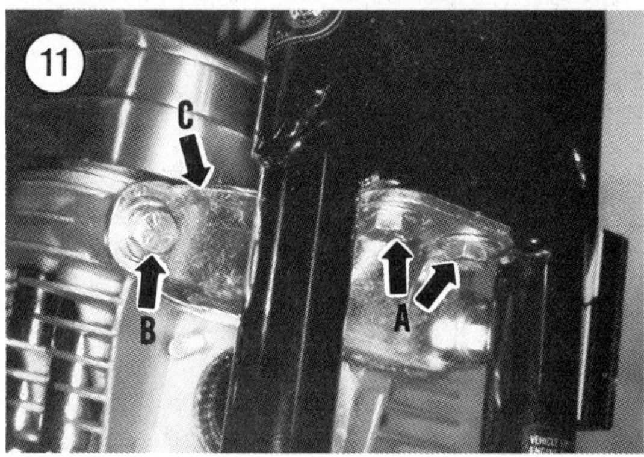

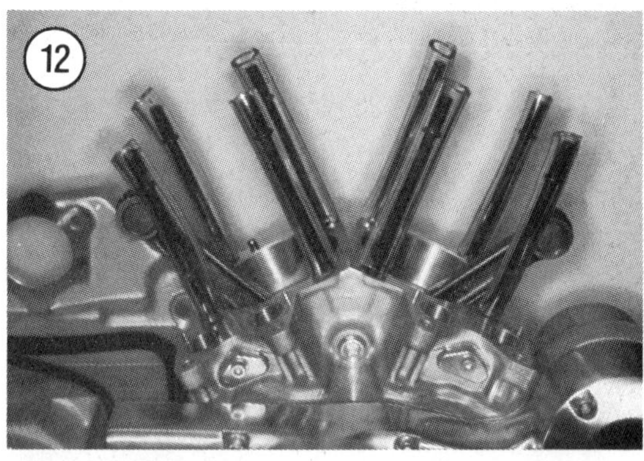

23. Disconnect the oil pressure switch electrical connector at the switch (**Figure 16**).

24. Disconnect the neutral switch electrical connector at the switch (**Figure 17**).

NOTE

***Figure 17** shows the neutral switch with the drive sprocket removed for clarity. You can disconnect the neutral switch connector with the drive sprocket mounted on the bike.*

25. Disconnect the ignition timer plate wires from the wiring harness (**Figure 18**, typical).

26. Disconnect the regulator/rectifier electrical connector(s) at the alternator stator connector. See **Figure 19** (1991-1993) or **Figure 20** (1994).

27. Disconnect the clutch cable from the handlebar.

28. Drain the engine oil tank as described in Chapter Three.

29. Label, then disconnect the oil feed, return and vent hoses at the oil tank. See **Figure 21** (1991-1993) or **Figure 22** (1994). Plug each hose and hose fitting to prevent oil leakage and contamination.

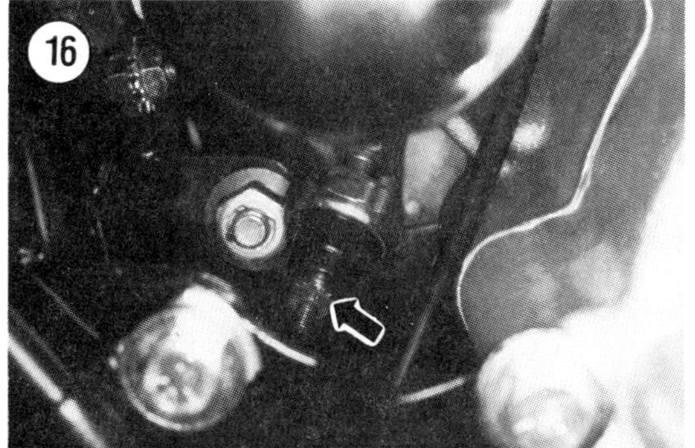

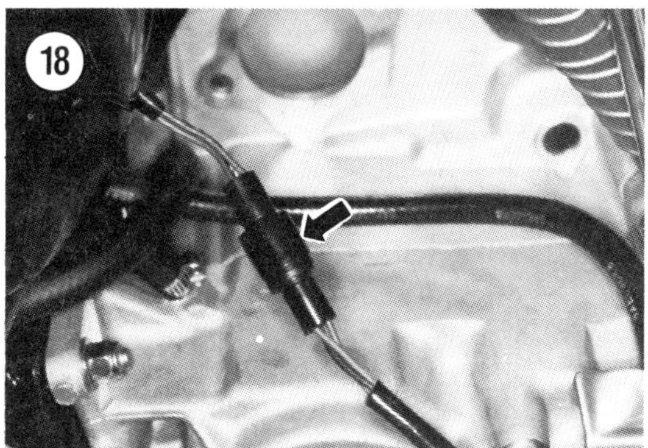

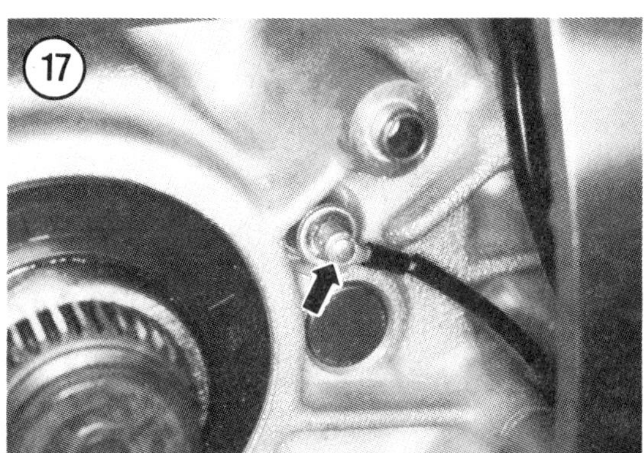

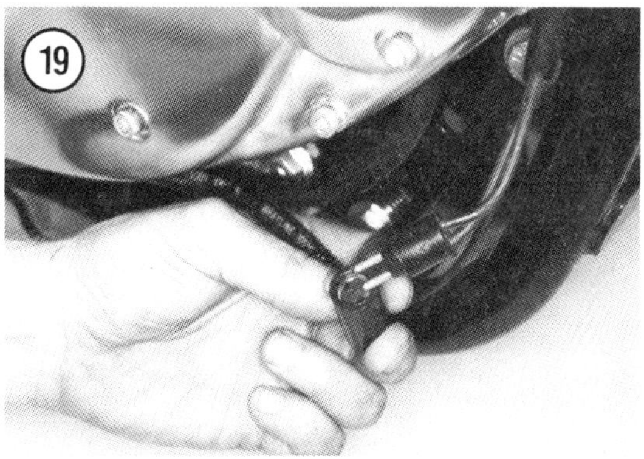

30. Place a jack and a piece of plywood under the engine. Do not place any tension against the engine until all of the engine mounting bolts and nuts have been loosened.
31. Loosen the left- and right-hand lower front engine mount bolts and nuts (**Figure 23**).
32. Disconnect the negative battery ground cable at the upper, left-hand rear engine mount bolt; see **Figure 24**.
33. Loosen the upper (**Figure 25**) and lower (**Figure 26**) rear engine mount bolts. See **Figure 27**.
34. Take some of the engine weight with the jack until the bolts can be removed by hand.
35. Remove the left- and right-hand lower front engine mount bolts, washers and nuts. Then remove the left- and right-hand mounting plates. See **Figure 23**.
36. Remove the rear engine mount bolts, lockwashers, flat washers and nuts. See **Figure 27**.
37. To avoid scratching the frame, wrap the exposed frame tubes with cardboard or plastic tubes.
38. Check the engine to make sure all wiring, hoses and other components have been disconnected or removed. If so, the engine is now ready to be removed from the frame.

NOTE
A minimum of 2 people must be used when removing the engine.

39. With an assistant's help, lift the engine up (**Figure 28**) and remove it from the right-hand side of the frame. If the cylinder heads are still mounted on the engine, tip the cylinder heads slightly off center to prevent them from hanging up on the upper frame rail.

CAUTION
Do not lay the engine on the left-hand side with the clutch installed or the clutch cable adjusting screw will be damaged.

40. Mount the engine in an engine stand or take it to a workbench for further disassembly.

Inspection

After the engine has been removed from the frame, perform the following.
1. Visually inspect the frame for cracks or other signs of damage. If damage is suspected or apparent,

VOLTAGE REGULATOR (1994)

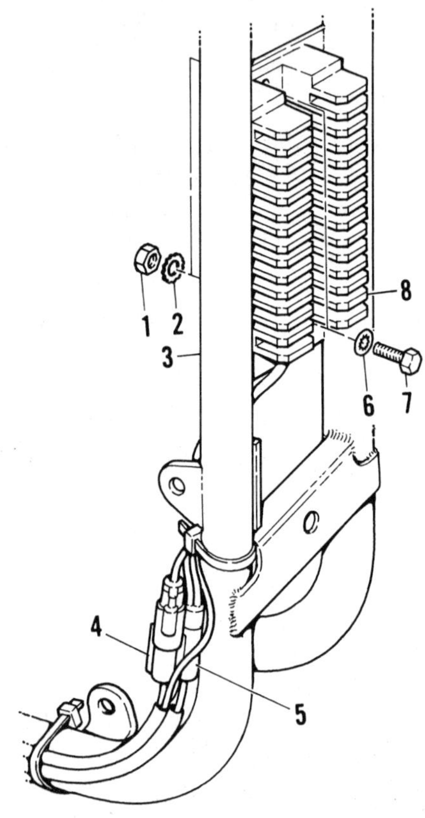

1. Nut
2. Lockwasher
3. Frame downtube
4. 1-pin connector (charging wire to main circuit breaker)
5. 2-pin connector (voltage regulator to alternator stator)
6. Lockwasher
7. Bolt
8. Voltage regulator

have the frame inspected by a Harley-Davidson dealer or frame alignment specialist.

2. Clean the frame before installing the engine.

3. If paint has been removed from the frame during engine removal or cleaning, touch up as required prior to installing the engine back in the frame.

4. While the engine is removed, remove the oil tank and thoroughly flush. Then reinstall the oil tank and plug the oil hoses to prevent contamination.

5. Replace any worn or damaged oil hoses and clamps.

6. Check the exposed hoses and cables for chafing or other damage. Replace loose, missing or damaged hose clamps and cable ties. See **Figure 29** and **Figure 30**.

7. Check all of the engine mounting fasteners for corrosion and thread damage. Clean each fastener in solvent to remove oil and Loctite residue. Replace worn or damaged fasteners before reassembly.

8. Check the flat washers for cupping; replace if necessary.

9. Check for damaged or weakened lockwashers; replace if necessary.

10. Check the wiring harness (**Figure 29** and **Figure 30**) for signs of damage that may have occurred when removing the engine. Repair or replace damaged wires as required.

11. On 1991-1993 models, disconnect and then spray each of the electrical connectors with electrical contact cleaner. Check the connector pins and sockets for damage. Reconnect the connectors.

NOTE
The Deutsch connectors used on 1994 models should not need cleaning.

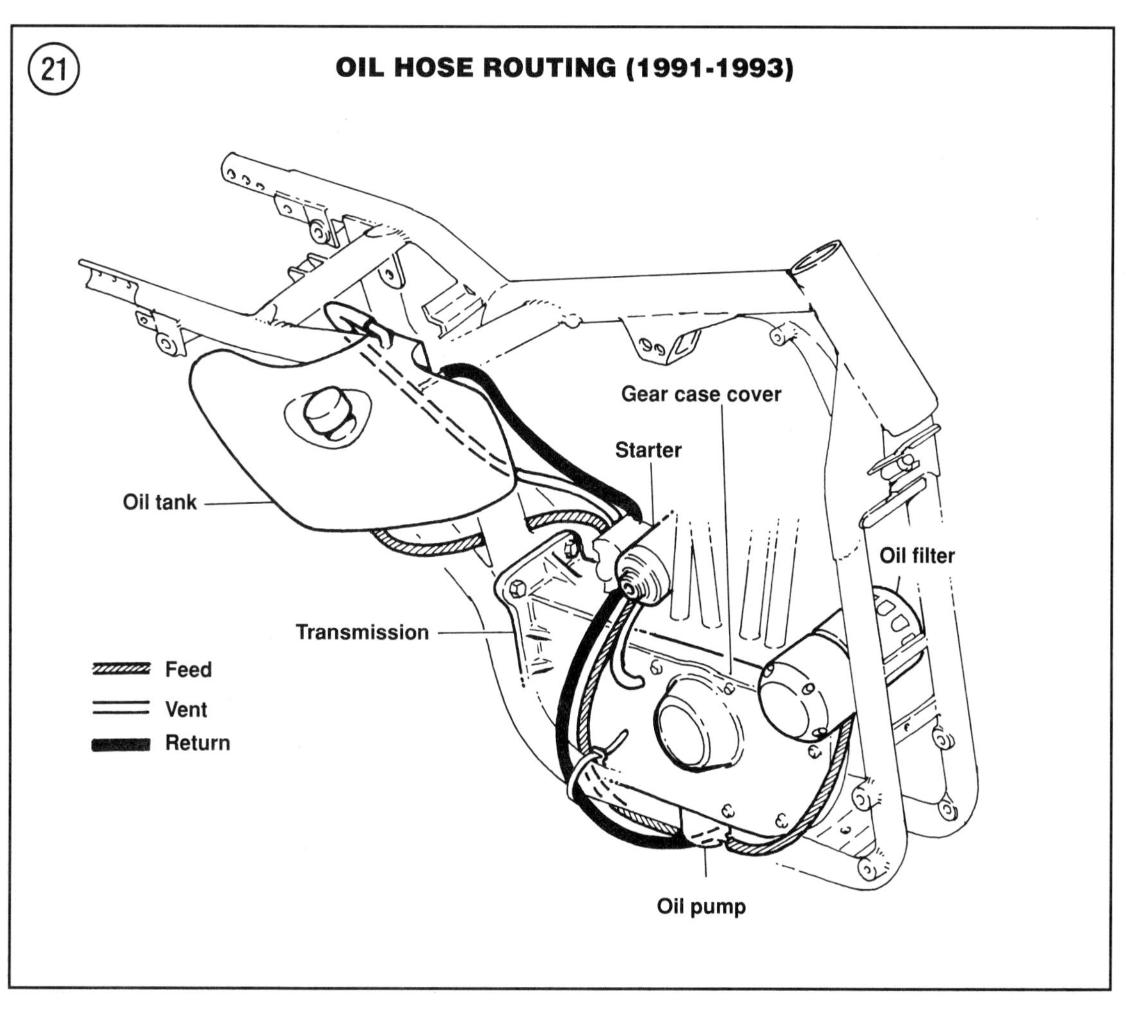

ENGINE INSTALLATION

NOTE
*Perform the **Inspection** procedures listed under **Engine Removal** in this chapter.*

1. Make sure the frame is supported properly before installing the engine. The jack and piece of plywood will not be required until after the engine is resting in the frame.
2. Lay out the engine mount plates and fasteners in the order shown in **Figure 23** (lower front engine mount) and **Figure 27** (rear engine mount).
3. If the plastic or cardboard frame protectors were removed, install them now so that you don't scratch or otherwise damage the frame when installing the engine.
4. Position all of the wiring connectors and hoses so that they are out of the way when installing the engine.
5. With your assistant, place the engine in the frame from the right-hand side.
6. Slide the jack (with the piece of plywood) underneath the engine. Position and then operate the jack to align the rear engine-to-frame mounting holes. Insert the lower engine dowel pins into the rear frame engine mount bracket as shown in **Figure 31**.

7. Apply an anti-seize lubricant, such as Permatex Ant-Seize, to all of the engine mounting bolts prior to installation.

8. To install the rear engine mount assembly (**Figure 27**), perform the following:

   a. Install a flat washer on the 2 upper engine mount bolts and install the bolts through the frame and engine. Install the locknut and washer on the right-hand bolt. Install the hex nut and washer on the left-hand bolt. Do not install the battery ground cable at this time.

   b. Install a lockwasher and flat washer on the 2 lower engine mount bolts and install the bolts through the frame and thread into the engine hand-tight.

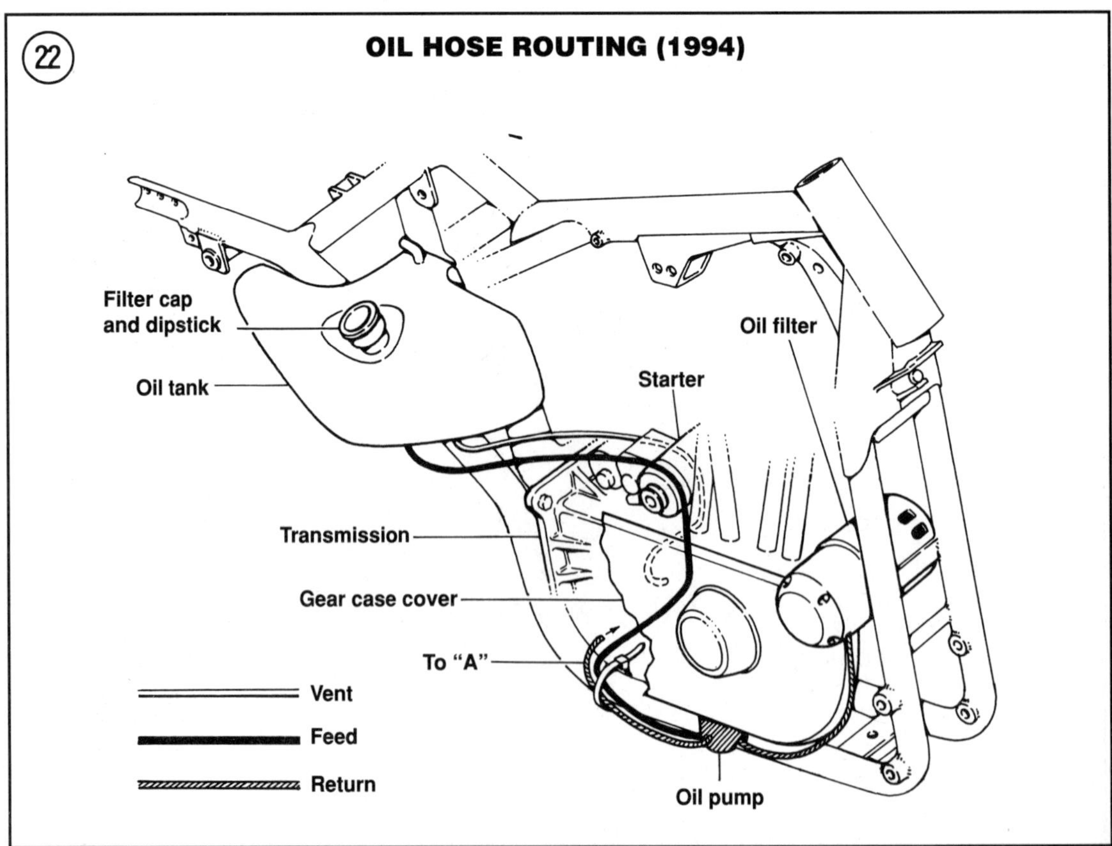

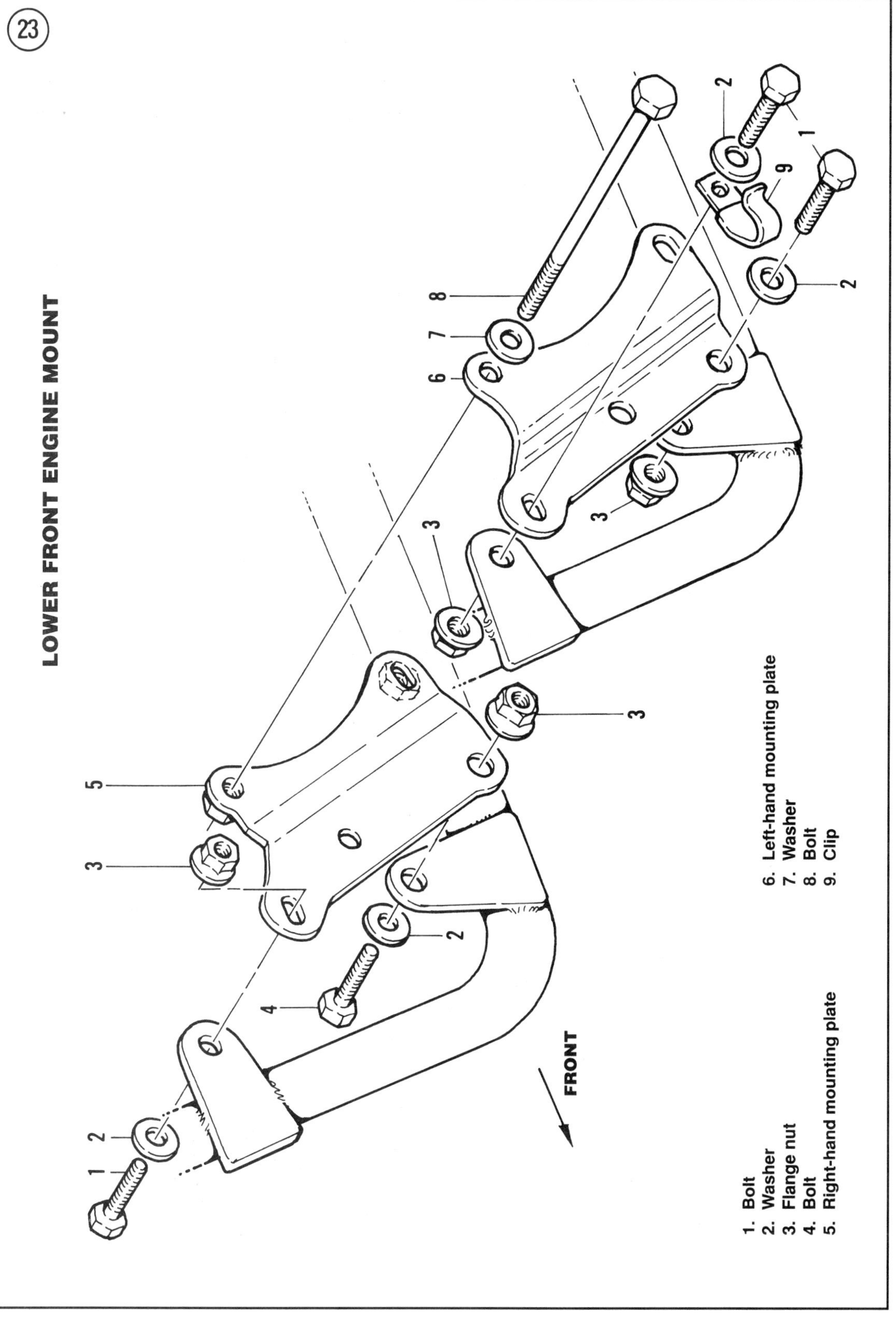
23
LOWER FRONT ENGINE MOUNT
FRONT
1. Bolt
2. Washer
3. Flange nut
4. Bolt
5. Right-hand mounting plate
6. Left-hand mounting plate
7. Washer
8. Bolt
9. Clip

9. Install the left- and right-hand lower front engine mount plates, bolts, washers and nuts as shown in **Figure 23**. Tighten the bolts hand-tight.

10. Tighten the rear engine mounting bolts and nuts (**Figure 27**) to the torque specification in **Table 4**.

11. Tighten the lower front engine bolts (A, **Figure 32**) to the torque specification in **Table 4**. Tighten the lower front frame bolts (B, **Figure 32**) to the torque specification in **Table 4**.

12. If the engine top end was not installed prior to installing the engine bottom end, install the top end components now as described in this chapter.

13. Install the top center engine mount assembly (**Figure 33**) as follows:

   a. Install the upper top center engine mount bolts and washers through the engine mount.
   b. Place the shim (if used) onto the top center engine mount bolts as shown in **Figure 33**.

NOTE
Three different shim thicknesses are available: 0.030 in. (0.76 mm), 0.060 in. (1.52 mm) and 0.090 in. (2.27 mm). When installing an engine that did not have any major components replaced

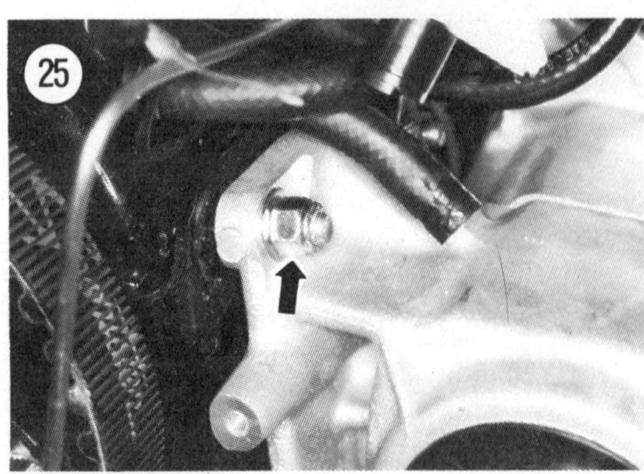

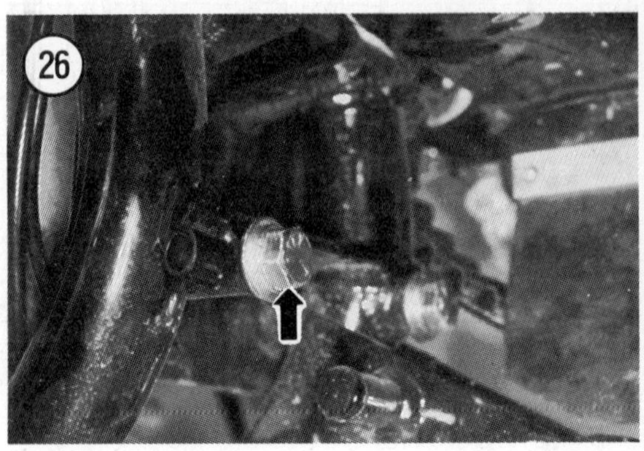

REAR ENGINE MOUNT

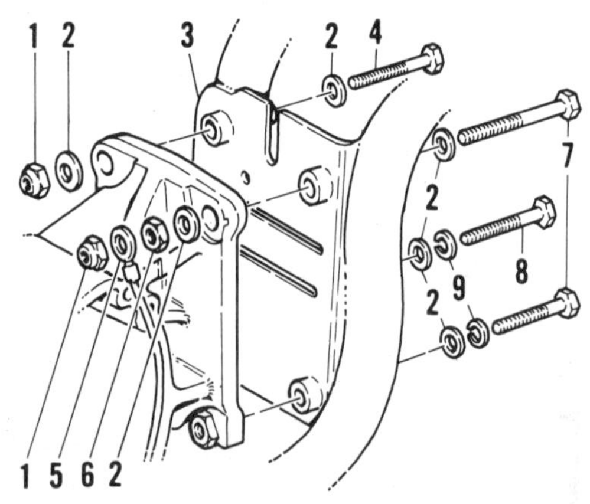

1. Locknut
2. Washer
3. Frame
4. Bolt
5. Battery ground cable
6. Nut
7. Bolt
8. Bolt
9. Lockwasher

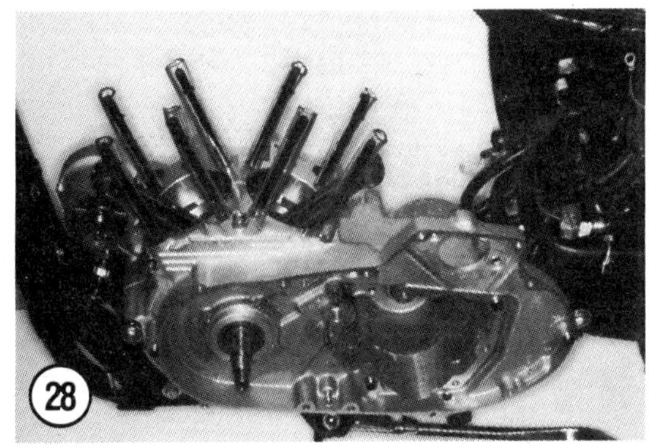

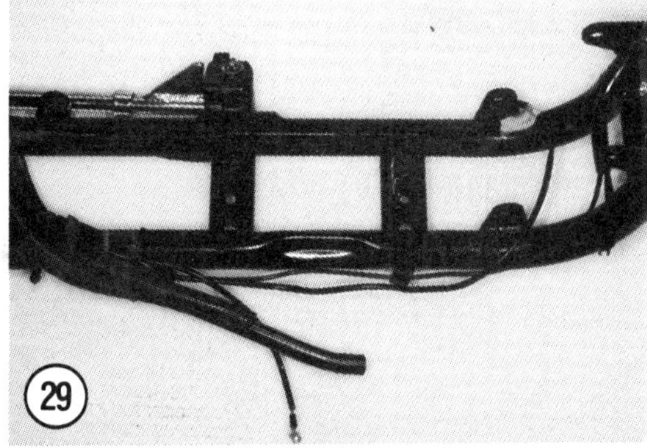

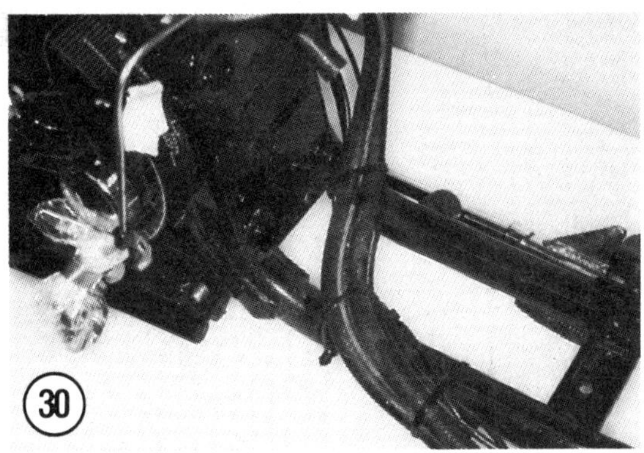

(engine cases, cylinder heads, top center engine mount or frame), the original thickness shim can be installed. If one of these major components was replaced, a different thickness shim may be required.

c. Install the top center engine mount onto the engine. Insert the 2 engine mount bolts through the frame so that the shim does not fall off.

d. Place the nut plate into position (**Figure 33**) and thread the engine mount bolts into the nut plate hand tight.

e. Install the VOES and the ignition switch.

f. Tighten the engine bolts to the torque specification in **Table 4**.

g. Tighten the frame bolts to the torque specification in **Table 4**.

14. Install the top front engine mount bracket (**Figure 34**) as follows:

a. Install the front upper mounting bracket and fasteners as shown in **Figure 34**. Tighten all of the bolts hand-tight only.

b. Tighten the engine bolts to the torque specification listed in **Table 4**.

c. Tighten the frame bolts to the torque specification listed in **Table 4**.

15. Slide a new hose clamp onto the oil feed, return and vent hoses and connect the hoses to the oil tank; see **Figure 21** (1991-1993) or **Figure 22** (1994).

16. Connect the battery ground wire to the crankcase bolt (**Figure 24**).

17. Connect the battery positive cable and the 18-gauge green wire to the starter motor.

18. Reconnect the regulator/rectifier electrical connector at the alternator stator connector. See **Figure 19** (1991-1993) or **Figure 20** (1994).

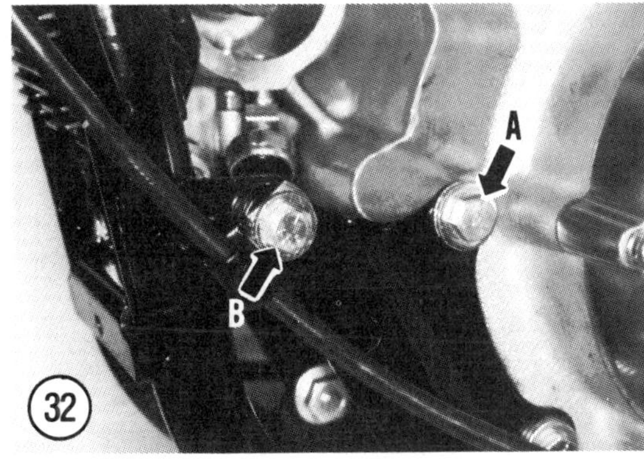

19. Reconnect the ignition timer plate wires at the wiring harness connectors (**Figure 18**, typical).

20. Reconnect the neutral switch electrical connector at the neutral switch (**Figure 17**).

21. Connect the oil pressure switch electrical connector at the oil pressure switch (**Figure 16**).

22. Reconnect the clutch cable at the handlebar. Adjust the clutch as described in Chapter Three.

23. Install the carburetor and intake manifold as described in Chapter Seven.

24. Reconnect the throttle and choke cables at the carburetor. Adjust both cables as described in Chapter Three.

25. Install enrichener knob bracket (**Figure 5**).

26. Install the rear chain or drive belt (**Figure 15**) over the front sprocket.

27. Install the rear sprocket cover as follows:

   a. Install the rear sprocket cover (A, **Figure 13**) together with the rear brake pedal and linkage assembly.

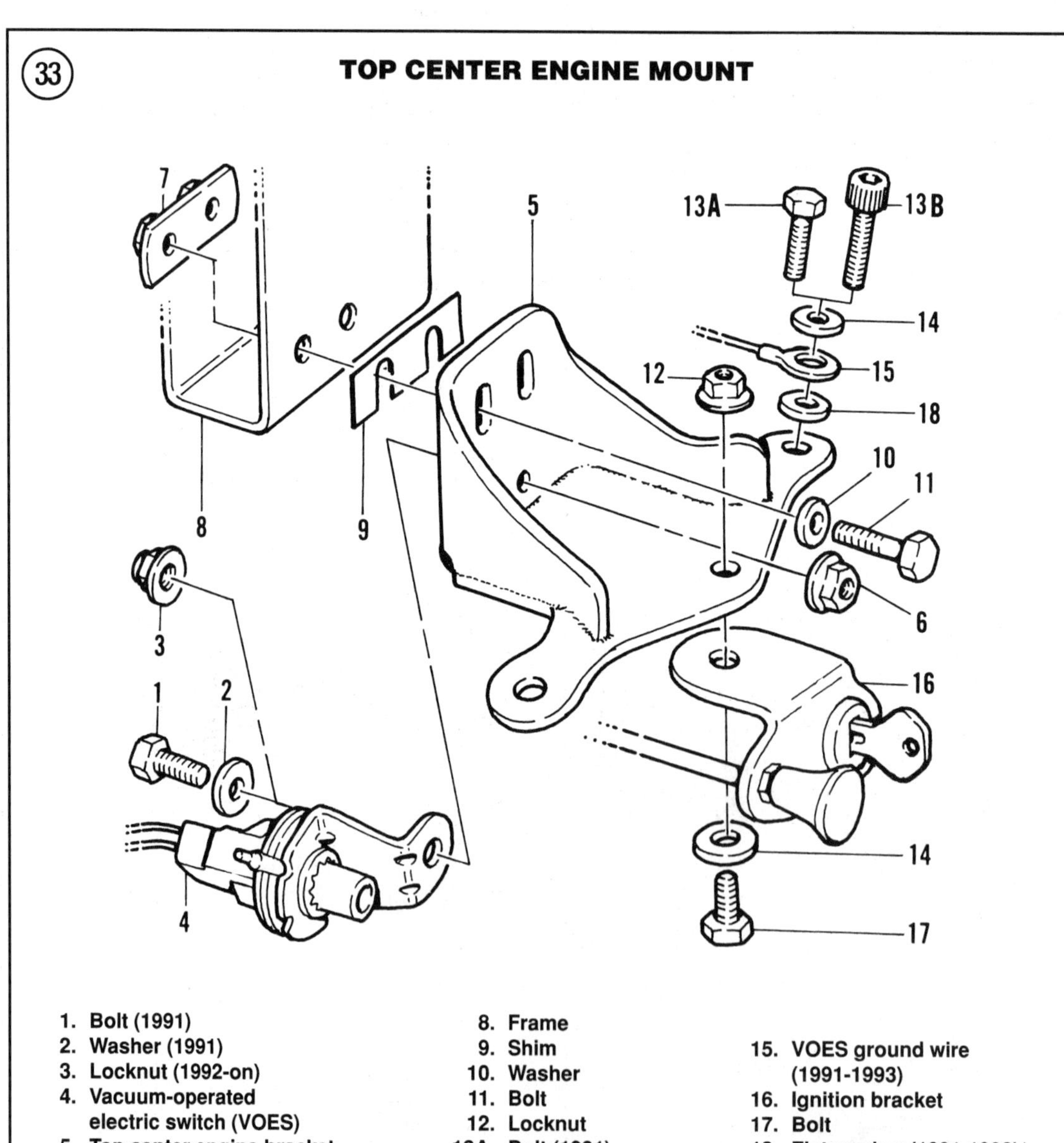

1. Bolt (1991)
2. Washer (1991)
3. Locknut (1992-on)
4. Vacuum-operated electric switch (VOES)
5. Top center engine bracket
6. Locknut
7. Nut plate
8. Frame
9. Shim
10. Washer
11. Bolt
12. Locknut
13A. Bolt (1991)
13B. Bolt (1992-on)
14. Washer
15. VOES ground wire (1991-1993)
16. Ignition bracket
17. Bolt
18. Flat washer (1991-1992)/ external tooth lockwasher (1993-on)

b. Install the rear sprocket cover mounting bolts and washers; tighten the bolts securely.
c. Reconnect the brake linkage to the master cylinder (**Figure 14**).
d. Install the rear master cylinder bolts (B, **Figure 13**) and washers and secure the master cylinder to the sprocket cover.
e. Secure the brake line with the clip and screw (C, **Figure 13**).

28. Adjust the rear brake pedal as described in Chapter Three.
29. Reconnect the VOES electrical connector at the ignition module.
30. Reconnect the VOES hose (**Figure 3**) at the carburetor.
31. Reinstall the ignition coil bracket and the throttle cable clip.
32. Install the ignition coil as described in Chapter Eight.
33. Install the horn as described in Chapter Eight.
34. Reconnect the spark plug wires.
35. Install the backplate and air filter assembly as described in Chapter Three.
36. Install the exhaust system as described in Chapter Seven.
37. Install the fuel tank as described in Chapter Seven. Secure the fuel hose with new hose clamps, if necessary.

NOTE
If you haven't done so, clean the battery and check the electrolyte level as described in Chapter Eight. The battery should be in good condition and fully

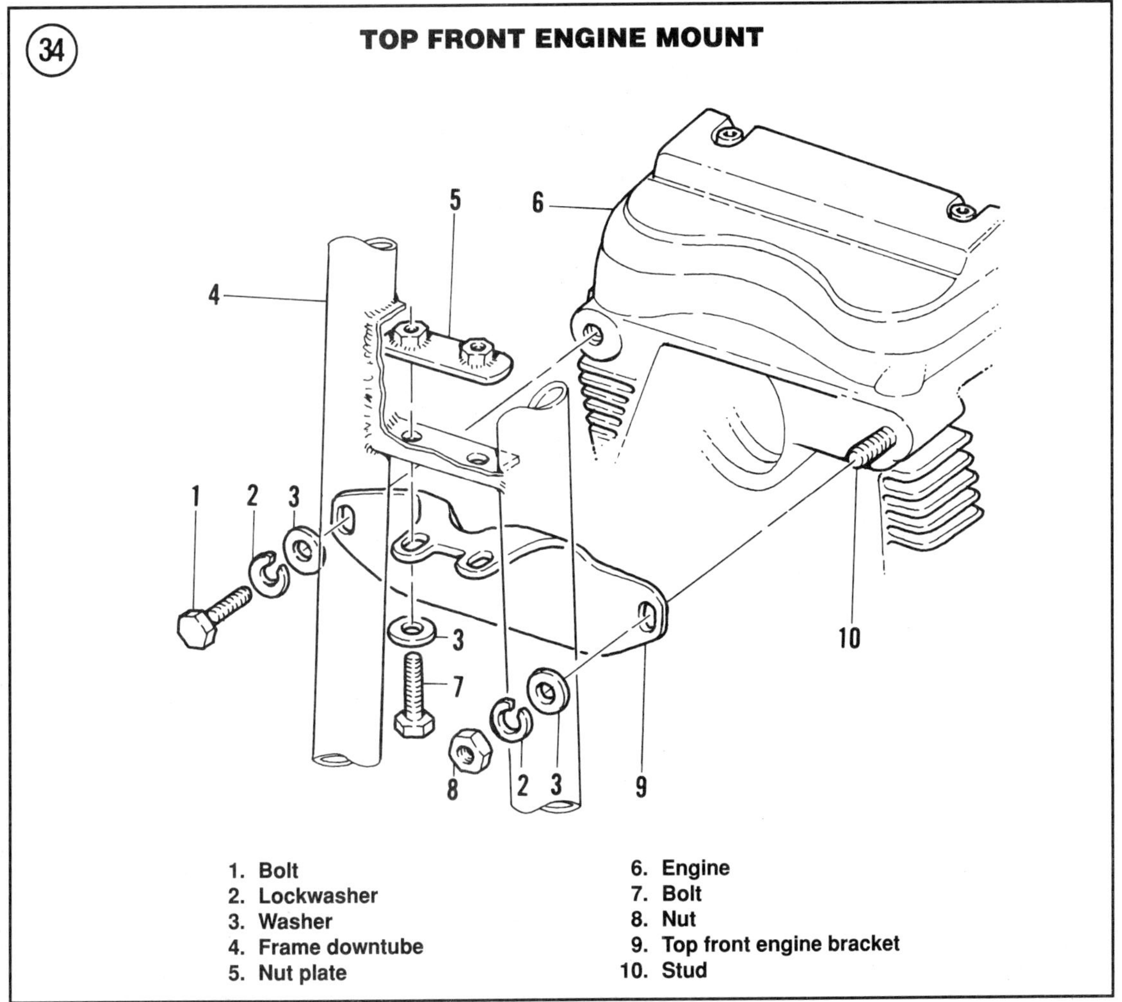

charged prior to installing it in the frame.

38. Install the battery tray and battery as described in Chapter Eight.
39. Install a new oil filter and engine oil as described in Chapter Three.
40. Install new transmission oil as described in Chapter Three.
41. Reconnect the positive battery cable, then the negative cable.

CAUTION
*Check the battery breather tube routing to prevent battery mist from damaging exposed parts. Refer to **Battery** in Chapter Eight.*

42. Adjust the drive chain or belt as described in Chapter Three.
43. Install the seat and seat bolt. Tighten the bolt securely.
44. Before starting the engine, perform the following:
    a. Recheck the engine tank oil level; see Chapter Three.
    b. Check the oil tank hoses for leaks.
    c. Recheck the transmission oil level.
    d. Check that the throttle moves smoothly and snaps back when released.
    e. Check that the fuel tank has an adequate supply of gasoline. If the bike has been sitting for some time, drain the tank and fill with fresh gasoline. Refer to *Fuel Tank.*
    f. Turn off the fuel valve and check for leaks. Turn the fuel valve on.
    g. Wipe off the exhaust pipes with a clean rag to remove as much oil and grease residue as possible. This will prevent the pipes from smoking excessively when they become hot.
45. Start the engine and allow it to idle with the transmission in NEUTRAL. Note the following:
    a. Listen carefully for rattles or other abnormal sounds. These may indicate loose brackets or fasteners.
    b. When the engine reaches normal operating temperature, shut it off.
    c. Check engine oil tank capacity as described in Chapter Three.
    d. Check transmission oil level as described in Chapter Three.
46. If new parts were installed, the engine should be broken in as described under *Engine Break-in* in this chapter. This step is critical to provide proper seating in of the new components to reduce friction to normal levels.

CAUTION
Failure to follow proper break-in procedures will reduce engine longevity and performance.

47. Before riding your Sportster, perform the *Routine Safety Checks* in Chapter Three.

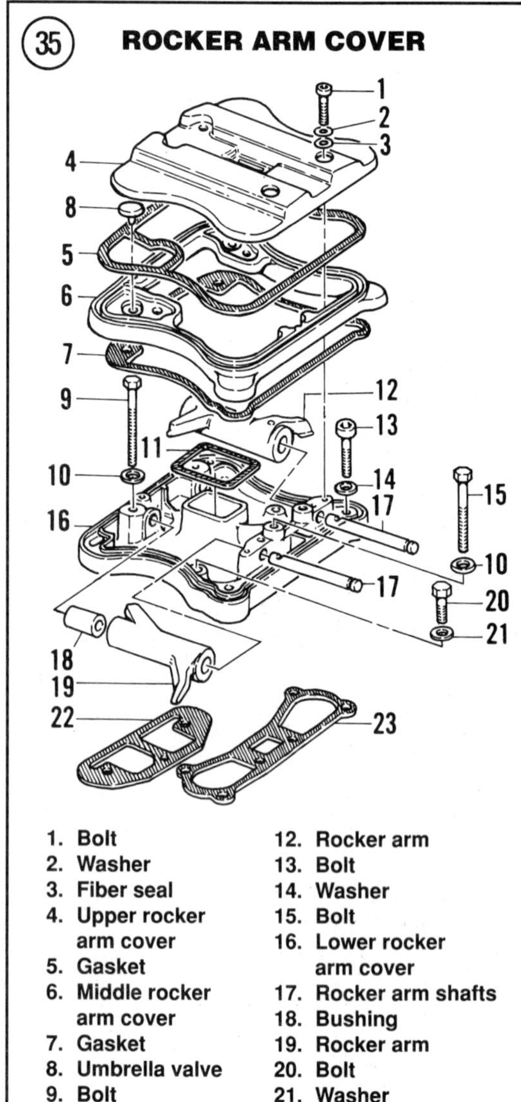

1. Bolt
2. Washer
3. Fiber seal
4. Upper rocker arm cover
5. Gasket
6. Middle rocker arm cover
7. Gasket
8. Umbrella valve
9. Bolt
10. Washer
11. Gasket
12. Rocker arm
13. Bolt
14. Washer
15. Bolt
16. Lower rocker arm cover
17. Rocker arm shafts
18. Bushing
19. Rocker arm
20. Bolt
21. Washer
22. Gasket
23. Gasket

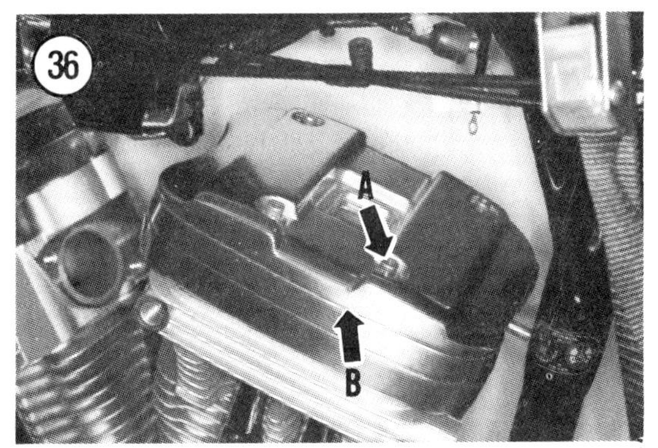

36

37

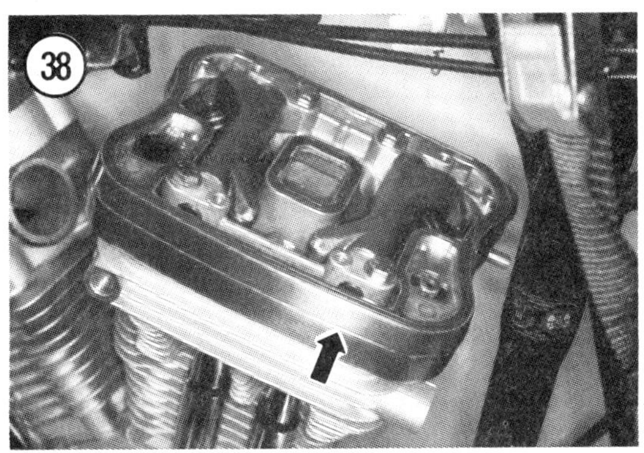

38

39

ROCKER ARM COVER/ CYLINDER HEAD

The front and rear rocker box and cylinder head assemblies can be removed with the engine installed in the frame.

Refer to **Figure 35** when performing the following procedures.

Rocker Box Removal

The rocker box assembly consists of the upper rocker cover, middle rocker cover and lower rocker arm cover.

1. Perform Steps 1-19 under *Engine Removal.*
2. Remove the spark plugs.
3. Remove the upper rocker arm cover bolts (A, **Figure 36**), steel washers (if used) and fiber washers. See **Figure 37**.
4. Remove the upper rocker arm cover (B, **Figure 36**).
5. Remove and discard the outer and inner gaskets (**Figure 38**).
6. Remove the middle rocker arm cover (**Figure 38**).
7. Remove and discard the outer and inner gaskets (**Figure 39**).

NOTE
Steps 8A and 8B describe 2 methods for turning the engine over by hand. When performing Step 8A, the bike must be supported with the rear wheel off the ground.

8A. Shift the transmission into fifth gear. While watching the rocker arms, pull in the clutch lever and turn the rear wheel until both valves are closed on the cylinder head being removed.

8B. Remove the primary cover as described in Chapter Five. While watching the rocker arms, turn the engine sprocket nut (with a socket and ratchet) until both valves are closed on the cylinder head being removed.

9. Loosen, then remove the 2 rocker arm mounting bolts and washers next to the pushrods (**Figure 40**).
10. Remove the remaining lower rocker arm cover mounting bolts and washers (**Figure 41**).

11. Remove the lower rocker arm cover (**Figure 42**). Discard both gaskets.

Cylinder Head Removal

Refer to **Figure 43** when performing this procedure.

NOTE
Identify and store the pushrods in a container so that they can be reinstalled in their original positions.

1. Label and then remove both pushrods (A, **Figure 44**).

CAUTION
Failure to loosen and remove the cylinder head mounting bolts properly can damage the cylinder head and cylinder studs.

2. Loosen the cylinder head mounting bolts 1/8 turn at a time in the order shown in **Figure 45**. Continue loosening the bolts 1/8 turn at a time until they are all loose. Then remove the bolts and washers.
3. Lift the cylinder head (B, **Figure 44**) off the cylinder. If the head is tight, tap it with a soft-faced hammer, then remove it.
4. Remove and discard the cylinder head gasket.
5. Remove the dowel pins and O-rings from the cylinder. Discard the O-rings.
6. To remove the pushrod cover (**Figure 46**):
   a. Loosen, then remove the pushrod rod retainer Allen bolt and washer.
   b. Remove the pushrod retainer, cover and O-ring.
7. To remove the valve tappets, refer to *Valve Tappets* in this chapter.

Rocker Arm Removal/Inspection/Installation

Label all parts prior to disassembly so that they will be installed in their original positions. Refer to **Figure 35** for this procedure.

1. Before removing the rocker arms, measure rocker arm end clearance as follows:
   a. Insert a feeler gauge between the rocker arm and the inside rocker arm cover boss as shown in **Figure 47**.
   b. Record the measurement.
   c. Repeat for each rocker arm.
   d. Replace the rocker arm and/or the lower rocker arm cover if the end clearance exceeds the service limit in **Table 2**.
2. Using a soft-faced punch, tap each rocker arm shaft (**Figure 48**) out of the lower rocker arm cover.
3. Remove the rocker arms (**Figure 48**).
4. Clean the rocker covers, rocker arms and shafts in solvent. Then clean with hot, soapy water and rinse with clear, cold water. Dry with compressed air.

5. Blow compressed air through all oil passages to make sure they are clear.

6. Examine the rocker arm pads (area that contacts the valve). See A, **Figure 49**. The pad on each rocker arm should be shiny and convex—curving outward. Replace the rocker arm if the pad shows signs of pitting, grooves or excessive wear.

7. Examine the rocker arm socket (area that retains the pushrod). See B, **Figure 49**. The socket will show wear but it should be smooth without any sign of a step or lip. Replace the rocker arm if the socket is severely worn, cracked or has a step or lip.

8. Examine the rocker arm shaft (**Figure 50**) for scoring, ridge wear or other damage. If these conditions are present, replace the rocker arm shaft. If the shaft does not show any visual wear or damage, perform Step 9.

9. Measure the rocker arm shaft outside diameter with a micrometer (**Figure 51**) where it rides in the rocker arm and in the lower rocker arm cover. Record both measurements.

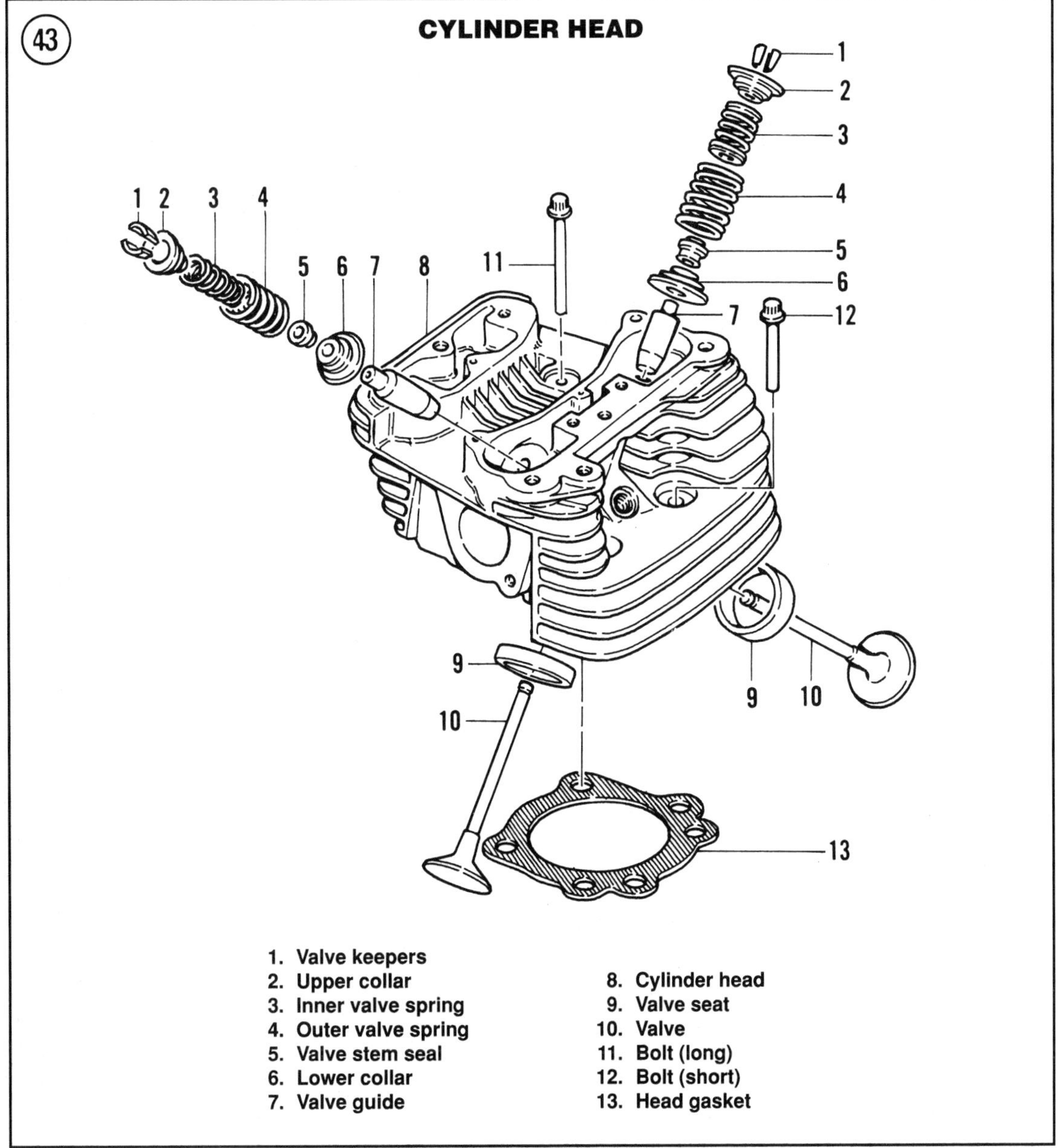

10. Measure the rocker arm bushing inside diameter (**Figure 52**) and the lower rocker arm cover bore diameter where the shaft rides (**Figure 53**). Record both measurements.

11. Subtract the measurements taken in Step 9 from those in Step 10 to obtain the following rocker arm shaft clearance measurements:

a. Shaft fit in rocker cover.

b. Shaft fit in rocker arm bushing.

12. Replace the rocker arm bushings or the lower rocker arm cover if the clearance exceeds the specifications in **Table 2**. Also, replace any parts which are worn beyond the service limit specification in **Table 2**. Rocker arm bushing replacement is described in this chapter.

13. Install the rocker arms into their original positions (**Figure 54**).

14. Align the notch (A, **Figure 55**) in the rocker arm shaft with the bolt hole (B, **Figure 55**) in the lower rocker arm cover and install the rocker arm shaft. Repeat for the opposite rocker arm shaft. See **Figure 56**.

Rocker Arm Bushing Replacement

Each rocker arm is equipped with 2 bushings (**Figure 52**). Replacement bushings must be reamed with the Harley-Davidson rocker arm bushing reamer (part No. HD-94804-57). If you do not have the correct size reamer, refer all service to a Harley-Davidson dealer.

NOTE
Because new bushings must be reamed, remove only one bushing at a time. The opposite bushing will be used as a guide when reaming the first bushing.

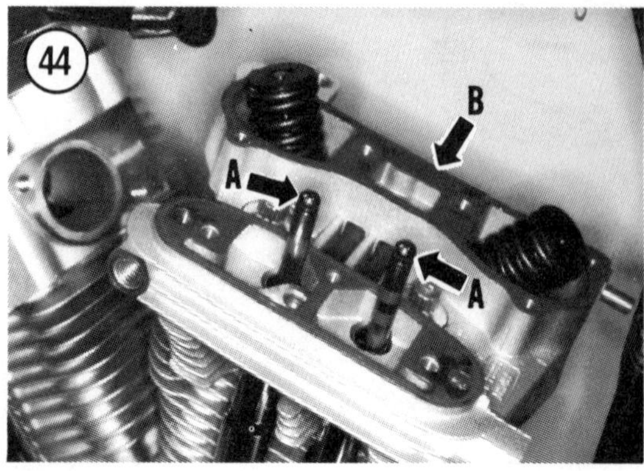

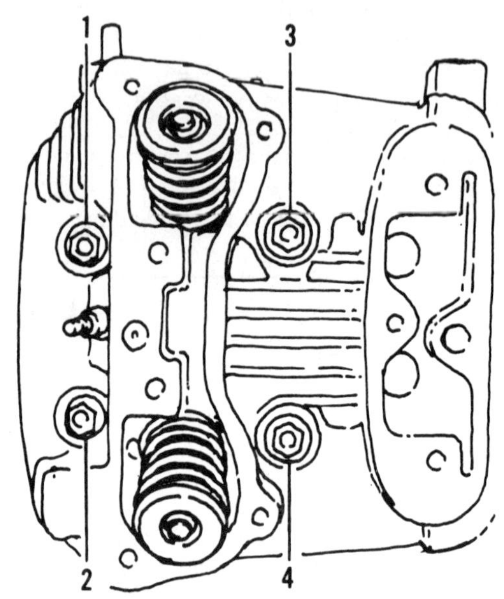

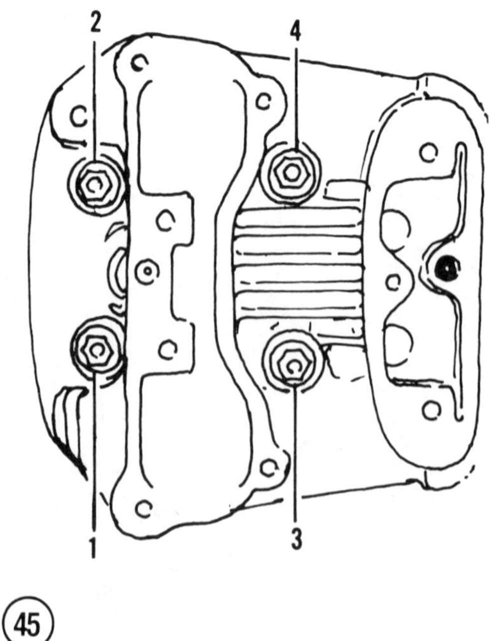

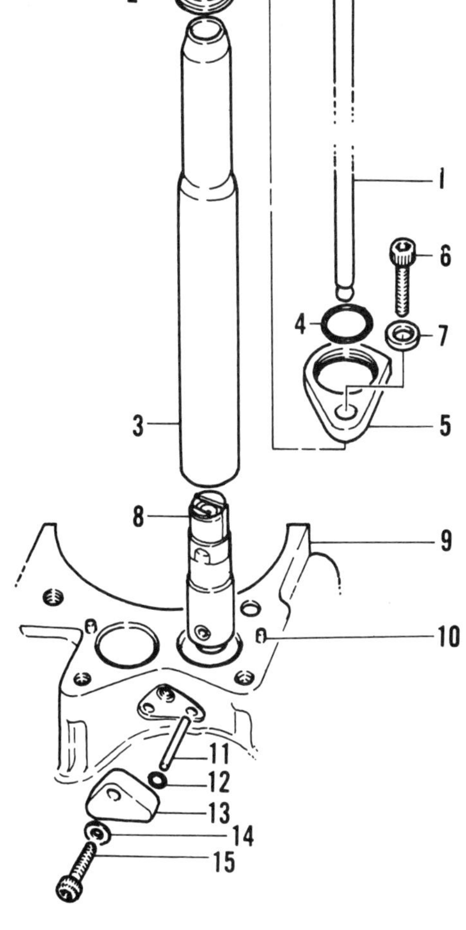
46
PUSHROD/TAPPET ASSEMBLY
1
2
3
4
5
6
7
8
9
10
11
12
13
14
15
1. Pushrod
2. Seal
3. Cover
4. O-ring
5. Seal plate
6. Bolt
7. Washer
8. Tappet
9. Crankcase
10. Locating pin
11. Pin
12. O-ring
13. Plate
14. Washer
15. Allen bolt

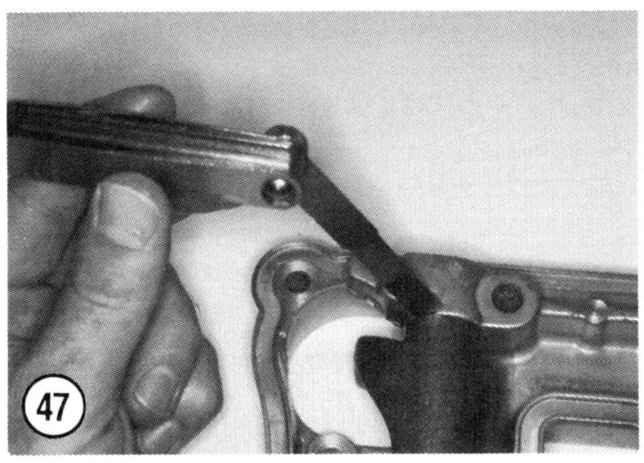
47

4

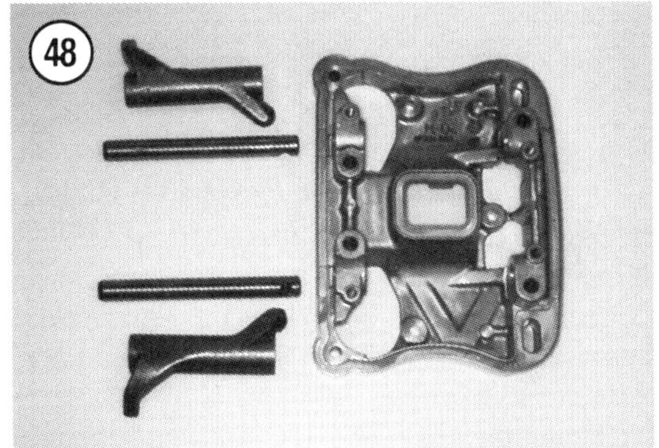
48

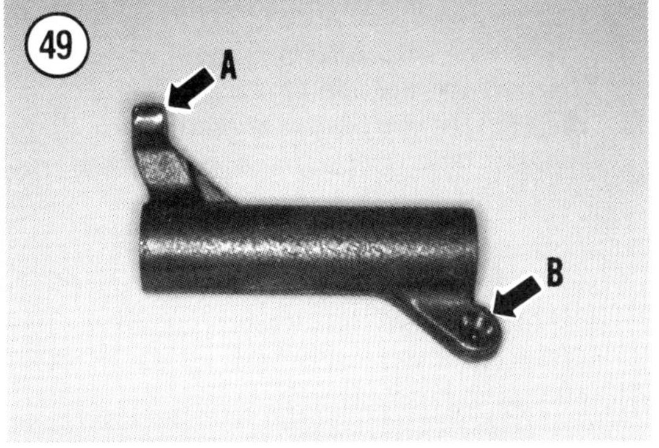
49
A
B

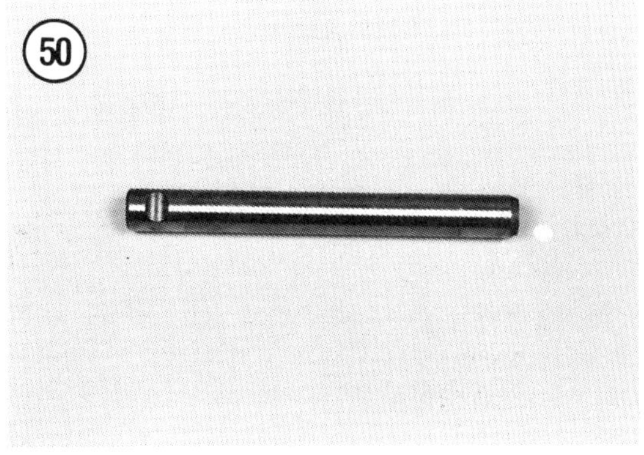
50

1. Press or drive one of the bushings from the rocker arm (**Figure 35**). Do *not* remove the second bushing. If the bushing is difficult to remove, perform the following:

   a. Thread a 9/16-18 in. tap into the bushing to be removed.
   b. Support the rocker arm in a press so that the tap is at the bottom.
   c. Insert a mandrel through the top of the rocker arm and seat it on top of the tap.
   d. Press on the mandrel to force the bushing/tap out of the rocker arm. Don't let the tap fall to the floor where it can shatter.
   e. Remove the tap from the bushing and discard the bushing.

2. Press in the new bushing (with its split portion facing toward the top of the rocker arm) until its outer surface is flush with the rocker arm bore inside surface (**Figure 52**).
3. Ream the new rocker arm bushing with the Harley-Davidson rocker arm bushing reamer (part No. 94804-57) as follows:

   a. Mount the rocker arm in a vise with soft jaws so that the new bushing is at the bottom.

CAUTION
The reamer must be turned clockwise only. Do not turn the reamer backwards (counterclockwise) or you may damage the reamer.

   b. Mount a tap handle on top of the reamer and insert the reamer into the bushing. Turn the reamer clockwise until it passes through the new bushing and remove it from the bottom side. The old bushing left in the rocker arm is used as a guide for the reamer.

4. Remove the rocker arm from the vise and repeat Steps 1-3 to replace the second bushing. The first bushing will now act as a guide for the reamer.
5. When both bushings have been replaced and reamed, clean the rocker arm and bushings in solvent. Then clean with hot, soapy water and rinse with clear, cold water. Dry with compressed air.
6. Measure the inside diameter of each bushing with a snap gauge. When properly reamed, the bushings should provide 0.0005-0.0020 in. (0.012-0.050 mm) shaft clearance.

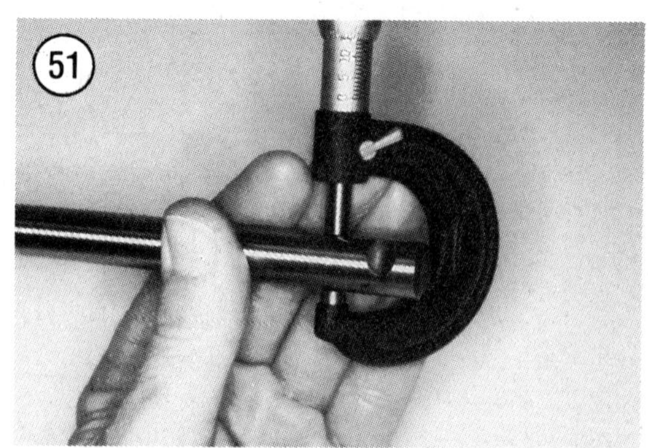

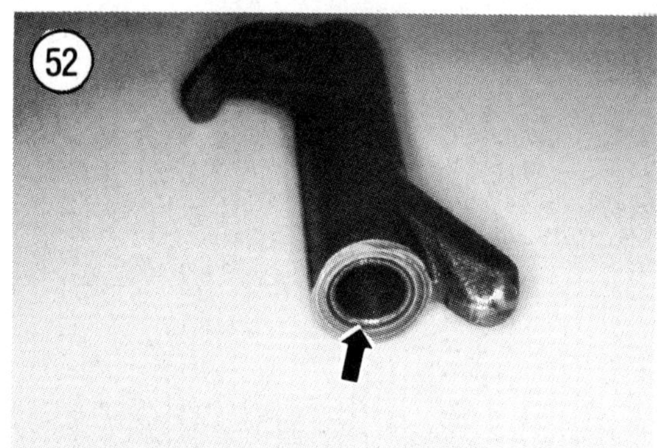

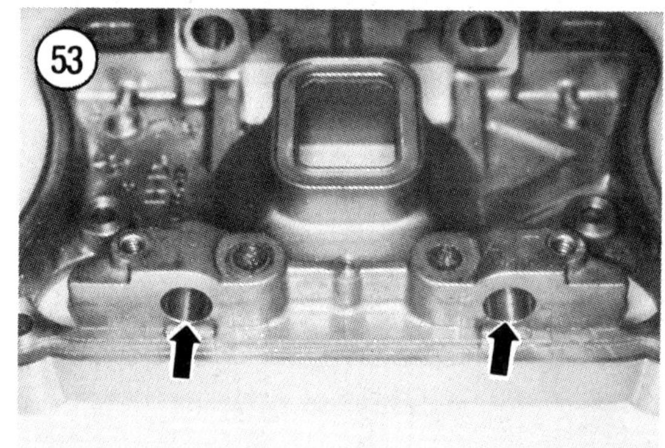

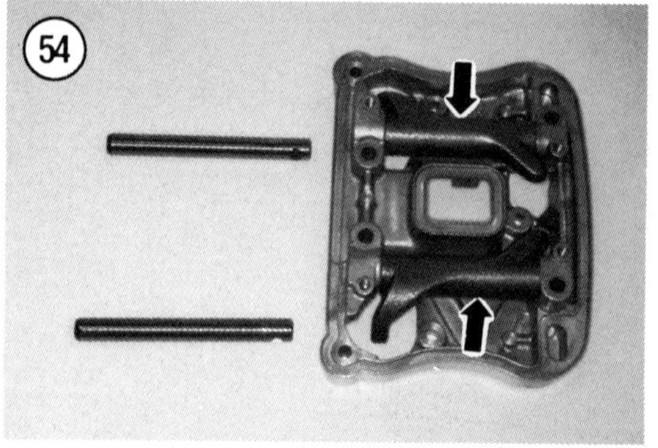

Cylinder Head Inspection

While this section and subsequent sections in this chapter describe cylinder head and valve service, you may want to farm out cylinder head work to a qualified Harley-Davidson dealer or Harley-Davidson performance specialist. We say this because complete and accurate cylinder head work requires a number of special tools: valve spring compressor, spring tester, valve-seat grinder and stones and valve grinder. This doesn't include the experience required to use them. If you are going to send the heads to a performance specialist, contact them first for suggested shipping methods and charges. Compare service rates by referring to the different companies that advertise in the popular motorcycle and Harley-Davidson magazines and newspapers.

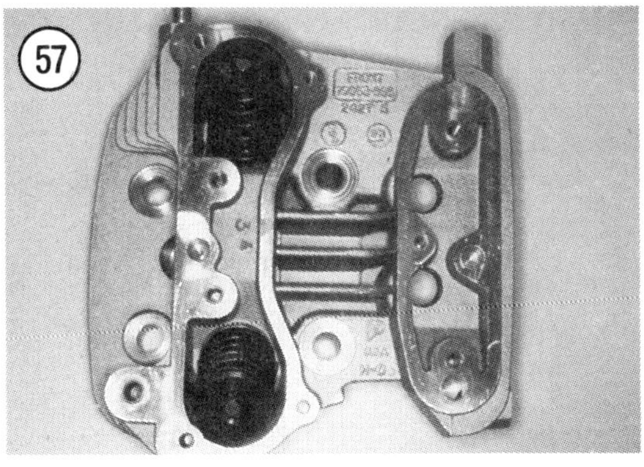

The aluminum cylinder head (**Figure 57**) can be nicked or gouged if mishandled. Handle the cylinder head carefully when cleaning and servicing it in the following procedures.

NOTE

If you are preparing your 883 cc Sportster for AMA Twin Sports racing, order a copy of the most recent AMA CCS rule book. The rules are specific about what you can and can not do when preparing an 883 cc cylinder head for competition. For a CCS rule book, write AMA Championship Cup Series, P.O. Box 447, Skyland, NC 28776.

CAUTION

If the combustion chambers are cleaned while the valves are removed, make sure to keep the scraper or wire brush away from the valve seats to prevent damaging the seat surfaces. A damaged or even slightly scratched valve seat will cause poor valve seating.

1. Remove and inspect the valves and valve seats as described under *Valves and Valve Components* in this chapter. Fabricate a cardboard or wooden holder to store the valves as they are removed.
2. Clean the cylinder head. A thorough cleaning is required to inspect the cylinder head accurately for wear and damage. Because of cylinder head construction, materials and operating conditions, different cleaning techniques and procedures will be required.
   a. First scrape the upper and lower gasket surfaces. Work slowly and carefully, making sure you do not scratch or gouge these surfaces. Damage could cause the head to leak when it is returned to service.
   b. Soak the head in a solvent tank. This will help to soften the carbon buildup in the combustion chambers and exhaust port and to remove oil and grease from the head surfaces. If you do not have access to a solvent tank, spray the head with an aerosol cleaner, following the manufac-

turer's instructions. Then wash the head in hot, soapy water and rinse with clear, cold water. Dry with compressed air, if available.

CAUTION
*Substep c describes cleaning of the combustion chambers (**Figure 58**). Do not use a power-driven wire brush to clean the combustion chambers. The bristles may leave scratches that could become hot spots when the head is returned to service.*

c. Bead-blasting is the most efficient way of removing deposits from the combustion chamber. If you choose to scrape or wire brush the combustion chambers, work carefully around the valve seats. A damaged or even slightly scratched valve seat will cause poor valve seat seating. Send your cylinder heads to a Harley-Davidson dealer for bead-blasting.

NOTE
After bead-blasting a head, clean it thoroughly to remove all blasting residue. This step is critical because the residue collects easily in corners and pockets and is difficult to remove. A bead-blasted head should be initially washed and soaked in a solvent tank, cleaned with hot soapy water, rinsed in cold water and then dried with a thorough blasting of compressed air. Even if the dealer or machine shop cleaned the head, you should reclean it yourself. Blasting residue that is not removed will get into the lubrication system and cause premature and rapid engine wear. When you are convinced the head is clean, clean it one more time.

3. Place a straightedge across the gasket surface at several points (**Figure 59**). Measure warp by inserting a feeler gauge between the straightedge and cylinder head at each location. If the warpage meets or exceeds the service limit in **Table 2**, take the head to a dealer for resurfacing or replace it.

4. Examine the spark plug threads in the cylinder head for damage. If damage is minor or if the threads are dirty or clogged with carbon, use a spark plug thread tap to clean the threads following the manufacturer's instructions. If thread damage is severe and cannot be repaired with the thread tap, install the correct size steel insert from a spark plug repair kit.

5. Check for cracks in the combustion chamber, exhaust port (**Figure 60**) and valve guide (**Figure 61**). If a crack is found, refer repair to a qualified service shop or replace the cylinder head.

6. Measure the rocker arm shaft bore diameter as described under *Rocker Arm Inspection* in this chapter.

7. Inspect the pushrods as described under *Pushrod Inspection* in this chapter.

58

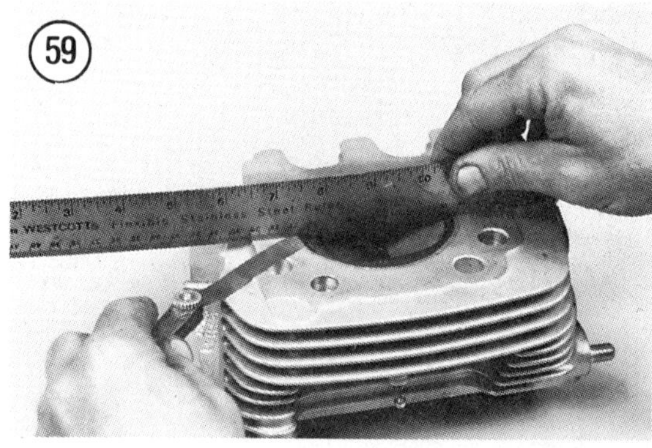

59

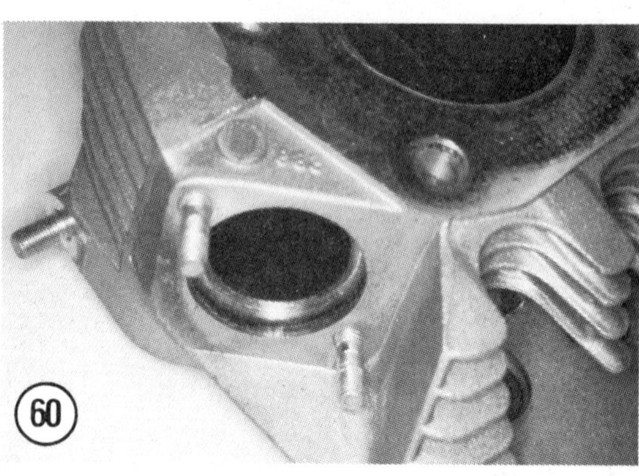
60

8. Inspect the following components as described under *Valves and Valve Components* in this chapter:
   a. Valve guides.
   b. Valve springs.
   c. Valve seats.
   d. Valves.
9. After the cylinder head has been thoroughly cleaned of all carbon, valve grinding compound and bead-blasting residue, install new valve guides (if necessary), valve spring and valves as described under *Valves and Valve Components* in this chapter.

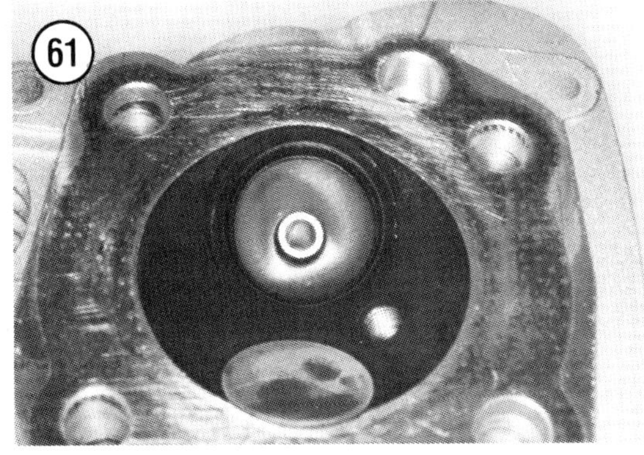

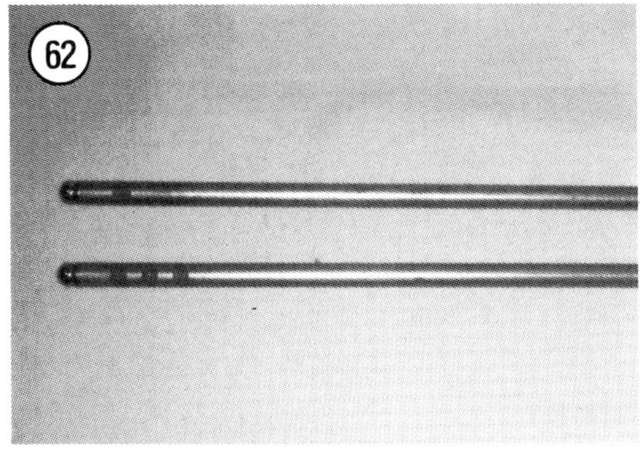

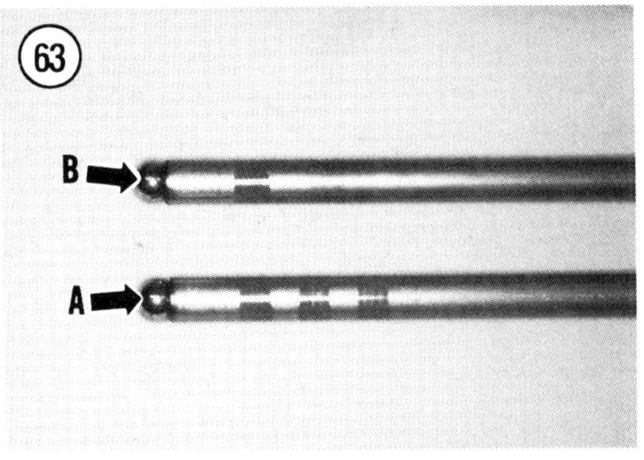

Pushrod Inspection and Replacement

1. Clean the pushrods in fresh solvent. Blow dry with compressed air.
2. Check pushrods (**Figure 62**) for:
   a. Bending.
   b. Cracks.
   c. Cracked or severely worn ball heads.
3. The exhaust and intake pushrods are different lengths. To identify or replace pushrods, note the following:
   a. Front and rear *exhaust* pushrods are 10.800 in. (274.32 mm) long.
   b. Front and rear *intake* pushrods are 10.746 in. (272.94 mm) long.
   c. Exhaust and intake pushrods are color coded for visual identification. Exhaust pushrods have a 3 band-pink code; see A, **Figure 63**. Intake pushrods have a 1 band-brown code; see B, **Figure 63**.

4

Head and Base Gaskets

While the stock Harley-Davidson gaskets are more than adequate for stock engines, they should not be installed on engines with modified squish areas (area between the cylinder head and piston) or for engines used for all-out racing.

The stock 1991 and later base gaskets are made out of paper. The thicknesses are approximately 0.017 in. uncompressed (new) and 0.015 in. compressed (installed).

When researching gasket kits, you will find a number of variations in gasket material and thicknesses. These aftermarket gasket kits will allow you to vary the deck height according to the engine's use. When installing aftermarket gaskets, follow the manufacturer's installation procedures, if included, as these kits have been developed through many hours of testing, under both street and race conditions.

When installing an aftermarket gasket, follow the manufacturer's instructions as to sealant type, if any, and other service or installation requirements.

CYLINDER HEAD, PUSHROD AND ROCKER BOX

Installation

The following tools will be required to install the cylinder heads:

a. New gaskets and O-rings.
b. New engine oil.
c. Torque wrench.
d. Marking pen.

Refer to **Figure 43**.

1. Lubricate the cylinder studs and cylinder head bolts as follows:
   a. Clean the cylinder studs and cylinder bolts.
   b. Apply clean engine oil to the cylinder stud threads and to the flat shoulder surface on the cylinder head bolts (**Figure 64**).
   c. Remove all excess oil from both parts with a lint-free cloth or compressed air. You only want to leave an oil film on these surfaces.

CAUTION
Excessive oil left on the cylinder studs can collect inside the top of cylinder head bolt, causing an oil lock and preventing the bolt from being correctly torqued. This will cause a blown head gasket and oil leak.

2. Install the pistons, rings and cylinders as described in this chapter.
3. Install the cylinder dowel pins (**Figure 65**).
4. Install a new O-ring over each dowel pin.

CAUTION
Because the O-rings help to center the head gasket on the cylinder block, the

64

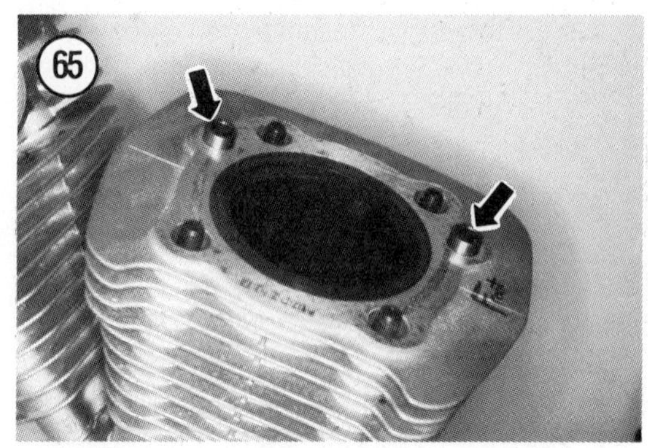

65

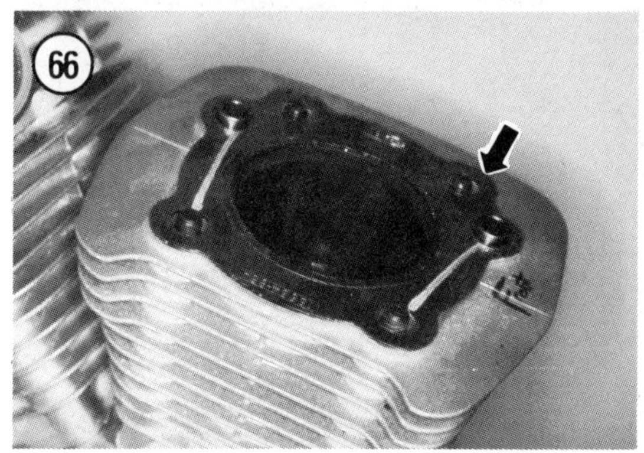

66

67

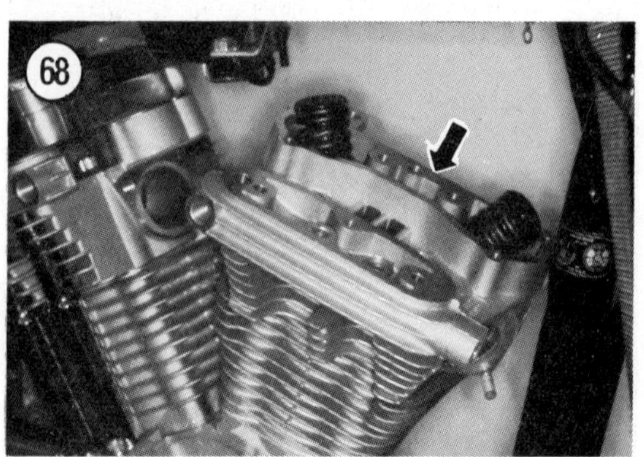

68

69

FRONT CYLINDER HEAD

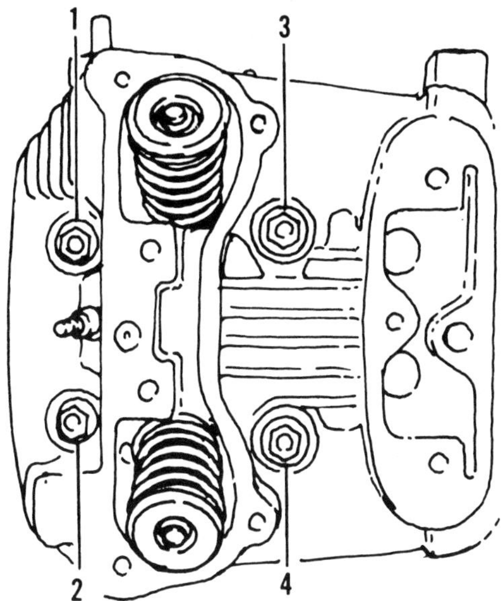

REAR CYLINDER HEAD

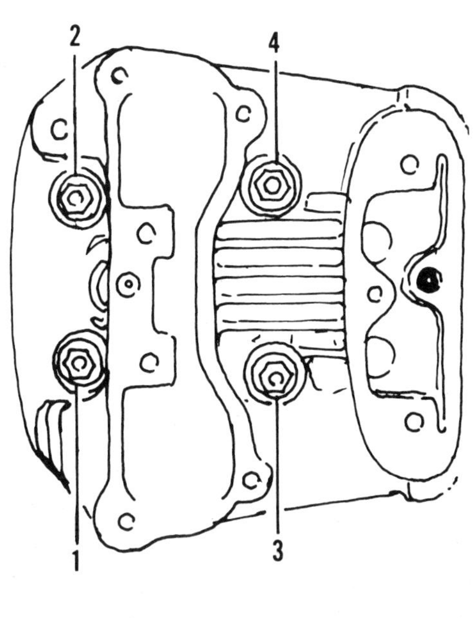

*O-rings must be installed **before** the head gasket.*

5. Install a new cylinder head gasket (**Figure 66**).

CAUTION
Do not put any type of sealer on stock head gaskets. If you are using an after-market head gasket, follow the manufacturer's instructions for gasket installation.

NOTE
*Cylinder heads can be identified by the "Front" and "Rear" marks cast into the bottom side of the head; see **Figure 67**.*

6. Install the cylinder head (**Figure 68**) onto the cylinder dowel pins and studs. Position the head carefully so that you don't knock the head gasket out of alignment.
7. Install the cylinder head bolts and run them down finger-tight. Install the long bolts in the center bolt holes; install the short bolts in the outer bolt holes (next to the spark plug hole).

CAUTION
Failure to follow the torque pattern and sequence in Step 8 may cause cylinder head distortion and gasket leakage.

8. Torque the cylinder head bolts as follows:
   a. Using a torque wrench, tighten bolt No. 1 to 7-9 ft.-lb. (9-12 N•m). Then continue and tighten bolts, 2, 3 and 4 in numerical order. **Figure 69** identifies the bolt numbers for the front and rear cylinder heads.
   b. Tighten bolt No. 1 to 12-14 ft.-lb. (16-19 N•m). Then continue and tighten bolts 2, 3 and 4 in numerical order.
   c. Using a pen (**Figure 70**), make a vertical mark on the No. 1 bolt head and a matching mark on the cylinder head. Repeat for each bolt. See **Figure 71**.
   d. Following the torque sequence in **Figure 69**, turn each bolt head 1/4 turn (90°) clockwise (**Figure 72**), using the match marks as a guide.
   e. Repeat for the opposite cylinder head.
9. If the valve tappets were removed, install them as described under *Valve Tappets* in this chapter.
10. Rotate the engine until both tappets from the cylinder head being serviced are installed on the lowest position (base circle) on the cam.

4

11. Install the pushrod covers (**Figure 73**) as follows:

a. Slide a new seal (2, **Figure 73**) down the pushrod cover.

b. Slide the retainer plate (**Figure 74**) down the pushrod cover.

c. Install a new O-ring (4, **Figure 73**) onto the top of the pushrod cover.

d. Tilt the pushrod cover (**Figure 75**) and install it through the pushrod cover hole in the cylinder head; see **Figure 76**. Then align the bottom of

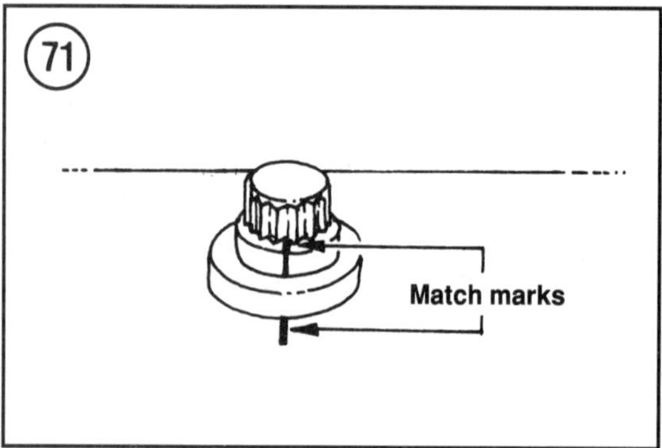

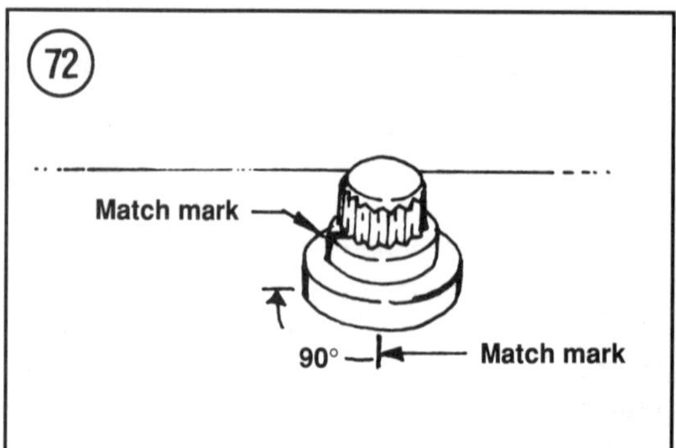

PUSHROD/TAPPET ASSEMBLY

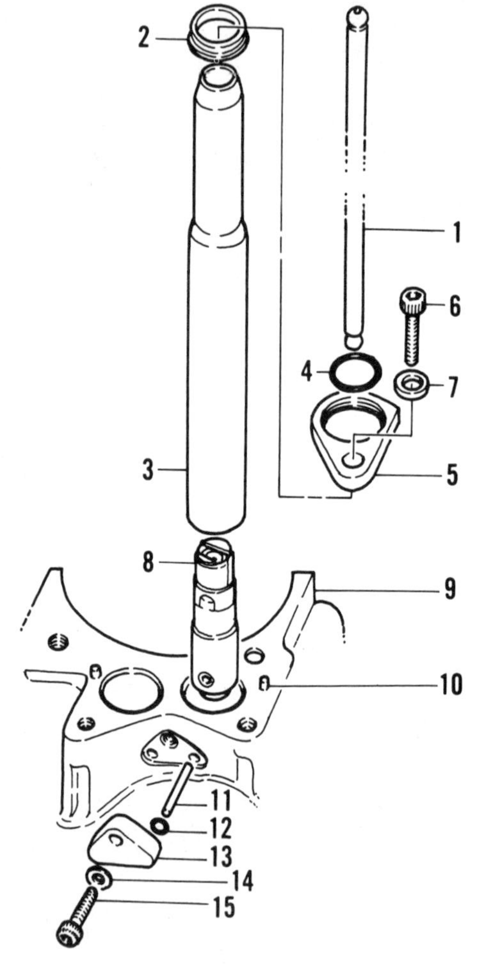

1. Pushrod
2. Seal
3. Cover
4. O-ring
5. Seal plate
6. Bolt
7. Washer
8. Tappet
9. Crankcase
10. Locating pin
11. Pin
12. O-ring
13. Plate
14. Washer
15. Allen bolt

the pushrod cover with the tappet hole and install the cover into the hole.

e. Slide the seal and the pushrod seal plate down the pushrod cover. Seat the seal into the seal plate.

f. Align the crankcase locating pin with the pushrod seal plate and position the plate (**Figure 77**) on the crankcase. Install the pushrod seal plate bolt and washer and tighten to the torque specification listed in **Table 4**.

12. Install the pushrods as follows:

a. If you labeled the pushrods during removal, install each pushrod in its original position.

b. If the pushrods were not labeled, or if you are installing new pushrods, identify them as follows.

c. The exhaust pushrods are marked with 3 pink bands (A, **Figure 63**) and are 10.800 in. (274.32 mm) long.

d. The intake pushrods (B, **Figure 63**) are marked with a single brown band and are 10.746 in. (272.94 mm) long.

e. Confirm pushrod length with a vernier caliper.

f. Make sure that each pushrod is seated in the top of its respective tappet (**Figure 78**).

13. Install new lower rocker arm cover gaskets (**Figure 79**) with the sealer bead on each gasket facing up.

14. Place the lower rocker cover into position (A, **Figure 80**), while at the same time inserting the pushrods into the rocker arm sockets; see B, **Figure 80**.

15. Install the lower rocker arm cover bolts and washers in their respective bolt holes.

4

NOTE
The rocker arm shafts have cutouts in them. The cutouts must align with the rocker arm cover bolt holes.

NOTE
When the lower rocker cover mounting bolts are tightened, the rocker arms will be pulled down at the same time. The rocker arms will in turn force the pushrods down, bleeding the lifters.

To ensure proper installation and tappet bleeding, the bolts must be tightened in a crisscross pattern and to specific torque specifications. This helps to distribute stress evenly through the rocker arms.

16. Starting with the 5/16 in. rocker cover bolts, finger-tighten each bolt one turn at a time. When you can no longer turn the bolts by hand, tighten the bolts gradually in a crisscross pattern to the torque specifications in **Table 4**.

CAUTION
Do not turn the engine over until all of the pushrods can be turned by hand. Otherwise, you may damage the rocker arms or pushrods.

17. Check that each pushrod can be turned by hand.
18. Install new center and outer gaskets (**Figure 81**) onto the lower rocker arm cover.
19. Install the middle rocker cover (A, **Figure 82**) onto the lower rocker cover.
20. Install a new gasket (B, **Figure 82**) onto the middle rocker cover.
21. Install the upper rocker cover (**Figure 83**) onto the middle rocker cover.
22. Slide on a steel washer (if used) and fiber seal onto each rocker cover mounting bolt (**Figure 84**).
23. Install the upper rocker cover mounting bolts and tighten to the torque specification in **Table 4**.
24. Repeat for the other cylinder head and rocker box assembly.
25. Reverse Steps 1-19 under *Engine Installation* to complete assembly.
26. If new top end components were installed, the engine must be broken in. Refer to *Engine Break-in* in this chapter.

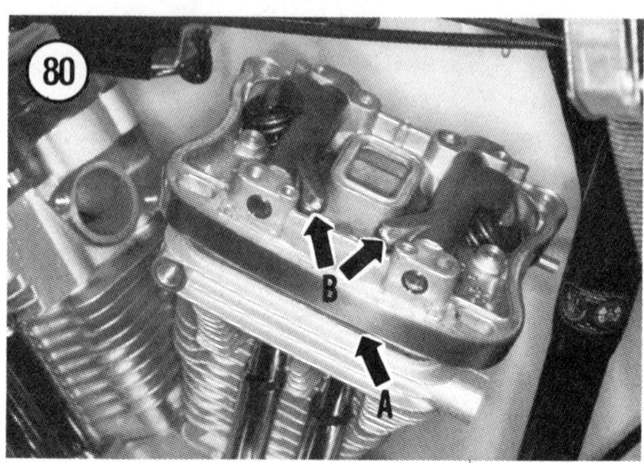

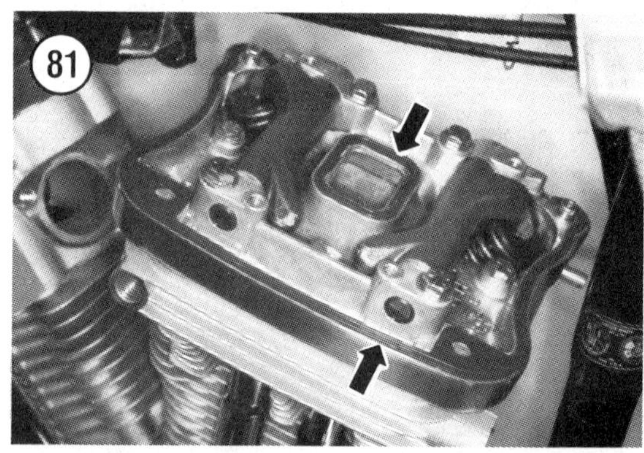

VALVES AND VALVE COMPONENTS

While this section and subsequent sections in this chapter describe cylinder head and valve service, you may want to farm out cylinder head work to a qualified Harley-Davidson dealer or Harley-Davidson performance specialist. This is because complete and accurate cylinder head work requires a number of special tools: valve spring compressor, spring tester, valve-seat grinder and stones, valve grinder and an assortment of valve related hand tools. This doesn't include the experience required to use them. If you are going to send the heads to a performance specialist, contact them first for suggested shipping methods and charges. Compare service rates by referring to the different service ads listed in the popular motorcycle and Harley-Davidson magazines and newspapers.

The aluminum cylinder head can be nicked or gouged if mishandled. Handle the cylinder head carefully when servicing it in the following procedures.

NOTE

If you are preparing your 883 cc Sportster for AMA Twin Sports racing, order a copy of the most recent AMA CCS rule book. The rules are specific about what you can and can not do when preparing an 883 cc cylinder head for class racing. For a CCS rule book, write AMA Championship Cup Series, P.O. Box 447, Skyland, NC 28776.

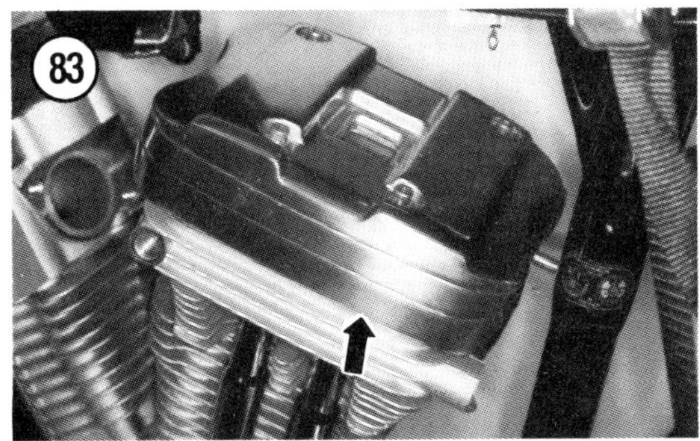

Removal

Refer to **Figure 85** for this procedure.

CAUTION

All component parts of each valve assembly must be kept together. Do not mix with like components from other valves or excessive wear may result.

1. Remove the cylinder head(s) as described in this chapter.
2. Install a valve spring compressor squarely over the valve retainer with other end of tool placed against valve head (**Figure 86**).
3. Tighten valve spring compressor until split valve keeper separates. Lift out split keeper with needlenose pliers (**Figure 87**).
4. Gradually loosen valve spring compressor and remove from head. Lift off valve collar (**Figure 88**).
5. Remove the outer and inner valve springs (**Figure 89**).

CAUTION

*Remove any burrs from the valve stem grooves before removing the valve (**Figure 90**); otherwise, the valve guides will be damaged.*

6. Remove the valve and the lower valve collar (**Figure 91**).
7. Repeat Steps 2-6 and remove remaining valves.
8. Support a wide-blade screwdriver with a shop cloth (**Figure 92**) and pry off the valve guide oil seal.
9. Repeat Step 8 for each oil seal.

Inspection

1. Clean valves with a wire brush and solvent.
2. Inspect the contact surface of each valve for burning (**Figure 93**). Minor roughness and pitting can be removed by lapping the valve as described in this chapter. Excessive unevenness to the contact

(85)

CYLINDER HEAD

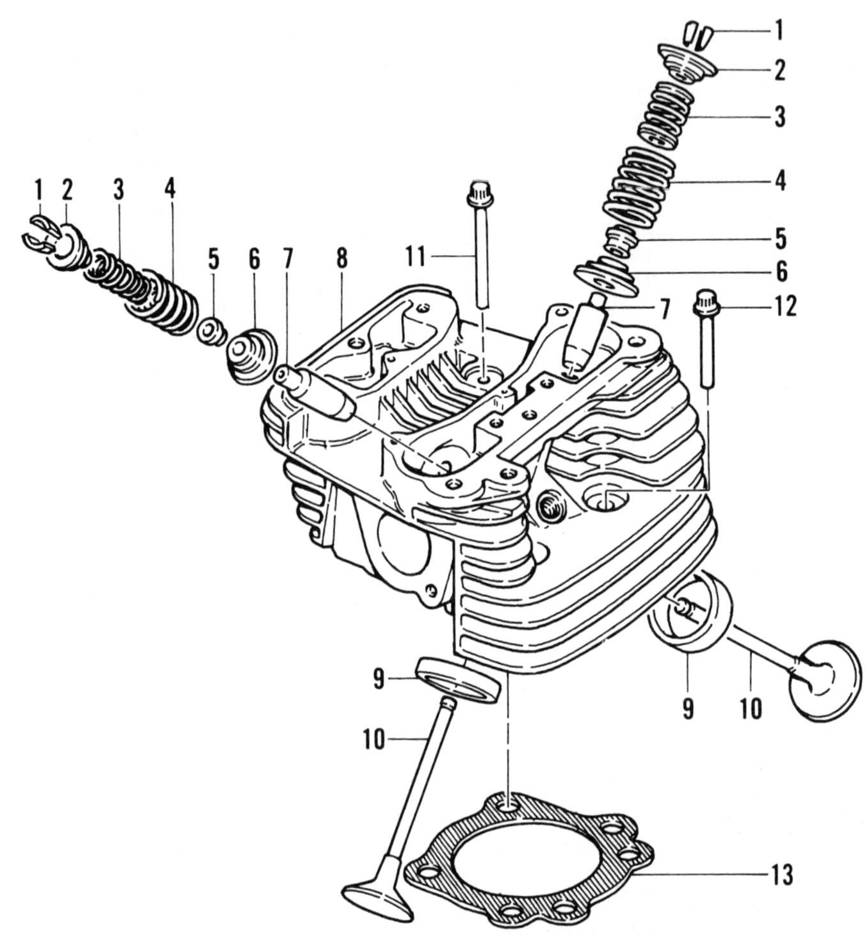

1. Valve keepers
2. Upper collar
3. Inner valve spring
4. Outer valve spring
5. Valve stem seal
6. Lower collar
7. Valve guide
8. Cylinder head
9. Valve seat
10. Valve
11. Bolt (long)
12. Bolt (short)
13. Head gasket

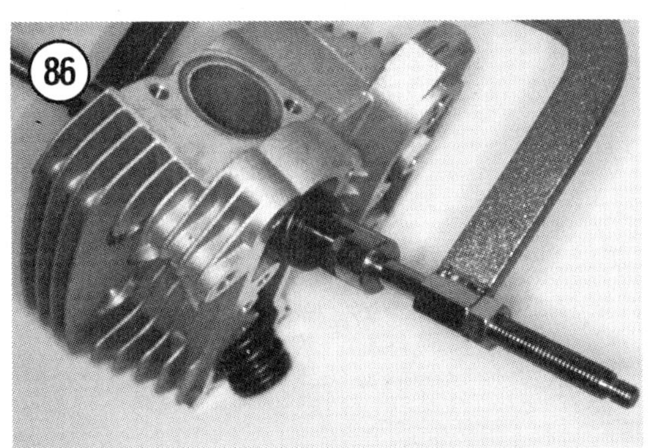
86

87

88

89

90

91

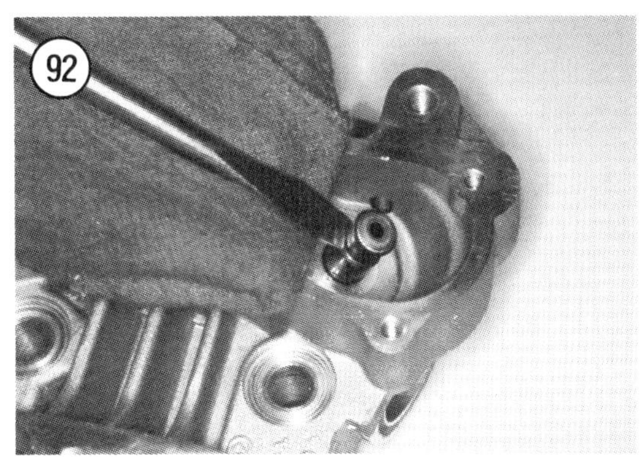
92

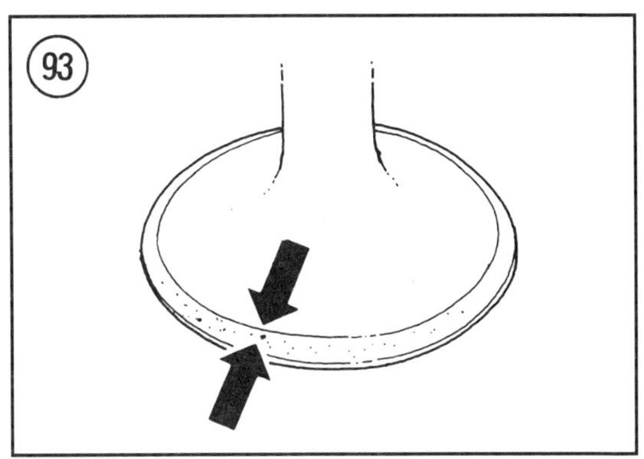
93

surface is an indication that the valve is not serviceable. The contact surface of the valve may be ground on a valve grinding machine, but it is best to replace a burned or damaged valve with a new one.

3. Inspect the valve stems for wear and roughness.
4. Measure valve stem O.D. with a micrometer (**Figure 94**). Record O.D. for each valve.
5. To clean the valve guides, perform the following:
   a. Lightly hone the valve guide with the Harley-Davidson Valve Guide Hone (part No. HD-34723). Lubricate the hone with honing oil—do not use motor oil. Drive the hone with an electric drill (500-1,200 rpm).
   b. Soak the head in hot, soapy water and clean the guides with the Harley-Davidson Valve Guide Brush (part No. HD-34751).
   c. Repeat for each valve guide.
   d. Rinse head in cold water and blow dry.
6. Measure each valve guide (A, **Figure 95**) at top, center and bottom with a bore gauge or small hole gauge. Record I.D. for each valve guide.
7. Subtract the measurement made in Step 4 from the measurement made in Step 6 above. The difference is the valve guide-to-valve stem clearance. See specifications in **Table 2** for specified clearance. Replace any guide and valve that is not within tolerance.

NOTE
Harley-Davidson does not list specific valve guide I.D. and valve stem O.D. measurements. Service wear is determined by measuring the valve stem clearance measurement.

8. Place the spring on a flat surface and check it for squareness with a combination square as shown in **Figure 96**. The spring should be parallel to the scale. If not, replace the spring.
9. Measure the valve spring free length with a vernier caliper (**Figure 97**). Replace the spring if it has sagged to the service limit dimension in **Table 2**.
10. Measure valve spring compression with a compression tool (**Figure 98**) and compare to specifications in **Table 3**. Replace weak or damaged springs.
11. If any one valve has a spring that is worn or damaged as determined in Steps 8-10, replace the valve springs as a set.
12. Check the valve spring retainers and split keepers. Replace worn or damaged parts as required.

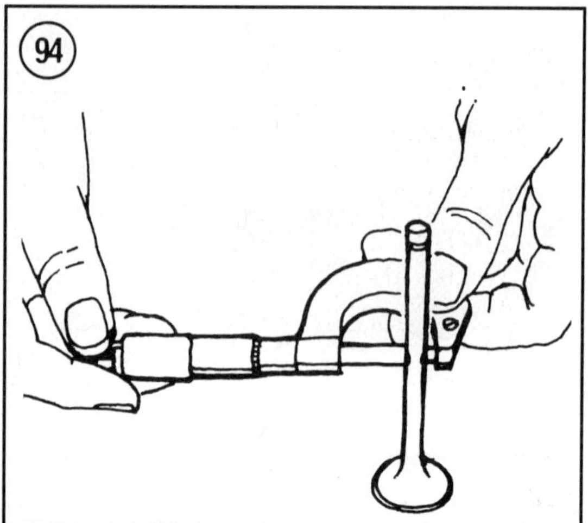

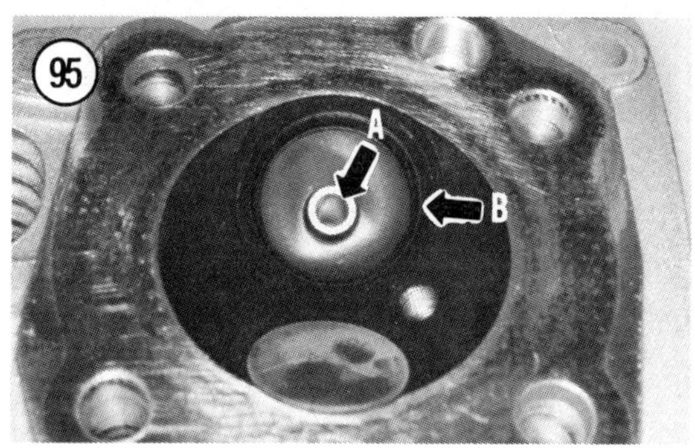

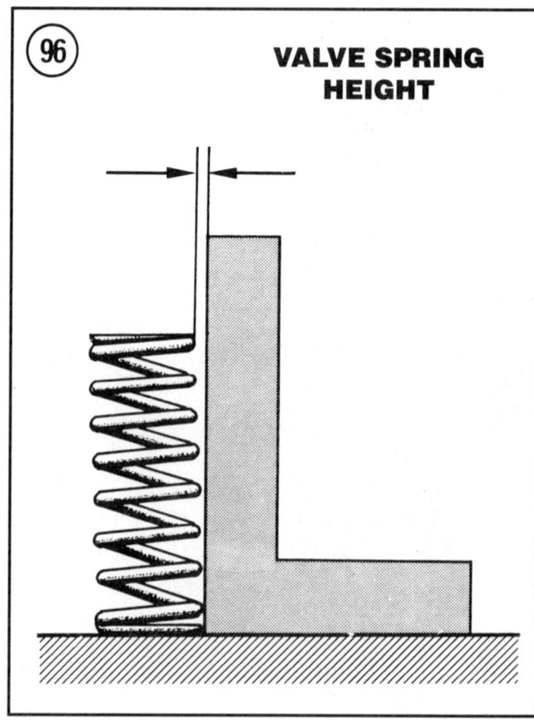

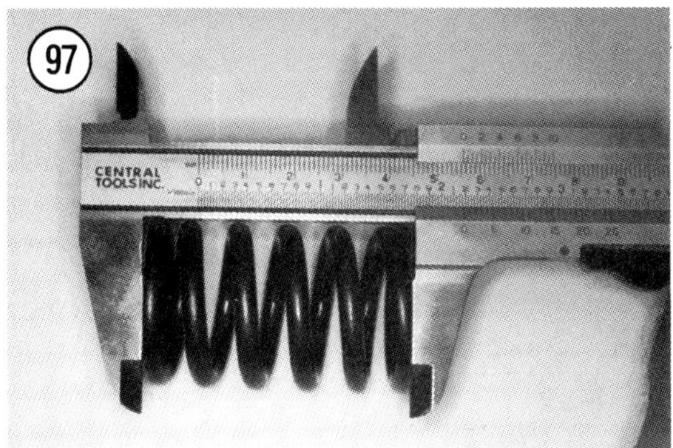

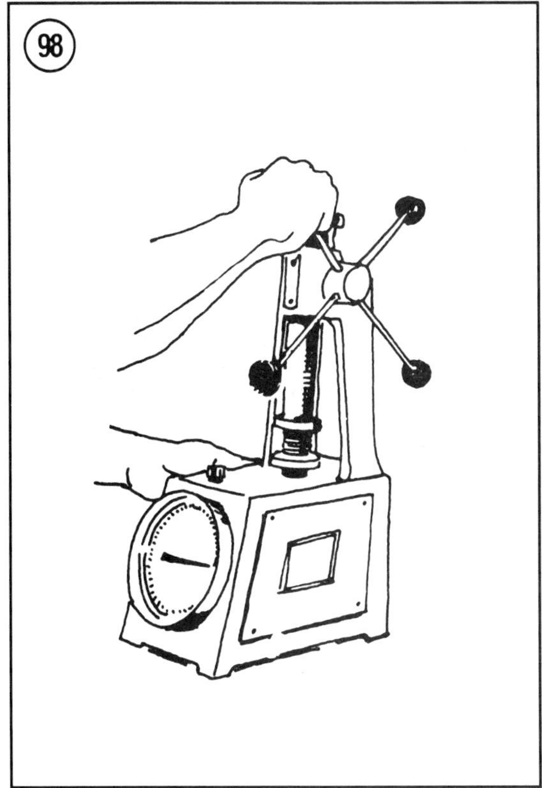

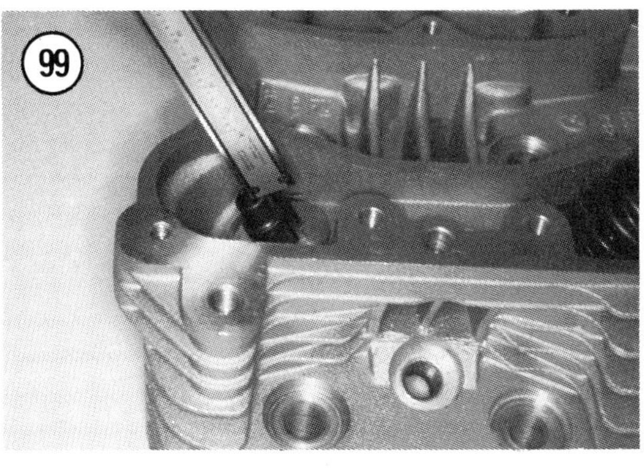

13. Inspect valve seats (B, **Figure 95**). If worn or burned, they must be reconditioned. This should be performed by your dealer or local machine shop. Seats and valves in near-perfect condition can be reconditioned by lapping with fine carborundum paste.

Valve Guide Replacement

When guides are worn so that there is excessive stem-to-guide clearance or valve tipping, they must be replaced. Replace all of the guides at the same time.

The following tools will be required to replace the valve guides:

NOTE
The following part numbers are all factory Harley-Davidson numbers.

a. Driver Handle and Remover (part No. HD-34740) or equivalent. By itself, this tool is used to remove the valve guides. This tool, along with the Valve Guide Installation Tool, is used to install the valve guides.
b. Valve Guide Installation Tool (part No. HD-34731) or equivalent.
c. Valve Guide Reamer (part No. HD-94810-80C) or equivalent. This tool is used to ream the valve guides after they have been installed in the cylinder head.
d. Valve Guide Hone (part No. HD-34723). This tool is used to hone the valve guides after reaming them to size.
e. Valve Guide Brush (part No. HD-34751). This tool is used to clean the valve guides after honing them.
f. Honing oil. Only honing oil should be used when honing the valve guides.

1. Place the cylinder head on a wooden surface so that the combustion chamber faces down.
2. Shoulderless valve guides are used. Before removing the guides, note and record the shape of the guide that projects into the combustion chamber. If you are not going to use the valve guide installation tool when installing the guide, measure the distance from the face of the guide to the cylinder head surface with a vernier caliper as shown in **Figure 99**; record this distance for each valve guide so that the guides can be installed to the same dimension.

4

3. The guides can be either driven or pressed out. Remove the valve guides as follows:

CAUTION

The correct size valve guide removal tool must be used when removing the valve guides; otherwise, the tool may mushroom the end of the guide. A mushroomed guide will widen the guide bore in the cylinder head as it passes through it.

a. Support the cylinder head so that the combustion chamber faces down. If you are driving the guides out, place the cylinder head on a piece of wood. If you are pressing the guides out, support the cylinder head in a press so that the valve guide is perpendicular to the press table.
b. Insert the driver handle and remover in the top of the valve guide.
c. Press or drive the valve out through the combustion chamber.
d. Repeat to remove the remaining valve guides.

4. Clean the valve guide bores in the cylinder head.
5. Because the valve guides are a press fit in the cylinder head, the new guide's O.D. must be sized with the valve guide bore in the cylinder head. This is because the guide bore in the cylinder is sometimes enlarged during guide removal. Determine valve guide sizes as follows:

a. Measure the valve guide bore I.D. in the cylinder head with a bore gauge or snap gauge. Record the bore I.D.
b. The new valve guide O.D. must be 0.0020-0.0033 in. (0.050-0.083 mm) larger than the guide bore in the cylinder head. When purchasing new valve guides, measure the new guide's O.D. with a micrometer. If the new guide's O.D. is not within these specifications, oversize valve guide(s) will be required. See your dealer for available sizes.

6. Apply a thin coating of molylube or white grease to the valve guide O.D. prior to installation.

CAUTION

When installing oversize valve guides, make sure to match each guide to its respective bore in the cylinder head.

7. Install the new guide with the Harley-Davidson driver handle and valve guide installation tools or equivalent aftermarket tools. Press or drive the guide into the cylinder head until the valve guide installation tool bottoms out on the cylinder head surface. When the tool bottoms out, the valve guide has been installed to the correct height. If you don't have the driver handle tool, install the valve to the same height recorded prior to removing the valve guide; measure the valve guide's installed height with a vernier caliper (**Figure 99**) when installing it.
8. Because replacement valve guides are sold with their I.D. smaller than the valve stem, each guide must be reamed to fit the valve stem. Use the Harley-Davidson valve guide reamer. Use cutting oil on the reamer when reaming the guide. Ream the guide to within 0.0010 in. (0.025 mm) of the finished valve guide I.D.; see **Table 2** for valve stem clearances and service limits.

CAUTION

When honing the valve guides in Step 9, keep in mind that you only have 0.0015-0.0033 in. (0.038-0.084 mm) (exhaust) and 0.0008-0.0026 in. (0.020-0.066 mm) (intake) valve stem clearance to work with. Excessive valve stem clearance reduces engine performance while increasing oil blowby and consumption.

9. Lightly hone the valve guide with the Harley-Davidson Valve Guide Hone (part No. HD-34723) or equivalent. Lubricate the hone with honing oil—do not use motor oil. Drive the hone with an electric drill (500-1,200 rpm). Hone the guide until the valve stem clearance specified in **Table 2** is obtained and with a crosshatch pattern of 60°.
10. Repeat for each valve guide.
11. Soak the cylinder head in a container filled with hot, soapy water. Then clean the valve guides with the Harley-Davidson valve guide brush or an

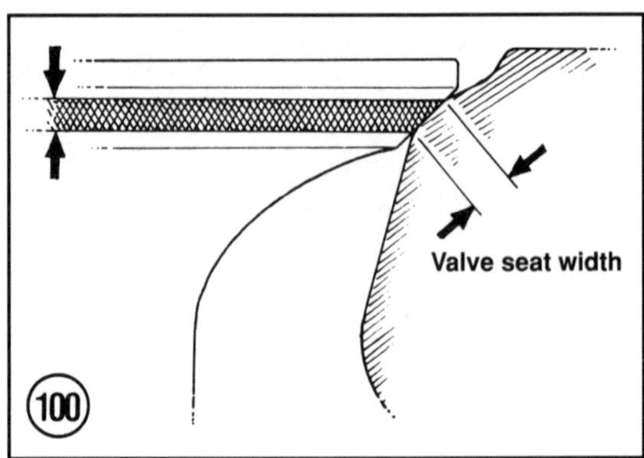

equivalent bristle brush—do not use a steel brush. Do not use cleaning solvent, kerosene or gasoline, as these chemicals will not remove all of the abrasive and minute particles produced during the honing operation. Repeat this step a few times until all of the valve guides have been thoroughly cleaned, rinse the cylinder head and valve guides in clear, cold water and dry with compressed air.

12. After cleaning and drying the valve guides, apply clean engine oil to the guides to prevent rust.

13. Reface the valve seats to make them concentric with the new valve guides. Refer to *Valve Seat Reconditioning* in this chapter.

Valve Seat Inspection

1. Clean the valves of all carbon, then rinse in solvent as described under *Valve Inspection* in this chapter.

2. The most accurate method of checking the valve seat width and position is to use Prussian blue or machinist's dye, available from auto parts stores. To check the valve seat with Prussian blue or machinist's dye, perform the following:

NOTE
Install the valves in their original locations when performing the following.

a. Thoroughly clean the valve face and valve seat with contact cleaner.
b. Spread a thin layer of Prussian Blue or machinist's dye evenly on the valve face.

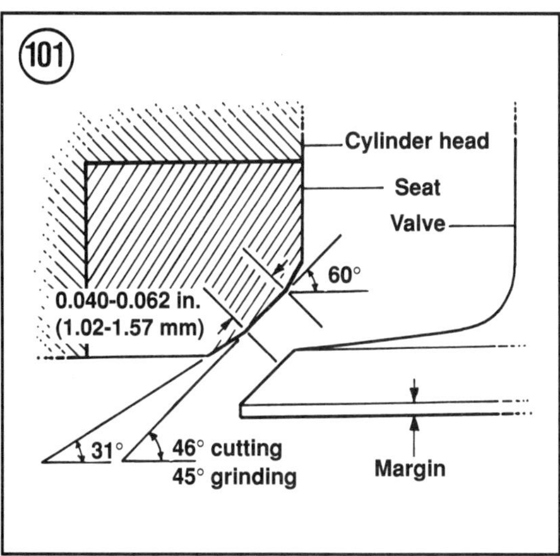

c. Insert the valve into its guide and turn it with a valve lapping tool.
d. Remove the valve and examine the impression left by the Prussian Blue or machinist's dye. If the impression left in the dye (on the valve or in the cylinder head) is not even and continuous and the valve seat width (**Figure 100**) is not even and continuous within the specified tolerance in **Table 2**, the cylinder head valve seat must be reconditioned.

3. Closely examine the valve seat in the cylinder head (**Figure 100**). It should be smooth and even with a polished seating surface.

4. If the valve seat is okay, install the valve as described in this chapter.

5. If the valve seat is not correct, recondition the valve seat as described in this chapter.

4

Valve Seat Reconditioning

Special valve seat cutter tools and considerable experience are required to recondition the valve seats in the cylinder head properly. You can save considerable money by removing the cylinder head and taking both cylinder heads to a dealer or machine shop and having the valve seats ground.

The following procedure is provided if you choose to perform this task yourself.

While the valve seat for both the intake valves and exhaust valves are machined to the same angles, different cutter sizes are required. The Neway Valve Seat Cutter Set (part No. HD-35758) can be used to cut the valve seats.

NOTE
Follow the manufacturer's instructions while using valve facing equipment.

The valve seat angles are shown in **Figure 101**. Note that Harley-Davidson specifies a 45° seat when grinding seats and a 46° seat when cutting seats.

1. Clean the valve guides as described under *Inspection* in this chapter.

2. Carefully rotate and insert the solid pilot into the valve guide. Make sure the pilot is correctly seated.

CAUTION
Valve seat accuracy will depend on a correctly sized and installed pilot.

3. Using the 45° (stone) or 46° (cutter) tool, descale and clean the valve seat with one or two turns.

CAUTION
*Measure the valve seat contact in the cylinder head (**Figure 100**) after each cut to make sure the contact area is correct and to avoid removing too much material. Overgrinding will sink the valves too far into the cylinder head, requiring replacement of the valve seat.*

4. If the seat is still pitted or burned, turn the 45° cutter additional turns until the surface is clean. Refer to the previous CAUTION to avoid removing too much material from the valve seat.
5. Remove the pilot from the valve guide.
6. Apply a small amount of valve lapping compound to the valve face and install the valve. Rotate the valve against the valve seat with a valve lapping tool. Remove the valve.
7. Measure the valve seat with a vernier caliper (**Figure 100** and **Figure 101**). Record the measurement to use as a reference point when performing the following.

CAUTION
The 31° cutter removes material quickly. Work carefully and check your progress often.

8. Install the 31° cutter onto the solid pilot and lightly cut the seat to remove 1/4 of the existing valve seat.
9. Install the 60° cutter onto the solid pilot and lightly cut the seat to remove the lower 1/4 of the existing valve seat.
10. Measure the valve seat with a vernier caliper. Then fit the 45 or 46° cutter onto the solid pilot and cut the valve seat to the specified seat width listed in **Table 2**.
11. When the valve seat width is correct, check valve seating as follows.
12. Remove the solid pilot from the cylinder head.
13. Inspect the valve seat-to-valve face impression as follows:
   a. Clean the valve seat with contact cleaner.
   b. Spread a thin layer of Prussian Blue or machinist's dye evenly on the valve face.
   c. Insert the valve into its guide.
   d. Support the valve with your fingers and turn it with a valve lapping tool.
   e. Remove the valve and examine the impression left by the Prussian Blue or machinist's dye.
   f. Measure the valve seat width (**Figure 100** and **Figure 101**). Refer to **Table 2** for the correct seat width.
   g. The valve contact area should be approximately in the center of the valve seat area.
14. If the contact area is too high on the valve, or if it is too wide, use the 31° cutter and remove a portion of the top area of the valve seat material to lower or narrow the contact area.
15. If the contact area is too low on the valve, or if it is too wide, use the 60° cutter and remove a portion of the lower area to raise and widen the contact area.
16. After the desired valve seat position and angle is obtained, use the 45° (stone) or 46° (cutter) tool and very lightly clean off any burrs that may have been caused by the previous cuts.
17. When the contact area is correct, lap the valve as described in this chapter.
18. Repeat Steps 1-17 for all remaining valve seats.
19. Thoroughly clean the cylinder head and all valve components in solvent, then clean with detergent and hot water and finish with a final rinsing in cold water. Dry with compressed air. Then apply a light coat of engine oil to all non-aluminum metal surfaces to prevent any rust formation.

Valve Lapping

Valve lapping is a simple operation which can restore the valve seal without machining if the amount of wear or distortion is not too great.

1. Smear a light coating of fine grade valve lapping compound on seating surface of valve.
2. Insert the valve into the head.
3. Wet the suction cup of the lapping stick and stick it onto the head of the valve. Lap the valve to the seat by spinning tool between hands while lifting and moving valve around seat 1/4 turn at a time.
4. Wipe off valve and seat frequently to check progress of lapping. Lap only enough to achieve a precise seating ring around valve head.
5. Closely examine valve seat in cylinder head. It should be smooth and even with a smooth, polished seating "ring."
6. Thoroughly clean the valves and cylinder head in solvent to remove all grinding compound. Any compound left on the valves or the cylinder head will end

up in the engine and cause premature and rapid engine wear.

7. After the lapping has been completed and the valve assemblies have been reinstalled into the head, the valve seal should be tested. Check the seal of each valve by pouring solvent into each of the intake and exhaust ports. There should be no leakage past the seat. If leakage occurs, combustion chamber will appear wet. If fluid leaks past any of the seats, disassemble that valve assembly and repeat the lapping procedure until there is no leakage.

VALVE SEAL INSTALLATION

1. Drive handle
2. Valve seal installation tool
3. Valve guide seal
4. Valve guide
5. Lower collar

(102)

Valve Seat Replacement

Valve seat replacement requires considerable experience and equipment. Refer this work to a Harley-Davidson dealer or machine shop.

Installation

The following tools will be required to install the valves:

a. Valve spring compressor.
b. Harley-Davidson Valve Seal Installation Tool (part No. HD-34643A) or equivalent.
c. Harley-Davidson Driver Handle (part No. HD-34740) or equivalent.

1. Lap valves as described in this chapter.

CAUTION

The cylinder heads, valve seats and valves must be thoroughly cleaned of all abrasive lapping compound before reassembling the cylinder head. Any lapping compound left in the engine will result in excessive engine wear.

2. Coat a valve stem with oil and insert the valve into its valve guide in cylinder head.
3. Install the lower collar so that its flat side faces down. See **Figure 91**.
4. Install new valve guide seals as follows:

a. Place a protective cover over the end of the valve stem (covering the valve keeper groove on valve stem).

CAUTION

The protective cover used in substep b prevents the valve stem keeper groove from tearing the valve stem seal.

b. Wipe the protective cover with clean engine oil and place a new valve guide seal on the cover.
c. Tap the seal into place with the Harley-Davidson valve seal installation tool and driver handle; see **Figure 102**. The oil seal is installed when the installation tool bottoms out on the lower collar. If you do not have the special tools, use a socket and hammer and tap the seal into place until it bottoms out against the lower collar. See **Figure 90**.
d. If you have to remove an oil seal after installing it, discard the seal and install a new one.

5. Install valve springs (**Figure 89**). Then install the upper valve spring collar (**Figure 88**).

6. Push down on upper valve spring collar with the valve spring compressor (**Figure 86**) and install valve keepers (**Figure 87**). After releasing tension from the compressor, lightly tap the upper retainer with a plastic hammer to make sure the keepers (**Figure 103**) are seated.

7. Repeat to install the remaining valve guide seals and valves.

103

104

PISTON/CYLINDER ASSEMBLY

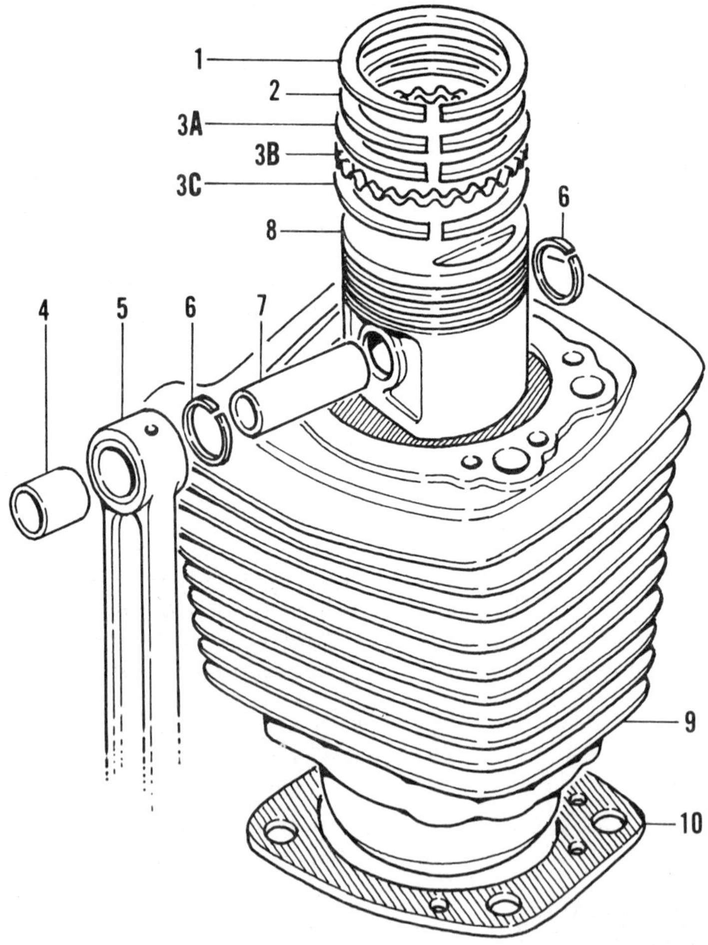

1. Upper compression ring
2. Lower compression ring
3A. Upper oil ring
3B. Spacer
3C. Lower oil ring
4. Bushing
5. Connecting rod
6. Retaining rings
7. Piston pin
8. Piston
9. Cylinder
10. Base gasket

CAUTION
Do not remove the valve after installing it as it will damage the valve seal. If you must remove the valve, install a new seal.

CYLINDER

Both cylinders can be removed with the engine mounted in the frame.

Removal

Refer to **Figure 104** when performing the following.

1. Remove all dirt and foreign material from both cylinders.
2. Remove the cylinder head as described in this chapter.
3. Remove the 2 dowel pins and O-rings (**Figure 105**) from the top of the cylinder.
4. Turn the engine over until the piston is at bottom dead center (BDC).
5. Loosen the cylinder by tapping around the perimeter with a rubber or plastic mallet.
6. Pull the cylinder straight up and off the piston and cylinder studs.
7. Stuff clean shop rags into the crankcase opening to prevent objects from falling undetected into the crankcase.
8. Install a hose over each stud to protect the piston and studs from damage.

CAUTION
While the cylinder is removed, use care when working around the cylinder studs to avoid bending or damaging them. The slightest bend could cause a stud failure later during engine operation.

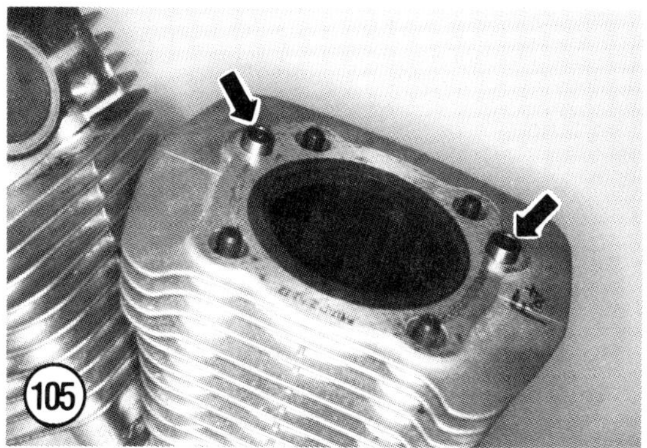

9. Remove the pistons and rings as described under *Pistons and Piston Rings* in this chapter.
10. Repeat Steps 1-9 for the other cylinder.

Inspection

The factory pistons cannot be accurately measured with standard measuring instruments and techniques. This is because the piston has a complex shape due to its design and manufacturing. Furthermore, the piston bore is offset. Piston-to-cylinder clearance is checked by measuring the cylinder bore only. If a cylinder is worn, the cylinder must be bored to specific factory specifications—not to match a particular piston size as with conventional methods.

The following procedure requires the use of highly specialized and expensive measuring instruments. If such instruments are not readily available, have the measurements performed by a dealer or qualified machine shop.

NOTE
*Harley-Davidson recommends that you clamp the cylinder between torque plates (HD-33446) (**Figure 106**) when making cylinder measurements and when boring and honing the cylinders. This arrangement simulates the distortion imparted on a cylinder when it is torqued down by the cylinder head and cylinder bolts. Measurements made without the engine torque plate can vary by 0.001 in. (0.025 mm). If you do not have access to the torque plates, refer service to a Harley-Davidson dealer.*

1. Carefully remove all gasket residue from both cylinder gasket surfaces.
2. Thoroughly clean the cylinder with solvent and dry with compressed air. Lightly oil the cylinder bore to prevent rust after performing Step 3.
3. Check the top (**Figure 107**) and bottom cylinder block gasket surfaces with a straightedge and feeler gauge. Replace the cylinder and piston if the following warpage limits are exceeded:
   a. *Top cylinder surface*: 0.006 in. (0.152 mm).
   b. *Bottom cylinder surface*: 0.008 in. (0.203 mm).
4. Install a new cylinder head and base gasket onto the cylinder and clamp the cylinder between the

4

torque plates (**Figure 106**). Install the torque plate bolts, making sure they engage the gaskets properly. Tighten the torque plate bolts following the procedure and torque specification given for the cylinder heads as described in this chapter.

5. Measure the cylinder bore with a bore gauge or inside micrometer at the points shown in **Figure 108**. Initial measurement should be made at a distance of 0.500 in. (12.7 mm) below the top (**Figure 109**) of the cylinder. The 0.500 in. (12.7 mm) depth represents the start of the ring path area; do not take readings that are out of the ring path area.

6. Measure in 2 axes—in line with the piston pin and at 90° to the pin. If the taper or out-of-round is greater than specifications (**Table 2**), the cylinders must be rebored to the next oversize and new pistons and rings installed. Rebore both cylinders even though only one may be worn.

7. Check the cylinder walls for scuffing, scratches or other damage; if evident, the cylinders should be rebored and the pistons replaced.

8. Have your dealer confirm all cylinder measurements before you order replacement parts or have the cylinders honed or bored.

9. After the cylinders have been serviced, wash each cylinder in hot, soapy water. This is the only way to clean the cylinder walls of the fine grit material left from the boring or honing job. After washing the cylinder bore, run a clean white cloth through it. If the cloth shows traces of grit or oil, the cylinder is not clean enough. Repeat until the cloth comes out clean. When the cylinder wall is clean, dry with compressed air and then lubricate with clean engine oil to prevent the cylinder wall from rusting. Repeat for the other cylinder.

CAUTION

The combination of hot soapy water described in Step 9 is the only solution that will completely clean the cylinder walls. Solvent and kerosene cannot wash fine grit out of the cylinder crevices. Grit left in the cylinder wall will

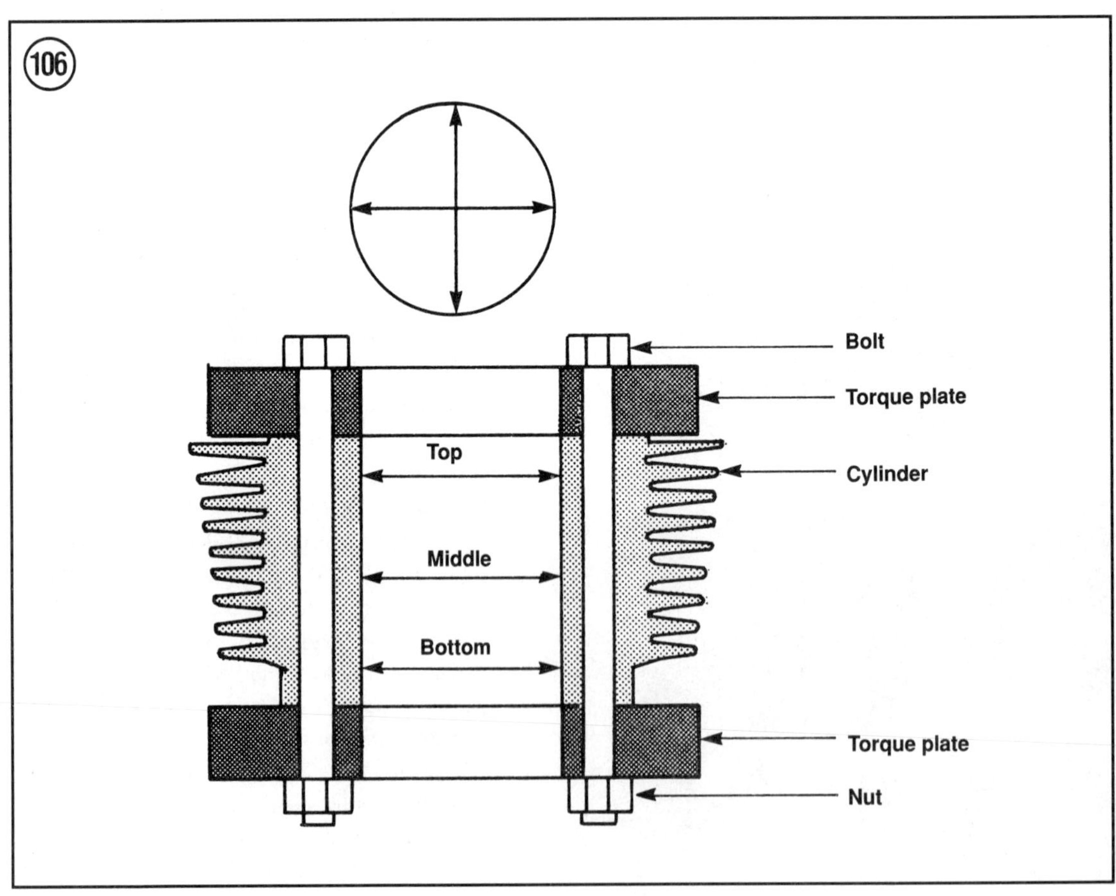

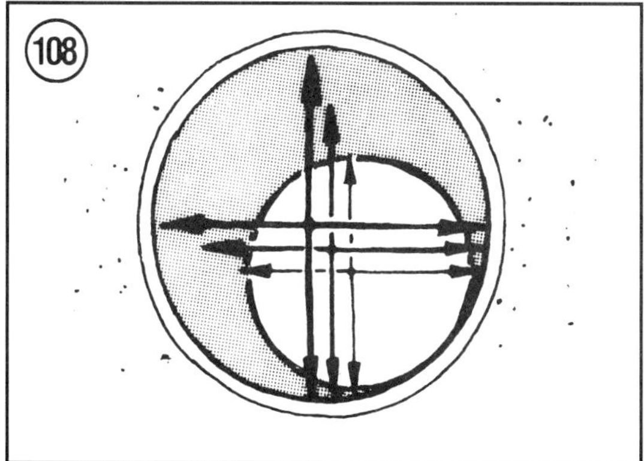

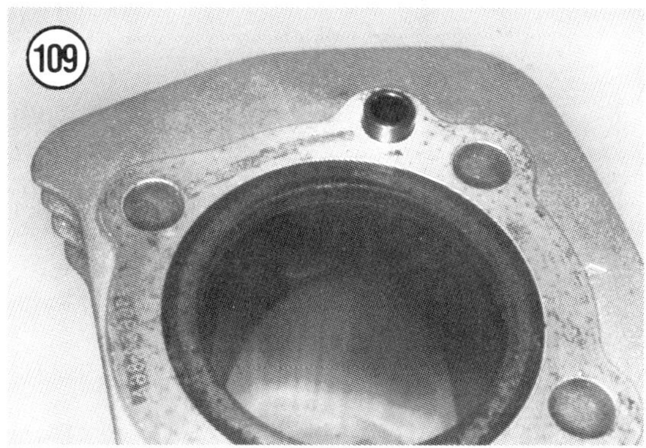

act as an abrasive grinding compound and cause premature wear to the engine components.

Installing New Pistons

Because the pistons cannot be accurately measured (see *Inspection*), the actual bore size will determine piston selection.

Cylinder Studs and Cylinder Head Bolts Inspection and Cleaning

The cylinder studs and cylinder head bolts must be in good condition and properly cleaned prior to installing the cylinders and cylinder heads. Otherwise, damaged or dirty studs may cause cylinder head distortion and gasket leakage.

1. Examine the cylinder head bolts (**Figure 110**) for head or thread damage. Replace if necessary.
2. Examine the cylinder studs for bending, looseness or damage. Replace loose or damaged studs as described under *Cylinder Stud Replacement* in this chapter. If the studs are in good condition, perform Step 3.

CAUTION
The cylinder studs, cylinder head bolts and washers are made of hardened material. Do not substitute these items with a part made of a lower grade material. If replacement is required, purchase new parts from a Harley-Davidson dealer.

3. Cover both crankcase openings with shop rags to prevent abrasive dust from falling into the engine.
4. Remove all carbon residue from the cylinder studs and cylinder head bolts as follows:
   a. Apply solvent to the cylinder stud and mating cylinder head bolt threads and thread the bolt onto the stud.
   b. Hand turn the cylinder head bolt back and forth to loosen and remove carbon residue from the threads. Remove the bolt from the stud. Blow both thread sets with compressed air.
   c. Repeat until both thread sets are free of all carbon residue.
   d. Spray the cylinder stud and cylinder head bolt with electrical contact cleaner and blow dry.

4

e. Set the cleaned bolt aside and install it on the same stud when installing the cylinder head.

5. Repeat Step 4 for each cylinder stud and cylinder head bolt set.

Installation

Refer to **Figure 104** when performing this procedure.

1. Install the pistons and rings as described in this chapter.
2. Check that all of the piston pin retaining rings have been properly installed (**Figure 111**).
3. Remove all gasket residue and clean the cylinders as described under *Inspection* in this chapter.
4. Install the dowel pin (A, **Figure 112**), if removed.

5A. Install a new factory cylinder base gasket (B, **Figure 112**) onto the crankcase. Make sure all holes line up properly.

5B. Install aftermarket aluminum or copper base gasket following the manufacturer's guidelines. If specified by the manufacturer, apply gasket sealer to the gasket prior to installation.

6. Turn the engine over until the piston is at top dead center (TDC).
7. Lubricate the cylinder bore and piston liberally with clean engine oil.
8. Slide the protective hoses off of the cylinder studs.
9. Stagger the piston ring end gaps so that they are 180° apart.
10. Compress the rings with a ring compressor (**Figure 113**).

NOTE
Install the cylinders in their original positions.

11. Carefully align the cylinder (front side facing forward) with the cylinder studs and slide it down (**Figure 114**) until it is over the top of the piston. Then continue sliding the cylinder down and past the rings (**Figure 115**). Once the rings are positioned in the cylinder, remove the ring compressor.
12. Continue to slide the cylinder down until it bottoms out on the crankcase.
13. Repeat to install the opposite cylinder.
14. Install the cylinder heads as described in this chapter.

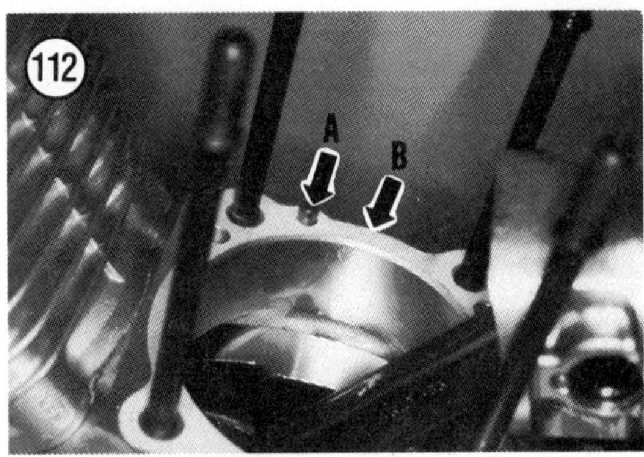

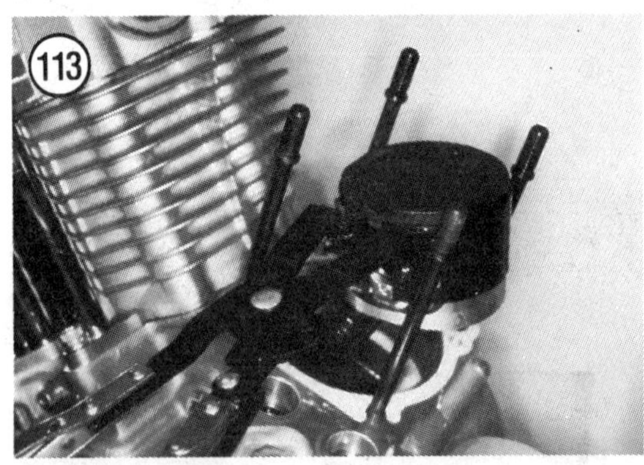

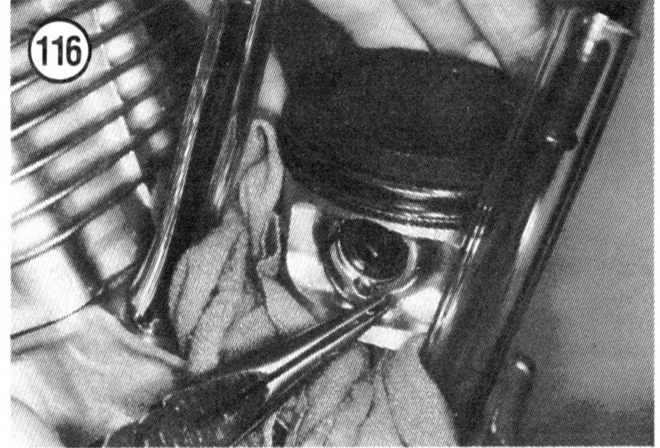

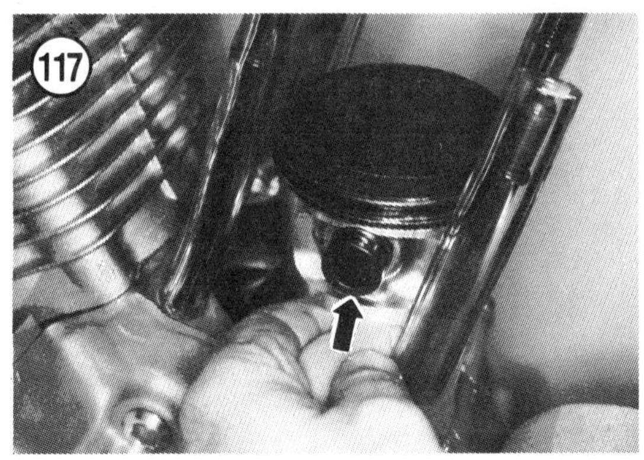

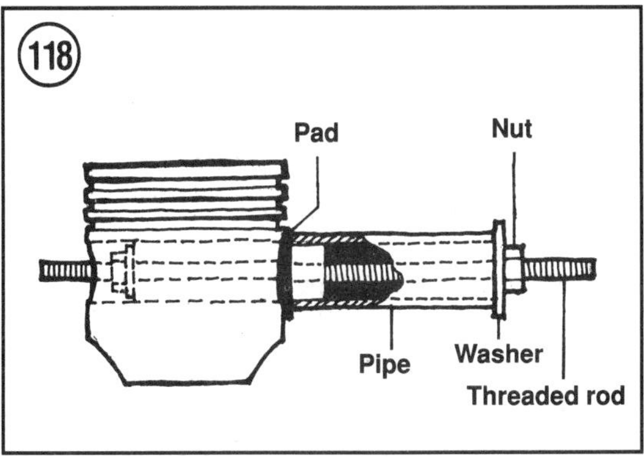

PISTONS AND PISTON RINGS

Refer to **Figure 104** when servicing the pistons and piston rings in this section.

Piston and Piston Rings Removal

1. Remove the cylinder head and cylinder as described in this chapter.
2. Cover the crankcase opening with clean shop rags to prevent objects from falling into the crankcase.
3. Lightly mark the pistons with an F (front) or R (rear) so they will be installed into the correct cylinder.

WARNING
Because the piston pin retaining rings are highly compressed in the piston pin ring groove, safety glasses must be worn during their removal and installation.

4. Using a suitable tool, pry the piston pin retaining rings (**Figure 116**) out of the piston. Place your thumb over the hole to help prevent the rings from flying out during removal.

NOTE
The piston pins should be marked so that they can be reinstalled in their original connecting rods.

5. Support the piston and push out the piston pin (**Figure 117**). If the piston is difficult to remove, use a homemade tool as shown in **Figure 118**.

NOTE
If you intend to reuse the piston rings, identify and store the rings in a container so that they can be reinstalled in their original ring grooves and on their original pistons.

6. Remove the old rings with a ring expander tool (**Figure 119**) or spread them with your fingers (**Figure 120**) and remove them.
7. Inspect the pistons, piston pins and pistons rings as described in this chapter.

4

Piston Inspection

1. Carefully clean the carbon (**Figure 121**) from the piston crown with a soft scraper. Do not remove or damage the carbon ridge around the circumference of the piston above the top ring.

CAUTION
Do not wire brush piston skirts.

2. Using a broken piston ring, remove all carbon deposits from the piston ring grooves (**Figure 122**). Make sure you do not remove aluminum from the piston ring grooves when cleaning them.
3. Examine each ring groove for burrs, dented edges and wear. Pay particular attention to the top compression ring groove, as it usually wears more than the others.
4. Measure cylinder clearance as described in this chapter. Replace worn or damaged parts as required.

Piston Pin Inspection

Factory 883 cc and 1200 cc piston pins are different. The 1200 cc piston pins are marked with a "12" or have a V-groove in one end of the pin (**Figure 123**). The 883 cc pins are not marked. When purchasing replacement piston pins, note these differences.

1. Clean the piston pin in solvent and dry thoroughly.
2. Replace the piston pins if cracked, pitted or scored.
3. If the piston pins are visually okay, check their clearance as described in *Piston Pin Bushing Inspection/Replacement* in this chapter.

Piston Pin Bushing Inspection

All models are equipped with a bushing (**Figure 104**) at the small end of the connecting rod. These bushings are reamed to provide correct piston pin clearance (clearance between piston pin and bushing). This clearance is critical in preventing pin knock and severe top end damage.

1. Inspect the piston pin bushings (**Figure 104**) for severe wear or damage (pit marks, scoring or wear grooves). Also check the bushings for a loose fit; the bushings must be a tight fit in the connecting rods.
2. Measure the piston pin O.D. with a micrometer where it rides in the bushing. Then measure the piston pin bushing I.D. with a snap gauge or bore gauge. Subtract the pin O.D. from bushing I.D. to obtain piston pin clearance. Replace the pin and bushing if the clearance meets or exceeds the service limit in **Table 2**.

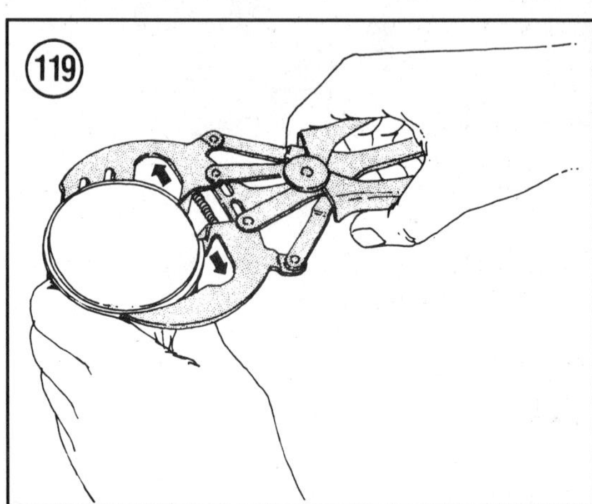

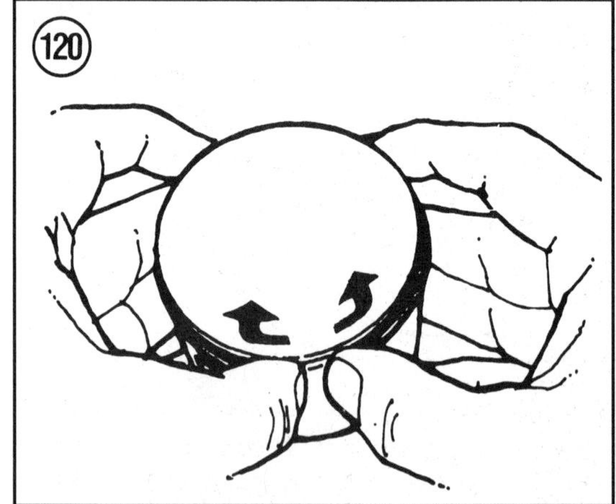

Piston Pin Bushing Replacement

The piston pin bushings can be replaced with the engine cases assembled and installed on the bike. If you do not have the required special tools, refer bushing replacement to a Harley-Davidson mechanic.

The following special tools will be required to replace and ream the piston pin bushings:

NOTE
All of the following part numbers are factory Harley-Davidson part numbers. Aftermarket tools are available.

a. Rod clamping fixture (part No. HD-95952-33A). This tool is required if the bushings are going to be replaced with the engine cases assembled.
b. Piston pin bushing tool (part No. HD-95984-32C).
c. Piston pin bushing reamer (part No. HD-94800-26A).
d. Connecting rod bushing hone (part No. HD-35102).

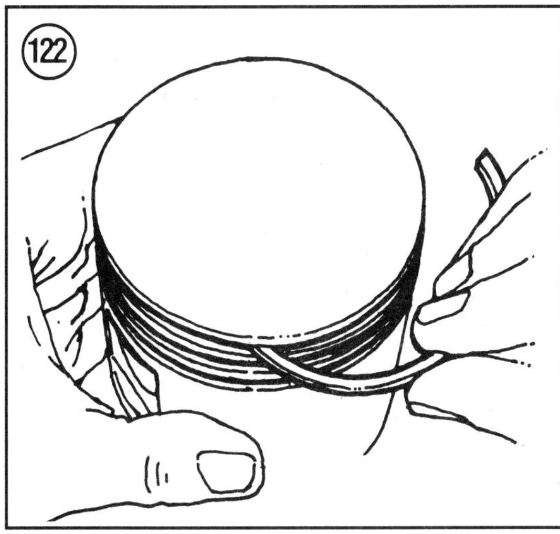

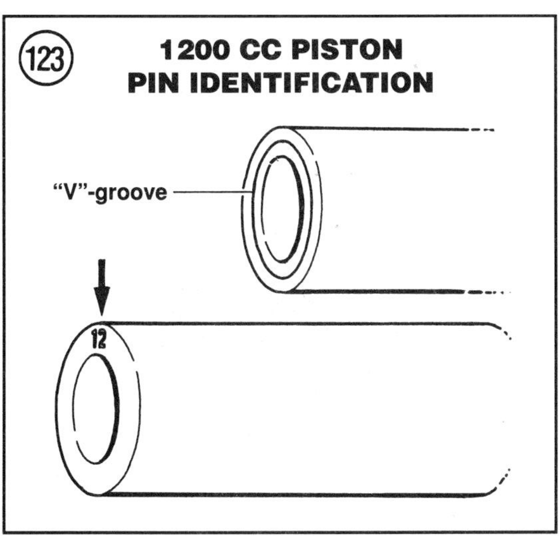

1. Remove 2 of the plastic hoses (protecting the cylinder studs) and slide the rod clamping fixture over the studs. Reinstall the 2 hoses.
2. Cover the crankcase opening with clean shop rags to keep bushing particles and abrasive dust from falling into the engine.
3. Wrap some brass shim stock around the rod and then tighten the 2 thumb screws on the rod clamping fixture against the rod to hold it in place.

NOTE
When installing the new bushing, align the oil hole in the bushing with the oil hole in the connecting rod.

4. Replace the bushing with the piston pin bushing tool, following the tool manufacturer's instructions. The bushing should be flush with both sides of the rod.
5. Check that the bushing and connecting rod oil holes align.
6. Turning the reamer clockwise, undercut the new bushing so that the piston pin clearance is 0.00125-0.00175 in. (0.031-0.044 mm).
7. Hone the new bushing to obtain the piston pin clearance specified in **Table 2**. Use honing oil—not engine oil—when honing the bushing to size.
8. Install the piston pin through the bushing. The pin should move through the bushing smoothly with no binding or roughness. Confirm pin clearance with a micrometer and snap gauge.

CAUTION
If the bushing clearance is less than 0.00125 in. (0.0317 mm), the pin may seize on the rod, causing severe engine damage.

9. Carefully remove the shop rags from the crankcase openings and replace them with clean rags.

4

Piston Ring Inspection

1. Clean the piston ring grooves of all carbon residue as described under *Piston Inspection* in this chapter.
2. Inspect ring grooves for burrs, nicks, or broken or cracked lands. Replace piston if necessary.
3. Insert one piston ring into the top of its cylinder and tap it down about 1/2 in. (12.7 mm) with the piston to square it in the bore. Measure the ring end gap with a feeler gauge and compare with specifications in **Table 2**. Replace the piston rings as a set if any one ring end gap measurement is excessive. Repeat for each ring.
4. Roll each compression ring around its piston groove as shown in **Figure 124**. The ring should move smoothly with no binding. If a ring binds up in its groove, check the groove for damage. Replace the piston if necessary.

Piston Ring Installation

Each piston is equipped with 3 piston rings: 2 compression and 1 oil ring assembly (**Figure 104**). The top compression ring is not marked. The second compression must be installed with its dot mark facing up.

Used piston rings must be installed on their original pistons and in their original grooves.

NOTE
When installing oversize compression rings, check the number to make sure the correct rings are being installed. The ring numbers should be the same as the piston oversize number.

1. Wash the piston in hot, soapy water. Then rinse with cold water and blow dry. Make sure the oil control holes in the lower ring groove are clear and open.
2. Clean the piston rings carefully and dry with compressed air.
3. Install the oil ring assembly as follows:
   a. The oil ring consists of 3 rings: a ribbed spacer ring and 2 steel rings.
   b. Install the spacer ring into the lower ring groove. Butt the spacer ring ends together. Do *not* overlap the ring ends.

CAUTION
Do not expand the steel rings when installing them.

   c. Insert one end of the first steel ring into the lower groove so that it is below the spacer ring. Then spiral the other end over the piston crown and into the lower groove. See **Figure 104**. To protect the ring end from scratching the side of the piston, place a piece of shim stock or a thin, flat feeler gauge between the ring and piston.
   d. Repeat sub-step c to install the other steel ring above the spacer ring.

NOTE
*When installing the compression rings, use a ring expander as shown in **Figure 119**. Do not expand the rings any more than necessary to install them.*

4. Install the second compression ring as follows:
   a. The second compression ring has a dot mark.
   b. Install the second compression ring so that its dot mark faces upward.
5. Install the top compression ring as follows:

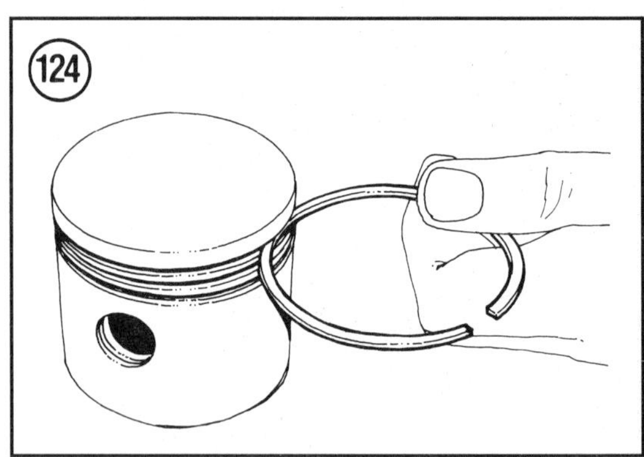

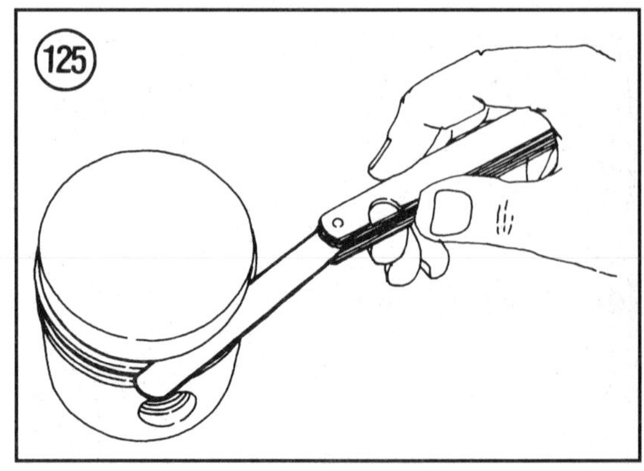

a. The top compression ring is not marked.
b. New upper compression rings can be installed with either side facing up. Used upper compression rings should be installed with their original top side facing up.

6. Check ring side clearance with a feeler gauge as shown in **Figure 125**. Check side clearance in several spots around the piston. If clearance meets or exceeds service limit in **Table 2**, note the following:

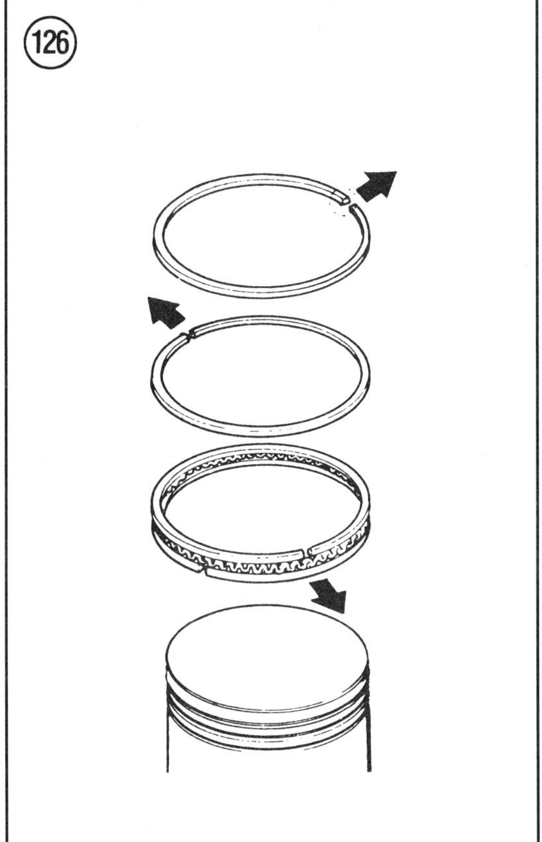

a. If the ring grooves were not cleaned, remove the rings and clean the grooves. Then reinstall rings and recheck clearance.
b. If reusing the old rings, replace the rings and or the piston.
c. If using new rings, replace the piston.

7. Stagger the ring gaps around the piston as shown in **Figure 126**. Harley-Davidson specifies that the ring gaps must not be within 10° of the piston's thrust face centerline.

Piston Installation

1. Cover both crankcase openings with clean paper towels to avoid dropping a retaining ring or dirt into the engine.
2. Install a *new* piston pin retaining ring into one groove in the piston. Make sure the ring seats in the groove completely.
3. Coat the connecting rod bushing and piston pin with assembly oil.

NOTE
The piston markings described in Step 4 are for factory Harley-Davidson pistons. If you are using aftermarket pistons, follow the manufacturer's directions for piston alignment and installation.

4. Place the piston over the connecting rod with its arrow mark facing *forward*. Install used pistons on their original connecting rods; refer to the marks you made on the piston during removal. Oversize pistons must be installed in the cylinder (front or rear) that they were originally fitted to during the boring process.
5. Insert the piston pin (**Figure 117**) through the piston. Hold the rod so that the lower end does not take any shock.
6. Install the other new piston pin retaining ring (**Figure 116**). Make sure it seats in the groove completely. See **Figure 127**.
7. Install cylinders as described under *Cylinder Installation* in this chapter.

VALVE TAPPETS

All models are factory equipped with hydraulic tappets and solid pushrods. The tappets consist of a piston, cylinder and check valve. During operation, tappets pump full of engine oil, thus taking up all play in the valve train. When the engine is off, the tappets will "leak down" as oil escapes from the hydraulic unit. When the engine is started, it is normal for the tappets to click until they refill with oil. If the tappets stop clicking after the engine is run for a few minutes, they are working properly.

Refer to **Figure 128** when servicing the pushrods and tappets.

PUSHROD/TAPPET ASSEMBLY

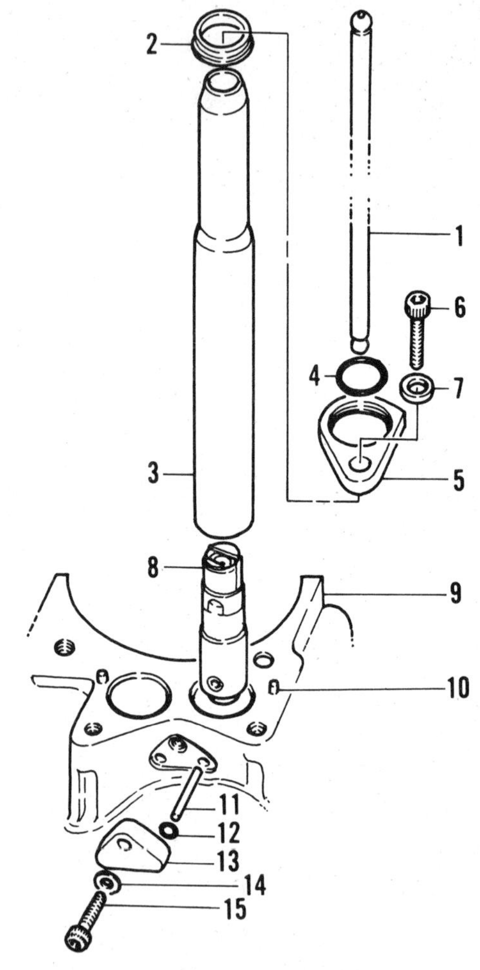

1. Pushrod
2. Seal
3. Cover
4. O-ring
5. Retainer
6. Bolt
7. Washer
8. Tappet
9. Crankcase
10. Locating pin
11. Pin
12. O-ring
13. Plate
14. Washer
15. Allen bolt

Removal

1. Remove the pushrods as described under *Cylinder Head Removal* in this chapter.
2. If you are not going to remove the cylinder heads, loosen, then remove the pushrod rod retainer Allen bolt and washer (**Figure 129**).
3. Remove the pushrod retainer, cover and O-ring (**Figure 130**).
4. Repeat for each pushrod.
5. Remove the lifter plate Allen bolt and washer and remove the plate (**Figure 131**).
6. Remove the tappet pin and its O-ring (**Figure 132**).
7. Remove the tappet (**Figure 133**) from the crankcase bore. Store the tappets in a container of oil in such a way that they can be installed in their original tappet bores.

NOTE

Cover the tappet storage container so that dirt and other abrasive materials cannot contaminate the oil.

8. Repeat for each tappet.

Cleaning and Inspection

CAUTION

Tappets must be stored and handled carefully to prevent contamination from dirt or other abrasive materials. When storing tappets, leave them in the container of oil they were placed in during removal. When measuring or inspecting tappets, place them on a clean, lint-free cloth.

1. Clean the pushrod covers in solvent and dry with compressed air. Do not clean the tappets in solvent or with any other type of cleaner. Leave the tappets

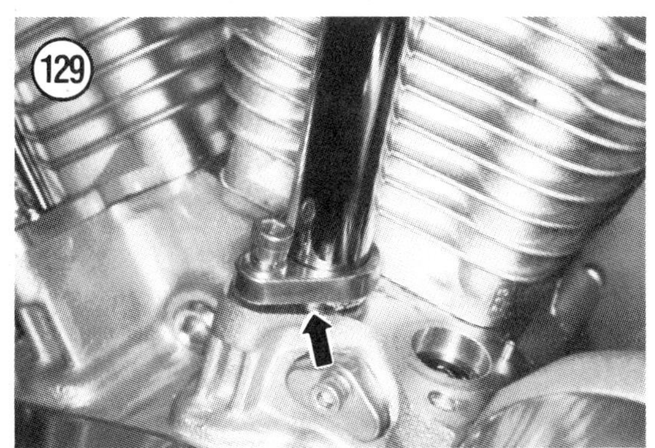

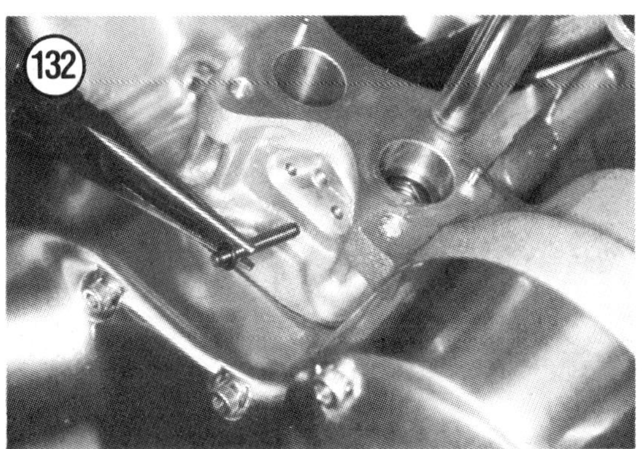

in the container of oil except when inspecting and installing them.

2. Check the tappet rollers (**Figure 134**) for pitting, scoring, galling or excessive wear. If the rollers are worn excessively, check the cam lobes for the same wear conditions. The cam lobes can be observed through the tappet guide hole in the crankcase. Replace the cam, if necessary, as described in this chapter.

3. Measure the valve tappet O.D. (**Figure 135**) with a micrometer. Record O.D. for each tappet.

4. Measure tappet bore I.D. with a bore gauge. Record I.D. for each tappet bore.

5. Subtract the measurement made in Step 3 from the measurement made in Step 4. The difference is the tappet-to-guide clearance. See **Table 2** for specified clearance. Correct excessive clearance by replacing tappet and/or crankcase.

6. Measure tappet roller end clearance. If end clearance is worn to the service limit specification in **Table 2**, replace the tappet.

7. Measure tappet roller fit on pin. If clearance meets or exceeds service limit in **Table 2**, replace the tappet.

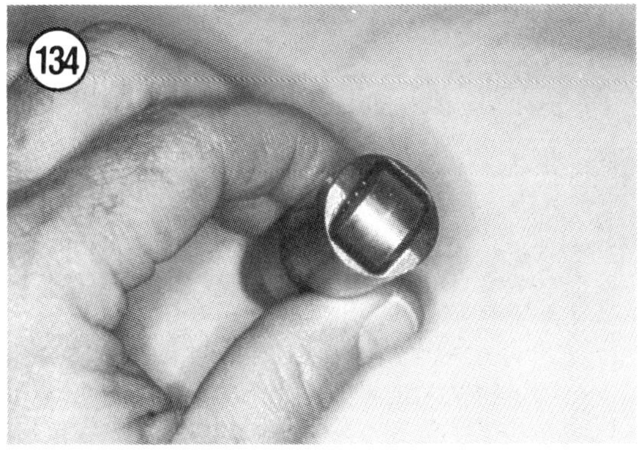

Installation

1. Rotate the engine counterclockwise so that the cam lobes for the tappets being installed are positioned with their base lobes facing up.
2. Soak each tappet in clean engine oil prior to installation. Make sure the roller needles (**Figure 134**) are well lubricated. This step will ensure smooth tappet operation and lubrication during initial engine start-up.
3. Install the tappet (**Figure 133**) into its original crankcase tappet bore; refer to your identification notes made during removal. Align the tappet so that the flats on the tappet face toward the front and rear of the engine; see **Figure 136**.
4. Insert the pins (**Figure 132**) through the crankcase holes.

NOTE
If the pins cannot be installed into the tappet body, the tappet is installed incorrectly.

5. Place a new O-ring over the end of the pin as shown in **Figure 137**.
6. Repeat Steps 1-5 to install the remaining tappets.
7. Install the plate (**Figure 131**), washer and screw. Tighten the tappet plate screw to the torque specification in **Table 4**.
8. Install the pushrod covers as follows:
   a. Slide a new seal (2, **Figure 128**) down the pushrod cover.
   b. Slide the retainer plate (**Figure 138**) down the pushrod cover.
   c. Install a new O-ring onto the top of the pushrod cover; see **Figure 4**, **Figure 128**.
   d. Tilt the pushrod cover (**Figure 130**) and install it through the pushrod cover hole in the cylinder head. Then align the bottom of the pushrod cover with the tappet hole and install the cover into the hole.
   e. Slide the seal and the pushrod seal plate down the pushrod cover. Seat the seal into the tappet hole.
   f. Align the crankcase locating pin with the pushrod seal plate and position the plate (**Figure 129**) on the crankcase. Install the pushrod seal plate bolt and washer and tighten to the torque specification listed in **Table 4**.
9. Install the pushrods as described under *Cylinder Head Installation* in this chapter.

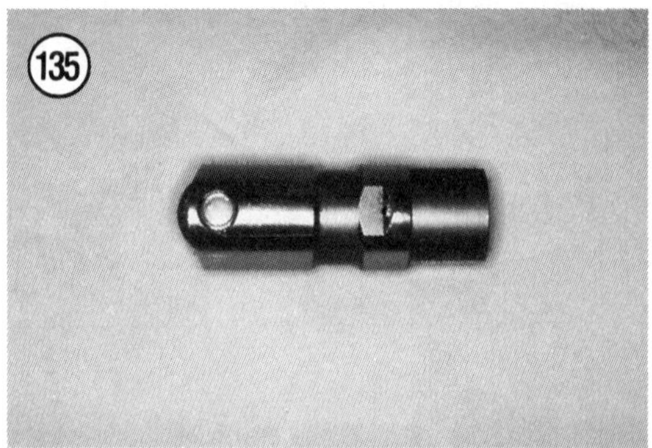

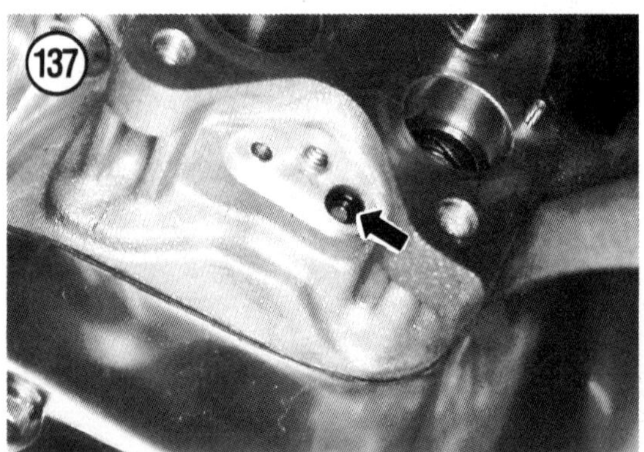

GEARCASE COVER AND TIMING GEARS

The gearcase assembly consists of the following components (**Figure 139**):

a. Four cam gears.

b. Four cam gear bushings (installed in right crankcase half).

c. Four cam gear bushings (installed in gearcase cover).

d. Pinion gear.

e. Oil pump drive gear.

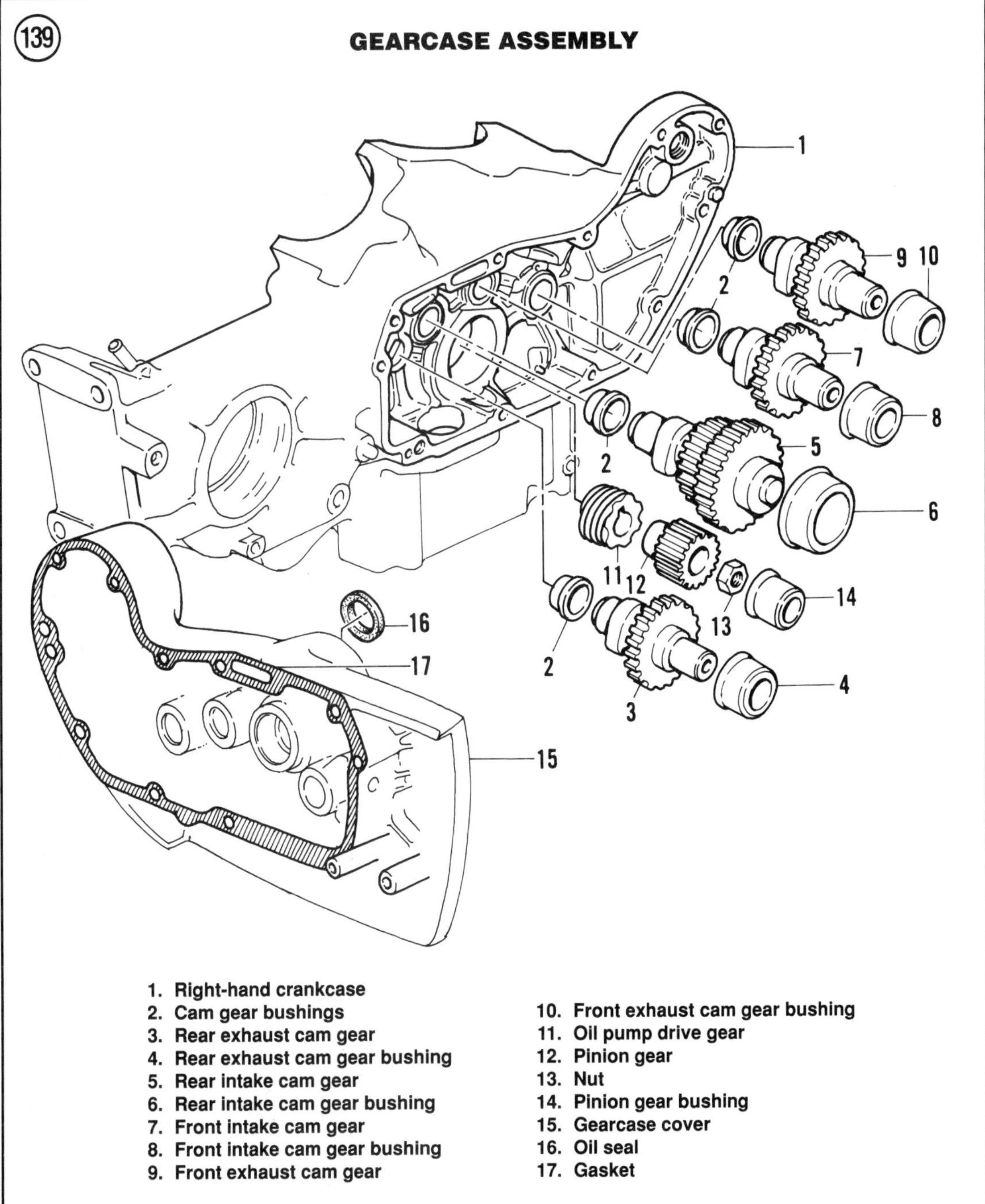

1. Right-hand crankcase
2. Cam gear bushings
3. Rear exhaust cam gear
4. Rear exhaust cam gear bushing
5. Rear intake cam gear
6. Rear intake cam gear bushing
7. Front intake cam gear
8. Front intake cam gear bushing
9. Front exhaust cam gear
10. Front exhaust cam gear bushing
11. Oil pump drive gear
12. Pinion gear
13. Nut
14. Pinion gear bushing
15. Gearcase cover
16. Oil seal
17. Gasket

f. Oil seal (installed in gearcase cover).

The cam gears have been closely matched at the factory for optimum operation and performance.

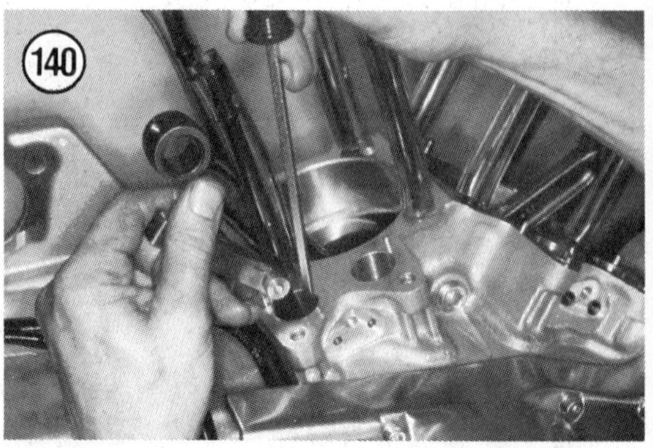

Removal

Refer to **Figure 139** for this procedure.

1. Remove the exhaust system as described in Chapter Seven.
2. Remove the footpeg assembly.
3. Remove the pushrods and valve tappets as described under *Valve Tappets* in this chapter.
4. Before removing the gearcase cover, check cam gear end play as follows:
   a. Rotate the engine counterclockwise so that the cam being checked has its lobe facing up.
   b. Pry the cam gear toward the gearcase cover with a wide-blade screwdriver.
   c. Measure the gap between the cam gear shaft thrust face and the bushing in the crankcase with a feeler gauge (**Figure 140**). This gap is cam gear end play. Write down the end play measurement.
   d. Repeat for each cam gear.
   e. If the end clearance is incorrect, replace the bushing and/or cam gear as described in this section.
5. Remove the ignition system sensor plate and rotor as described in Chapter Eight.
6. Place an empty oil pan underneath the crankcase cover.
7. Disconnect and plug the oil line at the crankcase cover (**Figure 141**).

NOTE

Because different length gearcase cover mounting screws are used, punch each screw through a piece of cardboard. Align the screws in the shape of the gearcase so that they can be installed in their original positions.

8. Remove the gearcase cover mounting screws.
9. Remove the gearcase cover (**Figure 142**) from the engine. If the cover is stuck in place, tap the cover lightly with a soft-faced hammer to free it from the gasket or sealer.
10. Remove and discard the gasket.
11. Remove the dowels (**Figure 143**), if necessary.

NOTE
As soon as you remove each cam gear, label and then place it in a container so that it can be reinstalled in its original position.

12. Remove and identify each cam gear:
    a. Rear exhaust cam gear (A, **Figure 144**).
    b. Rear intake cam gear (B, **Figure 144**).
    c. Front intake cam gear (C, **Figure 144**).
    d. Front exhaust cam gear (D, **Figure 144**).

NOTE
Loctite 262 was originally applied to the pinion gear nut.

13. Loosen, then remove the pinion gear nut (A, **Figure 145**). Then slide the pinion gear (B, **Figure 145**) and oil pump drive gear (**Figure 146**) off of the pinion shaft.

Inspection

1. Thoroughly clean gearcase compartment, cover and components with solvent. Blow out all oil passages with compressed air. Make sure that all traces of gasket compound are removed from the gasket mating surfaces.
2. Check the pinion gear and cam gear bushings in the gearcase cover for grooving, pitting or other wear; see **Figure 147**. If the bushings appear visibly worn, they must be replaced.
3. Inspect the cam gears (**Figure 148**) for cracks, deep scoring or excessive wear. The gears will show signs of pattern polish (**Figure 149**) but there should be no other apparent wear or damage.

Cam Gear Identification

The cam gear group consists of the following:

a. Rear exhaust cam gear (A, **Figure 144**).
b. Rear intake cam gear (B, **Figure 144**).
c. Front intake cam gear (C, **Figure 144**).
d. Front exhaust cam gear (D, **Figure 144**).
e. Pinion gear (B, **Figure 145**).

The cam lobes are stamped with a number (1, 2, 3 or 4) followed by the letter "D"; see **Figure 150**, typical. The number identifies the cam gear's engine position and function. The letter "D" identifies the model year application. For all models in this book, the letter "D" represents all 1991-1994 Sportster 5-speed models. The cam lobe markings are as follows:

a. 1D (rear exhaust cam gear).
b. 2D (rear intake cam gear).
c. 3D (front intake cam gear).
d. 4D (front exhaust cam gear).

Due to the critical nature of matching the cam gears during manufacturing, each gear is color coded with one paint dot; see **Figure 150**. This code is based on each gear's overall diameter as measured with 0.108 in. (2.74 mm) gauge pins (see *Measuring Cam gear Wear*) in this chapter. When replacing cam and pinion gears, the same color code gear must be used. For example, **Table 5** lists the cam and pinion gear color code and diameter specifications for each gear. When reading the table, note that there are 7 different gear diameters for each separate cam and pinion gear.

Measuring Cam Gear Wear

Harley-Davidson uses the pin method for determining cam gear wear. This method is accurate and easily performed in motorcycle service departments and home workshops. The only tools required are the correct size micrometer and the Harley-Davidson gauge pin set (part No. HD-38361) which consists of two 0.108 in. (2.74 mm) diameter gauge pins. To make this test, the gauge pins are placed in diametrically opposite gear tooth spaces as shown in **Figure 151**. You then measure across the gauge pins with a micrometer and compare with the gear sizes listed in **Table 5**.

1. Identify each cam gear by engine position, function and color code as described under *Cam Gear Identification*.

149

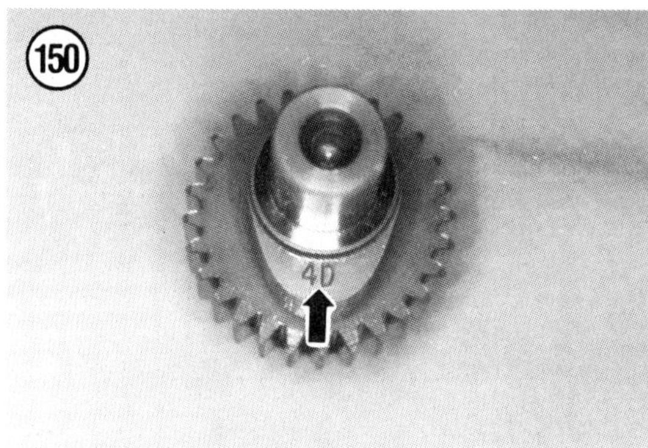

150

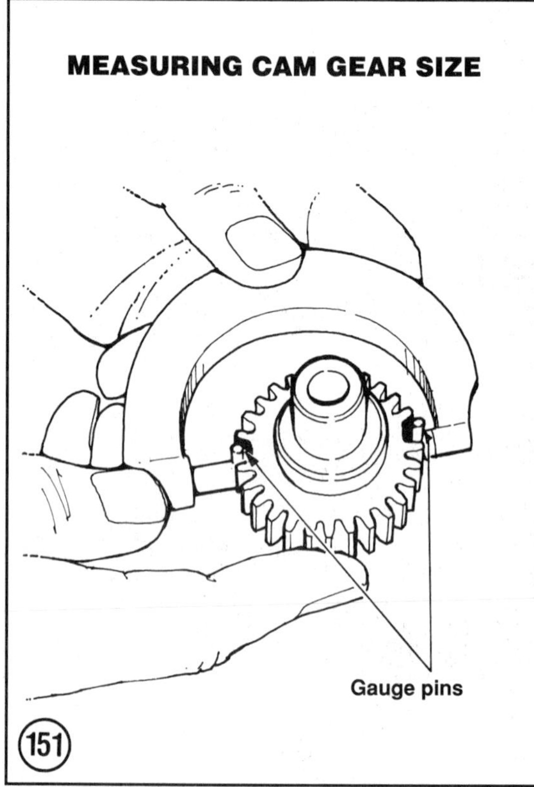

151

2. Place the two 0.108 in. (2.74 mm) diameter gauge pins between opposite gear teeth as previously described. Measure across the pins with a micrometer to determine the gear's diameter. Write down the measurement you obtain and repeat by moving the gauge pins 90°.

3. Compare your measurements with the gear diameter sizes listed in **Table 5**. If a cam gear measurement is not within the gear diameter range listed in **Table 5**, replace the cam gear with one that has the *same* color code.

CAUTION

Do not change the cam gear and pinion gear color codes. The cam and pinion gears in your engine were originally determined at the factory with the use of an elaborate temperature control environment and computer system. Preassembly procedures feed data to a computer which then selects the cam and pinion gears for each individual crankcase.

Measuring Cam Gear and Pinion Gear Bushing Wear

Excessive cam gear and pinion gear bushing clearance can cause excessive cam gear backlash.

1. Measure the cam/pinion gear O.D. with a micrometer (**Figure 149**). Write down the O.D. measurement.
2. Measure the corresponding bushing I.D. with a bore gauge or small hole gauge. Write down the I.D. measurement.
3. Subtract the measurement made in Step 2 from the measurement made in Step 1. The difference is the cam gear- or pinion gear-to-bushing clearance. See **Table 2** for the cam and pinion gear clearances. If clearance is excessive, replace the bushing as described in this chapter.

4

Bushing Removal

Gearcase cover (**Figure 147**) and crankcase (**Figure 152**) bushing replacement requires a number of special tools, including reamers for reaming the new bushings. Incorrect bushing installation will cause increased gear noise and premature wear. Refer all bushing service to a Harley-Davidson dealer or service shop.

Gearcase Cover Oil Seal Replacement

1. Inspect the oil seal (**Figure 153**) for severe wear, hardness, cracks or other damage.
2. Remove the oil with a seal puller or similar tool.
3. Pack the lip of the new oil seal with a waterproof bearing grease prior to installation.
4. Press in the oil seal (**Figure 153**) so that its manufacturer's name and size code faces out.

Installation

1. Apply engine oil to the pinion shaft, oil pump drive gear and pinion shaft gear.
2. Clean the pinion shaft threads and the pinion shaft nut of all threadlock residue.
3. Install the oil pump drive gear Woodruff key (**Figure 154**), if removed.
4. Slide the oil pump drive gear (**Figure 146**) onto the pinion shaft.

5. Align the pinion gear timing mark (**Figure 155**) with the center of the pinion shaft keyway and install the gear.

6. Apply Loctite 262 (red) to the pinion shaft nut (A, **Figure 145**) prior to installation. Install the nut and tighten to the torque specification in **Table 4**.

7. Identify the cam gears as described under *Cam Gear Identification* in this chapter.

8. Apply engine oil to the bushings, gears and gear shafts prior to installation.

9. Aligning the cam gear timing marks as shown in **Figure 156**, install the cam gears in the following order:

a. Rear exhaust cam gear (A, **Figure 157**).
b. Front intake cam gear (B, **Figure 157**).
c. Rear intake cam gear (**Figure 158**).
d. Front exhaust cam gear (**Figure 159**).
e. Double check that all of the cam gear timing marks are properly aligned (**Figure 156**).

10. Install the dowel pins (**Figure 143**), if removed.

156

CAM AND PINION GEARS

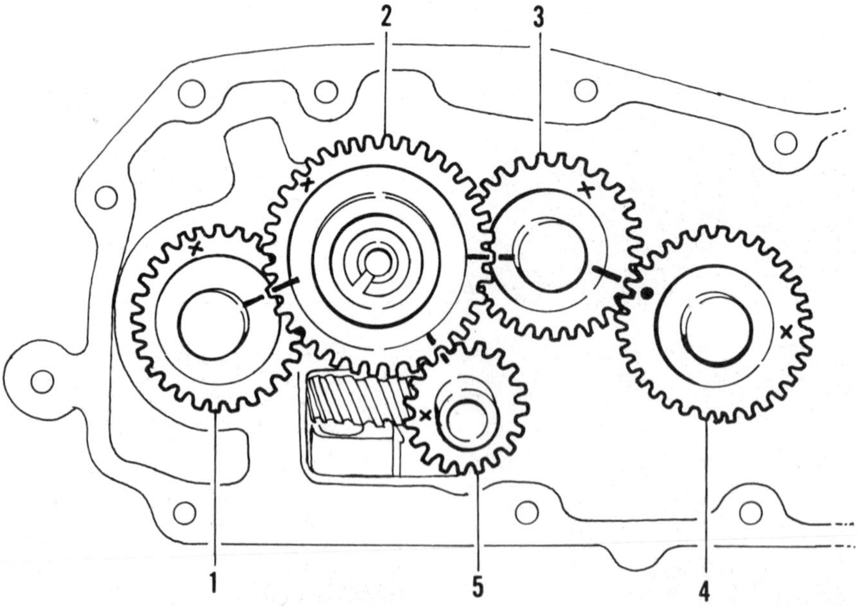

1. Rear exhaust cam gear
2. Rear intake cam bear
3. Front intake cam gear
4. Front exhaust cam gear
5. Pinion gear

11. Install a new gearcase cover gasket.
12. Install the gearcase cover (**Figure 142**).
13. Install the gearcase cover screws into their correct mounting positions. Tighten the screws finger-tight at first, then tighten in a crisscross pattern (**Figure 160**) to the torque specification listed in **Table 4**.
14. Check the cam gear end play for each cam gear as described under *Removal*.
15. Install the ignition components as described in Chapter Eight.

16. Install the valve tappets as described under *Valve Tappets* in this chapter.
17. Install the footpeg assembly.
18. Install the exhaust system as described in Chapter Seven.

OIL PUMP

The oil pump (**Figure 161**) is mounted underneath the front of the engine and can be removed with the engine installed in the frame and without removing the gearcase cover.

The oil pump consists of 2 sections: a feed pump which supplies oil under pressure to the engine components, and a scavenger pump which returns oil to the oil tank from the engine.

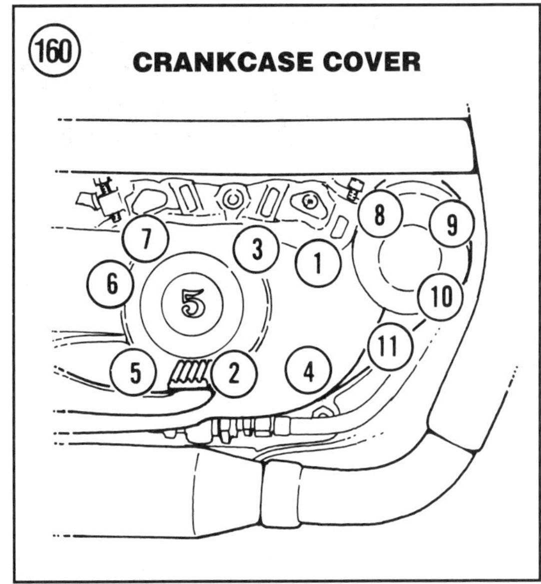

Removal

Refer to **Figure 162** for this procedure.

NOTE
Label all gears and Woodruff keys during removal so that they can be installed in their original positions.

1. Drain the oil tank as described in Chapter Three.
2. Wipe off each oil line and fitting at the oil pump.
3. Label each oil line (**Figure 161**) prior to disconnecting it.
4. Disconnect the oil lines from the oil pump. Plug the open end of each line to prevent oil leakage and contamination.
5. Loosen the oil pump mounting bolts (**Figure 163**). Then remove the bolts and oil pump from the engine. See **Figure 164**.
6. Remove and discard the oil pump gasket.
7. Cover the oil pump opening to keep dirt and other abrasive dust from entering the engine.

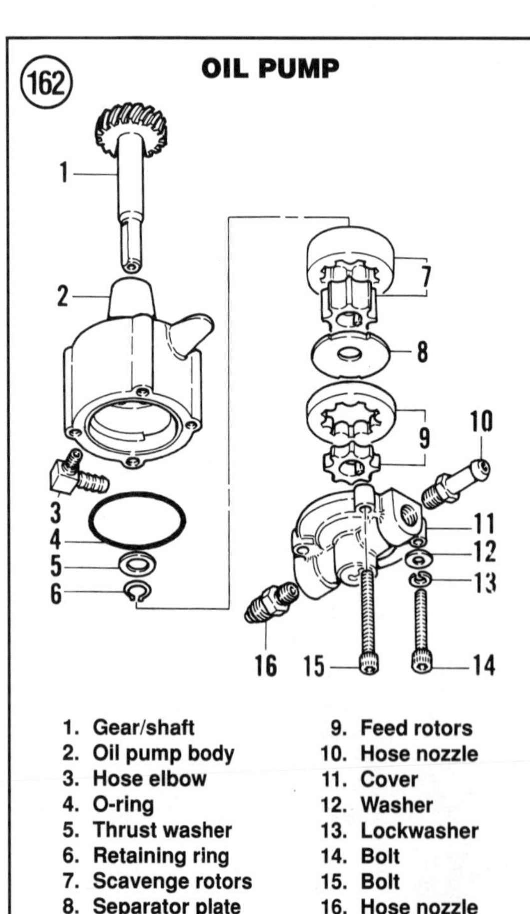

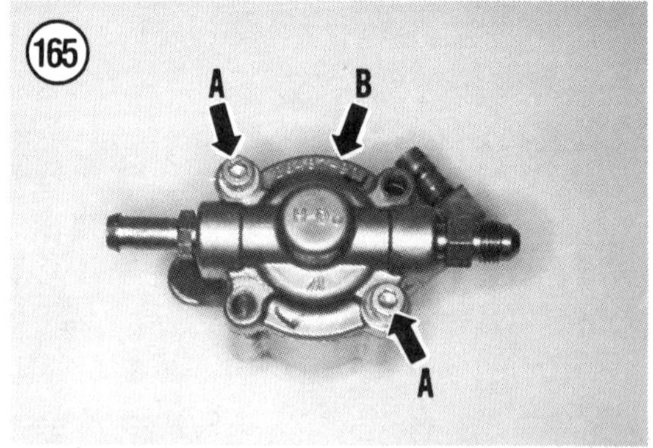

167

168

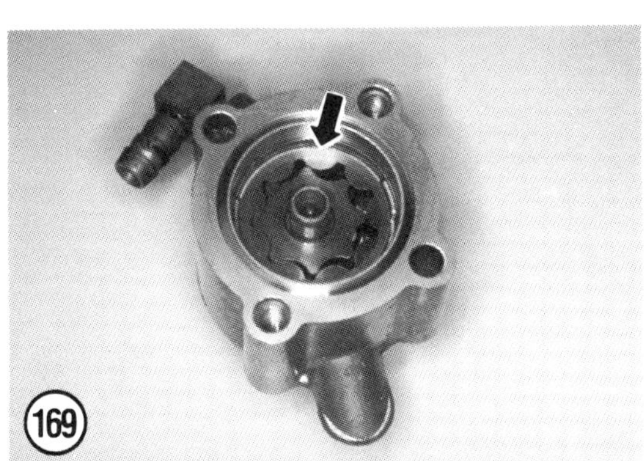
169

170

8. Store the oil pump in a plastic bag until disassembly or installation.

Disassembly

Refer to **Figure 162** when disassembling the oil pump.

1. Remove the oil pump housing screws (A, **Figure 165**), lockwashers and flat washers.
2. Remove the oil pump cover (B, **Figure 165**).
3. Remove and discard the O-ring (**Figure 166**).
4. Slide off the feed rotor assembly (**Figure 167**).
5. Remove the separator plate (**Figure 168**).
6. Slide off the scavenge rotor assembly (**Figure 169**).
7. Remove and discard the retaining ring (**Figure 170**).
8. Remove the thrust washer (**Figure 171**).
9. Remove the oil pump gear shaft (**Figure 172**).

Inspection

1. Thoroughly clean all parts in solvent and blow dry. Blow out all oil passages with compressed air.

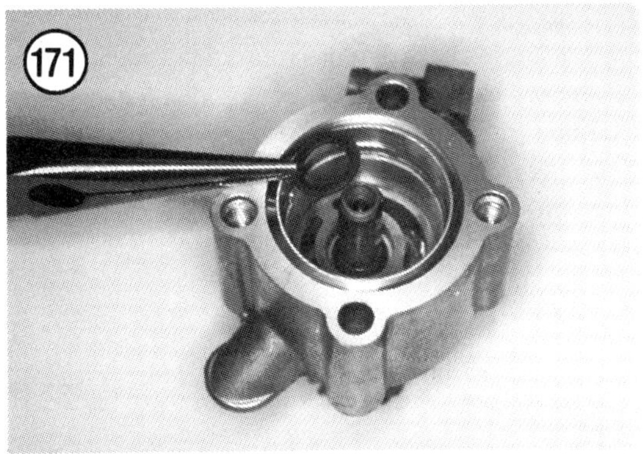
171

172

Place cleaned parts on a clean, lint-free cloth during inspection and reassembly.
2. Inspect the cover and body (**Figure 173**) for scratches, scoring or severe wear. Both rotor inside surfaces will show some scoring but it should not be excessive. If these areas are heavily scored, replace the oil pump assembly.
3. Inspect the gear shaft assembly (**Figure 174**) for wear. The gear will show signs of pattern polish but there should be no other apparent wear or damage.
4. Check the fit of the gear shaft where it passes through the oil pump body (**Figure 172**). The shaft should turn smoothly with no binding or excessive play.
5. Inspect the separator plate (**Figure 175**) for warpage, cracks or other damage.
6. Check both rotor sets for scoring, cracks or excessive wear. See **Figure 176**.
7. Measure the thickness of each feed rotor with a micrometer (**Figure 177**). Both rotors must be the same thickness. If they are not the same thickness, replace the feed rotors as a set.
8. Assemble the feed rotors and measure the clearance between the gear teeth with a feeler gauge as shown in **Figure 178**. If the gear clearance is worn to the service limit in **Table 2**, replace the feed rotors as a set.
9. Assemble the scavenge rotors and measure the clearance between the gear teeth with a feeler gauge as shown in **Figure 179**. If the gear clearance is worn to the service limit in **Table 2**, replace the scavenge rotors as a set.

173

174

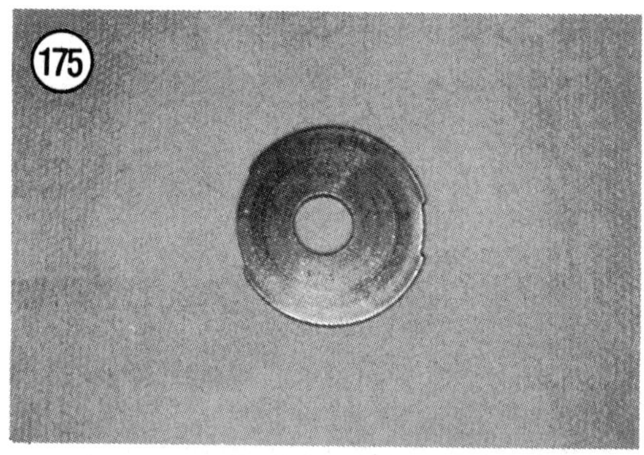
175

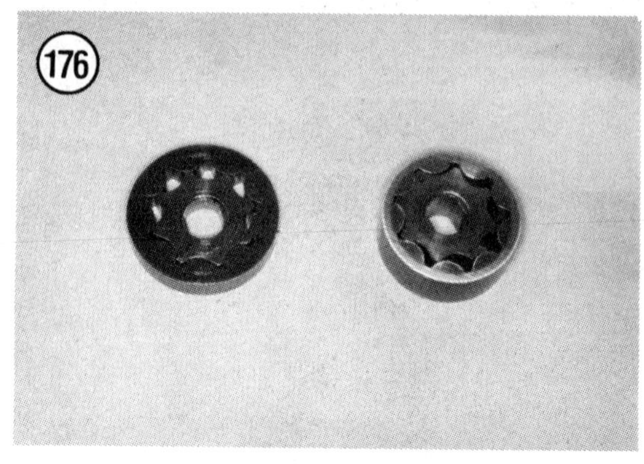
176

Reassembly

Refer to **Figure 162** when assembling the oil pump assembly.

NOTE
All parts must be spotlessly clean prior to assembly. If necessary, reclean as described under Inspection.

1. Coat all moving parts with clean engine oil prior to assembly.
2. Install the gear shaft (**Figure 172**) through the bottom of the oil pump body.
3. Install the thrust washer (**Figure 171**) onto the gear shaft.
4. Install a *new* retaining ring into the gear shaft groove (**Figure 170**). Make sure the ring seats in the

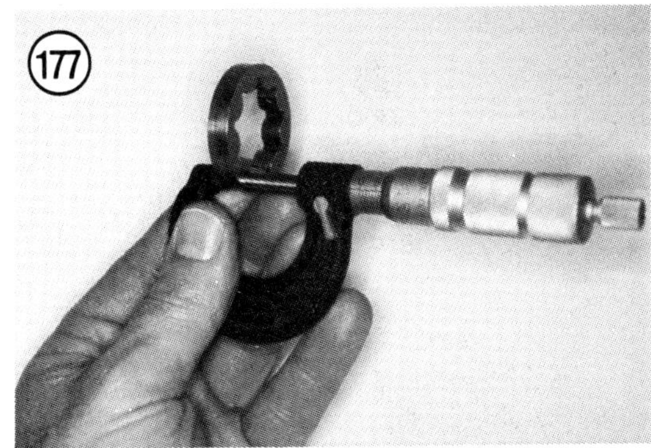

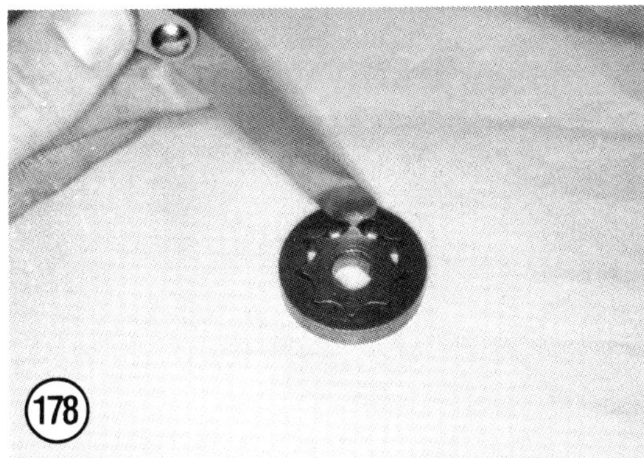

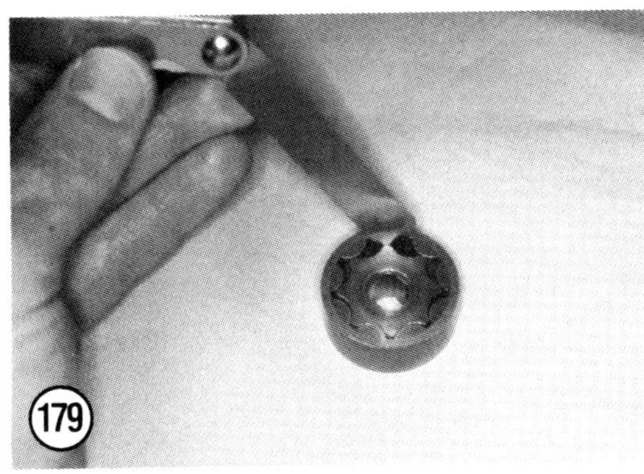

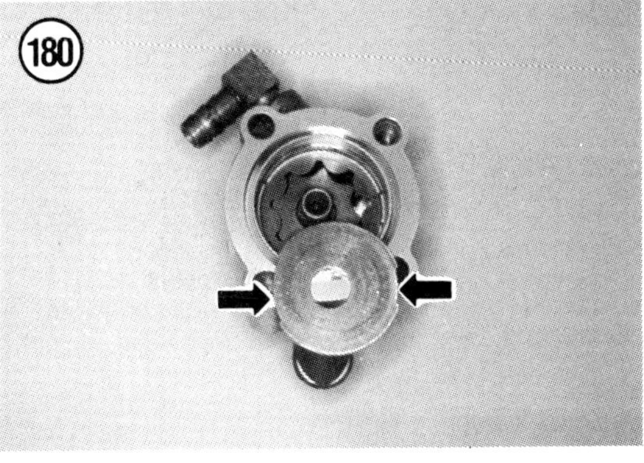

groove completely. Turn the gear shaft by hand; the shaft should turn smoothly with no binding or excessive play.

5. Install the inner, then the outer scavenge rotors. See **Figure 169**.

6. Install the separator plate (**Figure 180**) into the oil pump body; align the separator plate slots with the tabs inside the pump body. See **Figure 168**.

7. Install the feed rotors (**Figure 167**) over the gear shaft.

8. Install a *new* O-ring into the oil pump cover groove (**Figure 166**).

9. Install the pump cover (B, **Figure 165**) onto the pump body. Install oil pump screws, lockwashers and flat washers (A, **Figure 165**). Tighten the screws to the torque specification listed in **Table 4**.

10. Turn the gear shaft by hand; the pump should turn smoothly.

NOTE

If the oil hose fittings were removed from the oil pump, apply Hylomar or Teflon Pipe Sealant to the fitting threads prior to installation.

Installation

1. Thoroughly clean the oil pump and engine case gasket surfaces.

2. Install a new oil pump gasket. Then install the oil pump (**Figure 164**) onto the crankcase. Install the oil pump mounting screws and tighten to the torque specification in **Table 4**.

3. Unplug, then reconnect the oil hoses at the oil pump. Secure each hose with new hose clamps. See **Figure 161**.

NOTE

If the oil hose fittings were removed from the oil pump, apply Hylomar or Teflon Pipe Sealant to the fitting threads prior to installation.

4. Refill the oil tank as described in Chapter Three.

OIL FILTER MOUNT

The oil filter mount is part of the right-hand crankcase half. The oil filter mount houses the oil filter, check ball and spring, oil pressure switch and feed hose. See **Figure 181**.

Disassembly

1. Place a clean oil pan underneath the oil filter.
2. Drain the oil tank and remove the oil filter as described in Chapter Three.
3. Loosen and remove the oil filter adapter from the oil filter mount. Then remove the check ball and spring.
4. Disconnect the electrical wire at the oil pressure switch.
5. Loosen and remove the oil pressure switch.

Inspection

1. Remove thread sealant residue from all threaded parts.
2. Clean the check ball, spring and oil filter adapter in solvent and dry thoroughly.

Reassembly

1. Apply Hylomar or Teflon Pipe Sealant to the feed hose threads prior to installation. Install and tighten the feed hose securely.
2. Apply Hylomar or Teflon Pipe Sealant to the oil pressure switch threads prior to installation. Install the switch and tighten to the torque specification in **Table 4**.
3. Install the oil filter adapter as follows:
   a. The ends on the oil filter adapter are symmetrical; either end may be installed into the oil filter mount.
   b. Apply Loctite 242 (blue) onto the oil filter adapter threads that will be installed into the oil filter mount. Do *not* install thread sealant on the oil filter side.
   c. Install the spring, then the check ball into the hole in the center of the oil filter mount. Then push the oil filter adapter (Loctite end) against the check ball and thread it into the oil filter mount. Tighten the oil filter adapter to the torque specification in **Table 4**.
4. Reconnect the electrical wire onto the oil pressure switch.
5. Pour approximately 4 oz. (120 ml) of clean engine oil into the oil filter. Coat the oil filter gasket with engine oil (**Figure 182**).
6. Screw the oil filter onto the adapter until the filter gasket contacts the oil filter mount surface, then tighten an additional 1/4-1/2 turn.
7. Refill the engine oil tank as described in Chapter Three.
8. Start the engine and check visually for oil leaks.

CRANKCASE AND CRANKSHAFT

Crankcases must be disassembled to service the crankshaft, connecting rod bearings, pinion shaft bearing and sprocket shaft bearing. This section describes basic checks and procedures that can be performed in the home shop. More specialized service procedures, such as bearing and crankshaft service, should be referred to a Harley-Davidson dealer or service shop. A number of special tools and procedures are required. A press and the Harley-Davidson sprocket shaft bearing/seal installation tool (part

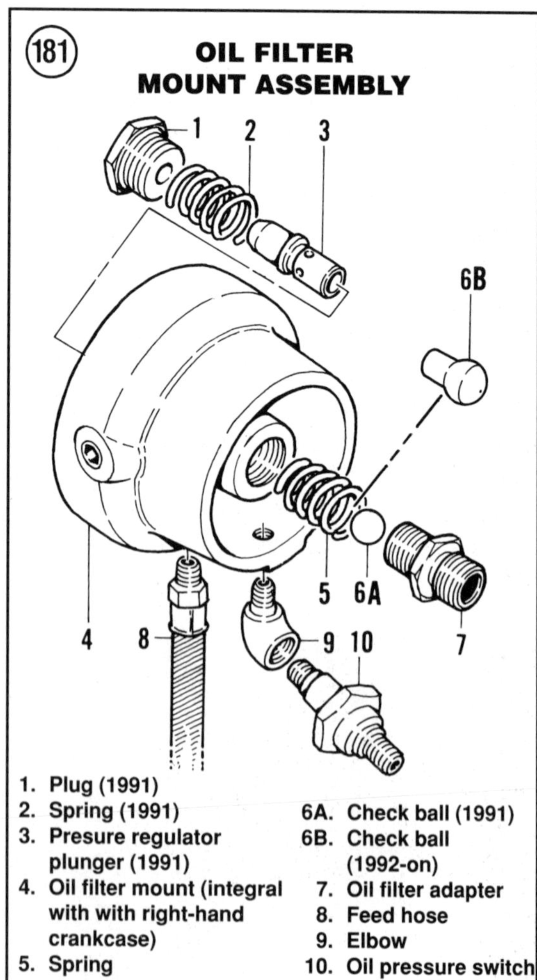

181 **OIL FILTER MOUNT ASSEMBLY**

1. Plug (1991)
2. Spring (1991)
3. Presure regulator plunger (1991)
4. Oil filter mount (integral with with right-hand crankcase)
5. Spring
6A. Check ball (1991)
6B. Check ball (1992-on)
7. Oil filter adapter
8. Feed hose
9. Elbow
10. Oil pressure switch

No. HD-37047A) are required to perform the following service procedures.

Refer to **Figure 183** and **Figure 184** when servicing the crankcases and crankshaft in the following procedures.

Crankshaft End Play Check

Crankshaft end play is a measure of sprocket shaft bearing wear. Crankshaft end play is controlled by a shim placed on the crankshaft sprocket shaft; see 8, **Figure 184**. Crankshaft end play should be measured prior to disassembling the crankcases.

NOTE
In Harley-Davidson terminology, the crankshaft's left-hand shaft is referred to as the sprocket shaft; the right-hand shaft is referred to as the pinion shaft.

When measuring end play, the crankshaft must be moved in and out. To do this, a special tool must be fabricated prior to checking end play. The special tool can be easily made by welding 2 handles onto a spare sprocket shaft nut.

1. Remove the engine from the frame as described in this chapter.
2. Remove the gearcase cover as described under *Gearcase Cover and Timing Gears* in this chapter.
3. Remove the primary chain and sprocket as described in Chapter Five.
4. Secure the crankcase to a workstand or workbench.
5. Attach a dial indicator so that the plunger touches against the end of the crankshaft as shown in **Figure 185**.

NOTE
The sprocket shaft bearings (left-hand side) must be preloaded when measuring crankshaft end play.

6. Install the engine sprocket onto the sprocket shaft. Then thread the sprocket nut (with handles) onto the sprocket shaft and tighten to 150-165 ft.-lb. (203-224 N•m).
7. Pull the sprocket shaft (**Figure 185**) in and out and note the flywheel end play reading on the dial indicator. If the total indicator reading is not within the flywheel end play specification listed in **Table 2**, the inner shim (8, **Figure 184**) must be replaced. Select the correct size shim from **Table 6**.
8. Remove the dial indicator, sprocket shaft nut and engine sprocket.

4

Crankcase Disassembly

This procedure describes crankcase disassembly and crankshaft removal. A press will be required to remove the crankshaft.

1. Remove the engine from the frame as described in this chapter.

CAUTION
*After removing the cylinders, slip rubber hoses (**Figure 186**) over the cylinder studs to avoid damaging them during the following service procedures. In addition, do not lift the crankcase assembly by grabbing the cylinder studs. Bent or damaged cylinder studs may cause oil leakage.*

2. Disassemble and remove the gearcase assembly as described in this chapter.
3. Check the crankshaft end play as described in this chapter.
4. Loosen, then remove the crankcase bolts and washer (**Figure 183**).
5. Lay the crankcase assembly on wood blocks so that the right-hand side (**Figure 187**) faces up.
6. Tap the crankcase with a plastic mallet and remove the right-hand crankcase half.
7. Remove the dowel pins.

WARNING
A press is required to remove the crankshaft in Step 8. To prevent eye damage

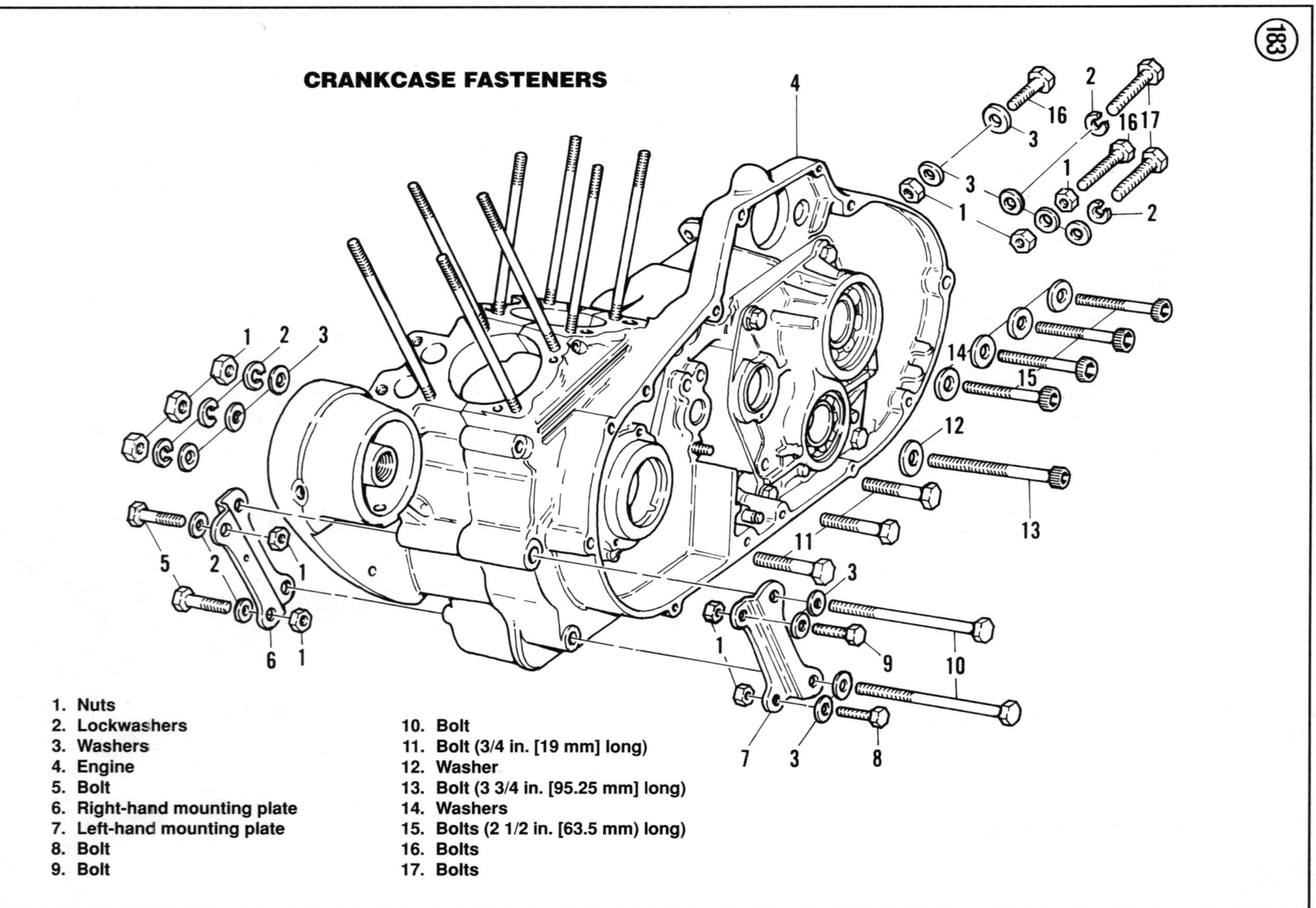

(183)

CRANKCASE FASTENERS

1. Nuts
2. Lockwashers
3. Washers
4. Engine
5. Bolt
6. Right-hand mounting plate
7. Left-hand mounting plate
8. Bolt
9. Bolt
10. Bolt
11. Bolt (3/4 in. [19 mm] long)
12. Washer
13. Bolt (3 3/4 in. [95.25 mm] long)
14. Washers
15. Bolts (2 1/2 in. [63.5 mm] long)
16. Bolts
17. Bolts

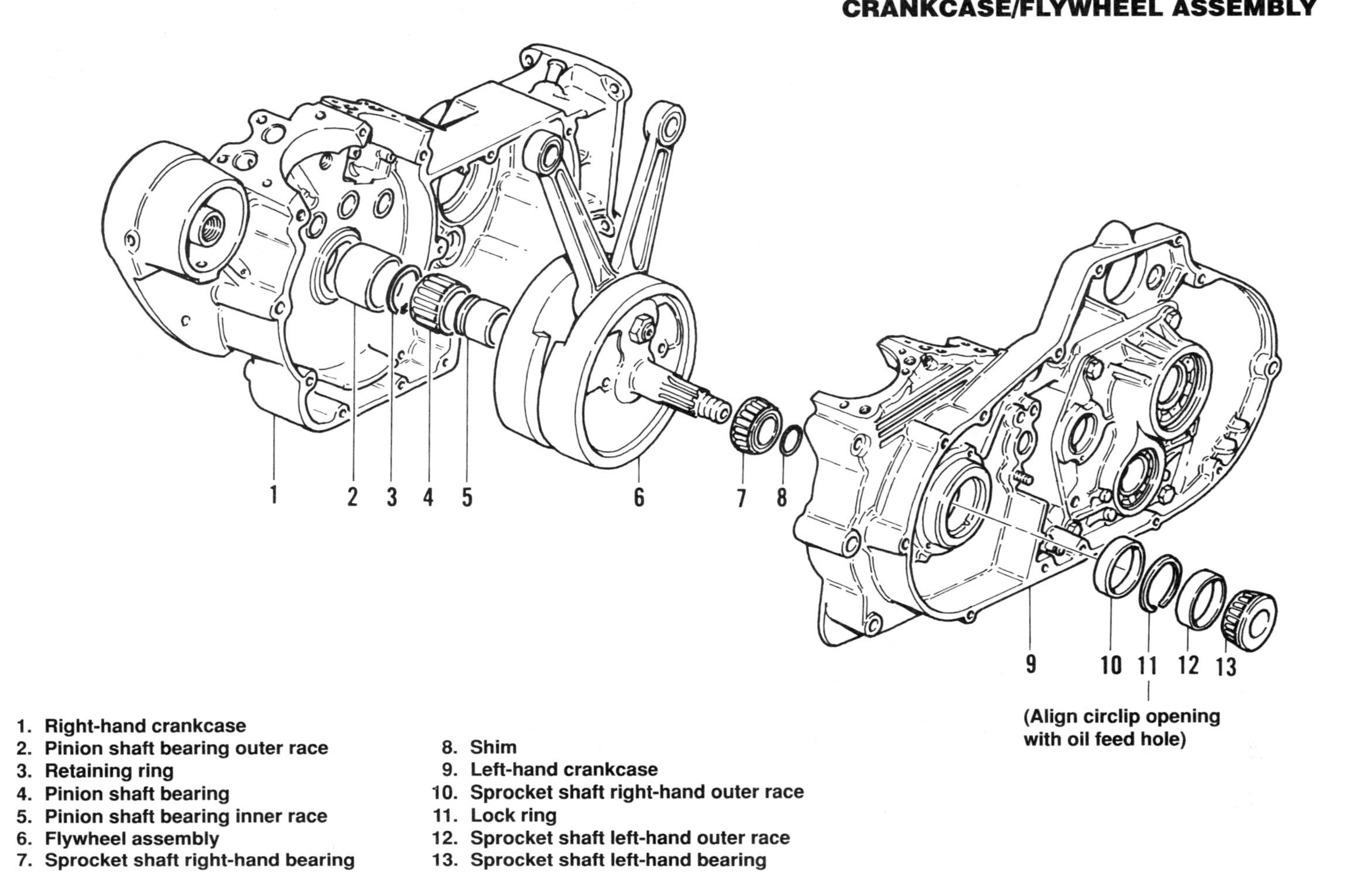
184
CRANKCASE/FLYWHEEL ASSEMBLY
1
2
3
4
5
6
7
8
9
10
11
12
13
(Align circlip opening
with oil feed hole)
1. Right-hand crankcase
2. Pinion shaft bearing outer race
3. Retaining ring
4. Pinion shaft bearing
5. Pinion shaft bearing inner race
6. Flywheel assembly
7. Sprocket shaft right-hand bearing
8. Shim
9. Left-hand crankcase
10. Sprocket shaft right-hand outer race
11. Lock ring
12. Sprocket shaft left-hand outer race
13. Sprocket shaft left-hand bearing

from parts flying out while under pressure, safety glasses must be worn.

8. Press the crankshaft out of the left-hand crankcase as follows:
   a. Support the left-hand crankcase in a press with parallel bars or wood blocks as shown in **Figure 188**. Check that there is adequate room for the crankshaft and connecting rods as the crankshaft is being pressed out.
   b. Center the press ram with sprocket shaft, then press the crankshaft from the case half. Support the bottom of the crankshaft to prevent it from falling to the floor.

CAUTION

Do not attempt to remove the crankshaft by driving it out with a hammer. The force may knock the flywheels out of alignment and damage the sprocket shaft threads.

Inspection

1. Measure connecting rod side play with a feeler gauge as shown in **Figure 189**. If the side play is not within the specifications in **Table 2**, refer service to a Harley-Davidson dealer.
2. Inspect the piston pin bushings (**Figure 190**) for severe wear or damage. Replace the bushings as described under *Piston Pin Bushing Replacement*.
3. Visually inspect the connecting rods (**Figure 191**) for damage.

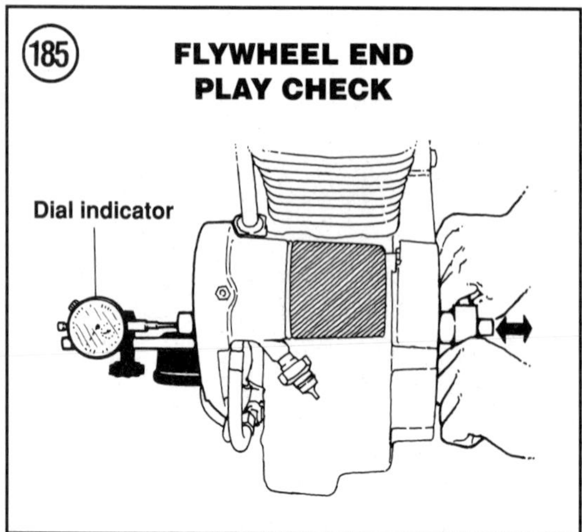

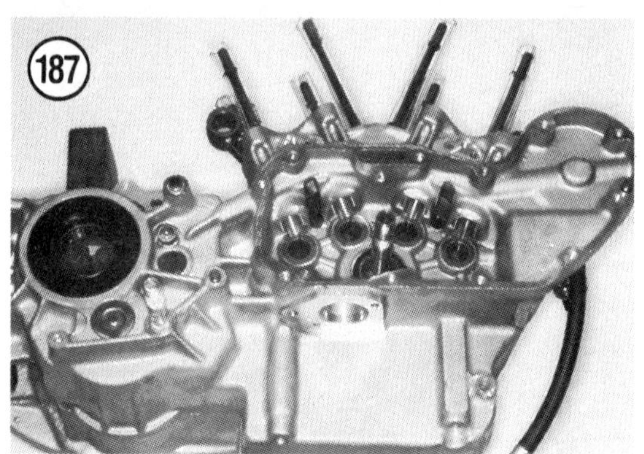

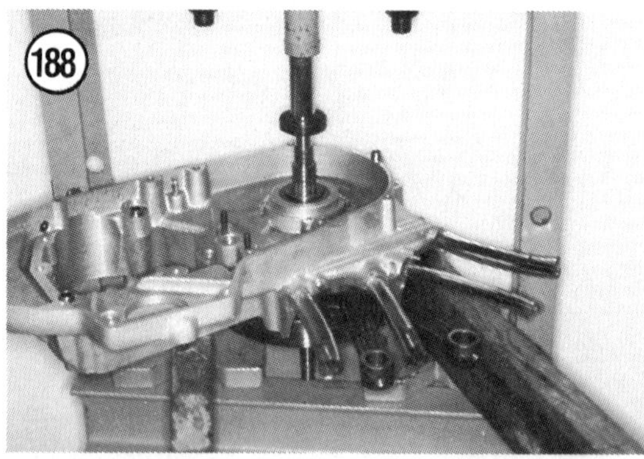

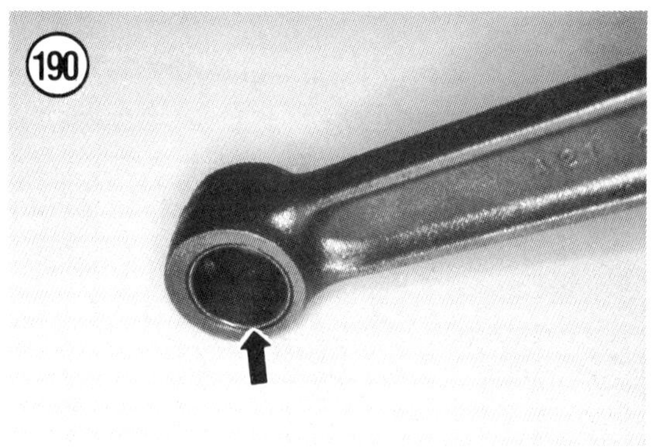

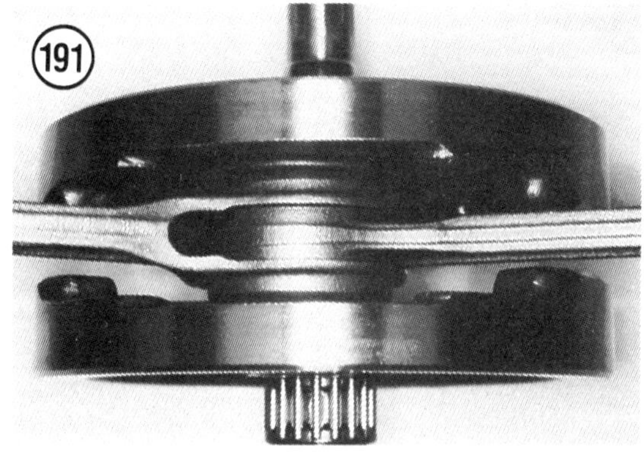

4. Inspect the motor shaft (A, **Figure 192**) and pinion shaft (B, **Figure 192**) for severe wear or damage. If damage is noted, refer replacement to a Harley-Davidson dealer.

5. Inspect the motor shaft bearing (**Figure 193**) for severe wear or damage.

6. Inspect the pinion shaft needle bearing (**Figure 194**) for severe wear or damage.

7. If either bearing is severely worn or damaged, refer replacement to a Harley-Davidson dealer.

8. Support the crankshaft on a truing stand or in a lathe and check runout with a dial indicator and compare to runout limit in **Table 2**. If runout is excessive, refer service to a Harley-Davidson dealer.

9. Remove the left-hand crankcase oil seal as follows:

   a. Remove the spacer (**Figure 195**), if used.

   b. Pry the oil seal out of the crankcase with a wide-blade screwdriver (**Figure 196**).

10. Remove the left-hand sprocket bearing (**Figure 197**).

11. Inspect the bearing and race for damage. If the bearing or race is damaged, refer replacement to a Harley-Davidson dealer.

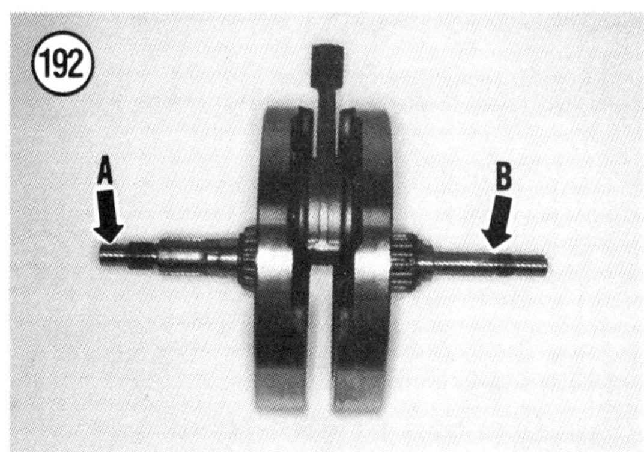

Crankshaft Installation/ Crankcase Assembly

The sprocket shaft bearing/seal installation tool (part No. HD-37047A) will be required to install the sprocket shaft bearing and oil seal.

Refer to **Figure 184** when performing this procedure.

1. If necessary, have a Harley-Davidson dealer or service shop install the pinion shaft and motor shaft bearings and bearing races.
2. Lubricate all parts with new engine oil prior to installation.
3. Position the crankshaft in a vise with soft jaws so that the sprocket shaft (**Figure 198**) faces up.
4. Place the left-hand crankcase over the crankshaft (**Figure 199**).
5. Install the end play shim (8, **Figure 184**) over the sprocket shaft.
6. Install the left-hand bearing (13, **Figure 184**) over the sprocket shaft.
7. Assemble the sprocket shaft bearing/seal installation tool (**Figure 200**) onto the sprocket shaft and pull the crankshaft into position as follows:
   a. Slide the 0.75 in. spacer (2, **Figure 200**) over the sprocket shaft so that its flat side faces downward.
   b. Thread the nut driver (1, **Figure 200**) onto the sprocket shaft threads until it bottoms out.
   c. Remove the nut driver and spacer from the sprocket shaft.
   d. Install the following spacers onto the sprocket shaft so that their flat sides face down: 1.2 in., 1.6 in. and 2.06 in.
   e. Install the nut driver (1, **Figure 200**) onto the sprocket shaft. Then tighten the nut driver until the left- and right-hand bearings (7 and 13, **Figure 184**) and end play shim (8, **Figure 184**) are drawn together. See **Figure 199**.
   f. Remove the nut driver and the spacer assembly.

8A. To install the left-hand crankcase oil seal on 1991-1992 models:
   a. Pack the oil seal lip with a waterproof grease prior to installation.
   b. Install the oil seal over the sprocket shaft so that its closed side faces out. Rest the seal against the crankcase.

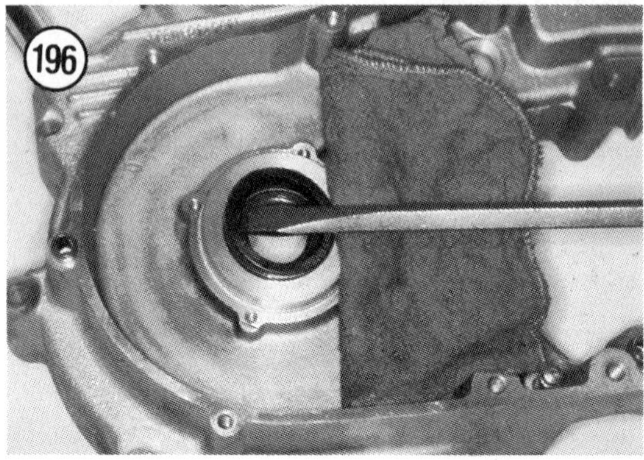
196

197

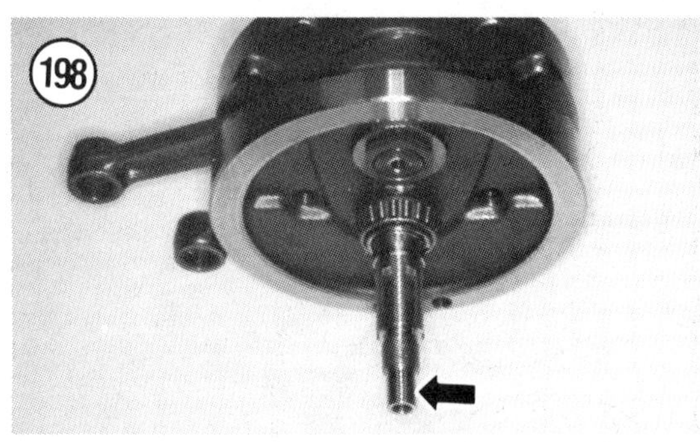
198

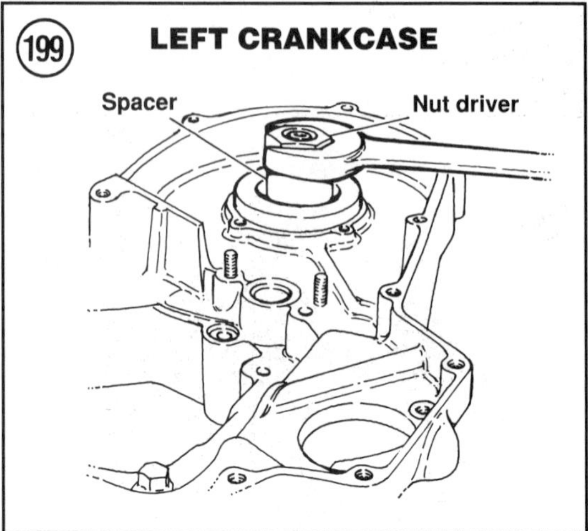

199 LEFT CRANKCASE

c. Center a driving tool over the oil seal. Then drive in the oil seal until its outer surface is flush with the oil seal bore inside surface.

8B. To install the left-hand crankcase oil seal on 1993-on models:

a. Pack the oil seal lip with a waterproof grease prior to installation.

b. Install the spacer in the seal.

c. Install the oil seal over the sprocket shaft so that its closed side faces out. Rest the seal against the crankcase.

HARLEY DAVIDSON SPROCKET SHAFT BEARING/SEAL INSTALLATION TOOL

1
2
3
4
5
6
7
8

200

d. Install the seal/spacer driver (7, **Figure 200**) over the sprocket shaft so that its smaller outer diameter side seats between the seal wall and the garter spring.

e. Fit the driver handle (8, **Figure 200**) over the seal/spacer driver and drive the seal and spacer into the bore until the spacer contacts the bearing cage. Remove the drive handle and the seal/spacer driver.

CAUTION
Do not remove the spacer after installing it. Removal will damage the new oil seal and the seal will have to be replaced.

9. Support the left-hand/crankshaft assembly on wood blocks as shown in **Figure 201**.

10. Install the crankcase dowel pins (**Figure 202**).

11. Coat the crankcase mating surfaces with Dow Corning Silastic or 3-M #800 sealant.

12. Align the crankcase halves and install the right-hand crankcase (**Figure 203**).

13. Install the crankcase bolts and washers (**Figure 204**).

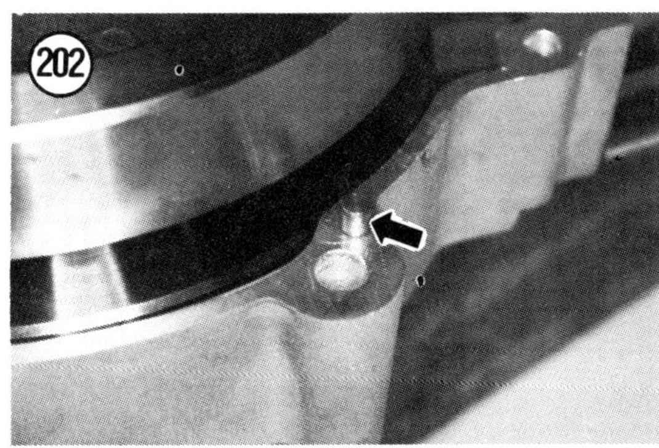

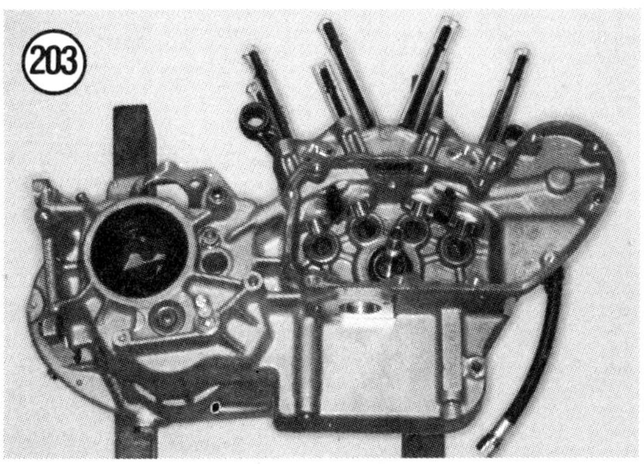

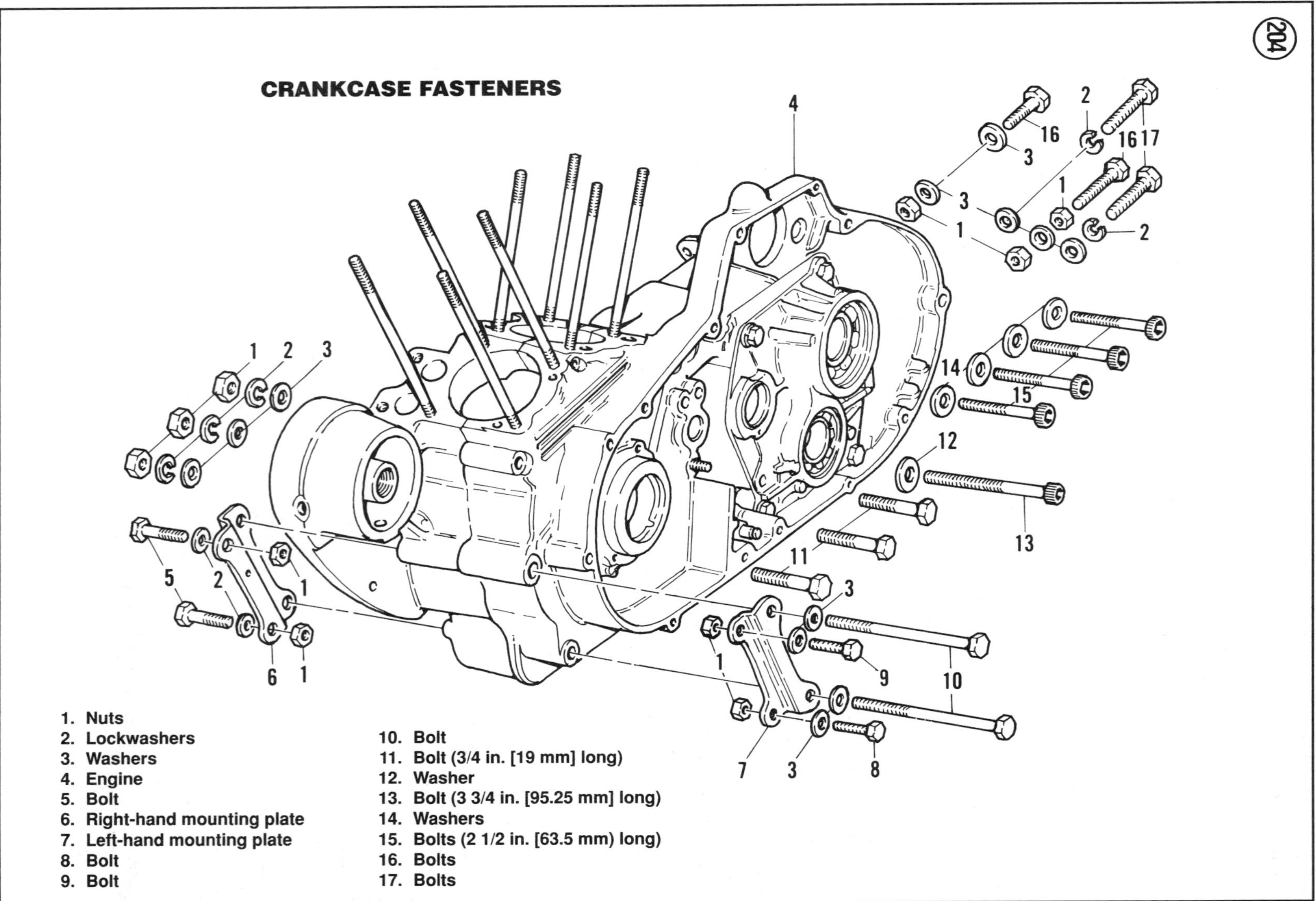
204
CRANKCASE FASTENERS
1. Nuts
2. Lockwashers
3. Washers
4. Engine
5. Bolt
6. Right-hand mounting plate
7. Left-hand mounting plate
8. Bolt
9. Bolt
10. Bolt
11. Bolt (3/4 in. [19 mm] long)
12. Washer
13. Bolt (3 3/4 in. [95.25 mm] long)
14. Washers
15. Bolts (2 1/2 in. [63.5 mm) long)
16. Bolts
17. Bolts

14. Tighten the 1/4 in. bolts to the torque specification in **Table 4**.

15. Tighten the 5/16 in. bolts to the torque specification in **Table 4**.

16. If the pinion shaft bearing (4, **Figure 184**) was removed, install it as follows:

a. Lubricate the pinion shaft bearing with new engine oil.

b. Slide the bearing onto the pinion shaft and into the outer bearing race in the right-hand crankcase.

c. Install a new retaining ring (3, **Figure 184**) in the groove in the pinion shaft bearing inner race (5, **Figure 184**).

17. Install the engine in the frame as described in this chapter.

18. Install all of the engine sub-assemblies as described in this chapter.

19. If new engine components were installed, perform the *Engine Break-In* in this chapter.

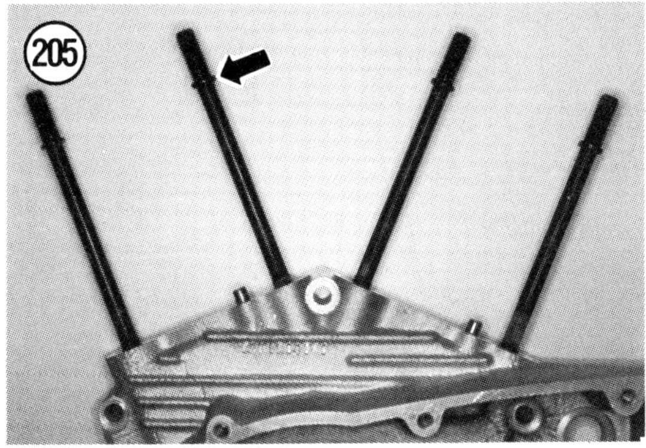

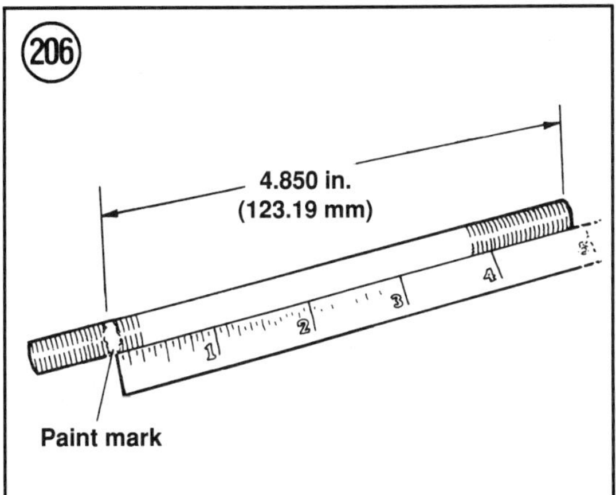

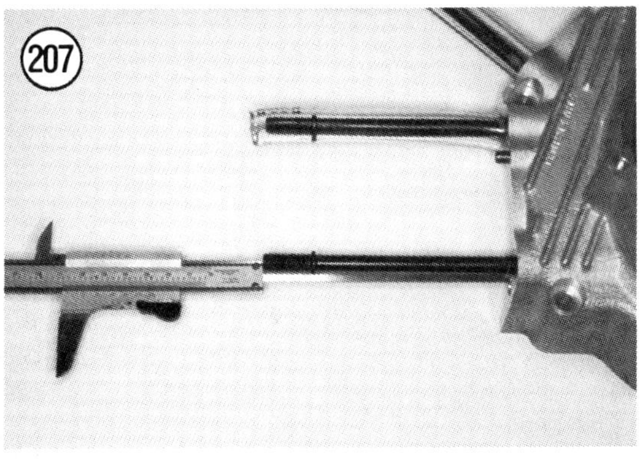

4

Cylinder Stud Replacement

Improper stud replacement can cause oil leakage. If you do not have all of the tools required to install the studs, have a dealer install the studs.

1. If the engine is assembled, stuff some clean shop rags into the crankcase opening to prevent abrasive particles from falling into the engine.
2. Remove the damaged stud with a stud remover.
3. Clean the crankcase threads and the new stud with solvent or contact cleaner. Blow dry.

NOTE

*The cylinder studs have a shoulder on the upper end; see **Figure 205**.*

4. Measuring from the top of the stud, paint a mark that is 4.850 in. (123.2 mm) down the stud; see **Figure 206**.
5. Drop a small steel ball into a cylinder head bolt and thread the bolt onto the top of the new stud.
6. Hand-thread the new stud into the crankcase, then install it with an air gun until the paint mark on the stud aligns with the crankcase base gasket surface.
7. Remove the cylinder head bolt and steel ball from the cylinder stud.
8. Measure the stud's installed height with a vernier caliper (**Figure 207**). The stud's installed height should be 4.770-4.870 in. (121.1-123.7 mm).
9. Place a protective hose over the stud.
10. Repeat Steps 2-9 for each stud.

ENGINE BREAK-IN

Following cylinder servicing (boring, honing, new rings, etc.) and major lower end work, the engine should be broken in just as though it were new. The performance and service life of the engine depend greatly on a careful and sensible break-in.

1. For the first 50 miles, maintain engine speed below 2,500 rpm in any gear. However, make sure you do not lug the engine. Do not exceed 50 mph during this period.

2. From 50 to 500 miles, vary the engine speed. Prolonged, steady running at one speed, no matter how moderate, is to be avoided. During this period, engine rpm may be increased to 3,000 rpm. Do not exceed 55 mph during this period.

3. If your model does not have a tachometer, use the information in **Table 7** as a guide to proper shifting.

4. After the first 500 miles, engine break-in has been completed.

Table 1 GENERAL ENGINE SPECIFICATIONS

Engine	OHV V2 Evolution
Piston displacement	
883 cc	53.9 cu. in. (883 cc)
1200cc	73.3 cu. in. (1201 cc)
Horsepower	
883 cc	55 hp @ 6,000 rpm
1200 cc	65 hp @ 5,200 rpm
Bore x stroke	
883 cc	3.000 × 3.812 in. (76.2 × 96.8 mm)
1200 cc	3.498 × 3.812 in. (88.85 × 96.8 mm)
Compression ratio	
All models	9.0:1
Torque	
883 cc	
1991-1992	55 ft.-lb. @ 4,500 rpm
1993-on	50 ft.-lb. @ 4,600 rpm
1200 cc	
1991-1992	71.5 ft.-lb. @ 4,000 rpm
1993-on	71 ft.-lb. @ 4,000 rpm

Table 2 ENGINE SERVICE SPECIFICATIONS

	New in. (mm)	Service limit [1] in. (mm)
Rocker arm		
Shaft fit in bushing	0.0005-0.0020 (0.012-0.050)	0.0035 (0.088)
End clearance	0.003-0.013 (0.076-0.330)	0.025 (0.635)
Bushing fit in rocker arm	0.004-0.002 (0.101-0.050)	—
Rocker arm shaft		
Shaft fit in rocker arm bushing	0.0007-0.0022 (0.017-0.055)	0.0035 (0.088)

(continued)

Table 2 ENGINE SERVICE SPECIFICATIONS (continued)

	New in. (mm)	Service limit [1] in. (mm)
Cylinder head		
Gasket surface flatness	0.006 (0.152)	0.006 (0.152)
Valve guide fit in head	0.0033-0.0020 (0.083-0.050)	—
Valve seat fit in head	0.0035-0.0010 (0.088-0.025)	—
Valves		
Guide-to-valve stem clearance		
Intake	0.0008-0.0026 (0.020-0.066)	0.0035 (0.088)
Exhaust	0.0015-0.0033 (0.038-0.083)	0.0040 (0.101)
Seat width	0.040-0.062 (1.016-1.574)	0.090 (2.286)
Stem protrusion from cylinder valve pocket	1.975-2.011 (50.165-51.079)	2.031 (51.587)
Valve springs free length[2]		
Outer springs	2.105-2.177 (53.467-55.295)	2.105 (53.467)
Inner springs	1.926-1.996 (48.92-50.69)	1.926 (48.92)
Valve spring compression specifications	See Table 3	
Piston (883 cc)		
Compression ring end gap	0.010-0.023 (0.254-0.584)	0.032 (0.812)
Oil control ring rail end gap	0.010-0.053 (0.254-1.346)	0.065 (1.651)
Compression ring side clearance		
Top	0.0020-0.0045 (0.050-0.114)	0.0065 (0.165)
2nd	0.0020-0.0045) (0.050-0.114)	0.0065 (0.165)
Oil control ring side clearance	0.0014-0.0074 (0.035-0.187)	0.0094 (0.238)
Piston (1200 cc)		
Compression ring end gap	0.007-0.020 (0.177-0.508)	0.032 (0.812)
Oil control ring rail end gap	0.009-0.052 (0.228-1.320)	0.065 (1.651)
Compression ring side clearance		
Top	0.0020-0.0045 (0.050-0.114)	0.0065 (0.165)
2nd	0.0016-0.0041 (0.040-0.104)	0.0065 (0.165)
Oil control ring side clearance	0.0016-0.0076 (0.040-0.187)	0.0094 (0.238)
Cylinder		
Taper		0.002 (0.050)
Out-of-round		0.003 (0.076)
Gasket surface (warpage limit)		
Top		0.006 (0.152)

(continued)

4

Table 2 ENGINE SERVICE SPECIFICATIONS (continued)

	New in. (mm)	Service limit [1] in. (mm)
Cylinder (continued)		
Gasket surface (warpage limit) (continued)		
Bottom		0.008 (0.203)
Bore diameter (883 cc) [3]		
Standard	3.0005 (76.212)	3.0035 (76.288)
Oversize		
0.005 in. (0.13 mm)	3.0048 (76.321)	3.0078 (76.398)
0.010 in. (0.25 mm)	3.0098 (76.448)	3.0128 (76.525)
0.020 in. (0.51 mm)	3.0198 (76.702)	3.0228 (76.779)
0.030 in. (0.76 mm)	3.0298 (76.956)	3.0328 (77.033)
0.040 in. (1.02 mm)	3.0398 (77.210)	3.0428 (77.287)
Bore diameter (1200 cc) [3]		
Standard	3.4978 (88.844)	3.5008 (88.920)
Oversize		
0.005 in. (0.13 mm)	3.502 (88.950)	3.505 (89.027)
0.010 in. (0.25 mm)	3.507 (89.077)	3.510 (89.154)
0.020 in. (0.51 mm)	3.517 (89.331)	3.520 (89.408)
0.030 in. (0.76 mm)	3.527 (89.585)	3.530 (89.662)
Tappets		
Clearance in guide	0.0008-0.0023 (0.020-0.058)	0.003 (0.076)
Roller fit on pin	0.0006-0.0013 (0.015-0.033)	—
Roller end clearance	0.010-0.014 (0.254-0.355)	0.026 (0.660)
Oil pump		
Shaft-to-pump clearance	0.0025 (0.063)	—
Feed/scavenge inner/outer rotor clearance	0.003 (0.076)	0.004 (0.101)
Gearcase		
Cam gear shaft bushing clearance	0.0007-0.0022 (0.017-0.055)	0.003 (0.076)
Cam gear shaft end play (minimum)		
Rear intake cam gear	0.006-0.024 (0.152-0.609)	0.040 (1.016)
All other cam gears	0.005-0.024 (0.127-0.609)	0.025 (0.635)
Connecting rods		
Side play @ crankshaft	0.005-0.025 (0.127-0.635)	0.030 (0.762)
Piston pin fit (clearance)	0.00125-0.00175 (0.031-0.044)	0.00200 (0.050)

(continued)

Table 2 ENGINE SERVICE SPECIFICATIONS (continued)

	New in. (mm)	Service limit [1] in. (mm)
Connecting rods (continued)		
Fit on crankpin	0.0004-0.0017 (0.010-0.043)	0.0027 (0.068)
Crankshaft		
Runout @ flywheel rim	0.000-0.010 (0.000-0.254)	0.010 (0.254)
Runout @ shaft	0.000-0.002 (0.000-0.050)	0.002 (0.050)
End play	0.001-0.005 (0.025-0.127)	0.005 (0.127)
Sprocket shaft bearing		
Outer race fit in crankcase	0.0004-0.0024 (0.010-0.060)	—
Bearing inner race fit on shaft	0.0002-0.0015 (0.005-0.038)	—
Pinion shaft bearings		
Pinion shaft journal diameter [2]	1.2500-1.2496 (31.750-31.739)	1.2494 (31.734)
Outer race diameter in right-hand crankcase	1.5646-1.5652 (39.740-39.756)	1.5672 (39.806)
Fit in cover bushing	0.0023-0.0043 (0.058-0.109)	0.0050 (0.127)
Bearing running clearance	0.00012-0.00088 (0.003-0.022)	—

1 Part should be considered worn if measurement exceeds service limit specification, unless otherwise noted; see below.
2 Part should be considered worn if measurement is less than the service limit specification.
3 ± 0.0002 in. (0.005 mm).

Table 3 VALVE SPRING COMPRESSION SPECIFICATIONS

	Compression length* in. (mm)	Pressure lbs.	kg
Outer springs			
Intake			
Closed	1.751-1.848 (44.47-46.94)	72-92	33-42
Open	1.286-1.383 (32.66-35.12)	183-207	83-94
Exhaust			
Closed	1.751-1.848 (44.47-46.94)	72-92	33-42
Open	1.332-1.429 (33.83-36.29)	171-195	77.6-88.5
Inner springs			
Intake			
Closed	1.577-1.683 (40.05-42.74)	38-49	17.24-22.23
Open	1.112-1.218 (28.24-30.93)	98-112	44.45-50.80

(continued)

4

Table 3 VALVE SPRING COMPRESSION SPECIFICATIONS (continued)

	Compression length* in. (mm)	Pressure lbs.	kg
Exhaust			
Closed	1.577-1.683 (40.05-42.74)	38-49	17.24-22.23
Open	1.158-1.264 (29.41-32.10)	91-106	41.3-48.1

* A valve spring compression tool is required; see text for measurement procedures.

Table 4 ENGINE TIGHTENING TORQUES

	ft.-lb.	N•m
Spark plug	11-18	15-24.4
Cylinder head mounting bracket fasteners		
Engine mount-to-engine	25-30	34-40.7
Engine mount-to-frame	30-35	40.7-47.5
Engine center mount-to-engine	28-35	38-47.5
Lower rocker cover bolts		
5/16 in.	15-18	20.3-24.4
1/4 in.	10-13	13.6-17.6
Crank pin nut	150-185	203.4-251
Pinion shaft nut	35-45	47.5-61
Oil tank mounting locknuts	3-5	4.1-6.8
Pushrod tube seal plate bolts	15-18	20.3-24.4
Rear engine mount bolts		
Frame to crankcase	25-30	34-41
Lower front engine mount bracket		
Engine bolts	25-30	34-41
Frame bolts	25-30	34-41
Upper front engine mount bracket		
Engine bolts	25-30	34-41
Frame bolts	30-35	41-47
Top center engine mount bracket		
Engine bolts	25-30	34-41
Frame bolts	30-35	41-47
Oil pressure switch	5-7	7-9
Oil filter adapter	8-12	11-16
Crankcase mounting bolts		
1/4 in.	see below	
5/16 in.		
1991-1992	16-26	22-35
1993-on	15-18	20-24
Upper rocker cover bolts	10-13	14-18
	in.-lb.	**N•m**
Crankcase mounting bolts		
1/4 in.	70-110	7.9-12.4
Oil pump assembly and mounting screws	125-150	14.1-16.9
Gearcase cover screws	80-110	9-12.4
Tappet plate screws	80-110	9-12.4
Rotor bolt	43-48	4.9-5.4
Timer screws		
Inner cover and sensor plate	15-20	1.7-2.3

Table 5 CAM AND PINION GEAR COLOR CODE AND OUTSIDE DIAMETER

GEAR NO. & POSITION	1	2 INBOARD	2 OUTBOARD	3	4	5
COLOR CODE (1 paint dot)	Rear exhaust	Rear intake	Rear intake	Front intake	Front exhaust	Pinion
BROWN	1.9010-1.9014 (48.285-48.296)	1.9040-1.9044 (48.362-48.372)	2.4026-2.4030 (61.026-61.036)	1.9010-1.9014 (48.285-48.296)	1.9040-1.9044 (48.362-48.372)	1.2758-1.2761 (32.405-32.413)
BLUE	1.9015-1.9019 (48.298-48.308)	1.9035-1.9039 (48.349-48.359)	2.4031-2.4035 (61.039-61.049)	1.9015-1.9019 (48.298-48.308)	1.9035-1.9039 (48.349-48.359)	1.2754-1.2757 (32.395-32.403)
RED	1.9020-1.9024 (48.311-48.321)	1.9030-1.9034 (48.336-48.346)	2.4036-2.4040 (61.051-61.062)	1.9020-1.9024 (48.311-48.321)	1.9030-1.9034 (48.336-48.346)	1.2750-1.2753 (32.385-32.393)
WHITE	1.9025-1.9029 (48.323-48.334)	1.9025-1.9029 (48.323-48.334)	2.4041-2.4045 (61.064-61.074)	1.9025-1.9029 (48.323-48.334)	1.9025-1.9029 (48.323-48.334)	1.2746-1.2749 (32.375-32.382)
GREEN	1.9030-1.9034 (48.336-48.346)	1.9020-1.9024 (48.311-48.321)	2.4046-2.4050 (61.077-61.087)	1.9030-1.9034 (48.336-48.346)	1.9020-1.9024 (48.311-48.321)	1.2742-1.2745 (32.365-32.372)
YELLOW	1.9035-1.9039 (48.349-48.359)	1.9015-1.9019 (48.298-48.308)	2.4051-2.4055 (61.089-61.100)	1.9035-1.9039 (48.349-48.359)	1.9015-1.9019 (48.298-48.308)	1.2738-1.2741 (32.354-32.362)
BLACK	1.9040-1.9044 (48.362-48.372)	1.9010-1.9014 (48.285-48.296)	2.4056-2.4060 (61.102-61.112)	1.9040-1.9044 (48.362-48.372)	1.9010-1.9014 (48.285-48.296)	1.2734-1.2737 (32.344-32.352)

4

Table 6 FLYWHEEL END PLAY SHIM THICKNESS

Harley-Davidson part number	in.	mm
9155	0.0975-0.0985	2.476-2.502
9142	0.0995-0.1005	2.527-2.553
9143	0.1015-0.1025	2.578-2.603
9144	0.1035-0.1045	2.629-2.654
9145	0.1055-0.1065	2.680-2.705
9146	0.1075-0.1085	2.730-2.756
9147	0.1095-0.1105	2.781-2.807
9148	0.1115-0.1125	2.832-2.857
9149	0.1135-0.1145	2.883-2.908

Table 7 GEAR CHANGES FOR ENGINE BREAK-IN (MODELS WITHOUT TACHOMETERS)

Gear Change	Vehicle speed
Acceleration	
1st to 2nd	15 mph (25 km/h)
2nd to 3rd	25 mph (40 km/h)
3rd to 4th	40 mph (65 km/h)
4th to 5th	50 mph (80 km/h)
Deceleration	
5th to 4th	40 mph (65 km/h)
4th to 3rd	30 mph (50 km/h)
3rd to 2nd	20 mph (30 km/h)
2nd to 1st	10 mph (15 km/h)

CHAPTER FIVE

CLUTCH AND PRIMARY DRIVE

This chapter describes service procedures for the clutch and primary drive. **Table 1** and **Table 2** are at the end of the chapter.

PRIMARY COVER

Removal (1991-1993)

Refer to **Figure 1**.

1. Disconnect the negative battery cable.
2. Place a drain pan under the primary cover and remove the oil drain plug (**Figure 2**). Allow the oil to drain.
3. Loosen the locknut (A, **Figure 3**) and turn the primary chain adjuster screw (B, **Figure 3**) counterclockwise to loosen the chain.
4. Remove the clutch inspection cover (**Figure 4**).
5. Remove the spring and lockplate (**Figure 5**).
6. Turn the clutch adjusting screw clockwise (**Figure 6**) until the nut can be removed, then remove the nut (**Figure 7**).
7. Remove the shift lever and left-hand footpeg assembly (**Figure 8**).

NOTE

Different length screws are used to secure the primary chain cover. After removing each screw, punch the screw through a piece of cardboard, following the primary cover outline, for reassembly reference.

8. Remove the primary chain cover (**Figure 9**) and gasket.
9. Remove the dowel pins (**Figure 10**), if necessary.
10. If necessary, remove the clutch mechanism as described in this chapter.
11. If necessary, service the following components as described in this chapter:
    a. Clutch mechanism adjuster.
    b. Primary chain adjuster.
    c. Shift shaft oil seal.

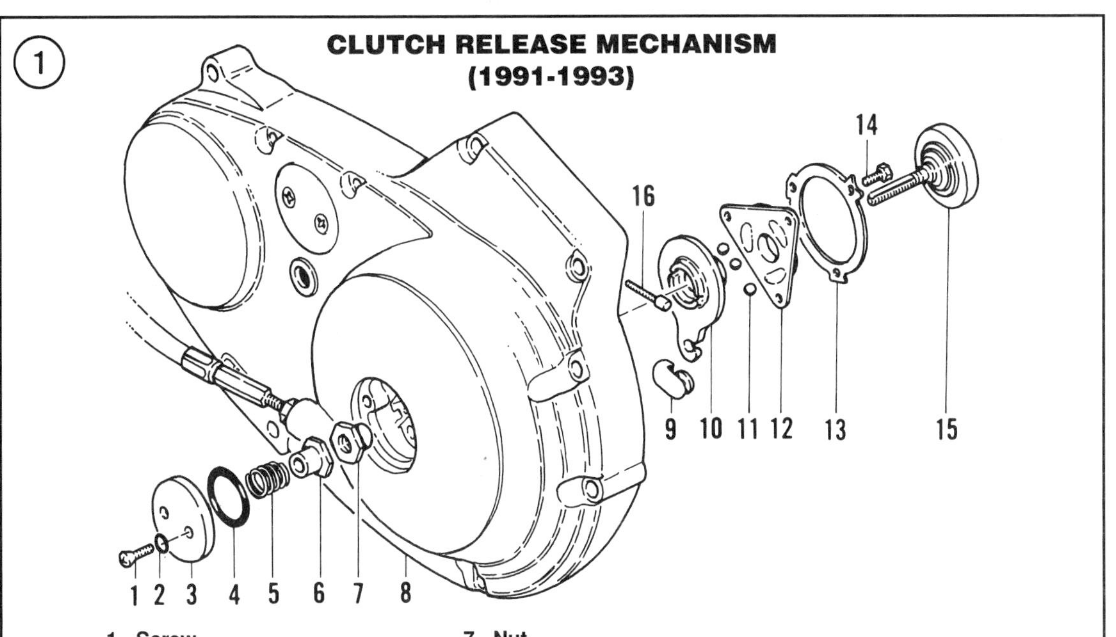

1. Screw
2. O-ring
3. Clutch inspection cover
4. O-ring
5. Spring
6. Lockplate
7. Nut
8. Primary cover
9. Cable coupling
10. Outer ramp
11. Ball (3)
12. Inner ramp
13. Lockplate
14. Bolt
15. Clutch adjusting screw assembly
16. Clutch cable

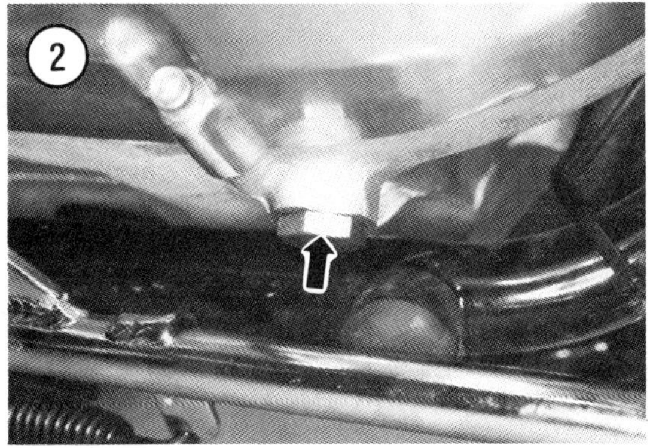

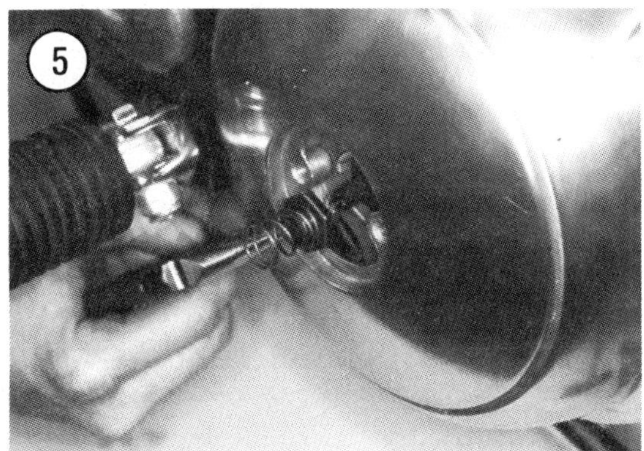

Installation (1991-1993)

Refer to **Figure 1**.

1. Clean the primary cover and engine crankcase gasket surfaces.

2. Clean the cover in solvent and dry thoroughly.

3. Clean the magnetic drain plug and reinstall it into the primary cover. Tighten the drain plug to the torque specification in **Table 2**.

4. Assemble the clutch mechanism assembly and connect the clutch cable as described under *Clutch Mechanism Assembly* in this chapter.

5. Install the dowel pins (**Figure 10**), if removed.

6. Using a new gasket, install the primary chain cover onto the crankcase. Install the cover mounting screws and tighten to the torque specification in **Table 2**. If necessary, use the bolt diagram in **Figure 11** to install the different length bolts into their correct positions.

7. Thread the nut (**Figure 7**) onto the clutch adjusting screw until the screw slot is accessible with a screwdriver. Then align and install the hex portion on the nut into the outer ramp recess. Turn the clutch adjusting screw (**Figure 6**) counterclockwise until the nut cannot be removed.

8. Adjust the clutch as described in Chapter Three. The spring and lockplate shown in **Figure 5** will be installed during the clutch adjustment procedure.

9. Adjust the primary chain as described in Chapter Three.

10. Refill the transmission oil as described in Chapter Three.

11. Install the shift lever (**Figure 8**) and tighten its pinch bolt to the torque specification in **Table 2**.

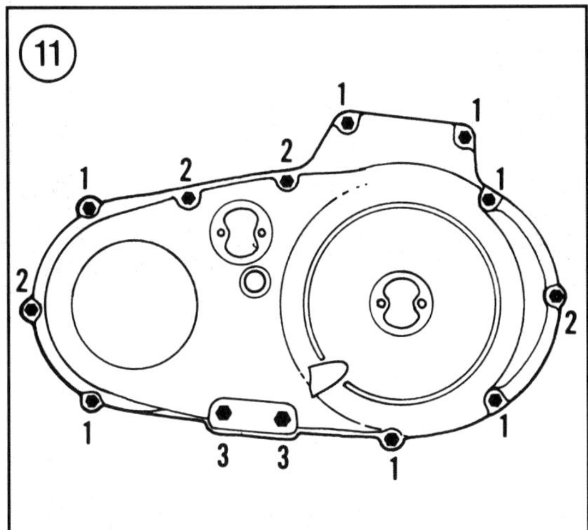

PRIMARY COVER (1991-1993)

1. 1/4-20 × 1 3/4 in. bolt with washers
2. 1/4-20 × 2 1/4 in. bolt with washers

LEFT FOOTREST SUPPORT

3. 5/16-18 × 3 1/2 in. bolt

12. Install the left-hand footpeg and tighten its mounting bolts to the torque specification in **Table 2**.

13. Reconnect the negative battery cable.

Removal (1994)

Refer to **Figure 12**.

1. Disconnect the negative battery cable.
2. Place a drain pan under the primary cover and remove the oil drain plug (**Figure 2**). Allow the oil to drain.
3. Loosen the locknut (A, **Figure 3**) and turn the primary chain adjuster screw (B, **Figure 3**) counterclockwise to loosen the chain.
4. Remove the clutch inspection cover. Remove the quad ring.
5. Remove the spring and lockplate.
6. Turn the clutch adjusting screw clockwise and release the ramp and coupling mechanism.

(12)

CLUTCH RELEASE MECHANISM (1994)

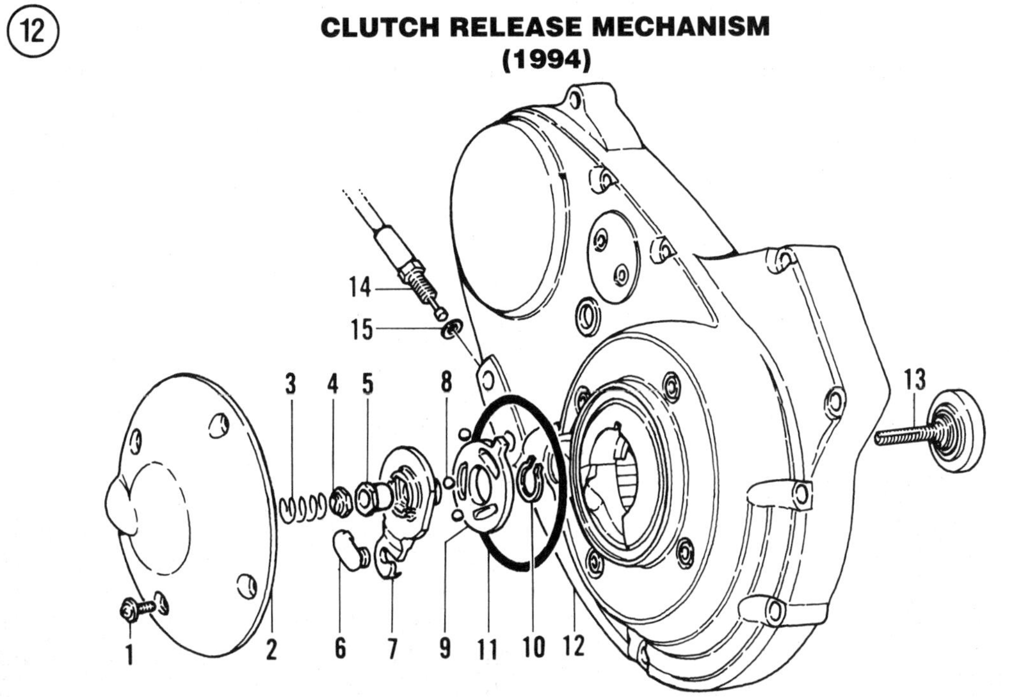

1. Torx screw and washer
2. Clutch inspection cover
3. Spring
4. Lockplate
5. Nut
6. Coupling
7. Outer ramp
8. Ball (3)
9. Inner ramp
10. Retaining ring
11. Quad ring
12. Primary cover
13. Clutch adjusting screw assembly
14. Clutch cable
15. O-ring

7. Turn the clutch adjusting screw clockwise to move the ramp assembly forward. Then unscrew the nut from the end of the adjusting screw and remove it.
8. Pivot the hook on the ramp to the rear of the cable end coupling. Then disconnect and remove the clutch cable from the slot in the coupling. Remove the coupling and ramp assembly.
9. Remove the shift lever and left-hand footpeg assembly.

NOTE
Different length screws are used to secure the primary chain cover. After removing each screw, punch the screw through a piece of cardboard, following the primary cover outline, for reassembly reference.

10. Remove the primary chain cover (**Figure 9**) and gasket.
11. Remove the dowel pins (**Figure 10**), if necessary.
12. If necessary, remove the clutch mechanism as described in this chapter.
13. If necessary, service the following components as described in this chapter:
   a. Clutch mechanism adjuster.
   b. Primary chain adjuster.
   c. Shift shaft oil seal.

Installation (1994)

Refer to **Figure 12**.
1. Clean the primary cover and engine crankcase gasket surfaces.
2. Clean the cover in solvent and dry thoroughly.
3. Clean the magnetic drain plug and reinstall it into the primary cover. Tighten the drain plug to the torque specification in **Table 2**.
4. Using a new gasket, install the primary chain cover onto the crankcase. Install the cover mounting screws and tighten to the torque specification in **Table 2**. If necessary, use the bolt diagram in **Figure 13** to install the different length bolts into their correct positions.
5. Fit the coupling over the clutch cable with the rounded side facing outward and the ramp connector button facing inward. With the retaining side of the ramp facing inward, install the ramp hook around the coupling button. Then rotate the assembly counterclockwise until the tang on the inner ramp fits into the primary cover slot.
6. Thread the nut onto the clutch adjusting screw until the slot in the end of the screw is accessible with a screwdriver. Then align and install the hex portion on the nut into the outer ramp recess. Turn the clutch adjusting screw counterclockwise until resistance is felt, then back off 1/4 turn.
7. Adjust the clutch as described in Chapter Three. The spring and lockplate shown in **Figure 12** will be installed during the clutch adjustment procedure.
8. Adjust the primary chain as described in Chapter Three.

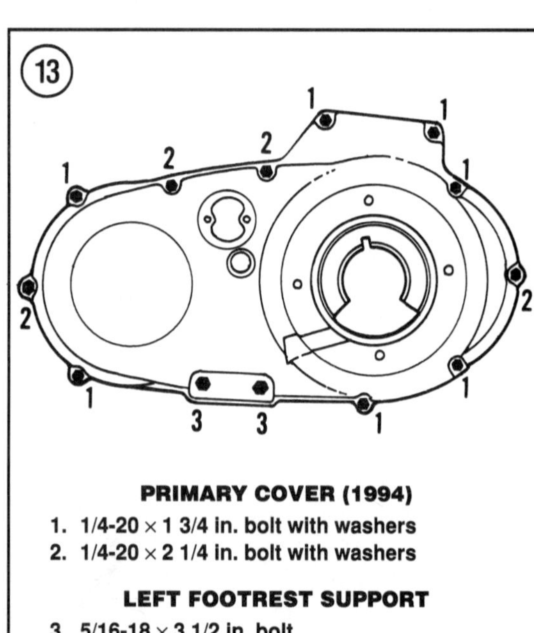

PRIMARY COVER (1994)
1. 1/4-20 × 1 3/4 in. bolt with washers
2. 1/4-20 × 2 1/4 in. bolt with washers

LEFT FOOTREST SUPPORT
3. 5/16-18 × 3 1/2 in. bolt

14

A B C

9. Refill the transmission oil as described in Chapter Three.
10. Install the shift lever (**Figure 8**) and tighten its pinch bolt to the torque specification in **Table 2**.
11. Install the left-hand footpeg and tighten its mounting bolts to the torque specification in **Table 2**.
12. Reconnect the negative battery cable.

CLUTCH RELEASE MECHANISM (1991-1993)

Removal

Refer to **Figure 1**.
1. Remove the primary cover as described in this chapter.
2. Pry the lockplate tabs (A, **Figure 14**) away from the mounting screws and remove the lockplate and screws.
3. Remove the clutch mechanism from the cover and disconnect the cable (B, **Figure 14**) from the ramp and coupling. Remove the clutch mechanism (C, **Figure 14**).

Inspection

1. Wash the clutch release mechanism in solvent and dry thoroughly.
2. Check the balls and ramp sockets (**Figure 15**) for pitting, severe wear or other damage.
3. Check the adjusting screw (**Figure 16**) for thread or bearing damage.
4. Replace the lockplate if the tabs are weak or broken.
5. Replace severely worn or damaged parts as required.

Installation

Refer to **Figure 1**.
1. Install the cable coupling onto the end of the clutch cable. Place the coupling in the ramp.
2. Apply grease to the ball and ramp surfaces (**Figure 15**) and insert the balls into the ramp sockets.
3. Assemble the inner and outer ramps and install on the primary cover (C, **Figure 14**). Install the lockplate and the ramp mounting screws. Tighten screws securely. Bend the lockplate tabs over the screws to lock them in place.
4. Install the primary cover as described in this chapter.
5. Adjust the clutch as described in Chapter Three.

CLUTCH RELEASE MECHANISM (1994)

Removal

Refer to **Figure 12**.
1. Loosen the clutch cable as follows:
   a. Slide the rubber boot away from the clutch cable adjuster.
   b. Hold the cable adjuster (A, **Figure 17**) and loosen the locknut (B, **Figure 17**).
   c. Loosen the cable adjuster to provide as much cable slack as possible.
2. Remove the left-hand footpeg.
3. Remove the clutch inspection cover screws and remove the cover.

NOTE
When removing the clutch inspection cover, work carefully to avoid removing or damaging the quad ring in the primary cover; see ***Figure 12****.*

5

4. Remove the spring and lockplate.
5. Turn the clutch adjusting screw clockwise and release the ramp and coupling mechanism.
6. Turn the clutch adjusting screw clockwise to move the ramp assembly forward. Then unscrew the nut from the end of the adjusting screw and remove it.
7. Pivot the hook on the ramp to the rear of the cable end coupling. Then disconnect and remove the clutch cable from the slot in the coupling. Remove the coupling and ramp assembly.
8. Remove the retaining ring securing the inner and outer ramp halves. Then remove the ramps and balls.

Inspection

1. Wash the clutch release mechanism in solvent and dry thoroughly.
2. Check the balls and ramp sockets (**Figure 15**) for pitting, severe wear or other damage.
3. Check the adjusting screw (**Figure 16**) for thread or bearing damage.
4. Replace the lockplate if the tabs are weak or broken.
5. Replace severely worn or damaged parts as required.

Installation

Refer to **Figure 12**.

1. Apply grease to the ball and ramp surfaces (**Figure 15**) and insert the balls into the outer ramp sockets.
2. Install the inner ramp on the outer ramp hook with its tang facing 180° from the hook of the outer ramp; see **Figure 12**.
3. Fit the coupling over the clutch cable with the rounded side facing outward and the ramp connector button facing inward. With the retaining side of the ramp facing inward, install the ramp hook around the coupling button. Then rotate the assembly counterclockwise until the tang on the inner ramp fits into the primary cover slot.
4. Thread the nut onto the clutch adjusting screw until the slot in the end of the screw is accessible with a screwdriver. Then align and install the hex portion on the nut into the outer ramp recess. Turn the clutch adjusting screw counterclockwise until resistance is felt, then back off 1/4 turn.
5. Adjust the clutch as described in Chapter Three. The spring and lockplate shown in **Figure 12** will be installed during the clutch adjustment procedure.

PRIMARY CHAIN ADJUSTER

The primary chain adjuster assembly (**Figure 18**) is mounted inside the primary cover.

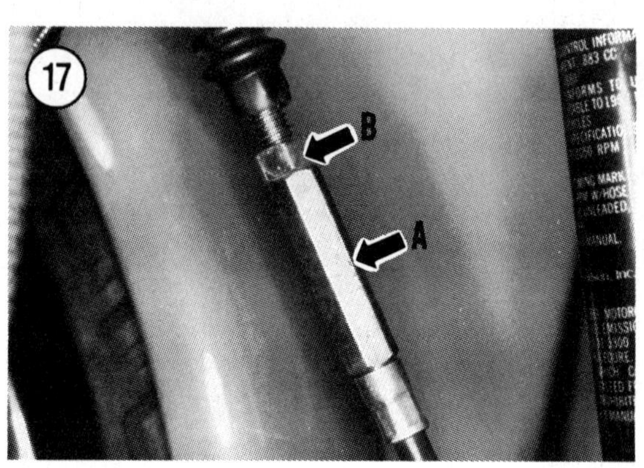

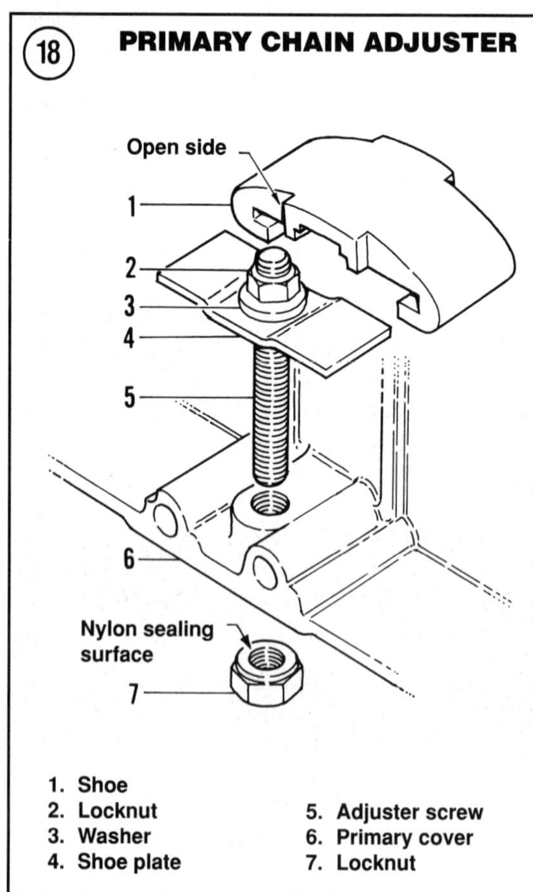

Removal

Refer to **Figure 18**.

1. Remove the primary cover as described in this chapter.
2. Remove the adjuster screw locknut (A, **Figure 19**).
3. Turn the adjuster screw (B, **Figure 19**) to remove it from the threaded boss in the primary cover (**Figure 18**).
4. Slide the adjuster shoe (C, **Figure 19**) off of the shoe plate.
5. Remove the upper locknut and shoe plate.

Inspection

1. Clean all parts in solvent and dry thoroughly.
2. Replace the adjuster shoe (C, **Figure 19**) if severely worn or damaged.
3. Replace the shoe plate if bent or otherwise damaged.
4. Replace the locknut(s) and adjuster screw if thread damage is apparent.

Installation

Refer to **Figure 18**.

1. Install the shoe plate over the top of the adjuster screw.
2. Place the spacer over the top of the adjuster screw and rest it on top of the shoe plate.
3. Thread the upper primary chain adjuster locknut onto the top of the adjuster screw. Tighten the upper locknut to the torque specification in **Table 2**.
4. Slide the open side of the adjuster shoe over the shoe plate (**Figure 18**) until the upper locknut is positioned against the closed side of the shoe.

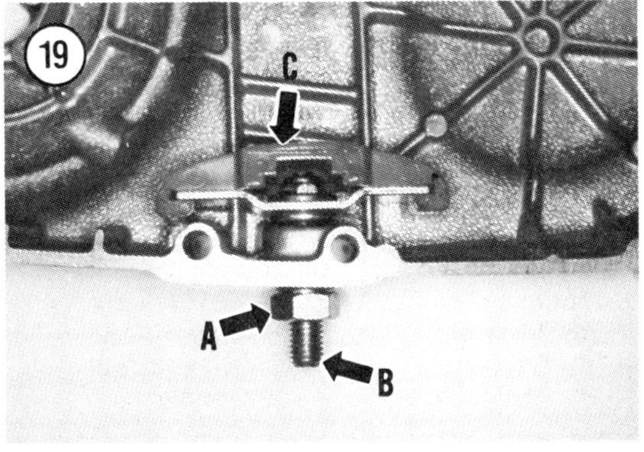

5. Place the adjuster assembly into the primary cover so that the closed side of the adjuster shoe faces toward the primary cover (C, **Figure 19**).
6. Thread the adjuster screw (B, **Figure 19**) into the boss at the bottom of the primary cover.
7. Thread the lower locknut (C, **Figure 19**) onto the adjuster screw.
8. Install the primary cover as described in this chapter.
9. Adjust the primary chain as described in Chapter Three.

PRIMARY DRIVE/CLUTCH

Refer to **Figure 20** when servicing the clutch.

5

Preliminary Steps

Complete disassembly of the clutch will require the use of the Harley-Davidson Spring Compression Tool (part No. HD-38515) or equivalent; see **Figure 21**. If you do not have access to the compression tool, you can remove the clutch intact from the bike and then take it to a Harley-Davidson dealer or service shop for disassembly and service. Do not attempt to disassemble the clutch without the special tool. Observe the *WARNING* in the following procedures.

Clutch/Primary Chain/Engine Sprocket Removal (Clutch is Not Disassembled)

This procedure describes removal of the clutch, primary chain and engine sprocket. If you wish to remove and then disassemble the clutch, perform this procedure and then perform *Clutch Disassembly*. If you wish to disassemble the clutch while it is installed on the bike, refer to *Clutch Disassembly on Bike* in this chapter.

1. Shift the transmission into 5th gear.
2. Disconnect the negative battery cable.
3. Remove the primary cover as described in this chapter.
4. Install the Harley-Davidson sprocket locking link (part No. HD-38362) or equivalent between the engine sprocket and clutch shell as shown in **Figure 22**.

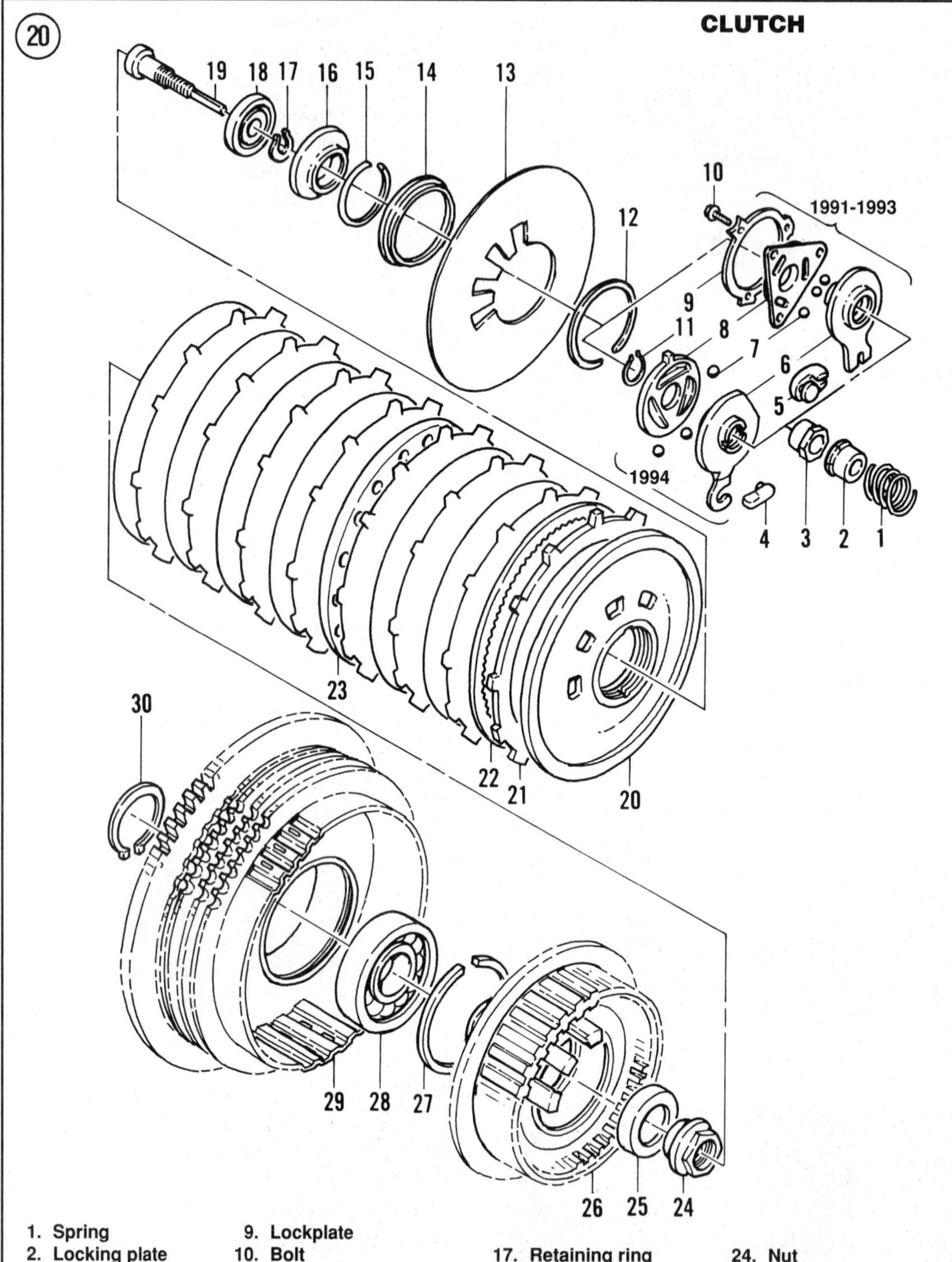

1. Spring
2. Locking plate
3. Well nut
4. Coupling
5. Coupling
6. Outer ramp
7. Balls (3)
8. Inner ramp
9. Lockplate
10. Bolt
11. Circlip
12. Snap ring
13. Diaphragm spring
14. Spring seat
15. Retaining ring
16. Release plate
17. Retaining ring
18. Bearing
19. Adjusting screw
20. Pressure plate
21. Friction plate
22. Steel plates
23. Spring plate
24. Nut
25. Washer
26. Clutch hub
27. Retaining ring
28. Bearing
29. Clutch shell/ring gear
30. Retaining ring

5. Loosen and remove the engine sprocket nut (A, **Figure 23**).

6. Loosen the engine sprocket by pulling it outward (do not remove it). If the engine sprocket is tight, break it loose with a puller and 2 bolts installed on the sprocket face (B, **Figure 23**).

7. Remove the retaining ring (**Figure 24**) holding the release plate/adjusting screw in position.

8. Remove the release plate/adjusting screw assembly (**Figure 25**).

NOTE
*The clutch nut (**Figure 26**) has left-hand threads.*

9. Turn the clutch nut (**Figure 26**) clockwise to loosen it. Then remove the clutch nut and washer (**Figure 27**).

10. Remove the locking link (**Figure 22**) installed during Step 4.

11. Remove the engine sprocket, primary chain and clutch as an assembly (**Figure 28**).

Clutch Disassembly on Bike

This procedure describes disassembly of the clutch (clutch plate removal) while it is mounted on the bike. Engine sprocket and primary chain removal is not required. Read this procedure completely through before starting disassembly.

1. Disconnect the negative battery cable.
2. Remove the primary cover as described in this chapter.

WARNING
*The Harley-Davidson Spring Compressing Tool (part No. HD-38515 [**Figure 21**]) or equivalent must be used when disassembling the clutch in the following steps. The clutch diaphragm spring is under considerable pressure and will fly off, possibly causing severe personal injury, if the tool is not used.*

3. To remove the diaphragm spring snap ring, perform the following:
   a. Thread the spring compression tool forcing screw onto the clutch adjusting screw as shown in **Figure 29**.
   b. Position the spring compression tool (**Figure 30**) against the diaphragm spring and thread the tool handle (**Figure 31**) onto the end of the forcing screw.

CAUTION
Turn the compression tool handle only the amount required to compress the diaphragm spring and remove the snap ring in substep c. Excessive compression of the diaphragm spring may damage the clutch pressure plate.

28

29

30

27

31

c. Hold the compression tool forcing screw with a wrench and turn the tool handle clockwise to compress the diaphragm spring.

d. Remove the snap ring (**Figure 32**) and spring seat (**Figure 33**) from the groove in the clutch hub.

e. Remove the diaphragm spring, pressure plate, clutch adjusting screw and spring compressing tool as an assembly; see **Figure 34**.

NOTE
Do not loosen the spring compressing tool to remove the diaphragm spring or pressure plate unless these parts require close inspection or replacement. Loosening and removing the compressing tool will require repositioning of the diaphragm spring during reassembly. This step will not be required as long as the compressing tool is not removed from these parts.

4. Remove the friction and steel clutch plates (**Figure 35**) (and the spring plate) from the clutch assembly in order shown in **Figure 20**. Note the spring plate installed between the 4th and 5th friction plates (**Figure 36**).

NOTE
Further removal steps are not required unless it is necessary to separate the clutch hub and shell assembly. Remove these parts as described under ***Clutch Removal (Clutch Not Disassembled)*** *in this chapter.*

Clutch Inspection

Refer to **Figure 20** when performing the following.

1. Clean all parts (except friction plates and bearing) in a non-oil based solvent and thoroughly dry with compressed air. Place all cleaned parts on lint-free paper towels.
2. Check each steel plate (A, **Figure 37**) for visual damage such as cracks or wear grooves. Then place each plate on a surface plate and check for warpage with a feeler gauge. Replace the steel plates as a set if any one plate is warped more than 0.006 in. (0.15 mm).

NOTE
A piece of plate glass can be used as a surface plate when measuring warpage in Step 2.

3. Inspect the friction plates (B, **Figure 37**) for worn or grooved lining surfaces; replace the friction plates as a set if any one plate is damaged. If the friction plates do not show visual wear or damage, wipe each plate thoroughly with a lint-free cloth to remove as much oil from the plates as possible. Then stack each of the 8 friction plates on top of each other and measure the thickness of the assembly with a vernier caliper or micrometer. Replace the friction plates as an assembly if the combined thickness of the 8 plates is less than 0.661 in. (16.79 mm).
4. Check the spring plate (C, **Figure 37**) for cracks or damage. Check for loose or damaged rivets. Replace the spring plate if necessary.
5. Check the diaphragm spring for cracks or damage. Check also for bent or damaged tabs. Replace the diaphragm spring if necessary.
6. A ball bearing is pressed into the clutch shell and the clutch hub is pressed into the bearing. Hold the clutch hub and rotate the clutch shell by hand. The shell should turn smoothly with no sign of roughness or tightness. If the clutch shell binds or turns roughly, the bearing is damaged and must be replaced. Refer to Step 10.
7. The steel clutch plate inner teeth mesh with the clutch hub splines. Check the splines for cracks or galling. They must be smooth for chatter-free clutch operation. If the clutch hub splines are damaged, the clutch hub must be replaced; refer to Step 10.
8. The friction plates (B, **Figure 37**) have tabs that slide in the clutch shell grooves. Inspect the shell grooves for cracks or wear grooves. The grooves must be smooth for chatter-free clutch operation. If the clutch shell grooves are damaged or worn severely, the clutch shell must be replaced; refer to Step 10.
9. Check the primary chain sprocket and the starter ring gear on the clutch shell for cracks, deep scoring, excessive wear or heat discoloration. If either the

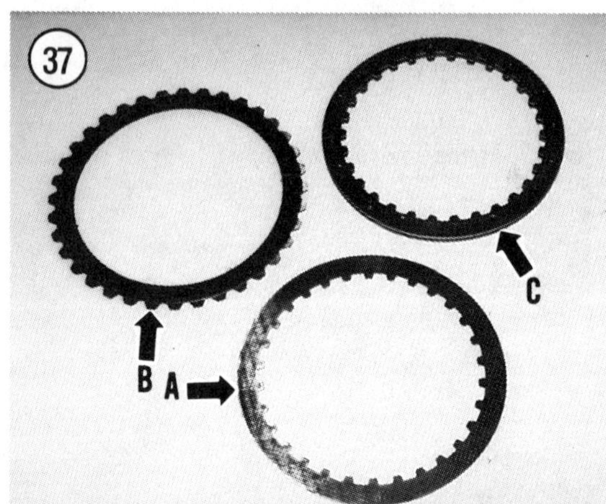

sprocket or ring gear is severely worn or damaged, replace the clutch shell; refer to Step 10. If the sprocket is worn, also check the primary chain and the engine sprocket as described in this chapter.

10. If the clutch hub, shell or bearing require replacement, refer to *Clutch Hub and Shell Disassembly/Reassembly* in this chapter.

Primary Chain

Replace the primary chain if severely worn or damaged. Do not attempt to repair the chain, as expensive engine damage will result if the chain breaks. If the primary chain is worn or damaged, check the engine sprocket and clutch shell sprocket for wear or damage. Replace parts as required.

Clutch Hub and Shell Disassembly/Reassembly

The clutch hub and shell should not be separated unless replacement of the hub, shell or bearing is required. Disassembly of the hub and shell will damage the ball bearing; bearing replacement will be required during reassembly. A press is required for this procedure.

Read this procedure completely through before starting disassembly. Refer to **Figure 20** when performing this procedure.

1. Remove the clutch plates from the clutch hub and shell assembly, if they have not been previously removed. Refer to *Clutch Disassembly on Bike*.
2. Remove the circlip from the clutch hub groove with circlip pliers (**Figure 38**).
3. Support the clutch hub and shell in a press (**Figure 39**) and press the clutch hub out of the bearing. See **Figure 40**. Remove the clutch shell from the press.
4. Locate the circlip (**Figure 41**) securing the bearing in the clutch shell. Carefully remove the circlip from the clutch shell groove.

NOTE
When removing the bearing in Step 5, note that the bearing must be removed through the front side of the shell. The clutch shell is manufactured with a shoulder on the rear (primary chain) side.

5. Support the clutch shell in the press and press the bearing out of the shell. Discard the bearing.
6. Discard worn or damaged parts. Clean reusable and new parts (except bearing and circlips) in solvent and dry thoroughly.
7. Place the clutch shell into the press. Then align the bearing with the clutch shell and press bearing into shell until bearing bottoms out against lower shoulder. When pressing the bearing into the clutch shell, press only on the outer bearing race. Installing the bearing by pressing on its inner race will damage the bearing. Refer to *Ball Bearing Replacement* in Chapter One for additional information.
8. Install a new bearing circlip into the clutch shell groove (**Figure 41**). Make sure the circlip seats in the groove completely.
9. Press the clutch hub into the clutch shell as follows:
   a. Place the clutch shell in a press. Support the inner bearing race with a sleeve as shown in **Figure 42**.

CAUTION
Failure to support the inner bearing race properly will cause bearing and clutch shell damage. Refer to ***Figure 42***

5

to make sure the inner bearing race is supported properly.

b. Align the clutch hub with the bearing and press the clutch hub into the bearing until the clutch hub shoulder seats against the bearing.
c. Using circlip pliers, install a new clutch hub circlip (**Figure 38**). Make sure the circlip seats in the clutch hub groove completely.

10. After completing assembly, hold the clutch hub and rotate the clutch shell by hand. The shell should turn smoothly with no roughness or binding. If the clutch shell binds or turns roughly, the bearing may have been damaged during reassembly.

Clutch Assembly

This section describes clutch assembly. After assembly, the clutch will be installed back onto the bike. If you did not disassemble the clutch assembly, refer to *Clutch Installation*.

Refer to **Figure 20** when performing this procedure.

1. Soak all of the clutch plates in clean transmission oil for approximately 5 minutes before installing them.

NOTE
Before installing the clutch plates, count the number of each plate. You should have 8 friction plates, 6 steel plates and 1 spring plate.

2. Align the tabs on a friction plate with the clutch shell grooves and install the plate. Then align the inner teeth on a steel plate with the clutch hub grooves and install the plate. Repeat until all of the clutch plates have been installed. The spring plate (**Figure 36**) should be installed between the 4th and 5th friction plate. The last plate installed should be a friction plate.

NOTE
During clutch removal, you had the option of whether or not to remove the spring compressing tool from the diaphragm spring and pressure plate after removing the pressure plate assembly. If the spring compressing tool was not removed from the diaphragm spring and pressure plate, proceed to Step 4. If the spring compressing tool was removed and the diaphragm spring was separated from the pressure plate, continue with Step 3.

3. Assemble the pressure plate and diaphragm spring as follows:
a. Install the adjusting screw assembly (release plate, circlip, bearing and adjusting screw) into the pressure plate. Install the release plate by aligning its tabs with the slots in the pressure plate. Secure the release plate by installing the retaining ring into the pressure plate groove. Make sure the retaining ring seats in the groove completely.
b. The diaphragm spring is not flat, but instead it has a convex side (side that curves outward). Install the diaphragm spring onto the pressure plate so that the convex side faces *away* from the pressure plate—the convex side must face out.
c. Install the spring seat with its flat, larger outer diameter side facing toward the diaphragm spring.

WARNING
The following steps describe installation of the diaphragm spring circlip. Because of the force required to compress the diaphragm spring when installing the circlip, the Harley-Davidson Spring Compressing Tool (part No. HD-

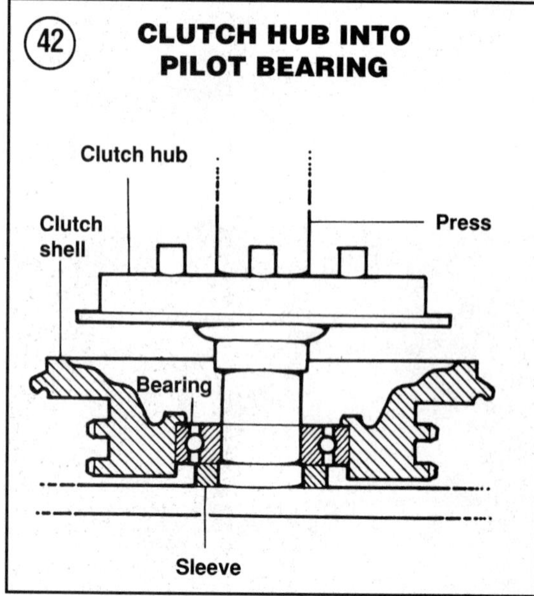

*38515 [**Figure 21**]) or equivalent must be used. Severe personal injury from the diaphragm spring flying out could occur if the special tool is not used.*

4. To install the diaphragm spring snap ring, perform the following:
   a. Thread the spring compression tool forcing screw onto the clutch adjusting screw.
   b. Position the spring compression tool against the diaphragm spring and thread the tool handle onto the end of the forcing screw. Do not apply pressure against the diaphragm spring at this time.
   c. Align the square holes in the pressure plate and diaphragm spring with the prongs on the face of the clutch hub. Then place the spring seat, snap ring, diaphragm spring, pressure plate, adjusting screw assembly and compressing tool onto the clutch hub (**Figure 34**).

CAUTION

Turn the compression tool handle only the amount required to compress the diaphragm spring and install the snap ring in substep e. Excessive compression of the diaphragm spring may damage the clutch pressure plate.

   d. Hold the compression tool forcing screw with a wrench and turn the tool handle clockwise to compress the diaphragm spring.
   e. Install the spring seat and snap ring into the groove in the clutch hub prongs.
   f. After making sure the circlip is seated completely in the clutch hub groove, slowly turn the compressing tool handle counterclockwise while checking that the clutch spring seat lip seats inside the circlip. After all tension has been removed from the compressing tool, remove it from the release plate.

5. Remove the release plate retaining ring. Then remove the adjusting screw assembly (release plate, retaining ring, bearing and adjusting screw).

5

43

44

Clutch Installation

1. Assemble the clutch assembly as described in the previous section.
2. The engine sprocket, primary chain and clutch are installed as an assembly. Assemble the engine sprocket, clutch and primary chain as shown in **Figure 43**.

CAUTION

The rotor is mounted on the engine sprocket. Carefully inspect the inside of the rotor for small bolts, washers or other metal "debris" that may have been picked up by the magnets. These small metal bits can cause severe damage to the alternator stator assembly.

3. Lift the primary drive assembly as a unit and slide the engine sprocket and clutch into the primary chaincase. See **Figure 44**.
4. Install the Harley-Davidson sprocket locking link (part No. HD-38362) or equivalent between the engine sprocket and clutch shell as shown in **Figure 45**.

CAUTION

The engine sprocket is tightened to a high torque specification. Make sure you hold the sprocket securely when tightening the nut in Step 5.

5. Apply 2-3 drops of Loctite 262 (red) to the engine sprocket nut threads and thread the nut (**Figure 46**) onto the sprocket shaft. Tighten the engine sprocket nut to the torque specification in **Table 2**.
6. Install the clutch nut washer onto the mainshaft so that the word "OUT" on the washer faces outward.

NOTE
The clutch nut uses left-hand threads.

7. Apply 2-3 drops of Loctite 262 (red) to the clutch nut threads and thread the nut onto the mainshaft by turning the nut *counterclockwise*. Using a torque wrench, tighten the clutch nut (**Figure 47**) to the torque specification in **Table 2**.
8. Remove the sprocket locking link (**Figure 45**).
9. Install the adjusting screw assembly (**Figure 48**) by aligning the 2 tabs on the release plate perimeter with the 2 recesses in the pressure plate.
10. Install a new retaining ring (**Figure 49**).
11. Install the primary cover as described in this chapter.
12. Adjust the primary chain as described in Chapter Three.
13. Refill the primary chain housing with the correct type and quantity oil as described in Chapter Three.
14. Reconnect the negative battery cable.

CLUTCH CABLE

Replacement (1991-1993)

Refer to **Figure 50**.
1. Remove the primary cover as described in this chapter.

2. Pry the lockplate tabs (A, **Figure 51**) away from the mounting screws and remove the lockplate and screws.
3. Remove the clutch mechanism from the cover and disconnect the cable (B, **Figure 51**) from the ramp and coupling. Remove the clutch mechanism (C, **Figure 51**).
4. Turn the clutch cable (**Figure 52**) counterclockwise and remove it from the primary cover.
5. Remove the O-ring (**Figure 53**) from the lower cable end fitting.
6. At the clutch lever, remove the pivot pin circlip and remove the pivot pin (2, **Figure 54**).
7. Slide the clutch lever out of its bracket (**Figure 54**).
8. Remove the clutch cable and disconnect the clutch cable from the lever (**Figure 54**).

(50)

CLUTCH RELEASE MECHANISM (1991-1993)

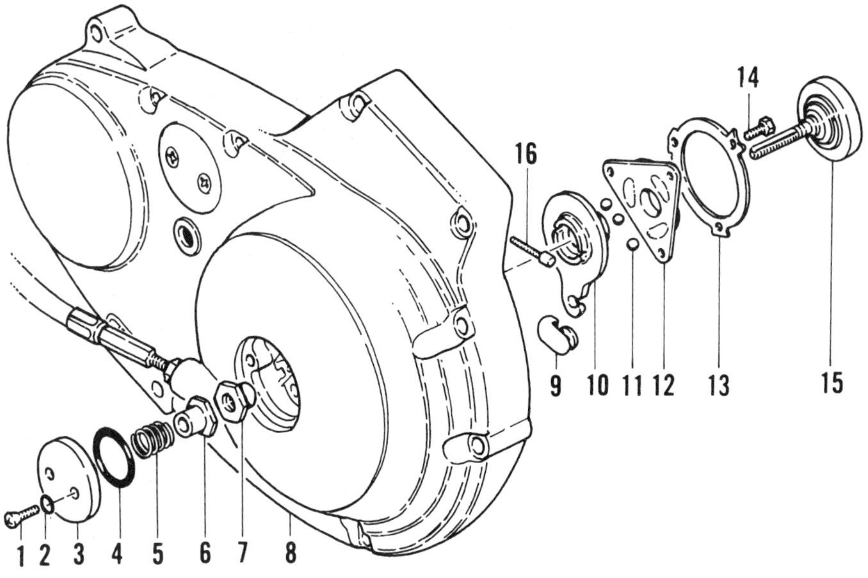

1 2 3 4 5 6 7 8 9 10 11 12 13 14 15 16

1. Screw
2. O-ring
3. Clutch inspection cover
4. O-ring
5. Spring
6. Lockplate
7. Nut
8. Primary cover
9. Cable coupling
10. Outer ramp
11. Ball (3)
12. Inner ramp
13. Lockplate
14. Bolt
15. Clutch adjusting screw assembly
16. Clutch cable

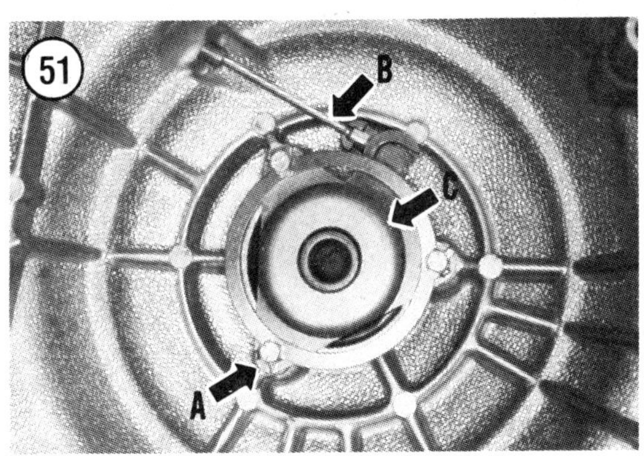

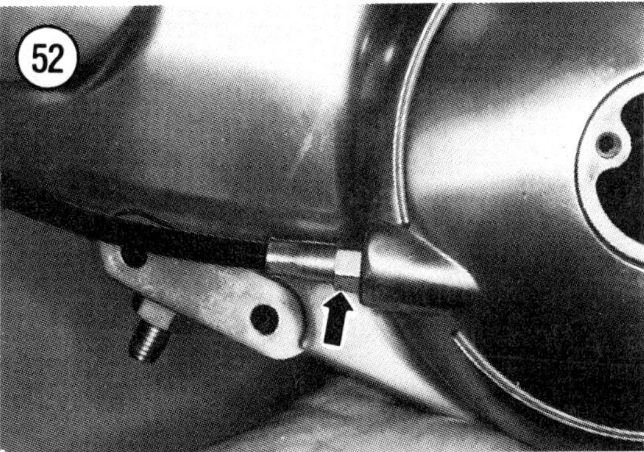

9. Remove the screw and anti-rattle spring from the bottom of the clutch lever (**Figure 54**).
10. Slide the clutch cable through the guide clip (**Figure 55**) and remove the clutch cable.
11. Slide the O-ring over the lower cable end fitting (**Figure 53**) and insert the cable into the primary cover. Turn the cable (**Figure 52**) clockwise and tighten it securely.
12. Connect the lower end of the clutch cable to the cable coupling. Connect the cable coupling to the outer ramp (**Figure 50**).

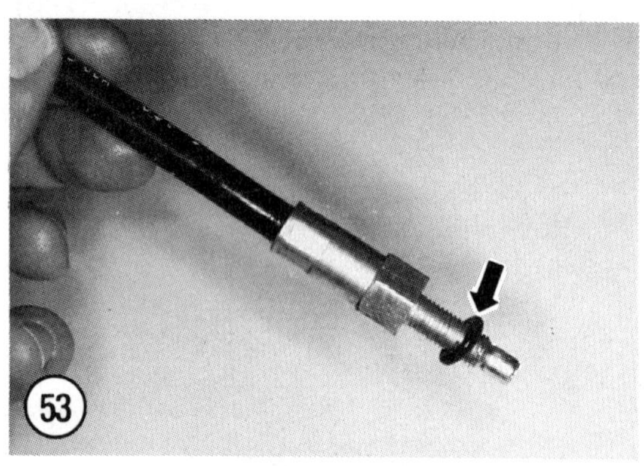

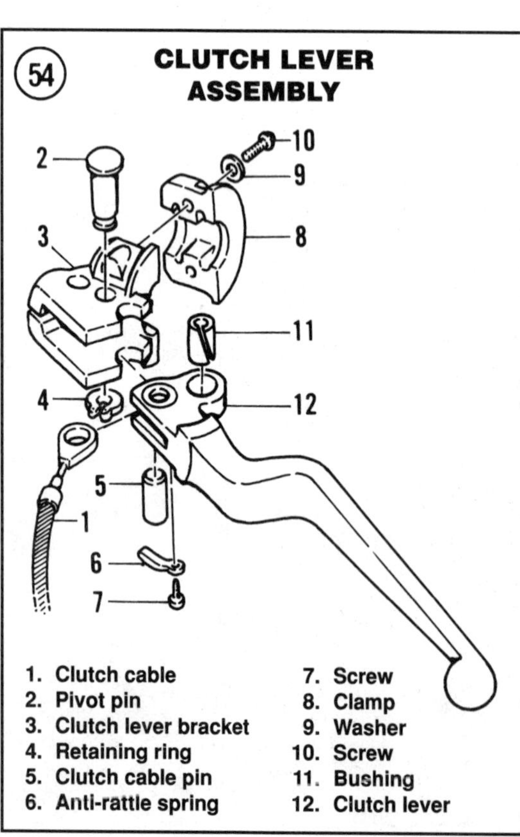

1. Clutch cable
2. Pivot pin
3. Clutch lever bracket
4. Retaining ring
5. Clutch cable pin
6. Anti-rattle spring
7. Screw
8. Clamp
9. Washer
10. Screw
11. Bushing
12. Clutch lever

13. Install the clutch release mechanism and lock-plate onto the primary cover with the mounting screws. Tighten the screws securely. Bend the lock-plate tabs over the screw heads to lock them.
14. Install the primary cover as described in this chapter.
15. Route the clutch cable as shown in **Figure 56**.

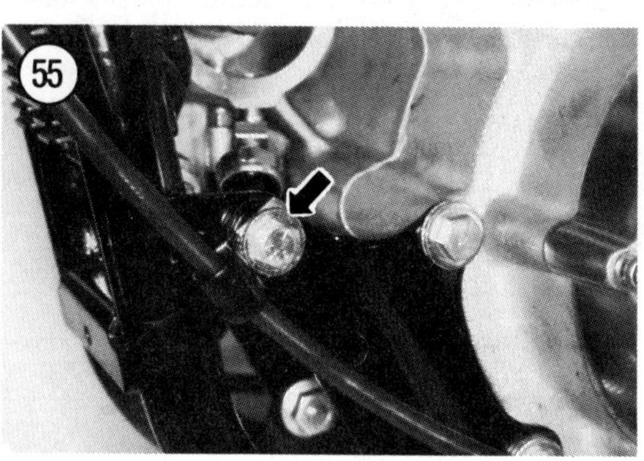

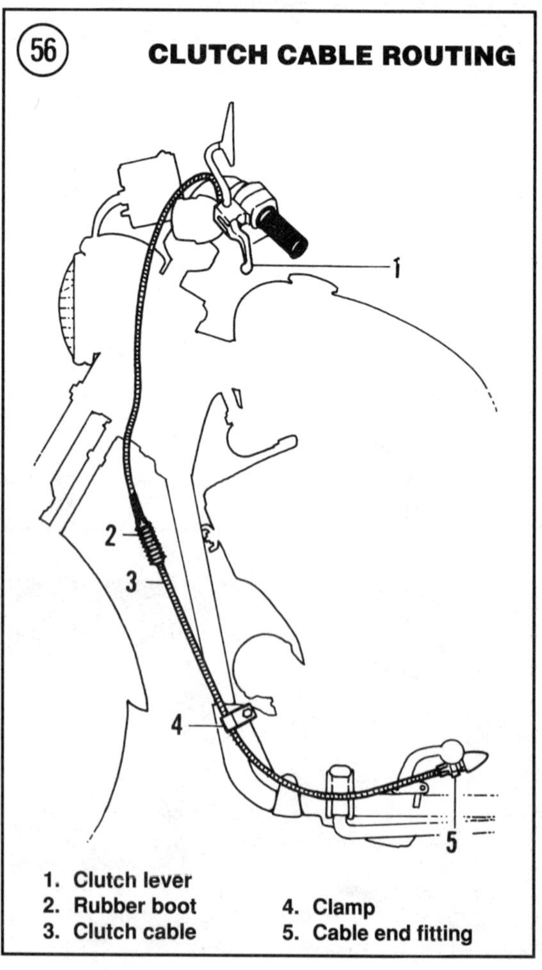

1. Clutch lever
2. Rubber boot
3. Clutch cable
4. Clamp
5. Cable end fitting

16. Install the anti-rattle spring and screw onto the clutch lever (**Figure 54**).

17. Connect the clutch cable to the clutch lever and secure it with the clutch cable pin (**Figure 54**).

18. Install the clutch lever into the bracket.

19. Wipe the pivot pin shoulder with a small mount of Loctite Anti-seize. Then install the pivot pin through the clutch bracket and lever and secure it with the circlip. See **Figure 54**.

20. Adjust the clutch as described in Chapter Three.

Replacement (1994)

Refer to **Figure 57**.

1. Remove the clutch inspection cover screws and remove the cover.

NOTE
*When removing the clutch inspection cover, work carefully to avoid removing or damaging the quad ring in the primary cover; see **Figure 57**.*

2. Remove the spring and lockplate.
3. Turn the clutch adjusting screw clockwise and release the ramp and coupling mechanism.
4. Turn the clutch adjusting screw clockwise to move the ramp assembly forward. Then unscrew the nut from the end of the adjusting screw and remove it.
5. Pivot the hook on the ramp to the rear of the cable end coupling. Then disconnect and remove the clutch cable from the coupling slot.
6. Turn the clutch cable (**Figure 52**) counterclockwise and remove it from the primary cover.
7. Remove the O-ring (**Figure 53**) from the lower cable end fitting.

5

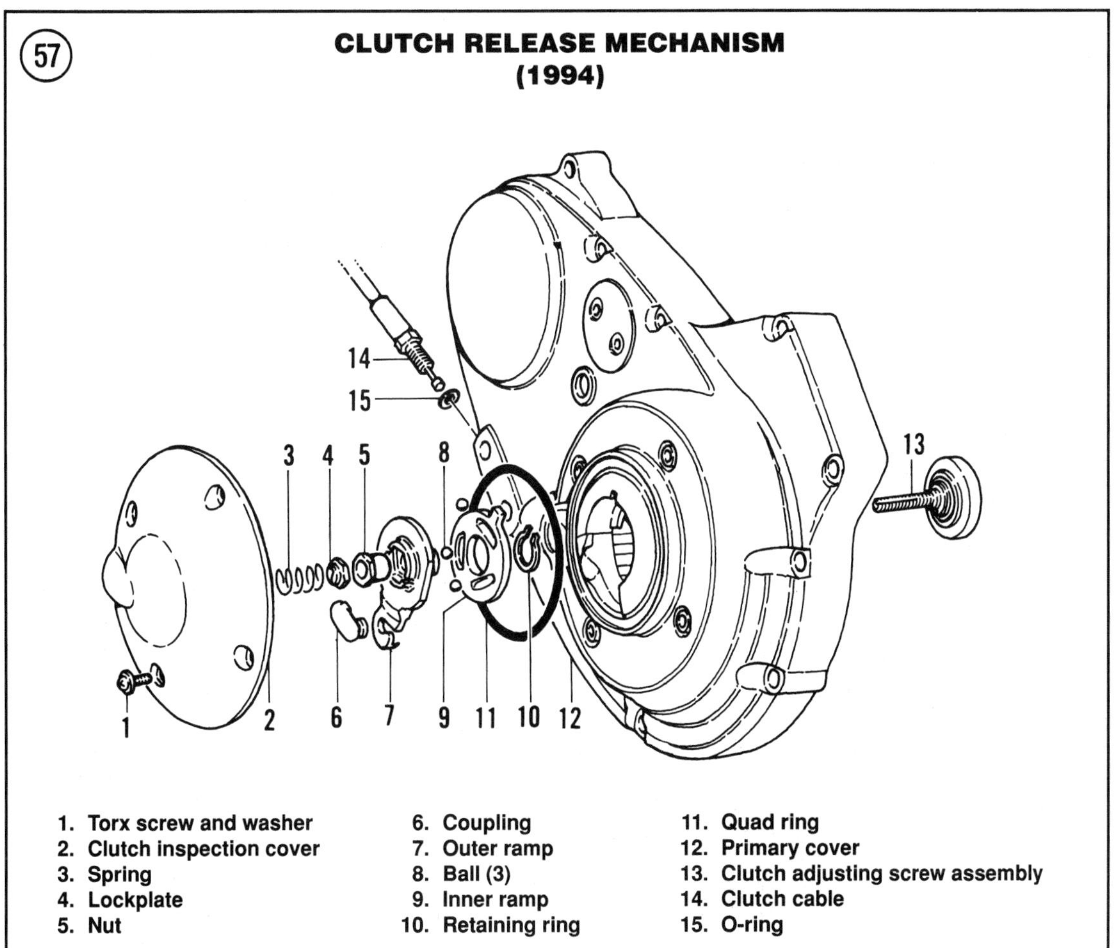

1. Torx screw and washer
2. Clutch inspection cover
3. Spring
4. Lockplate
5. Nut
6. Coupling
7. Outer ramp
8. Ball (3)
9. Inner ramp
10. Retaining ring
11. Quad ring
12. Primary cover
13. Clutch adjusting screw assembly
14. Clutch cable
15. O-ring

8. At the clutch lever, remove the pivot pin circlip and remove the pivot pin (2, **Figure 54**).
9. Slide the clutch lever out of its bracket (**Figure 54**).
10. Remove the clutch cable and disconnect the clutch cable from the lever (**Figure 54**).
11. Remove the screw and anti-rattle spring from the bottom of the clutch lever (**Figure 54**).
12. Slide the clutch cable through the guide clip (**Figure 55**) and remove the clutch cable.
13. Slide the O-ring over the lower cable end fitting (**Figure 53**) and insert the cable into the primary cover. Turn the cable (**Figure 52**) clockwise and tighten it securely.
14. Fit the coupling over the clutch cable with the rounded side facing outward and the ramp connector button facing inward. With the retaining side of the ramp facing inward, install the ramp hook around the coupling button. Then rotate the assembly counterclockwise until the tang on the inner ramp fits into the primary cover slot.
15. Thread the nut onto the clutch adjusting screw until the slot in the end of the screw is accessible with a screwdriver. Then align and install the hex portion on the nut into the outer ramp recess. Turn the clutch adjusting screw counterclockwise until resistance is felt, then back off 1/4 turn.
16. Adjust the clutch as described in Chapter Three. The spring and lockplate shown in **Figure 57** will be installed during the clutch adjustment procedure.
17. Route the clutch cable as shown in **Figure 56**.
18. Install the anti-rattle spring and screw onto the clutch lever (**Figure 54**).
19. Connect the clutch cable to the clutch lever and secure it with the clutch cable pin (**Figure 54**).
20. Install the clutch lever into the bracket.
21. Wipe the pivot pin shoulder with a small amount of Loctite Anti-seize. Then install the pivot pin through the clutch bracket and lever and secure it with the circlip. See **Figure 54**.
22. Adjust the clutch as described in Chapter Three.

Table 1 CLUTCH SPECIFICATIONS

	New in. (mm)	Wear limit in. (mm)
Friction plates		
Thickness		
Individual plates	0.0835-0.0897 (2.121-2.277)	— —
Friction plate pack*	—	0.661 (16.79)
Steel plate thickness	0.0609-0.0649 (1.547-1.647)	—
Friction and steel plates warpage		0.0059 (0.149)

* See text for measurement procedure.

Table 2 CLUTCH TIGHTENING TORQUES

	ft.-lb.	N•m
Drain plug	14-21	19-28.5
Clutch nut	70-80	95-108.5
Engine sprocket nut	150-165	203-224
Footpeg mounting bolts	16-28	22-38
Chain tensioner stud nut	20-25	27.1-34
Primary chain adjuster locknuts		
Upper	10-12	14-16
Lower*	20-25	27-34

(continued)

Table 2 CLUTCH TIGHTENING TORQUES (continued)

	in.-lb.	N•m
Inspection cover screws	40-60	4.5-6.8
Primary cover fasteners	80-110	9-12.4
Oil level plug	90-110	10.2-12.4
Clutch release mechanism screws	22-40	2.5-3.4
Shift lever pinch bolt	80-110	9-12.4

* This adjuster locknut is mounted underneath the primary cover.

CHAPTER SIX

TRANSMISSION

This chapter describes service procedures for the 5-speed transmission, shifter pawl, main drive gear and transmission bearings. A hydraulic press will be required to service many of the transmission components described in this chapter. Do not attempt to disassemble or remove parts without a press; otherwise, severe damage will result.

All repairs related to the primary drive and clutch are covered in Chapter Five.

Transmission gear ratios are listed in **Table 1**. **Table 2** lists transmission tightening torques. **Table 1** and **Table 2** are at the end of the chapter.

TRANSMISSION

The transmission can be removed and installed through an access door in the left-hand side of the crankcase. Transmission removal does not require engine removal or crankcase disassembly.

Removal

Refer to **Figure 1** when performing this procedure.

1. Remove the exhaust system as described in Chapter Seven.
2. Drain the transmission oil as described in Chapter Three.
3. Remove the drive sprocket as described in Chapter Nine.
4. Remove the engine sprocket, clutch and primary drive chain as described in Chapter Five.
5. Shift the transmission into 1st gear.
6. Disconnect the detent lever spring (**Figure 2**) from the post groove.
7. Remove the retaining ring (A, **Figure 3**) from the groove in the end of the shift drum. Discard the retaining ring as a new one must be installed during reassembly.
8. Slide the detent plate (B, **Figure 3**) off of the shift drum pins.
9. Loosen the 2 shifter shaft locknuts (A, **Figure 4**). Then remove the locknuts and washers.
10. Remove the shifter shaft assembly (B, **Figure 4**) from the crankcase.
11. Loosen the countershaft retainer screw (**Figure 5**). Then remove the screw and countershaft retainer collar (**Figure 6**).
12. Loosen the transmission access door mounting bolts (**Figure 7**). Then remove the bolts and washers.
13. Remove the access cover with the transmission and shift mechanism attached. See **Figure 8**.

(1)

SHIFT ASSEMBLY

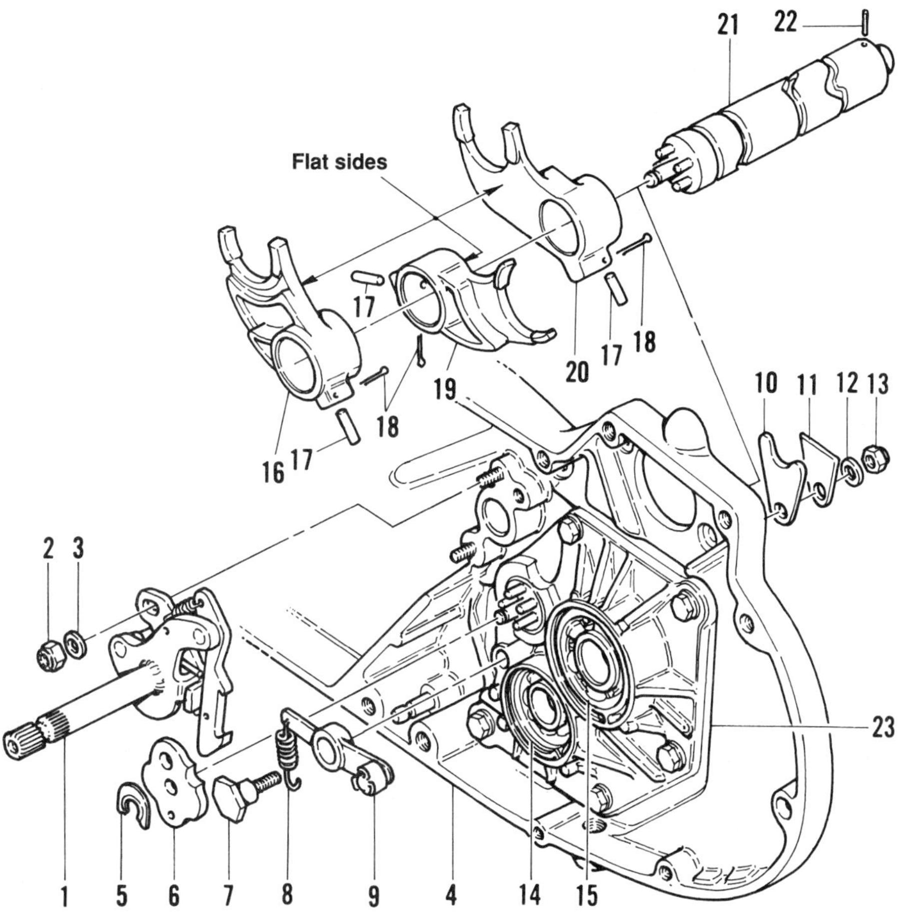

Flat sides

1. Shifter shaft assembly
2. Locknut
3. Washer
4. Right-hand crankcase
5. Detent plate retaining ring
6. Detent plate
7. Detent screw
8. Spring
9. Detent arm
10. Shifter drum locating plate
11. Reinforcing plate
12. Washer
13. Locknut
14. Countershaft bearing
15. Mainshaft bearing
16. 4th gear shift fork
17. Shift fork pins
18. Cotter pins
19. 1st and 2nd gear shift fork
20. 3rd and 5th gear shift fork
21. Shift drum
22. Pin (neutral indicator)
23. Access door

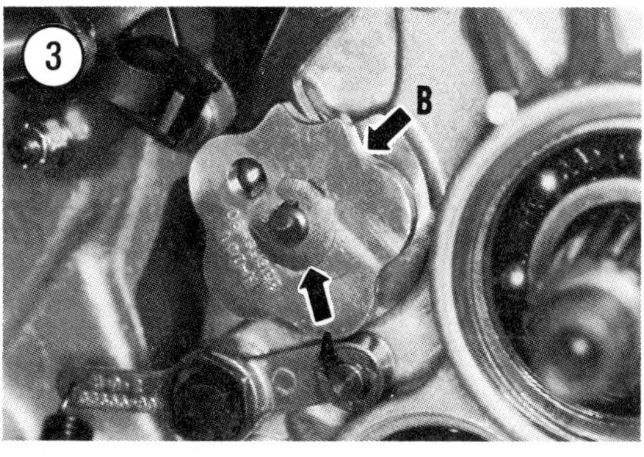

14. Remove the 2 dowel pins (**Figure 9**).
15. If further disassembly is necessary, perform the following as described in this chapter:
   a. *Shift Forks and Shift Drum Assembly.*
   b. *Transmission Disassembly.*
16. If necessary, remove the main drive gear as described under *Main Drive Gear Removal* in this chapter.

Inspection

1. Clean the transmission cavity (**Figure 9**) with cleaning solvent and dry with compressed air.
2. Inspect the access door bearings as described in this chapter.
3. Remove all thread sealant residue from the drive sprocket nut and main drive gear threads.

Transmission Installation

A No. 32 (0.116 in.) drill bit will be required when installing the transmission assembly.

Refer to **Figure 1** when installing the transmission.

1. If the shift forks, shift drum and transmission were removed and disassembled, assemble them onto the access door as described under the following sections described in this chapter:
   a. *Transmission Assembly* in this chapter.
   b. *Shift Forks and Shift Drum Assembly.*
2. If removed, install the main drive gear as described under *Main Drive Gear Installation* in this chapter.
3. Lubricate the transmission gears and shifter assembly with clean transmission oil prior to installation.
4. Install the 2 dowel pins (**Figure 9**), if removed.

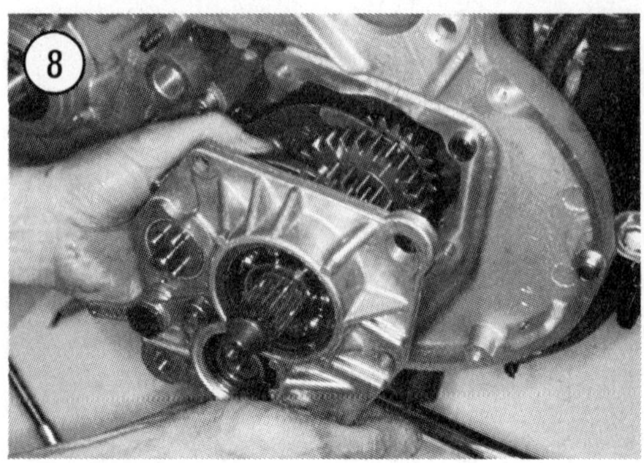

5. Align the transmission assembly with the access door opening and install the transmission/shifter assembly (**Figure 8**) while noting the following:

a. The mainshaft (**Figure 10**) should enter 5th gear (**Figure 11**).

b. The drum shifter shaft and countershaft should enter their respective crankcase bearings.

6. Apply Loctite 242 (blue) to the transmission access door mounting bolts prior to installation. Install the bolts (**Figure 7**) and washers and tighten to the torque specification in **Table 2**.

7. Install the countershaft retainer collar (**Figure 5**) as follows:

a. The retainer collar has one flat side and one beveled side.

b. Install the retainer collar, with its beveled side facing outward, onto the countershaft (**Figure 6**).

c. Shift the transmission into 1st gear.

d. Apply Loctite 242 (blue) onto the retainer collar Torx screw prior to installation. Install the countershaft retainer collar screw and tighten to the torque specification listed in **Table 2**.

8. Install the shifter shaft assembly by first lifting the shift pawl (**Figure 12**) over the shift drum studs and then aligning the shifter shaft mounting holes with the 2 crankcase studs (A, **Figure 4**). Install the 2 washers and nuts (A, **Figure 4**); tighten the nuts hand-tight only.

9. Connect the detent arm spring onto the post groove as shown in **Figure 2**.

10. Make sure the shift pawl spring is connected to the pawl (**Figure 13**).

11. Install the detent plate onto the shift drum, aligning the holes in the plate with the pins in the drum (**Figure 14**).

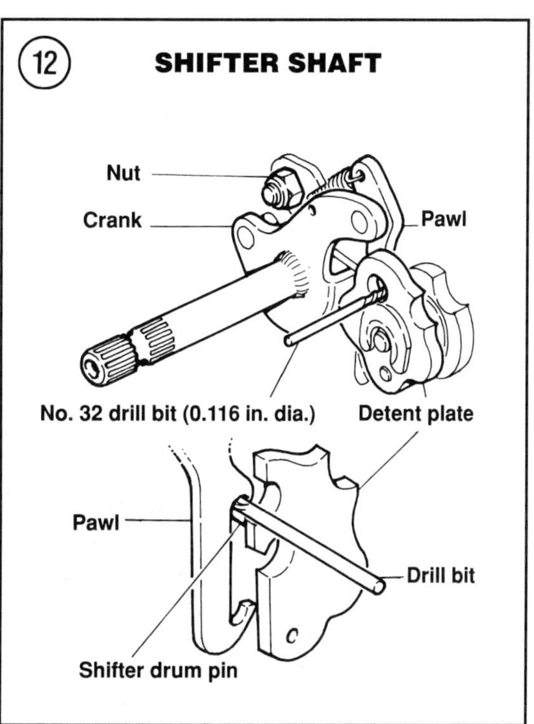

6

12. Install a *new* detent plate retaining ring (**Figure 15**) into the groove in the end of the shift drum. Use the TRUARC installation tool (No. PR-0310) or equivalent to install the new retaining ring. Make sure the retaining ring is correctly seated in the shift drum groove.

13. Adjust the shifter pawl as follows:
   a. Shift the transmission into 3rd gear.
   b. Install a No. 32 drill bit (0.116 in.) through the hole in the detent plate and between the shift pawl and drive pin (at the end of the shift drum shaft) as shown in **Figure 12** and A, **Figure 16**.
   c. Press down on the top of the shift shaft crank (**Figure 12**) to remove all clearance between the drill bit and shift pawl.

NOTE

Pressing down on the shift shaft crank helps to algin the shift pawl with the shift drum pins. However, do not push excessively as this may cause the shift drum to rotate.

   d. While applying pressure to the shift shaft crank, tighten the *lower* shifter shaft locknut (B, **Figure 16**) to 90-110 in. (10.2-12.4 N•m).
   e. Tighten the *upper* shifter shaft nut (C, **Figure 16**) to 90-110 in.-lb. (10.2-12.4 N•m).
   f. Remove the No. 32 drill bit.

14. Install the engine sprocket, clutch and primary drive chain as described in Chapter Five.

15. Refill the transmission oil as described in Chapter Three.

16. Install the drive sprocket and the drive chain or drive belt as described in Chapter Eleven.

17. Install the exhaust system as described in Chapter Seven.

18. Start the engine and check for oil leaks.

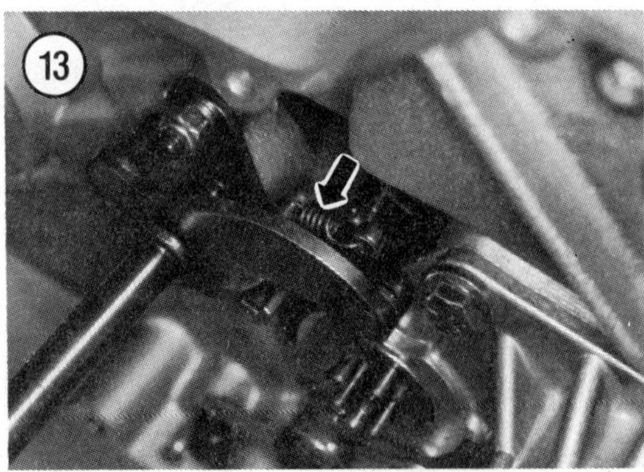

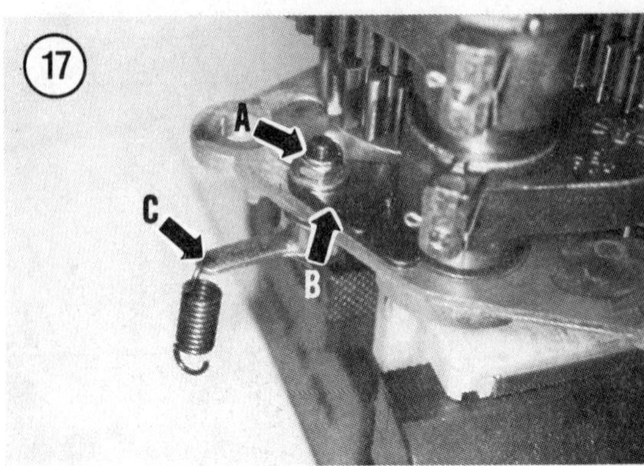

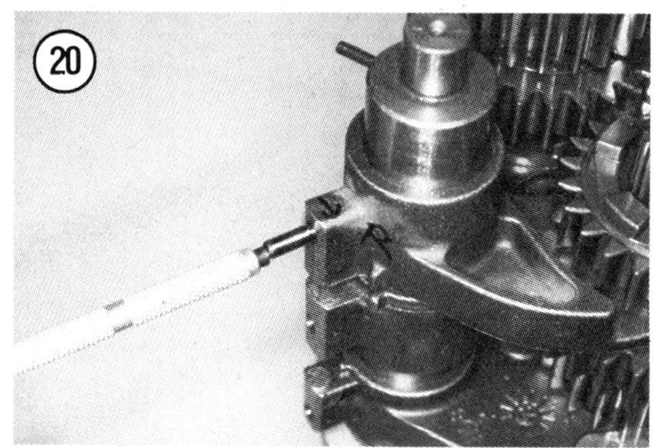

19. Test drive the bike slowly, checking that the transmission shifts properly.

SHIFT FORKS AND SHIFT DRUM

Disassembly

Refer to **Figure 1** when performing this procedure.

1. Remove the transmission assembly as described under *Transmission Removal* in this chapter.
2. Secure the transmission access door in a vise with soft jaws (**Figure 10**). Then remove the following parts:
   a. Detent nut and washer (A, **Figure 17**).
   b. Reinforcing plate (B, **Figure 17**).
   c. Detent screw, arm and spring (C, **Figure 17**).
   d. Shift drum locating plate (**Figure 18**).
3. Remove the cotter pin (**Figure 19**) from each shift fork. Discard the cotter pins.
4. Remove the shift fork pin from each shift fork with a small magnet (**Figure 20**).
5. Slide the shift drum (**Figure 21**) out of the access door and remove it.
6. Remove the 3 shift forks (**Figure 22**).

6

Inspection

1. Clean all of the parts in solvent (except the access door bearings) and dry with compressed air.
2. Inspect each shift fork (**Figure 23**) for severe wear, cracks, bending or other damage. Check that each shift fork slides on the shift drum smoothly (**Figure 24**).
3. Check for any arc-shaped wear or burned marks on the shift forks. This wear pattern indicates that the shift fork has come in contact with the gear. The

fork fingers have become excessively worn and the fork must be replaced.

4. Check the shift drum grooves (A, **Figure 25**) for wear or roughness. If any groove profile shows excessive wear or damage, replace the shift drum.
5. Check the shift drum pins (**Figure 26**) for cracks or severe wear.
6. Check the shift fork pins for cracks or severe wear.
7. Roll the shift drum on a flat surface such as a piece of plate glass and check it for any warpage or damage.
8. Inspect the shifter shaft assembly (**Figure 27**) for the following defects:
   a. Bent shifter shaft (A, **Figure 27**).
   b. Damaged shifter shaft splines (B, **Figure 27**).
   c. Worn or damaged shift pawl (**Figure 28**).
   d. Weak or damaged return springs.
9. Inspect the detent arm assembly (**Figure 29**) for the following defects:
   a. Worn or damaged detent screw (A, **Figure 29**).
   b. Worn or damaged detent arm (B, **Figure 29**).
   c. Worn or damaged shift drum locating plate (C, **Figure 29**).
   d. Worn or damaged reinforcing plate (D, **Figure 29**).
10. Check the detent plate (**Figure 30**) for severe wear or damage.
11. Refer to *Access Door Bearings* in this chapter to clean, inspect and replace bearings.
12. Replace worn or damaged parts as required.

Assembly

Refer to **Figure 1** when performing the following procedure.

1. Clamp the transmission access door in a vise with soft jaws.
2. Lubricate each shift fork bore with transmission oil prior to installation.

NOTE
*Refer to **Figure 31** when identifying and installing the shift forks.*

3. Install shift fork No. 1 (3rd and 5th gear), with its flat side facing toward the access door, into the mainshaft second gear groove (A, **Figure 32**).
4. Install shift fork No. 2 (1st and 2nd gear), with its flat side facing away from the access door, into the countershaft third gear groove (B, **Figure 32**).

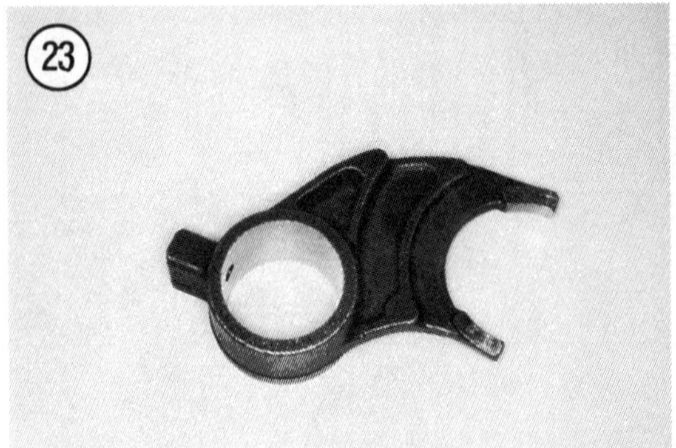

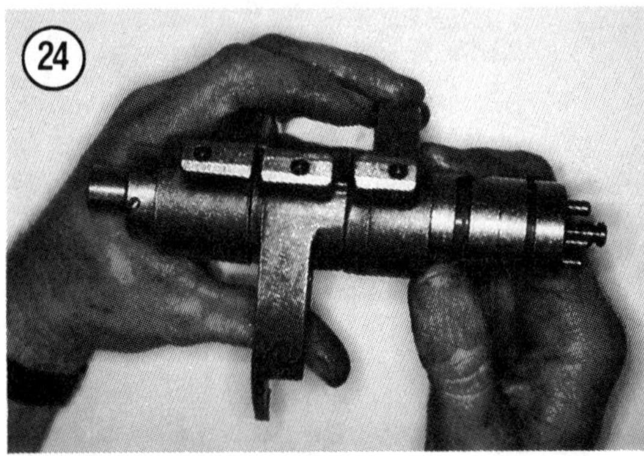

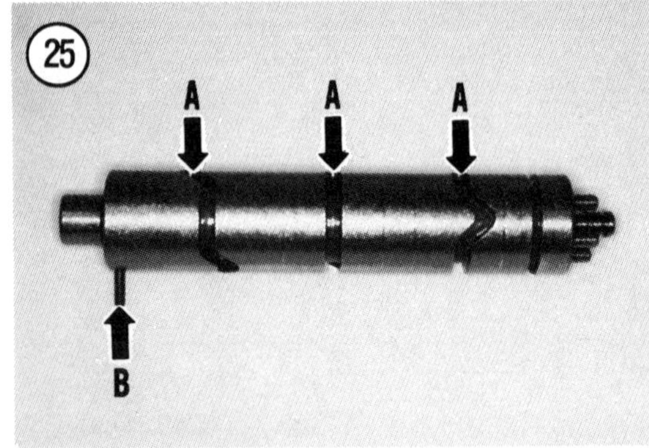

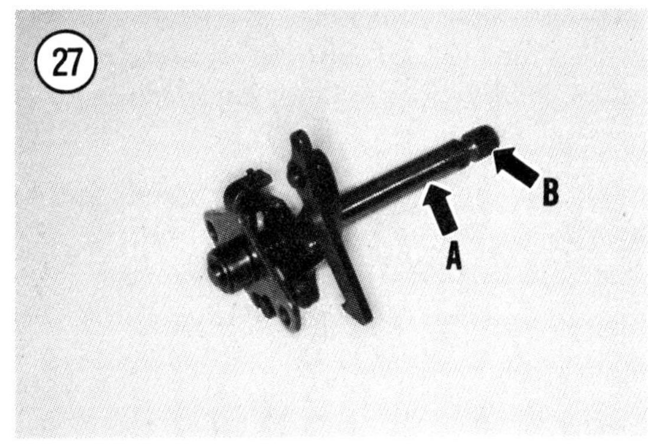

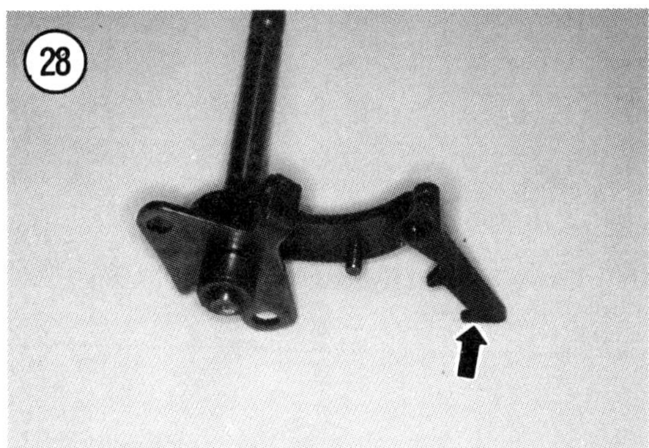

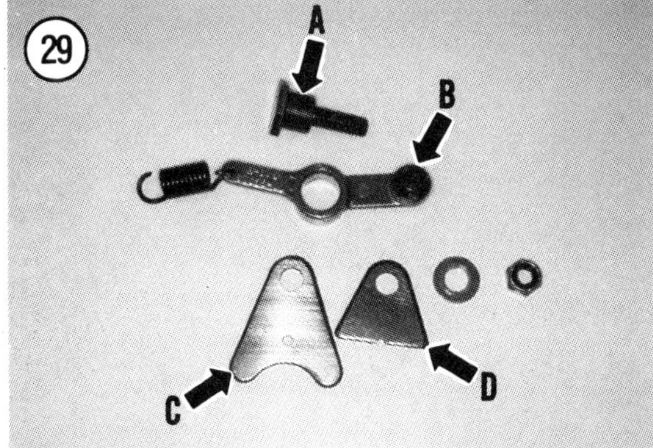

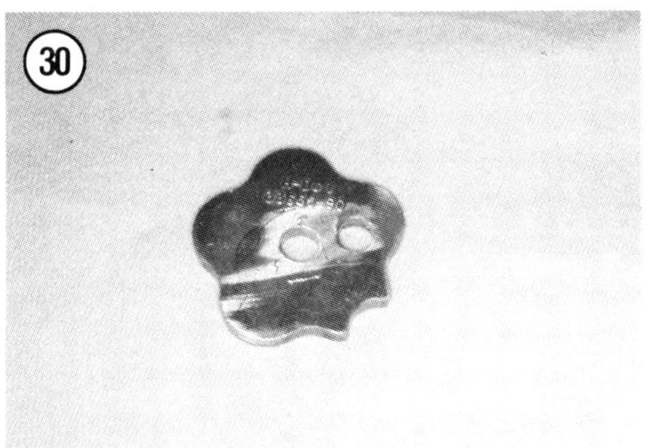

5. Install shift fork No. 3 (4th gear), with its flat side facing away from the access door, into the mainshaft first gear groove (C, **Figure 32**).

6. Align the shift drum, with its neutral indicator pin (B, **Figure 25**) facing up, with the shift forks. Then insert the shift drum (**Figure 21**) through the shift forks and through the bearing in the access door.

7. Lubricate the shift fork pins with transmission oil prior to installation.

CAUTION

*The cotter pins must be installed through the shift forks as shown in **Figure 33**. Otherwise, the cotter pins may be damaged during transmission operation.*

8. Align the lower shift drum groove (A, **Figure 34**) with the pin hole in shift fork No. 3 (4th gear); see C, **Figure 32**. Install the shift fork pin through the shift fork so that it drops into the shift drum groove; turn the shift drum while pushing on the pin with a

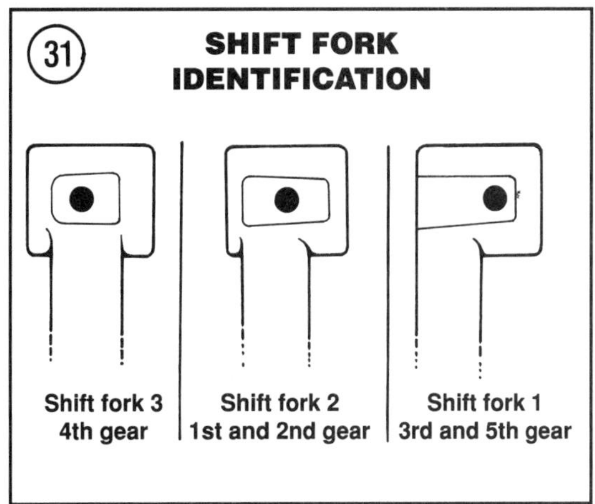

6

small screwdriver. Then install a *new* cotter pin and bend its ends over to lock it in place.

9. Align the center shift drum groove (B, **Figure 34**) with the pin hole in shift fork No. 2 (1st and 2nd gear); see B, **Figure 32**. Install the shift fork pin through the shift fork so that it drops into the shift drum groove; turn the shift drum while pushing on the pin with a small screwdriver. Then install a *new* cotter pin and bend its ends over to lock it in place.

10. Align the upper shift drum groove (C, **Figure 34**) with the pin hole in shift fork No. 1 (3rd and 5th gear); see A, **Figure 32**. Install the shift fork pin through the shift fork so that it drops into the shift drum groove; turn the shift drum while pushing on the pin with a small screwdriver. Then install a *new* cotter pin and bend its ends over to lock it in place.

NOTE

*Refer to **Figure 33** and **Figure 35** for the correct installation of the shift fork cotter pins.*

11. Install the shift drum locating plate (**Figure 36**) into the shift drum groove, making sure the hole in the plate fits over the roll pin in the access door (**Figure 37**).

12. Install the reinforcing plate (A, **Figure 38**) on top of the shift drum locating plate, making sure to engage the notch in the reinforcing plate with the roll pin in the access door.

13. Slide the detent screw (A, **Figure 39**) through the detent arm (B, **Figure 39**). Then insert the detent screw through the access door and through the 2 plates previously installed; see **Figure 38**. Install the washer and nut (B, **Figure 39**). Tighten the detent screw to the torque specification in **Table 2**.

NOTE

*Do not install the detent plate (6, **Figure 1**) and retaining ring (5, **Figure 1**) at this time. These parts are installed during transmission installation and shift pawl adjustment.*

14. Install the transmission assembly as described in this chapter.

COTTER PIN INSTALLATION

Cotter pins

33

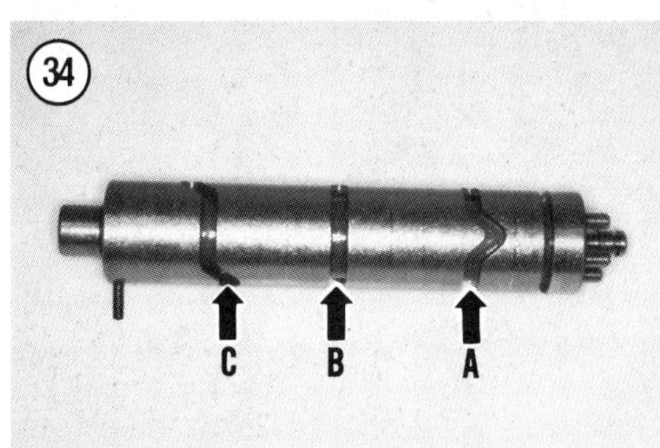

MAINSHAFT AND COUNTERSHAFT

Refer to **Figure 40** when performing the following procedures.

A press is required to disassemble and reassemble the transmission assembly.

Disassembly

1. Remove the transmission assembly as described in this chapter.

37

38

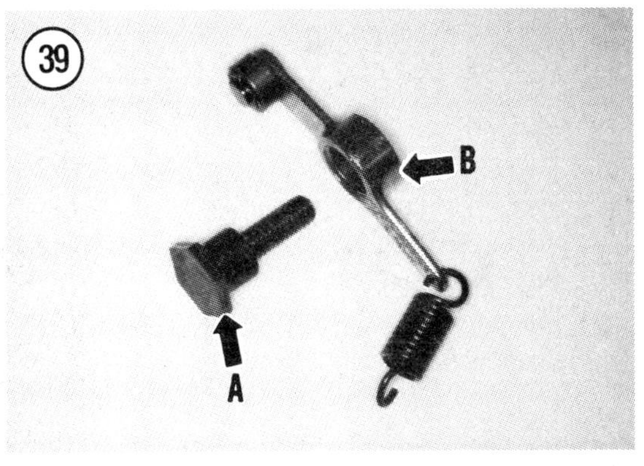

39

2. Remove the shift forks and shift drum as described in this chapter.
3. Clamp the transmission in a vise with soft jaws as shown in **Figure 41**. The transmission shafts are identified as follows:
   a. Countershaft (A, **Figure 41**).
   b. Mainshaft (B, **Figure 41**).

NOTE

Identify and then store all parts as they are disassembled so that they will be installed in their same locations.

4. Remove the retaining ring (**Figure 42**) positioned next to countershaft 5th gear.
5. Remove the following gears in order:
   a. Countershaft 5th gear (**Figure 43**).
   b. Mainshaft 2nd gear (**Figure 44**).
   c. Countershaft 2nd gear (**Figure 45**).
6. Remove the countershaft 2nd gear split bearing (**Figure 46**).
7. Remove the countershaft thrust washer (**Figure 47**).
8. Remove the retaining ring (**Figure 47**) positioned next to countershaft 3rd gear.
9. Remove countershaft 3rd gear (**Figure 48**).
10. Remove the retaining ring and thrust washer (**Figure 49**) located next to mainshaft 3rd gear. See **Figure 50**.
11. Remove mainshaft 3rd gear (**Figure 51**).
12. Remove mainshaft 3rd gear split bearing (**Figure 52**).
13. Remove the mainshaft thrust washer (**Figure 53**).
14. Press the countershaft out of its access door bearing as follows:
   a. Remove the access door from the vise and install the Harley-Davidson countershaft gear support plate (part No. 37404) under countershaft 4th gear as shown in **Figure 54**.
   b. Support the countershaft gear support plate on some metal blocks in a press so that the countershaft can be pressed out without any interference. Center the countershaft under the press ram. See **Figure 55**.
   c. Place a mandrel on top of the countershaft and press the countershaft out of the access cover. Catch the countershaft assembly (**Figure 56**) so that it doesn't fall to the floor.
   d. Set the mainshaft/access door aside for now.

6

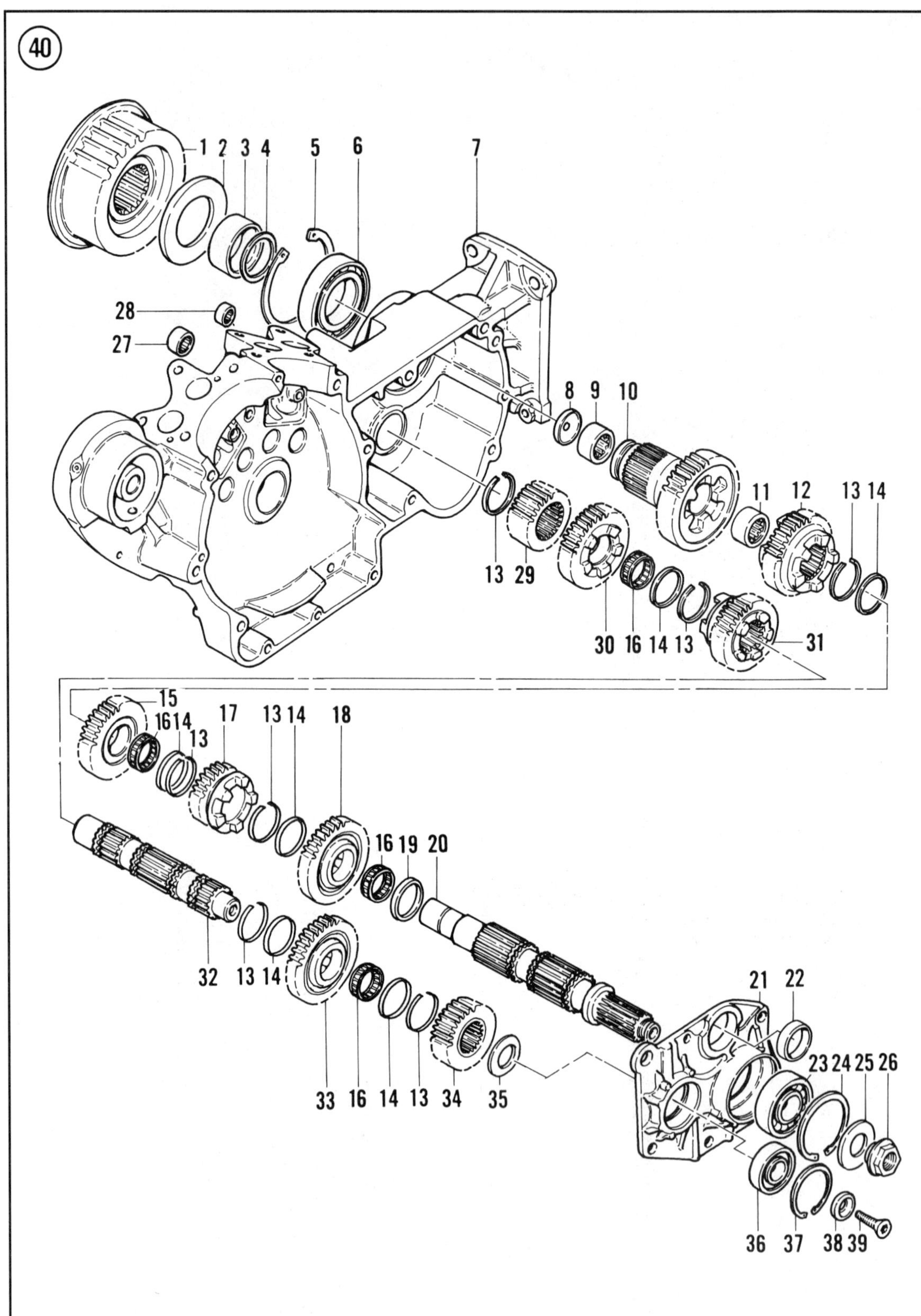
40
1 2 3 4 5 6 7
28
27
8 9 10
11 12 13 14
13 29
30 16 14 13 31
15
16 14 13
17
13 14
18
16 19 20
32 13 14
21 22
23 24 25 26
33 16 14 13 34 35
36 37 38 39

TRANSMISSION ASSEMBLY

1. Drive sprocket
2. Oil seal
3. Spacer (drive belt)
4. Quad ring
5. Retaining ring
6. Bearing
7. Right-hand crankcase
8. Seal
9. Needle bearing
10. Main drive gear
11. Needle bearing
12. Mainshaft 2nd gear
13. Retaining ring
14. Thrust washer
15. Mainshaft 3rd gear
16. Split bearing
17. Mainshaft 1st gear
18. Mainshaft 4th gear
19. Spacer
20. Mainshaft
21. Access door
22. Bushing
23. Bearing
24. Retaining ring
25. Spring washer
26. Mainshaft nut
27. Countershaft needle bearing
28. Shifter shaft needle bearing
29. Countershaft 5th gear
30. Countershaft 2nd gear
31. Countershaft 3rd gear
32. Countershaft
33. Countershaft 1st gear
34. Countershaft 4th gear
35. Bevel spacer
36. Bearing
37. Retaining ring
38. Retainer collar
39. Screw

6

15. Remove the following components from the countershaft:

a. Beveled spacer (**Figure 57**).

b. Countershaft 4th gear (**Figure 58**).

c. Retaining ring (A, **Figure 59**) and thrust washer (B, **Figure 59**) positioned next to 1st gear.

d. Countershaft 1st gear (C, **Figure 59**).

e. Split bearing (A, **Figure 60**).

f. Thrust washer (B, **Figure 60**).

g. Retaining ring (C, **Figure 60**).

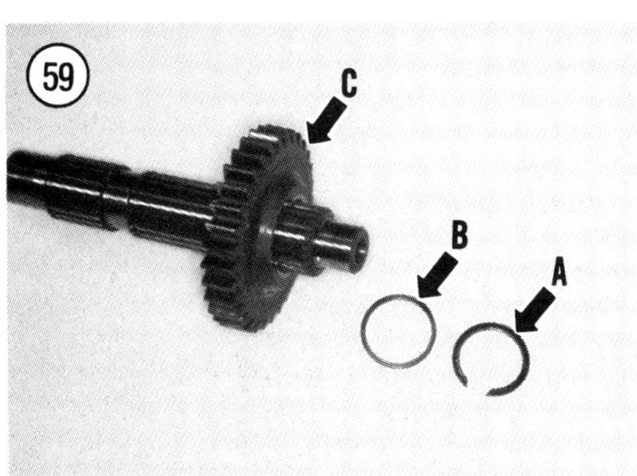

6

16. Remove the retaining ring and mainshaft 1st gear (**Figure 61**).
17. Press the mainshaft out of its access door bearing as follows:
   a. Support mainshaft 4th gear in a press as shown in **Figure 62**. Make sure the mainshaft can be pressed out without any interference. Center the mainshaft under the press ram.
   b. Place a mandrel on top of the mainshaft and press the mainshaft out of the access cover. Catch the mainshaft so that it doesn't fall to the floor.
18. Remove the following components from the mainshaft:
   a. Spacer (19, **Figure 40**).
   b. Mainshaft 4th gear (18, **Figure 40**).
   c. Split bearing (16, **Figure 40**).
   d. Thrust washer (14, **Figure 40**).
   e. Retaining ring (13, **Figure 40**).

Inspection

Harley-Davidson does not list service specifications for the transmission components. If you are experiencing transmission problems, and are not familiar with transmission inspection and repair, refer inspection to a qualified Harley-Davidson mechanic.

1. Clean all components in solvent and dry with compressed air.
2. Check each gear tooth for excessive wear, burrs, galling and pitting. Check each gear for missing teeth. Make sure the gear lugs (**Figure 63**) are in good condition.
3. Install each splined gear (**Figure 64**) on its respective shaft and check for excessive play or binding.

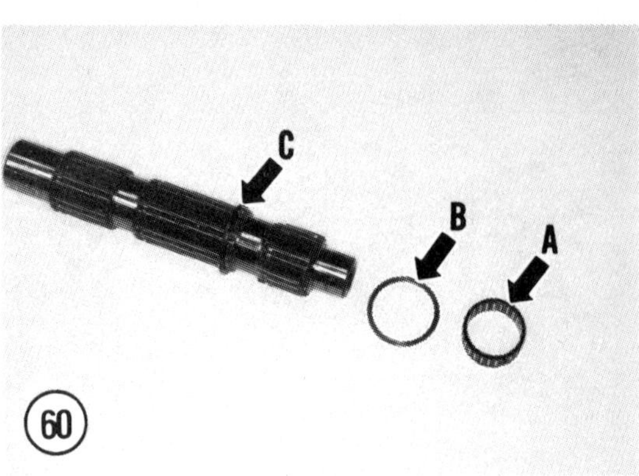

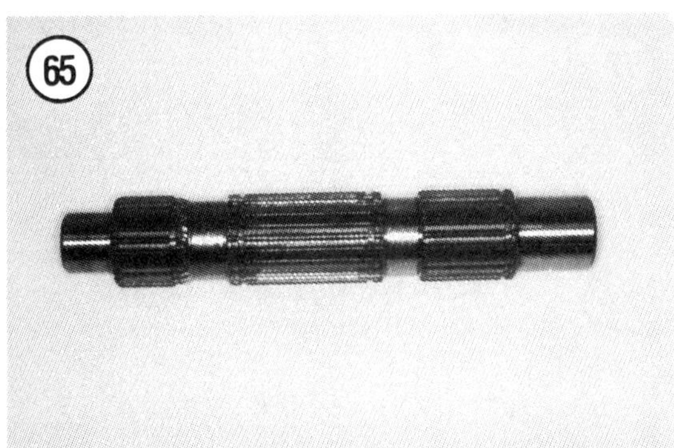
65

4. Check each free-wheeling gear (**Figure 63**) for scoring, galling or seizure marks. Spin the gear on its shaft; it should turn freely.

5. Check the groove in each sliding gear (**Figure 64**) for severe wear or damage. If the groove is severely worn or damaged, check the mating shift fork for damage. Replace the gear if necessary.

NOTE
Defective gears should be replaced. It is a good idea to replace the mating gears as a set.

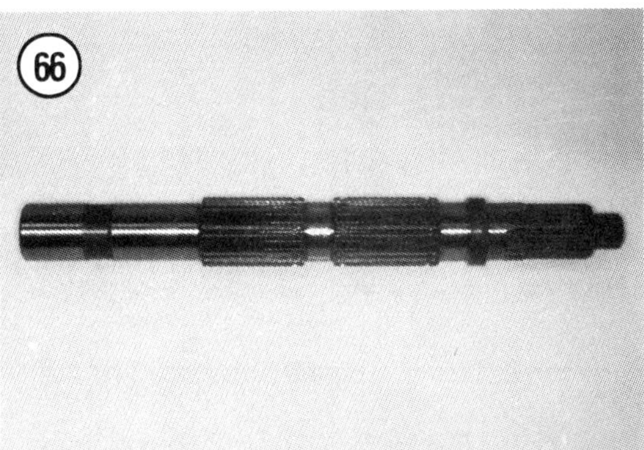
66

6. Check the bearing surface on each shaft. These surfaces must be smooth. See **Figure 65** (countershaft) and **Figure 66** (mainshaft).

7. Check the shaft splines (**Figure 67**) for severe wear or damage.

8. Inspect the retaining ring grooves (**Figure 68**) in each shaft. Each groove must have sharp square shoulders. If any are severely worn or damaged, the shaft(s) must be replaced. See the damaged splines in **Figure 69**.

9. Check the split bearings (**Figure 70**) for severe wear or damage.

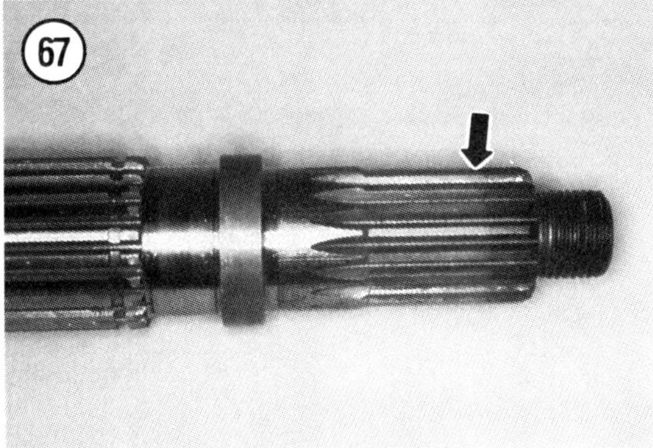
67

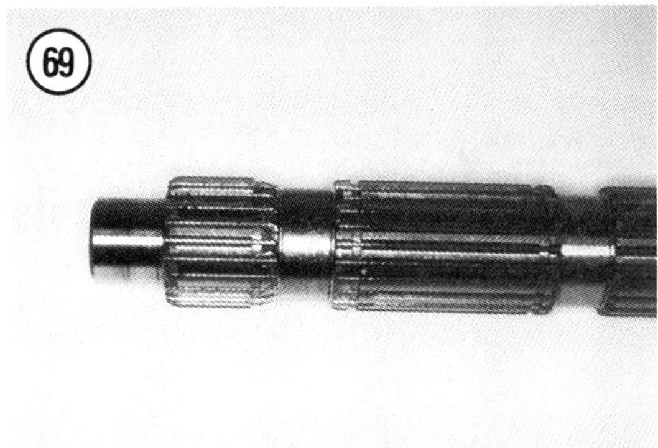
69

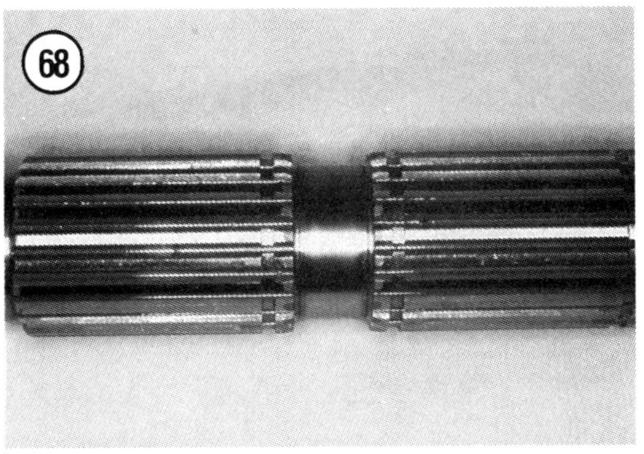
68

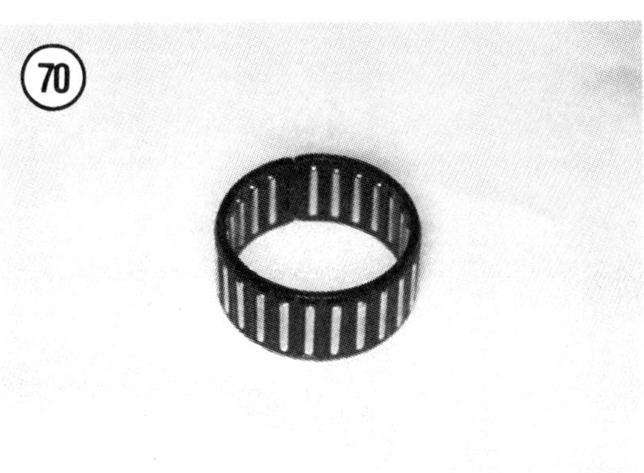
70

10. Check the thrust washers for galling, scoring, cracks or other damage. If the washers are not smooth, replace them.
11. Check the countershaft (**Figure 65**) and mainshaft (**Figure 66**) for bending, damaged splines or other abnormal wear.

Assembly

Refer to **Figure 40** when assembling the transmission shafts.

NOTE
All retaining rings should be replaced every time the transmission is disassembled to ensure proper gear alignment and engagement. Transmission retaining rings become worn with use and increase gear side play. In addition, retaining rings are normally distorted when removed. For this reason, always use new retaining rings when assembling the transmission shafts. Do not expand a retaining ring more than necessary to slide it over the shaft. If a retaining ring is expanded too far, it will be distorted and will not grip the shaft sufficiently, resulting in a loose fit.

1. Apply a light coat of clean transmission oil to all sliding gear and shaft sliding surfaces and split bearings (**Figure 70**) prior to installing any part.
2. If removed, install the access door bearings as described in this chapter.
3. Press the mainshaft into its bearing as follows:
   a. Place a piece of pipe in a press that matches the mainshaft bearing's inner race diameter as shown in A, **Figure 71**. Place the bearing inner

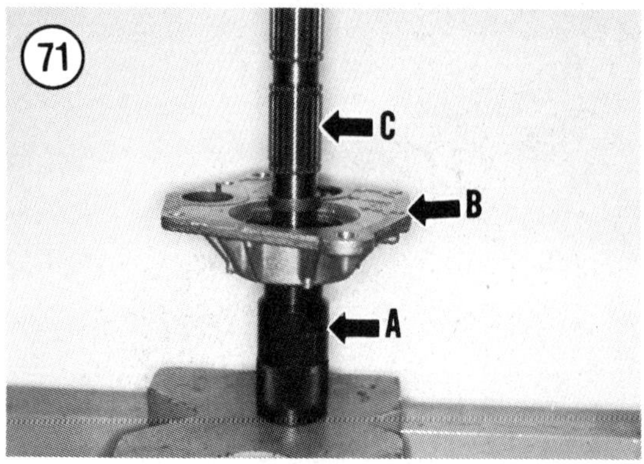

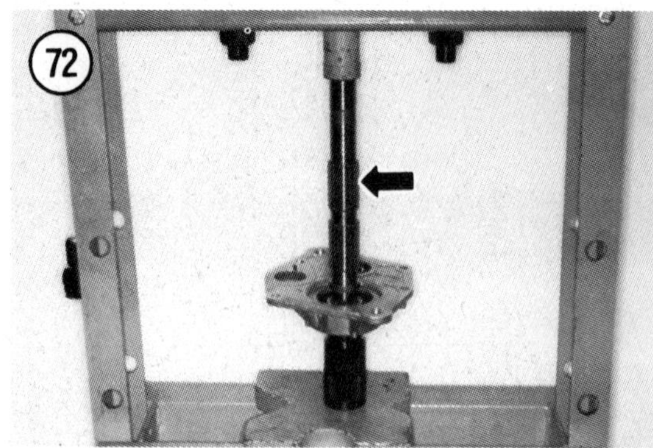

race on the pipe so that the access door inner surface faces up as shown in B, **Figure 71**.

b. Insert the mainshaft (splined end) (C, **Figure 71**) through the bearing and center it with the press ram (**Figure 72**).

c. Press the mainshaft into the bearing until the mainshaft shoulder bottoms out against the bearing.

d. Remove the mainshaft/access door assembly and support it in a vise with soft jaws.

4. Slide the spacer (**Figure 73**) down the mainshaft and seat it against the bearing (A, **Figure 74**).

5. Install the mainshaft 4th gear split bearing and seat it next to the spacer (B, **Figure 74**)

6. Install mainshaft 4th gear with its shoulder (**Figure 75**) facing toward the access door bearing. Slide the gear over the bearing (**Figure 76**).

7. Install the thrust washer (**Figure 77**) and retaining ring. Seat the retaining ring in the groove next to 4th gear (**Figure 78**). Because of the gear's recess, you may have to push the circlip into its groove with a screwdriver.

8. Install mainshaft 1st gear (**Figure 79**) so that its gear dogs face toward the access door.

NOTE

Set the mainshaft aside and begin countershaft assembly with Step 9.

9. Install a retaining ring into the second countershaft groove that is on the end of the shaft with the internal threads; see **Figure 80**.

10. Install the thrust washer next to the retaining ring as shown in A, **Figure 81**.

11. Install the split bearing next to the thrust washer as shown in B, **Figure 81**.

12. Install countershaft 2nd gear so that the gear's shoulder faces toward the open retaining ring

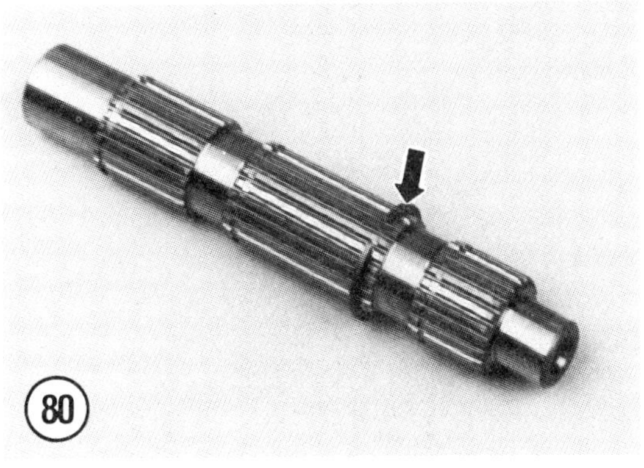

6

groove. Slide the gear over the bearing. See **Figure 82**.

13. Install the thrust washer (A, **Figure 83**) and seat it next to the gear.
14. Install the retaining ring (B, **Figure 83**) into the groove next to the thrust washer. See **Figure 84**.
15. Install countershaft 4th gear (A, **Figure 85**) so that the side with the single radial groove faces toward the thrust washer installed in Step 14.
16. Install the beveled washer over the countershaft so that its beveled side faces away from the gear. Seat the washer next to 4th gear (B, **Figure 85**).
17. Press the countershaft (**Figure 86**) into its access door bearing as follows:
    a. Support the countershaft in a press so that the assembled gear end faces up. Place the bottom of the countershaft on a press block. See A, **Figure 87**.
    b. Place the access door (B, **Figure 87**) countershaft bearing over the countershaft while at the same time meshing the countershaft and mainshaft gears. Hold both gear shafts straight up.
    c. Place a socket or hollow bearing driver (C, **Figure 87**) over the *inner* countershaft bearing race. Center the socket or bearing driver underneath the press ram.

CAUTION
The socket or bearing driver must press against the countershaft inner bearing race or bearing damage will result.

    d. Bring the press ram into position over the countershaft, checking that both shafts are straight up and that both gear sets are properly meshed, then press the bearing onto the countershaft

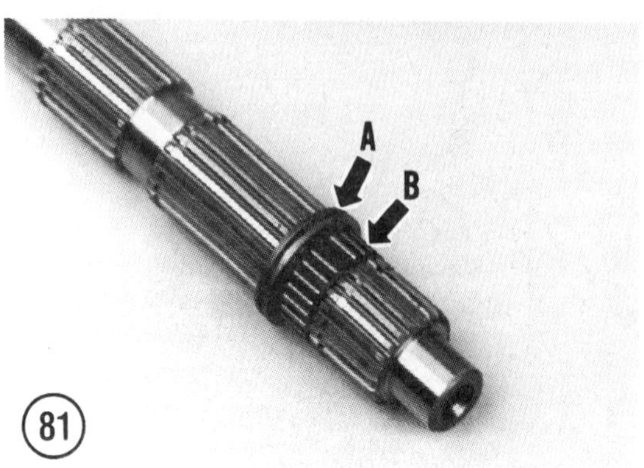

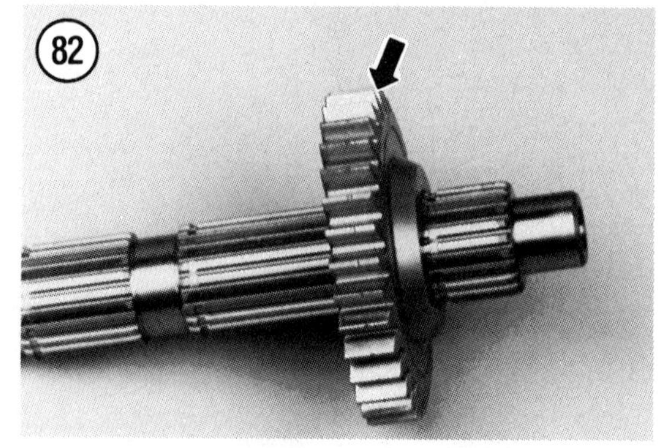

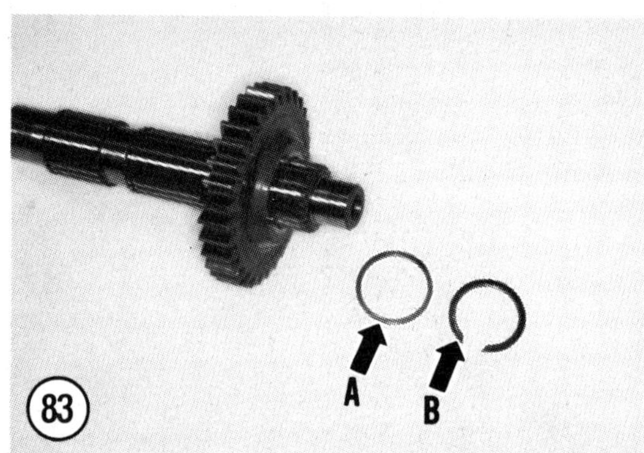

86

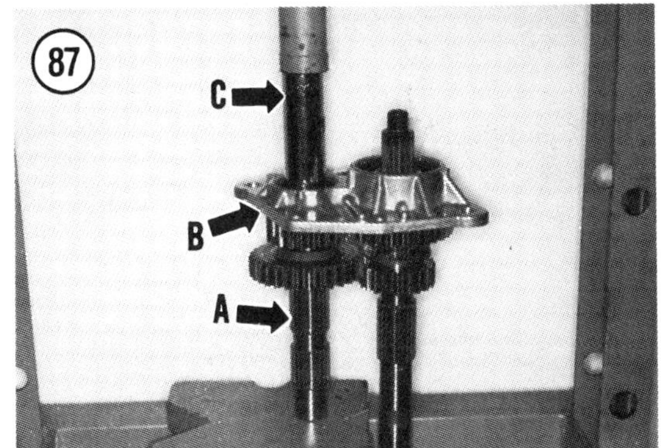

87

until the beveled spacers bottom out against the bearing.

e. Release the press ram and check countershaft 4th gear. When properly installed, countershaft 4th gear should have zero end play.

18. Secure the access door in a vise with soft jaws.

19. Install the retaining ring and thrust washer (**Figure 88**) onto the mainshaft. Seat the retaining ring in the groove next to mainshaft 1st gear.

20. Install the mainshaft 3rd gear split bearing (**Figure 89**) next to the thrust washer.

21. Install mainshaft 3rd gear (**Figure 90**) over the split bearing so that the gear dogs face up.

22. Install the thrust washer and retaining ring. Seat the retaining ring in the groove next to mainshaft 3rd gear (**Figure 91**).

23. Install countershaft 3rd gear (**Figure 92**) so that its gear dogs face away from the access cover.

24. Install the countershaft retaining ring and thrust washer (**Figure 93**). Seat the retaining ring in the groove next to the countershaft 3rd gear.

25. Install the countershaft split bearing (**Figure 94**) next to countershaft 3rd gear.

88

90

89

91

26. Install countershaft 2nd gear (**Figure 95**) over the split bearing. Install the gear so that its gear dogs face toward the access cover.
27. Install mainshaft 2nd gear (**Figure 96**) so that its gear dogs face toward the access cover.
28. Install countershaft 5th gear (**Figure 97**).
29. Install the retaining ring into the groove next to countershaft 5th gear (**Figure 98**).
30. Install the shift forks and shift drum as described in this chapter.

92

MAIN DRIVE GEAR

Two special tools are required to remove and install the main drive gear from the right-hand crankcase. Removing the main drive gear without these special tools, may cause crankcase and/or main drive gear damage.

The special tools are as follows:

a. Harley-Davidson main drive gear remover and installer (part No. HD-35316A). See **Figure 99** and A, **Figure 100**.
b. Harley-Davidson cross plate (part No. HD-35316-91). See B, **Figure 100**.

These tools will be called out by name in the following procedures.

Refer to **Figure 101** for this procedure.

93

Removal

1. Remove the transmission assembly as described in this chapter.
2. Remove the quad ring (A, **Figure 102**) and spacer (B, **Figure 102**) from the main drive gear.
3. Tap out the seal (A, **Figure 103**) that is mounted in the end of the main drive gear. Use a drift inserted through the main drive gear as shown in B, **Figure 103**. Discard the seal.
4. Assemble the Harley-Davidson main drive gear remover and installer and the cross plate as shown in **Figure 104**. See **Figure 105** and **Figure 106**.

94

NOTE

*Insert the 2 cross plate pins (**Figure 105**) into the pin holes in the transmission housing. This will center the cross plate with the main drive gear.*

5. Tighten the puller nut (B, **Figure 106**) to push the main drive gear from the main drive gear bearing. Then remove the nut and puller bolt and remove the

95

main drive gear (**Figure 107**) from the transmission portion of the engine crankcase. Disassemble and remove the puller and support plate assembly.

6. Pry the main drive gear oil seal (2, **Figure 101**) out of the right-hand crankcase.

NOTE

Because the main drive gear inner bearing race (6, ***Figure 101****) was not supported when the main drive gear was removed in Step 4, the bearing is damaged. Whenever the main drive gear is removed, the main drive gear bearing must be replaced, as it is no longer serviceable.*

7. Replace the main drive gear bearing as described under *Right-Hand Transmission Case Bearings*.

Inspection

1. Clean the main drive gear in solvent and dry with compressed air.

2. Check each gear tooth (**Figure 108**) for excessive wear, burrs, galling and pitting. Check for missing gear teeth.

3. Check the gear splines for severe wear, galling or other damage.

4. Inspect the 2 main drive gear needle bearings (**Figure 109**) for severe wear or damage. Insert the mainshaft into the main drive gear to check bearing wear. If necessary, replace the bearings as described in this section.

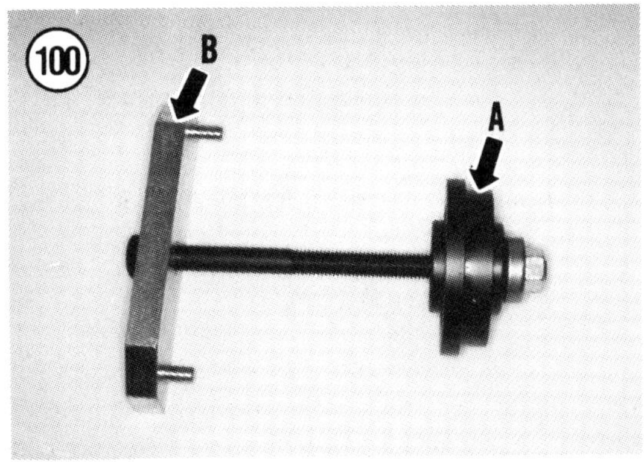

MAIN DRIVE GEAR ASSEMBLY (101)

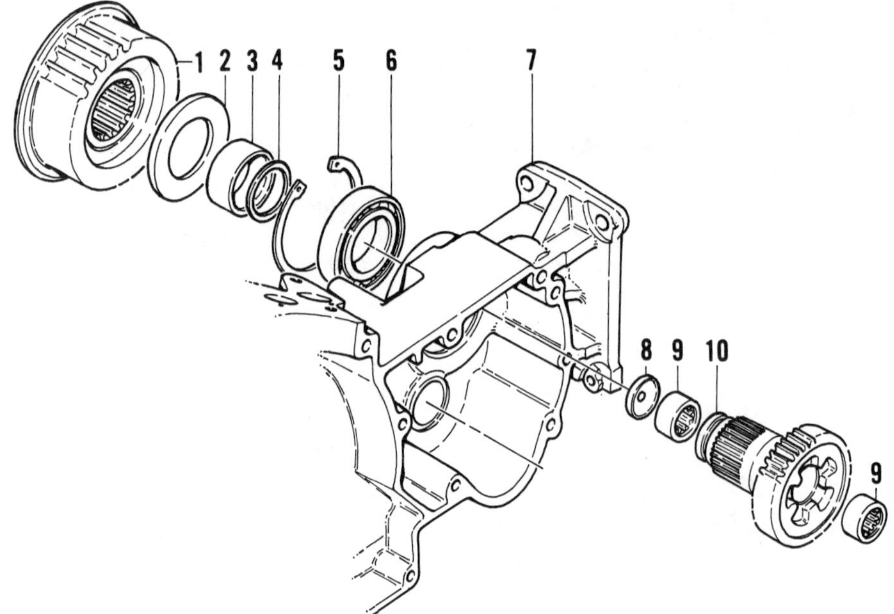

1. Drive sprocket
2. Oil seal
3. Spacer (drive belt)
4. Quad ring
5. Retaining ring
6. Bearing
7. Right-hand crankcase
8. Seal
9. Needle bearing
10. Main drive gear

Main Drive Gear Needle Bearing Replacement

Both main drive gear needle bearings (9, **Figure 101**) must be installed to a specific depth; see **Figure 110**. Bearing installation can be easily performed with the Harley-Davidson inner/outer main drive gear needle bearing installation tool (part No. HD-37842). If you do not have this tool, you will have to measure the bearings when installing them.

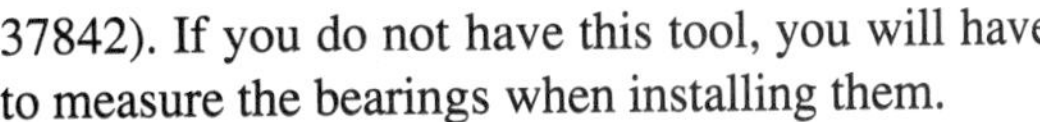

(104)

MAIN DRIVE GEAR REMOVAL

Crankcase
Thrust washer
Bolt
Nut
Cross plate
5th gear
Driver

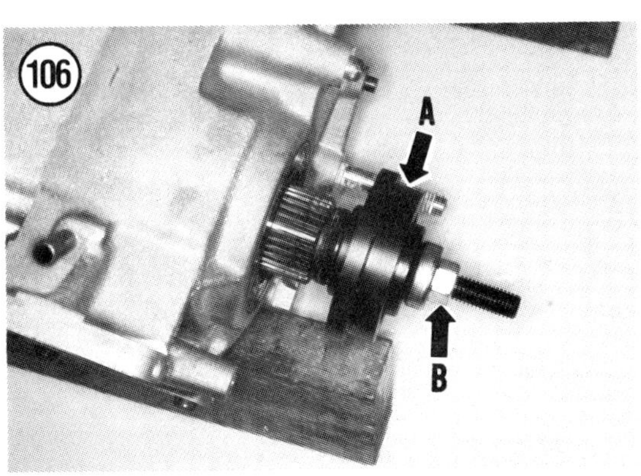

Always replace both main drive gear needle bearings at the same time.

CAUTION
Do not install a main drive gear needle bearing that has been removed. Removal damages the bearings and they are no longer serviceable.

6

1. Support the main drive gear in a press and press out both needle bearings.
2. Clean the bearing bore in solvent and dry thoroughly.

NOTE
Install both needle bearings with their manufacturer's name and size code facing out.

3A. Installing bearing with the Harley-Davidson inner/outer main drive gear needle bearing installation tool: This tool is stamped with two sets of numbers. The side stamped 0.080 is for pressing in the inner end bearing. The side stamped 0.285 is for pressing in the outer end bearing. **Figure 110** identifies the main drive gear inner and outer ends.

a. Install the main drive gear in a press with the outer end facing up. Align the new bearing with the main drive gear and install the installation tool with the side marked 0.285 inserted into the bearing. Operate the press until the tool bottoms out.
b. Turn the main drive gear over so that the inner end faces up. Align the new bearing with the main drive gear and install the installation tool with the side marked 0.080 inserted into the bearing. Operate the press until the tool bottoms out.

3B. If you are installing the bearings without the installation tool, perform the following. **Figure 110** identifies the main drive gear inner and outer ends.

a. Using a suitable mandrel, press in the outer end bearing to a depth of 0.270-0.300 in. (6.86-7.62 mm). See **Figure 110**.
b. Using a suitable mandrel, press in the inner end bearing to a depth of 0.080 in. (2.032 mm). See **Figure 110**.

110 MAIN DRIVE GEAR

Outer end
Main drive gear
Inner end
0.03-0.06 in. (0.76-1.52 mm)
Plug seal
Needle bearings
0.27-0.30 in. (6.86-7.62 mm)
(0.080 in. (2.032 mm)

Main Drive Gear Installation

1. Replace the main drive gear bearing (6, **Figure 101**) as described under *Right-hand Crankcase Bearings* in this chapter.

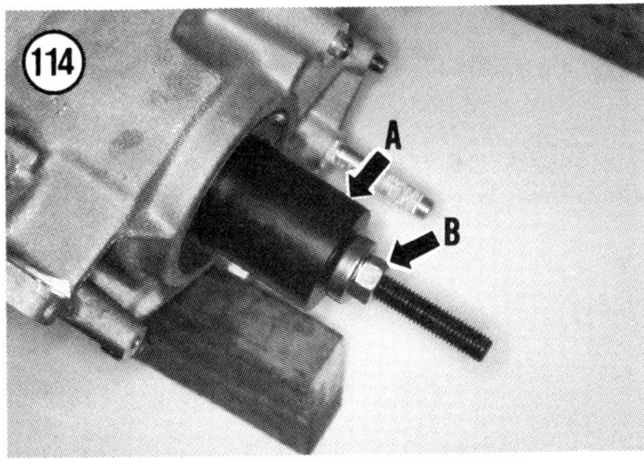

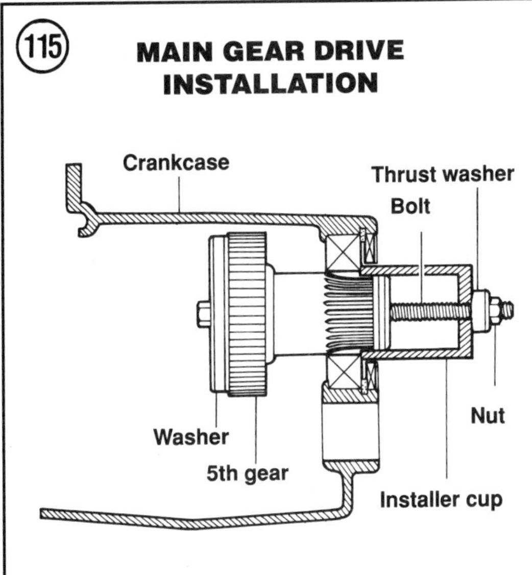

2. Coat the oil seal lips with transmission oil prior to installation.
3. Slide the oil seal (2, **Figure 101**), with its lips facing toward the crankcase, over the spacer. Tap the oil seal into the crankcase until its outer surface (**Figure 111**) is flush with or slightly below (0.030 in. [0.76 mm] maximum) the oil seal bore inside surface.
4. Insert the main drive gear (**Figure 107**) into the main drive gear bearing in the transmission portion of the engine crankcase as far as it will go (**Figure 112**). Then hold it in place and assemble the Harley-Davidson main drive gear remover and installer tool as shown in **Figure 113** and A, **Figure 114**.

CAUTION
*Note how the installer cup, shown in **Figure 115**, supports the main drive gear bearing inner race. If you are installing the main drive gear with a different tool setup, make sure the inner bearing race is supported in the same way. Otherwise, the bearing will be damaged when the main drive gear is pressed into place.*

5. Tighten the puller nut (B, **Figure 114**) to pull the main drive gear through the bearing. Continue until the gear's shoulder bottoms out against the inner bearing race.
6. Disassemble and remove the installer tool assembly.
7. Tap a new seal (**Figure 116**) into the end of the main drive gear until its outer surface is 0.03-0.06 in. (0.76-1.52 mm) below the bearing bore inside surface as indicated in **Figure 110**.
8. Install a *new* quad ring (A, **Figure 117**) over the threaded portion of 5th gear and position it next to the gear taper.
9. Slide the spacer (B, **Figure 117**), with its chamfered end facing toward the quad ring, over 5th gear and seat it against the bearing. See **Figure 118**.
10. Install the transmission assembly as described in this chapter.

ACCESS DOOR BEARINGS

The access door is equipped with the following bearings:

a. Mainshaft bearing (A, **Figure 119**).
b. Countershaft bearing (B, **Figure 119**).

c. Shift drum bushing (C, **Figure 119**).

Mainshaft/Countershaft Bearings Inspection

1. Clean both bearings in kerosene. Hold the inner bearing race with your fingers and dry the bearing with compressed air.

WARNING
Do not spin the bearings with compressed air. Compressed air will spin the bearings at speeds far in excess of their designed capacity. This may cause the bearing to fly apart and throw metal debris into the air, which may cause eye damage or other injuries on contact.

2. Turn the inner bearing race slowly with your finger. The bearing should turn smoothly with no roughness, binding or excessive play. If these conditions are noted, reclean and dry the bearing. If these conditions still persist, replace the bearing as described in this chapter.

3. If the bearing turns smoothly, check for visible damage. Check for overheating, cracked races, pitting and galling. Also check the bearing fit in the bearing bore; both bearings must be a tight fit. If the bearing is a loose fit, check the access door for cracks or other damage.

4. Replace the bearings, if necessary, as described in this chapter.

5. If the bearings can be reused, lubricate them thoroughly with transmission oil, then place the access door in a plastic bag and seal it until transmission reassembly.

Shift Drum Bushing Inspection

1. Clean the bushing (C, **Figure 119**) with solvent or kerosene. Dry with compressed air.

2. Inspect the bushing for scoring, overheating, galling or excessive wear.

3. Replace the bushing, if necessary, as described in this chapter.

Mainshaft/Countershaft Bearing Replacement

This procedure can be used to replace both bearings.

1. Remove the bearing circlip.

2. Support the access door, with its inside surface facing up, in a press.

3. Using a suitable mandrel or bearing driver, press the bearing out of the access door.

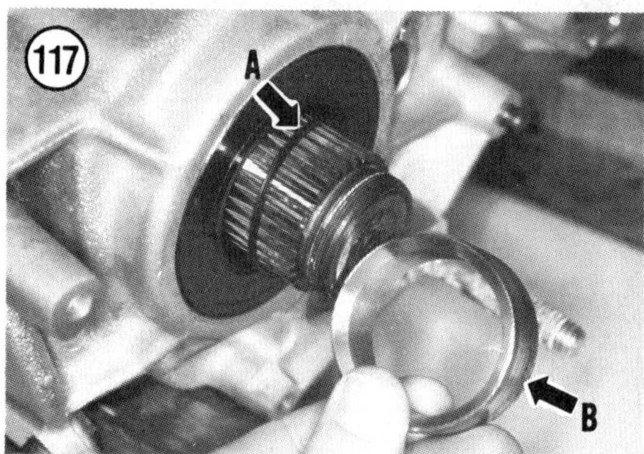

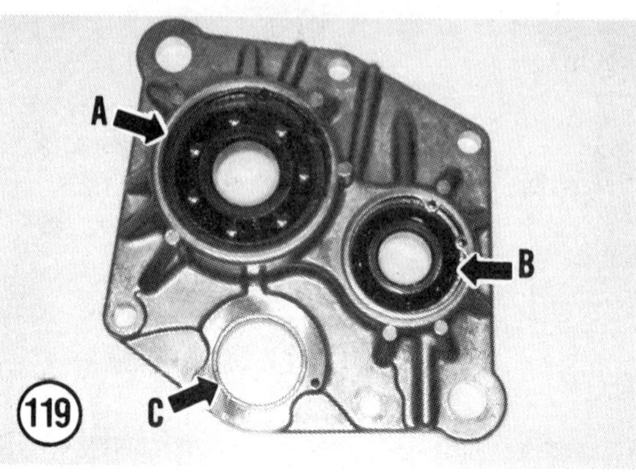

4. Clean the bearing bore and dry with compressed air.

5. Check the circlip groove for severe wear, cracks or other damage. If the groove is damaged, replace the access door.

CAUTION
Make sure the access door is positioned so that it is not resting on the shift drum retaining pin. Otherwise, the access door will be damaged when pressure is applied to it.

6. Support the access door, with its outside surface facing up, in a press.

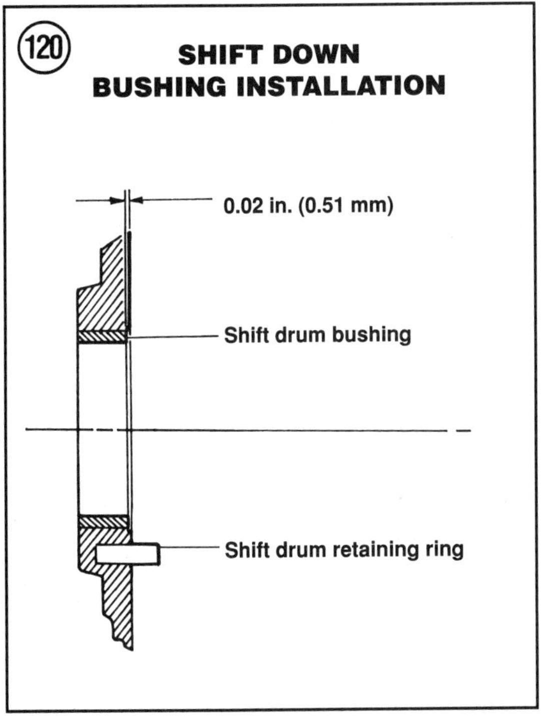

NOTE
Install both bearings with their manufacturer's name and size code facing out.

7. Place a socket or bearing driver on the outer bearing race and press the bearing into the access cover until the bearing bottoms out.

8. Install a new circlip, with its beveled side facing away from the bearing, into the access door groove. Make sure the circlip is fully seated in the groove.

9. Repeat for the opposite bearing.

Shift Drum Bushing Replacement

1. Support the access door in a press and press out the bushing from either side.

2. Clean the bushing bore in kerosene and dry with compressed air.

3. Support the access door, with its outside surface facing down, in a press.

4. Press in the bushing until its outer surface is flush with or 0.02 in. (0.51 mm) below the bushing bore inside surface as shown in **Figure 120**.

RIGHT-HAND TRANSMISSION CASE BEARINGS

The right-hand transmission case is equipped with the following bearings:

a. Main drive gear bearing (**Figure 121**).

b. Countershaft needle bearing (A, **Figure 122**).

c. Shift drum needle bearing (B, **Figure 122**).

Each of these bearings can be replaced with the engine crankcase assembled and installed in the frame.

Main Drive Gear Bearing Inspection

Because the main drive gear bearing (**Figure 121**) is damaged when the main drive gear is removed, do not attempt to reuse the bearing. Replace the bearing as described in this section.

6

Countershaft and Shift Drum Needle Bearings Inspection

1. Clean both needle bearings (A and B, **Figure 122**) in kerosene and dry with compressed air.
2. Check the needle bearings for severely worn, loose or damaged rollers. Check the roller cage and outer shell for damage.
3. Check each bearing for a loose fit in its bore; both bearings must be a tight fit. If the bearing is a loose fit, check the access door for cracks or other damage.
4. Replace the bearings, if necessary, as described in this chapter.
5. If the bearings can be reused, lubricate them thoroughly with transmission oil.

Main Drive Gear Bearing Replacement

Refer to **Figure 101** when replacing the main drive gear bearing.

1. Pry the main drive gear bearing oil seal (**Figure 123**) out of the crankcase with a wide-blade screwdriver. Pad the screwdriver to avoid damaging the crankcase.
2. Remove the circlip (**Figure 121**) from the crankcase groove. This circlip is located behind the main drive gear oil seal.
3. Drive the main drive gear bearing out of the crankcase, working from inside the transmission housing, with a suitable bearing driver. Discard the bearing.
4. Clean the bearing bore and dry with compressed air. Check the bore for nicks or burrs. Check the circlip groove for damage.

NOTE

The Harley-Davidson main drive gear remover and installer and cross plate tool, used to remove the main drive gear, are used to install the new bearing. Refer to **Main Drive Gear** *for further information on these tools.*

NOTE

When assembling the new bearing on the installation tool and installing it into the crankcase, install it with the manufacturer's name and size code facing out.

5. Install the new bearing onto the Harley-Davidson main drive gear remover and installer and cross plate tools as shown in **Figure 124**.

NOTE

*Insert the 2 cross plate pins into the pin holes in the transmission housing (***Fig-**

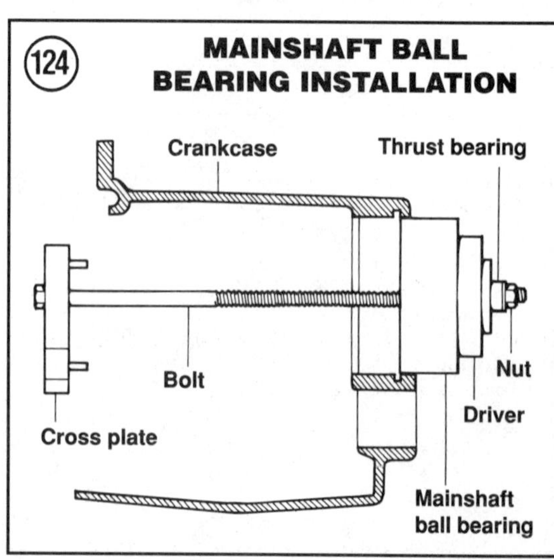

ure 125). This will center the cross plate with the main drive gear bearing.

6. Tighten the puller nut to pull the bearing into the crankcase. Continue until the bearing bottoms out against the bearing bore surface.
7. Disassemble and remove the puller tool assembly.
8. Install the circlip, with its beveled side facing out, into the crankcase groove. Make sure the circlip is fully seated in the groove.

NOTE
The main drive gear bearing oil seal is installed during the transmission installation procedure. Refer to ***Transmission Installation*** *in this chapter.*

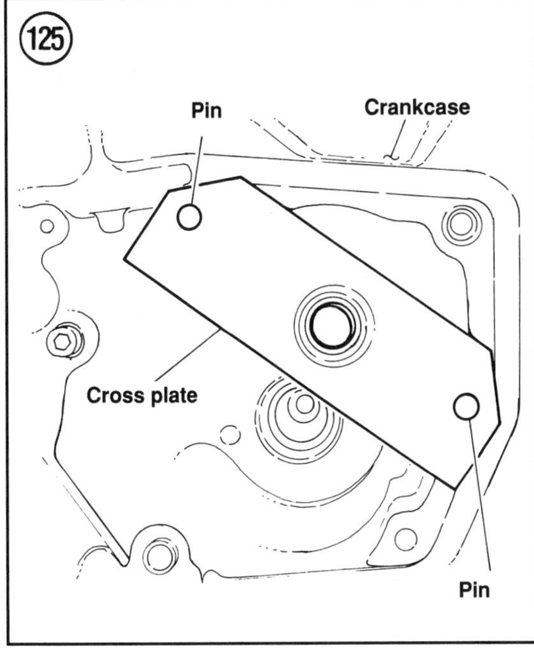

9. Lubricate the bearing with transmission fluid.

Countershaft Needle Bearing Replacement

1. Drive the countershaft needle bearing (A, **Figure 122**) out of the crankcase, working from inside the transmission housing, with a suitable bearing driver. Discard the bearing.
2. Clean the bearing bore and dry with compressed air. Check the bearing bore for nicks or burrs.
3. Align the new bearing, with its closed side facing out, with the crankcase bearing bore.
4. Drive in the new bearing until its outer surface is flush with or 0.030 in. (0.76 mm) below the bushing bore inside surface.
5. Lubricate the bearing with transmission fluid.

6

Shift Drum Needle Bearing Replacement

1. Drive the shift drum needle bearing (B, **Figure 122**) out of the crankcase, working from inside the transmission housing, with a suitable bearing driver. Discard the bearing.
2. Clean the bearing bore and dry with compressed air. Check the bearing bore for nicks or burrs.
3. Align the new bearing, with its closed side facing out, with the crankcase bearing bore.
4. Drive in the new bearing until its outer surface is flush with or 0.030 in. (0.76 mm) below the bushing bore inside surface.
5. Lubricate the bearing with transmission fluid.

Table 1 TRANSMISSION SPECIFICATIONS

Primary drive sprockets (engine-to-transmission)	
Number of gear teeth	
Engine sprocket	35
Clutch sprocket	56
Ratio	1.60:1
Final drive sprockets (transmission-to-rear wheel)—1991-1992	
Number of sprocket teeth	
Transmission sprocket	
Chain drive	21
Belt drive	
883 cc	27
1200 cc	29

(continued)

Table 1 TRANSMISSION SPECIFICATIONS (continued)

Final drive sprockets (transmission-to-rear wheel)--1991-1992 (continued)	
Number of sprocket teeth	
Rear wheel sprocket	
Chain drive	48
Belt drive	61
Gear ratio	
883 Standard and Hugger	2.29:1
883 Deluxe	2.26:1
1200	2.10:1
Secondary drive belt	
Number of teeth	
883 Deluxe	
1991 (yellow color code)	127
1992-on (orange color code)	128
1200 (orange color code)	128
Final drive sprockets (transmission-to-rear wheel)—1993-on	
Number of sprocket teeth	
Transmission sprocket	
883 cc	27
1200 cc	29
Rear wheel sprocket	
All models	61
Gear ratio	
883 cc	2.26:1
1200 cc	2.10:1
Internal gear ratios	
1st gear	2.78
2nd gear	2.03
3rd gear	1.49
4th gear	1.22
5th gear	1.00
Overall gear ratios (U.S. models)	
1991-1992 883 Standard and Hugger	
1st	10.16
2nd	7.41
3rd	5.44
4th	4.45
5th	3.66
1991-1992 883 Deluxe and all 1993-on 883 cc	
1st	10.04
2nd	7.32
3rd	5.38
4th	4.39
5th	3.61
1991-on 1200	
1st	9.35
2nd	6.82
3rd	5.01
4th	4.09
5th	3.36
Overall gear ratios (European models)	
1993-on 883 cc models	
1st	9.71
2nd	7.12
3rd	5.18
4th	4.26
5th	3.61

(continued)

Table 1 TRANSMISSION SPECIFICATIONS (continued)

Overall gear ratios (European models) (continued)	
1993-on 1200 cc models	
1st	9.04
2nd	6.62
3rd	4.82
4th	3.97
5th	3.36
Overall gear ratios (Switzerland)	
1993-on 883 cc models	
1st	9.05
2nd	6.60
3rd	4.85
4th	3.96
5th	3.25
1993-on 1200 cc models	
1st	8.43
2nd	6.14
3rd	4.51
4th	3.68
5th	3.03

6

Table 2 TRANSMISSION TIGHTENING TORQUES

	ft.-lb.	N•m
Transmission access door bolts	13-17	17.6-23
Transmission sprocket nut*	110-120	149-162.7
Countershaft retainer collar screw	13-17	17.6-23
Detent screw/nut	13-17	17.6-23
	in.-lb.	**N•m**
Sprocket cover screws	90-110	10.2-12.4
Shift lever pinch bolt	90-110	10.2-12.4
Transmission sprocket nut lockplate screws		
1991 (1 screw)	50-60	5.7-6.8
1992		
Chain drive (1 screw)	50-60	5.7-6.8
Belt drive (2 screws)	90-110	10.2-12.4
1993-on	90-110	10.2-12.4
Shift shaft locknuts	90-110	10.2-12.4

* Left-hand threads.

CHAPTER SEVEN

FUEL, EXHAUST AND EMISSION CONTROL SYSTEMS

This chapter includes service procedures for all parts of the fuel, exhaust and emission control system.

Carburetor specifications are listed in **Table 1**. **Tables 1-3** are found at the end of the chapter.

AIR FILTER

The air filter must be cleaned or replaced at the intervals specified in Chapter Three (or more frequently in dusty areas).

Air filter service is described in Chapter Three.

CARBURETOR

Service

Major carburetor service (removal and cleaning) should be performed when poor engine performance and/or hesitation is observed. Alterations in jet size, cylinder cutaway, etc., should be attempted only if you're experienced in this type of "tuning" work; a bad guess could result in costly engine damage or, at best, poor performance.

If, after servicing the carburetors and making adjustments as described in this chapter, the motorcycle does not perform correctly (and assuming that other factors affecting performance are correct, such as ignition timing and condition, valve adjustment, etc.), the motorcycle should be checked by a dealer or a qualified performance tuning specialist.

Vacuum Piston Inspection

If you suspect that the vacuum piston is not operating properly (failing to rise or close properly), perform the following procedures before removing the carburetor.

1. Check vacuum piston rise as follows:
   a. Remove the air filter and its backplate (Chapter Three) so that you can see the vacuum piston. See **Figure 1**.

WARNING

*When you are checking vacuum piston operation with the engine running as described in substep b, **protect** your eyes from a possible back-fire by **wearing safety glasses** and standing a safe distance away from the carburetor. Have an assistant operate the throttle;*

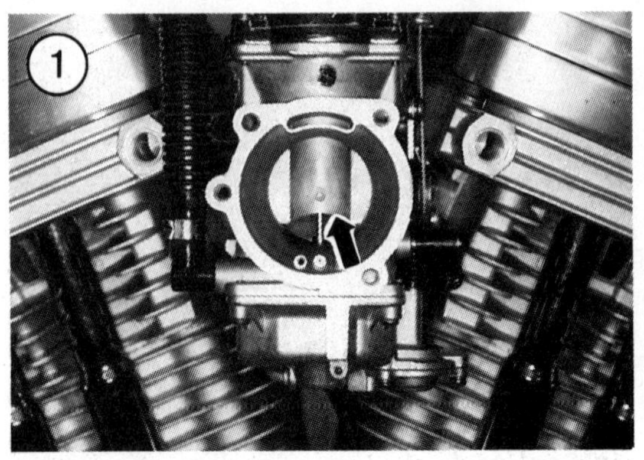

do not operate the throttle and watch the vacuum piston at the same time. You will be too close to the carburetor.

b. With the engine running and properly warmed up, have an assistant open and close the throttle several times while you watch vacuum piston operation. The vacuum piston should rise and lower when the throttle is opened and closed. Turn the engine off.
c. With the engine off, lift the vacuum piston all the way up the carburetor bore with your finger and release it. Note how the piston traveled upward in the bore. The piston should move smoothly with no roughness or binding.

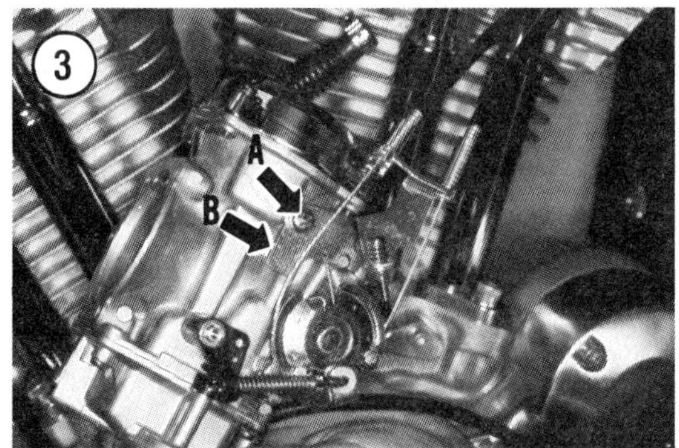

2. Check piston closing as follows:
   a. With the engine off, lift the vacuum piston all the way up the carburetor bore with your finger and release it. Note how the piston drops in the bore. It should drop smoothly and come to a stop at the bottom of the bore.
   b. Without touching the piston after releasing it in substep a, observe the bottom of the piston in relation to the piston bore. The lower edge of the piston should align or rest with the horizontal groove at the bottom end of the piston bore.
3. If the vacuum piston failed to operate properly as described in these steps, refer to Chapter Two for carburetor troubleshooting.

Carburetor Removal/Installation

1. Remove the air filter and backplate as described in Chapter Three.
2. Turn the fuel valve off.
3. Remove the enrichener bracket mounting screw (**Figure 2**) and allow the bracket to rest on top of the intake manifold.

NOTE
It is easier to remove the enrichener cable while it is attached to the carburetor.

4. Remove the fuel tank as described in this chapter. Plug the fuel hose to prevent dirt from entering.
5. Label the 2 throttle cables at the carburetor if you are going to disconnect them.
6. Identify and label all carburetor hoses for correct reinstallation. Then disconnect the hoses from the carburetor.
7. Pull the carburetor off of its seal ring and manifold (**Figure 3**).
8. Remove the 2 throttle cable bracket screws and lockwasher (A, **Figure 3**, typical) and remove the bracket (B, **Figure 3**) from the carburetor. See **Figure 4**.
9. Remove the carburetor seal ring (**Figure 5**).
10. If necessary, remove the intake manifold as described in this chapter.

NOTE
Drain the gasoline from the carburetor assembly and place it in a heavy-duty

plastic bag to keep it clean until it is worked on or reinstalled.

11. Inspect the carburetor seal ring (**Figure 5**) for severe wear, hardness, cracks or other damage. Replace if necessary.
12. Install the seal ring (**Figure 5**) onto the intake manifold so that the channel in the back of the ring fits into the intake manifold lip as shown in **Figure 6**.
13. If removed, connect the throttle cables to the throttle cable bracket as shown in **Figure 4**.
14. Install the throttle cable bracket (B, **Figure 3**) onto the carburetor so that the notch in the bracket engages with the pin on the carburetor. Install the 2 screws and lockwashers (A, **Figure 3**, typical) and tighten securely.

NOTE
Check that the throttle cables are routed properly.

NOTE
To ease carburetor installation, lightly wipe the carburetor seal ring inner diameter (part that contacts the carburetor spigot) with liquid dish soap detergent or tire mounting lube.

15. Insert the enrichener cable (**Figure 2**) between the cylinders and above the intake manifold. Then align the carburetor with the intake manifold and push the carburetor into the seal ring until it bottoms out (**Figure 7**). Position the carburetor so that it is straight up (**Figure 1**).
16. Secure the enrichener bracket to the cylinder head bracket with its mounting screw (**Figure 2**).
17. Reconnect the VOES hose to the VOES fitting on the carburetor (**Figure 8**).
18. Install the air filter backplate and air filter as described in Chapter Three.

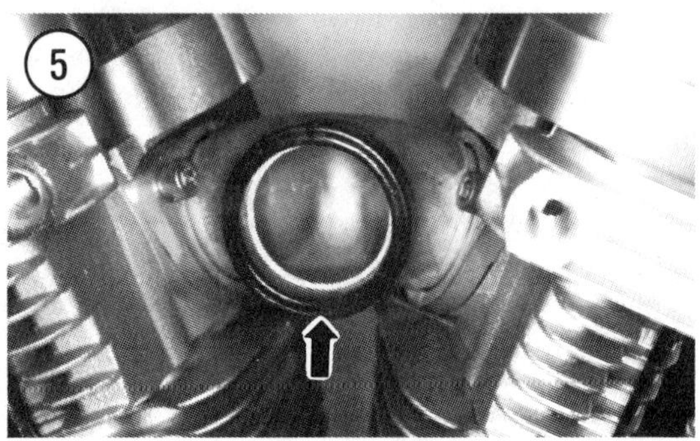

19. If the intake manifold was removed, tighten the 4 Allen bolts to the torque specification in **Table 2**.
20. On California models, reconnect all evaporative emissions control system hoses following your notes made prior to disassembly. Then refer to *Evaporative Emissions Control System* in this chapter to confirm the correct connection of each hose.

CAUTION
Interchanging the vacuum hose connections will reduce engine performance

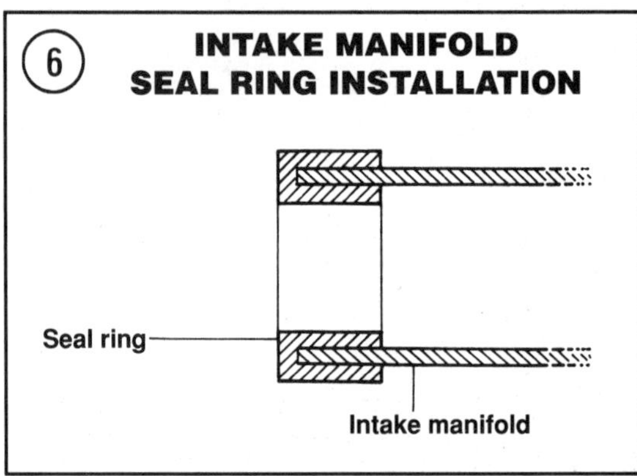

9 INTAKE MANIFOLD

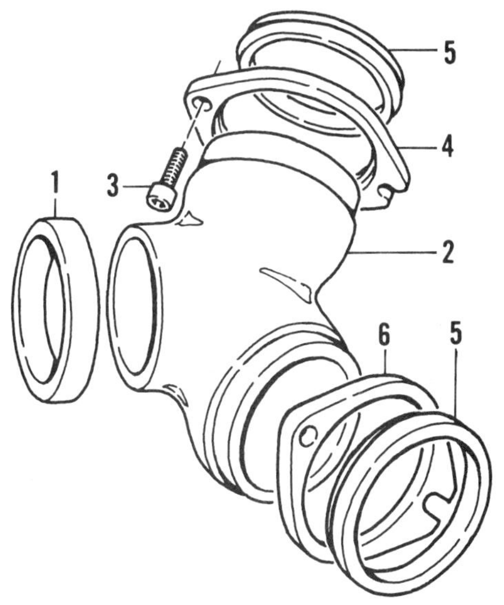

1. Seal ring
2. Intake manifold
3. Bolt
4. Rear mounting flange
5. Seal
6. Front mounting flange

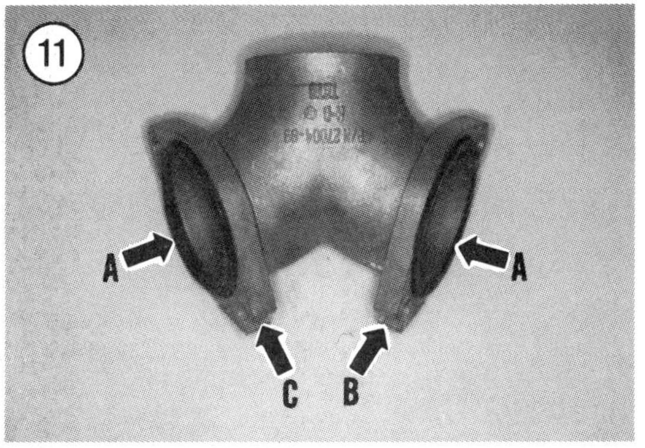

WARNING

Make sure that all evaporative emission control hoses are routed in such a way that they cannot contact any hot engine or exhaust component. These hoses contain flammable vapors. If a hose melts from contacting a hot part, leaking vapors may ignite, causing severe bike damage and rider injury.

21. Install the fuel tank as described in this chapter.
22. Adjust the throttle and enrichener cables as described in Chapter Three.

Intake Manifold Removal/Installation

The front and rear intake manifold flanges (**Figure 9**) have different part numbers. Identify the flanges during removal so that you don't mix them up during reassembly.

1. Loosen the intake manifold Allen bolts. Then remove the 2 right-hand Allen bolts (A, **Figure 10**).
2. Remove the intake manifold, 2 flanges and 2 manifold seals (**Figure 9**).
3. Check the intake manifold seals (A, **Figure 11**) for wear, deterioration or other damage. Replace the seals if necessary.
4. Install the front (B, **Figure 11**) and rear (C, **Figure 11**) flanges onto the intake manifold so that the slot in each flange aligns with the 2 left-hand intake manifold Allen bolts.
5. Insert an intake manifold seal (A, **Figure 11**) into each manifold flange—chamfered edge first.
6. Install the 2 left-hand intake manifold Allen bolts (**Figure 12**) so that 3-4 threads engage with the cylinder head threads.
7. Align the intake manifold flange slots with the 2 Allen bolts (**Figure 12**) and install the intake mani-

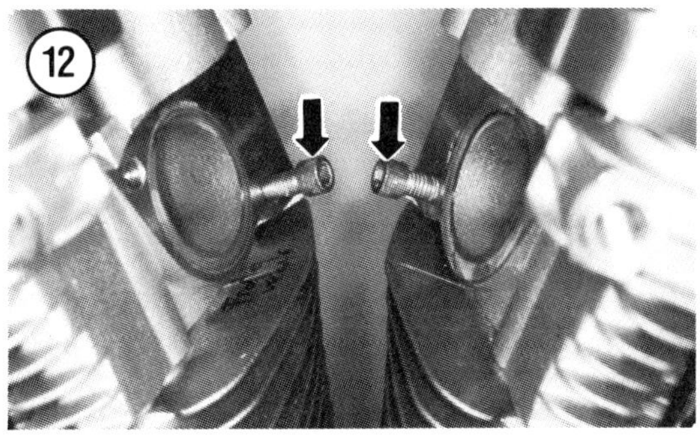

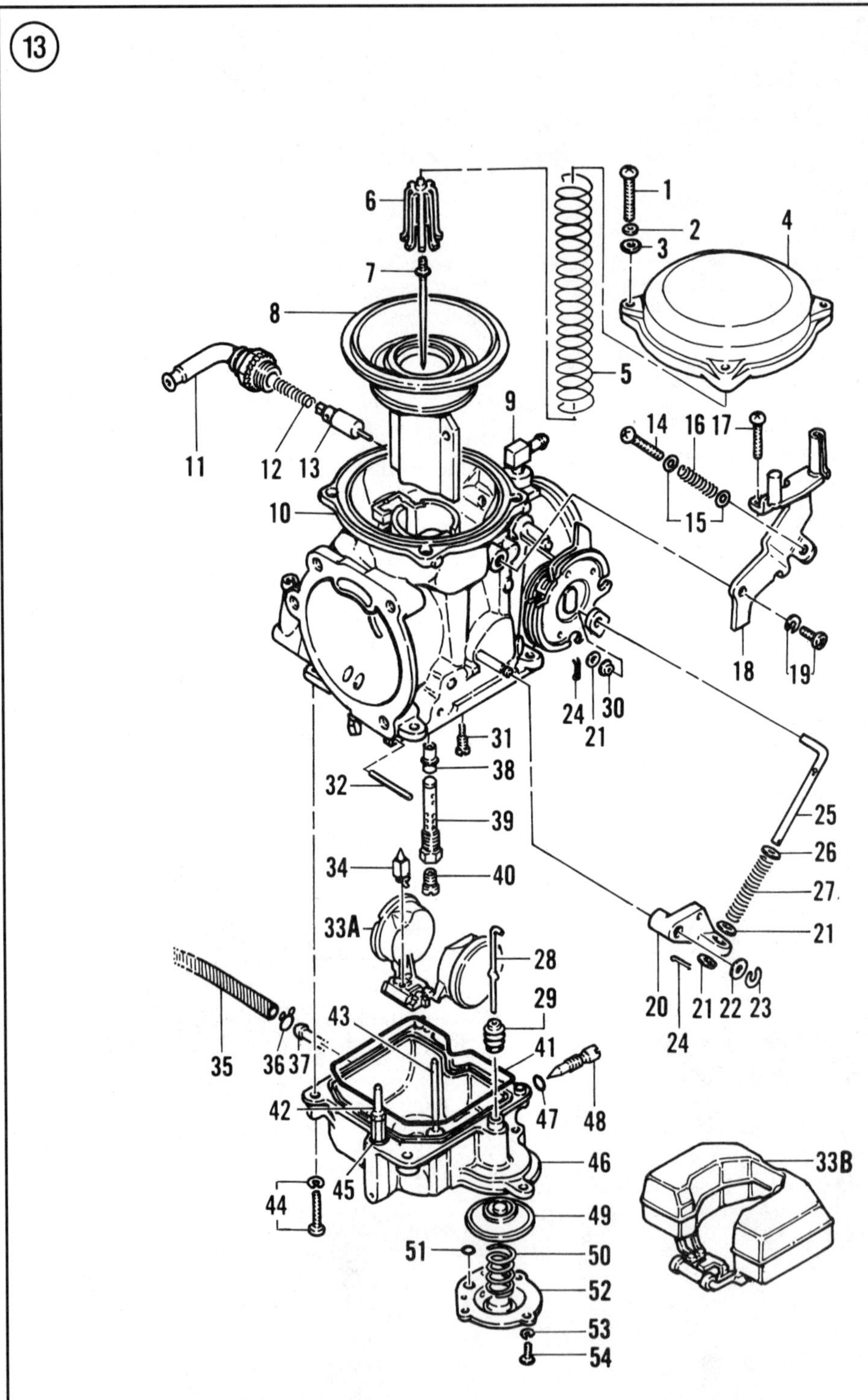
13
1
2
3
4
5
6
7
8
9
10
11
12
13
14
15
16
17
18
19
20
21
22
23
24
25
26
27
28
29
30
31
32
33A
33B
34
35
36
37
38
39
40
41
42
43
44
45
46
47
48
49
50
51
52
53
54

CARBURETOR

1. Screw
2. Lockwasher
3. Flat washer
4. Top cover
5. Spring
6. Spring seat
7. Jet needle
8. Vacuum piston
9. VOES nozzle
10. Housing
11. Cable guide
12. Spring
13. Enrichener valve
14. Idle speed adjust screw
15. Washer
16. Spring
17. Screw
18. Throttle cable bracket
19. Screw and lockwasher
20. Lever
21. Washer
22. Washer
23. E-clip
24. Cotter pin
25. Pump linkage
26. Washer
27. Spring
28. Accelerator pump rod
29. Boot
30. Collar
31. Pilot jet
32. Float rod

33A. Float (1991)

33B. Float (1992-on)

34. Fuel valve
35. Hose
36. Clip
37. Overflow pipe
38. Needle jet
39. Needle jet holder
40. Main jet
41. O-ring
42. Accelerator pump nozzle
43. Overflow pipe
44. Screw and lockwasher
45. O-ring
46. Float bowl
47. O-ring
48. Drain screw
49. Diaphragm
50. Spring
51. O-ring
52. Accelerator pump housing
53. Lockwasher
54. Screw

fold (B, **Figure 10**). Install the 2 right-hand Allen bolts (A, **Figure 10**). Tighten all of the intake manifold bolts finger-tight only.

8. Install the carburetor as described in this chapter.
9. Install the air filter backplate and air filter as described in this chapter.
10. Tighten the intake manifold bolts to the torque specification in **Table 2**.

Disassembly

When servicing the carburetor, you will be working with a number of small parts that can easily become lost. As the carburetor is disassembled, store the parts in a metal pan or tray.

Refer to **Figure 13** for this procedure.

1. Unscrew and remove the enrichener cable (**Figure 14**).
2. If not previously removed, remove the throttle cable bracket screw and lockwasher and remove the bracket (**Figure 15**).
3. Remove the float bowl as follows:
   a. Remove the screws and washers securing the float bowl (**Figure 16**) to the carburetor. Re-

7

move the float bowl from the carburetor while allowing the pump rod (**Figure 17**) to withdraw from the boot on the bowl.

b. Disconnect the pump rod from the lever assembly on the carburetor (**Figure 18**).

c. Carefully pull the boot (**Figure 19**) off of the float bowl.

4A. On 1991 models, remove the float pin (**Figure 20**) and lift off the float and needle valve assembly (**Figure 21**).

4B. On 1992-on models, remove the float pin (**Figure 22**) and lift off the float and needle valve assembly (**Figure 23**).

5. The main jet is screwed into the top of the needle jet holder. Either remove the main jet (**Figure 24**) and then the needle jet holder (**Figure 25**) or remove the needle jet holder with the main jet attached.

6. Remove the needle jet from the needle jet bore in the carburetor (**Figure 26**).

7. Remove the pilot jet (**Figure 27**).

CAUTION

If the screwdriver used to remove the pilot jet is too small, you may break the slots at the top of the jet and damage it.

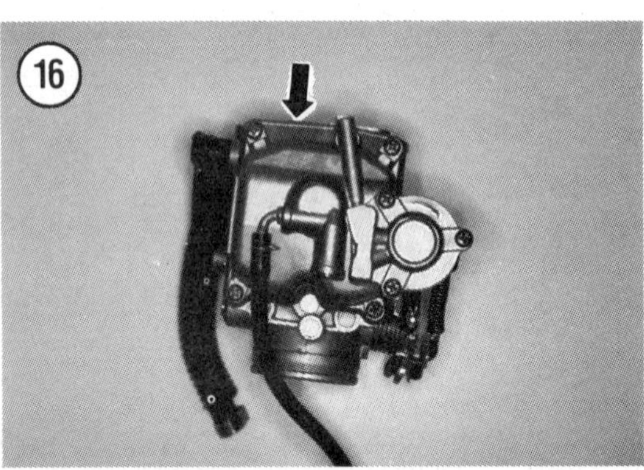

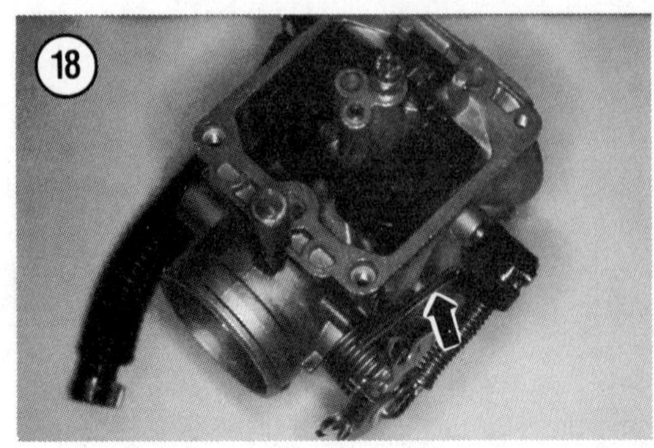

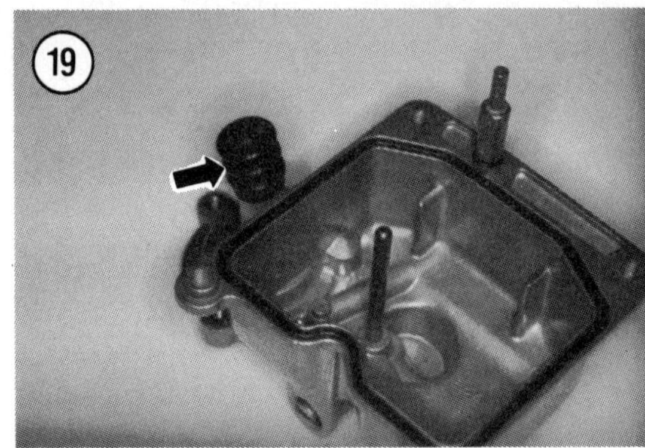

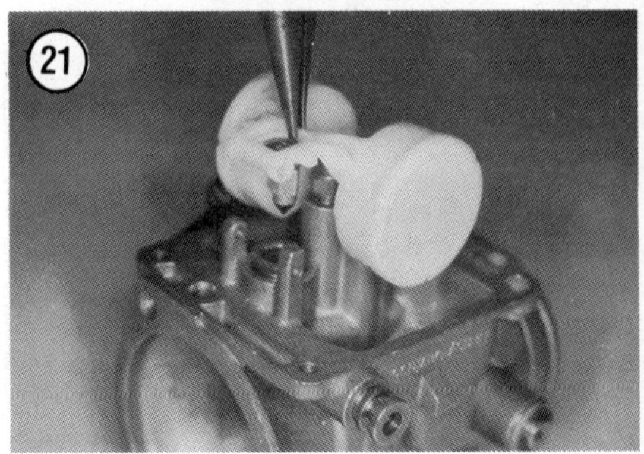

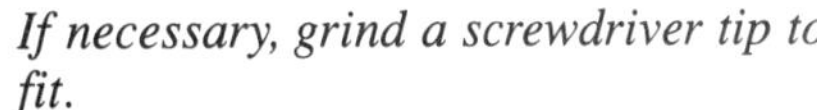
If necessary, grind a screwdriver tip to fit.

8. Remove the remaining cover screws and washers and remove the cover (**Figure 28**) and spring (**Figure 29**).

9. Remove the vacuum piston (**Figure 30**) from the carburetor housing. Do not damage the jet needle sticking out of the bottom of the vacuum piston.

10. Remove the spring seat (A, **Figure 31**) and jet needle (B, **Figure 31**) from the vacuum piston.

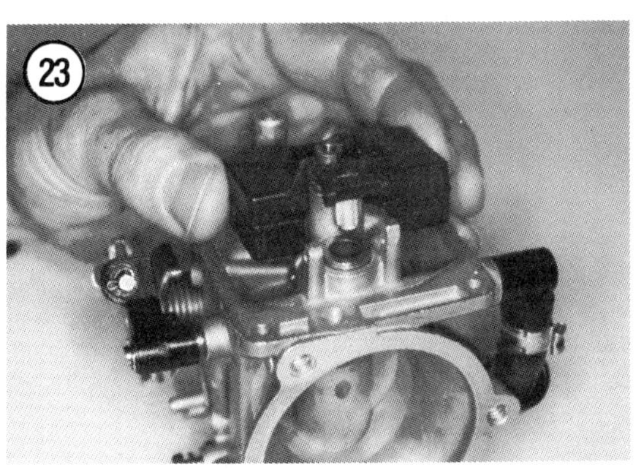

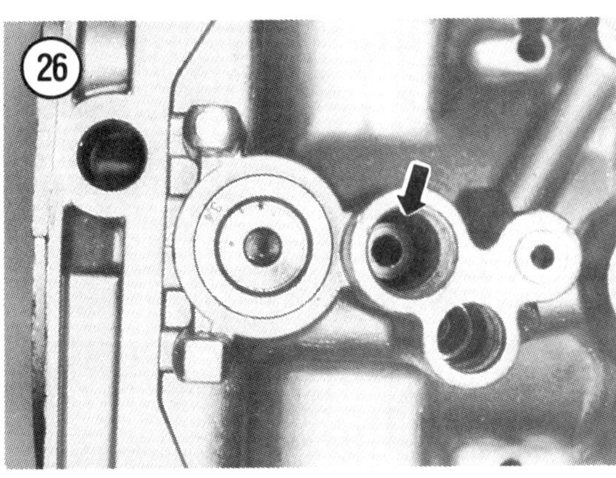

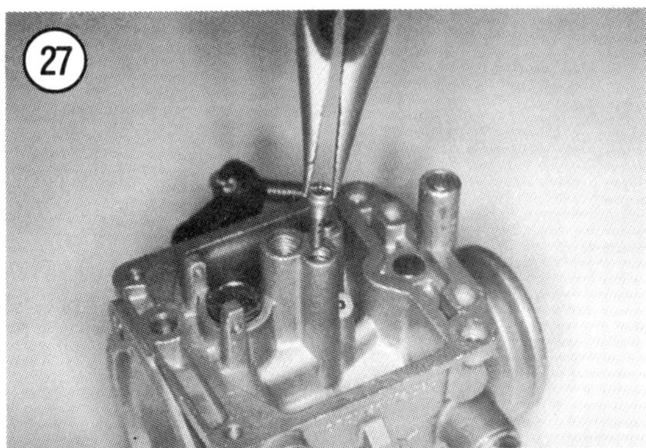

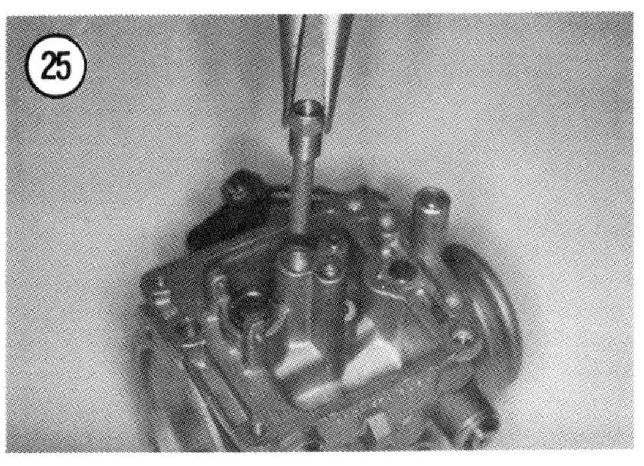

NOTE
An accelerator pump diaphragm is installed in a separate chamber on the bottom side of the float bowl. The accelerator pump reduces engine hesitation by injecting a fine spray of fuel into the carburetor intake passage during sudden acceleration. Because the pump is synchronized with the throttle plate, note the position of the throttle and pump rods when removing the float bowl in the following steps.

11. Remove the accelerator pump diaphragm as follows:
   a. Remove the screws and lockwashers holding the pump cover (**Figure 32**) to the float bowl and remove the cover.
   b. Remove the small pump cover O-ring (**Figure 33**).
   c. Remove the spring (A, **Figure 34**) and diaphragm (B, **Figure 34**).

NOTE
*Replacement parts are not available for the throttle plate (**Figure 35**) assembly. Do not loosen the screws or remove the throttle plate.*

Inspection

CAUTION
Before cleaning plastic or rubber components, make sure that the cleaning agent is compatible with these materials. Some types of solvents can cause permanent damage. Carburetor cleaner use is described in Step 1.

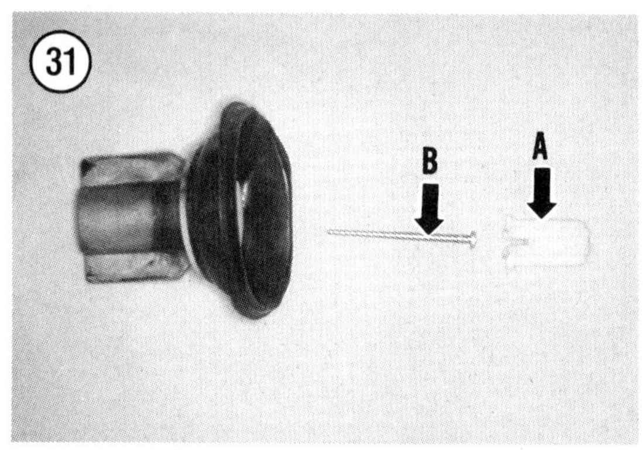

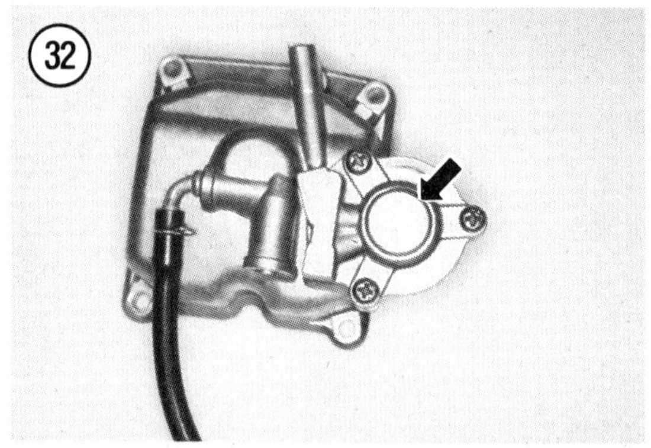

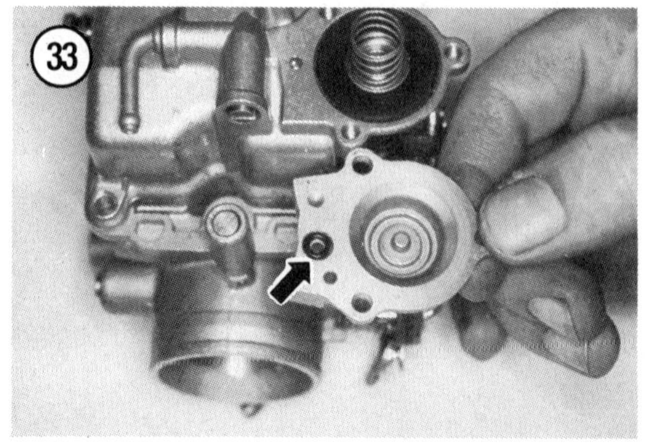

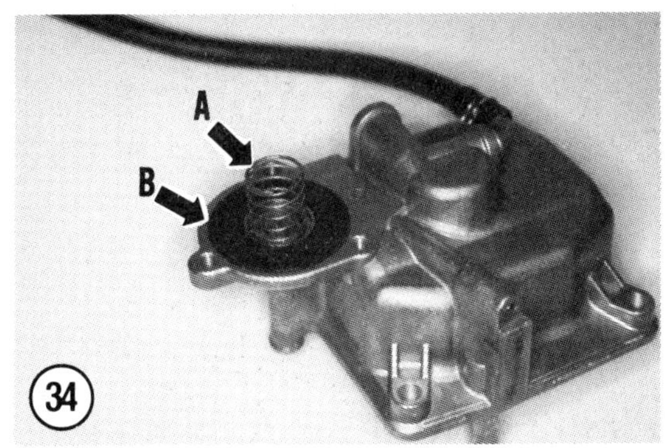

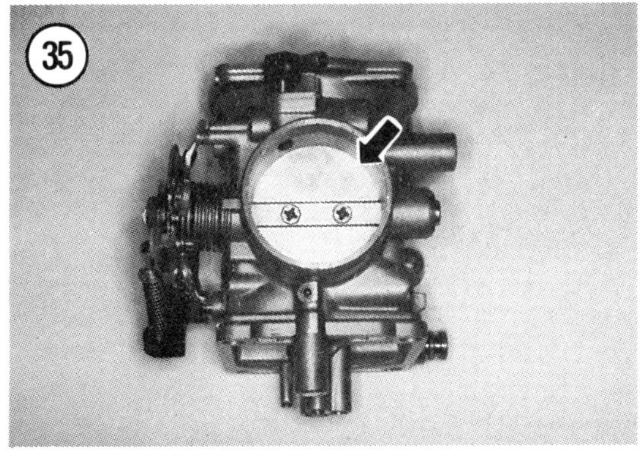

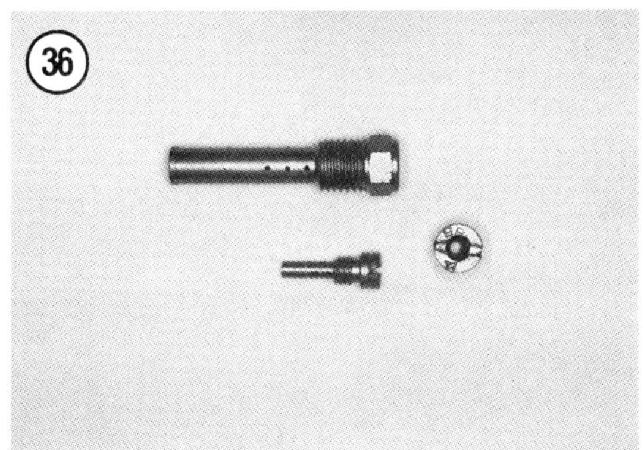

1. Clean all metal parts that were removed from the carburetor body in a good grade of carburetor cleaner. This solution is available at most automotive supply stores, in a small, resealable tank with a dip basket. If it is tightly sealed when not in use, the solution will last for several cleanings. Follow the manufacturer's instructions for correct soaking time.

CAUTION

Do not soak the carburetor body in a tank of carburetor cleaner. The cleaner can damage the non-removable rubber seals used at the throttle plate shaft assembly.

2. Remove all parts from the cleaner and blow dry with compressed air. Blow out the jets (**Figure 36**) with compressed air. *Do not* use a piece of wire to clean them, as minor gouges in a jet can alter the flow rate and upset the air/fuel mixture.
3. Make sure that the needle jet holder (**Figure 36**) bleed tube orifices are clear.
4. Make sure all fuel and air openings are clear. Blow out with compressed air if necessary.
5. Check the float assembly for leaks; see A, **Figure 37** (1991) or **Figure 38** (1992-on). Place the float in a container full of water and push it down. There should be no bubbles. Replace the float assembly if it leaks.
6. Check the float needle (B, **Figure 37**) and seat (**Figure 39**) contact areas closely. Both contact surfaces should appear smooth without any gouging or other apparent damage. Replace the needle if damaged. The seat is a permanent part of the carburetor housing; if damaged the housing must be replaced.
7. A damaged accelerating pump diaphragm (**Figure 40**) will cause poor acceleration. Hold the dia-

7

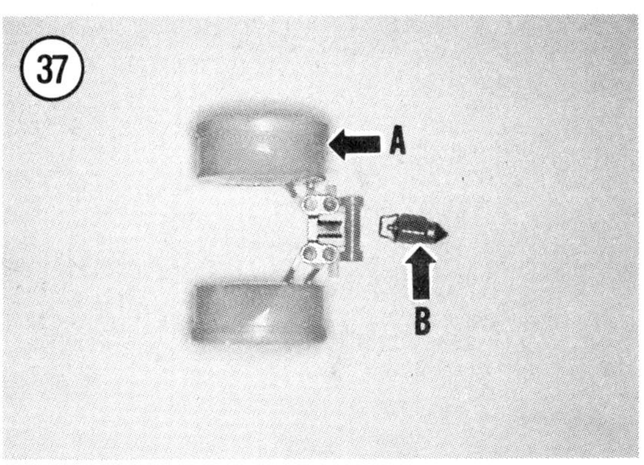

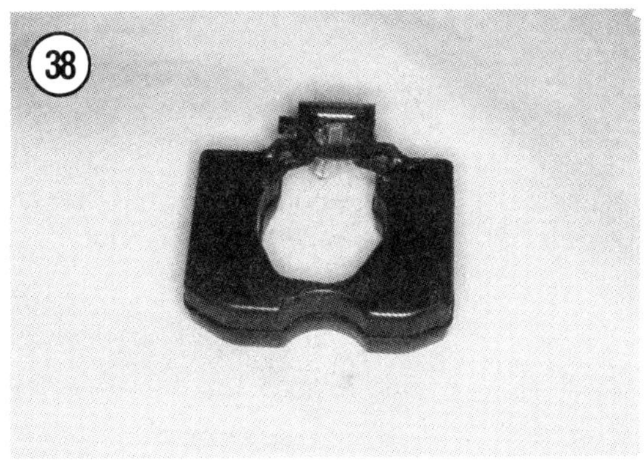

phragm up to a strong light and check the diaphragm for pin holes, cracks or other damage. Replace if necessary.

8. Remove the accelerator pump nozzle and its O-ring (**Figure 41**) from the float bowl. Clean the nozzle with compressed air.

9. Replace the pump rod if bent or worn.

10. O-rings tend to become hardened after prolonged use and heat and therefore lose their ability to seal properly. Inspect all O-rings and replace if necessary. When replacing an O-ring, make sure the new O-ring fits in its groove properly. See **Figure 42**, typical.

11. Inspect the pilot jet (**Figure 36**) for wear or damage that may have occurred during removal. Check the slot in the top of the jet for cracks or breakage. Do not install a damaged pilot jet, as you may not be able to remove it.

NOTE

Step 12 describes bench checks that should be performed to the vacuum piston. Operational checks with the vacuum piston installed in the carburetor and with the engine running are described in this chapter.

12. Bench check the vacuum piston as follows:
   a. Check the spring (**Figure 29**) for fatigue, stretching, distortion or other damage.
   b. Check the vacuum passage through the bottom of the piston (**Figure 43**) for contamination. Clean passage if blocked.
   c. The sides of the piston (**Figure 43**) ride in grooves machined in the carburetor bore. Check these sides for roughness, nicks, cracks or distortion. If the piston sides are damaged, check the mating grooves in the carburetor for dam-

40

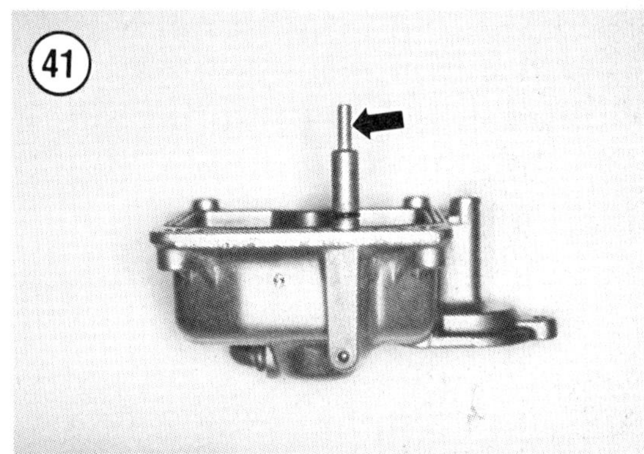
41

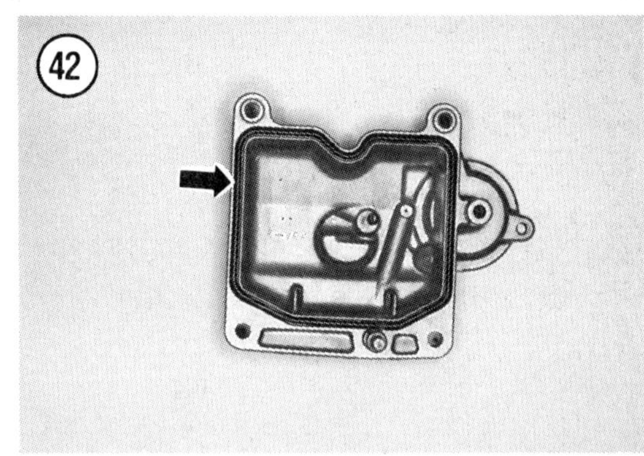
42

39

43

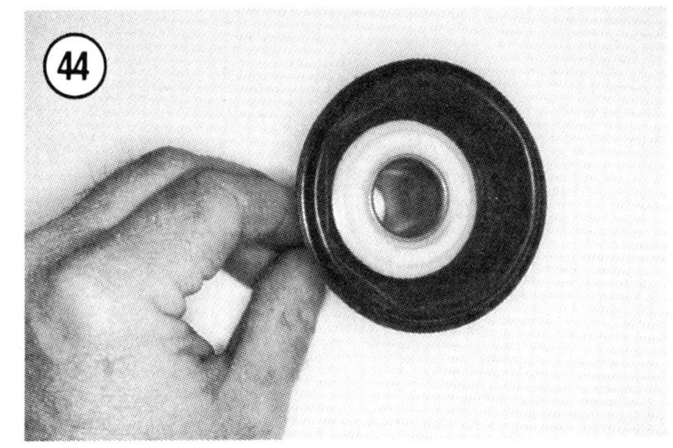

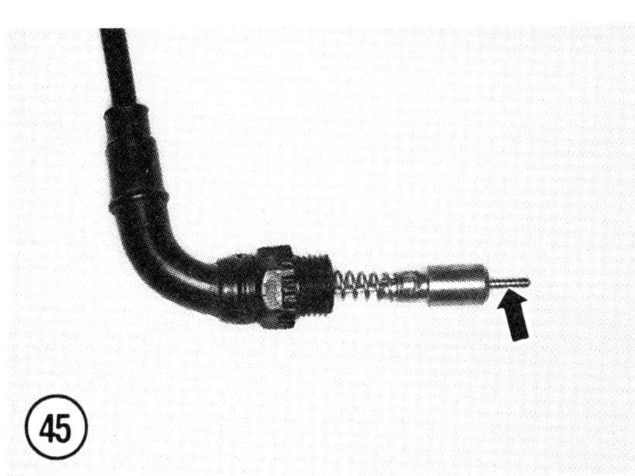

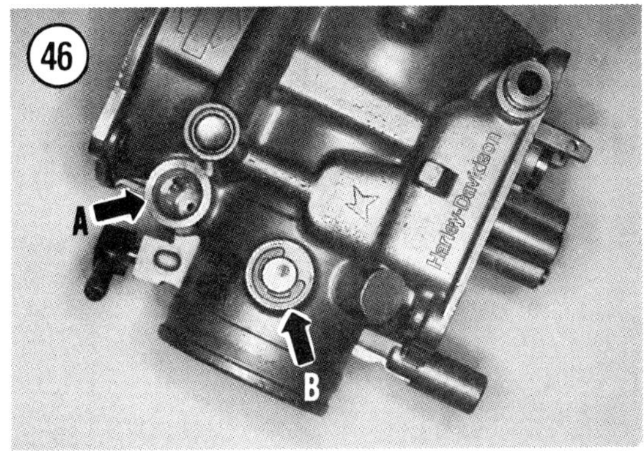

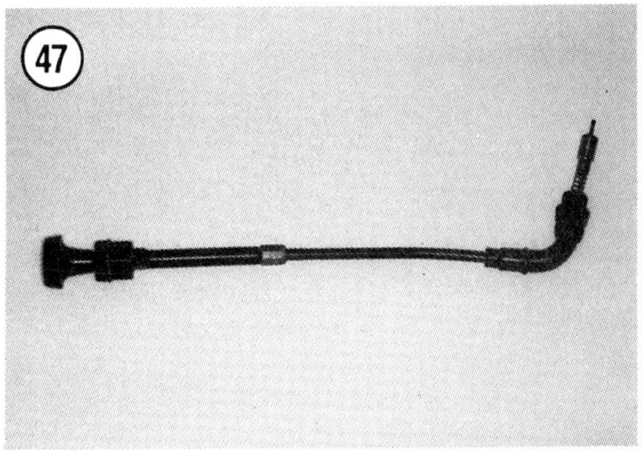

age. Minor roughness can be removed with emery cloth or by buffing. If the sides are severely damaged, the vacuum piston will have to be replaced.

d. Hold the vacuum piston up to a light and check the diaphragm (**Figure 44**) for pin holes, tearing, cracks, age deterioration or other damage. Check the diaphragm where it is mounted against the piston. If the diaphragm is damaged, the vacuum piston must be replaced.

e. Check jet needle (B, **Figure 31**) for bending or damage.

13. A plugged, improperly seating or contaminated enrichener system will cause hard starting as well as poor low and high speed performance. Check the following:

a. Check for a rough or damaged enrichener valve. Check the needle (**Figure 45**) on the end of the enrichener valve for bending or contamination.

b. Check the enrichener valve spring for fatigue, stretching or distortion.

c. The enrichener valve chamber (A, **Figure 46**) in the carburetor must be clean. Clean the chamber carefully, making sure the enrichener valve air inlet and the air/fuel passages are clear.

d. Check the enrichener valve cable (**Figure 47**) for kinks or other damage.

14. Check the throttle rod (**Figure 48**) and all external carburetor components for missing or damaged parts.

15. Check that the throttle valve shaft E-clip (B, **Figure 46**) is properly secured in the groove on the end of the shaft.

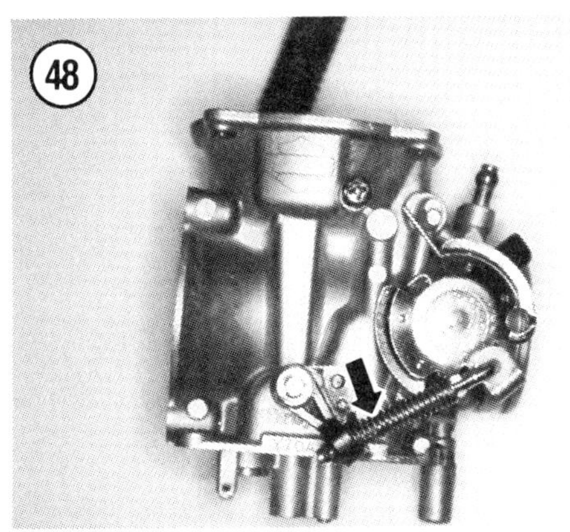

Assembly

Refer to **Figure 13** when performing this procedure.

1. Prior to assembly, perform the *Inspection* procedure to make sure all worn or damaged parts have been repaired or replaced. All parts should be thoroughly cleaned before assembly.

NOTE
*Before installing new jets, check the jet size and compare it to the old jet. If you are not rejetting the carburetor, make sure to install the same size jet(s). See **Table 1** for stock jet sizes.*

2. Drop the pilot jet (**Figure 49**) into the passage and tighten it with the same screwdriver used during removal.
3. The needle jet has 2 different sides and can be installed incorrectly. Install the needle jet into its passage (**Figure 50**) so that the end with the larger opening faces up toward the vacuum piston chamber.
4. Install the needle jet holder (**Figure 51**) into the main jet passage and tighten it securely.
5. Install the main jet (**Figure 52**) onto the end of the needle jet holder and tighten securely.

6A. On 1991 models, install the float as follows:

a. Install the fuel valve onto the float (**Figure 53**) and position the float onto the carburetor so that the valve drops into its seat.
b. Align the float pivot arm with the 2 carburetor mounting posts and slip the pin through the float pivot arm and mounting posts (**Figure 54**).

6B. On 1992-on models, install the float as follows:

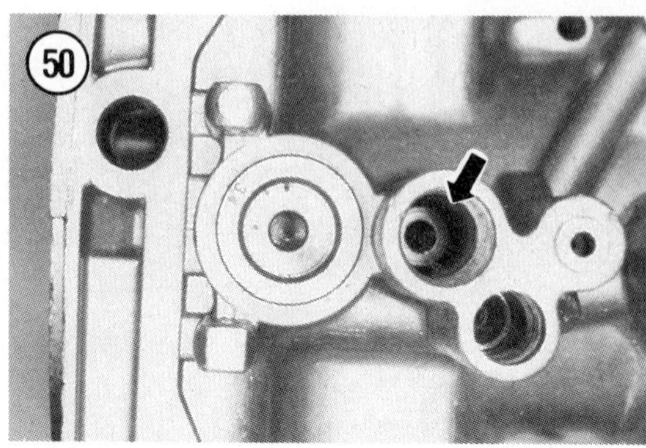
50

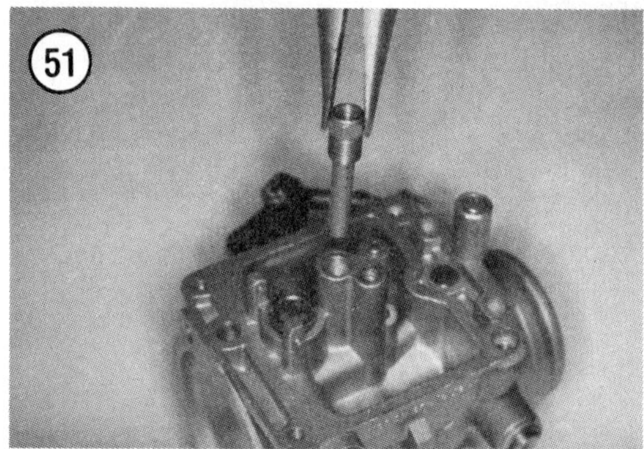
51

52

49

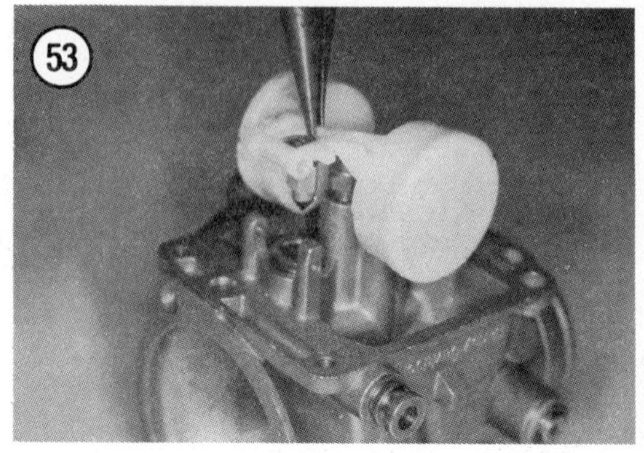
53

54

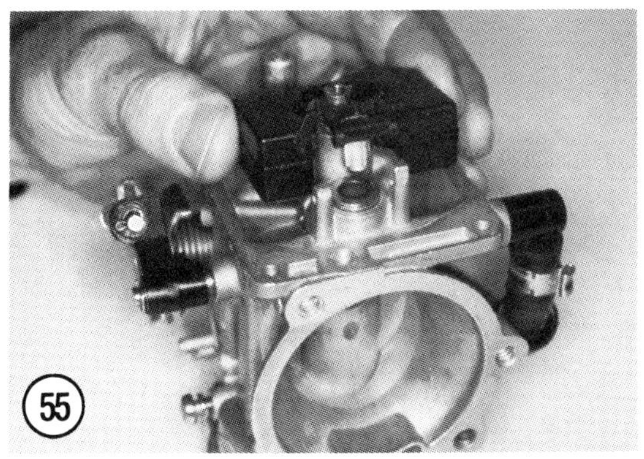
55

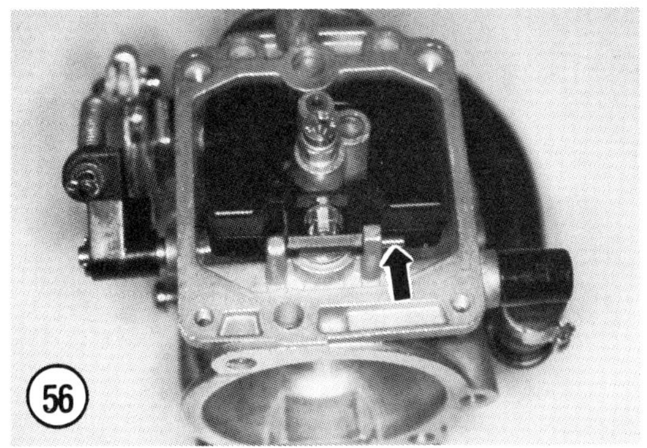
56

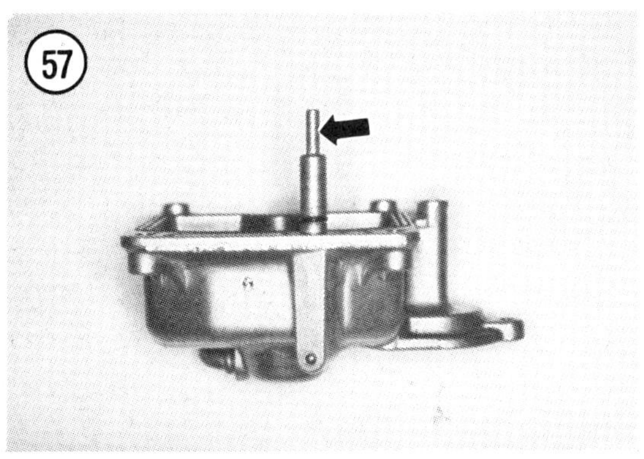
57

a. Install the fuel valve onto the float (**Figure 55**) and position the float onto the carburetor so that the valve drops into its seat.
b. Align the float pivot arm with the 2 carburetor mounting posts and slip the pin through the float pivot arm and mounting posts (**Figure 56**).

7. Check float level as described in this chapter.
8. Assemble and install the float bowl as follows:

a. Insert the accelerator pump nozzle into the float bowl. Install the O-ring onto the nozzle. See **Figure 57**.
b. Install the rubber boot (A, **Figure 58**) and O-ring (B, **Figure 58**) onto the float bowl.
c. Connect the pump rod onto the lever assembly on the carburetor (**Figure 59**).
d. Insert the pump rod through the boot on the float bowl and engage the rod with the diaphragm while installing the float bowl (**Figure 60**) onto the carburetor. Then check that the pump rod is still attached to the lever assembly as shown in **Figure 61**. Check also to see if the pump rod is visible through the hole in the pump chamber in the float bowl (**Figure 62**). If not, remove and reinstall the float bowl and pump rod.

7

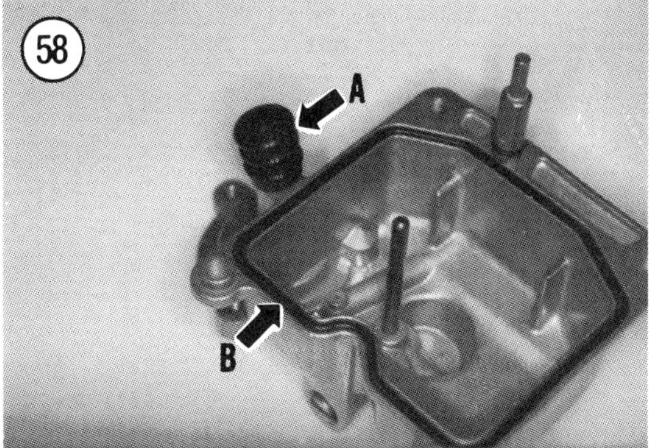

58

59

  e. Install the float bowl screws and washers and tighten securely in a crisscross pattern.

9. Install the accelerator pump diaphragm assembly as follows:
  a. Insert the accelerator pump diaphragm into the bottom of the float bowl. Make sure the diaphragm seats around the bowl groove evenly (**Figure 63**).
  b. Install the spring into the center of accelerator pump diaphragm (**Figure 64**).
  c. Install the O-ring into the cover passageway hole (**Figure 65**).
  d. Align the cover assembly with the diaphragm and bowl and install the cover assembly. Install the screws and lockwashers and tighten securely. See **Figure 66**.

10. Drop the jet needle (B, **Figure 67**) through the center hole in the vacuum piston. Insert the spring seat (A, **Figure 67**) over the top of the needle to secure it.

11. Align the slides on the vacuum piston with the grooves in the carburetor bore and install the vacuum piston (**Figure 68**). The slides on the piston are offset, so the piston can only be installed one way. When installing the vacuum piston, make sure the jet needle drops through the needle jet.

12. Seat the outer edge of the vacuum piston into the groove at the top of the carburetor piston chamber.

13. Insert the spring (**Figure 69**) into the vacuum piston so that the end of the spring fits over the spring seat.

14. Align the free end of the spring with the carburetor top and install the top onto the carburetor, compressing the spring.

15. Hold the carburetor top in place and lift the vacuum piston with your finger. The piston should

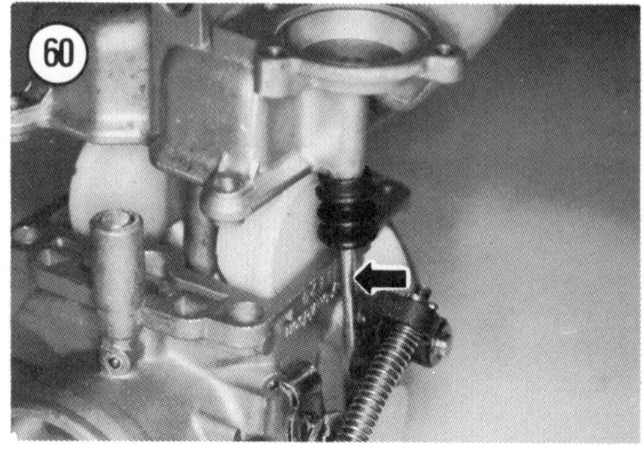
60

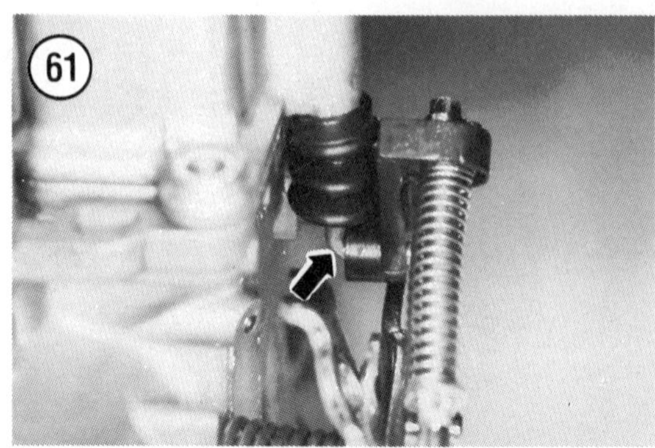
61

62

63

64

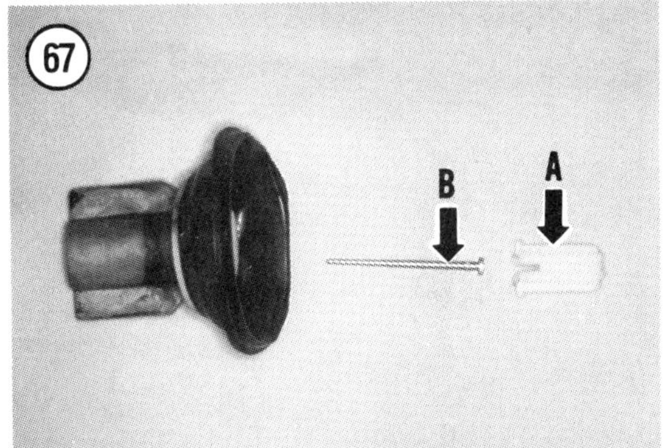

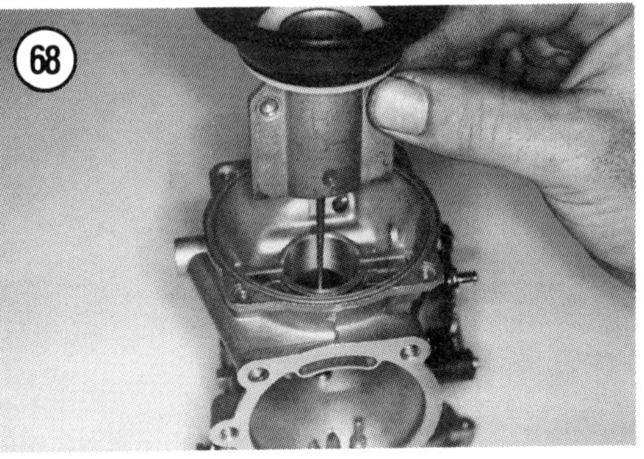

move smoothly. If the piston movement is rough or sluggish, the spring may be improperly installed. Remove the top and reinstall the spring.

16. Install the 3 carburetor top screws, lockwashers and flat washers securely.

NOTE

*If you want to install the throttle cable bracket prior to installing the carburetor on the engine, perform Step 17. Otherwise, you can connect the cables to the throttle cable bracket and then install the bracket onto the carburetor; see **Carburetor Removal/Installation** in this chapter.*

17. Install the throttle cable bracket (A, **Figure 70**) onto the carburetor so that the end of the idle speed screw engages the top of the throttle cam stop (B, **Figure 70**). Hold the bracket in place and install the bracket's side mounting screw and washer; tighten screw securely. Then install the upper bracket mounting screw (**Figure 71**), lockwasher and flat washer finger-tight. Tighten the remaining carburetor cap screw securely.

7

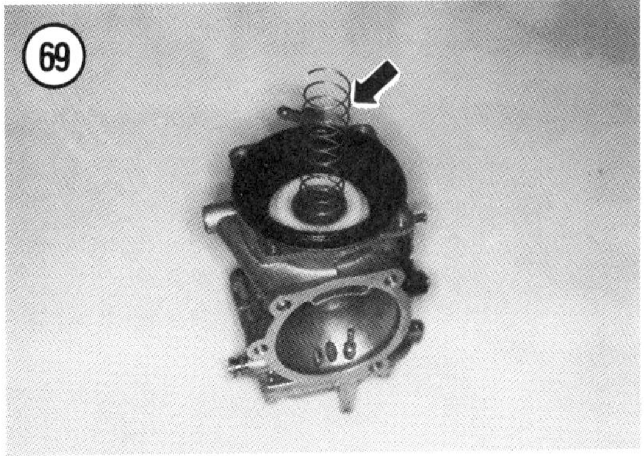

18. Align the enrichener valve needle with the needle passage in the carburetor (**Figure 72**) and install the enrichener valve. Tighten the valve nut securely.
19. Install the float bowl overflow hose and secure it with its clamp.

Float Level Adjustment (1991)

An incorrect float level can cause flooding as well as poor fuel economy and acceleration.

The carburetor must be removed and partially disassembled for this adjustment.

1. Remove the carburetor as described in this chapter.
2. Remove the float bowl as described in this chapter.
3. One-piece floats are used in the carburetor. Before checking the float level, check that the 2 float halves (**Figure 73**) are aligned at an equal height with each other. If the float halves are not in alignment, remove the float and check it for damage.
4. Turn the carburetor to position the float bowl as shown in **Figure 74**. Measure the float height from the face of the bowl mounting flange surface to the bottom float surface (**Figure 74**). Do not apply pressure to the float when measuring. The correct float height is 0.690-0.730 in. (17.5-18.5 mm).
5. If the float level is incorrect, remove the float pin and float. With a screwdriver, bend the tab on the float hinge that contacts the fuel valve.
6. Reinstall the float and the float pin and recheck the float level. Repeat until the float level is correct.
7. Reinstall the float bowl and carburetor as described in this chapter.

Float Adjustment (1992-on)

An incorrect float level can cause flooding as well as poor fuel economy and acceleration.

The carburetor must be removed and partially disassembled for this adjustment.

1. Remove the carburetor as described in this chapter.
2. Remove the float bowl as described in this chapter.
3. One-piece floats are used in the carburetor. Before checking the float level, check that the 2 float halves (**Figure 75**) are aligned at an equal height

71

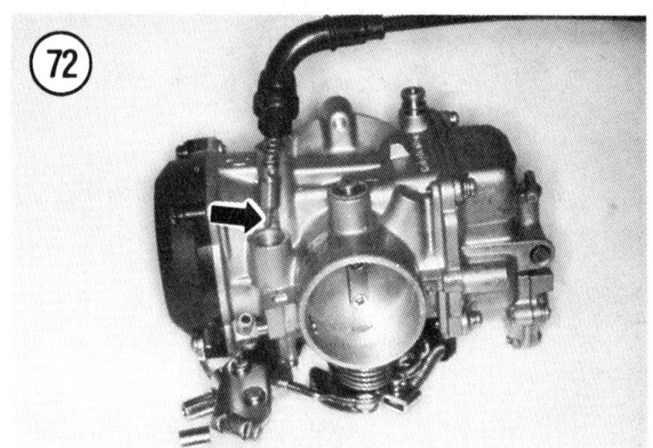
72

73

74 FLOAT HEIGHT

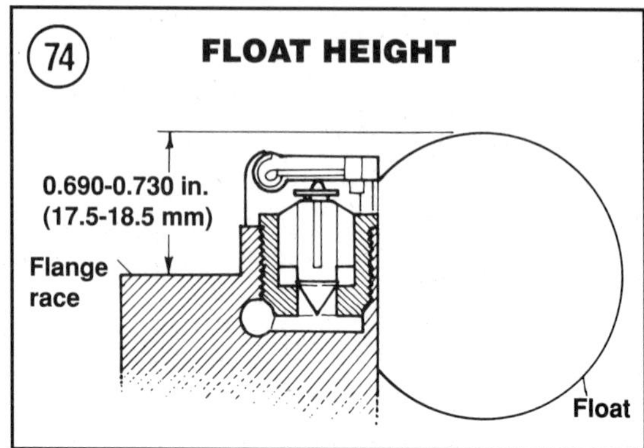

75

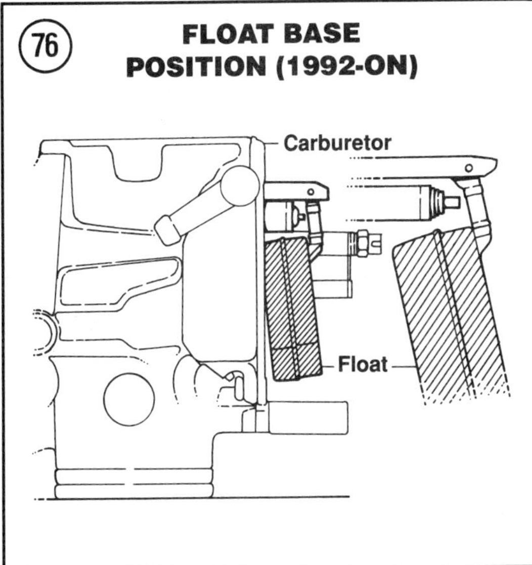

76
FLOAT BASE POSITION (1992-ON)

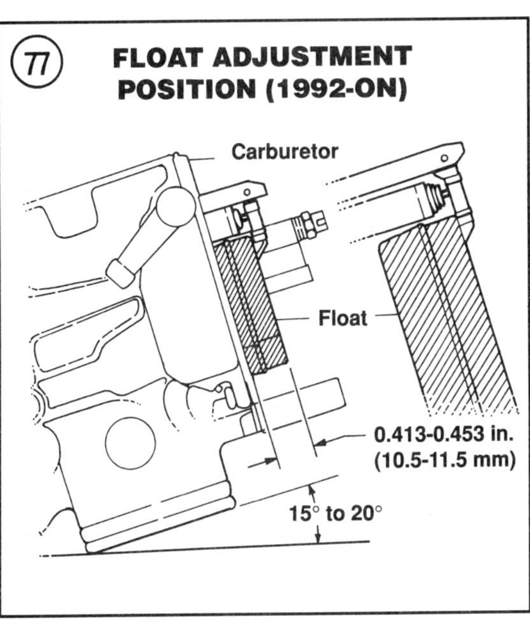

77
FLOAT ADJUSTMENT POSITION (1992-ON)

with each other. If the float halves are not in alignment, remove the float and check it for damage.

4. Place the carburetor intake spigot on a flat surface as shown in **Figure 76**. This is the base position.

5. Tilt the carburetor counterclockwise 15-20° as shown in **Figure 77**. At this position, the float will come to rest as the float pin compresses without compressing the pin return spring.

NOTE
If the carburetor is tilted less than 15° or more than 20°, the following carburetor measurements will be incorrect.

6. Measure from the carburetor flange surface to the top of the float with a caliper or float gauge as shown in **Figure 77**. When measuring float level, make sure you do not compress the float. The correct float level measurement is 0.413-0.453 in. (10.5-11.5 mm).

7. If the float level is incorrect, remove the float pin and float. With a screwdriver, bend the tab on the float hinge that contacts the fuel valve.

8. Reinstall the float and the float pin and recheck the float level. Repeat until the float level is correct.

9. Reinstall the float bowl and carburetor as described in this chapter.

CARBURETOR REJETTING

Do not try to solve a poor running engine problem by rejetting the carburetor if all of the following conditions hold true.

1. The engine has held a good tune in the past with the standard jetting.

2. The engine has not been modified (this includes the addition of accessory exhaust systems).

3. The motorcycle is being operated in the same geographical region under the same general climatic conditions as in the past.

4. The motorcycle was and is being ridden at average highway speeds.

If those conditions all hold true, the chances are that the problem is due to a malfunction in the carburetor or in another component that needs to be adjusted or repaired. Changing carburetor jet size probably won't solve the problem. Rejetting the carburetor may be necessary if any of the following conditions hold true.

1. A non-standard type of air filter element is being used.

2. A non-standard exhaust system is installed on the motorcycle.
3. Any of the following engine components have been modified: pistons, cams, valves, compression ratio, etc.

NOTE
When installing accessory engine equipment, manufacturers often enclose guidelines on rejetting the carburetor.

4. The motorcycle is in use at considerably higher or lower altitudes or in a considerably hotter or colder climate than in the past.
5. The motorcycle is being operated at considerably higher speeds than before and changing to colder spark plugs does not solve the problem.
6. Someone has previously changed the carburetor jetting.
7. The motorcycle has never held a satisfactory engine tune.

NOTE
If it is necessary to rejet the carburetor, check with a dealer or motorcycle performance tuner for recommendations as to the size of jets to install for your specific situation.

THROTTLE AND IDLE CABLE REPLACEMENT

All models use a dual cable arrangement. The throttle cable is installed into the right-hand anchor slot at the top of the throttle housing. The idle cable is installed into the left-hand anchor slot at the top of the throttle housing. See **Figure 78**, typical.

NOTE
You can identify the throttle and idle cables by checking the size of the threads used on each cable's threaded adjuster. The throttle cable uses a 5/16-18 in. threaded adjuster. The threaded adjuster on the idle cable uses 1/4-20 in. threads.

1. Remove the air filter and backplate as described in Chapter Three.
2. Slide the rubber boot (**Figure 79**) on each cable away from its cable adjuster.

HANDLEBAR THROTTLE CONTROL ASSEMBLY

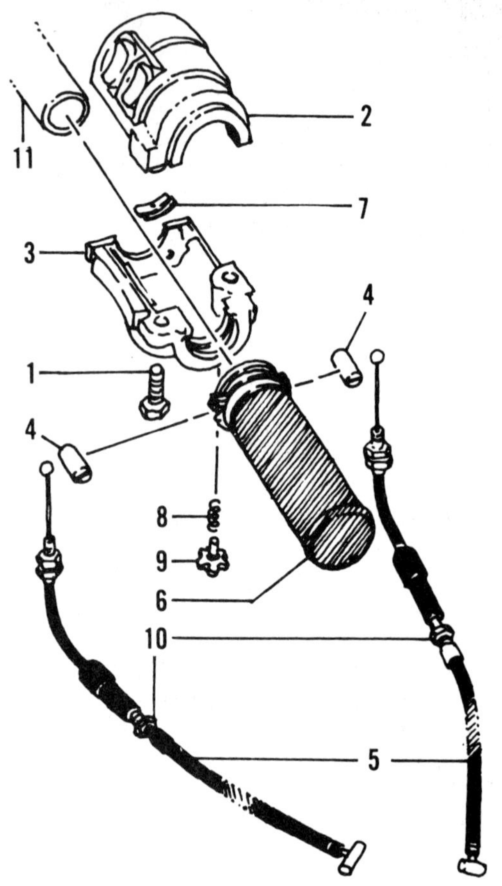

1. Screw
2. Upper housing
3. Lower housing
4. Ferrule
5. Control cable
6. Throttle grip
7. Friction spring
8. Spring
9. Adjusting screw
10. Adjusting nut
11. Handlebar

78

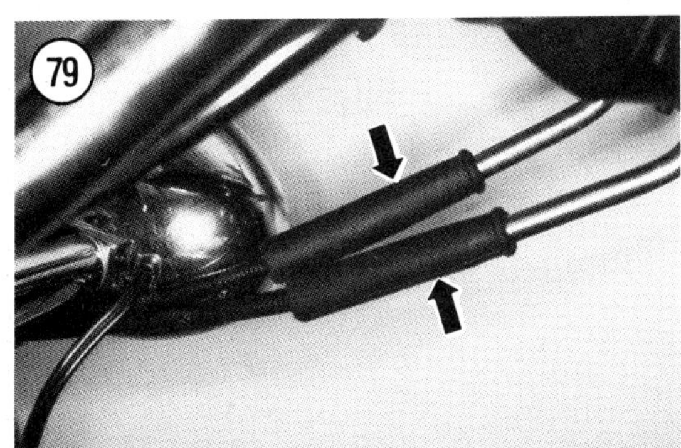

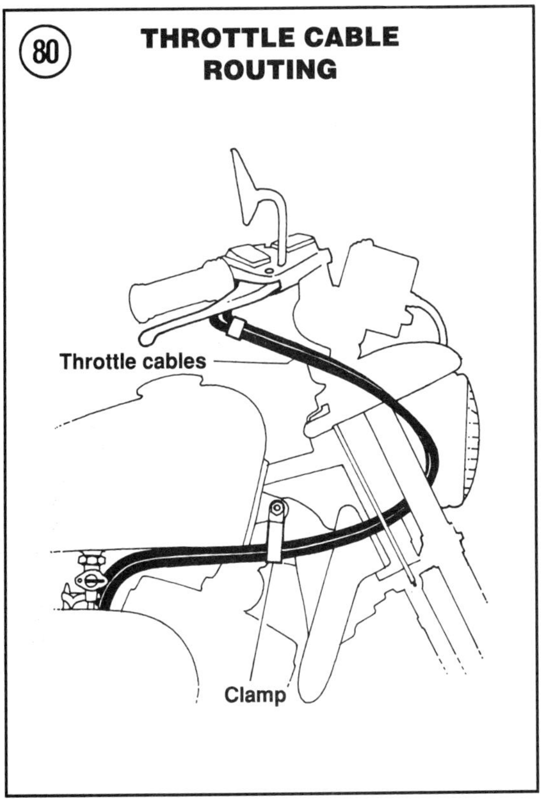

80

THROTTLE CABLE ROUTING

Throttle cables

Clamp

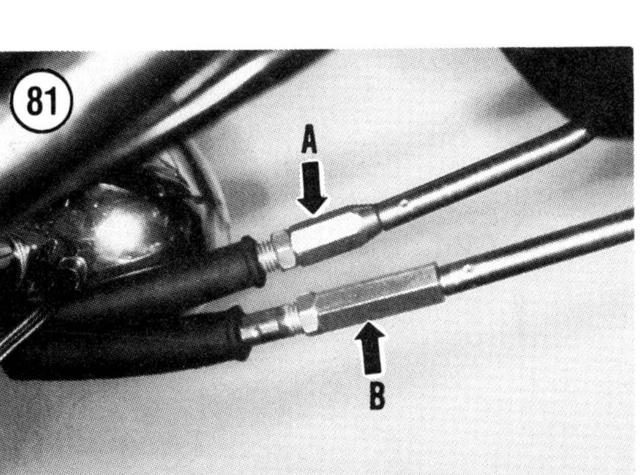

NOTE
Compare the routing of both cables with the routing path shown in ***Figure 80****. If necessary, make a diagram of the routing path for reassembly.*

3. Loosen the cable adjust nuts and turn the cable adjusters to obtain as much cable slack as possible. See A and B, **Figure 81**.
4. Remove the screws securing the upper and lower right-hand switch/throttle housing (**Figure 82**) together and separate the housing from the handlebar.
5. Loosen the cable locknuts at the lower switch housing.
6. Unhook the cables from the throttle grip and remove the ferrule from the end of each cable.
7. Unscrew each cable and remove it from the lower housing assembly.
8. At the carburetor, hold the lever up with one hand and disengage the cable end. Slip the cable out through the carburetor bracket. Repeat for the other cable. **Figure 83** shows the throttle cables with the carburetor removed for clarity.
9. Pass both cables through the bracket mounted on the front fuel tank mounting bolt (**Figure 84**).

10. Remove the cables from the bike.

11. Clean the throttle grip in solvent and dry thoroughly. Check the throttle slots for cracks or other damage. Replace the throttle if necessary.

12. The friction adjust screw is secured to the lower switch housing with a circlip. If necessary, remove the friction spring, circlip, spring and friction adjust screw. Check these parts for wear or damage. Replace damaged parts and reverse to install. Make sure the circlip seats in the friction screw groove completely.

13. Clean the throttle area on the handlebar with solvent or electrical contact cleaner.

14. Lightly wipe the throttle area on the handlebar with graphite.

NOTE
*The throttle cable (A, **Figure 81**) uses a 5/16-18 in. threaded cable adjuster.*

15. Screw the throttle cable into the lower switch housing and fit the ferrule onto the end of the cable. Then insert the ferrule into the right-hand anchor slot at the top of the throttle.

NOTE
*The idle cable (B, **Figure 81**) uses a 1/4-20 in. threaded cable adjuster.*

16. Screw the idle cable into the lower switch housing and fit the ferrule onto the end of the cable. Then insert the ferrule into the left-hand anchor slot at the top of the throttle.

17. Assemble the upper and lower switch housings and slide the throttle grip onto the handlebar. Install the housing screws and tighten securely. Operate the throttle and make sure both cables move in and out properly.

18. Route the throttle cables from the throttle grip to the carburetor as shown in **Figure 80**. Pass both cables through the fuel tank bracket as shown in **Figure 84**.

19. Install the throttle cable (A, **Figure 81**) into the shorter, outboard cable guide on the carburetor bracket; see A, **Figure 83**.

20. Install the idle cable (B, **Figure 81**) into the longer, inboard cable guide on the carburetor bracket; see B, **Figure 83**.

21. Operate the throttle grip and make sure the carburetor throttle linkage is operating correctly and with no binding. If operation is incorrect or there is

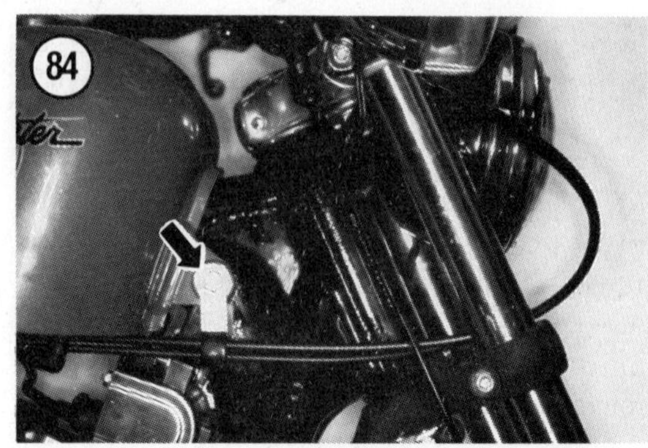

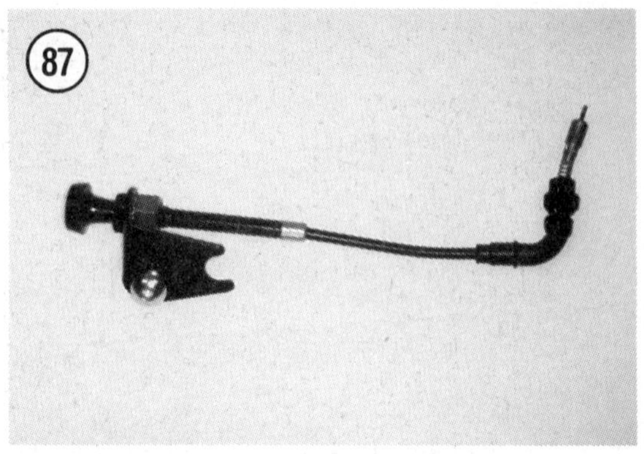

binding, carefully check that the cables are attached correctly and there are no tight bends in the cables.

22. Adjust the throttle and idle cables as described in Chapter Three.

23. Start the engine and allow it to idle in NEUTRAL. Then turn the handlebar from side-to-side. Do not operate the throttle. If the engine speed increases as the handlebar assembly is turned, the throttle cables are routed incorrectly. Recheck cable routing and adjustment.

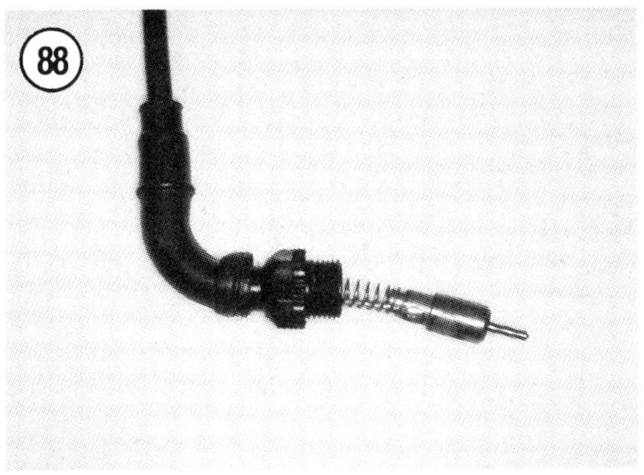

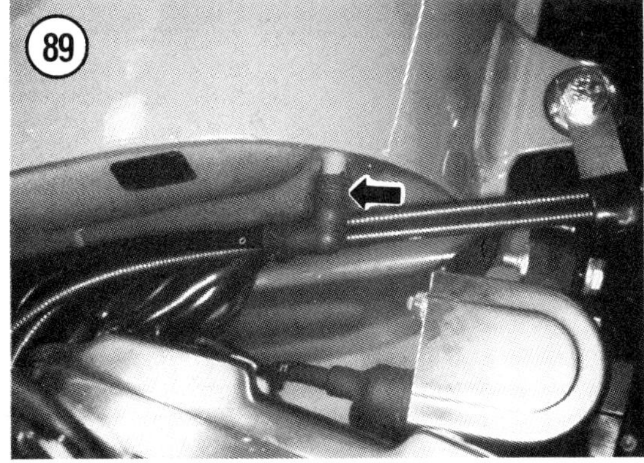

WARNING
Do not ride the motorcycle until the throttle cables are properly adjusted.

ENRICHENER CABLE REPLACEMENT

1. Remove the air filter and backplate as described in Chapter Three.
2. Remove the enrichener bracket mounting screw (**Figure 85**) and allow the bracket to rest on top of the intake manifold.
3. Unscrew the enrichener from the carburetor. **Figure 86** shows the enrichener cable with the carburetor removed for clarity.
4. Remove the enrichener cable (**Figure 87**) from the motorcycle.
5. Remove the bracket from the enrichener cable.
6. Reverse these steps to install the enrichener cable while noting the following.
7. Align the enrichener valve needle with the needle passage in the carburetor (**Figure 88**) and install the enrichener valve. Tighten the valve nut securely.
8. Adjust the enrichener cable as described in Chapter Three.

FUEL TANK

The fuel tank is bolted to the upper frame tube. A 3-way fuel shutoff valve is mounted on the bottom of the tank on the right-hand side.

Depending on model year and state, fuel tank venting is as follows:

a. On 1991 non-California models, the filler cap is equipped with a pressure/vacuum relief valve for fuel tank venting.
b. On 1991 California models, refer to *Evaporative Emission Control System* for fuel tank venting information.
c. On 1992-on models, the fuel tank is vented through a standpipe installed inside the fuel tank. A hose is connected to the standpipe nozzle (**Figure 89**) at the bottom of the tank. This tube is routed along the frame and connected to a vapor valve (**Figure 90**) mounted to the frame and located between the battery and oil tank. On non-California models, a hose connected to the bottom of the vapor valve connects to a fitting in the hollow frame member. On California models, a hose connected to the bottom of the vapor valve connects to the carbon canister.

WARNING
Make sure the fuel tank vapor hoses are routed in such a way that they cannot contact any hot engine or exhaust component. These hoses contain flammable vapors. If a hose melts from contacting a hot part, leaking vapors may ignite, causing severe bike damage and rider injury.

Removal/Installation

When removing the fuel tank in the following procedure, keep track of all fasteners and rubber bushings so that you don't lose or mix them up during installation. Installing the fasteners into their original mounting positions can help to prevent excessive tank vibration that could cause the tank to crack later on.

Refer to **Figure 91** (1991-1992) or **Figure 92** (1993-on).

WARNING
Gasoline is very volatile and presents an extreme fire hazard. Be sure to work in a well-ventilated area away from any open flames (including pilot lights on household appliances). Do not allow anyone to smoke in the area. Have a fire extinguisher rated for gasoline fires handy.

1. Disconnect the negative battery lead.
2. Disconnect the fuel supply hose at the fuel shutoff valve (**Figure 93**). Connect a longer hose to the shutoff valve fitting and place the open end of the hose into gasoline storage tank or can. Turn the shutoff valve to RESERVE and drain the fuel into the tank. Don't lose the fuel line insulator.
3. Remove the front (**Figure 94**) and rear (**Figure 95**) fuel tank mounting fasteners.
4. Disconnect the vapor vent hose from the fitting on the bottom of the fuel tank (**Figure 89**), if so equipped.

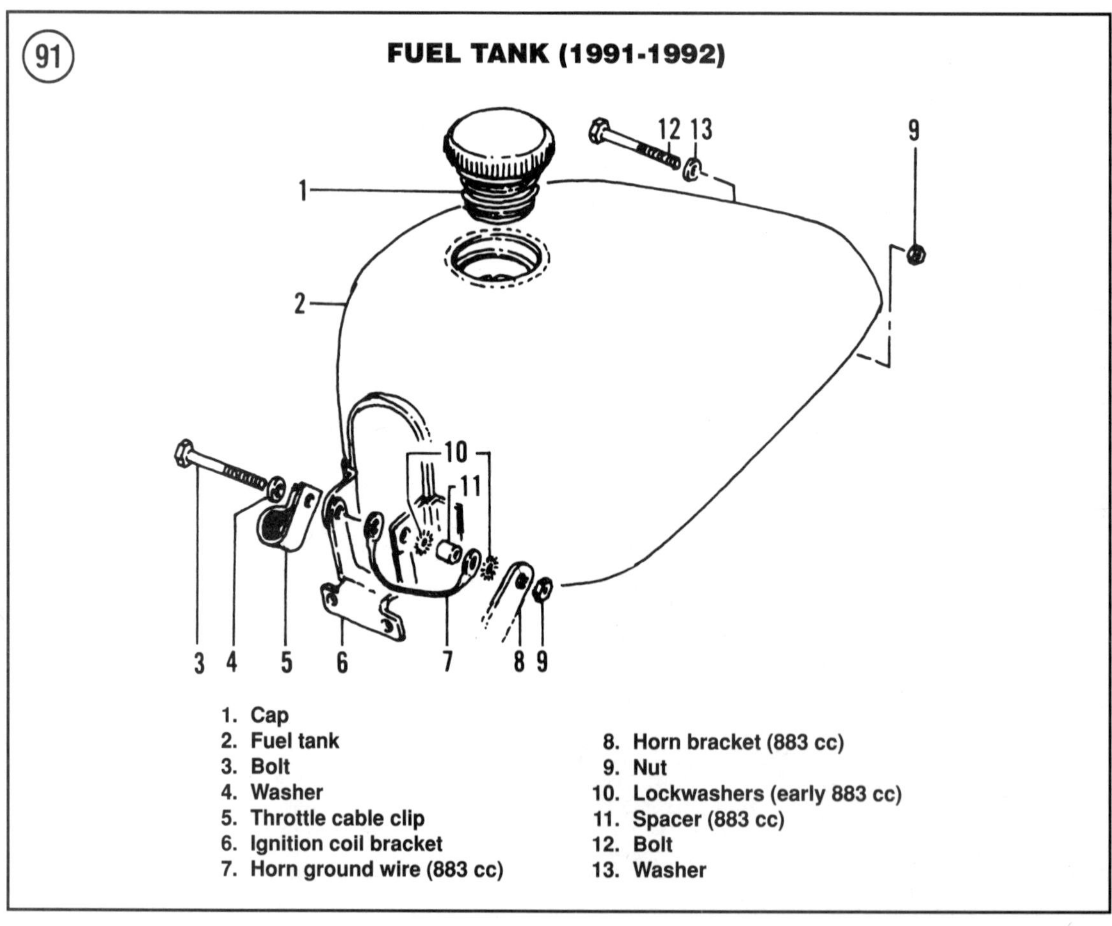

91 **FUEL TANK (1991-1992)**

1. Cap
2. Fuel tank
3. Bolt
4. Washer
5. Throttle cable clip
6. Ignition coil bracket
7. Horn ground wire (883 cc)
8. Horn bracket (883 cc)
9. Nut
10. Lockwashers (early 883 cc)
11. Spacer (883 cc)
12. Bolt
13. Washer

5. Remove the fuel tank.

NOTE
Store the fuel tank in a safe place—away from open flame or objects that could fall and damage it.

6. Drain any remaining fuel left in the tanks into the proper gasoline storage tank or can.
7. Installation is the reverse of these steps. Note the following.
8. Tighten the front and rear bolts to the tightening torque listed in **Table 2**.

NOTE
On 883 cc models, make sure the horn does not contact the frame or ignition coil bracket.

9. Reconnect the fuel supply hose (**Figure 93**) to the fuel valve and secure it with a new clamp.
10. Refill the tank and check for leaks.

Inspection

Refer to **Figure 91** or **Figure 92** for this procedure.

1. Inspect all of the fuel and vent lines for cracks, age deterioration or damage. Replace damaged lines with the same type and size materials. The fuel line must be flexible and strong enough to withstand engine heat and vibration.
2. Check the fuel line insulator for damage.
3. Check for damaged or missing rubber dampers.

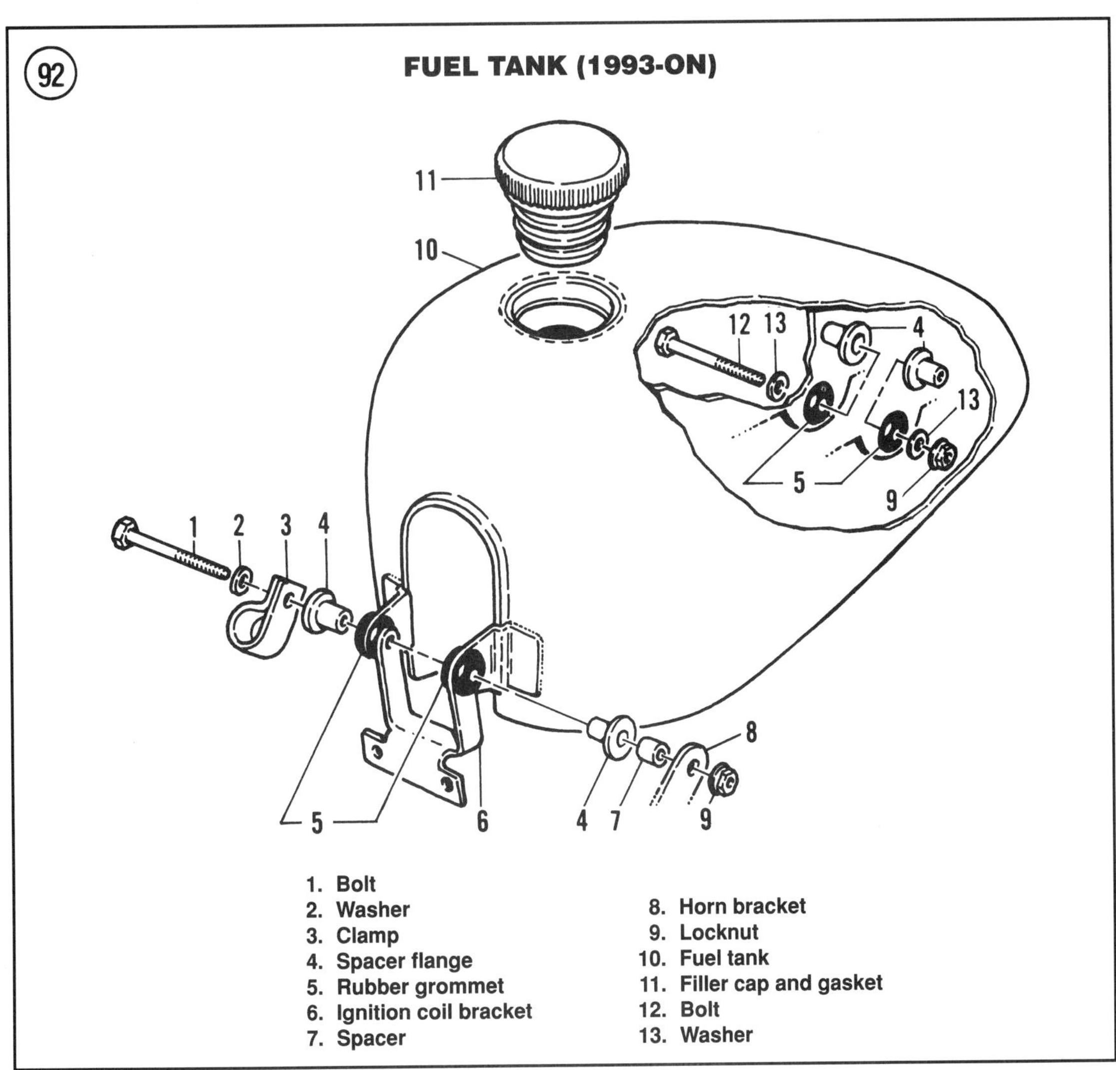

(92) **FUEL TANK (1993-ON)**

1. Bolt
2. Washer
3. Clamp
4. Spacer flange
5. Rubber grommet
6. Ignition coil bracket
7. Spacer
8. Horn bracket
9. Locknut
10. Fuel tank
11. Filler cap and gasket
12. Bolt
13. Washer

4. Remove the filler cap and inspect the inside of the tank for rust or contamination. If there is a rust buildup inside the tank, clean and flush the tank as described in this chapter.
5. Inspect the fuel tank for leaks.

Fuel Tank Flushing

While the fuel tank requires very little in the way of service, moisture inside the tank can cause the tank to rust. If allowed to go unchecked, rust will cause fuel supply and carburetor problems. If rust has formed in the tank, perform the following.

1. Remove and drain the fuel tank as described in this chapter.
2. Remove the fuel shutoff valve as described in this chapter. While the valve is off the tank, clean it as described in this chapter.
3. Plug all of the tank openings.

NOTE
The following steps describe the use of soap and water to clean the tank. If you plan to use a commercial fuel tank cleaning agent, follow the manufacturer's instructions.

4. To help break up the rust buildup, add a number of non-ferrous balls or pellets into the tank. Count the number of balls put into the tank so that you can be sure all of the balls are removed after cleaning.

WARNING
Do not use metal balls to loosen fuel tank deposits. Metal balls can produce a spark that could ignite fumes trapped in the tank, causing a serious explosion and possible personal injury.

5. Prepare a soap and water solution and pour it into the tank. Install the fuel cap and shake the tank to move the balls around and break up the rust deposits.
6. After cleaning the inside of the tank, pour the tank's contents into a container so that you can count the balls added previously.
7. If necessary, repeat Steps 5 and 6 until all of the rust has been removed. If the rust buildup is difficult to remove, you will have to use a commercial cleaning agent.

NOTE
If you are going to put the tank into storage, pour an equal amount of fuel and oil into the tank. This will prevent rust buildup during storage. Drain and flush the tank before starting the engine.

8. After all of the rust has been removed and the tank has been thoroughly flushed, allow it to air dry before installing it.

Repairing Minor Tank Leaks (Pin Hole Size)

Small pin hole size leaks can be repaired with a commercial fuel tank sealant. Follow the manufacturer's instructions. If the leak cannot be repaired with the sealant, refer further service to your dealer.

WARNING
Welding a metal tank is serious business, as any trace of fuel left in the tank can cause it to explode. If the tank must be welded, refer service to your dealer. Do not attempt this repair at home. A tank explosion can cause severe personal injury.

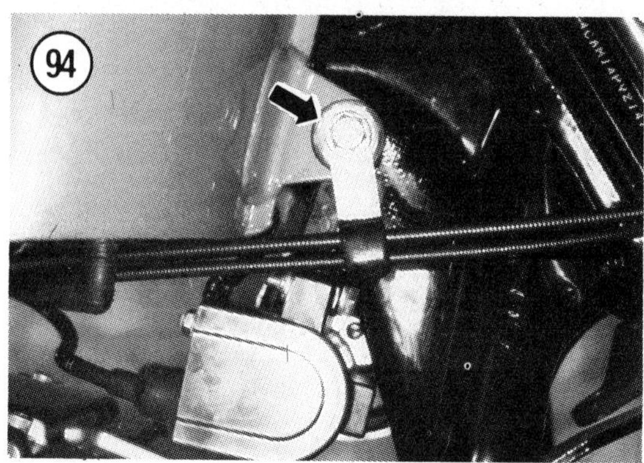

FUEL SHUTOFF VALVE

A 3-way fuel shutoff valve is mounted onto the left-hand fuel tank (**Figure 93**). A replaceable fuel strainer is mounted at the top of the shutoff valve.

Removal/Installation and Filter Cleaning

The fuel filter removes particles which might otherwise enter into the carburetor and possibly cause the float needle to remain in the open position.

Refer to **Figure 93** and **Figure 96** for this procedure.

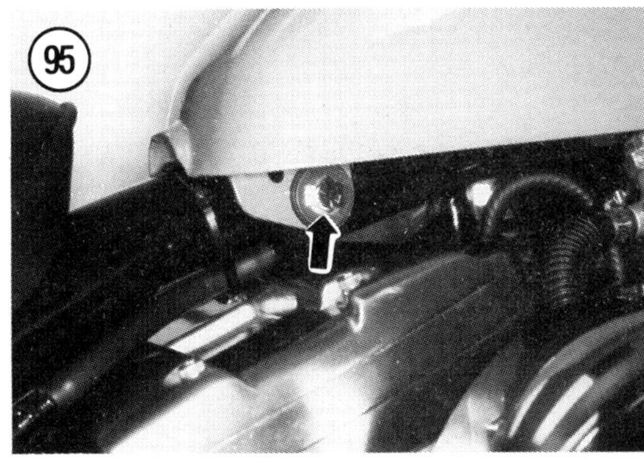

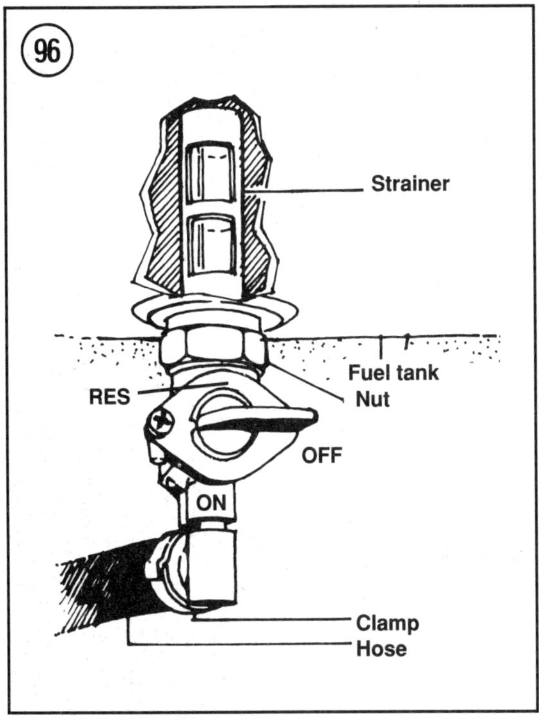

WARNING
Gasoline is very volatile and presents an extreme fire hazard. Be sure to work in a well-ventilated area away from any open flames (including pilot lights on household appliances). Do not allow anyone to smoke in the area and have a fire extinguisher rated for gasoline fires handy.

1. Disconnect the battery negative lead.
2. Turn the fuel valve to OFF.
3. Disconnect the fuel supply hose at the fuel shutoff valve. Connect a longer hose to the shutoff valve fitting and place the open end of the hose into a gasoline storage tank or can. Turn the shutoff valve to RESERVE and drain the fuel into the tank. Don't lose the fuel line insulator.
4. Loosen the shutoff valve fitting and remove the shutoff valve from the fuel tank. Catch any gas that may leak from the tank after the valve is removed.
5. Check the fuel strainer for contamination or damage. If the strainer cannot be thoroughly cleaned, replace it. Install a new gasket when installing a new strainer.

NOTE
*If the strainer is contaminated, the fuel tank may require cleaning and flushing. Refer to **Fuel Tank Flushing** in this chapter.*

6. Inspect the condition of the gasket; replace if necessary.
7. Clean the fuel tank threads of all sealant.
8. Coat the shutoff valve threads with Hylomar PL32/L25 and insert the valve into the tank. Tighten the valve fitting to secure the valve.
9. Remove the drain hose from the fuel tank and reconnect the fuel supply hose. Secure the fuel supply hose with a new hose clamp. Make sure the insulator is placed over the fuel supply hose before reconnecting it.
10. Refill the fuel tank and check for leaks.

EXHAUST SYSTEM

The stock exhaust system installed on all of the models covered by this manual is shown in **Figure 97**.

Each exhaust pipe clamps to its respective cylinder head exhaust port with a flange plate and 2 nuts.

Knitted steel gaskets are placed between the cylinder exhaust pipe and cylinder head to prevent exhaust leakage. The 5/16 in. O.D. exhaust pipe studs are threaded with a fine thread (5/16-24) on one end and a coarse thread (5/16-18) on the opposite end. The coarse thread end threads into the cylinder head. The fine thread end is used to secure the 2 exhaust pipe flange mounting nuts.

Removal

1. Secure the bike on a suitable stand.
2. The heat shields are held to the pipes with hose clamps. These clamps rust easily, so before removing them, spray each clamp with WD-40 or a similar lubricant to help prevent thread strippage when loosening them. You can hold a rag behind the clamp

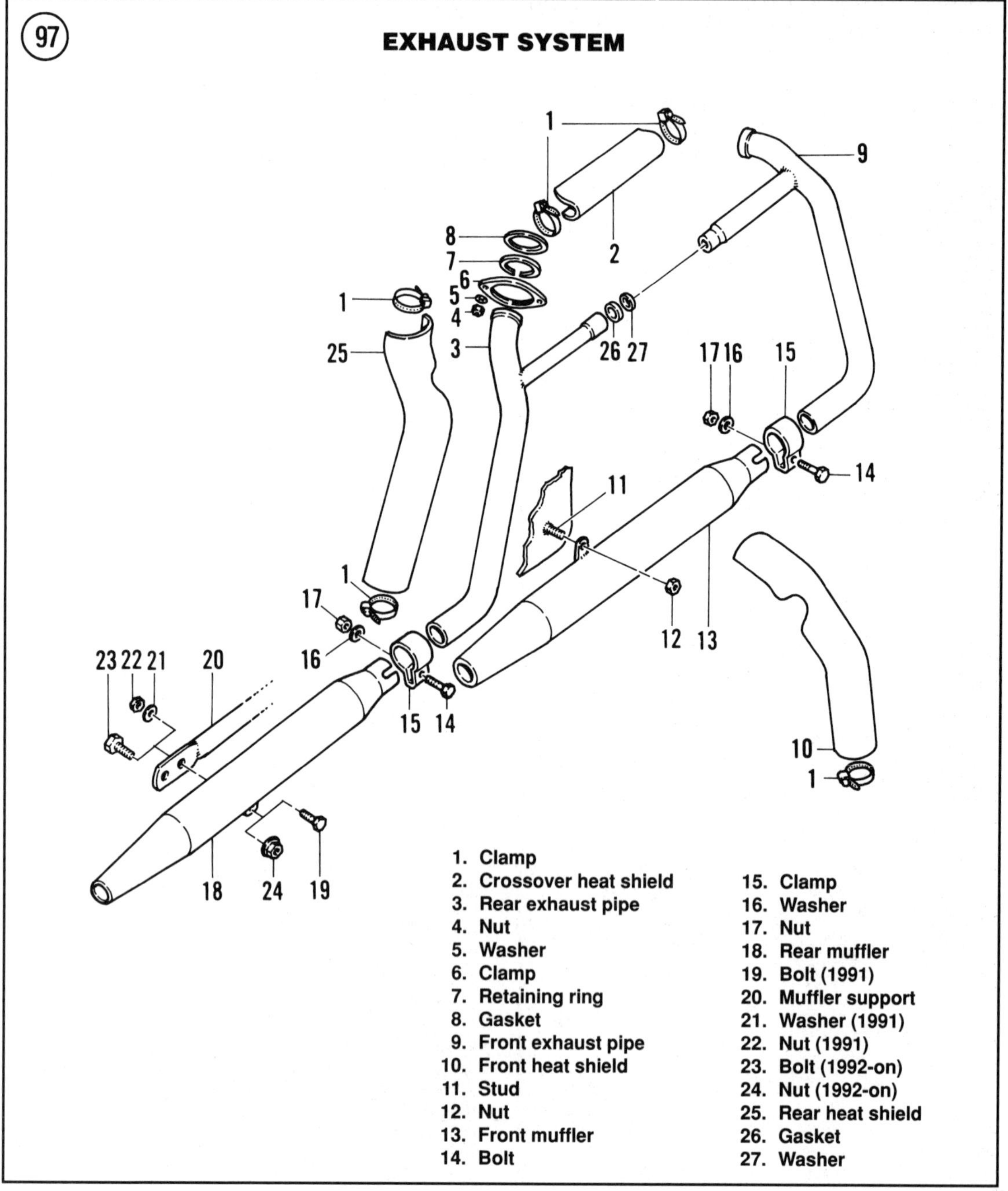

when spraying it to prevent the lubricant from contacting the engine or other components. Turn the hose clamp screws until the clamp is disconnected from around the pipe, then remove the heat shields.

3. Remove the nuts and washers securing the front and rear exhaust pipes to the cylinder heads; see **Figure 98**, typical.

4. To remove the front muffler locknut (**Figure 99**), perform the following:

   a. Remove the master cylinder mounting bolts (**Figure 100**) and lift the brake pedal upward.
   b. Loosen and remove the front muffler locknut (**Figure 99**).

5A. On 1991 models, remove the nut, washer and bolt which secures the rear muffler to the muffler support bracket.

5B. On 1992-on models, remove the locknut (**Figure 101**) and bolt which attaches the rear muffler to the muffler support bracket.

6. Slide the exhaust pipe clamps away from the cylinder head studs.

CAUTION

*If the exhaust pipe clamps (**Figure 102**) do not slide off of the cylinder head studs easily in Step 7, the clamp has bowed from the clamp nuts being overtightened. **Figure 103** shows a bowed clamp. If a clamp is like the one shown in **Figure 103**, the clamp will wedge against the studs when trying to remove and install it. If a clamp is tight, remove one of the cylinder head studs using the 2 nut technique (see Chapter One) before the stud threads are damaged, or if necessary, with a pair of vise-grip pliers. The stud can be reinstalled before installing the exhaust pipe. The clamp*

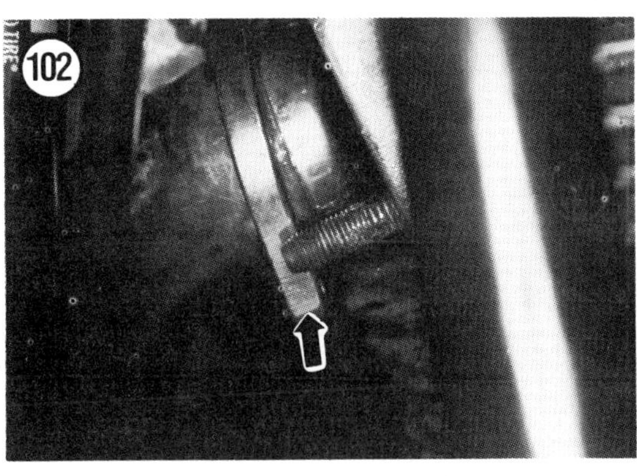

can either be removed from the exhaust pipe and flattened, or replaced.

7. Remove the exhaust as an assembly (**Figure 104**).
8. Remove and discard the exhaust port gaskets (**Figure 105**).
9. Loosen the muffler clamp bolts and remove the mufflers from the exhaust pipes.
10. Inspect the exhaust system as described in this chapter.

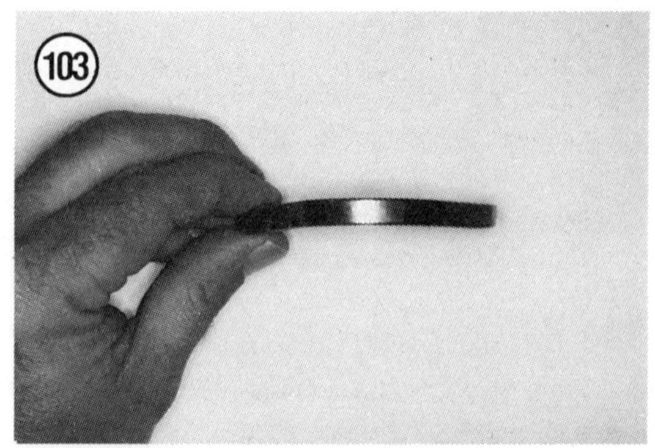

Installation

1. Before installing the new exhaust port gaskets, scrape the gasket and the pipe fitting surfaces in the port with a knife blade or similar tool to remove all carbon residue—removing the carbon will assure a good gasket fit. Wipe the port with a rag, then align the new gasket with the port and push it into place. The new gasket should fit snugly in the port (**Figure 106**). Repeat for the other exhaust port and gasket.
2. Before installing the exhaust pipes, check that the retaining rings (**Figure 107**) holding the clamps to the exhaust pipes fit tightly in the pipe grooves.

NOTE
*If you had to remove or discard an exhaust stud, install the stud now. Refer to **Stud Replacement** in Chapter One.*

3. Position the exhaust pipe assembly (without mufflers) so that the front and rear exhaust pipes fit into the front and rear cylinder head exhaust pipes. Slide the clamps over the mounting studs and install a washer and nut over each stud (**Figure 98**). Install the nuts finger-tight only.
4. Install the muffler clamps and their fasteners over the end of their respective exhaust pipes as shown in **Figure 97**. Then slide each muffler onto its respective exhaust pipe.
5. Turn the front muffler so that its mounting tab engages the stud as shown in **Figure 97** and **Figure 99**. Install the locknut finger-tight.
6A. On 1991 models, align the rear muffler tab with the muffler support bracket and install the bolt, washer and nut finger-tight.
6B. On 1992 models, align the rear muffler tab with the muffler support bracket and install the bolt and locknut (**Figure 101**) finger-tight.

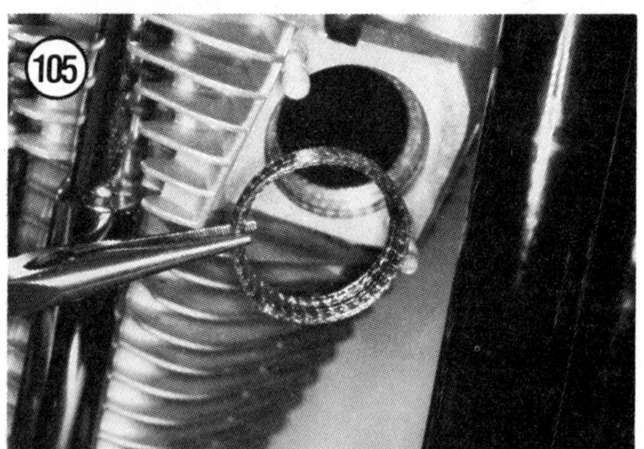

NOTE
*Make sure to install the rear muffler mounting bolt assembly in the direction shown in **Figure 97**.*

7. Tighten exhaust fasteners in the following order to the torque specification in **Table 3**:
   a. Cylinder head exhaust stud nuts (**Figure 98**).
   b. Front and rear muffler clamp nuts (**Figure 108**).
   c. Front muffler locknut (**Figure 99**).
   d. Rear muffler fasteners (**Figure 101**, typical).

107

108

109

   e. Rear master cylinder mounting bolts (**Figure 100**).
8. Wipe the exhaust pipes and mufflers with a clean rag to remove all traces of oil and grease, then polish the exhaust pipes.
9. Install the heat shields and secure with their mounting clamps. Clean and polish the heat shields.

NOTE
If you are installing new pipes, check with the pipe manufacturer and your dealer for information regarding tuning changes that may be required with the new pipes. You want the carburetor jetting and ignition timing to be as spot-on as possible before starting the engine to prevent exhaust pipe bluing. If the pipes are new (have not been installed on a running engine), you may want to consider coating the inside of the exhaust pipes with a special sealer, such as DYNO-KOTE Pipe Bluing Preventative before installing them. See your dealer for additional information.

10. Start the engine and check for leaks. Some smoke will be evident after starting, especially if WD-40 was used on the hose clamps (prior to removal) or if oil and grease residue was not wiped off of the exhaust pipes and mufflers.

Inspection

1. Check the exhaust pipe for cracks or spots that have rusted through. A damaged or leaking pipe should be replaced.
2. Remove all rust from all pipe and muffler mating surfaces.
3. Check all of the hoses for damage or severe rusting. Clean or repair clamps as required.
4. If the exhaust flange is distorted, you should repair or replace it before reinstalling it. Perform the following:
   a. Each exhaust flange is secured to its exhaust pipe with a retaining ring (**Figure 107**). Pry the ring out of its groove and remove the flange. Discard the ring. See **Figure 109**.
   b. Examine the flange for distortion or other damage; the flange must be flat to fit properly onto the exhaust studs. If the flange is not severely distorted, you may be able to hammer or press it flat. If not, install a new flange. Make sure you

do not damage the edges or holes in the flange when straightening it.

c. If you straightened a flange, check its fit on the exhaust studs before installing it onto the pipe.

d. Clean the end of the pipe to remove all rust and other debris. If you are reinstalling a used flange, clean the inside of the flange thoroughly.

e. Slide the flange on the exhaust pipe so that the shoulder on the flange faces toward the retaining ring groove. Install a new retaining ring and check its fit; it must be secure in its groove.

f. Repeat for the other exhaust pipe and flange, if required.

5. Replace worn or damaged heat shield clamps as required.

6. Store the exhaust pipes in a safe place until they are reinstalled.

Exhaust System Care

The exhaust system greatly enhances the appearance of any motorcycle. And more importantly, the exhaust system is a vital key to the motorcycle's operation and performance. As the owner, you should periodically inspect, clean and polish the exhaust system. Special chemical cleaners and preservatives compounded for exhaust systems are available at most motorcycle shops.

Severe dents which cause gas flow restrictions require the replacement of the damaged part.

Problems occurring within the exhaust pipes are normally caused by rust from the collection of water in the pipe. Periodically, or whenever the exhaust pipes are removed, turn the pipes to remove any trapped water.

EVAPORATIVE EMISSION CONTROL SYSTEM (CALIFORNIA MODELS)

All of the California models covered by this manual are equipped with an evaporative emission control system. This system is used to prevent gasoline vapors from escaping into the atmosphere. When the

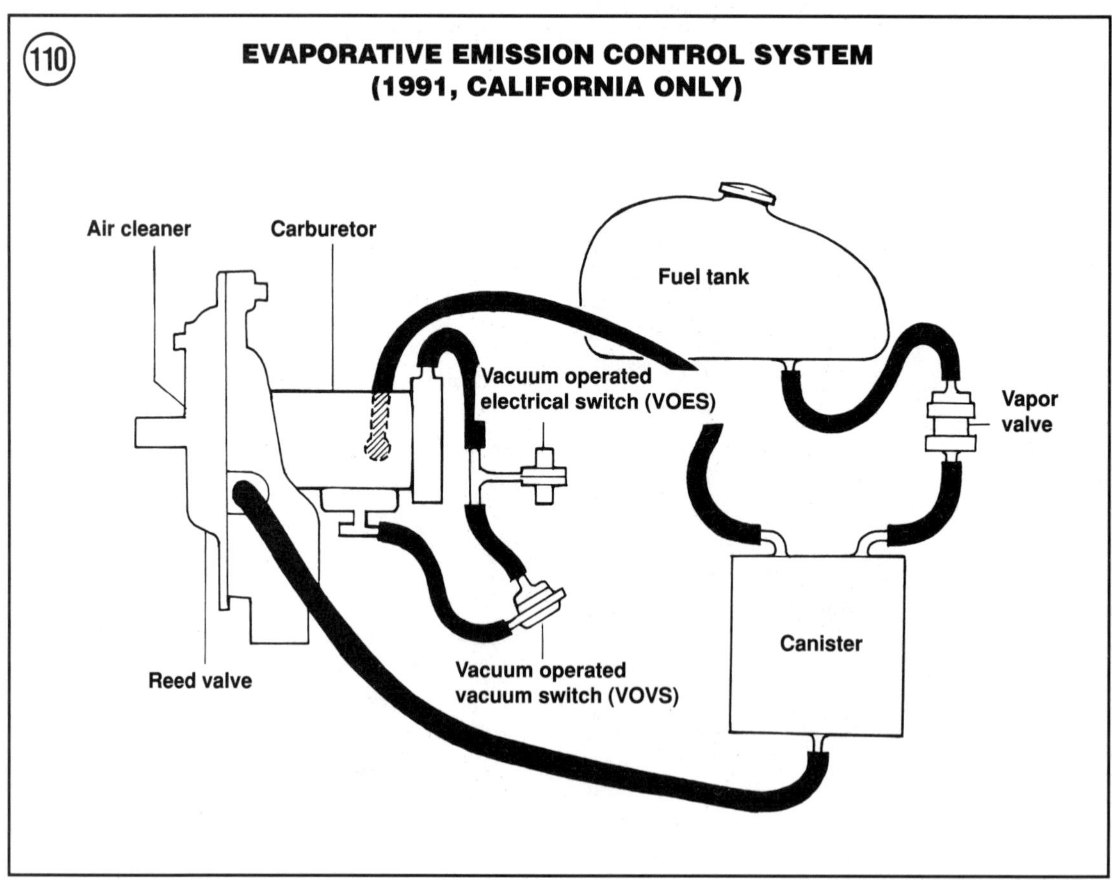

engine is not running, fuel vapor from the fuel tank is routed through the vapor valve and stored in a carbon canister. When the engine is running, these vapors are drawn through a purge hose and into the carburetor where they are to be burned in the combustion chambers. The vapor valve also prevents gasoline vapors from escaping from the carbon canister if the bike should fall onto its side.

Two evaporative emission control systems have been used on the California models covered by this manual.

Inspection/Replacement

Refer to **Figure 110** (1991) or **Figure 111** (1992-on) for the components and the hose routing to the various parts. Before removing the hoses from any of the parts, mark the hose and the fitting with a piece of masking tape and identify where the hose goes. There are so many hoses on some of these models, it can be very confusing where each one is supposed to be attached.

1. Check all emission control lines or hoses to make sure they are correctly routed and properly connected.

WARNING
Make sure the fuel tank vapor hoses are routed in such a way that they cannot contact any hot engine or exhaust component. These hoses contain flammable vapors. If a hose melts from contacting a hot part, leaking vapors may ignite, causing severe bike damage and rider injury.

2. Make sure that there are no kinks in the lines or hoses and that there are no signs of excessive wear or burning on lines that are routed near engine hot spots.

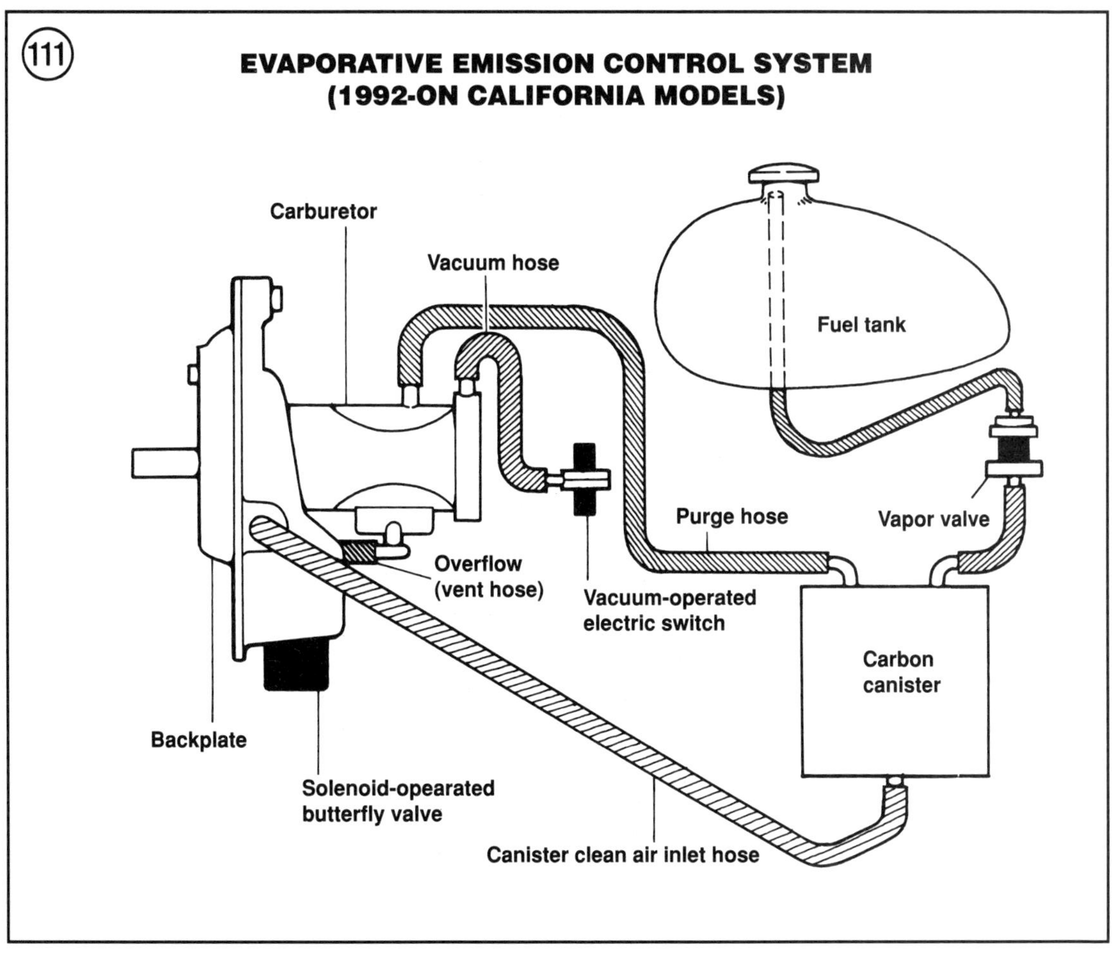

7

3. Check the physical condition of all lines and hoses in the system for cuts, tears or loose connections. These lines and hoses are subjected to various temperature and operating conditions and eventually become brittle and crack. Damaged lines or hoses should be replaced.

4. Check all components in the emission control system for visible signs of damage, such as broken fittings or broken nipples on the component.

5. When replacing one or more lines or hoses, refer to the diagram for your model. Disconnect one end of the line from the component, then connect one end of the new line to the component fitting. Disconnect the other end of the line and connect the other end of the new line. In this way, you will not make any mistakes and will be able to follow the routing of the old line, correcting any improper placement that carries the line near components where it might rub and wear or be burned by hot components.

EVAPORATIVE EMISSION CONTROL SYSTEM SERVICE

Refer to **Figure 110** (1991) or **Figure 111** (1992) when servicing the evaporative emission control system.

Vapor Valve Replacement

The vapor valve (**Figure 112**) is mounted on the frame tube between the battery and oil tank.

1. Remove the battery as described in Chapter Eight.

2. Label the hoses at the vapor valve and then disconnect them.

3. Note that one end of the vapor valve is longer than the other end. The longer end must face up when the vapor valve is installed on the bike. Remove and replace the vapor valve.

CAUTION
The vapor valve must be installed in a vertical position with the ***longer end*** *facing upward or excessive pressure will build in the fuel tank.*

4. Install by reversing these steps.

Carbon Canister Replacement

The carbon canister is mounted on the bottom side of the swing arm.

Refer to **Figure 113**.

1. Remove the canister guard mounting screws and remove the guard.
2. Cut the canister cable strap. Discard the strap.
3. Label and then disconnect the hoses at the canister. Plug the open end of each hose to prevent contamination.
4. Press the canister bracket locking tab and slide the canister toward the left-hand side of the bike and off of the bracket.
5. If necessary, remove the canister bracket mounting fasteners and mounting plate assembly and remove the canister bracket.
6. Install by reversing these steps.

CAUTION
Do not alter the carbon canister position. The canister must be mounted ***below*** *the carburetor to work correctly.*

Reed Valves (1991)

Whenever the air filter assembly is removed from the bike, check the reed valve assembly for broken reed valves. To replace damaged reed valves, perform the following.

1. Remove the air filter and backplate as described in Chapter Three.
2. Remove the screws securing the reed cover to the reed support and remove the cover (**Figure 114**).
3. Refer to **Figure 115**. Remove the screws securing the reed bottom to the reed support. Then remove the following parts:

a. Reed bottom.
b. Reed top.
c. Reed stop.

4. Check the reeds for cracks or debris that would prevent the reed from closing. Replace worn or damaged parts as required.
5. See **Figure 115**. Attach the reed bottom, reed top and the reed stop to the reed support cover. Secure with the attaching screws.
6. Install the reed support cover onto the reed support and secure with the attaching screws (**Figure 114**).
7. Install the air filter and backplate as described in Chapter Three.

Vacuum Operated Valve Switch Testing/Replacement (1991)

The vacuum-operated vacuum switch (VOVS) closes off the carburetor's float bowl vent passage when the engine is not running. This prevents fuel vapor from escaping when the engine is turned off.

A hand-operated vacuum pump (Harley-Davidson part No. HD-23738) or equivalent is required to test the VOVS.

1. Label and then disconnect the hoses from the VOVS; see **Figure 110** and **Figure 116**.
2. Attach a vacuum pump to port A in **Figure 116**.
3. Apply 1-2 in. HG vacuum to the valve while watching the pump gauge. The vacuum should remain steady. If vacuum reading decreases rapidly, the diaphragm is damaged.
4. If vacuum remains constant (Step 3), blow into port C; air should pass through the VOVS. If air cannot pass through, the VOVS is damaged.
5. Remove the vacuum pump and blow into port B; air should not pass through the VOVS. If air can pass through, the VOVS is damaged.
6. If the VOVS failed to react as described in Steps 3-5, replace it with a new one.

7

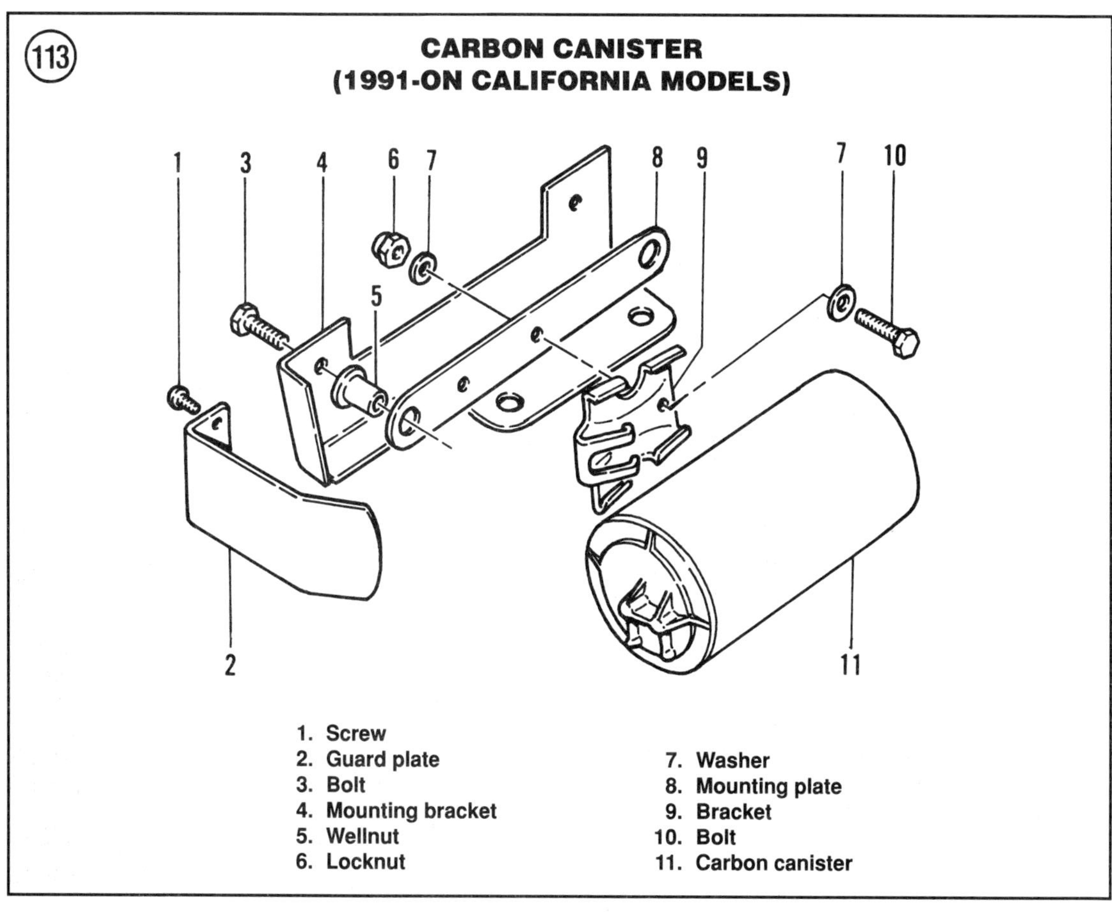

Solenoid-Operated Butterfly Valve Troubleshooting (1992-on)

On 1992-on California models, a solenoid-operated butterfly valve is installed in the air filter backplate to seal off the backplate when the ignition switch is turned off to prevent fuel vapors from escaping into the atmosphere. Turning the ignition switch to the ON or IGNITION position energizes the solenoid hold-in windings. When the start switch is operated, the solenoid pull-in windings are energized. The hold-in windings will keep the butterfly valve open until the ignition switch is turned off.

Test the solenoid-operated butterfly valve if the engine suffers from sluggish acceleration and the engine's top speed tops out at 40 mph.

1. First check that all of the hoses are properly connected; see **Figure 111**. If the hoses are okay, proceed with Step 2.
2. Butterfly valve is not opening due to an electrical malfunction:
   a. Check that the solenoid valve electrical connector is properly connected. If the connection is okay, disconnect the connector and check for dirty or loose-fitting terminals; clean and repair as required. If okay, continue with substep b.
   b. Test the solenoid as described under *Solenoid Testing* in this chapter.
3. Butterfly valve not opening and closing properly due to mechanical problem:
   a. Check the mechanical linkage assembly (**Figure 117**) for corroded, loose, broken or missing components. The butterfly valve linkage and

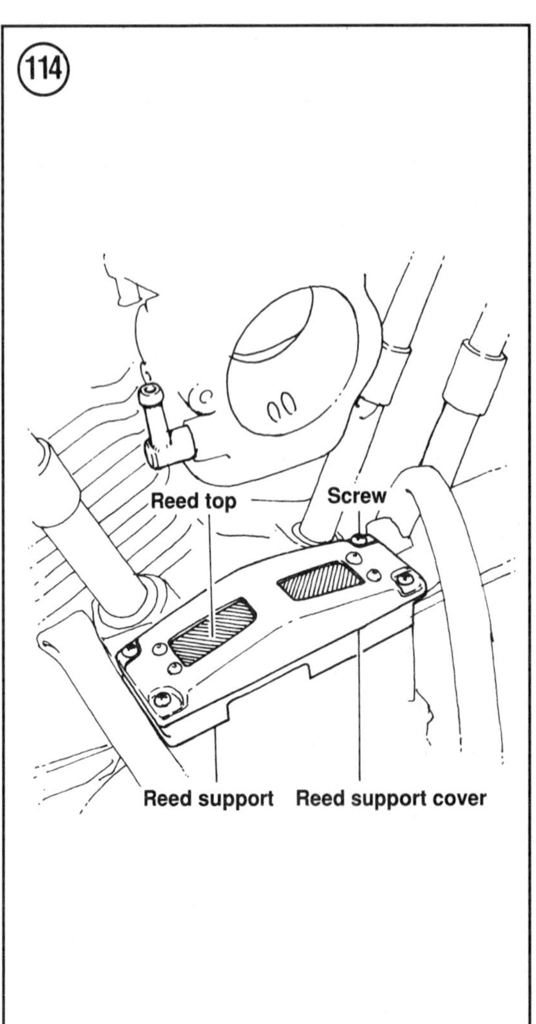

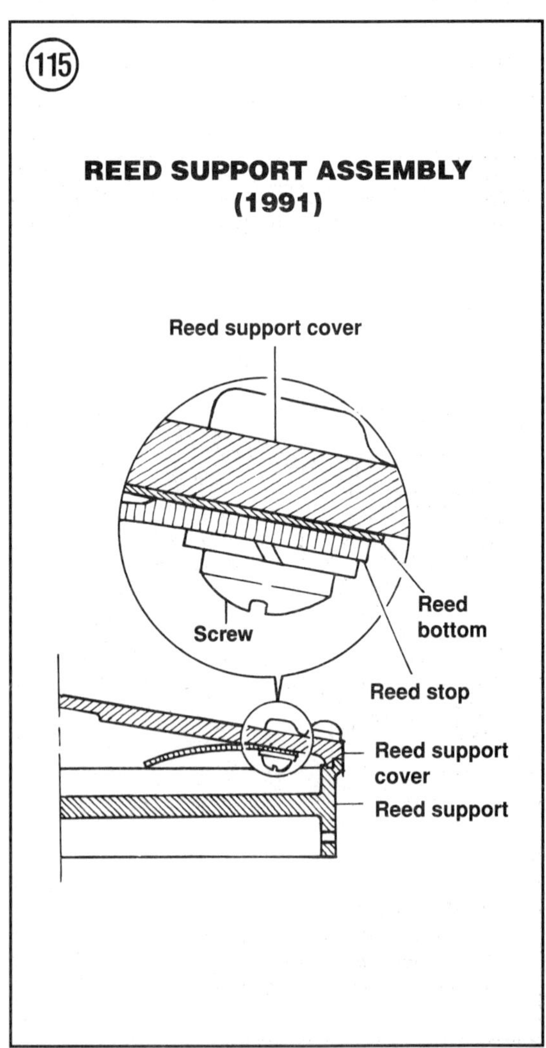

plunger should be cleaned every 5,000 miles as described in this chapter.

b. Check for a broken solenoid spring (**Figure 117**). If the spring is broken, replace the solenoid assembly. The spring cannot be replaced separately. Replace as described in this chapter.

Solenoid Valve Electrical Testing (1992-on)

Prior to testing the solenoid valve, fabricate the test harness shown in **Figure 118**. The part numbers listed on the drawing are Harley-Davidson part numbers.

Solenoid winding resistance test

1. Remove the air filter and backplate as described in Chapter Three.

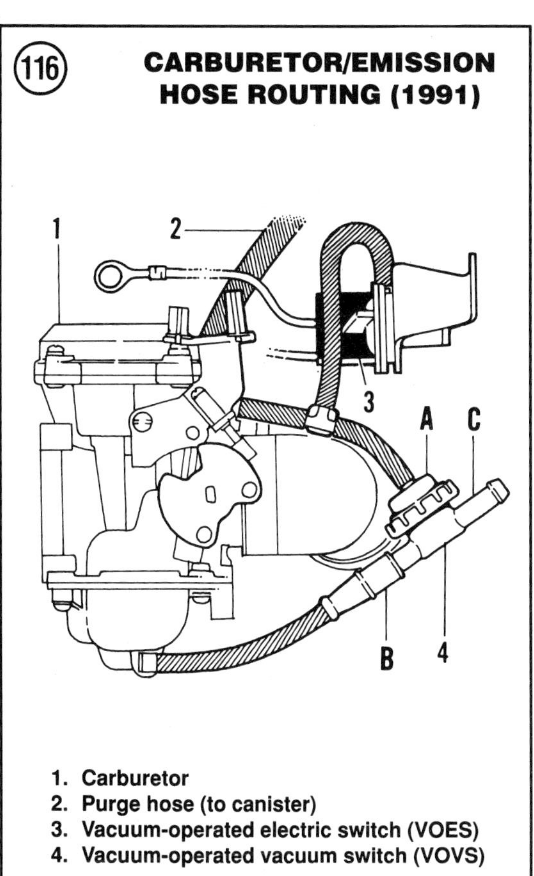

1. Carburetor
2. Purge hose (to canister)
3. Vacuum-operated electric switch (VOES)
4. Vacuum-operated vacuum switch (VOVS)

2. Disconnect the solenoid valve 4 prong electrical connector (**Figure 117**).
3. Check for dirty or loose-fitting terminals and connectors.
4. Connect the solenoid test connector to the solenoid connector (**Figure 119**).
5. Refer to **Figure 120** for test connections and values and compare your meter readings to the stated values. If any of the meter readings differ from the stated values, replace the solenoid as described in this chapter.
6. If the resistance readings are correct, proceed with the following test.

Pull-in coil test

A fully charged 12-volt battery is required for this test.

1. Remove the air filter and backplate as described in Chapter Three.
2. Disconnect the solenoid valve 4 prong electrical connector (**Figure 117**).
3. Check for dirty or loose-fitting terminals and connectors.
4. Connect the solenoid test connector to the solenoid connector (**Figure 119**).
5. Connect a 12-volt battery to the 2 solenoid test connector wires shown in **Figure 121**. The butterfly valve should open when battery voltage is applied. Disconnect the battery connections and note the following:
   a. If the butterfly valve now opens but did not open when originally connected to the wiring harness, perform Step 6.
   b. If the butterfly valve did not open, check the linkage for corroded, missing or damaged parts. If the linkage assembly appears okay, retest with a new solenoid.
6. Perform the following:
   a. Switch an ohmmeter to R × 1 and cross the test leads. Then check for ground at the grey/black connector pin in the solenoid 4-prong connector. The ohmmeter should read 1 ohm or less.
   b. Reconnect the solenoid 4-prong connector.
   c. Switch a voltmeter to the 12 VDC scale.
   d. Connect the positive voltmeter lead to the black/red lead in the 4-prong connector and the negative probe to a good engine ground. Press the start button while reading the voltage indicated on the voltmeter. It should be 12 volts.

7. If any of the meter readings differ from those specified in Step 6, there is a problem in the solenoid wiring harness. Use voltage and resistance checks to locate the damaged wire(s). After repairing the wire(s), repeat the above checks.

8. If the meter readings were correct as performed in Step 7, perform the following test.

Hold-in coil test

A fully charged 12-volt battery is required for this test.

1. Remove the air filter and backplate as described in Chapter Three.
2. Disconnect the solenoid valve 4 prong electrical connector (**Figure 117**).

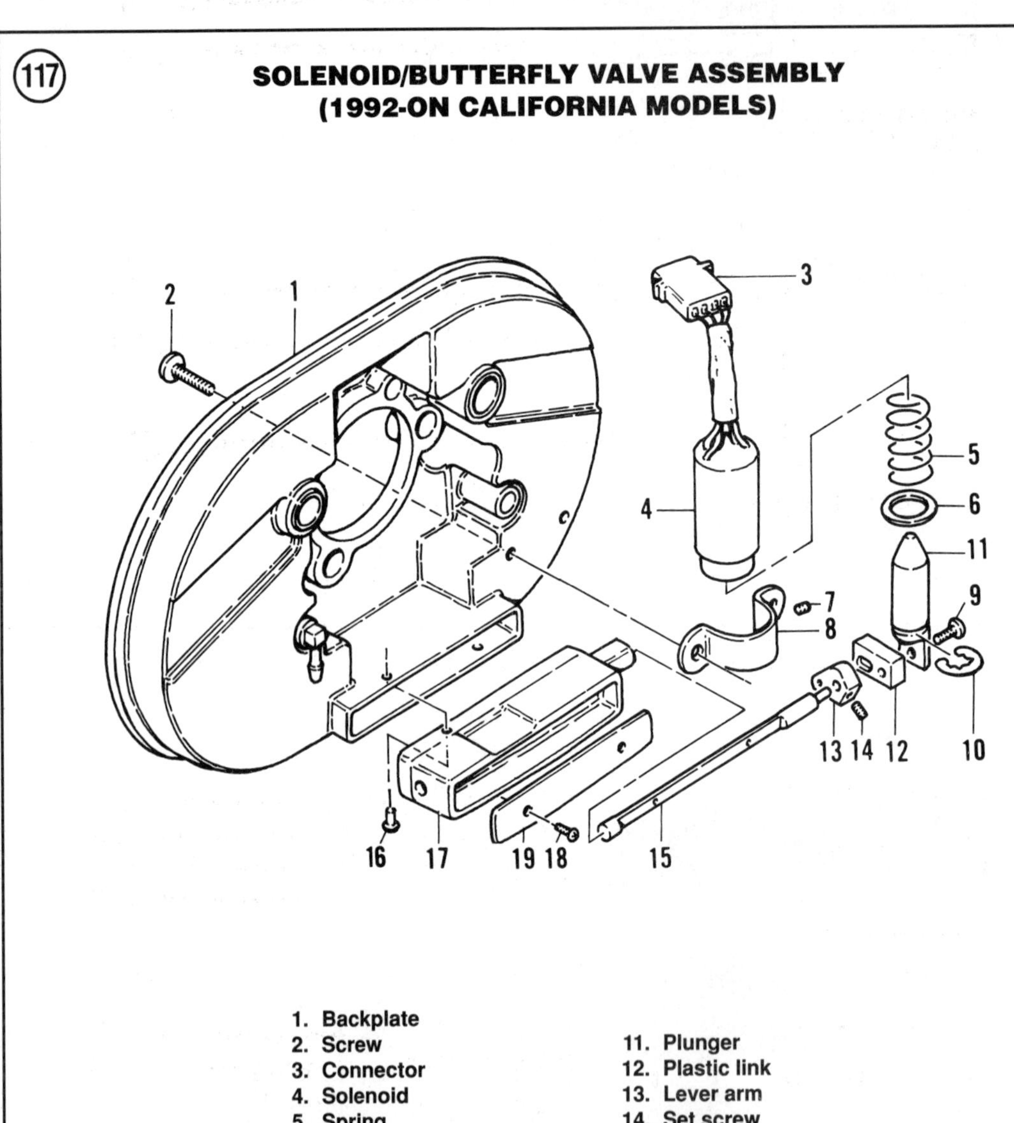

(118) **SOLENOID TEST CONNECTOR**

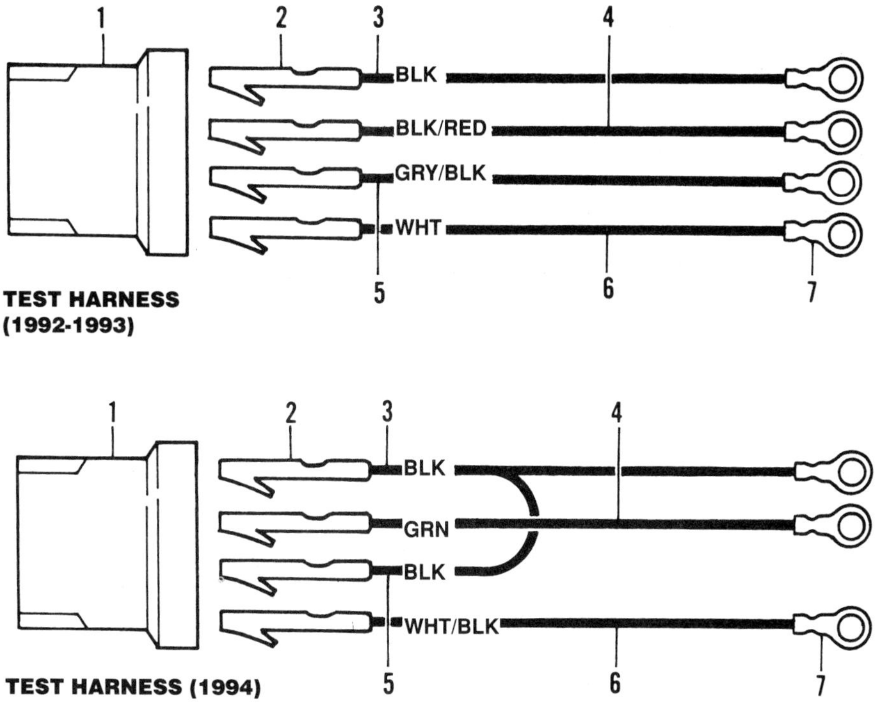

1
2
3
4
BLK
BLK/RED
GRY/BLK
WHT
5
6
7
TEST HARNESS (1992-1993)
1
2
3
4
BLK
GRN
BLK
WHT/BLK
5
6
7
TEST HARNESS (1994)

(119) **RESISTANCE TEST**

4 place socket connector
Solenoid
Solenoid test connector
BLK
BLK/RED
GRY/BLK
WHT
1992-1993
Solenoid
Solenoid test connector
BLK
GRN
BLK
WHT/BLK
1994
4
3
2
1
WHT/BLK
BLK
GRN
BLK
A
To cycle harness

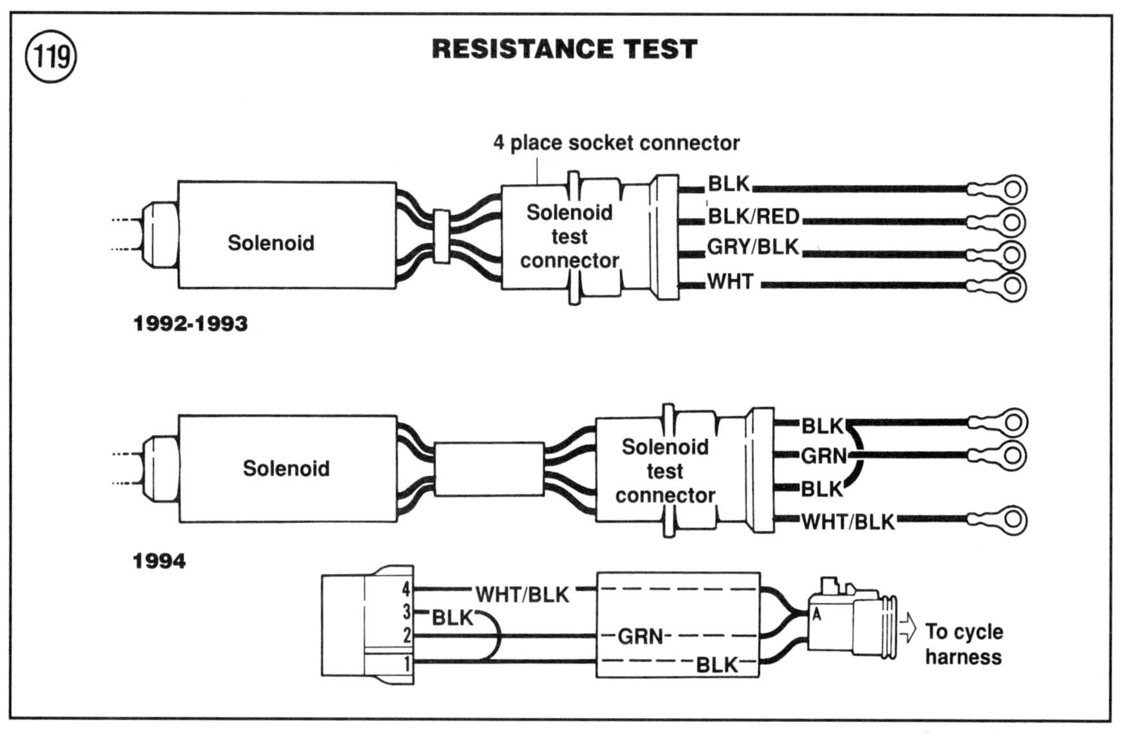

(120)

SOLENOID WINDING RESISTANCE

TEST	POSITIVE PROBE (+)	NEGATIVE PROBE (–)	RESISTANCE
1992-1993			
Pull-in	Back/Red	Gray/Black	4-6 Ohms
Hold-in	White	Black	21-27 Ohms
1994			
Pull-in	Green	Black	4-6 Ohms
Hold-in	White/Black	Black	21-27 Ohms

(121)

SOLENOID PULL-IN COIL TEST

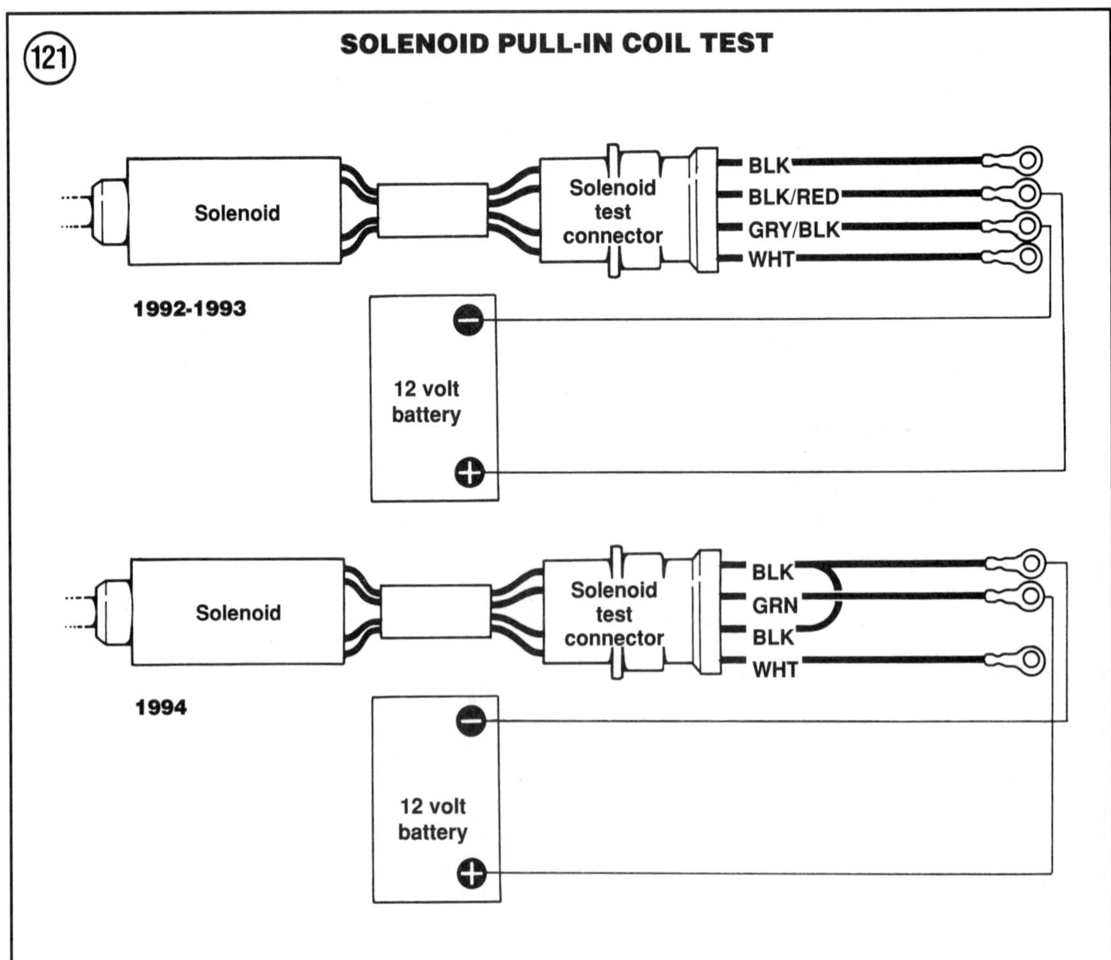

3. Check for dirty or loose-fitting terminals and connectors.
4. Connect the solenoid test connector to the solenoid connector (**Figure 119**).
5. Connect a 12-volt battery to the 2 solenoid test connector wires shown in **Figure 122** and perform the following:
   a. Open the butterfly valve carefully with a screwdriver by pushing inward on the top side of the butterfly valve.
   b. Remove the screwdriver. The butterfly valve should remain open as long as the solenoid hold-in windings are energized.
   c. Disconnect the negative battery cable from the solenoid test connector. The butterfly valve should close.
   d. If the butterfly valve operated as described in substeps b and c, the solenoid hold-in windings are operating correctly.

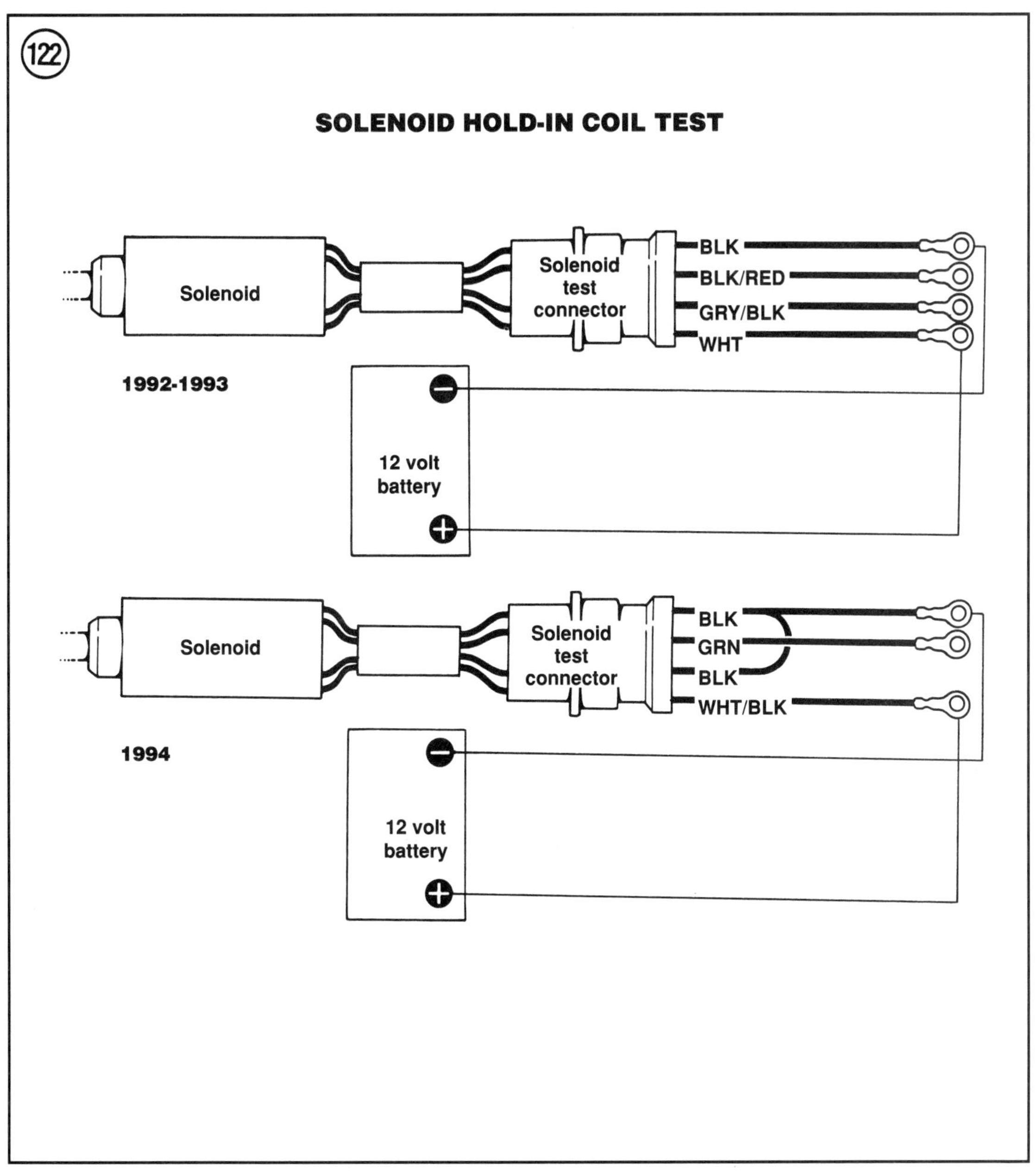

7

e. If the butterfly valve failed to operate properly, perform Step 6.

f. Disconnect the positive battery cable from the solenoid test connector.

6. If the butterfly valve did not remain open in Step 5, substep b, perform the following:

a. Switch an ohmmeter to R × 1 and cross the test leads. Then check for ground at the black connector pin in the solenoid 4-prong connector. The ohmmeter should read 1 ohm or less.

b. Reconnect the solenoid 4-prong connector.

c. Switch a voltmeter to the 12 VDC scale.

d. Connect the positive voltmeter lead to the white lead in the 4-prong connector and the negative probe to a good engine ground. Turn the ignition switch to the ON or IGNITION position and read the voltage indicated on the voltmeter. It should be 12 volts.

7. If any of the meter readings differ from those specified in Step 6, there is a problem in the solenoid wiring harness. Use voltage and resistance checks to locate the damaged wire(s). After repairing the wire(s), repeat the above checks.

8. If the solenoid test readings were correct but the butterfly valve does not work properly, perform Step 3 under *Solenoid-Operated Butterfly Valve Troubleshooting (1992-on).*

9. Remove all test equipment and reconnect the solenoid 4-prong connector.

Butterfly Valve and Solenoid Cleaning and Lubrication (1992-on)

Refer to **Figure 117**.

1. Remove the air filter and backplate as described in Chapter Three.

2. At every 2,500 mile (4,022 km) interval, inspect the butterfly valve and solenoid for proper operation.

3. At every 5,000 mile (8,045 km) interval, spray the butterfly valve and plunger with carburetor cleaner. Then, after the carburetor cleaner evaporates, lubricate the linkage and plunger with a dry film spray lubricant.

4. Reinstall the air filter and backplate as described in Chapter Three.

Butterfly Valve Solenoid Removal/Installation/Adjustment (1992-on)

Refer to **Figure 117**.

1. Remove the air filter and backplate as described in Chapter Three.

2. Remove the plunger mounting screw.

3. Loosen the lever arm set screw.

4. Slide the solenoid up to free it from the clamp and remove it.

5. Slide the solenoid into the clamp.

6. Apply Loctite 242 (blue) to the plunger mounting screw and lever arm set screw threads.

NOTE

When assembling the plunger and plastic link, the slot in the plastic link must face toward the pin on the lever arm.

(123) CARBURETOR/EMISSION HOSE ROUTING (1992-ON)

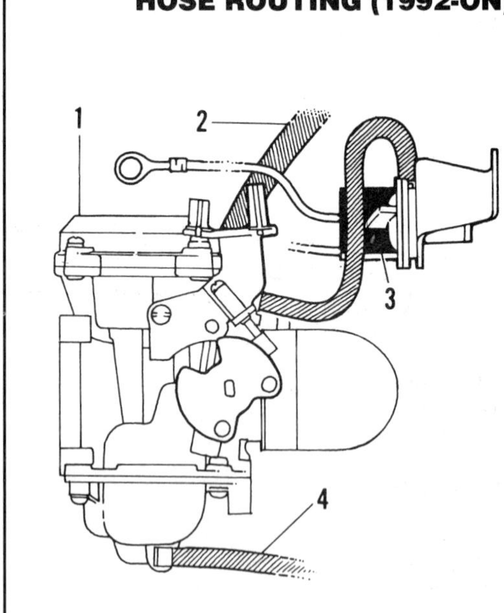

1. Carburetor
2. Purge hose to canister
3. Vacuum-operated electric switch (VOES)
4. Vent hose to air filter backplate

7. Align the deep flat side on the plunger with the plastic link, then install the plunger mounting screw. Tighten the screw securely.
8. Loosen the solenoid set screw.
9. Push the plunger upward until the butterfly valve opens fully and hold it in this position. Then position the solenoid body inside the clamp.
10. While still lifting the plunger upward (butterfly valve fully open), press downward on top of the solenoid until the bottom of the solenoid just touches the plastic washer. Tighten the solenoid set screw securely.
11. Release the plunger and check that the solenoid spring closes the butterfly valve completely. If not, readjust the plunger and solenoid.
12. Install the air filter and backplate as described in Chapter Three.

Emission/Carburetor Hose Routing (All Models)

Refer to **Figure 116** (1991) or **Figure 123** (1992-on) for emission hose routing at the carburetor.

7

Table 1 CARBURETOR SPECIFICATIONS

	883 cc	1200 cc
All non-California models		
Pilot (slow) jet		
1991	45	45
1992-on	40	40
Main jet		
1991	175	175
1992-on	160	170
California models		
Pilot (slow) jet		
1991	42	42
1992-on	40	40
Main jet		
1991	160	160
1992	160	170
1993-on	170	185
European models		
Pilot (slot) jet		
1993-on	40	40
Main jet		
1993-on	160	160

Table 2 FUEL SYSTEM TIGHTENING TORQUES

	ft.-lb.	N•m
Intake manifold	6-10	8-14
Fuel tank mounting bolts		
1991-1992	9	12.2
1993-on	8-16	11-22

Table 3 EXHAUST SYSTEM TIGHTENING TORQUES

	ft.-lb.	N•m
Cylinder head-to-exhaust stud nuts	6-8	8.1-10.8
Muffler clamp nuts	7	9.5
Front muffler locknut		
1991-1992	50-60	68-81.3
1993-on	20-40	27-54.2
Rear muffler bolt and nut or locknut		
1991-1992	19	25.7
1993-on	10-15	13.6-20.3
Rear master cylinder mounting bolts	155-190 in.-lb.	17.5-21.5

CHAPTER EIGHT

ELECTRICAL SYSTEM

All models covered in this manual are equipped with a 12-volt, negative-ground electrical system. Many electrical problems can be traced to a simple cause such as a loose or corroded connection or frayed wire. While these are easily corrected problems which may not appear important, they can quickly lead to serious difficulty if allowed to go uncorrected.

This chapter provides service procedures for the battery, charging system, ignition system, starter, lights, switches and circuit breakers. Tune-up procedures involving the ignition system are described in Chapter Three.

Tables 1-4 are found at the end of the chapter.

BATTERY

The battery is the single most important component in the motorcycle electrical system. Yet most electrical system troubles can be traced to battery neglect. In addition to checking and correcting the battery electrolyte level on a weekly basis, the battery should be cleaned and inspected at periodic intervals. Battery capacity is listed in **Table 1**.

Safety Precautions

When working with batteries, use extreme care to avoid spilling or splashing the electrolyte. This solution contains sulfuric acid, which can ruin clothing and cause serious chemical burns. If any electrolyte is spilled or splashed on clothing or skin, immediately neutralize with a solution of baking soda and water, then flush with an abundance of clean water.

WARNING

Electrolyte splashed into the eyes is extremely harmful. Safety glasses should always be worn while working with batteries. If electrolyte is splashed into the eyes, call a physician immediately, force the eyes open and flood with cool, clean water for approximately 15 minutes.

If electrolyte is spilled or splashed onto any surface, it should be immediately neutralized with baking soda and water solution and then rinsed with clean water.

While batteries are being charged, highly explosive hydrogen gas forms in each cell. Some of this gas escapes through filler cap openings and may form an explosive atmosphere in and around the battery. This condition can persist for several hours. Sparks, an open flame or a lighted cigarette can ignite the gas, causing an internal battery explosion and possible serious personal injury.

Take the following precautions to prevent an explosion:

1. Do not smoke or permit any open flame near any battery being charged or which has been recently charged.
2. Do not disconnect live circuits at battery terminals since a spark usually occurs when a live circuit is broken.
3. Take care when connecting or disconnecting any battery charger. Be sure its power switch is off before making or breaking connections. Poor connections are a common cause of electrical arcs which cause explosions.
4. Keep all children and pets away from charging equipment and batteries.

For maximum battery life, it should be checked periodically for electrolyte level, state of charge and corrosion. During hot weather periods, frequent checks are recommended. If the electrolyte level is below the bottom of the vent well in one or more cells, add distilled water as required. To assure proper mixing of the water and acid, operate the engine immediately after adding water. *Never* add battery acid instead of water—this will shorten the battery's life.

On all models covered in this manual, the negative side is grounded. When removing the battery, disconnect the negative (–) cable first, then the positive (+) cable. This minimizes the chance of a tool shorting to ground when disconnecting the "hot" positive cable.

WARNING
When performing the following procedures, protect your eyes, skin and clothing. If electrolyte gets into your eyes, flush your eyes thoroughly with clean water and get prompt medical attention.

Battery Removal

1. Remove the seat.
2. Remove the battery strap nut and washer and remove the battery strap (A, **Figure 1**).
3. Remove the battery top cover (B, **Figure 1**).
4. Disconnect the negative battery cable from the battery (**Figure 2**).

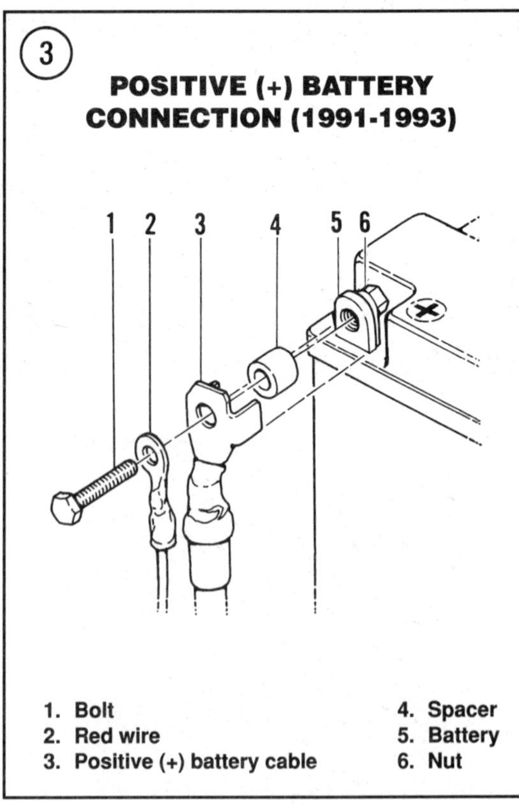

5A. On 1991-1993 models, remove the positive battery cable bolt, red wire (from main circuit breaker), positive battery cable and spacer (**Figure 3**).

5B. On 1994 models, remove the positive battery cable bolt, positive battery cable and spacer (**Figure 4**).

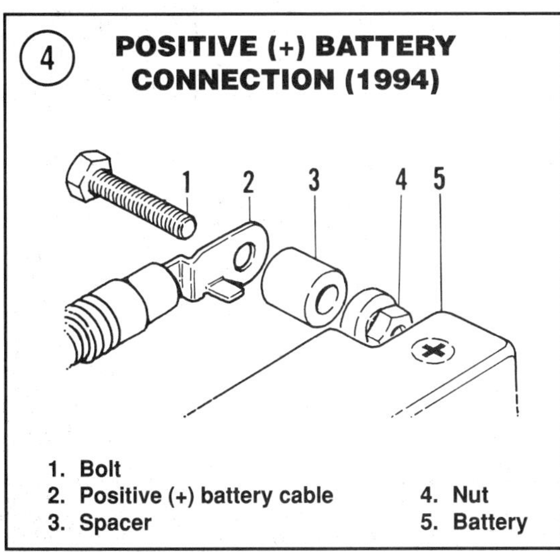

1. Bolt
2. Positive (+) battery cable
3. Spacer
4. Nut
5. Battery

6. Disconnect the battery vent tube at the battery.
7. Remove the battery.

CAUTION

Be careful not to spill battery electrolyte on painted or polished surfaces. The liquid is highly corrosive and will damage the finish. If it is spilled, wash it off immediately with soapy water and thoroughly rinse with clean water.

Cleaning and Inspection

1. Inspect the battery tray and cushion (**Figure 5**) for contamination or damage. Clean with a solution of baking soda and water.
2. Check the entire battery case (**Figure 6**) for cracks or other damage. If the battery case is warped, discolored or has a raised top, the battery has been suffering from overcharging or overheating.
3. Check the battery hold-down strap for acid damage, cracks or other damage. Replace strap if required.
4. Check the positive battery cable routing connection in the battery tray. Tighten the bolt, if necessary.
5. Check the battery terminal parts—bolts, spacers and nuts—for corrosion or damage. Clean parts thoroughly with a solution of baking soda and water. Replace severely corroded or damaged parts.

NOTE

Keep cleaning solution out of the battery cells or the electrolyte level will be seriously weakened.

6. Clean the top of the battery with a stiff bristle brush using the baking soda and water solution.
7. If necessary, remove the battery tray and clean and/or replace damaged parts.
8. Check the battery cable clamps for corrosion and damage. If corrosion is minor, clean the battery cable clamps with a stiff wire brush. Replace severely worn or damaged cables.

NOTE

Do not overfill the battery cells in Step 9. The electrolyte expands due to heat from charging and will overflow if the level is above the upper level line.

9. Remove the caps (**Figure 7**) from the battery cells and check the electrolyte level. Add distilled

8

water, if necessary, to bring the level within the upper and lower level lines on the battery case (**Figure 6**).

Battery Installation

1. Reposition the battery into the battery tray. Make sure the rubber cushion is installed in the bottom of the tray before installing the battery. Install the battery strap to secure the battery.
2A. On 1991-1993 models, install the spacer, positive battery cable, red wire and bolt (**Figure 3**). Tighten the bolt securely.
2B. On 1994 models, install the spacer, positive battery cable and bolt (**Figure 4**). Tighten the bolt securely.
3. Install and tighten the negative battery cable (**Figure 2**).

CAUTION
Be sure the battery cables are connected to their proper terminals. Connecting the battery backwards will reverse the polarity and damage the rectifier.

4. Coat the battery connections with dielectric grease or petroleum jelly.
5. Place the top cover (B, **Figure 1**) on the battery.
6. Attach the forward end of the battery strap (A, **Figure 1**) under the front side of the battery tray. Then lay the strap over and into the groove in the battery top. Insert the threaded stud on the rear end of the battery strap into the hole at the rear side of the battery tray. Install the washer and nut. Tighten the nut securely.
7. Reconnect the battery vent tube to the battery.

NOTE
If the battery vent tube was removed from the bike, refer to ***Battery Vent Tube Routing*** *in this chapter.*

WARNING
After installing the battery, make sure the vent tube is not pinched. A pinched or kinked tube would allow high pressure to accumulate in the battery and cause the battery to explode. If the vent tube is damaged, replace it.

8. Install the seat.

Battery Vent Tube Routing

The battery vent tube must be routed properly and not touch any moving parts. Proper routing will ensure that vent hose outlet (**Figure 8**) is positioned away from all metal components. Replace the vent tube if it becomes kinked or plugged.

Connect the vent tube onto the battery vent nipple. On all models covered by this manual, the vent nipple is on the forward side of the battery; see **Figure 7**. Following the transmission housing curve, route the tube past the transmission and insert the hose through the vent hose clip on the frame (**Figure 8**). On California models, continue by inserting the vent tube through the additional vent tube clip mounted on the rear muffler mount. On California models, the vent tube must extend 3 in. (76 mm) down from the bottom of the second clip. On all other models, the vent tube must extend 3 1/2 in. (89 mm) down from the bottom of the clip.

Testing

Hydrometer testing is the best way to check battery condition. Use a hydrometer with numbered

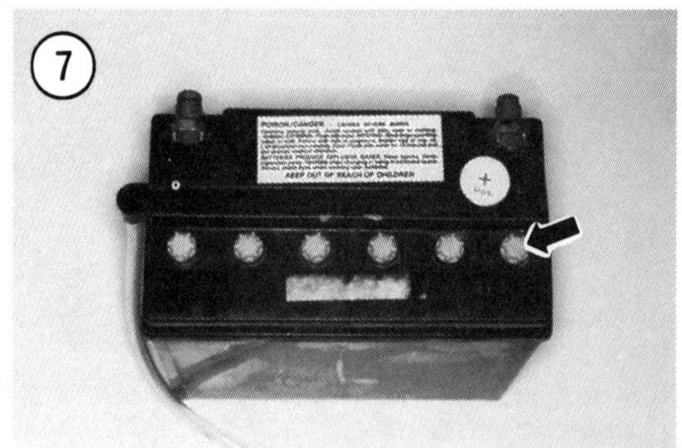

graduations from 1.100 to 1.300 rather than one with just color-coded bands. To use the hydrometer, squeeze the rubber ball, insert the tip into the cell and release the ball (**Figure 9**).

NOTE
Do not attempt to test a battery with a hydrometer immediately after adding water to the cells. Charge the battery for 15-20 minutes at a rate high to cause vigorous gassing and allow the water and electrolyte to mix thoroughly.

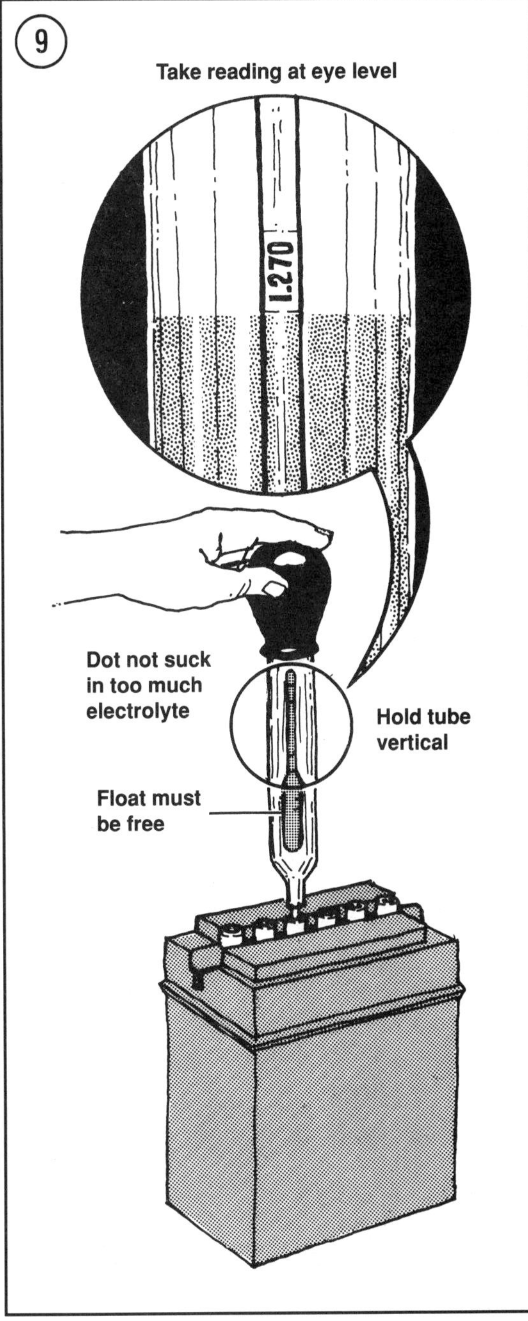

Draw enough electrolyte to float the weighted float inside the hydrometer. When using a temperature-compensated hydrometer, release the electrolyte and repeat this process several times to make sure the thermometer has adjusted to the electrolyte temperature before taking the reading.

Hold the hydrometer vertically and note the number in line with the surface of the electrolyte (**Figure 10**). This is the specific gravity for this cell. Return the electrolyte to the cell from which it came.

The specific gravity of the electrolyte in each battery cell is an excellent indication of that cell's condition (**Table 2**). A fully charged cell will read 1.275-1.280 while a cell in good condition reads from 1.225-1.250 and anything below 1.225 is dead. Charging is also necessary if the specific gravity varies more than 0.050 from cell to cell.

NOTE
If a temperature-compensated hydrometer is not used, add 0.004 to the specific gravity reading for every 10° above 80° F (25° C). For every 10° below 80° F (25° C), subtract 0.004.

8

Load Testing

A load test checks the battery's ability to provide current and to maintain a minimum amount of voltage.

A battery load tester is required for this procedure. When using a load tester, follow the manufacturer's instructions.

1. Remove the battery from the motorcycle as described in this chapter.
2. To perform this test, the battery must be fully charged. Use a hydrometer to check the battery specific gravity as described in this chapter, and bring the battery up to full charge, if required.

WARNING
The battery load tester must be turned OFF prior to connecting or disconnecting the test cables at the battery. Otherwise, a spark could cause the battery to explode, showering the area with sulfuric acid, causing serious injury.

CAUTION
Two basic requirements for preventing battery damage during load testing are: (1) do not attempt to load test a discharged battery; and (2) do not load test a battery for more than 20 seconds.

3. Connect the load tester cables to the battery following the manufacturer's instructions.
4. Adjust the load control knob until the ammeter reads 3 times the battery's ampere-hour rating. For example, the Sportster's 19-amp-hour battery should be loaded to 57 amperes.
5. Read the voltmeter scale. After 15 seconds, the voltage reading (with the load still applied) should be 9.6 volts or higher. Now quickly remove the load and turn the tester OFF.
6. If the voltage reading was 9.6 volts or higher, the battery output capacity is good. If the reading was below 9.6 volts, the battery is defective and must be replaced.
7. Install the battery as described in this chapter.

Charging

A good state of charge should be maintained in batteries used for starting. When charging the battery, note the following:

a. During charging, the cells will show signs of gas bubbling. If one cell has no gas bubbles or if its specific gravity is low, the cell is probably shorted.
b. If a battery not in use loses its charge within a week after charging or if the specific gravity drops quickly, the battery is defective. A good battery should only self-discharge approximately 1 percent each day.

CAUTION
Always remove the battery from the bike before connecting charging equipment.

WARNING
During charging, highly explosive hydrogen gas is released from the battery. The battery should be charged only in a well-ventilated area, and open flames and cigarettes should be kept away. Never check the charge of the battery by arcing across the terminals; the resulting spark can ignite the hydrogen gas.

1. Remove the battery from the bike as described in this chapter.
2. Connect the positive (+) charger lead to the positive battery terminal and the negative (–) charger lead to the negative battery terminal.
3. Remove all vent caps (**Figure 7**) from the battery, set the charger at 12 volts, and switch it on. Normally, a battery should be charged at a slow charge

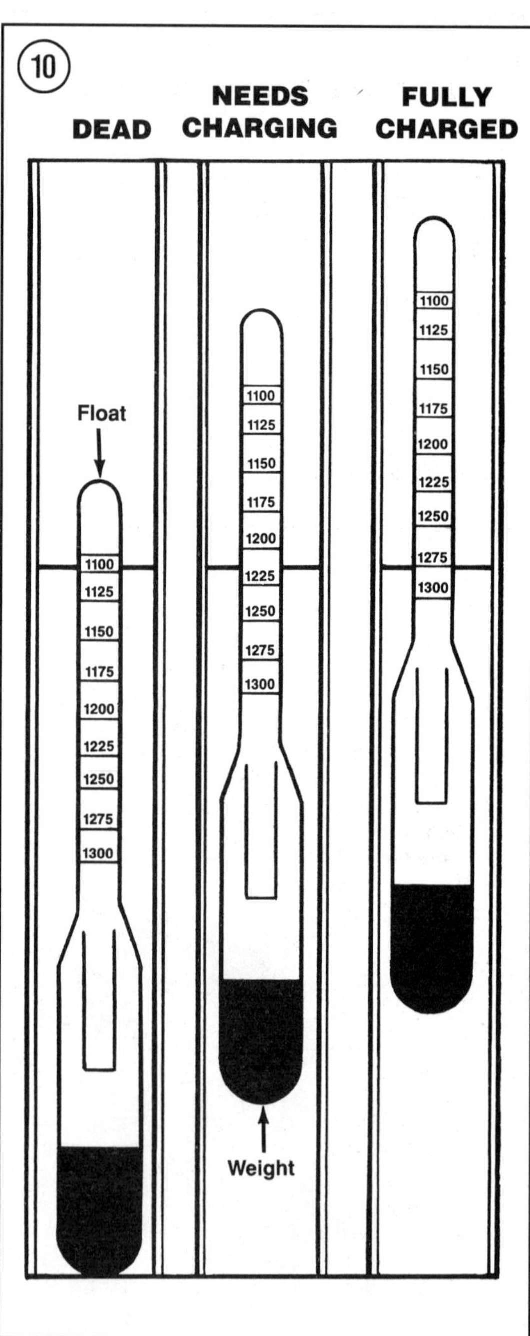

rate of 1/10 its given capacity. See **Table 1** for battery capacity.

CAUTION
The electrolyte level must be maintained at the upper level during the charging cycle; check and refill with distilled water as necessary.

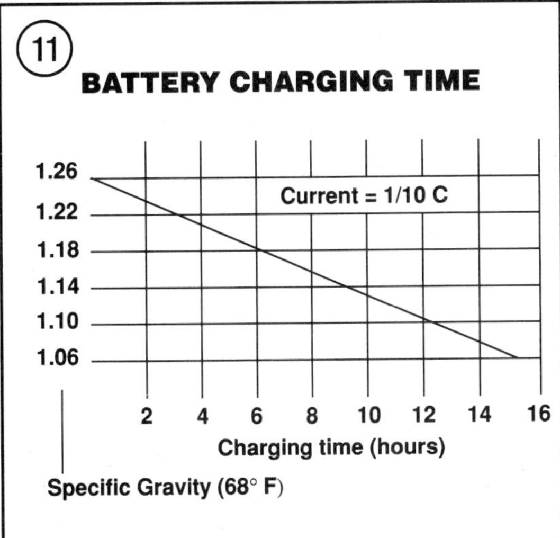

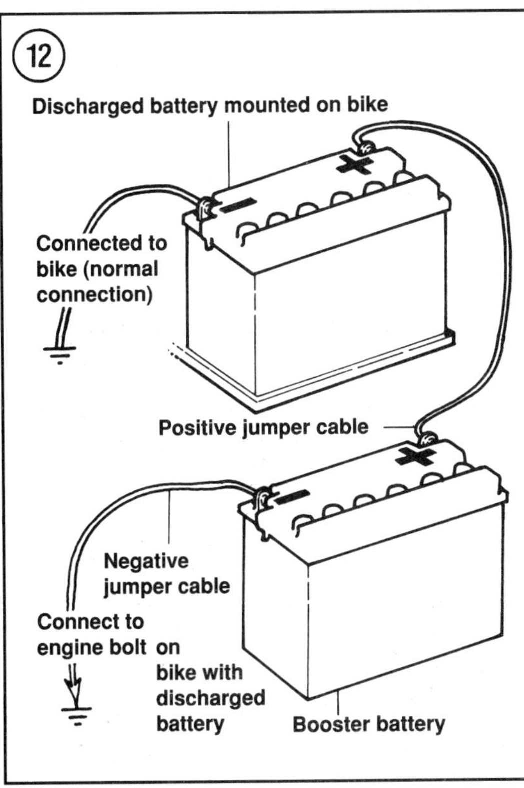

4. The charging time depends on the discharged condition of the battery. The chart in **Figure 11** can be used to determine approximate charging times at different specific gravity readings. For example, if the specific gravity of your battery is 1.180, the approximate charging time would be 6 hours.
5. After the battery has been charged for about 8 hours, turn the charger off, disconnect the leads and check the specific gravity. It should be within the limits specified in **Table 2**. If it is, and remains stable for one hour, the battery is charged.

New Battery Installation

When replacing the old battery with a new one, be sure to charge it completely (specific gravity, 1.260-1.280) before installing it. Failure to do so, or using the battery with a low electrolyte level will permanently damage the battery.

Jump Starting

If the battery becomes severely discharged, it is possible to start and run an engine by jump starting it from another battery. If the proper procedure is not followed, however, jump starting can be dangerous. Check the electrolyte level before jump starting any battery. If it is not visible or if it appears to be frozen, do not attempt to jump start the battery, as the battery may explode or rupture.

The booster battery must be a fully charged 12 volt battery.

WARNING
Use extreme caution when connecting a booster battery to one that is discharged to avoid personal injury or damage to the system.

Do not lean over the batteries when making the connections. Safety glasses should be worn when performing the following procedure.
1. Position the 2 vehicles so that the jumper cables will reach between batteries, but the vehicles do not touch.
2. Remove the seat to gain access to the dead battery. Remove parts as required to access the booster battery.
3. Make sure all electrical accessories are turned off.
4. Connect the jumper cables in the following order (**Figure 12**):

a. Connect the positive (+) jumper cable between the 2 battery positive terminals.
b. Connect one end of the negative (–) jumper cable to the booster battery negative terminal. Connect the opposite end to an unpainted engine case bolt on the bike with the dead battery. *Do not* connect the jumper cable to the negative battery terminal on the dead battery.

WARNING
*An electrical arc may occur when the final connection is made. This could cause an explosion if it occurs near the battery. For this reason, the final connection should be made to a good ground **away** from the battery and not to the battery itself. This includes keeping the connection away from the battery vent tube.*

NOTE
Do not connect the negative jumper cable to a chrome or painted part as the connection may discolor it.

5. Check that all jumper cables are out of the way.

NOTE
When attempting to start the engine in Step 6, do not operate the starter longer than 6 seconds. Excessive starter operation will overheat the starter and cause damage. Allow 15 seconds between starting attempts.

6. Start the engine. Once it starts, run it at a moderate speed.

CAUTION
Racing the engine may damage the electrical system.

7. Remove the jumper cables in the exact reverse order.

CHARGING SYSTEM

The charging system consists of the battery, alternator, regulator, ignition switch, circuit breaker and connecting wiring.

The alternator generates an alternating current (AC) which the rectifier converts to direct current (DC). The regulator maintains the voltage to the battery and load (lights, ignition, etc.) at a constant voltage regardless of variations in engine speed and load.

Service Precautions

Before servicing the charging system, observe the following precautions to prevent damage to any charging system component.

1. Never reverse battery connections. Instantaneous damage may occur.
2. Do not short across any connection.
3. Never attempt to polarize an alternator.
4. Never start the engine with the alternator disconnected from the voltage regulator/rectifier, unless instructed to do so in testing.
5. Never start or run the engine with the battery disconnected.
6. Never attempt to use a high-output battery charger to assist in engine starting.
7. Before charging battery, disconnect the negative battery lead.
8. Never disconnect the voltage regulator connector with the engine running.

9. Do not mount the voltage regulator/rectifier unit at another location.

10. Make sure the battery negative terminal is connected to both engine and frame.

Testing

A malfunction in the charging system generally causes the battery to remain undercharged. Perform the following visual inspection to determine the cause of the problem. If the visual inspection proves satisfactory, test the charging system as described in Chapter Two.

1. Make sure the battery cables are connected properly (**Figure 2**). The red cable must be connected to the positive battery terminal. If polarity is reversed, check for a damaged rectifier.

2. Inspect the terminals for loose or corroded connections. Tighten or clean as required.

3. Inspect the physical condition of the battery. Look for bulges or cracks in the case, leaking electrolyte or corrosion build-up.

4. Carefully check all connections at the alternator to make sure they are clean and tight.

5. Check the circuit wiring for corroded or loose connections. Clean, tighten or connect as required.

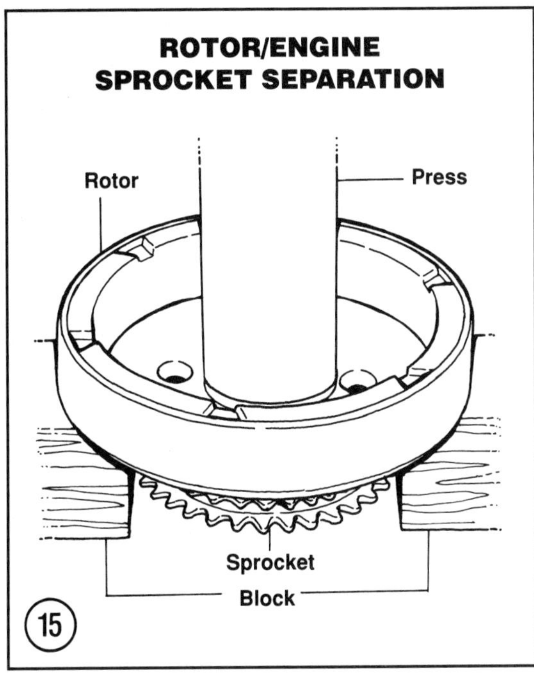

Rotor Removal/Installation

The rotor (A, **Figure 13**) is mounted on the engine sprocket (B, **Figure 13**).

1. Remove the primary chain, engine sprocket and clutch as described in Chapter Five.
2. If necessary, press the engine sprocket off of the rotor as described in this chapter.
3. Install the primary chain, engine sprocket and clutch as described in Chapter Five.

CAUTION
*Carefully inspect the inside of the rotor (A, **Figure 14**) for small bolts, washers or other metal "debris" that may have been picked up by the magnets. These small metal bits can cause severe damage to the alternator stator assembly.*

Rotor Disassembly/Reassembly

1. Remove the rotor-to-engine sprocket mounting bolts (B, **Figure 14**).
2. Support the rotor in a press as shown in **Figure 15**. Then press the engine sprocket off of the rotor.
3. Clean the engine sprocket, rotor and mounting bolts in solvent and dry thoroughly. Remove any Loctite residue from the sprocket and mounting bolt threads.
4. Place the rotor on top of the sprocket, aligning the holes in the rotor with the threaded holes in the sprocket.
5. Apply Loctite 242 (blue) to the mounting bolts prior to installation. Then install the bolts finger-tight only.
6. Support the sprocket in a press and place a piece of pipe between the rotor and press ram. Press the rotor onto the sprocket.
7. Tighten the rotor-to-engine sprocket mounting bolts to the torque specification in **Table 4**.

Inspection

1. Check the rotor (**Figure 16**) carefully for cracks or breaks.

WARNING
A cracked or chipped rotor must be replaced. A damaged rotor may fly apart

8

at high rpm, throwing metal fragments into the engine. Do not attempt to repair a damaged rotor.

2. Check the rotor magnets (A, **Figure 14**) for damage or looseness.
3. Replace the rotor, if necessary, as described in this chapter.

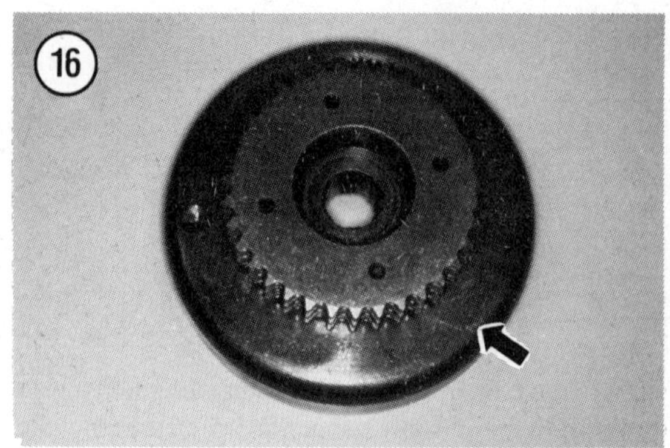

Stator Removal/Installation

The stator (**Figure 17**) is mounted behind the rotor and bolted to the left-hand crankcase. Torx screws with a locking adhesive applied are used to secure the stator. These Torx screws must be replaced after removal.

1. Remove the rotor as described in this chapter.
2. On a piece of paper, draw a diagram of the stator wiring harness frame routing path prior to removing the stator in the following steps.
3. Disconnect the electrical connector at the stator (**Figure 18**, typical).
4. Remove the cable straps from the stator wiring harness.
5. Remove the metal clamp plate (**Figure 19**).
6. Remove and discard the stator plate Torx screws (**Figure 20**).
7. Remove the stator wiring grommet from the crankcase.
8. Remove the stator assembly and its attached wiring harness (**Figure 21**).
9. Inspect the stator wires (**Figure 22**) for fraying or damage. Check the stator connector pins for looseness or damage. Replace the stator if necessary.
10. Installation is the reverse of these steps. Note the following.
11. Lightly coat the stator wiring grommet with engine oil. Then insert the grommet (**Figure 23**) into the crankcase.
12. Install *new* stator Torx screws and tighten to the torque specifications in **Table 4**.

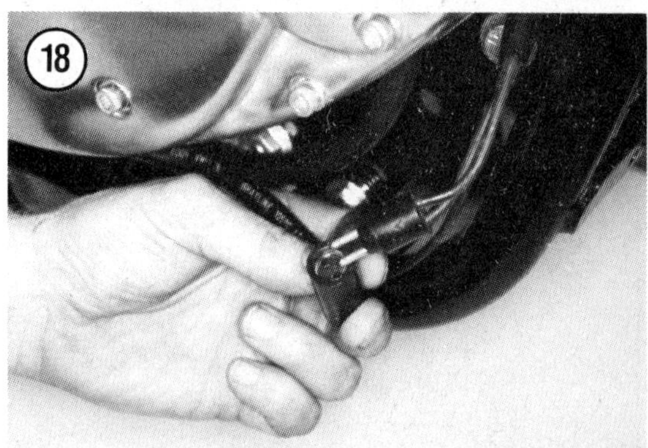

CAUTION

As described in Step 12, new Torx screws must be used. The thread locking compound originally applied to the Torx screws is sufficient for one time use only. A loose Torx screw would back out and cause severe alternator damage.

20

21

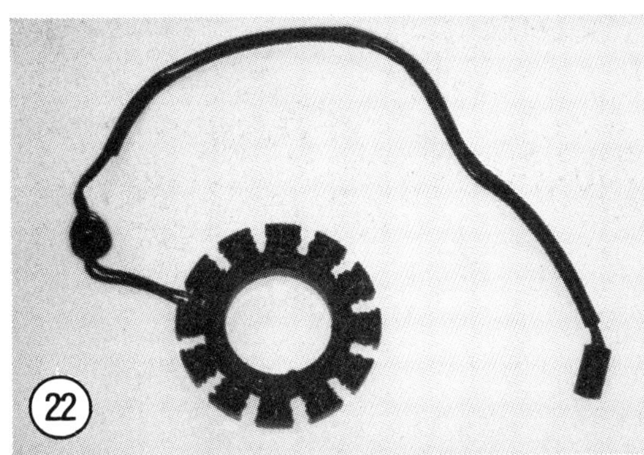
22

23

13. Following your routing diagram notes (Step 2), route the stator wiring harness along the frame. Secure the harness with the proper cable straps.

CAUTION

When bringing the wiring harness out from underneath the gearcase cover, the harness should be routed 1 1/2 in. (38 mm) forward of the rear gearcase edge. This distance is necessary to prevent the secondary drive chain/belt or sprocket from damaging the wiring harness.

14. Install the rotor as described in this chapter.

Voltage Regulator Removal/Installation

The voltage regulator is mounted on the front frame downtubes. See **Figure 24** (1991-1993) or **Figure 25** (1994).

The voltage regulator cannot be rebuilt; if damaged it must be replaced.

1. Disconnect the negative battery cable as described in this chapter.

2A. On 1991-1993 models, perform the following:
   a. Disconnect the voltage regulator-to-stator 2-pin wiring connector (**Figure 18**).
   b. Disconnect the voltage regulator-to-circuit breaker black wiring lead. This connector is mounted underneath the seat.
   c. On a piece of paper, draw a diagram of the voltage regulator wiring harness frame routing path prior to removing the voltage regulator.

2B. On 1994 models, perform the following:
   a. Disconnect the voltage regulator-to-circuit breaker 2-pin wiring connector.

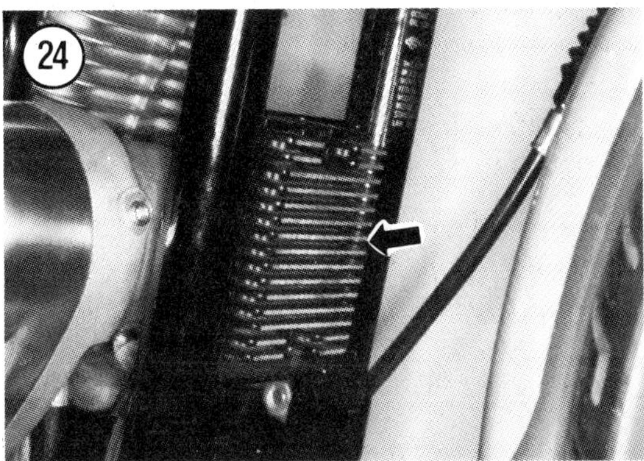
24

  b. Disconnect the voltage regulator-to-50 amp 1-pin Deutsch wiring connector (**Figure 25**).

3. Disconnect and remove the cable straps securing the voltage regulator wiring harness to the frame. Carefully pull the wiring harness away from the frame.
4. Remove the voltage regulator mounting fasteners and remove the voltage regulator.
5. Install by reversing these removal steps.

IGNITION SYSTEM

The ignition system (**Figure 26**) consists of a single ignition coil, 2 spark plugs, inductive pickup unit, ignition module and a vacuum operated electric switch (VOES). This system has a full electronic advance. The inductive pickup unit is driven by the engine and generates pulses which are routed to the solid-state ignition control module. This control module computes the ignition timing advance and ignition coil dwell time, eliminating the need for mechanical advance and routine ignition service.

The vacuum operated electric switch (VOES) senses intake manifold vacuum through a carburetor body opening. The switch is open when the engine is in low vacuum situations such as acceleration and high load. The switch is closed when engine vacuum is high as during a low engine load condition. The VOES allows the ignition system to follow 2 spark advance curves. A maximum spark curve can be used during a high-vacuum condition to provide improved fuel economy and performance. During heavy engine load and acceleration (low vacuum) conditions, the spark can be retarded to minimize ignition knock and still maintain performance.

The timing sensor is triggered by the leading and trailing edges of the 2 rotor slots. As rpm increases, the control module "steps" the timing in 3 stages of advance.

Refer to **Figure 27** (1991-1993) or **Figure 28** (1994) for a diagram of the ignition circuit.

Sensor Plate Removal/Installation

Refer to **Figure 27** (1991-1993) or **Figure 28** (1994).

1. Disconnect the negative battery lead.

NOTE

The sensor plate wiring harness connector must be removed from the end of the wiring harness prior to removing the wiring harness through the gearcase cover.

2. Disconnect the sensor plate wiring harness connector. Then remove the connector from the wiring harness as follows:
   a. On a piece of paper, record the position of each sensor plate wiring terminal in the end of the connector.
   b. On 1991-1993 models, remove the terminals from the end of the connector using the Cannon Connector Tool #201051.

25 VOLTAGE REGULATOR (1994)

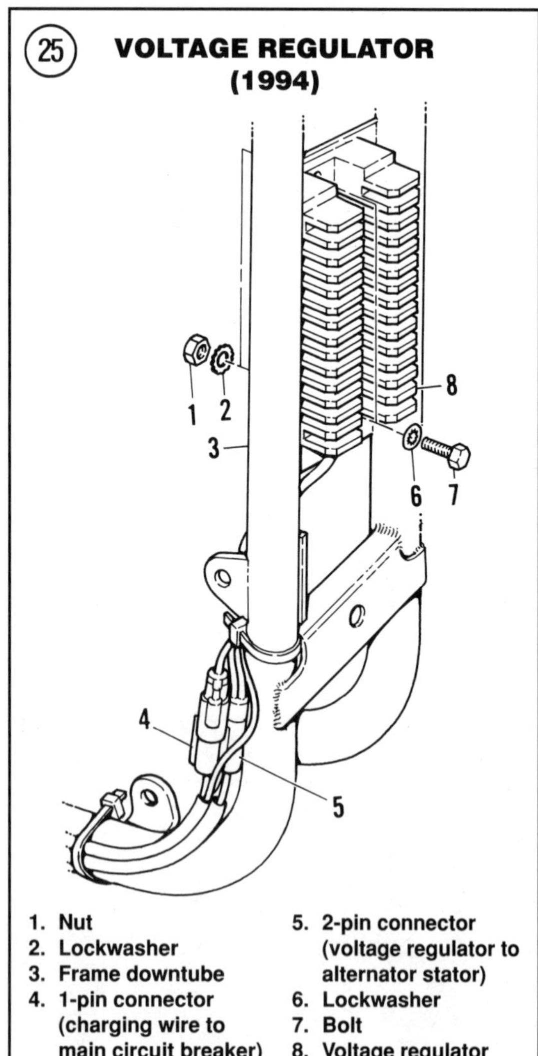

1. Nut
2. Lockwasher
3. Frame downtube
4. 1-pin connector (charging wire to main circuit breaker)
5. 2-pin connector (voltage regulator to alternator stator)
6. Lockwasher
7. Bolt
8. Voltage regulator

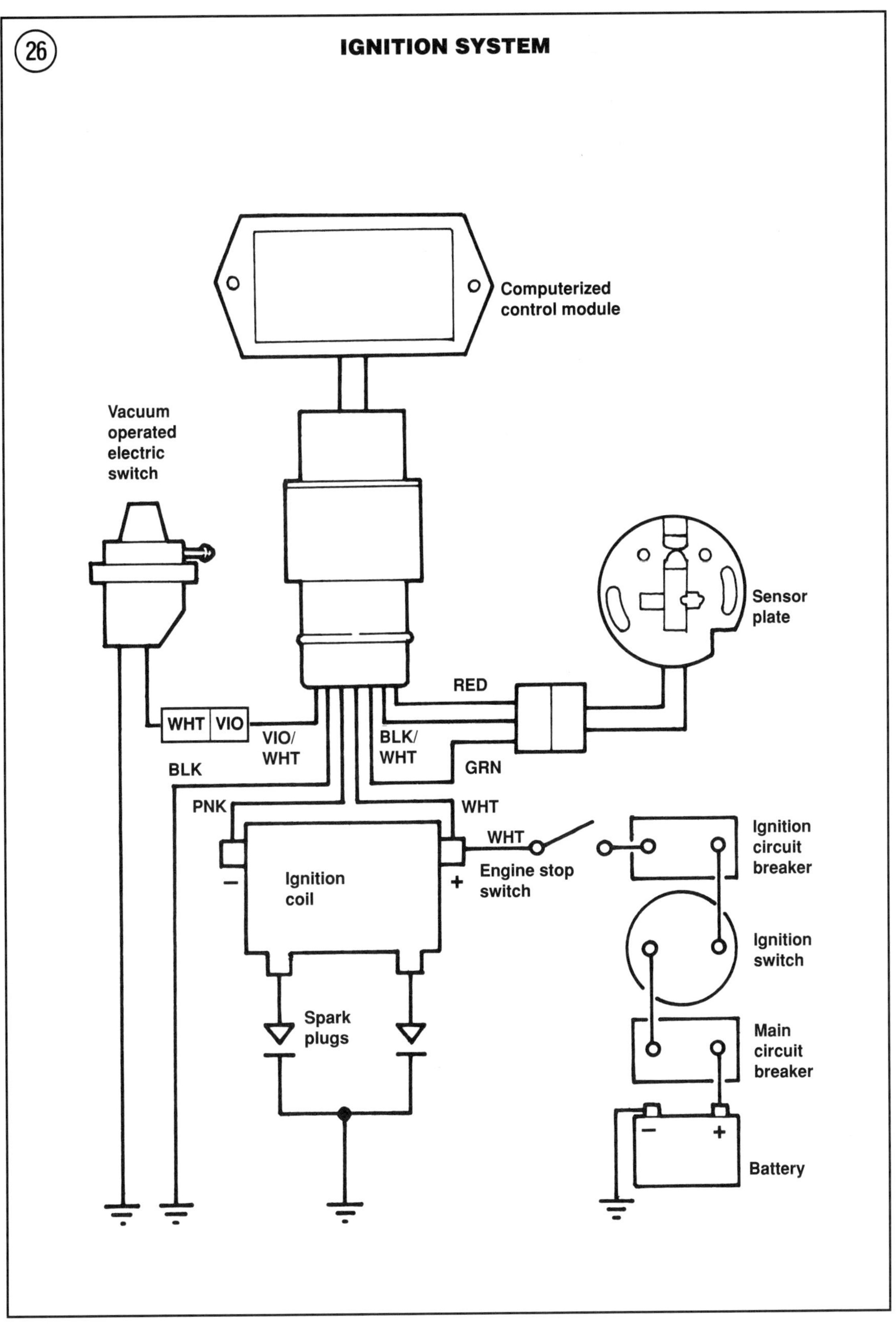
26
IGNITION SYSTEM
Computerized
control module
Vacuum
operated
electric
switch
Sensor
plate
RED
WHT
VIO
VIO/
WHT
BLK/
WHT
GRN
BLK
PNK
WHT
WHT
Ignition
circuit
breaker
–
Ignition
coil
+
Engine stop
switch
Ignition
switch
Spark
plugs
Main
circuit
breaker
–
+
Battery

c. On 1994 models, remove the terminals from the end of the connecting as described under *Deutsch Electrical Connectors* in this chapter.

3. Drill out the outer cover rivets with a 3/8 in. drill bit (**Figure 29**).

4. Using a punch, tap the rivets through the outer cover (**Figure 30**) and remove the outer cover.

5. Using a punch, tap the rivets through the inner cover.

6. Remove the inner cover Phillips screws (**Figure 31**) and remove the cover and gasket (**Figure 32**).

7. To help approximate ignition timing when installing the sensor plate, mark an alignment mark of

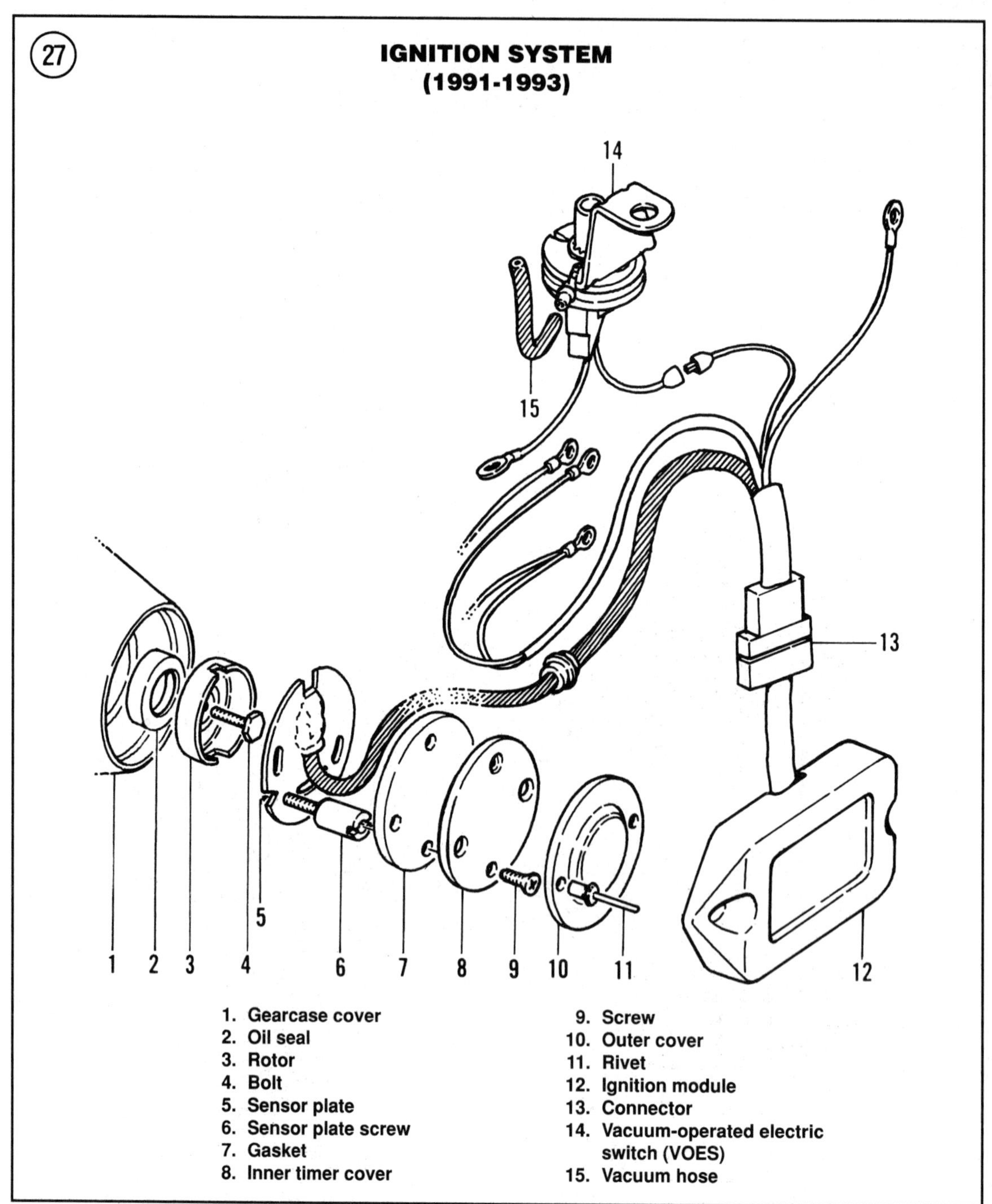

the sensor plate mounting screws position on the sensor plate.
8. Remove the screws (**Figure 33**) securing the sensor plate to the crankcase and pull the sensor plate out of the gearcase cover.
9. Withdraw the sensor plate wiring harness through the crankcase hole and remove the sensor plate.
10. Remove the rotor bolt (A, **Figure 34**) and rotor (B, **Figure 34**).
11. Installation is the reverse of these steps, noting the following.
12. To install the rotor:
   a. Align the tab on the back of the rotor (**Figure 35**) with the notch in the end of the crankshaft (**Figure 36**).

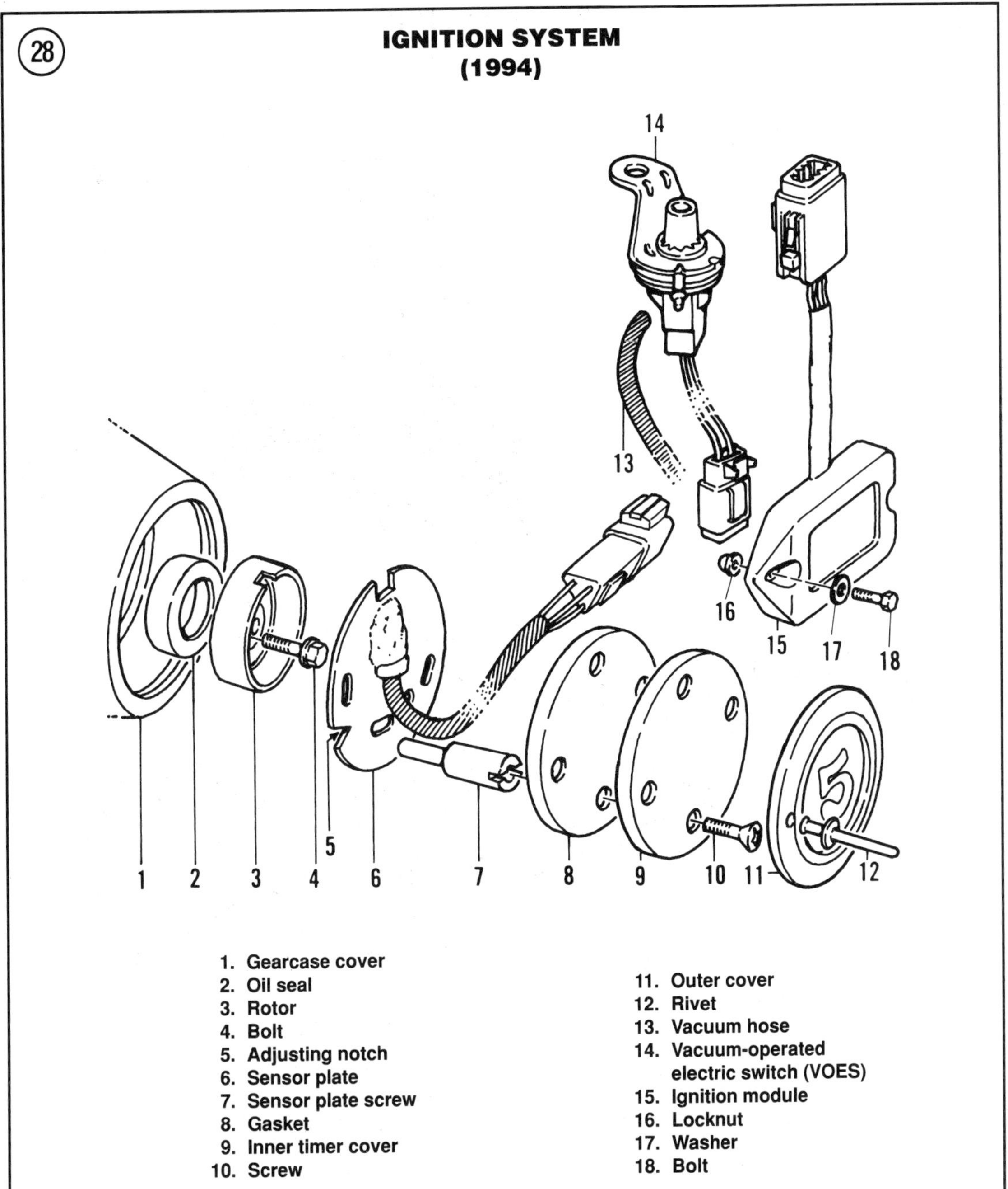

1. Gearcase cover
2. Oil seal
3. Rotor
4. Bolt
5. Adjusting notch
6. Sensor plate
7. Sensor plate screw
8. Gasket
9. Inner timer cover
10. Screw
11. Outer cover
12. Rivet
13. Vacuum hose
14. Vacuum-operated electric switch (VOES)
15. Ignition module
16. Locknut
17. Washer
18. Bolt

b. Apply Loctite 242 (blue) to the rotor bolt (A, **Figure 34**) and tighten it to the torque specification in **Table 4**.

13. Insert the sensor plate wires through the gearcase cover and route the wiring harness along its original path.

CAUTION
The sensor plate wiring harness should be routed approximately 1 1/2 in. (38 mm) forward of the gearcase rear edge. To exceed this measurement may allow the wiring harness to contact the secondary drive chain/belt and or sprocket, damaging the wiring harness.

14. Before riveting the cover in place, check the ignition timing as described in Chapter Three.

CAUTION
Make sure to use the correct rivets in Step 15. These are special timing cover rivets which do not have ends that will fall into the timing compartment and damage the ignition components.

15. Rivet the outer cover to the inner cover. Use only rivets (Harley-Davidson part number 8699) to secure the outer cover. See **Figure 37** and **Figure 29**.

Inspection

1. If necessary, follow the procedures in Chapter Two to troubleshoot the ignition system.
2. Check the ignition compartment for oil leakage. If present, remove the gearcase oil seal (**Figure 36**) by prying it out with a screwdriver or seal remover. Install a new seal by tapping it in place with a suitable size socket placed on the outside of the seal. Drive the seal in position so it is flush with the seal bore surface.

NOTE
If the gearcase oil seal is not installed all the way, it will leak.

Ignition Module Removal/Installation

The ignition module (**Figure 38**) is mounted on the left-hand side of the motorcycle, rearward of the battery.

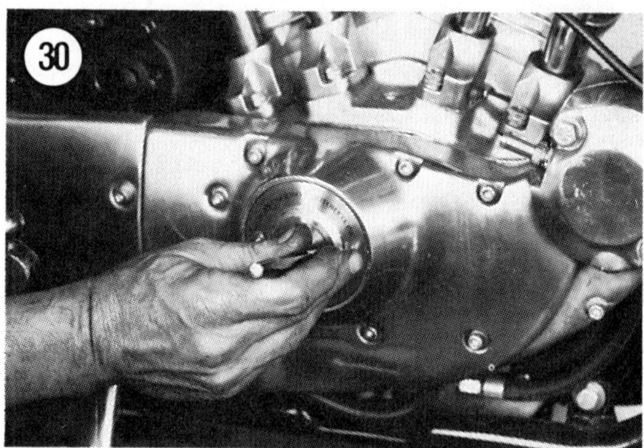

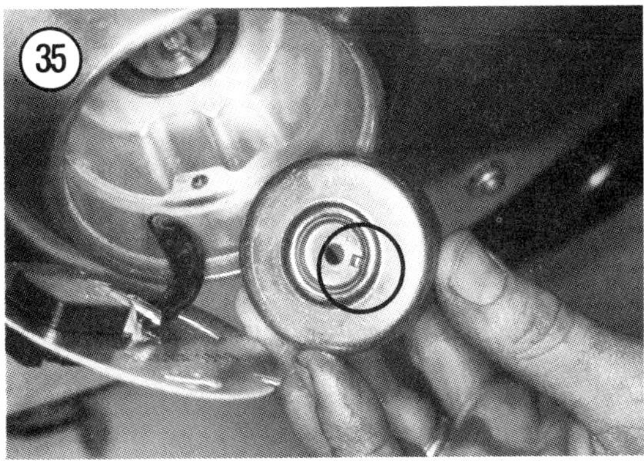

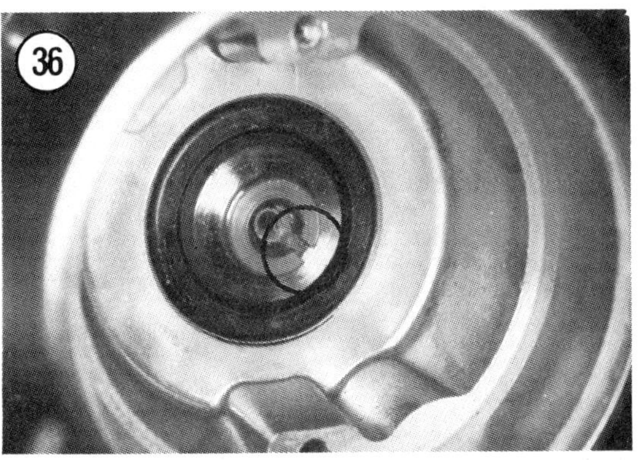

1. Disconnect the negative battery cable as described in this chapter.
2. Remove the ignition module cover.
3. Disconnect the ignition module wires at the ignition coil.
4. Loosen and remove the ground wire connection at the frame.
5. Remove the module mounting bolts and remove the module assembly (**Figure 38**).
6. Install by reversing these steps.

Vacuum-Operated Electric Switch (VOES) Bench Test

Refer to **Figure 39** when performing this procedure.

NOTE
*The VOES can be tested with a timing light while mounted on the bike. Refer to **Ignition Timing** in Chapter Three.*

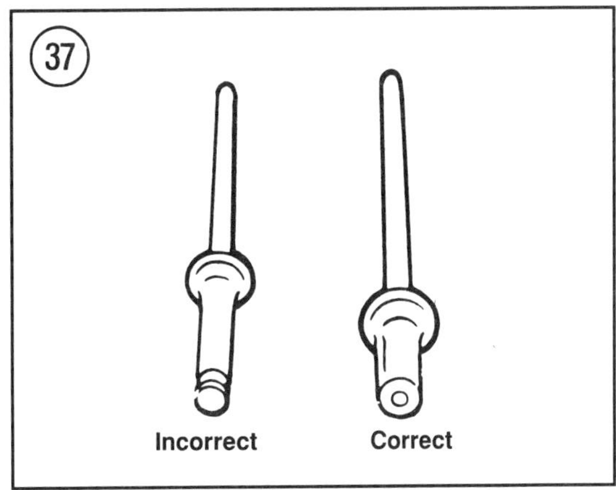

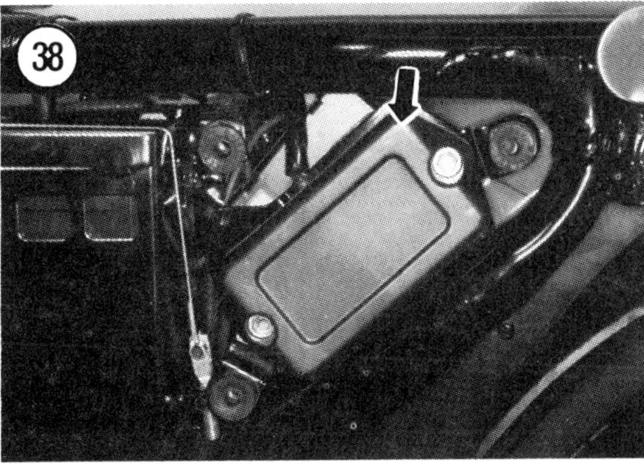

8

1. Remove the VOES as described in the following procedure.
2. Connect an ohmmeter to the 2 VOES electrical leads (1991-1993) or socket terminals (1994). Switch the meter to the R × 1 scale and zero the meter.
3. Connect a hand-operated vacuum pump to the VOES vacuum fitting.
4. Slowly operate the vacuum pump handle while reading the vacuum gauge and ohmmeter. The ohmmeter should read 0 ohms with a vacuum reading of 3.5-4.5 in./Hg (89-114 mm/Hg). If the vacuum reading falls outside this range when the ohmmeter reads 0 ohms, the VOES switch is faulty and must be replaced.

Vacuum-Operated Electric Switch (VOES) Replacement (1991-1993)

Refer to **Figure 39** for this procedure.

1. Remove the air filter and backplate as described in Chapter Three.
2. Remove the rear fuel tank mounting bolt.
3. Raise the rear of the fuel tank and disconnect the VOES wire from the ignition module. Remove the VOES cable strap.
4. Disconnect the vacuum hose from the VOES.
5. Remove the VOES ground wire bolt, washers and locknut.
6. Remove the VOES locknut and remove the VOES from the top center engine mount bracket.
7. Install by reversing these steps while noting the following.
8. Tighten the VOES locknut to the torque specification in **Table 4**.
9. Tighten the VOES ground wire bolt and locknut to the torque specification in **Table 4**.

CAUTION
Make sure that the VOES and its ground wire do not contact the engine rocker box. Engine vibration and heat can damage the switch and/or ground wire.

10. Tighten the fuel tank mounting bolt as described in Chapter Seven.

Vacuum-Operated Electric Switch (VOES) Replacement (1994)

1. Remove the air filter and backplate as described in Chapter Three.
2. Remove the rear fuel tank mounting bolt.
3. Raise the rear of the fuel tank and push the 2-pin Deutsch connector mounted on the top motor mount rearward to unsnap it from its T-stud clip.
4. Disconnect the 2-pin Deutsch connectors.
5. Remove the rubber cap mounted on the stud at the back of the top center engine mount. Loosen, then remove the locknut to free the VOES mounting bracket.

(39) **VACUUM-OPERATED ELECTRIC SWITCH**

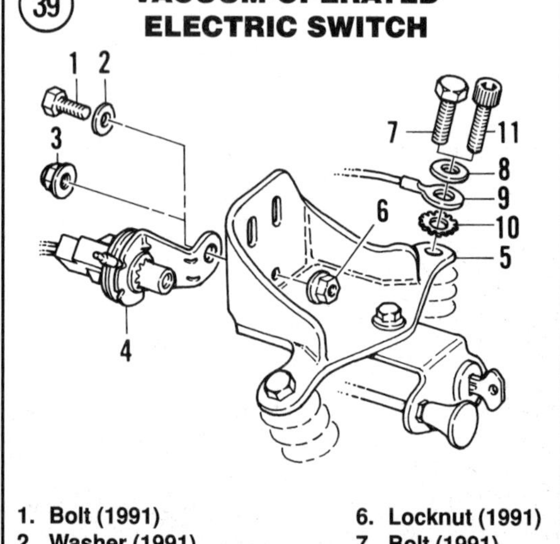

1. Bolt (1991)
2. Washer (1991)
3. Locknut (1992-1993)
4. Vacuum-operated electric switch (VOES)
5. Top center engine bracket
6. Locknut (1991)
7. Bolt (1991)
8. Washer
9. Ground wire
10. Lockwasher
11. Bolt (1992-1993)

(40)

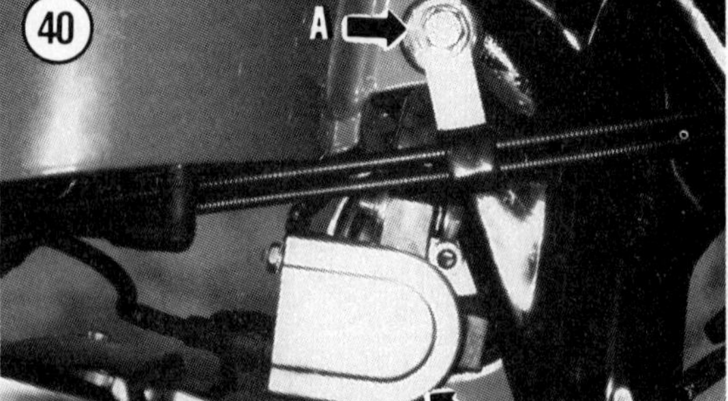

6. Pull the VOES out and disconnect the vacuum hose from the VOES.
7. Install by reversing these steps while noting the following.
8. Tighten the VOES mounting bracket locknut to the torque specification in **Table 4**.

CAUTION
Make sure that the VOES and its ground wire do not contact the engine rocker box. Engine vibration and heat can damage the switch and/or ground wire.

9. Tighten the fuel tank mounting bolt as described in Chapter Seven.

IGNITION COIL

The ignition coil is a form of transformer which develops the high voltage required to jump the spark plug gap. The only maintenance required is that of keeping the electrical connections clean and tight and occasionally checking to see that the coils are mounted securely.

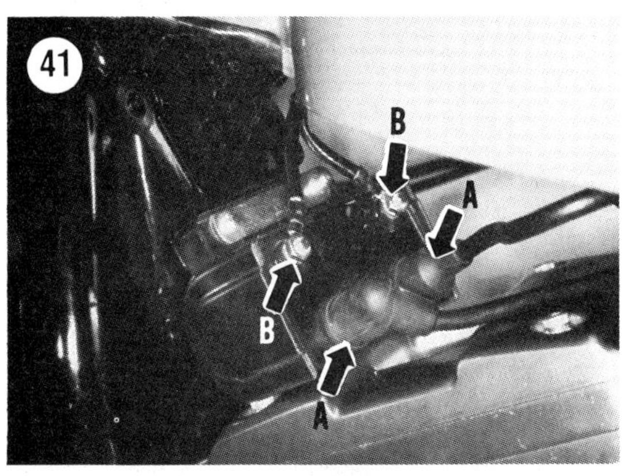

Removal/Installation

The ignition coil is mounted underneath the fuel tank.
1. Disconnect the negative battery cable as described in this chapter.
2. Remove the front fuel tank mounting bolt (A, **Figure 40**) and rest the ignition coil (B, **Figure 40**) on top of the cylinder head cover.

NOTE
Label all wiring connectors prior to disconnecting them in the following steps.

3. Disconnect the spark plug cables (A, **Figure 41**) at the ignition coil.
4. Disconnect the ring terminal wires (B, **Figure 42**) at the ignition coil.
5. Remove the coil cover, if so equipped.
6. Remove the ignition coil (with the fuel tank mounting bracket).
7. Installation is the reverse of these steps.

CAUTION
*When replacing an ignition coil, make sure the coil is marked **ELECTRONIC ADVANCE**. Installing an older type ignition coil could damage electronic ignition components.*

8

STARTER

The starting system consists of the starter motor, starter gears, solenoid and the starter button.

When the starter button is pressed, it engages the starter solenoid switch that completes the circuit allowing electricity to flow from the battery to the starter motor.

CAUTION
Never attempt to operate the starter by pushing the starter button for more than 5 seconds at a time. If the engine fails to start, wait a minimum of 10 seconds to allow the starter to cool. The starter can be damaged by failing to observe this caution.

Removal

1. Disconnect the negative battery cable.

2. Remove the primary cover as described in Chapter Five.

3. Remove the rear exhaust pipe as described in Chapter Seven.

4. Disconnect the electrical connectors at the starter motor. See **Figure 42**, typical.

5. Remove the bolts and washers (**Figure 43**) that hold the starter to the left-hand crankcase. Then withdraw the starter and its gasket from the crankcase and remove the starter from the right-hand side (**Figure 44**).

6. Service the starter as described in this chapter.

Installation

1. Install a new gasket onto the starter.

2. Insert the starter (and gasket) through the crankcase and loosely install the mounting bolts (**Figure 43**) and washers. Engage the starter motor gear with the clutch ring gear (if the clutch is installed on the bike) as shown in **Figure 45**.

3. Then tighten the starter mounting bolts to the torque specification in **Table 4.**

4. Clean, then reconnect the electrical connectors at the starter motor. See **Figure 42**, typical.

5. Install the primary cover as described in Chapter Five.

6. Install the rear exhaust pipe as described in Chapter Seven.

7. Reconnect the negative battery cable.

Disassembly

Refer to **Figure 46** and **Figure 47** for this procedure.

1. Clean all grease, dirt and carbon from the case and end covers.

2. Disconnect the solenoid wire (**Figure 48**).

3. Loosen and remove the 2 starter housing thru-bolts (A, **Figure 49**).

4. Remove the 2 screws (B, **Figure 49**) securing the end cover to the brush holder. Remove the end cover (C, **Figure 49**).

NOTE

The end cover screws on 1200 cc models are equipped with O-rings.

5. Lift the field coil brush springs out of their holders with a small hook and remove the brushes from their holders.

6. Slide the brush holder (**Figure 50**) off of the commutator.

7. Remove the armature (**Figure 51**) and field frame assembly (**Figure 52**).

8. If necessary, remove and disassemble the drive housing as follows:

a. Remove the 2 screws (**Figure 53**) and washers securing the drive housing (A, **Figure 54**) to the

43

44

45

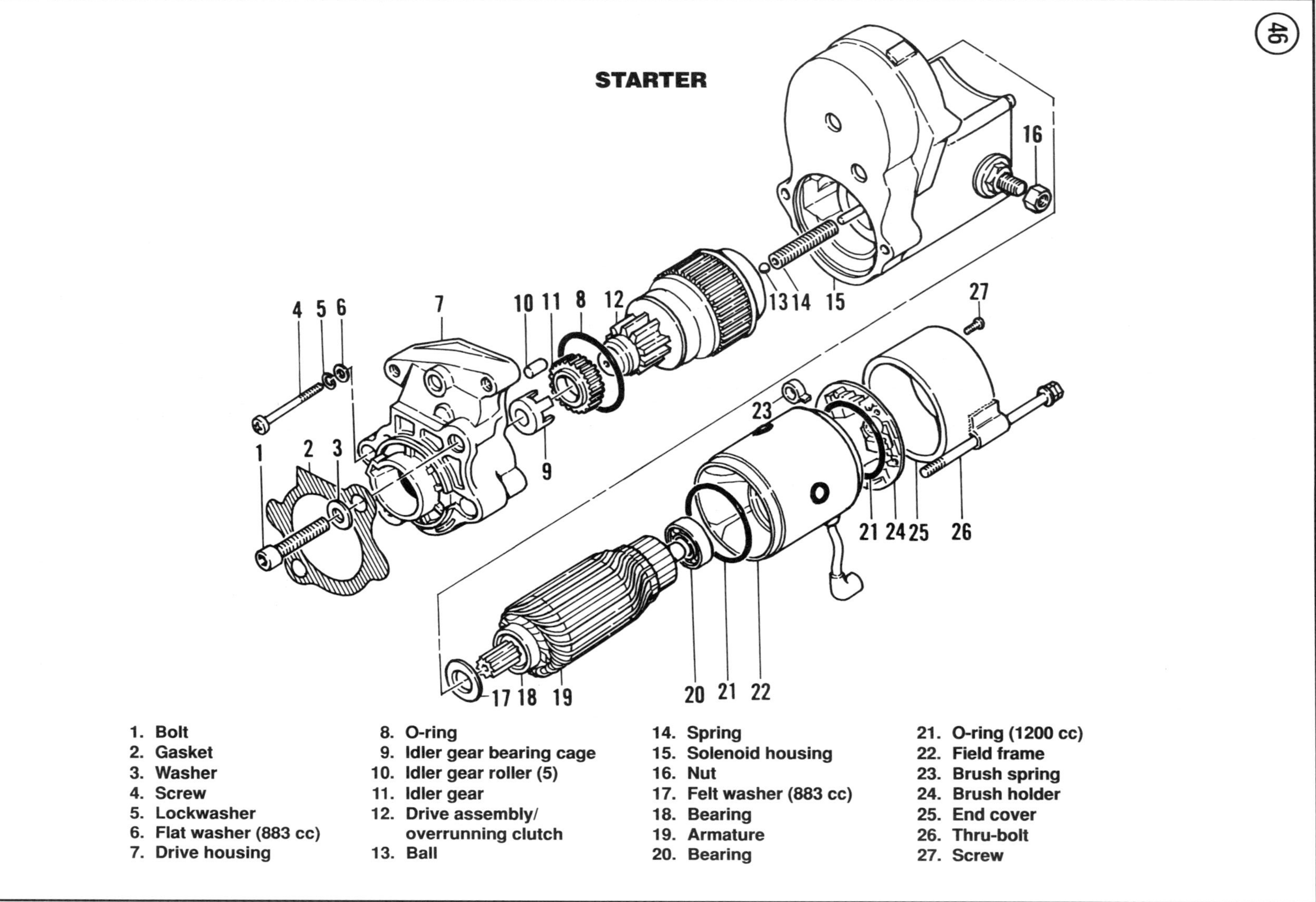
46
STARTER
1. Bolt
2. Gasket
3. Washer
4. Screw
5. Lockwasher
6. Flat washer (883 cc)
7. Drive housing
8. O-ring
9. Idler gear bearing cage
10. Idler gear roller (5)
11. Idler gear
12. Drive assembly/ overrunning clutch
13. Ball
14. Spring
15. Solenoid housing
16. Nut
17. Felt washer (883 cc)
18. Bearing
19. Armature
20. Bearing
21. O-ring (1200 cc)
22. Field frame
23. Brush spring
24. Brush holder
25. End cover
26. Thru-bolt
27. Screw

solenoid housing (B, **Figure 54**). O-rings are installed on these screws (**Figure 55**).

b. Remove the drive housing (A, **Figure 54**) from the solenoid housing.

c. Remove the ball and spring (**Figure 56**) from the solenoid housing.

d. Remove the drive assembly (A, **Figure 57**), idler gear (B, **Figure 57**) and the idler gear bearing assembly (**Figure 58**) from the drive housing.

e. Carefully pry the O-ring (**Figure 59**) out of the groove in the bottom of the drive housing.

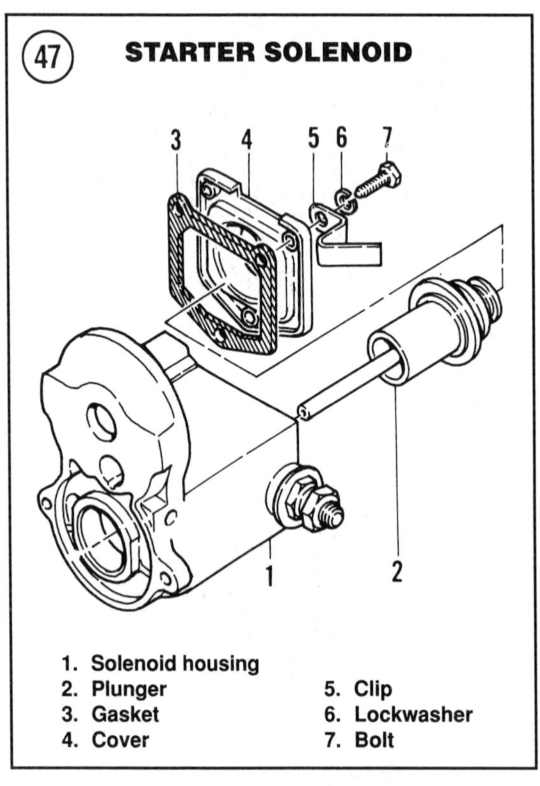

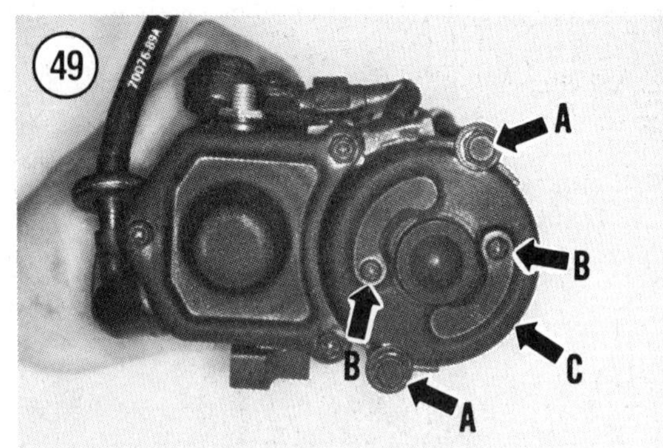

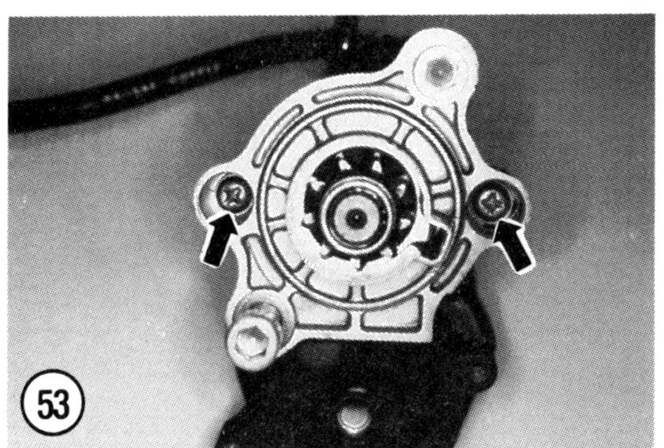

9. Inspect the starter assembly as described in this chapter.

Inspection (All Models)

1. The starter components should be cleaned thoroughly. Do not clean the field coils or armature in any cleaning solution that could damage the insulation. Wipe these parts off with a clean rag. Likewise, do not soak the overrunning clutch in any cleaning

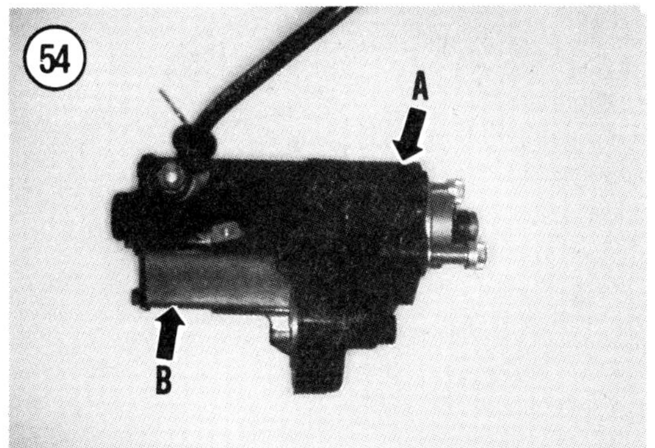

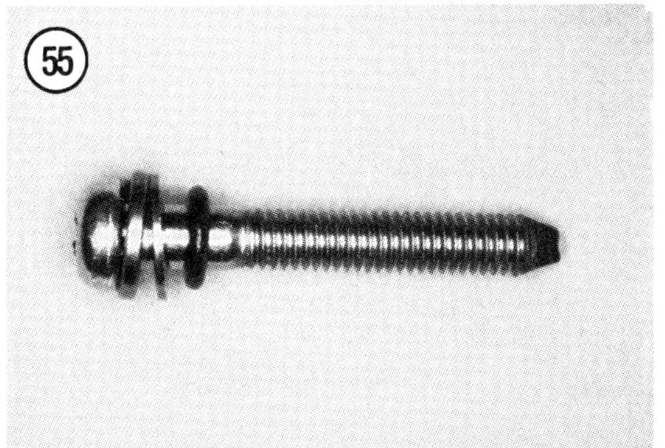

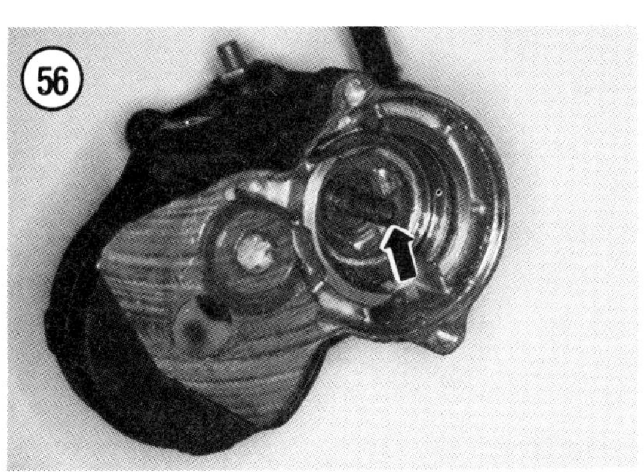

solution as the chemicals could dissolve the lubrication within the clutch and ruin it.

2. Measure the length of each brush with a vernier caliper (**Figure 60**). If the length is less than the minimum wear length specified in **Table 3**, it must be replaced. Replace the brushes in sets of four, even though only one may be worn to this dimension. See **Figure 61** (field coil) and **Figure 62** (brush holder).

NOTE

*The field coil brushes (**Figure 61**) are soldered in position. To replace, first apply heat to the brushes soldered joint to unsolder. Remove the old brushes. Solder the new brushes in place with rosin core solder—do not use acid core solder.*

3. Inspect the condition of the commutator (A, **Figure 63**). The mica in the commutator should be at least 0.008 in. (0.20 mm) undercut. If the mica undercut is less than this amount, undercut the mica with a piece of hacksaw blade to a depth of 1/32 in. (0.79 mm). This procedure can also be performed by a dealer or automotive specialist with a undercutting machine. When undercutting mica, each groove must form a right angle. Do not cut the mica so that a thin edge is left next to the commutator segment. **Figure 64** shows the proper angle. After undercutting the mica, remove burrs by sanding commutator lightly with crocus cloth.

4. Inspect the commutator copper bars for discoloration. If a pair of bars is discolored, grounded armature coils are indicated.

5. The armature can be checked for winding shorts with a growler. To do this, the mechanic inserts the armature into a growler (**Figure 65**). The growler is then turned on while a hacksaw blade is held close to but not touching the armature. The armature is then rotated slowly by hand; if the blade vibrates and

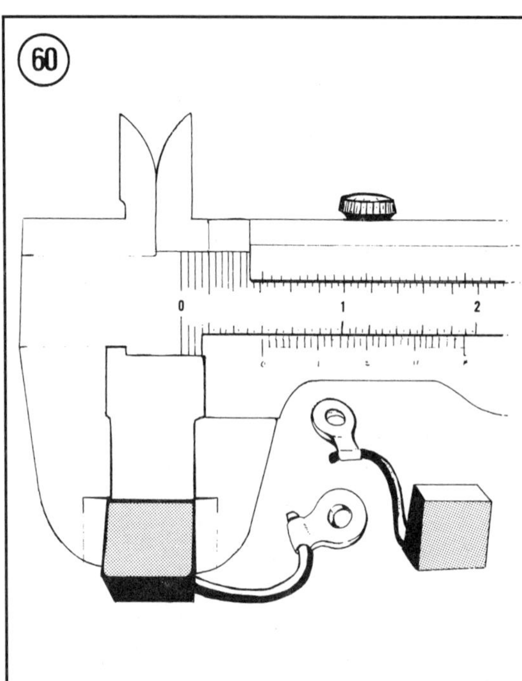

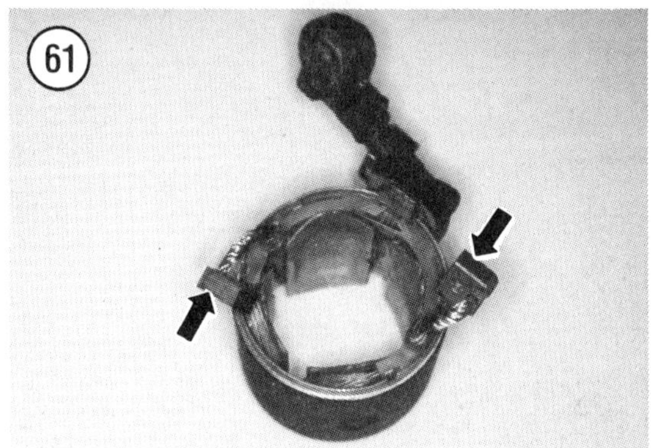

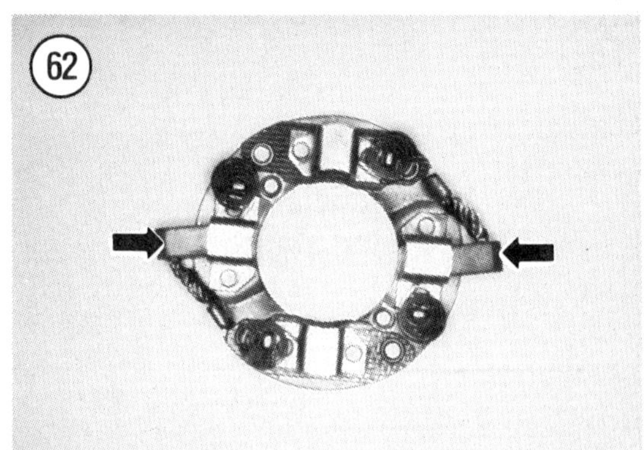

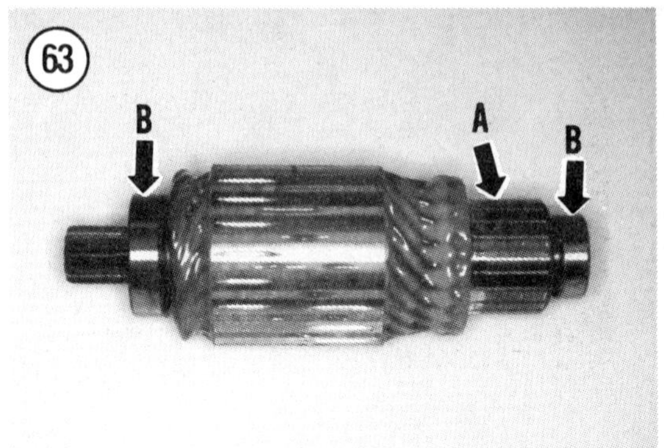

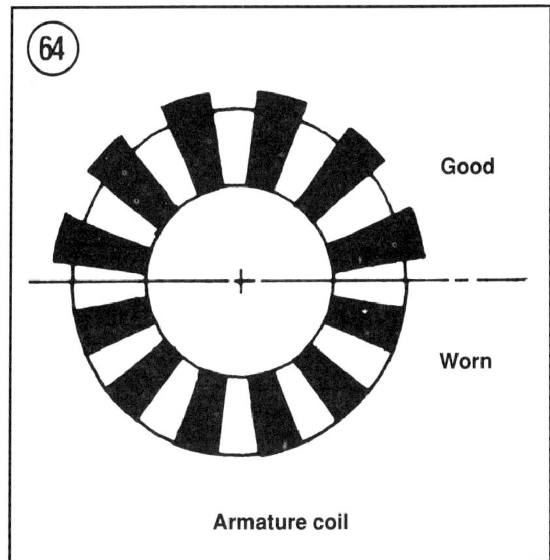

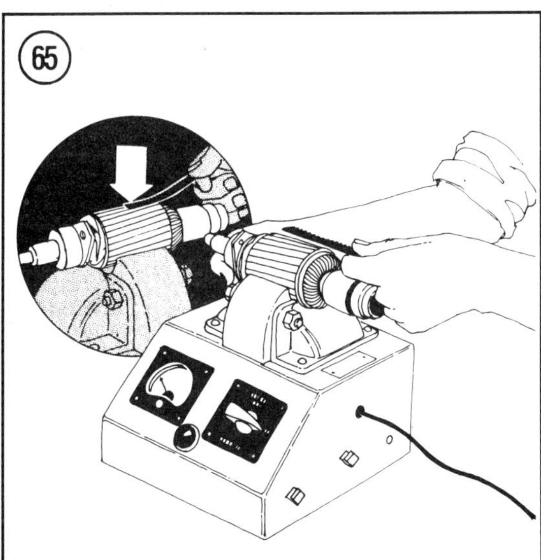

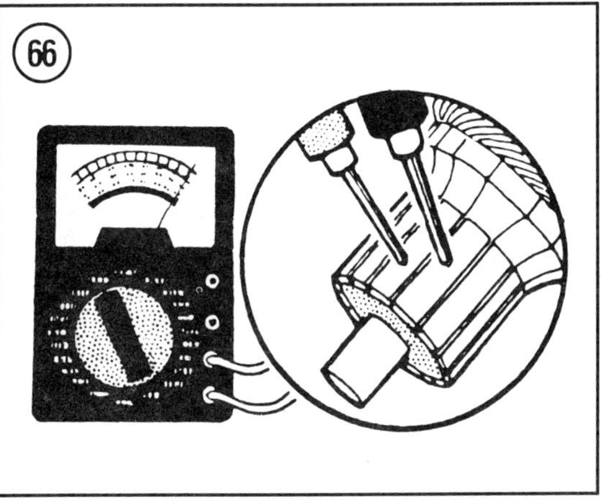

is attracted to the armature, an armature winding is shorted. If this is the case, the armature must be replaced. Refer this test to a Harley-Davidson dealer or automotive electrical specialist.

6. Place the armature in a lathe or between crankshaft centers and check commutator runout with a dial indicator. If runout exceeds 0.016 in. (0.41 mm), commutator should be trued on a lathe. When truing the commutator to eliminate the out-of-round condition, make the cuts as light as possible. Replace the armature if the commutator O.D. meets or is less than the wear limit listed in **Table 3**.

7. Use an ohmmeter and check for continuity between the commutator bars (**Figure 66**); there should be continuity between pairs of bars. If there is no continuity between pairs of bars, the armature is open. Replace the armature.

8. Connect an ohmmeter between any commutator bar and the armature core (**Figure 67**); there should

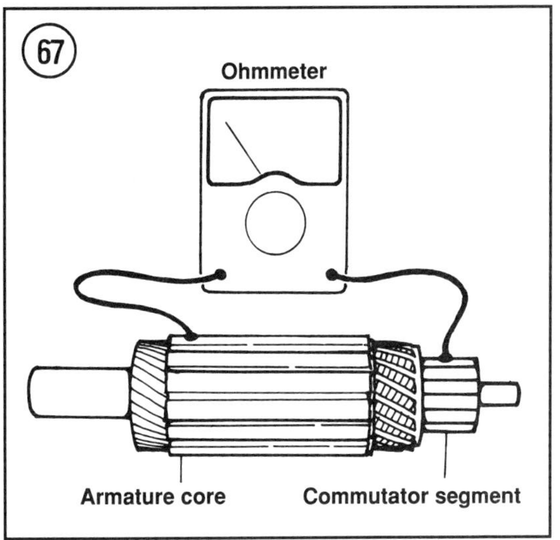

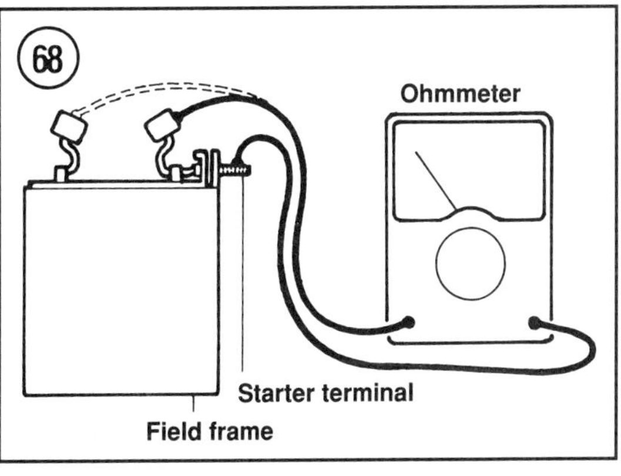

8

be no continuity. If there is continuity, the armature is grounded. Replace the armature.

9. Connect an ohmmeter between the starter cable terminal and each field frame brush (**Figure 68**); there should be continuity. If there is no continuity at either brush, the field windings are open. Replace the field frame assembly.

10. Connect an ohmmeter between the field frame housing and each field frame brush (**Figure 69**); there should be no continuity. If there is continuity at either brush, the field windings are grounded. Replace the field frame assembly.

11. Connect an ohmmeter between the brush holder plate and each brush holder (**Figure 70**); there should be no continuity. If there is continuity at either brush holder, the brush holder or plate is damaged. Replace the brush holder plate.

12. Service the armature bearings as follows:
   a. Check the bearings (B, **Figure 63**) on the armature shaft. If worn or damaged, remove and install new bearings with a bearing splitter and a press.

NOTE
Note that the 2 bearings installed on the armature shaft have different part numbers. When replacing the bearings, identify the old bearings before their removal in relationship to their position on the armature. This information can then be used to make sure the new bearings are installed correctly.

   b. Check the bearing bores in the end cover and solenoid housing. Replace the cover or housing if this area is severely worn or cracked.

13. The drive assembly is bolted onto the end of the solenoid housing. Inspect it as follows:
   a. Check the teeth on the idler gear (A, **Figure 58**) and drive assembly (A, **Figure 71**) for wear or damage.
   b. Check for chipped or worn bearing rollers (B, **Figure 58**). Damaged rollers would cause the pinion to turn roughly in the overrunning direction.
   c. Check the idler gear shaft in the drive housing for severe wear or damage.
   d. Replace worn or damaged parts as required.

14. Check the pinion gear (B, **Figure 71**) teeth for cracks, deep scoring or excessive wear.

15. Check the drive assembly bearings (C, **Figure 71**) for severe wear or damage.

Assembly

Refer to **Figure 46** or **Figure 47** for this procedure.

1. Prior to assembly, perform the *Inspection* procedure to make sure all worn or defective parts have

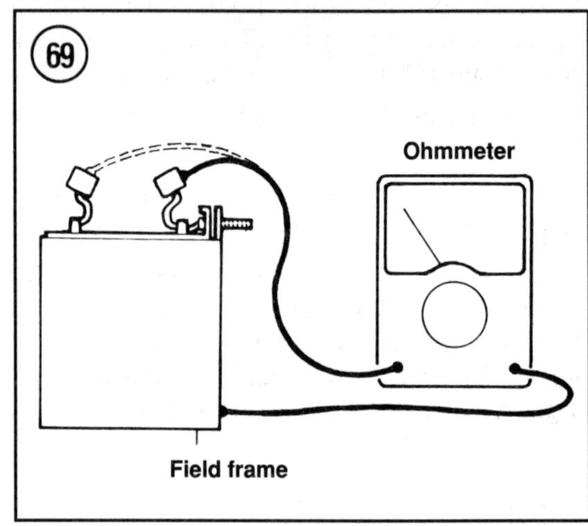

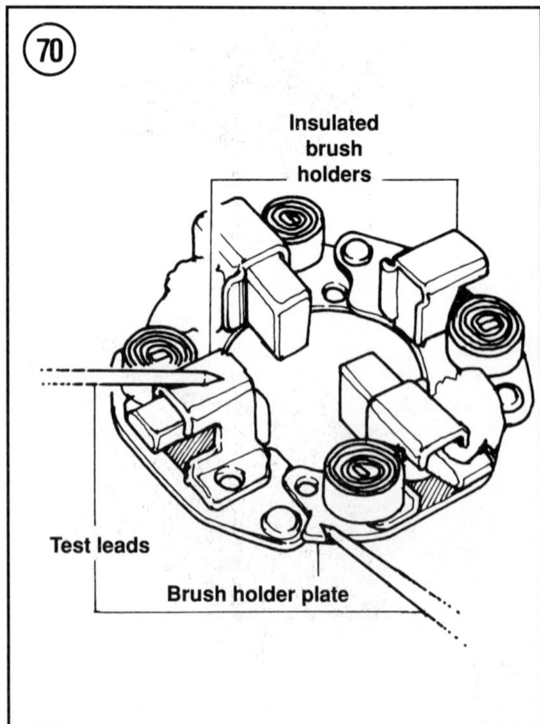

been repaired or replaced. All parts should be thoroughly cleaned before assembly.

2. Smear a thin film of Lubriplate 110 onto the drive housing O-ring and insert the O-ring into the groove in the bottom of the housing (**Figure 59**). Make sure that the O-ring seats squarely in the groove.

3. After the drive assembly components have been cleaned and dried, lubricate all components with Lubriplate 110.

4. Place the idler gear over the shaft in the drive housing. Then place the idler bearing cage in the gear so that the open cage end faces toward the solenoid; see B, **Figure 57**. Install the bearing pins in the cage.

5. Insert the drive assembly (A, **Figure 57**) into the drive housing.

6. Drop the ball into the shaft and slide the spring (**Figure 56**) over the solenoid plunger shaft.

7. Align the drive housing (A, **Figure 54**) with the solenoid housing (B, **Figure 54**) and assemble both housings. Secure the drive housing with the screws, lockwashers, flat washers and O-rings (**Figure 55**). Tighten the screws (**Figure 53**) securely.

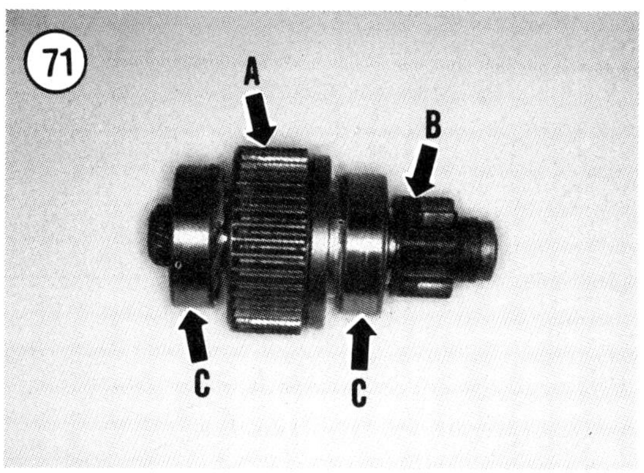

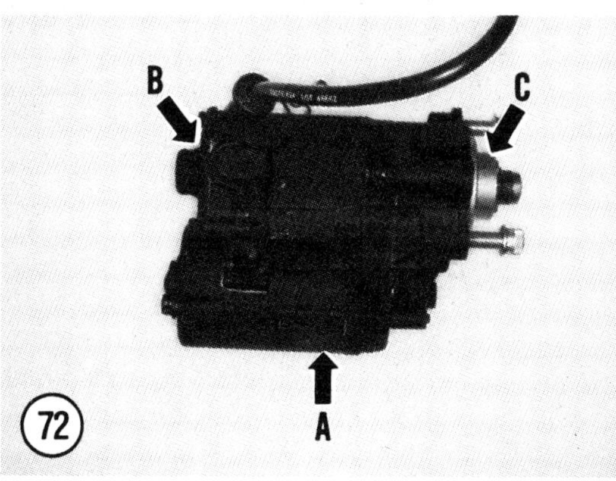

8. Pack the armature bearings with Lubriplate 110. Then install the field frame housing (**Figure 52**) onto the solenoid housing.

9. Install the armature into the drive housing as shown in **Figure 51**.

10. Install the brush plate (**Figure 50**) into the end of the field frame and install the 4 brushes so that they ride over the commutator.

11. Install the 2 positive brushes as follows:
   a. The positive brushes are soldered to the field coil assembly.
   b. Pull a positive brush out of its brush holder. A piece of wire bent to form a small hook on one end can be used to access the brushes.
   c. Insert the positive brush into its brush holder.
   d. Release the spring so that tension is applied against the brush.
   e. Repeat for the other positive brush.

12. Install the 2 negative brushes as follows:
   a. The negative brushes are mounted onto the brush holder.
   b. Pull a negative brush out of its brush holder. A piece of wire bent to form a small hook on one end can be used to access the brushes.
   c. Insert the negative brush into its brush holder.
   d. Release the spring so that tension is applied against the brush.
   e. Repeat for the other negative brush.

13. Align the slot in the rear cover with the terminal in the frame and install the rear cover (C, **Figure 49**). Install the thru-bolts (A, **Figure 49**) through the starter assembly. Tighten the starter thru-bolts to the torque specification in **Table 4**.

14. Secure the brush holder to the rear cover with the 2 screws (B, **Figure 49**) and washers. Tighten the screws securely.

15. Reconnect the solenoid wire (**Figure 48**).

STARTER SOLENOID

The starter solenoid (A, **Figure 72**), starter motor (B, **Figure 72**) and drive assembly (C, **Figure 72**) are assembled as one unit.

Disassembly/Reassembly

Refer to **Figure 73** for this procedure.

1. Remove the starter motor as described in this chapter.

2. Separate the solenoid (A, **Figure 72**) from the starter assembly as described in this chapter.

3. Remove the screws and washers (and clip) that hold the cover to the solenoid housing. Then remove the cover and gasket.
4. Remove the solenoid plunger from the solenoid housing.
5. Inspect the parts for severe wear or damage. Replace parts as required.
6. Installation is the reverse of these steps, noting the following.
7. Make sure the solenoid plunger shaft engages the spring in the drive assembly shaft.

LIGHTING SYSTEM

The lighting system consists of a headlight, taillight/brake light combination, turn signals, indicator lights and meter illumination lights.

Always use the correct wattage bulb. Harley-Davidson lists bulb sizes by part number. The use of a larger wattage bulb will give a dim light and a smaller wattage bulb will burn out prematurely. Replacement bulbs can be purchased through Harley-Davidson dealers by part number or by reading the number of the defective bulb and cross-referencing it with another supplier.

Headlight Replacement

Refer to **Figure 74** for this procedure.

WARNING
*If the headlight has just burned out or turned off it will be **Hot**! Don't touch the bulb until it cools off.*

1. Remove the outer molding ring pinch screws and remove the outer molding ring (**Figure 75**).
2. Carefully pry the headlight lens assembly (**Figure 76**) from the rubber mount.
3. Depress the locking tabs on both sides of the electrical connector (**Figure 77**). Then hold the locking tabs down and pull the connector off of the headlight terminals. Remove the headlight lens assembly.
4. Remove the socket cover (A, **Figure 78**) from the back of the headlight lens assembly.
5. Depress the ends of the bulb retaining clip and unhook the clip from the headlight assembly slots (A, **Figure 79**). Pivot the retaining clip away from the bulb.

CAUTION
*All models are equipped with a quartz halogen bulb (**Figure 80**). Do not touch the bulb glass with your fingers because traces of oil on the bulb will create temperature variances in the glass when the bulb is on; this may cause the bulb to fracture or will drastically reduce the life of the bulb. Clean any traces of oil from the bulb glass with a cloth moistened in alcohol or lacquer thinner. When handling the bulb, touch only the metal base or terminals.*

6. Lift the bulb (B, **Figure 79**) out of the headlight lens assembly.
7. Replace the retaining clip (A, **Figure 79**) if damaged.

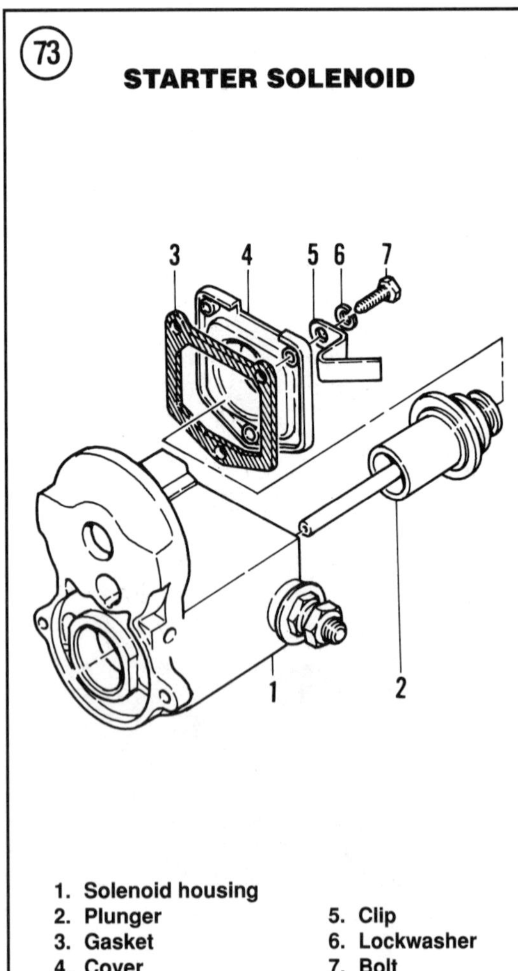

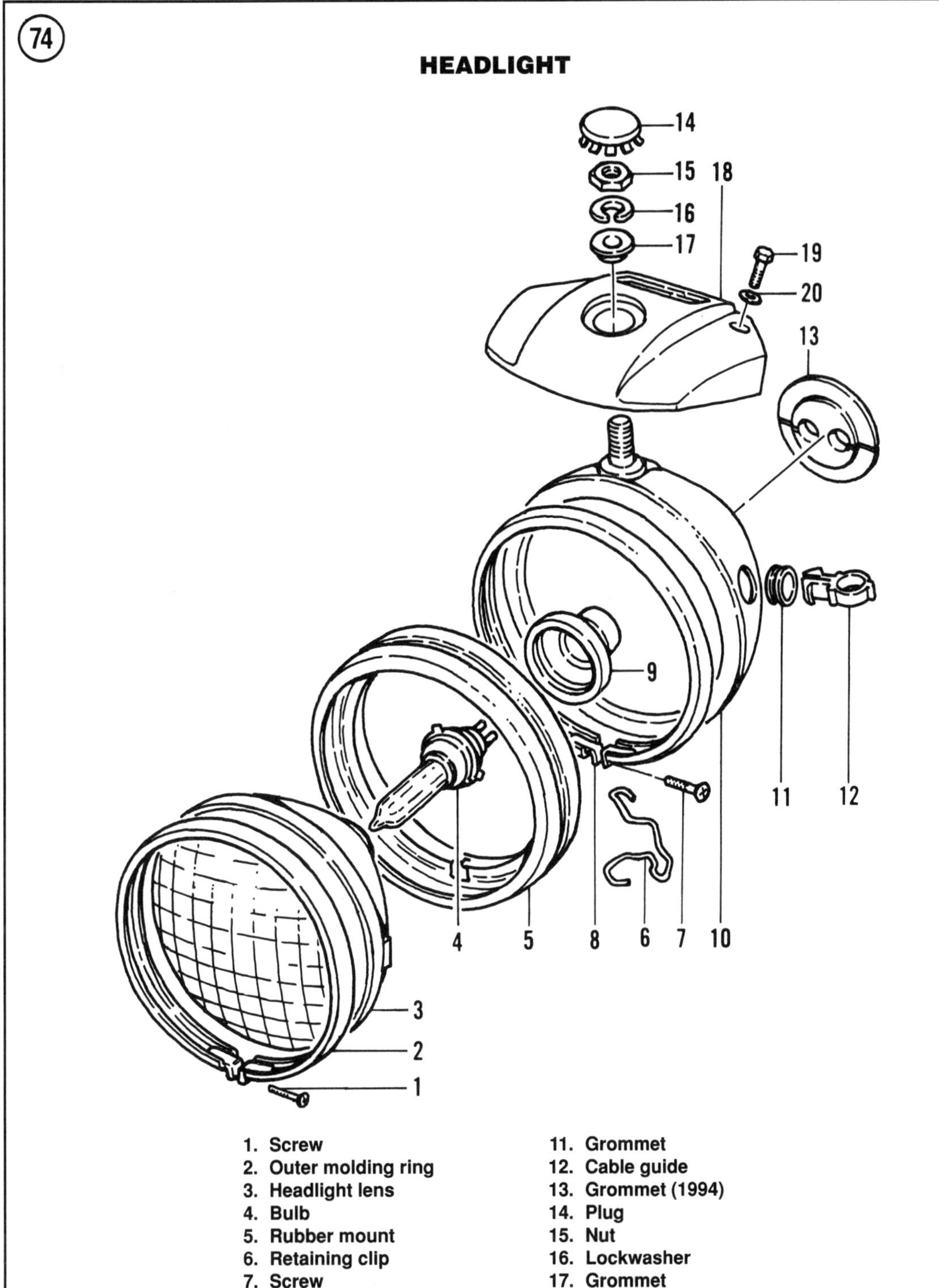

1. Screw
2. Outer molding ring
3. Headlight lens
4. Bulb
5. Rubber mount
6. Retaining clip
7. Screw
8. Inner molding ring
9. Socket cover
10. Headlight housing
11. Grommet
12. Cable guide
13. Grommet (1994)
14. Plug
15. Nut
16. Lockwasher
17. Grommet
18. Headlight bracket
19. Bolt
20. Washer

8. Install by reversing these steps while noting the following:

a. Read the previous CAUTION prior to handling the replacement bulb.

b. Install the bulb and make sure the projections on the bulb are meshed with the slots in the lens assembly; see B, **Figure 79**.

c. Position the socket cover with the "TOP" mark located at the top; see B, **Figure 78**. This ensures that the vent holes in the socket cover are positioned at the bottom. Push it on until it is completely seated.

d. Make sure the electrical connector (**Figure 81**) is free of corrosion and that all of the wiring in the headlight housing is pushed aside so that it cannot be pinched when the headlight lens is installed.

e. Make sure the electrical connector is pushed on tight (**Figure 77**).

f. Check that the headlight operates properly before riding the bike.

g. Check headlight adjustment as described in this chapter.

Headlight Adjustment

Adjust the headlight horizontally and vertically according to Department of Motor Vehicle regulations in your area.

1. Park the motorcycle on a level surface approximately 25 feet (7.62 m) from the wall (test pattern). Have a rider sit on the seat and make sure the tires are inflated to the correct pressure when performing this adjustment. See Chapter Three for tire pressure.

2. Draw a horizontal line on a wall which is 35 in. (889 mm) above the floor.

75

76

77

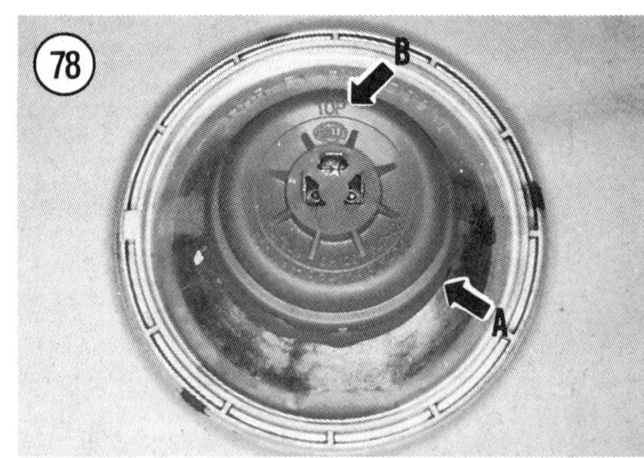

78

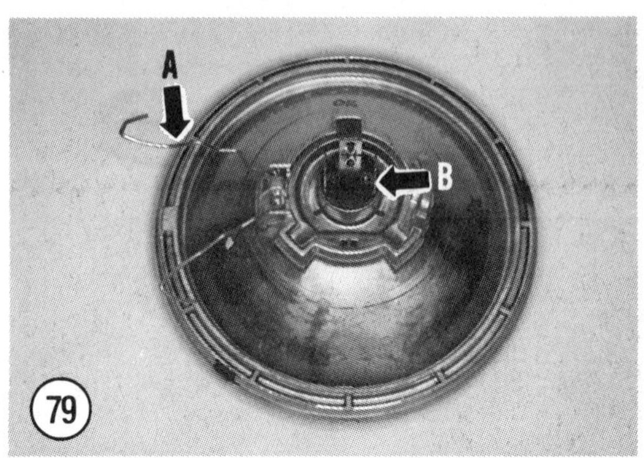

79

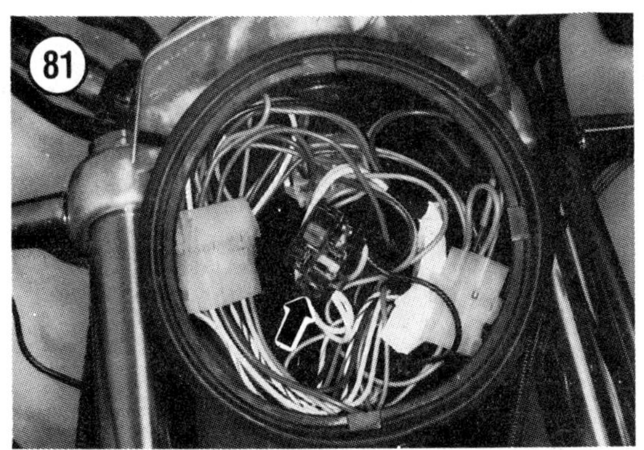

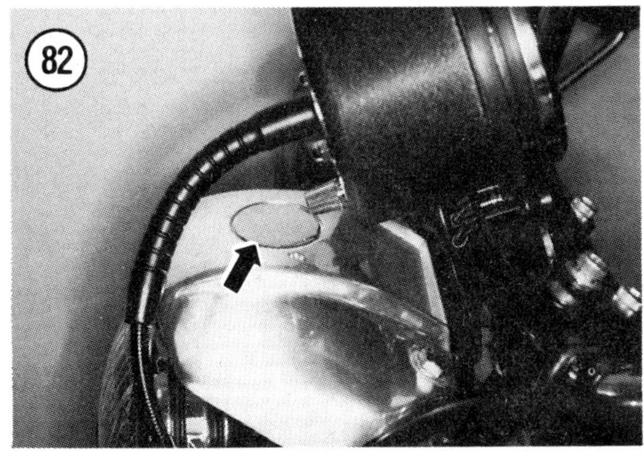

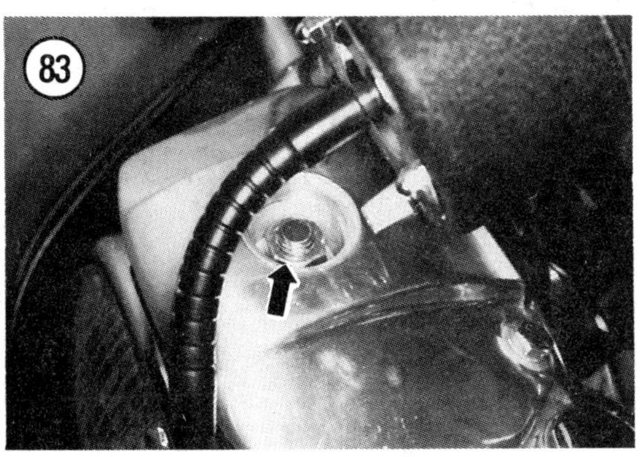

3. Aim the headlight at the wall and turn on the headlight. Switch the headlight to the high beam.
4. Check the headlight beam alignment. The broad, flat pattern of light (main beam of light) should be centered on the horizontal line (equal area of light above and below line).
5. Now check the headlight beam lateral alignment. With the headlight beam pointed straight ahead (centered), there should be an equal area of light to the left and right of center.
6. If the beam is incorrect as described in Steps 4 and/or 5, adjust as follows.
   a. Remove the plug (**Figure 82**) from the top of the headlight housing.
   b. Loosen the headlight clamp nut (**Figure 83**).
   c. With your hands, tilt the headlight assembly up or down to adjust the beam vertically while turning the assembly to the left- or right-hand sides to adjust the beam horizontally.
   d. When the beam is properly adjusted both horizontally and vertically, tighten the headlight adjust nut (**Figure 83**) to the torque specification in **Table 4**.
   e. Push the plug (**Figure 82**) into the headlight housing.

8

Taillight/Brake Light Replacement

1. Remove the rear lens and its gasket (**Figure 84**).
2. Push in on the bulb (**Figure 85**) and remove it.
3. Replace the lens gasket if torn or otherwise damaged.
4. Replace the bulb and install the lens.

Turn Signal Light Replacement

1. Remove the turn signal lens (**Figure 86**).

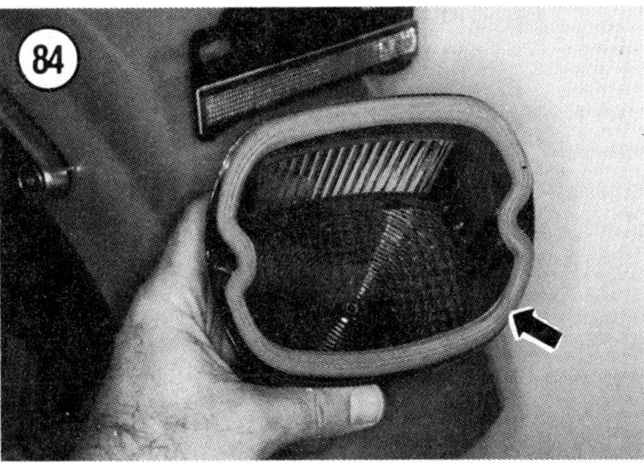

2. Push in on the bulb (**Figure 87**) and remove it.

3. Replace the bulb and install the lens.

Indicator Light Panel Replacement (1991-1993)

An indicator light panel (**Figure 88**) is used to monitor the headlight high beam, oil pressure, neutral position and turn signal lamps. The individual lamps do not have replaceable bulbs. If one of the lamps becomes faulty, the individual indicator lamp harness (**Figure 89**) must be replaced as an assembly.

1. On 1991 models, remove the speedometer and tachometer (1200 cc) as described in this chapter.

2. Remove the headlight lens assembly as described under *Headlight Bulb Replacement* in this chapter.

3. Remove the headlight adjust nut (**Figure 83**), lockwasher and washer securing the headlight housing to the headlight bracket. Then slide the headlight housing out of the headlight bracket. See **Figure 74**.

4. Disconnect the indicator lamp connector in the headlight housing. **Figure 90** shows the individual lamp positions.

5. Remove the indicator lamp leads from the connector using the Harley-Davidson terminal tool (part No. HD-97364-71 [**Figure 91**]) or equivalent.

NOTE
When replacing the left- or right-hand turn indicator or high beam indicator lamp harness, disconnect its ground wire from the upper fork bracket.

6. Using a sharp, pointed tool, carefully pry the trim cover (**Figure 90**) from the indicator lamp housing on the instrument bracket.

7. Working at the indicator lamp on the instrument bracket, push the indicator light harness through the indicator lamp housing and remove it. See **Figure 92**.

8. Install a new indicator light harness by reversing these steps. Note the following.

9. Check and adjust the headlight beam as described in this chapter. Then tighten the headlight adjust nut (**Figure 83**) to the torque specification in **Table 4**.

85

86

87

88

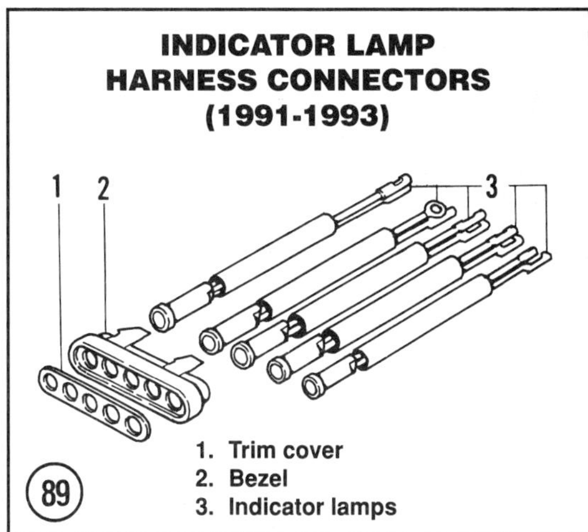

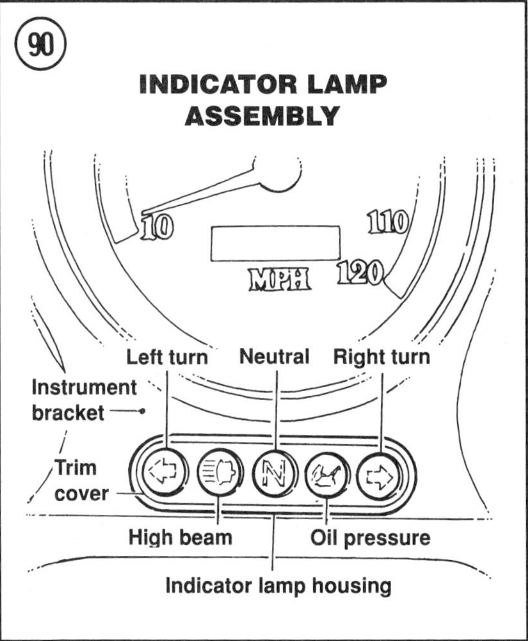

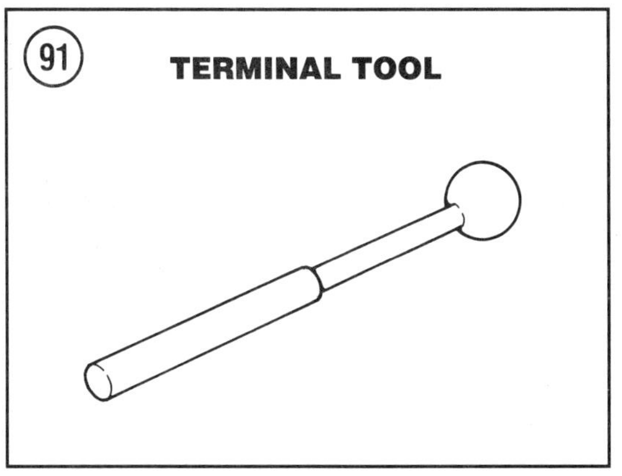

Indicator Light Panel Replacement (1994)

An indicator light panel (**Figure 88**) is used to monitor the headlight high beam, oil pressure, neutral position and turn signal lamps. The individual lamps do not have replaceable bulbs. If one of the lamps becomes faulty, the lamp assembly must be removed from the indicator light panel.

NOTE
Prior to replacing one or more of the indicator light panel lamp assemblies, review the information listed under ***Deutsch Electrical Connectors****. To properly separate and then reconnect the Deutsch connectors, special crimping procedures and crimping tools will be required. If you are not equipped to service these connectors, refer service to a Harley-Davidson dealer.*

1. Remove the headlight bracket bolts (A, **Figure 93**) and lockwashers and remove the headlight bracket (B, **Figure 93**) from the upper fork stem bracket.

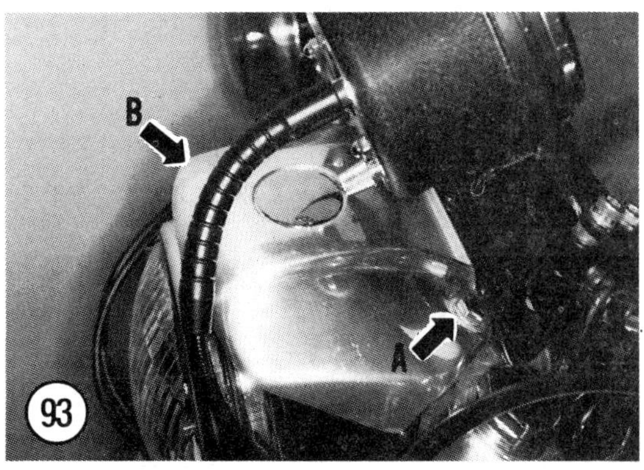

8

2. Disconnect the black 12-pin Deutsch connector located between the headlight lens assembly and the headlight bracket. See **Figure 94** (speedometer only) or **Figure 95** (speedometer and tachometer) for a schematic diagram of the 12-pin connector for your model. Also, refer to the wiring diagram for your model at the end of this manual.

NOTE
*Refer to **Deutsch Electrical Connectors** in this chapter for an exploded view diagram of the 12-pin Deutsch connector.*

3. Depress the 2 latches on the connector and disconnect the pin and socket halves.

4. Insert a wide-blade screwdriver between the socket housing and locking wedge at the point shown in **Figure 96**. Then turn the screwdriver 90° and pop the secondary locking wedge off the socket housing.

5. Depress the terminal latches mounted inside the socket housing and pull all of the sockets out through the rear wire seal.

6. Locate the cable strap on the wiring harness leading to the Deutsch connector. Then cut the cable strap and remove the conduit.

7. Using a sharp, pointed tool, carefully pry the trim cover (**Figure 90**) from the indicator lamp housing on the instrument bracket.

8. Using wire cutters, cut the wire from the bulb assembly approximately 1 1/2 in. (38.1 mm) above the wire splices. By cutting the wire at this distance, the splice and other bulb connections are left intact.

NOTE
The oil and neutral lamps lead to the 3-wire splice. The high beam and turn signal lamps lead to the 4-wire splice.

9. Push the bulb assembly through the front of the indicator lamp housing and discard.

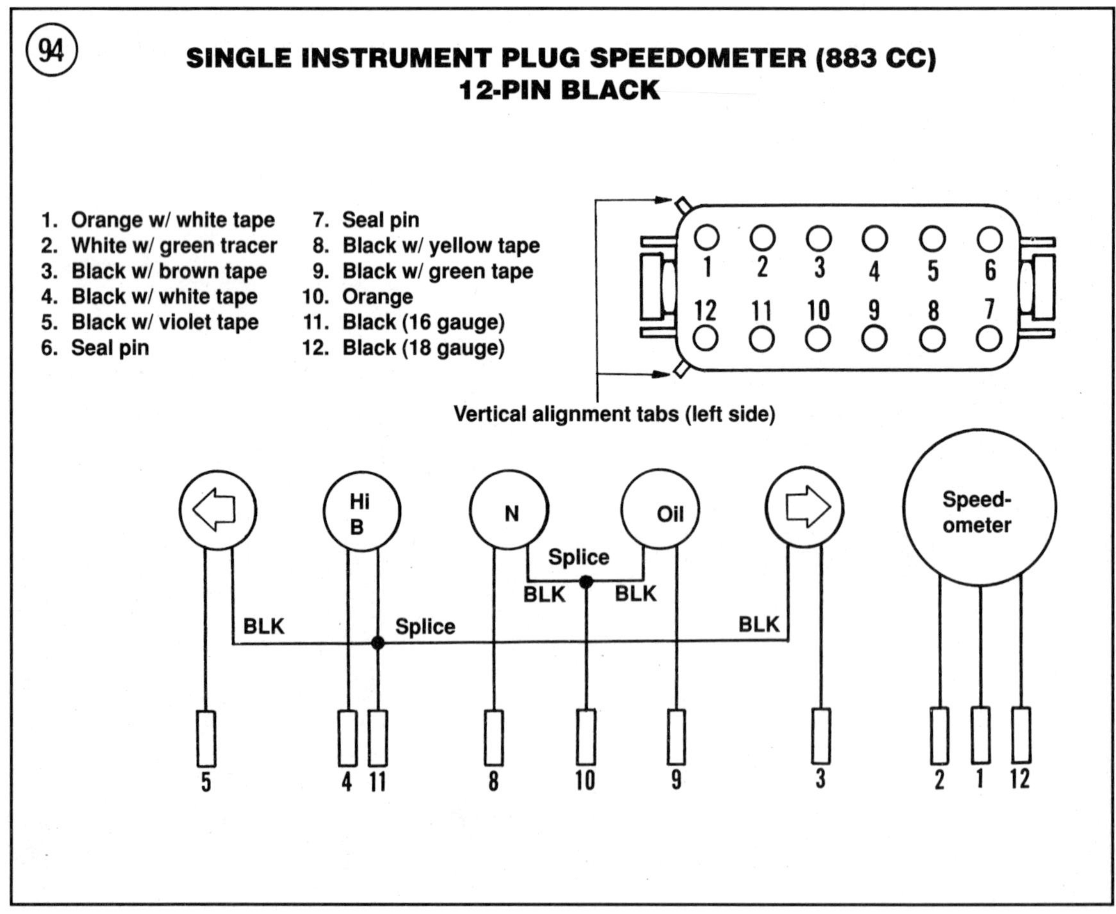

10. Trim the wires on the replacement bulb assembly to the same length as that on the discarded assembly.
11. Install a new Deutsch socket terminal to the head of the replacement bulb assembly. You can match the lead with the colored tape on the wire. To crimp the connectors, refer to *Deutsch Electrical Connectors* in this chapter.
12. Insert the replacement bulb—socket end first-through the front of the indicator lamp housing.
13. Align the trim cover (**Figure 90**) with the indicator lamp housing and snap it in place.
14. Install the butt connector to the remaining black, untaped wire on the replacement bulb assembly. Complete the butt splice as described under *Sealed Butt Connectors* in this chapter.
15. Slide the conduit over the butt splices and wire crimps and install a new cable strap to secure the conduit to the wiring harness.
16. Align and then install the rear wire seal into the back of the socket housing.
17. Hold the wire socket approximately 1 in. (25.4 mm) behind the contact barrel and push the socket through the holes in the wire seal and into its correct chamber until it clicks in place; see **Figure 94** or **Figure 95** for the individual wire positions. Lightly tug on the wire to verify that it is locked in place.
18. Install the internal seal onto the socket housing lip. Align and insert the tapered end of the secondary locking wedge into the center groove within the socket housing. Then press the wedge down until it locks in place.
19. Align the socket housing tabs with the pin housing grooves and push the connector halves together until they "click" in place.
20. Place the Deutsch connector underneath the bracket at the backside of the headlight assembly.
21. Align the headlight bracket holes with the mating holes in the upper steering stem bracket. Then install the headlight bracket bolts and lockwashers and tighten to the torque specification in **Table 4**.

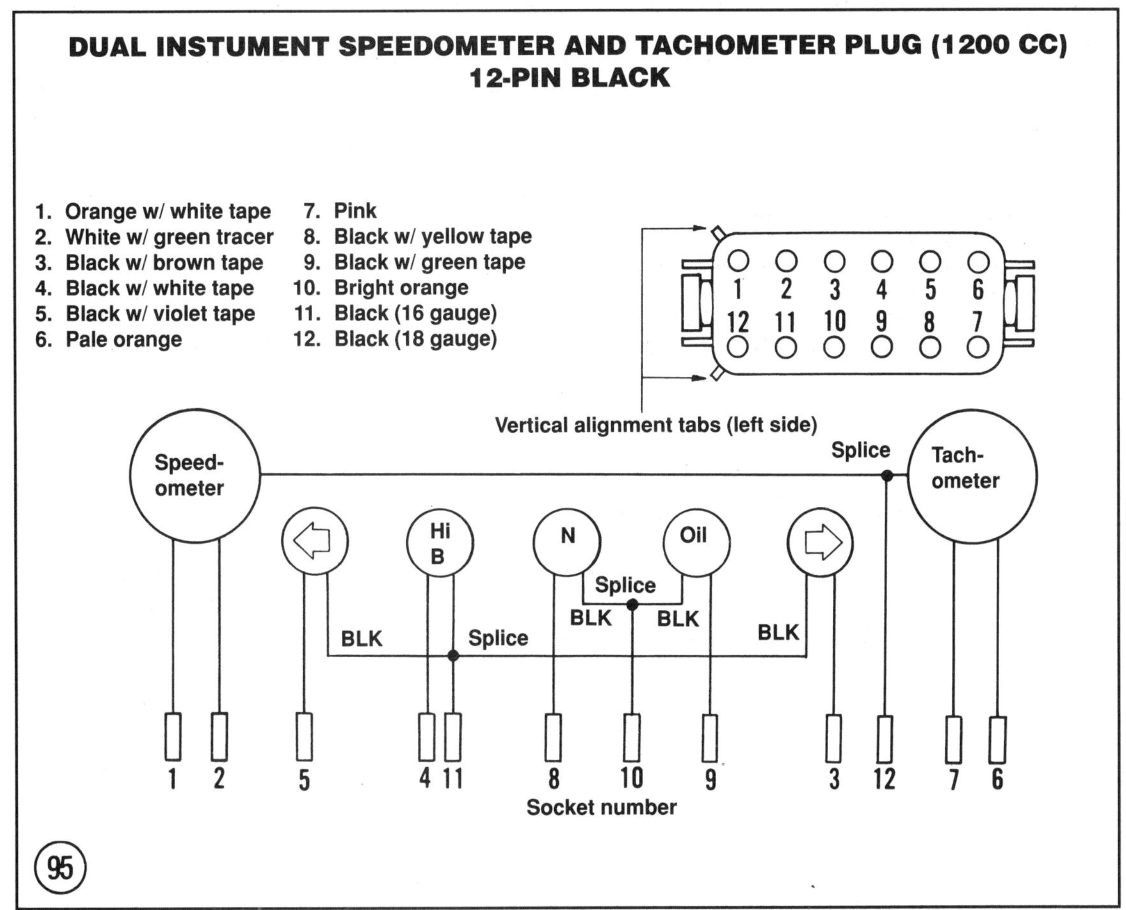

SWITCHES

Switches can be tested for continuity with an ohmmeter (see Chapter One) at the switch connector plug by operating the switch in each of its operating positions and comparing results with the switch operation. When testing switches, consider the following:

a. First check the circuit breaker.
b. Check the battery as described in this chapter and bring the battery to the correct state of charge, if required.
c. When separating 2 connectors, pull on the connector housings and not the wires.
d. After locating a defective circuit, check the connectors to make sure they are clean and properly connected. Check all wires going into a connector housing to make sure each wire is properly positioned and that the wire end is not loose.
e. To connect connectors properly, push them together until they click into place.

Handlebar Switch Replacement

The left-hand handlebar switch housing (**Figure 97**) is equipped with the following switches:

a. Headlight HI-LO beam.
b. Horn.
c. Left-hand turn signal.

The right-hand handlebar switch housing (**Figure 98**) is equipped with the following switches:

a. RUN-OFF.

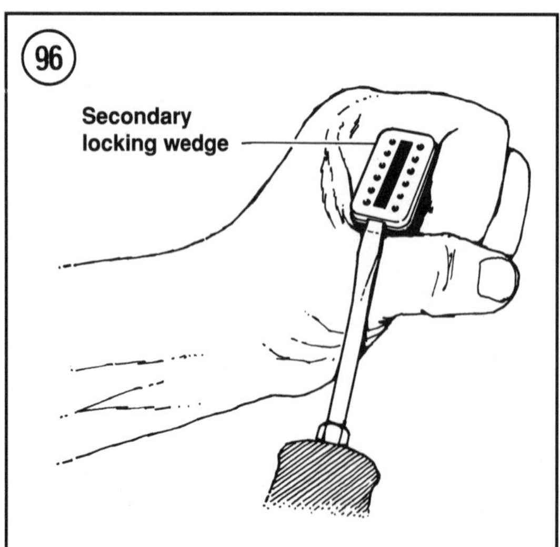

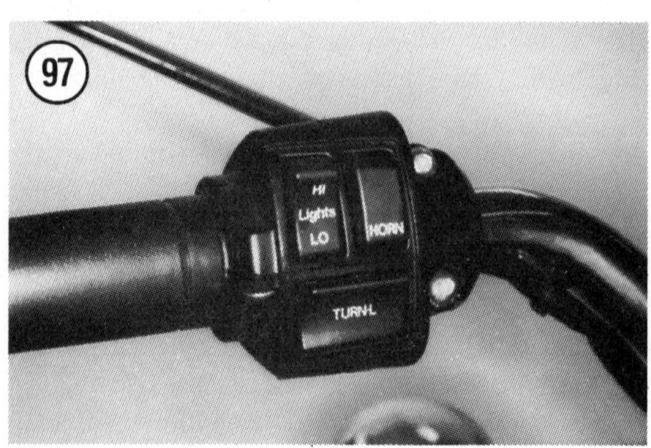

LEFT-HAND HANDLEBAR SWITCH

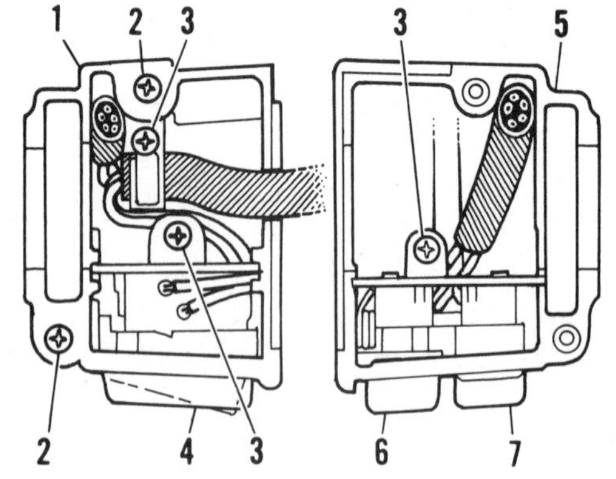

1. Lower housing
2. Screw
3. Machine screw
4. Left-hand turn signal switch
5. Upper housing
6. Dimmer switch (HI-LO)
7. Horn switch

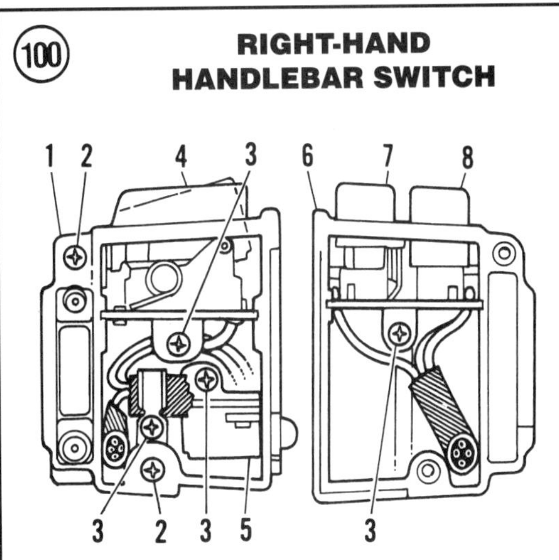

1. Lower housing
2. Screw
3. Machine screw
4. Right-hand turn signal switch
5. Brake light switch
6. Upper housing
7. Engine stop/run switch
8. Start switch

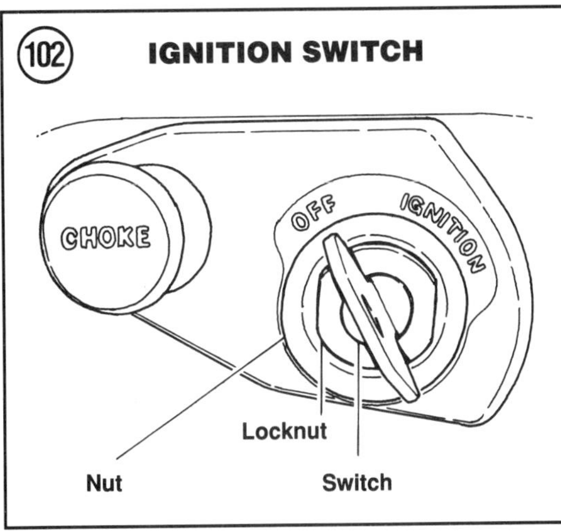

b. Start.
c. Brake light.
d. Right-hand turn signal.

Refer to **Figure 99** (left-hand) or **Figure 100** (right-hand) when replacing the individual switches.

1. Remove the screws securing the switch housing to the handlebar. Then carefully separate the switch housing (**Figure 101**) to gain access to the defective switch.
2. Disconnect the switch wire at the electrical connection.
3. Replace the defective switch by removing the holding screw. Then pull the switch out of the housing.
4. Installation is the reverse of these steps. Make sure to route the wires correctly to prevent damaging them when tightening the switch housing.

Ignition/Lighting Switch Removal/Installation

The ignition/light switch is non-repairable. If the switch is faulty, replace it as follows.

1991

1. Disconnect the negative battery cable.
2. Remove the ignition key.
3. Loosen and remove the outer chrome nut securing the ignition switch to the mounting plate (**Figure 102**).
4. Push the ignition switch through the cover (toward inside) and remove it from the mounting plate (**Figure 102**).
5. Label and disconnect the electrical connectors at the switch; see 1991 wiring diagram at end of book.
6. Remove the switch screws and washers and remove the switch.
7. Installation is the reverse of these steps.
8. Check the ignition/light switch for proper operation.

1992-1993

1. Disconnect the negative battery cable.
2. Remove the ignition key.
3. Loosen and remove the outer chrome nut (A, **Figure 103**) securing the ignition switch to the mounting plate.

8

4. Loosen the enrichener cable nut on the backside of the cable bracket (B, **Figure 103**). The remove the enrichener cable out of the cable slot in bracket.
5. Remove the top center engine mount bracket Torx screw (C, **Figure 103**) and remove the enrichener cable bracket (and horn/bracket on 1200 cc models).
6. Remove the ignition switch locknut (**Figure 104**). Then remove the switch, switch cover and trim plate off of the top center engine mount bracket.
7. Label and disconnect the electrical connectors at the switch; see the wiring diagram for your model at end of book.
8. Remove the ignition switch.
9. Installation is the reverse of these steps while noting the following.
10. Tighten the ignition switch locknut to the torque specification in **Table 4**.
11. Tighten the top center engine mount bracket Torx screw to the torque specification in **Table 4**.
12. Check the ignition/light switch for proper operation.

1994

1. Disconnect the negative battery cable.
2. Remove the ignition key.
3. Remove the fuel tank as described in Chapter Seven.
4. Cut the 2 main wiring harness cable straps. Discard the cable straps.

NOTE
The enrichener cable hex nut uses left-hand threads. Turn the nut ***clockwise*** *to remove it.*

5. Loosen the enrichener cable nut on the backside of the cable bracket. The remove the enrichener cable out of the cable slot in bracket.
6. Remove the top center engine mount bracket Torx screw and remove the enrichener cable bracket (and horn/bracket on 1200 cc models).
7. Loosen and remove the outer chrome nut (**Figure 105**) securing the ignition switch to the mounting plate.
8. Remove the ignition switch locknut and the ignition switch cover.
9. Remove the ignition switch from the switch cover.
10. If you are going to replace the ignition switch, remove the ignition switch harness cover and cut the switch wires 3 in. (76.2 mm) from the switch.
11. Install by reversing these removal steps. Note the following:
12. To reconnect the new ignition switch:
   a. Slide the replacement conduit onto the wiring harness.
   b. Match the ignition switch and wiring harness color codes, install new butt connectors to the wiring harness and ignition switch wires. Seal the butt splice connectors as described under *Seal Butt Connectors* in this chapter.
13. Install the ignition switch into the hole in the switch cover so that the "TOP" mark stamped on the switch body faces upward toward the switch position decal.
14. Tighten the ignition switch locknut to the torque specification in **Table 4**.
15. Tighten the top center engine mount bracket Torx screw to the tightening torque in **Table 4**.
16. Check the ignition/light switch for proper operation.

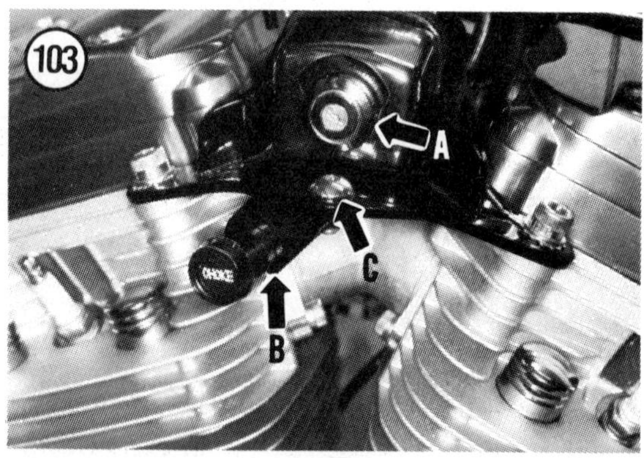

Oil Pressure Switch Testing/Replacement

The oil pressure switch (**Figure 106**) is mounted on the oil filter mount, directly below the oil filter. The oil pressure switch is a pressure-actuated diaphragm-type. When the oil pressure is low or when oil is not circulating through a running engine, spring tension inside the switch holds the switch contacts closed. This completes the signal light circuit and causes the oil pressure indicator lamp to light.

The oil pressure signal light should turn on when:

a. Turning the ignition switch on prior to starting the engine.

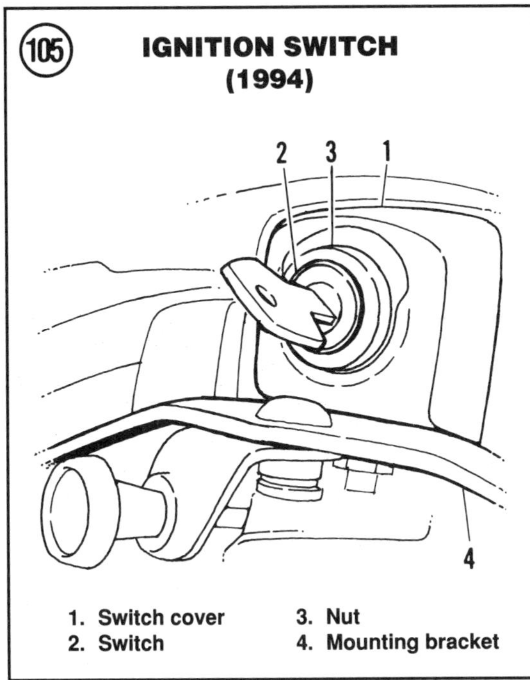

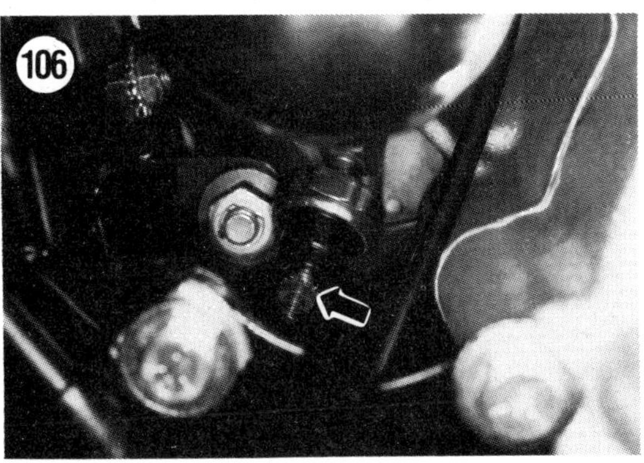

b. Engine idle is well below 1,000 rpm.
c. Engine is operating with low oil pressure.
d. Oil is not circulating through the running engine.

The oil pressure signal light should turn off when:

a. There is adequate oil pressure.
b. Engine rpm is 1,000 rpm or higher.

NOTE
The oil pressure signal light may not come on when the ignition switch is turned off and then back on immediately. This is due to the oil pressure retained in the oil filter housing.

The following procedures tests the electrical part of the oil pressure switch. If the oil pressure switch, indicator lamp and related wiring are okay, inspect the lubrication system as described in Chapter Two.

1. Remove the rubber boot and disconnect the electrical connector at the switch.
2. Turn the ignition switch ON.
3. Ground the switch wire to the engine.
4. The oil pressure indicator lamp on the instrument panel should light.
5. If the signal indicator lamp does not light, check for a burned-out indicator lamp and inspect all wiring between the switch and the indicator lamp. If necessary, replace the lamp as described in this chapter.

6A. If the problem was solved in Steps 3-5, attach the electrical connector to the pressure switch. Make sure the connection is tight and free from oil. Slide the rubber boot back into position.

6B. If the problem was not solved in Steps 3-5 and the warning light remains ON when the engine is running, shut the engine off. Check the engine lubrication system as described in Chapter Two.

7. To replace the switch, unscrew it from the engine and install a new one. Test the new switch as described in Steps 1-4. Tighten the oil pressure switch to the torque specification in **Table 4**.

Neutral Indicator Switch Testing/Replacement

The neutral indicator switch is mounted in the right-hand crankcase, directly forward of the main drive gear shaft (**Figure 107**). The neutral indicator light on the instrument panel should light when the

8

ignition is turned ON and the transmission is in NEUTRAL.

1. Remove the drive sprocket cover as described in Chapter Nine.
2. Disconnect the electrical connector at the neutral indicator switch.
3. Turn the ignition switch ON.
4. Ground the neutral indicator switch wire to the engine or any other suitable ground.
5. If the neutral indicator lamp lights, the neutral switch is faulty. Replace the neutral indicator switch and retest.
6. If the neutral indicator lamp does not light, check for a burned-out indicator lamp, faulty wiring or a loose or corroded connection. If necessary, replace the lamp as described in this chapter.

7A. If the problem was solved in Steps 3-6, attach the electrical connector to the neutral switch. Make sure the connection is tight and free from oil.

7B. If the problem was not solved in Steps 3-6, replace the neutral indicator switch as described in the following steps.

8. Remove the drive sprocket as described in Chapter Eleven.
9. Loosen and remove the switch from the right-hand crankcase.
10. Apply Loctite 242 (blue) to the neutral indicator switch thread prior to installation. Install the switch (**Figure 107**) and tighten to the torque specification in **Table 4**.
11. Install the drive sprocket cover as described in Chapter Nine.

Hand-lever Brake Light Switch Testing/Replacement

The hand-lever brake light switch is mounted in the right-hand handlebar switch assembly. Refer to *Handlebar Switch Replacement* in this chapter.

Foot-lever Brake Light Switch Testing/Replacement

A hydraulic, normally-open foot-lever brake light switch is used on all models. The foot-lever brake light switch threads into a hole intersecting a brake fluid passageway in the rear brake line tee fitting. This fitting connects the rear master cylinder and brake caliper hoses. A rubber boot keeps dirt and road debris off of the switch (**Figure 108**). When the ignition switch is turned ON and the foot-lever is released, the brake switch contacts are open and the brake light is off. When the foot-lever is applied, hydraulic pressure closes the switch contacts, providing a ground path for the brake light to come on.

If the brake light does not come on when the ignition is turned ON and the foot-lever is applied (with sufficient hydraulic pressure to lock the brake), perform the following.

1. Turn the ignition switch OFF.
2. Use an ohmmeter and check for continuity between the 2 terminals on the brake light switch connector. There should be no continuity (infinite resistance) with the foot-lever released. With the foot-lever applied there should be continuity (low resistance). If the brake switch fails either of these tests the switch must be replaced as follows.
3. Disconnect the electrical wires at the bottom of the switch body.
4. Stretch the rubber boot (**Figure 108**) and slip it off of the brake switch.

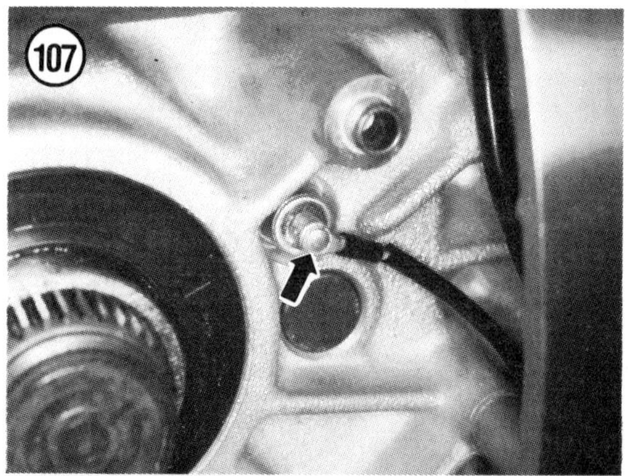

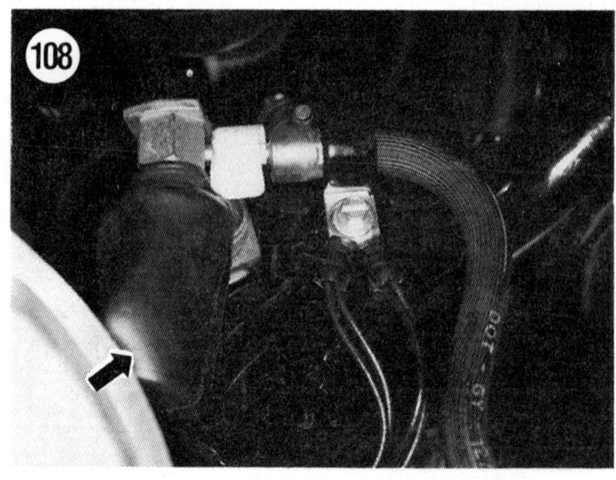

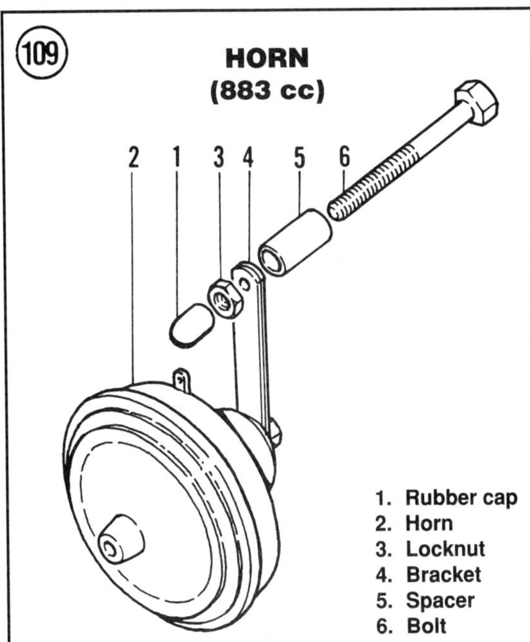

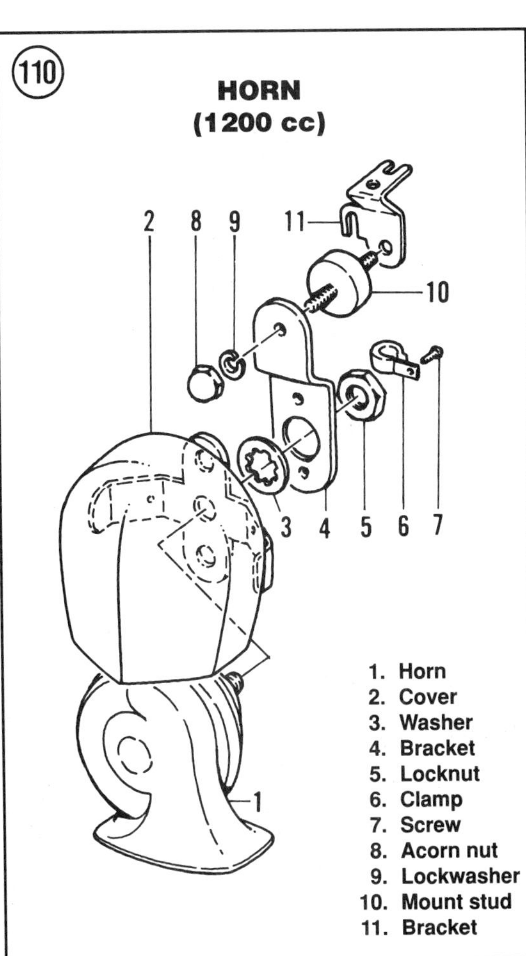

5. Loosen and remove the switch from the tee nut on the rear brake line.
6. Thread the new switch into the tee nut. Tighten the switch to the torque specification in **Table 4**.
7. Reconnect the switch electrical connectors.
8. Bleed the rear brake as described in Chapter Twelve.
9. Check the brake light with the ignition switch turned on and the foot-lever applied.

WARNING
Do not ride the motorcycle until the brakes and brake light are working properly.

HORN

The horn is an important safety device and should be kept in working order. If the horn is damaged, it should be replaced immediately.

If the horn fails to blow properly, check for broken or frayed horn wires. Also check the battery as described in this chapter.

Removal/Installation (883 cc)

Refer to **Figure 109**.

1. Label and then disconnect the horn electrical connectors at the horn spade terminals.
2. Remove the rubber cap from the front fuel tank mounting bolt.
3. Hold the front fuel tank mounting bolt and remove the horn locknut.
4. Remove the horn, horn bracket and spacer.
5. Install by reversing these removal steps while noting the following:
   a. Make sure the electrical connectors and horn spade terminals are free of corrosion.
   b. Hold the front fuel tank mounting bolt and tighten the horn locknut to the torque specification in **Table 4**.
   c. Check that the horn operates correctly.

Removal/Installation (1200 cc)

Refer to **Figure 110**.

1. Label and then disconnect the horn electrical connectors at the horn spade terminals.

8

2. Remove the Acorn nut and lockwasher securing the horn assembly to the rubber mount stud.
3. Remove the horn assembly and remove the wire clip from the backside of the horn bracket.
4. Remove the locknut from the recess in the horn bracket. Then remove the horn and tooth lockwasher.
5. Install by reversing these removal steps while noting the following:
   a. Make sure the electrical connectors and horn spade terminals are free of corrosion.
   b. Hold the front fuel tank mounting bolt and tighten the horn locknut to the torque specification in **Table 4**.
   c. Check that the horn operates correctly.

TURN SIGNAL MODULE

All models are equipped with a turn signal module, an electronic microprocessor that controls the turn signals and the 4-way hazard flasher. The turn signal module receives its information from the speedometer and turn signal switches.

On 1991-1993 models, the turn signal module (**Figure 111**) is mounted to the inboard side of the ignition module bracket. On 1994 models, the module (**Figure 112**) is mounted to the front right-hand side of the electrical bracket.

Performance Test (1991-1993)

If the turn signals are not working properly, perform the following performance test. A jumper wire, ohmmeter and voltmeter will be required.

1. Remove the turn signal module as described in this chapter.
2. After removing the module, identify the socket connector and module pin connectors on your bike with the diagram in **Figure 113**.
3. With ignition switch off, check for ground at pin No. 1.

NOTE
Following tests are made with ignition switch on.

4. Check for voltage at pin No. 2. Voltmeter should read 12 volts.
5. Connect a jumper wire between pins No. 2 and No. 4. The right-hand front and rear turn signal lights should illuminate.
6. Connect a jumper wire between pins No. 2 and No. 6. The left-hand front and rear turn signal lights should illuminate.
7. Connect a jumper wire between pins No. 4 and No. 8 and depress the right-hand turn signal switch button. The right-hand front and rear turn signal lights should illuminate.
8. Connect a jumper wire betweens pins No. 6 and No. 10 and depress the left-hand turn signal switch button. The left-hand front and rear turn signal lights should illuminate.

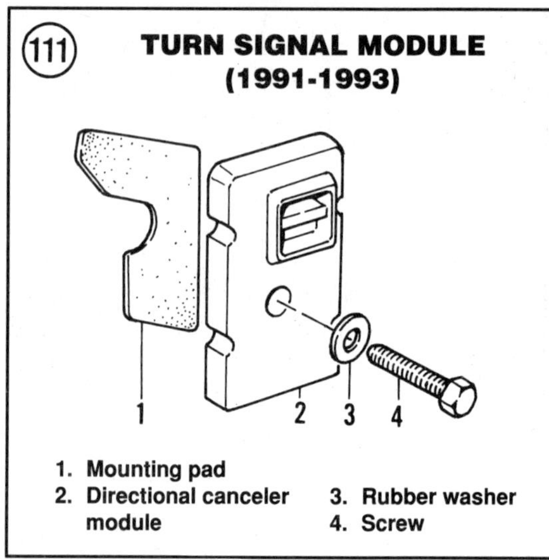

TURN SIGNAL MODULE (1991-1993)

1. Mounting pad
2. Directional canceler module
3. Rubber washer
4. Screw

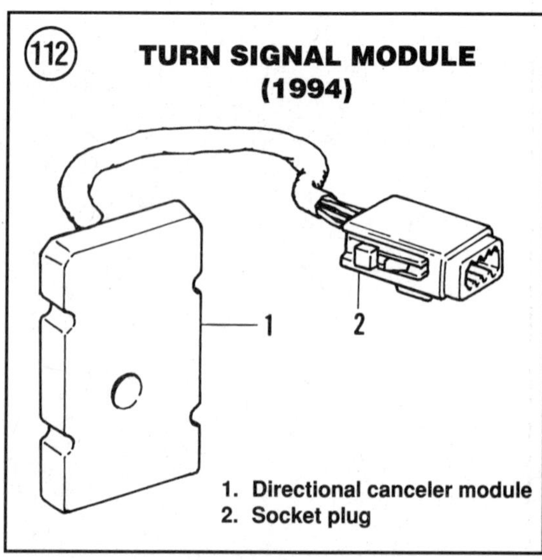

TURN SIGNAL MODULE (1994)

1. Directional canceler module
2. Socket plug

9. Remove the jumper wire and turn the ignition switch off.
10. If the module passed all 6 tests, install the module as described in this chapter. If the module failed one or more tests, refer to *Troubleshooting* in this section.

Performance Test (1994)

If the turn signals are not working properly, perform the following performance test. A jumper wire, ohmmeter and voltmeter will be required.
1. Remove the turn signal module as described in this chapter.
2. After removing the module, identify the socket connector and module pin connectors on your bike with the diagram in **Figure 114**.
3. With ignition switch off, check for ground at pin No. 1.

NOTE
Following tests are made with ignition switch on.

4. Check for voltage at pin No. 2. Voltmeter should read 12 volts.
5. Connect a jumper wire between pins No. 2 and No. 4. The right-hand front and rear turn signal lights should illuminate.

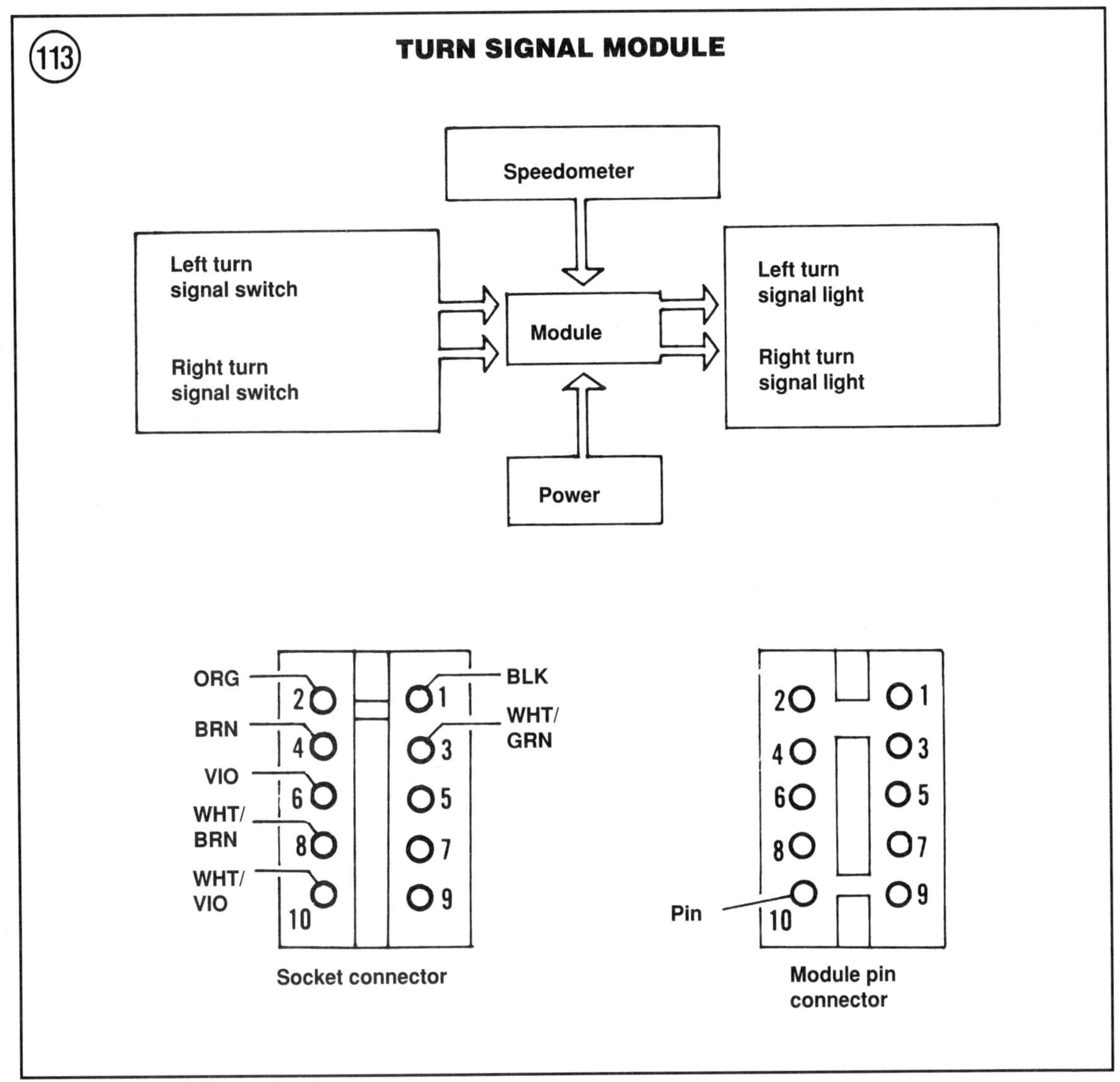

8

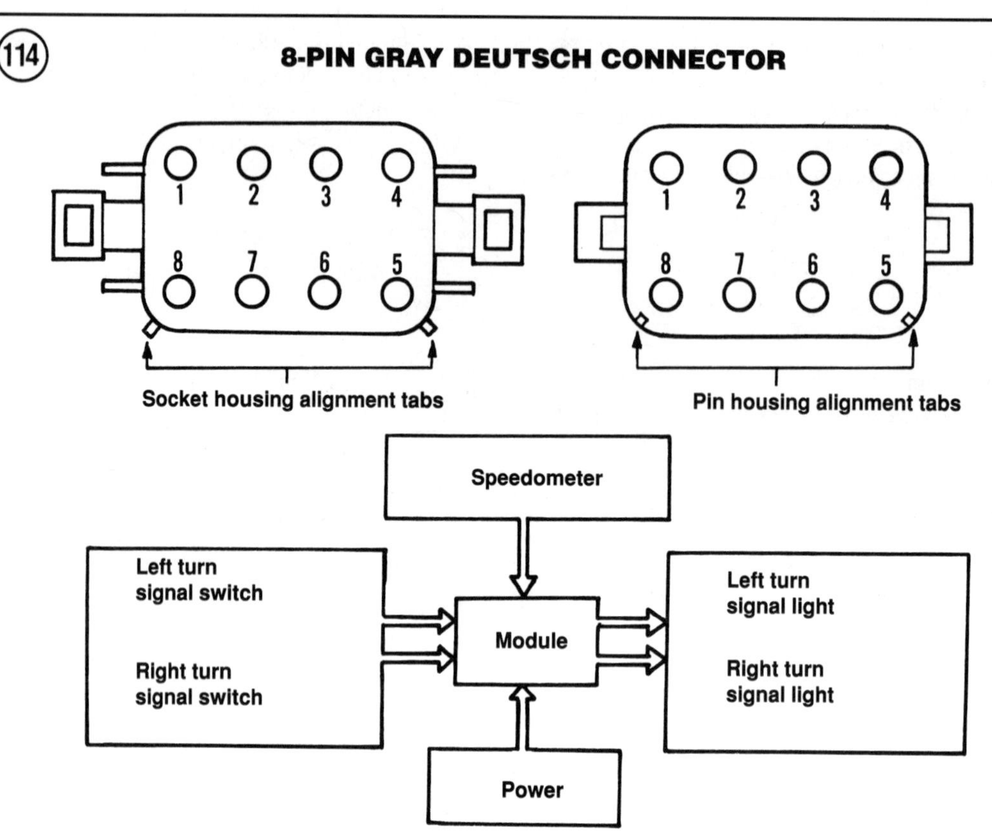

Pin number	Wire color	Description/function
1	BLK	Module ground to motorcycle
2	ORG/WHT	12vdc input from accessory circuit breaker
3	WHT/GRN	Speedometer reed switch input
4	BRN	Pulsed 12vdc for flashing right turn signal lights
5	VIO	Pulsed 12vdc for flashing left turn signal lights
6	WHT/BRN	12vdc from right turn signal switch (when pressed)
7	WHT/VIO	12vdc from left turn signal switch (when pressed)
8	—	Not used

6. Connect a jumper wire between pins No. 2 and No. 5. The left-hand front and rear turn signal lights should illuminate.

7. Connect a jumper wire between pins No. 4 and No. 6 and depress the right-hand turn signal switch button. The right-hand front and rear turn signal lights should illuminate.

8. Connect a jumper wire betweens pins No. 5 and No. 7 and depress the left-hand turn signal switch button. The left-hand front and rear turn signal lights should illuminate.

9. Remove the jumper wire and turn the ignition switch off.

10. If the module passed all 6 tests, install the module as described in this chapter. If the module failed one or more tests, refer to *Troubleshooting* in this section.

Troubleshooting

The following basic troubleshooting procedures will help isolate some specific problems to the module. If it is necessary to access the turn signal module, remove it as described in this chapter.

Refer to **Figure 113** (1991-1993) or **Figure 114** (1994) for socket and module pin connector identification.

One or both turn signals do not flash. Light on front or rear side is lit, but does not flash

1. Remove the lens and check for a burned out bulb. Replace bulb if necessary.
2. If the bulb is okay, check for one of the following problems:
   a. Check the bulb socket contacts for corrosion. Clean contacts and recheck. If you have a problem with corrosion building on the contacts, wipe the contacts with a dielectric grease before installing the bulb.
   b. Check for a broken bulb wire. Repair wire or connector.
   c. Check for a loose bulb socket where it is staked to the housing. If the bulb socket is loose, replace the light assembly.
   d. Check for a poor ground connection. If the ground is poor, scrape the ground mounting area or replace damaged ground wire(s), as required.

Turn signals do not operate on one side

1. Perform the checks listed under *One or both turns signals do not flash. Light on front or rear side is lit, but does not flash.* If these checks do not locate the problem, proceed to Step 2.
2. Inoperative handlebar directional switch. Perform the following:
   a. Turn the ignition switch ON.
   b. Disconnect the turn signal module electrical connector.
   c. Locate pin No. 8 or No. 10 (1991-1993) or pin No. 6 or No. 7 (1994) on the socket connector.
   d. With a voltmeter set on the DC scale, connect the negative lead to a good ground and the positive lead to one of the pin numbers specified in substep c for your model and press the turn signal switch. The voltmeter should read 12 volts when the switch is pressed in.
   e. If there is a 12 volt reading, proceed to Step 3.
   f. If there is no voltage reading, proceed to Step 4.
3. Inoperative module. If 12 volts were recorded in Step 2, and the lights and connecting wires are in good condition, the module may be damaged. Replace the module and retest.
4. Damaged directional switch wire circuit. If no voltage was recorded in Step 2, check the handlebar switch and related wiring for damage. Tests can be made by performing continuity and voltage checks.
5. Reconnect the turn signal module electrical connector.

Turn signals/hazard lights do not operate on both sides

1. If none of the turn signals or hazard flashers operate, check the module for proper ground with an ohmmeter. Using the wiring diagram at the end of this book for your model, trace the ground connection from the module to the frame tab. If a ground is not present, remove the ground wire at the frame and scrape the frame and clean the connector. Check the ground wire for breaks. Repair as required. If a ground is present, perform Step 2.

CAUTION
Do not operate the module without pin No. 1 grounded. Otherwise, the module will burn out.

2. Refer to the wiring diagram for your model and locate the accessory circuit breaker. Turn the ignition switch ON and check for voltage on the hot or load side of the circuit breaker with a voltmeter. If there is no voltage, check the following components:
   a. Accessory circuit breaker.
   b. Main circuit breaker.
   c. Starter relay.
   d. Ignition switch.
   e. Circuit wiring.

Turn signals do not cancel

1. Support the bike so that the front wheel clears the ground.
2. Connect an ohmmeter to the speedometer white/green wire and ground. Spin the front wheel and watch the ohmmeter scale. The ohmmeter should alternate between 0 ohms and infinity.
   a. If ohmmeter reading is correct, disconnect the module pin connector. With a voltmeter set on the DC scale, connect the negative lead to a good ground and the positive lead to the No. 3 pin socket connector. The voltmeter should read 12 volts. If ohm and volt readings are correct, the module is damaged.
   b. If ohmmeter reading is incorrect, check for damaged wiring from the speedometer white/green wire to the module. If wiring is okay, the reed switch in the speedometer may be damaged.

Removal/Installation (1991-1993)

On 1991-1993 models, the turn signal module (**Figure 111**) is mounted to the inboard side of the ignition module bracket.

1. Remove the seat.
2. Make sure the ignition switch is turned off.
3. Disconnect the harness connector from the module.
4. Remove the module screw and washer. Then remove the module and rubber pad.
5. Install by reversing these removal steps while noting the following:
   a. Make sure the electrical connectors are free of moisture.
   b. Tighten the screw securely.
   c. Check that the turn signal and flasher systems work properly.

Removal/Installation (1994)

On 1994 models, the turn signal module is mounted to the front right-hand side of the electrical bracket.

1. Remove the seat.
2. Make sure the ignition switch is turned off.
3. Remove the bolts securing the electrical bracket (**Figure 115**) to the frame. Lift the electrical bracket out of the frame.
4. Locate the 8-pin Deutsch connector on the left-hand side of the electrical bracket. Push the connector up and disconnect its clip from the T-stud.
5. Disconnect the turn signal module plug from its electrical connector.
6. Cut the cable straps securing the module to the electrical bracket. Note the position of the cable straps as they are routed through the electrical bracket for reassembly. Remove the module and discard the cable straps.

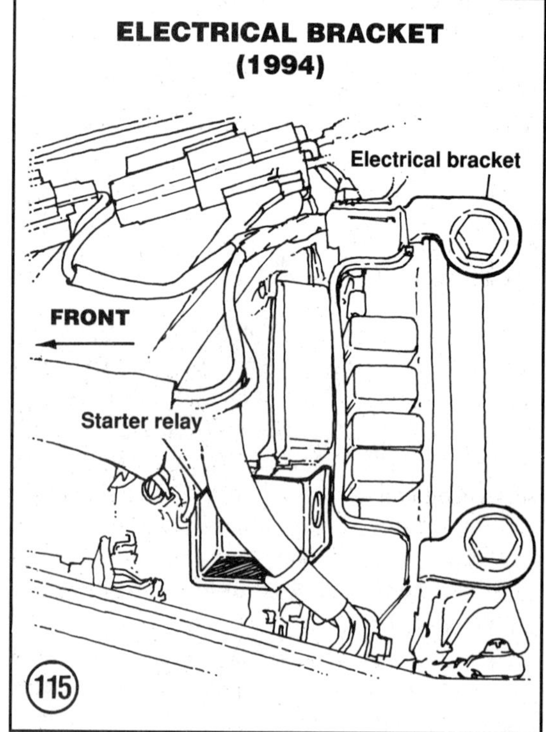

7. Position the new cable straps through the holes in the front of the electrical bracket.
8. Position the new turn signal module against the front of the electrical bracket so that its flat side faces out and its plug end facing down.
9. Wrap the cables around the 2 grooves in the side of the module, then connect and tighten the cables. Cut off cable excess.
10. Reconnect the turn signal module plug to its electrical connector.
11. Position the large end of the attachment clip end slot over the T-stud on the electrical bracket. Push the connector assembly down and engage small end of slot.
12. Install electrical bracket mounting bolts and tighten securely.
13. Check that the turn signal and flasher systems work properly.

DEUTSCH ELECTRICAL CONNECTORS (1994)

All 1994 Sportster models use Deutsch DT Series Electrical Connectors. These connectors are designed to provide a superior seal, as compared to conventional connectors, to prevent dirt and moisture from entering the connector and shorting out the pin connections. The Deutsch connectors also provide better connector retention.

The following section describes service procedures that are required to remove, disassemble and reconnect the Deutsch electrical connectors.

Connector Location and Disconnection

The pin housings on most connectors are secured with attachment clips. These clips are then fastened to T-studs on the frame that provide a more positive location when locating or routing the electrical connectors or wiring harness. This system improves serviceability and reduces electrical problems from chafing or other routing induced problems.

Figure 116 identifies the Deutsch connector locations and shows a diagram of each connector with color codes.

1. To remove a connector from its attachment clip, first push the connector toward the rear and lift the connector off the T-stud.

NOTE
The Deutsch connectors have 1 or 2 locking tabs. When disconnecting the connectors in Step 2, both locking tabs (if so equipped) must be pressed in simultaneously.

2. To separate the connector halves (pin and socket housings), depress the external latch on the socket housing with your fingers. Then, using a rocking motion, separate the socket halves.

Connector Removal/Installation

To remove or replace many of the electrical accessories, the Deutsch electrical connector must be partially disassembled and then reassembled.

Socket terminal removal/installation

This procedure describes how to remove and install the socket terminals from the socket housing connector half.

Refer to **Figure 117** or **Figure 118**.

NOTE
*This procedure is performed on a 12-pin Deutsch connector (**Figure 118**). Procedures can also be used for 2-, 3-, 4- and 6-pin connectors.*

1. Disconnect the connector housings.
2. Remove the secondary locking wedge (7, **Figure 118**) as follows:
   a. Locate the secondary locking wedge in **Figure 117** or **Figure 118**.
   b. Insert a wide-blade screwdriver between the socket housing and locking wedge and turn the screwdriver 90° to force the wedge up (**Figure 119**).
   c. Remove the secondary locking wedge (7, **Figure 118**).
3. Lightly press the terminal latches inside the socket housing and remove the socket terminal (14, **Figure 118**) through the holes in the rear wire seal.
4. Repeat Step 3 for each socket terminal.
5. Remove the wire seal (12, **Figure 118**), if necessary.

8

(116)

LEFT FRONT TURN SIGNAL AND HANDLEBAR CONTROLS 12-PIN GRAY

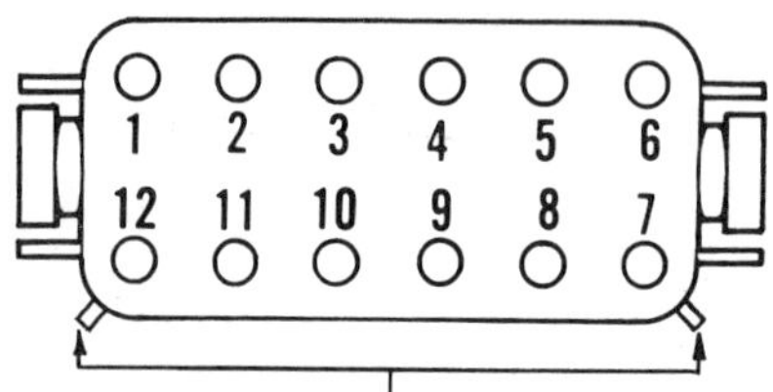

1 2 3 4 5 6
12 11 10 9 8 7
Horizontal alignment tabs (bottom)

1. Seal pin
2. Seal pin
3. Orange w/ white tracer
4. Yellow
5. Blue
6. White
7. White w/ violet tracer
8. Yellow w/ black tracer
9. Blue*
10. Violet
11. Black
12. Seal pin

* Seal pin on European models

RIGHT FRONT TURN SIGNAL AND HANDLEBAR CONTROLS 12-PIN BLACK

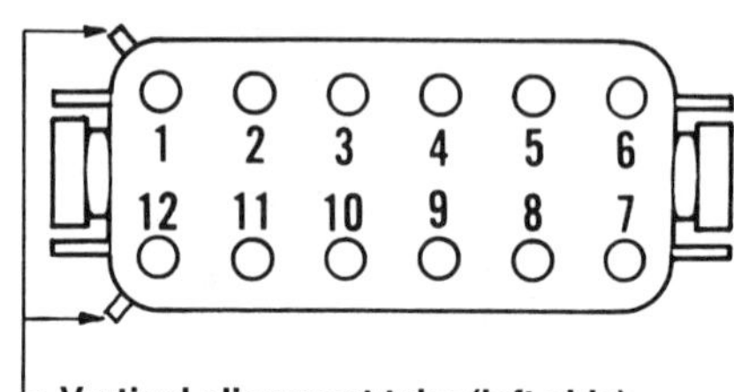

1 2 3 4 5 6
12 11 10 9 8 7
Vertical alignment tabs (left side)

1. Seal pin
2. Seal pin
3. Orange w/ white tracer
4. Red w/ yellow tracer
5. Gray
6. White w/ black tracer
7. White w/ brown tracer
8. Black w/ red tracer
9. Blue*
10. Violet
11. Black
12. Seal pin

* Seal pin on European models

INSTRUMENT LIGHTS 12-PIN BLACK

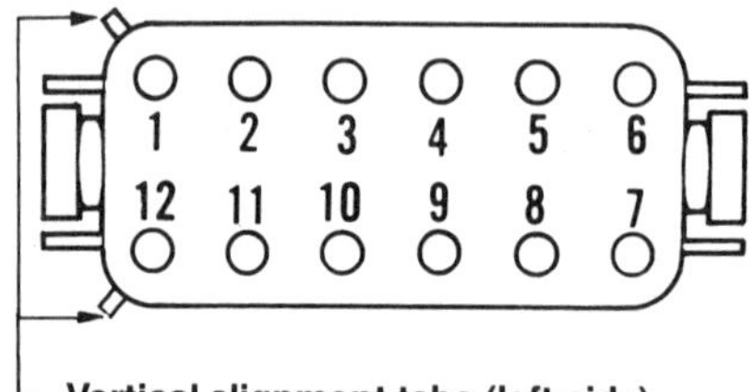

1 2 3 4 5 6
12 11 10 9 8 7
Vertical alignment tabs (left side)

1. Orange w/ white tape
2. White w/ green tracer
3. Black w/ brown tape
4. Black w/ white tape
5. Black w/ violet tape
6. Pale orange*
7. Pink*
8. Black w/ yellow tape
9. Black w/ green tape
10. Bright orange
11. Black (16 gauge)
12. Black (18 gauge)

* Seal pin on 883 cc

V.O.E.S. 2-PIN BLACK

External latch (top side)
1
2

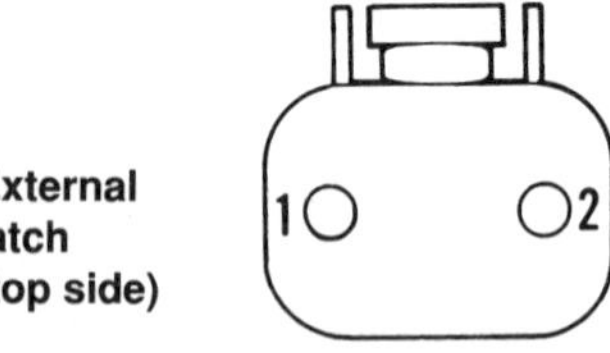

1. Black (violet w/ white tracer into harness)
2. Black (Black into harness)

(continued)

116 (continued)

CALIFORNIA AIR BOX
3-PIN BLACK

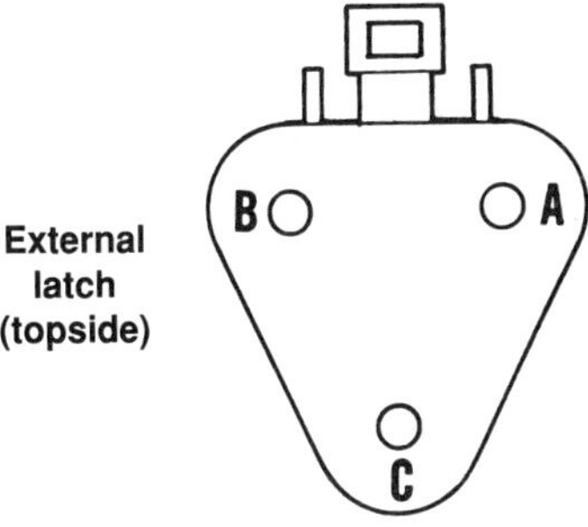

A. Green
B. White w/ black tracer
C. Black

TAILLIGHT/STOP
4-PIN BLACK

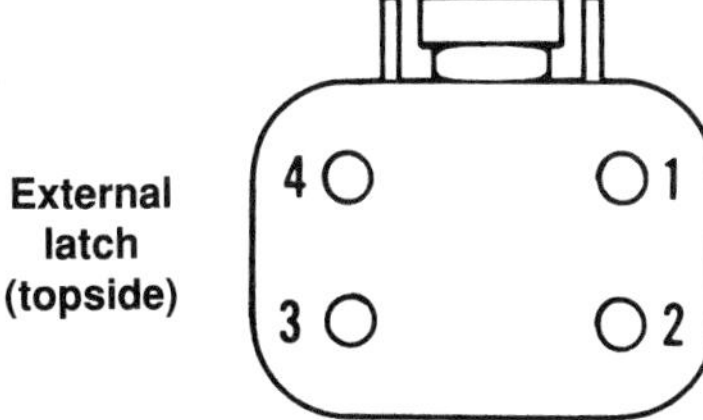

Domestic
1. Blue
2. Seal pin
3. Red w/ yellow tracer
4. Black

European
1. Seal pin
2. Orange w/ white tracer
3. Red w/ yellow tracer
4. Black

RIGHT REAR TURN SIGNAL
2-PIN BLACK

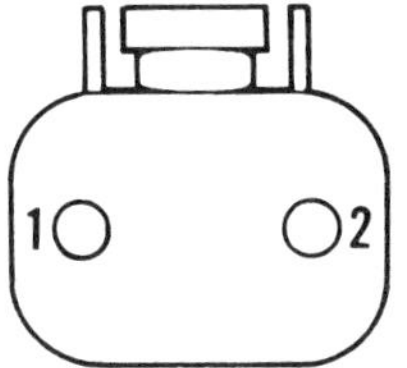

1. Violet
2. Black

LEFT REAR TURN SIGNAL
2-PIN GRAY

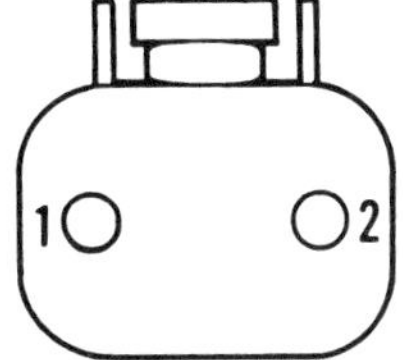

1. Violet
2. Black

(continued)

8

(116) (continued)

SELF-CANCELLING MODULE
8-PIN GRAY

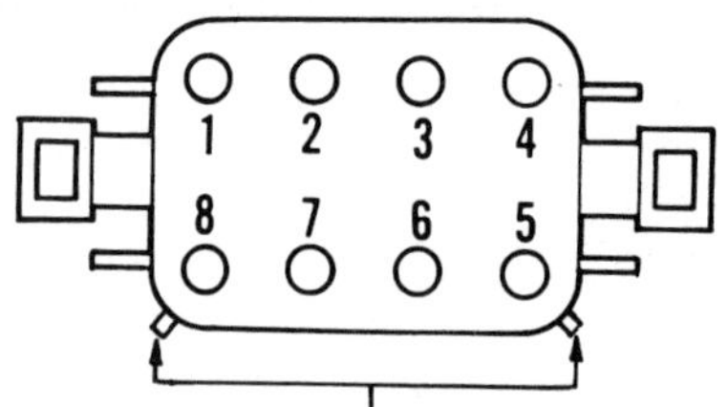

1. Black
2. Orange w/ white tracer
3. White w/ green tracer
4. Brown
5. Violet
6. White w/ brown tracer
7. White w/ violet tracer
8. Seal pin

IGNITION SENSOR
3-PIN BLACK

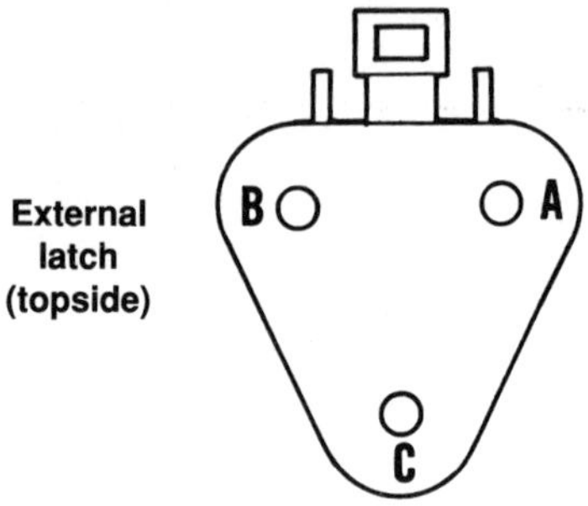

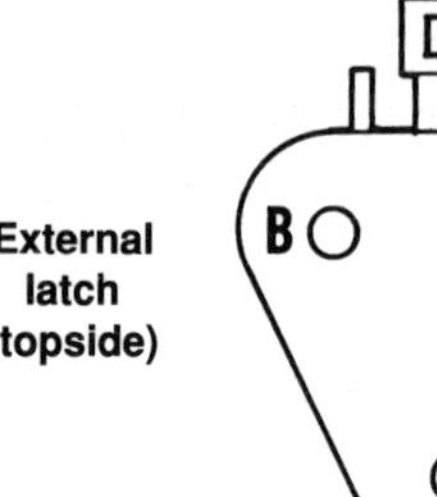

A. Red w/ white tracer
B. Green w/ white tracer
C. Black w/ white tracer

IGNITION MODULE
8-PIN BLACK

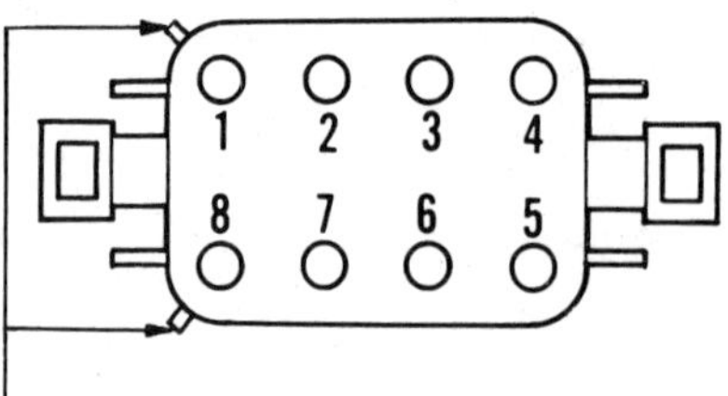

1. White w/ black tracer
2. Black w/ white tracer
3. Red w/ white tracer
4. Pink
5. Green w/ white tracer
6. Violet w/ white tracer
7. Black
8. Seal pin

VOLTAGE REGULATOR
CHARGING WIRE
1-PIN BLACK

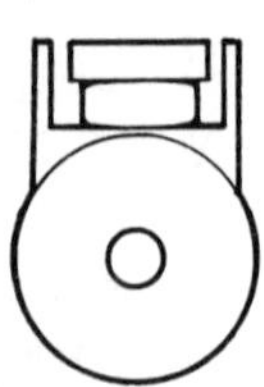

1. Black (red into harness)

NOTE
Reassemble the socket housing, starting with Step 6.

6. Install the wire seal (12, **Figure 118**) into the socket housing, if removed.
7. Hold the socket housing and insert the socket terminals (14, **Figure 118**) through the holes in the wire seal so that they enter their correct chamber holes as shown in **Figure 116** or **Figure 117**. Continue until the socket terminal clicks in place. Then lightly tug on the wire to make sure that it is locked in place.
8. If removed, seat the internal seal (8, **Figure 118**) onto the socket housing as shown in **Figure 118**.

NOTE
Except for the 3-pin Deutsch connector, all of the secondary locking wedges are symmetrical (both sides are the same). When assembling the 3-pin connector, the arrow on the secondary locking

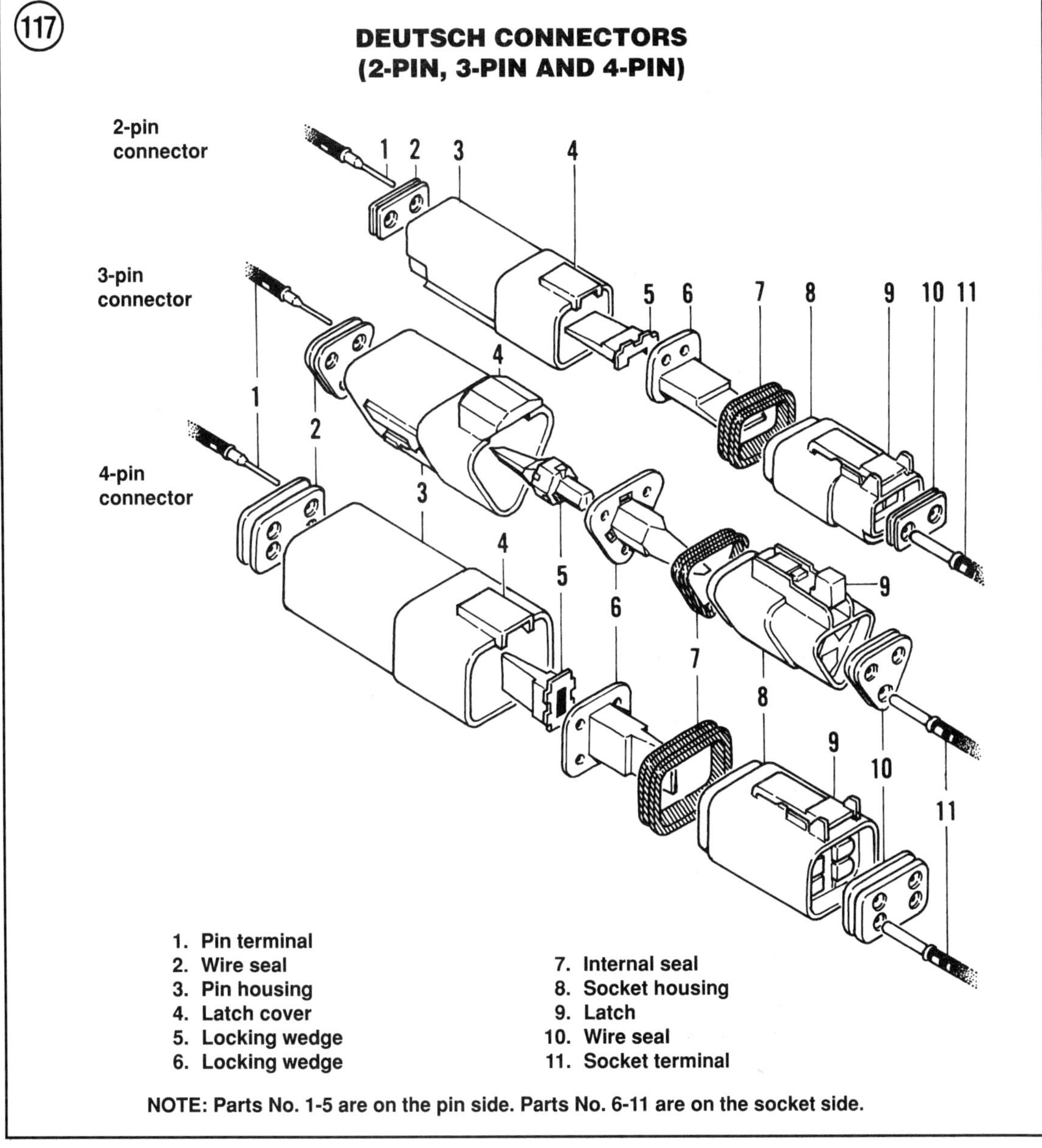

1. Pin terminal
2. Wire seal
3. Pin housing
4. Latch cover
5. Locking wedge
6. Locking wedge
7. Internal seal
8. Socket housing
9. Latch
10. Wire seal
11. Socket terminal

NOTE: Parts No. 1-5 are on the pin side. Parts No. 6-11 are on the socket side.

*wedge must be installed so that it is pointing toward the external latch; see **Figure 120**.*

9. Install the secondary locking wedge into the socket housing as shown in **Figure 117** or **Figure 118**. Press the secondary locking wedge down until it snaps in place.

NOTE
If the secondary locking wedge does not slide into position easily, one or more of the socket terminals is improperly installed.

Pin terminal removal/installation

This procedure describes how to remove and install the pin terminals from the pin housing (3, **Figure 118**) connector half.

Refer to **Figure 117** or **Figure 118**.

NOTE
*This procedure is performed on a 12-pin Deutsch connector (**Figure 118**). Procedures can also be used for 2-, 3-, 4- and 6-pin connectors.*

1. Disconnect the connector halves.
2. Remove the secondary locking wedge (6, **Figure 118**) with needlenose pliers or a piece of bent safety wire.
3. Lightly press the terminal latches inside the pin housing and remove the pin terminals (1, **Figure 118**) through the holes in the wire seal (2, **Figure 118**).
4. Repeat Step 3 for each pin terminal.
5. Remove the wire seal (2, **Figure 118**), if necessary.

118

DEUTSCH CONNECTOR (12-PIN)

1. Pin terminal
2. Wire seal
3. Pin housing
4. Latch cover
5. Alignment grooves
6. Locking wedge
7. Secondary locking wedge
8. Internal seal
9. Alignment tabs
10. External latch
11. Socket housing
12. Wire seal
13. Seal pin
14. Socket terminal

NOTE: Parts no. 1-6 are on the pin side. Parts No. 7-14 are on the socket side.

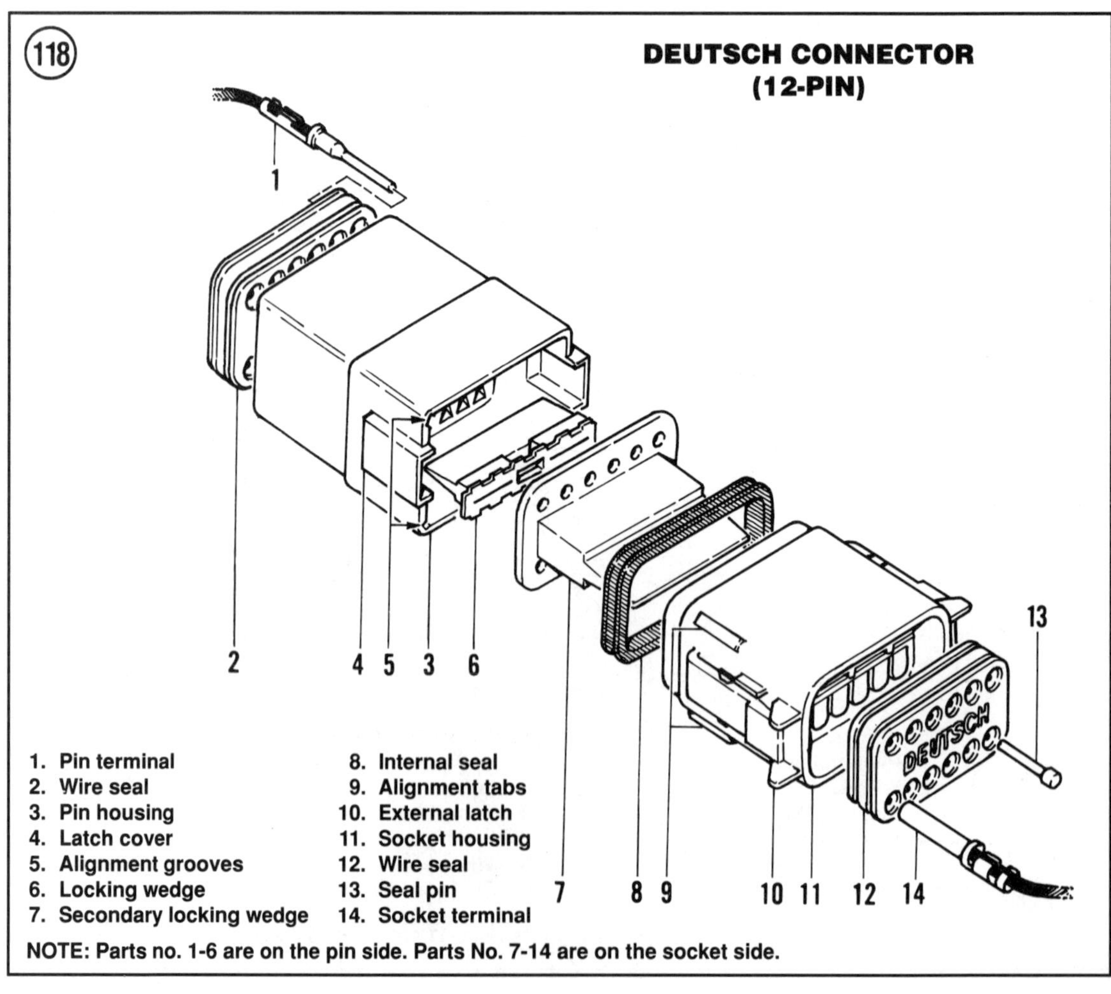

NOTE
Reassemble the pin housing, starting with Step 6.

6. Install the wire seal (2, **Figure 118**) into the socket housing, if removed.
7. Hold the pin housing and insert the pin terminals (1, **Figure 118**) through the holes in the wire seal so that they enter their correct numbered holes as shown in **Figure 116**. Continue until the pin terminal clicks in place. Then lightly tug on the wire to make sure that it is locked in place.

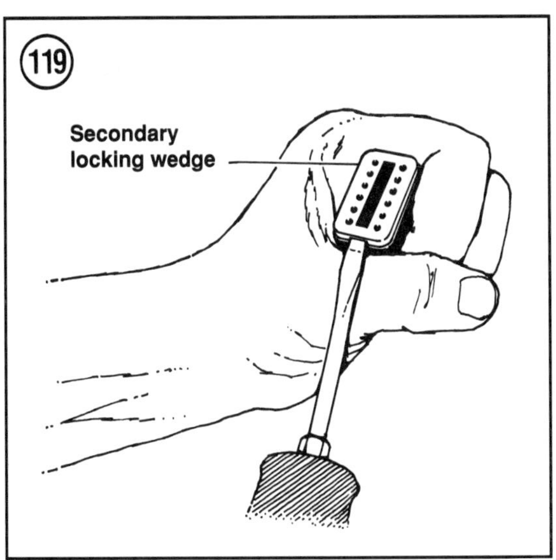

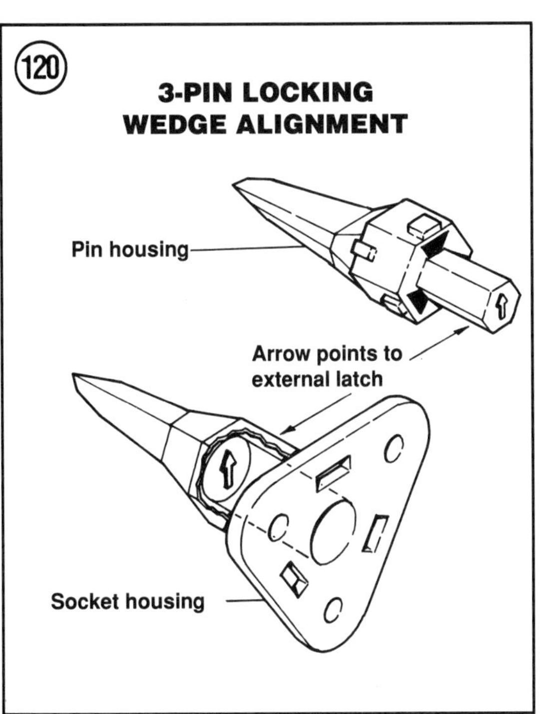

NOTE
*Except for the 3-pin Deutsch connector, all of the secondary locking wedges are symmetrical (both sides are the same). When assembling the 3-pin connector, the arrow on the secondary locking wedge must be installed so that it is pointing toward the external latch; see **Figure 120**.*

8. Install the secondary locking wedge into the pin housing as shown in **Figure 117** or **Figure 118**. Press the secondary locking wedge down until it snaps in place. When properly installed, the wedge will fit into the pin housing center groove.

NOTE
If the secondary locking wedge does not slide into position easily, one or more of the pin terminals is improperly installed.

Deutsch Pin and Socket Crimping Procedures

The Harley-Davidson electrical terminal crimp tool (part No. HD-39965) will be required to install new pin (1, **Figure 118**) and socket (14, **Figure 118**) terminals. Use the instructions included with the crimp tool.

When stripping the wire insulation prior to installing the socket or pin terminals, strip away 5/32 in. (3.96 mm) of wire insulation. This ensures that the exposed wires will fill the terminal barrel.

After crimping the terminal and wire, tug lightly on the wire to make sure the crimp holds. **Figure 121** shows a properly crimped terminal and wire.

Sealed Butt Connectors

When replacing the ignition switch or the indicator lamp(s) on 1994 models, sealed butt connectors will be required to join the new part to the main wiring harness; see **Figure 122**. When installing butt connectors on adjacent wires, stagger the connectors so that they are not side-by-side.

CIRCUIT BREAKERS

All models use circuit breakers to protect the electrical circuit. Circuit breaker ratings for the different circuits are listed in **Table 1**.

Whenever a failure occurs in any part of the electrical system, each circuit breaker is self-resetting and will automatically return power to the circuit when the electrical fault is found and corrected.

CAUTION
If the electrical fault on circuit breaker equipped models is not found and corrected, the breakers will cycle on and off continuously. This will cause the motorcycle to run erratically and eventually the battery will lose its charge.

Usually the trouble can be traced to a short circuit in the wiring connected to the circuit breaker. This may be caused by worn-through insulation or by a wire which has worked loose and shorted to ground. Occasionally, the electrical overload which causes the fuse to blow may occur in a switch or motor. By following the wiring diagrams at the end of the book,

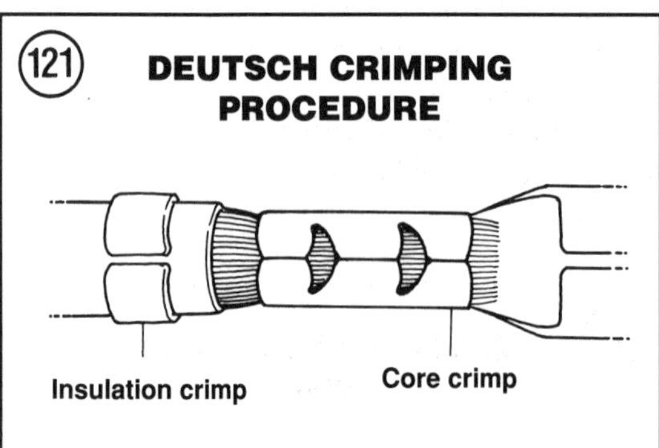

SEALED BUTT CONNECTOR INSTALLATION

STEP 1
Metal insert
Insert stripped wire ends into connector

STEP 2
Crimp wire ends

STEP 3
Heat and allow connector to cool
Melted sealant

122

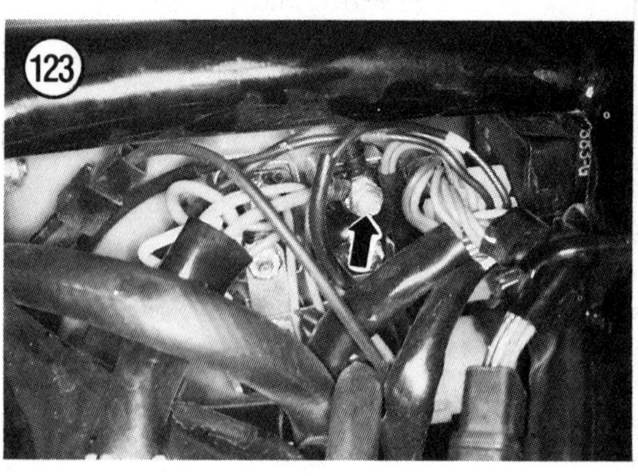

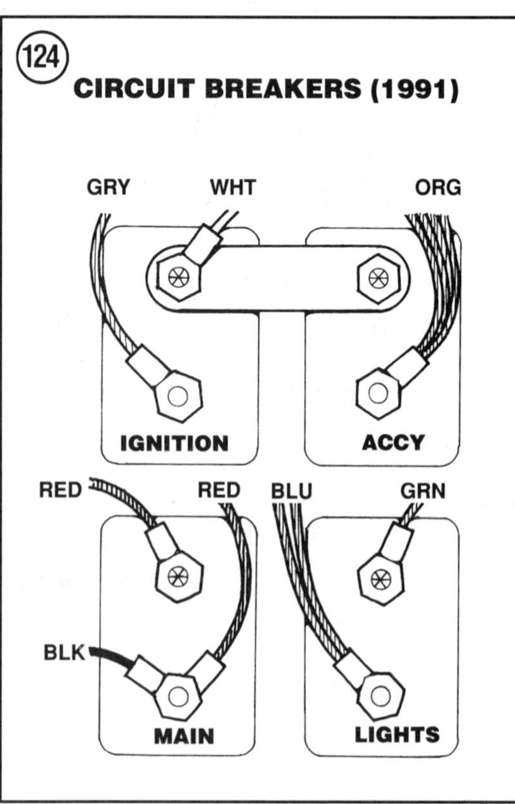

the circuits protected by each circuit breaker can be determined.

A tripped circuit breaker should be treated as more than a minor annoyance; it should serve also as a warning that something is wrong in the electrical system.

Replace a defective circuit breaker by disconnecting the wire and pulling it out of its holder. Reverse to install.

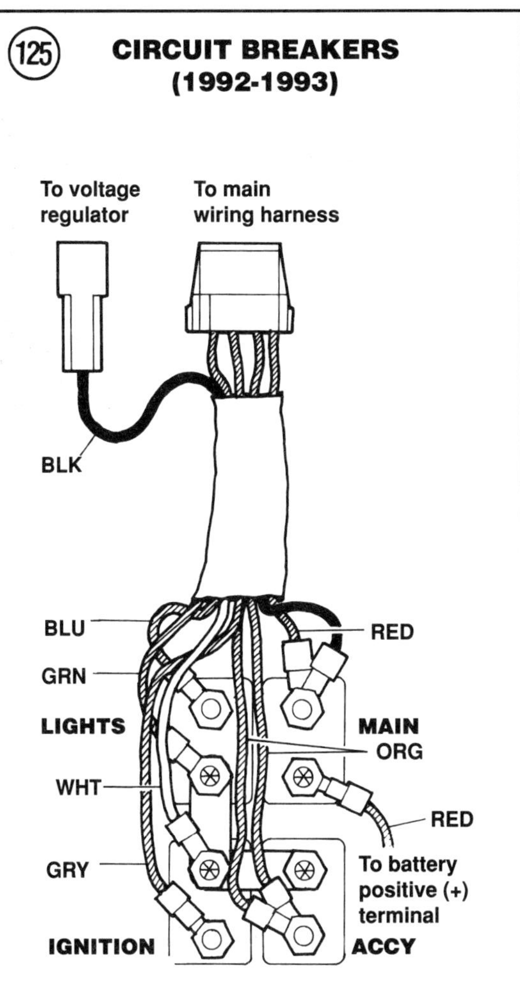

1991-1993

1991-1993 models have 4 circuit breakers mounted on the front side of the rear fender underneath the seat (**Figure 123**). Refer to **Figure 124** (1991) or **Figure 125** (1992-1993). Disconnect the negative battery cable prior to servicing the circuit breakers.

1994

1994 models have 5 circuit breakers. The ignition, instruments, lights and accessories circuit breakers are mounted in the circuit breaker block installed in the electrical bracket mounted underneath the seat (**Figure 126**). The main circuit breaker is mounted in the electrical bracket on the right-hand side of the circuit breaker block (**Figure 115**). Disconnect the negative battery cable prior to servicing the circuit breakers.

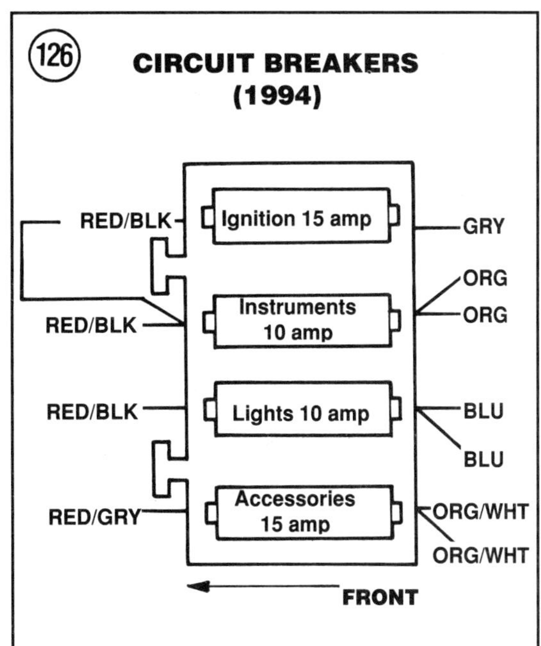

Tables 1-4 are on the following pages.

8

Table 1 ELECTRICAL SPECIFICATIONS

Battery	12 volt, 19 amp-hours
Circuit breakers	
1991-1993	
Main	30 amp
Accessory	15 amp
Ignition	15 amp
Lights	15
1994	
Main	50
Accessory	15
Ignition	15
Lights	10
Instruments	10

Table 2 BATTERY STATE OF CHARGE

1.110-1.130	Discharged
1.140-1.160	Almost discharged
1.170-1.190	One-quarter charged
1.200-1.220	One-half charged
1.230-1.250	Three-quarters charged
1.260-1.280	Fully charged

Table 3 ELECTRIC STARTER SPECIFICATIONS

Starter identification	
883 cc	Yellow paint dot on drive housing
1200 cc	Blue paint dot on drive housing
Free current	90 amp (max) @ 11.5 V
Free speed	3,000 rpm (min) @ 11.5 V
Stall current	
883 cc	300 amp (max) @ 2.5 V
1200 cc	400 amp (max) @ 2.4 V
Stall torque	
883 cc	5 ft.-lb. (min) @ 2.5 V
1200 cc	8.1 ft.-lb. (min) @ 2.4 V
Starter brush minimum wear length	
883 cc	0.354 in. (8.9 mm)
1200 cc	
1991-1992	0.413 in. (10.4 mm)
1993-on	0.354 in. (8.9 mm)
Commutator minimum outer diameter	1.141 in. (28.9 mm)

Table 4 TIGHTENING TORQUES

	ft.-lb.	in.-lb.	N•m
Starter thru-bolts			
883 cc		20-25	2.3-2.8
1200 cc		39-65	4.4-7.3
Cable nuts		65-80	7.3-9.0
Stator Torx screws		30-40	3.4-4.5
Rotor bolt		43-48	4.9-5.4

(continued)

Table 4 TIGHTENING TORQUES (continued)

	ft.-lb.	in.-lb.	N•m
Timer screws			
Inner cover and sensor plate		15-20	1.7-2.3
Rotor-to-engine sprocket bolts		90-110	10.2-12.4
Rotor (ignition)		75-80	8.5-9.0
Stator torx screws		30-40	3.4-4.5
Starter mounting bolts	13-20		17.6-27.1
Headlight adjust nut	10-20		14-27
Headlight bracket bolts	10-16		14-22
Ignition switch locknut			
1991-1993	6		8
1994	3-7		4-9
Top center engine bracket torx screw	5-10		7-14
Oil pressure switch	5-7		7-9
Neutral indicator switch	3-5		4-7
Brake light switch	7-10		9-14
Horn locknut			
883 cc	8-16		11-22
1200 cc	5-10		7-14
Vacuum operated electric switch			
1991-1993			
Mounting bracket locknut	5-12		7-16
Ground wire bolt	25-30		34-41
1994			
Mounting bracket locknut	5-12		7-16

CHAPTER NINE

WHEELS, HUBS AND TIRES

This chapter describes disassembly and repair of the front and rear wheels, hubs and tire service. For routine maintenance, see Chapter Three.

Tire service is a critical aspect to the overall operation and safety of your motorcycle. Tires should be properly mounted, balanced and maintained while in service.

Tables 1-11 are found at the end of the chapter.

FRONT WHEEL

Proper front wheel maintenance and inspection is critical to the safe operation of your Harley. The following section describes complete service to the front wheel. Service to the front hub and bearings is described later in this chapter.

Removal

1. Support the bike so that the front wheel clears the ground.
2. Remove the brake caliper mounting bolts (**Figure 1**) and lift the caliper away from the brake disc. Support the caliper with a cord so that the weight of the caliper is not supported by the brake line.

NOTE

*Insert a piece of wood or vinyl in the caliper between the brake pads (**Figure 2**). That way, if the brake lever is inadvertently squeezed, the piston will not be forced out of the cylinder. If this does happen, the caliper might have to be disassembled to reseat the piston and the system will have to be bled.*

3. Remove the axle nut (**Figure 3**), lockwasher and flat washer.
4. Loosen the front axle pinch bolt nut (A, **Figure 4**). Do not remove the pinch bolt.

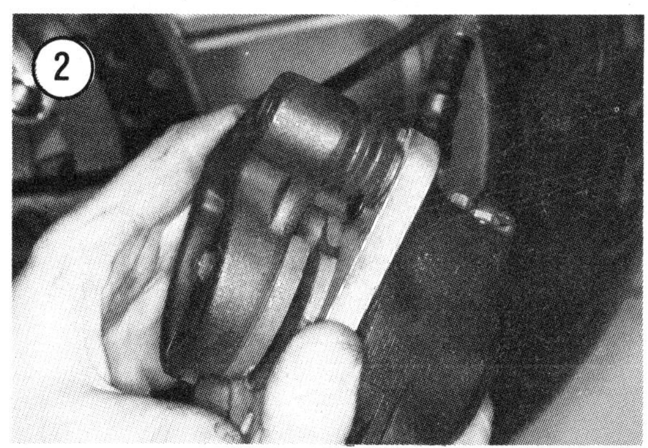

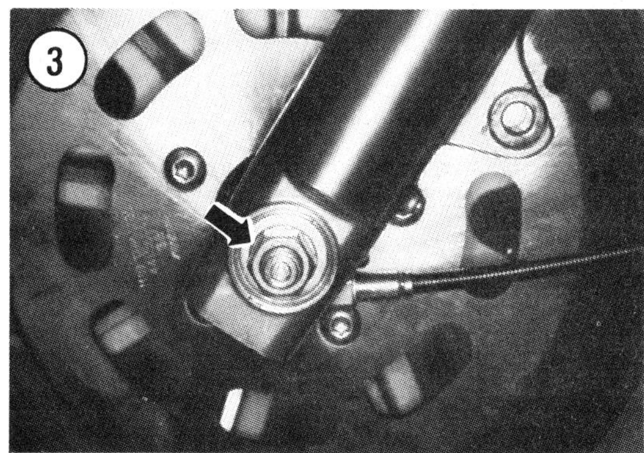

5. Tap the end of the axle with a soft faced mallet and remove it from the wheel (B, **Figure 3**). If the axle is tight, tap the end of the axle with a brass or aluminum drift.

6. Pull the wheel away from the fork sliders slightly and remove the speedometer drive gear (with attached felt seal) from the wheel. See **Figure 5**.

7. Remove the right-hand axle spacer (**Figure 6**), if necessary.

CAUTION

Do not set the wheel down on the disc surface, as it may be scratched or warped. Either lean the wheel against a wall or place it on a couple of wood blocks.

8. When servicing the wheel assembly, install the washer and nut on the axle to prevent their loss.

9. Inspect the front wheel assembly as described in this chapter.

Installation

1. Clean the axle in solvent and dry thoroughly. Make sure the axle bearing surfaces on both fork sliders and the axle are free from burrs and nicks.

2. Apply a light coat of wheel bearing grease to the axle shaft prior to installation.

3. Install the right-hand axle spacer (**Figure 6**), if removed.

4. Install the felt seal (**Figure 5**) onto the speedometer drive, if removed.

5. Install the speedometer drive pin into the brake disc notch as shown in **Figure 7**.

6. Hold the speedometer drive in position and install the wheel between the fork tubes.

7. Insert the axle (B, **Figure 4**) through the front forks and wheel from the right-hand side.
8. Install the flat washer, lockwasher and axle nut (**Figure 3**) finger-tight.
9. Insert a rod through the axle hole and tighten the axle nut (**Figure 3**) to the torque specification in **Table 8**.
10. Tighten the front axle pinch bolt nut (A, **Figure 4**) to the torque specification in **Table 8**.
11. Perform the *Front Axle End Play Check* in this chapter.
12. Remove the vinyl tubing or pieces of wood from the brake caliper. Then *carefully* insert the disc between the pads when installing the brake caliper. Be careful not to damage the leading edge of the brake pads when installing the brake caliper. Tighten the brake caliper bolts (**Figure 1**) to the torque specification in **Table 8**.
13. After the wheel and brake is completely installed, rotate it several times and apply the front brake a couple of times to make sure the wheel rotates freely and that the brake pads are against the disc correctly.

Inspection

1. Remove any corrosion on the front axle with a piece of fine emery cloth.
2. Install the wheel in a wheel truing stand and spin the wheel. Visually check the wheel for excessive wobble or runout. If it appears that the wheel is not running true, remove the tire from the rim as described later in this chapter. Then remount the wheel into the truing stand and measure axial and lateral runout (**Figure 8**) with a pointer or dial indicator. Compare actual runout readings with service limit specifications listed in **Table 1**. Note the following:

a. Cast wheels: If the runout meets or exceeds the service limit (**Table 1**), check the wheel bearings as described under *Front Hub* in this chapter. If the wheel bearings are okay, cast wheels will have to be replaced as they cannot be serviced. Inspect the wheel for signs of cracks, fractures, dents or bends. If it is damaged in any way, it must be replaced.

b. Laced wheels: If the wheel bearings, spokes, hub and rim assembly are not damaged, the runout can be removed by accurately truing the wheel. Refer to *Spoke Adjustment* in this chapter. If the rim is dented or damaged in any way, the rim should be replaced and the wheel respoked and trued by a Harley-Davidson dealer or a qualified repair shop familiar with rebuilding Harley wheels.

WARNING
Do not try to repair any damage to cast wheels as it will result in an unsafe riding condition.

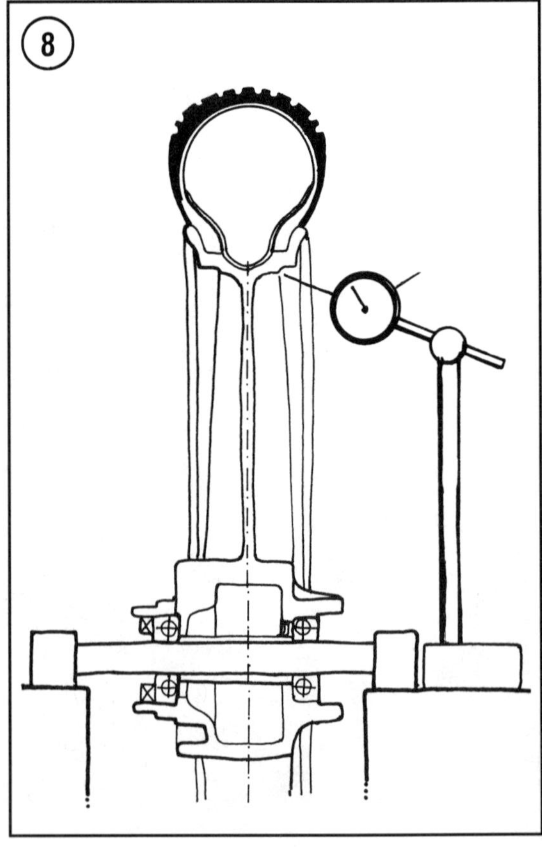

3. While the wheel is off, check the tightness of the brake disc bolts. Refer to the tightening torques listed at the end of Chapter Twelve.

Front Wheel Bearing End Play Check

Front wheel bearing end play must be maintained within certain specifications. On early 1991 models, end play is set by the length of the spacer sleeve installed between the wheel bearings. On late 1991 and later models, end play is set by spacer shims installed between the spacer sleeve and shoulder washer. See **Figure 9** or **Figure 10**. Excessive end play can cause bearing side loading and premature bearing failure. Wear in this critical area can be gauged by checking front wheel bearing end play each time the front wheel is removed. When the end play is incorrect, the spacer sleeve (early 1991) or spacer shim (late 1991-on) must be replaced with one that will bring the end play back to within the specified range.

After tightening the axle nut, check the front wheel bearing end play as follows.

NOTE
The front wheel should be installed on the bike and off of the ground when performing the following. Make sure that the bike is supported securely.

1. Tighten the front axle to the tightening torque listed in **Table 8**.
2. Mount a dial indicator so that the plunger contacts the end of the axle (**Figure 11**). Then grasp the wheel and attempt to move the wheel back and forth by pushing and pulling it along the axle center line. Measure axle end play by observing the dial indicator needle.

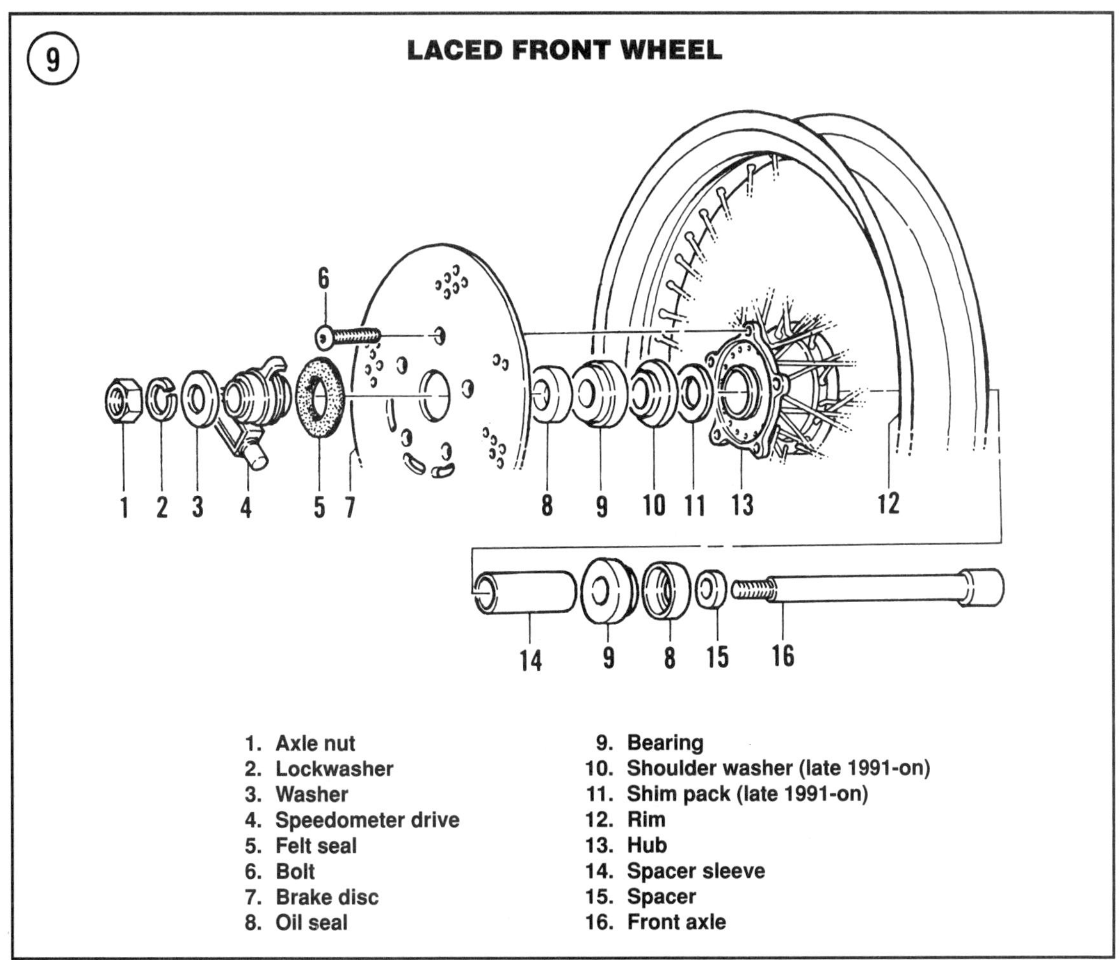

9

3. If the end play exceeds the specifications in **Table 1**, double check front wheel installation. If the end play is incorrect, note the following:

a. On early 1991 models, replace the spacer sleeve with a longer or shorter one. See **Table 2** for spacer sleeve lengths.

b. On late 1991-on models, replace spacer shim with a thicker or thinner one. See **Table 3** for spacer shim thicknesses.

c. On all models, remove the wheel and disassemble the front hub as described under *Front Hub* in this chapter.

d. Reassemble the hub and install the front wheel. Then recheck the bearing end play measurement.

FRONT HUB

Tapered roller bearings are installed on each side of the hub. Oil seals are installed on the outside of each bearing to protect them from dirt and other contaminants. The bearings can be removed from the hub after removing the outer oil seals. The bearing races are pressed into the hub and should not be removed unless they require replacement.

Disassembly/Inspection/Reassembly

Refer to the following for your model when performing this procedure:

a. Laced wheel: **Figure 9**.

b. Cast wheel: **Figure 10**.

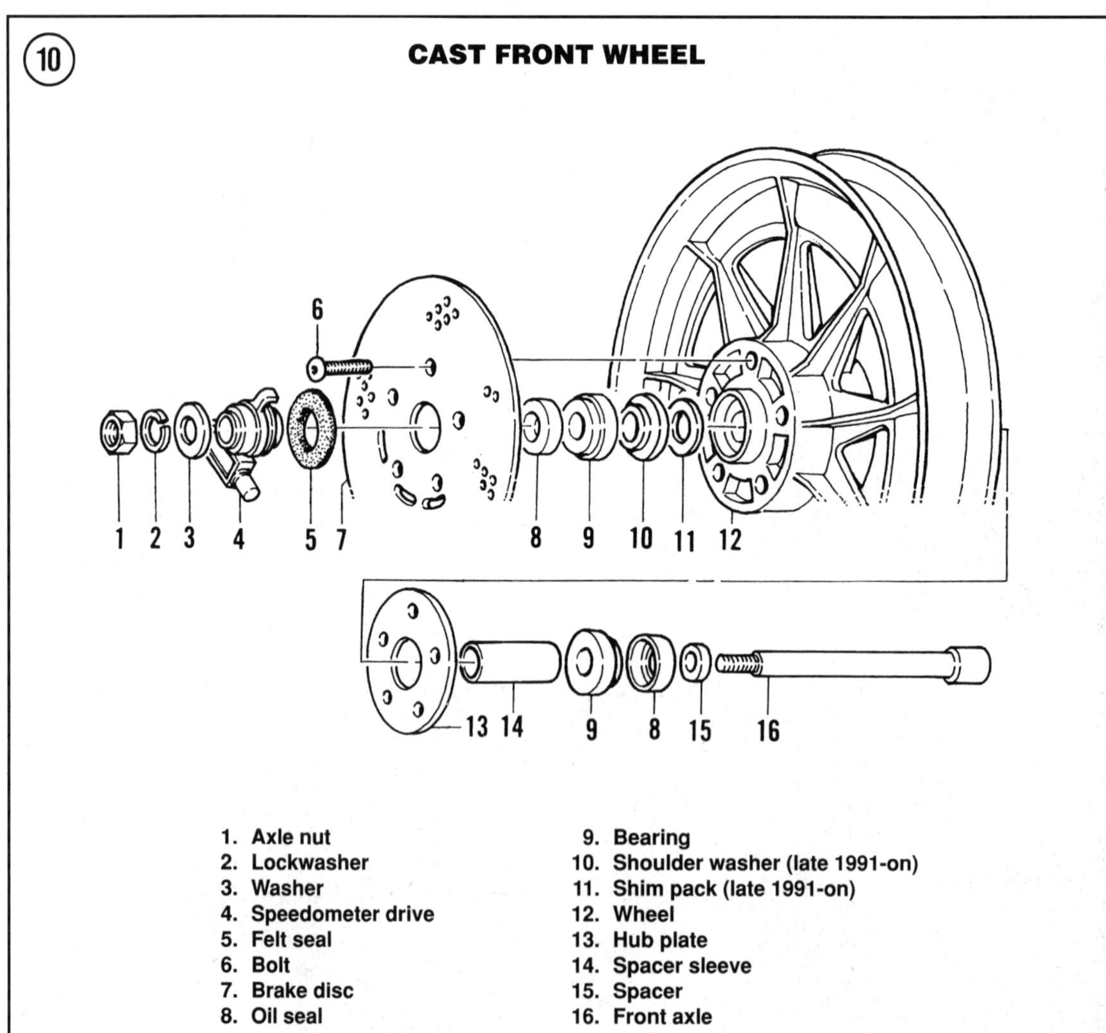

NOTE
The bearings and races are matched pairs. Label all parts so that they may be returned to their original positions.

1. Remove the front wheel as described in this chapter.

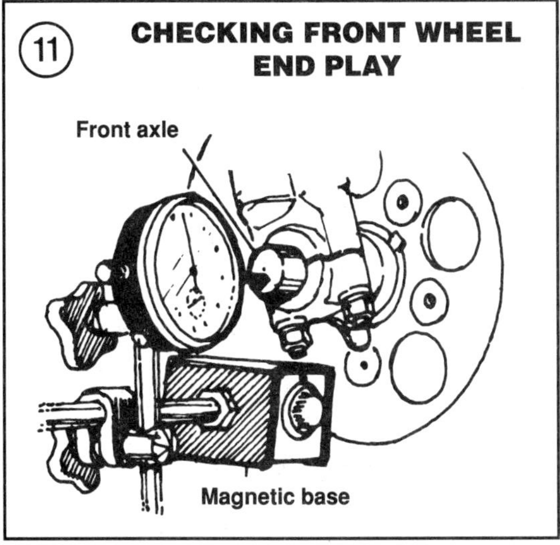

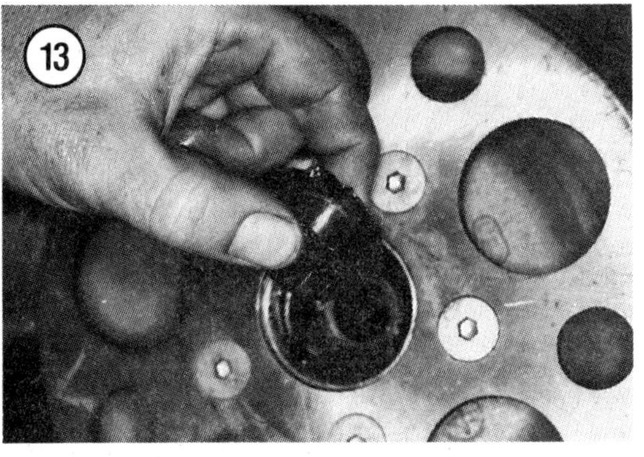

2. If necessary, remove the brake disc as described in Chapter Twelve.
3. If necessary, remove the hub plate on cast wheels.
4. Pry the oil seals out of the hub (**Figure 12**). If you are using a screwdriver, place a rag underneath the screwdriver to avoid damaging the hub.
5. Remove the bearing assemblies (**Figure 13**) and spacer sleeve. On late 1991-on models, remove the shoulder washer and spacer shim(s).
6. Wash the bearings thoroughly in clean solvent and dry with compressed air. Wipe the bearing races off with a clean rag dipped in solvent. Then check the roller bearings and races for wear, pitting or excessive heat (bluish tint). Replace the bearing and races as a complete set. Replace the bearing races as described in Step 7. If the bearing and its race do not require replacement, proceed to Step 8. If you are going to reinstall the original bearing(s), pack the bearing thoroughly with grease and wrap it in a clean, lint-free cloth or wax paper. Wipe a film of grease across the bearing race.
7. Replace the bearing races (**Figure 14**) as follows:
   a. A universal bearing remover should be used to remove the races from the hub. If this tool is unavailable, insert a drift punch through the hub and tap the race out of the hub with a hammer. Move the punch around the race to make sure the race is driven squarely out of the hub. Do not allow the race to bind in the hub as this can damage the race bore in the hub. Severe damage to the race bore will require replacement of the hub.
   b. Clean the inside and outside of the hub with solvent. Dry with compressed air.
   c. Wipe the outside of the new race with oil and align it with the hub. Using a bearing driver or socket with an outside diameter slightly smaller

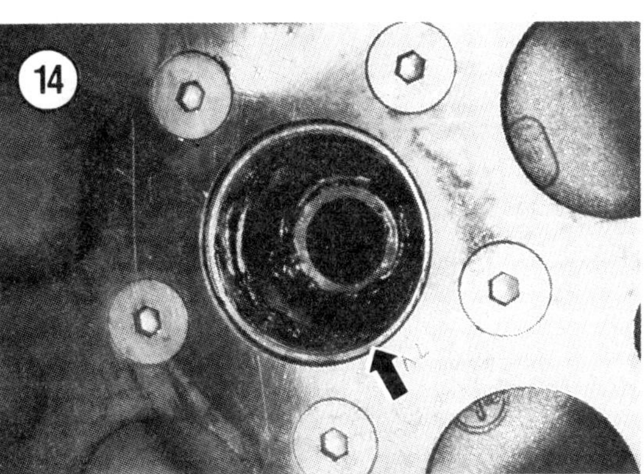

than the bearing race, drive the race into the hub until it bottoms out on the hub shoulder. As you begin to drive the race into the hub, stop and check your work often to make sure the race is square with the hub bore. Do not allow the race to bind during installation.

NOTE

If you do not have the proper size tool to drive the race into the hub, have a Harley-Davidson dealer or independent repair shop install the race. Do not attempt to install the race by driving it into the hub with a small diameter punch or rod.

8. Blow any dirt or foreign matter out of the hub prior to installing the bearings.
9. Wipe the ends of the spacer sleeve with grease and install it into the hub.
10. On late 1991-on, perform the following:
  a. Install the spacer shim(s) into the left-hand side of the hub and rest it against the hub counterbore.
  b. Install the shoulder washer into the hub, with its shoulder side facing out, and seat it against the spacer shim(s).
11. Wipe each bearing race with grease.
12. Pack the bearings with grease and install them in the bearing races.
13. Pack the seal lip cavity of each seal with grease.
14. The oil seals should have the same part number and can be installed on either side. Confirm this with your dealer.
15. Install the oil seals using a bearing driver or socket with an O.D. slightly smaller than the oil seal (**Figure 15**). Carefully drive the oil seals into the hub until they are flush with the hub or recessed 0.020 in. (0.51 mm) below the hub surface.
16. If the brake disc was removed, refer to Chapter Twelve for correct procedures and tightening torques.
17. If the hub plate was removed on cast wheels, install the hub and secure it with *new* Torx screws. Tighten the hub plate Torx screws to the torque specification in **Table 8**.
18. After the wheel is installed on the bike and the front axle tightened to the specified torque specification, the bearing end play should be checked as described in this chapter.
19. If the hub on spoke wheels is damaged, the hub can be replaced by removing the spokes and having a dealer assemble a new hub. If the hub on cast wheels is damaged, the wheel assembly must be replaced; it cannot be repaired.

REAR WHEEL

Proper rear wheel maintenance and inspection is critical to the safe operation of your Harley. The following section describes complete service to the

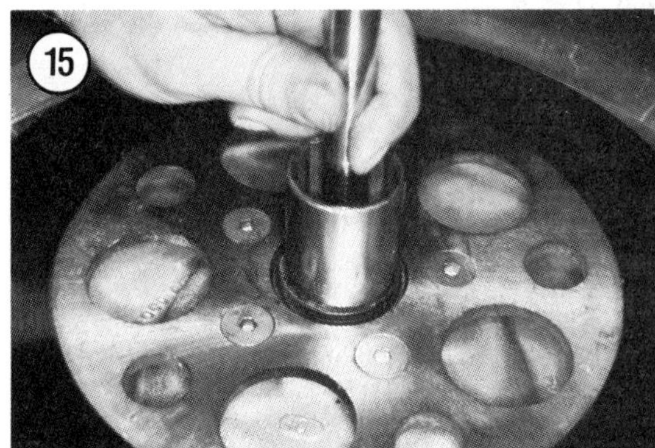

rear wheel. Service to the rear hub and bearings is described later in this chapter.

Removal

1. Support the bike so that the rear wheel clears the ground.
2. Remove and discard the rear axle cotter pin (A, **Figure 16**).
3. Loosen the drive chain or belt adjusting locknuts and adjuster bolts (B, **Figure 16**).
4. Loosen and remove the axle nut (C, **Figure 16**) and washer.

5. Slide the axle out of the wheel (**Figure 17**) and allow the wheel to drop to the ground.
6. Remove the outer right-hand axle spacer (**Figure 18**).

NOTE
The shoulders on the inner left- and right-hand axle spacers are inserted through the oil seal. These spacers should not fall out when the wheel is removed.

7. Lift the drive chain or belt off of the sprocket and remove the rear wheel (**Figure 19**).

NOTE
Insert a piece of wood or vinyl tubing in the caliper between the brake pads in place of the disc. That way, if the brake pedal is inadvertently depressed, the piston will not be forced out of the cylinder. If this does happen, the caliper might have to be disassembled to reseat the piston and the system will have to be bled. By using the wood or vinyl tubing, bleeding the brake should not be necessary when installing the wheel.

8. If the wheel is going to be off for any length of time, or if it is to be taken to a shop for repair, install the spacer on the axle along with the axle nut and washer to prevent losing any parts.

CAUTION
Do not set the wheel down on the disc surface, as it may be scratched or warped. Either lean the wheel against a wall or place it on a couple of wood blocks.

9. Inspect the rear wheel assembly as described in this chapter.

Installation

1. Clean the axle in solvent and dry thoroughly. Make sure the axle bearing surfaces on the axle are free from burrs and nicks.
2. Apply a thin film of waterproof bearing grease to the axle shaft prior to installation.
3. Make sure the inner left- and right-hand axle spacers are inserted through the oil seal as shown in **Figure 20**. If necessary, install the spacers and oil seals as described under *Rear Hub* in this chapter.

4. Remove the vinyl tubing from the brake caliper. Then position the rear wheel into the swing arm, through the drive chain or belt, and position the right-hand axle spacer (**Figure 18**) between the swing arm and wheel.

5. Lift the wheel into position and install the axle (**Figure 17**) from the right-hand side.

6. Install the washer and nut (**Figure 16**).

7. Adjust the drive chain or belt as described in Chapter Three.

8. Tighten the axle nut to the torque specification listed in **Table 9**.

NOTE
If it is necessary to tighten the axle nut a bit more to line up the axle nut slot with the cotter pin hole in the axle, make sure you do not exceed the maximum torque specification listed in ***Table 9***.

9. Perform the *Rear Axle End Play Check* in this chapter.

10. Install a new cotter pin and bend its arms over to lock it.

11. Rotate the wheel several times to make sure it rotates freely and that the brakes work properly.

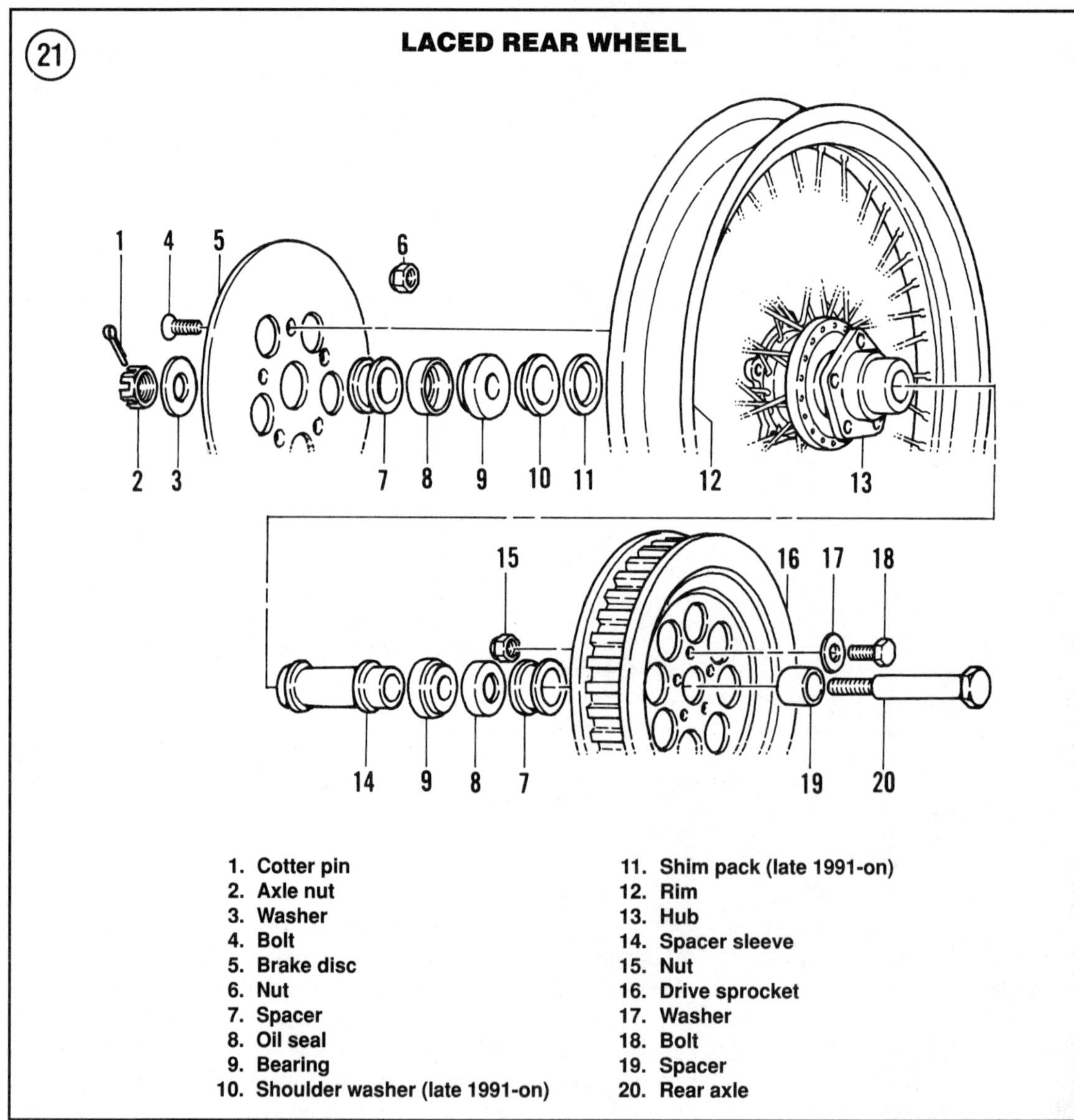

1. Cotter pin
2. Axle nut
3. Washer
4. Bolt
5. Brake disc
6. Nut
7. Spacer
8. Oil seal
9. Bearing
10. Shoulder washer (late 1991-on)
11. Shim pack (late 1991-on)
12. Rim
13. Hub
14. Spacer sleeve
15. Nut
16. Drive sprocket
17. Washer
18. Bolt
19. Spacer
20. Rear axle

Inspection (All Models)

1. Remove any corrosion on the rear axle with a piece of fine emery cloth.
2. Install the wheel in a wheel truing stand and spin the wheel. Visually check the wheel for excessive wobble or runout. If it appears that the wheel is not running true, remove the tire from the rim as described later in this chapter. Then remount the wheel into the truing stand and measure axial and lateral runout (**Figure 8**) with a pointer or dial indicator. Compare actual runout readings with service limit specifications listed in **Table 4**. Note the following:
   a. *Cast wheel:* If the runout meets or exceeds the service limit (**Table 4**), check the wheel bearings as described under *Rear Hub* in this chapter. If the wheel bearings are okay, the cast wheel will have to be replaced as it cannot be serviced. Inspect the wheel for signs of cracks, fractures, dents or bends. If it is damaged in any way, it must be replaced.
   b. *Laced wheel:* If the wheel bearings, spokes, hub and rim assembly are not damaged, the runout can be removed by accurately truing the wheel. Refer to *Spoke Adjustment* in this chapter. If the rim is dented or damaged in any way, the rim should be replaced and the wheel respoked and trued by a Harley-Davidson dealer or a qualified repair shop familiar with rebuilding Harley wheels.

WARNING
Do not try to repair any damage to cast wheels as it will result in an unsafe riding condition.

3. While the wheel is off, check the tightness of the brake disc bolts. Refer to the tightening torque listed at the end of Chapter Twelve.

Rear Wheel Bearing End Play Check (All Models)

Rear wheel bearing end play must be maintained within certain specifications. On early 1991 models, end play is set by the length of the spacer sleeve installed between the wheel bearings. On late 1991 and later models, end play is set by spacer shims installed between spacer sleeve and shoulder washer. See **Figure 21** or **Figure 22**. Excessive end play can cause bearing side loading and premature bearing failure. Wear in this critical area can be gauged by checking rear wheel bearing end play each time the rear wheel is removed. When the end play is incorrect, the spacer sleeve (early 1991) or spacer shim (late 1991-on) must be replaced with one that will bring the end play back to within the specified range.

After tightening the axle nut, check the rear wheel bearing end play as follows.

NOTE
The rear wheel should be installed on the bike and off of the ground when performing the following. Make sure that the bike is supported securely.

1. Tighten the rear axle to the tightening torque listed in **Table 9**.
2. Mount a dial indicator so that the plunger contacts the end of the axle (**Figure 11**). Then grasp the wheel and attempt to move the wheel back and forth by pushing and pulling it along the axle center line. Measure axle end play by observing the dial indicator needle.
3. If the end play exceeds the specifications in **Table 4**, double check rear wheel installation. Check that the right-hand spacer (**Figure 20**) is properly installed. If the end play is still incorrect, note the following:
   a. On early 1991 models, replace the spacer sleeve with a longer or shorter one. See **Table 5** or **Table 6** for spacer sleeve lengths.
   b. On late 1991-on models, replace spacer shim with a thicker or thinner one. See **Table 7** for spacer shim thicknesses.
   c. On all models, remove the wheel and disassemble the rear hub as described under *Rear Hub* in this chapter.
   d. Reassemble the hub and install the rear wheel. Then recheck the end play measurement.

REAR HUB

Tapered roller bearings are installed on each side of the hub. Oil seals installed on the outside of each bearing protect them from dirt and other contaminants. The bearings can be removed from the hub after removing the outer oil seals. The bearing races are pressed into the hub and should not be removed unless they require replacement.

Disassembly/Inspection/Reassembly

Refer to the following for your model when performing this procedure:

a. Laced wheel: **Figure 21**.

b. Cast wheel: **Figure 22**.

NOTE
The bearings and races are matched pairs. Label all parts so that they may be returned to their original positions.

1. Remove the rear wheel as described in this chapter.
2. If necessary, remove the brake disc as described in Chapter Twelve.
3. If necessary, remove the driven sprocket as described in this chapter.
4. Remove the inner spacers (**Figure 23**).
5. Pry the oil seals out of the hub (**Figure 24**). If you are using a screwdriver, place a rag underneath the screwdriver to avoid damaging the hub. Remove the spacer from the oil seal, if so equipped. Then identify and remove the bearing from its race.
6. On late 1991-on models, remove the spacer shim(s) and shoulder washer.
7. Remove the spacer sleeve from the hub and wash it thoroughly in solvent.
8. Repeat to remove the opposite bearing. Remember, the bearings are matched to their races; label the bearings if they are going to be reused.
9. Wash the bearings thoroughly in clean solvent and dry with compressed air. Wipe the bearing races off with a clean rag dipped in solvent. Then check the roller bearings and races for wear, pitting or excessive heat (bluish tint). Replace the bearing and races as a complete set. Replace the bearing races as

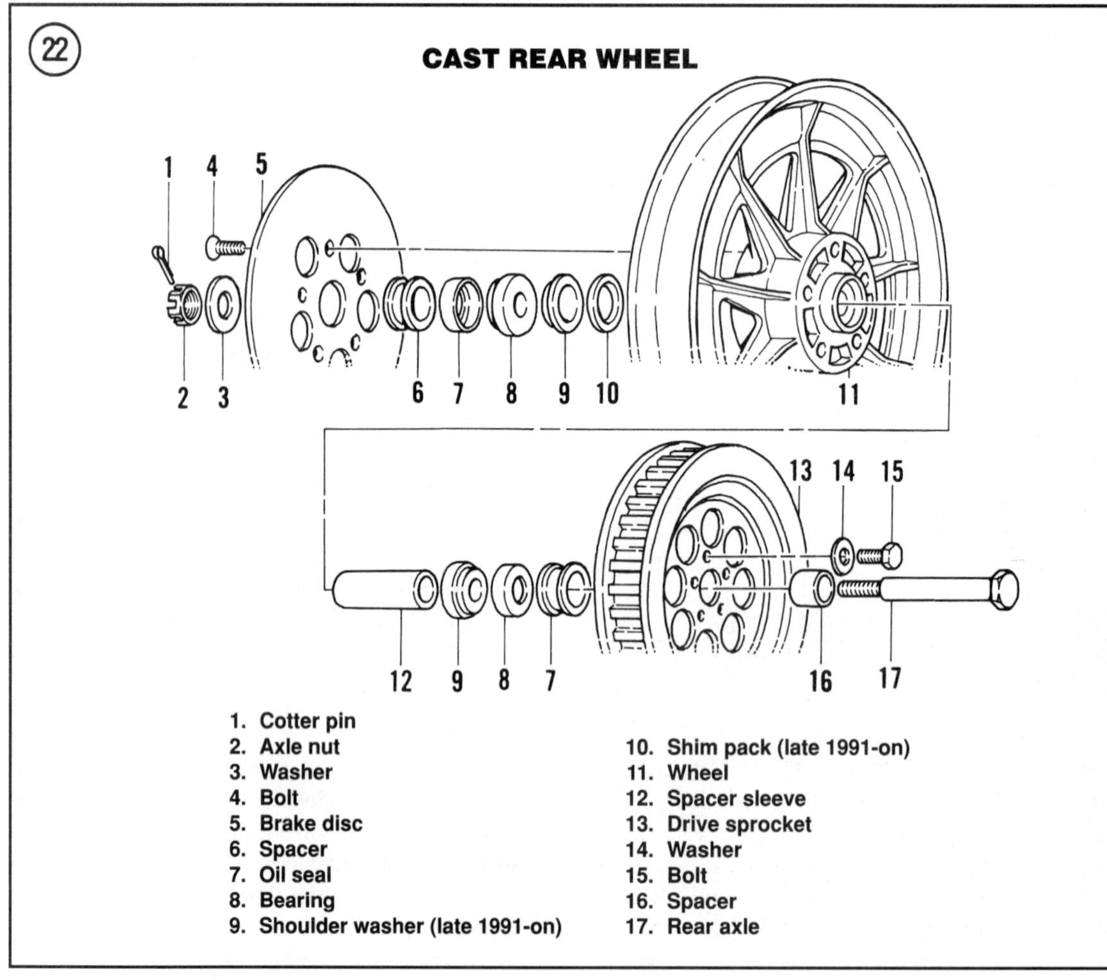

described in Step 10. If the bearing and its race do not require replacement, proceed to Step 11. If you are going to reinstall the original bearing(s), pack the bearing thoroughly with grease and wrap it in a clean, lint-free cloth or wax paper. Wipe a film of grease across the bearing race. If the bearings and races are not lubricated after cleaning them, they may begin to rust.

10. Replace the bearing races (**Figure 14**) as follows:
   a. A universal bearing remover should be used to remove the races from the hub. If this tool is unavailable, insert a drift punch through the hub and tap the race out of the hub with a hammer. Move the punch around the race to make sure the race is driven squarely out of the hub. Do not allow the race to bind in the hub as this can damage the race bore in the hub. Severe damage to the race bore will require replacement of the hub.
   b. Clean the inside and outside of the hub with solvent. Dry with compressed air.
   c. Wipe the outside of the new race with oil and align it with the hub. Using a bearing driver or socket with an outside diameter slightly smaller than the bearing race, drive the race into the hub until it bottoms out on the hub shoulder. As you begin to drive the race into the hub, stop and check your work often to make sure the race is square with the hub bore. Do not allow the race to bind during installation.

NOTE

If you do not have the proper size tool to drive the race into the hub, have a Harley-Davidson dealer or independent repair shop install the race. Do not attempt to install the race by driving it into the hub with a small diameter punch or rod.

11. Blow any dirt or foreign matter out of the hub prior to installing the bearings.
12. Wipe the ends of the spacer sleeve with grease and install it into the hub.
13. On late 1991-on, perform the following:
   a. Install the spacer shim(s) into the left-hand side of the hub and rest it against the hub counterbore.
   b. Install the shoulder washer into the hub, with its shoulder side facing out, and seat it against the spacer shim(s).
14. Wipe each bearing race with grease.
15. Pack the bearings with grease and install them in the bearing races.
16. Install new oil seals as follows:
   a. Pack the seal lip cavity of each seal with grease.
   b. The oil seals have the same part number and can thus be installed into either side.
   c. Install the oil seals so that their closed side faces out.
   d. Use a bearing driver or socket with an O.D. slightly smaller than the oil seal (**Figure 22**) to install the oil seals.
   e. On laced wheels, install the oil seals until their outer surface is 0.26-0.28 in. (6.6-7.1 mm) below the hub surface.
   f. On cast wheels, install the oil seals until their outer surface is 0.31 in. (7.9 mm) below the hub surface.
17. If the brake disc was removed, refer to Chapter Twelve for correct procedures and tightening torques.
18. If the driven sprocket was removed, install it as described in this chapter.

19. After the wheel is installed on the bike and the rear axle tightened to the specified torque specification, the bearing end play should be check as described in this chapter.
20. If the hub on spoke wheels is damaged, the hub can be replaced by removing the spokes and having a dealer assemble a new hub. If the hub on cast wheels is damaged, the wheel assembly must be replaced; it cannot be repaired.

DRIVE CHAIN AND SPROCKETS

Drive chains (**Figure 25**) were originally installed on 1991-1992 standard and Hugger Sportster models. O-ring drive chains were installed on 1992 models.

Refer to Chapter Three for drive chain inspection, cleaning and adjustment procedures.

Drive Chain Size

The standard drive chain size is No. 530 (3/8 in. wide) × 110 links.

Drive Chain Removal/Installation

A chain breaker will be required to remove the master link.
1. Support the bike so that the rear wheel is off the ground.
2. Turn the rear wheel and drive chain until the master link is accessible.
3. Remove the master link spring clip with a pair of pliers.
4. Using a chain breaker, press the connecting link out of the side plate. When disconnecting an O-ring chain, remove the 4 O-rings (**Figure 26**, typical).

NOTE
If you plan on reusing the drive chain, mark the chain's installation position (side and top positions). That way, the chain can be installed so that it will operate in the same position.

5. If installing a new drive chain, or if you have an old drive chain, connect this chain to your original chain with the old master link. Pull the new chain around the front sprocket.
6. Disconnect the original chain from the new or old chain.
7. If you are going to reuse the original chain, service it as required, then connect it to the old chain and pull it around the front sprocket. Disconnect the both chains.
8. Install by reversing these removal steps, noting the following.
9. If you are using an O-ring chain, install the 4 O-rings onto the master link as shown in **Figure 26**.
10. If you are assembling the chain with a press fit master link, refer to *Press Fit Master Link* to press the side plate onto the connecting link.

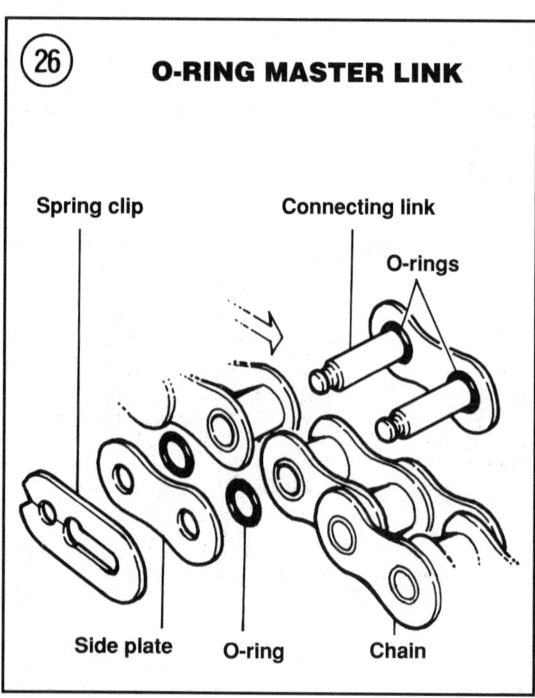

11. Install the spring clip on the master link so that the closed end of the clip is facing the direction of chain travel (**Figure 27**).

12. Lubricate and adjust the drive chain as described in Chapter Three.

Press Fit Master Link

Many of the new drive chains are designed so that the master link side plate is installed with a press fit. To install this type of master link, a press-fit chain tool is required; **Figure 28** illustrates one type of chain press tool that is available on the aftermarket. To disconnect the chain, first remove the outer clip from the master link, then use a chain breaker to separate the side plate from the connecting link.

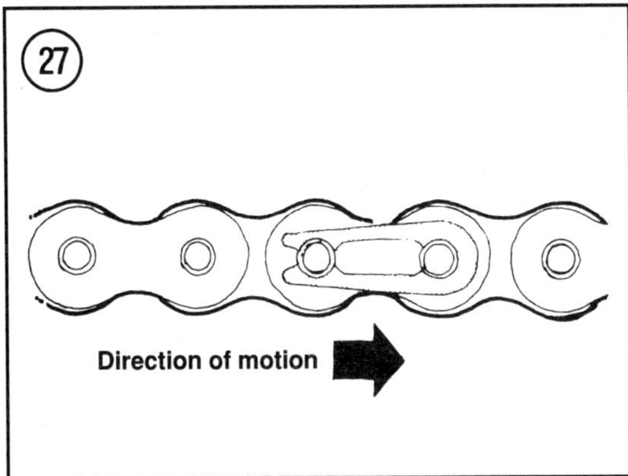

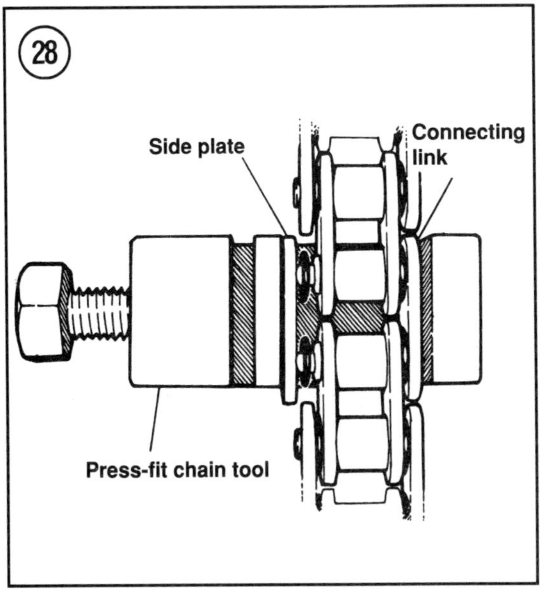

NOTE

Most commercial press-fit chain tools are designed to press the side plate onto the connecting link to its correct depth. If the side plate is pressed on too far, it will bind the chain where it is joined at the master link. If the side plate is not pressed on far enough, the spring clip cannot be installed correctly and will probably come off. What you are trying to do is to press the side plate onto the connecting link so that the slide plate is flush with both pin seating grooves in the connecting link.

CAUTION

Attempting to install a press-fit master link without the proper tools will generally damage the master link and parts of the chain.

Cutting A Drive Chain To Length

The standard drive chain size is No. 530 (3/8 in. wide) × 110 links. If your replacement drive chain is too long, cut it to length as follows.

1. Remove the new chain from its box and stretch it out on your workbench. Set the master link aside for now.

2. Count out 110 links on the new chain. Make a chalk mark on the 2 chain pins where you want to cut it. Count the chain links one more time just to make sure you are correct.

WARNING

A bench grinder or hand-operated high-speed grinding tool will be required to grind the chain pins when cutting the chain. When using this equipment in the following steps, safety glasses must be worn.

3. Grind the head of two pins flush with the face of the side plate with a grinder or suitable grinding tool.

4. Next, use a chain breaker or a punch and hammer and lightly tap the pins out of the side plate; support the chain carefully when doing this. If the pins are still tight, grind more material from the end of the pins and then try again.

5. Remove the side plate and push out the connecting link.

Service and Inspection

For service and inspection of the drive chain, refer to *Drive Chain/Cleaning, Inspection, and Lubrication* in Chapter Three.

Drive Sprocket Removal/Installation

The drive sprocket (front) is mounted on the end of mainshaft fifth gear.

1. Remove the exhaust pipes as described in Chapter Seven.
2. Remove the rear master cylinder bolts (A, **Figure 29**) and remove the footpeg and brake pedal assembly (B, **Figure 29**). It is not necessary to disconnect the brake line at the master cylinder.
3. Remove the master cylinder hose clip (A, **Figure 30**).
4. Remove the sprocket cover (B, **Figure 30**).
5. Remove the drive sprocket lockscrew (**Figure 31**).
6. Loosen the rear axle nut and loosen the chain adjusters (**Figure 32**).

NOTE
The drive sprocket nut has left-hand threads.

7. Turn the drive sprocket nut (**Figure 33**) clockwise and remove it.
8. Remove the drive sprocket from the transmission mainshaft.
9. Installation is the reverse of these steps, noting the following.
10. Remove all thread locking compound from the sprocket nut and mainshaft threads.
11. Install the drive sprocket (**Figure 33**) onto the mainshaft.
12. Apply Loctite 262 (red) to the sprocket nut threads and thread the nut onto the mainshaft by turning it counterclockwise. Tighten the nut to the torque specification in **Table 9**.
13. Determine which one of the three drive sprocket lockscrew sprocket holes aligns with a nut flat; see **Figure 31**. If none of the holes align with a nut flat, tighten the nut until one of the lockscrew holes aligns with a nut flat.

CAUTION
If the drive sprocket nut requires additional tightening, do not exceed 150 ft.-lb. (203 N•m). Do not loosen the drive sprocket nut to align the screw hole.

14. Apply Loctite 242 (blue) to the drive sprocket lockscrew threads. Then install the lockscrew into

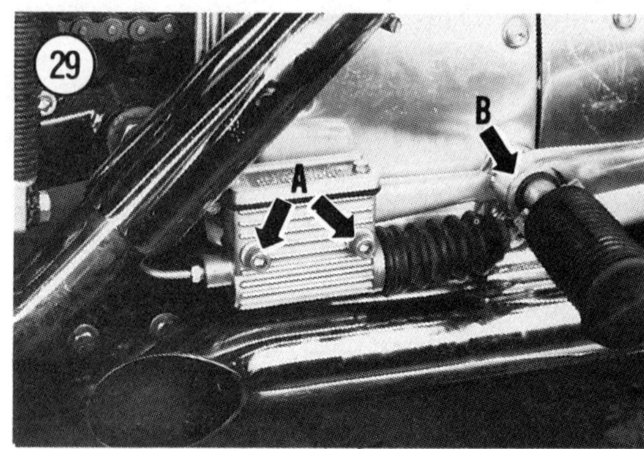

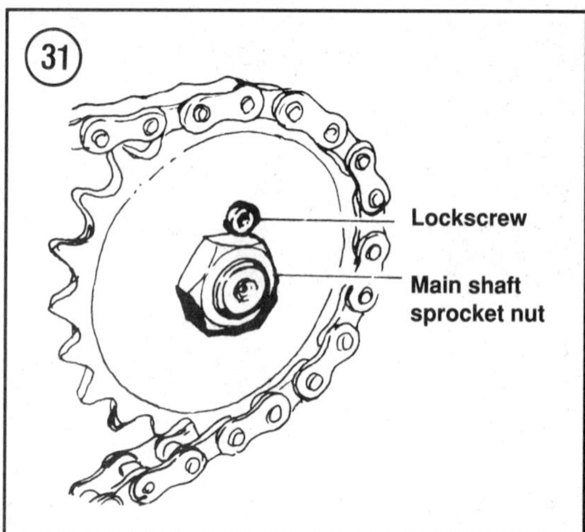

the correct sprocket hole so that it rests against the nut flat (**Figure 31**) and tighten to the torque specification in **Table 9**.

15. Reverse Steps 1-3 to complete assembly. Tighten the drive sprocket cover and rear master cylinder screws to the torque specifications in **Table 9**.

16. If you loosened the rear master cylinder pushrod locknut, adjust the rear brake as described in Chapter Three.

WARNING

Check that the rear brake is operating properly before riding the bike.

17. Adjust the drive chain as described in Chapter Three.

Driven Sprocket Removal/Installation

The driven sprocket (rear) is bolted to the rear wheel (**Figure 32**).

1. Remove the rear wheel as described in this chapter.

2. Remove the bolts and nuts securing the sprocket to the hub and remove the sprocket.
3. Replace worn or damaged sprocket fasteners as required.
4. Installation is the reverse of these steps. Tighten the sprocket nuts and bolts to the torque specification in **Table 9**.

Inspection

Inspect the sprocket teeth. If the teeth are visibly worn, replace both the drive and driven sprockets and the drive chain. Never replace any one sprocket or chain as a separate item; worn parts will cause rapid wear of the new component. Refer to *Drive Chain Adjustment* in Chapter Three for additional information.

SECONDARY DRIVE BELT AND SPROCKETS

O.E.M. drive belt assemblies are installed on all 1991-1992 883 Standard and Deluxe models, 1991-1992 1200 models and all 1993 and later models. O.E.M. drive belts can be identified by number of teeth and color code; see **Table 1** in Chapter Six.

Drive Belt Removal/Installation

The drive belt should be replaced when severely worn or damaged.

1. Remove the rear wheel as described in this chapter.
2. Remove the rear sprocket cover (A, **Figure 34**) as follows:
   a. Using an Allen wrench, loosen then remove the rear brake master cylinder mounting bolts (B, **Figure 34**) and washers.

NOTE

It is not necessary to disconnect the brake line at the master cylinder.

   b. Remove the clevis pin cotter pin at the rear brake pedal. Then remove the clevis pin (**Figure 35**) to disconnect the brake pedal from the brake rod end.
   c. Remove the screw and clip (C, **Figure 34**) securing the brake line to the sprocket cover.

d. Loosen then remove the Allen bolts and washers securing the sprocket cover to the engine. Remove the sprocket cover (A, **Figure 34**) together with rear brake pedal and linkage assembly.

3. Remove the cotter pin and loosen the rear axle nut (A, **Figure 36**) and the rear drive belt adjusters (B, **Figure 36**).
4. Remove the lower right-hand shock absorber mounting bolt and belt guard.
5. Mark the belt with a chalk mark so that it can be installed in its original operating position.

CAUTION
When removing the drive belt in Step 6, do not bend the belt backwards or twist it into loops smaller than 5 in. (127 mm). Otherwise, the belt cords will be damaged and you will have to replace the belt.

6. Slide the drive belt (**Figure 37**) off the drive sprocket and remove it from the bike.
7. Installation is the reverse of these steps. Adjust the drive belt tension and tighten the rear axle nut as described in Chapter Three.
8. Make sure the rear brake is operating correctly. If the brake line was disconnected, bleed the rear brake as described in Chapter Twelve.

Inspection

The drive belt has a built-in polyethylene lubricant coating that burnishes off during break-in. Do not apply lubricants. Inspect the drive belt for wear or damage. Replace any belt that appears questionable. See **Figure 38**.

CAUTION
When handling a drive belt, never bend the belt sharply as this will weaken the belt and cause premature failure.

Drive Sprocket Removal/Installation

1. Remove the rear wheel as described in this chapter.
2. Shift the transmission into 1st gear.
3. Remove the rear sprocket cover (A, **Figure 34**) as follows:

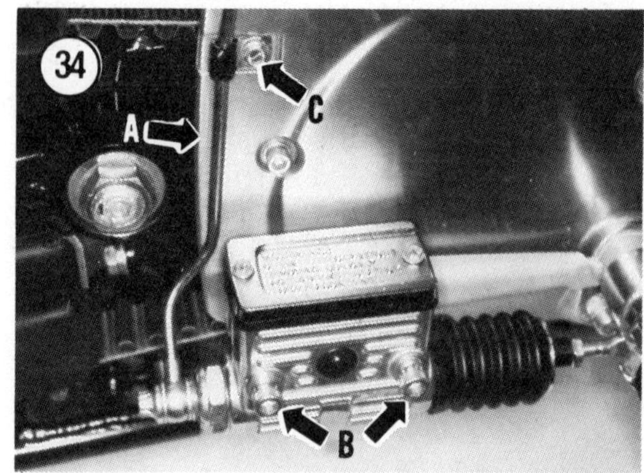

(38)

DRIVE BELT INSPECTION

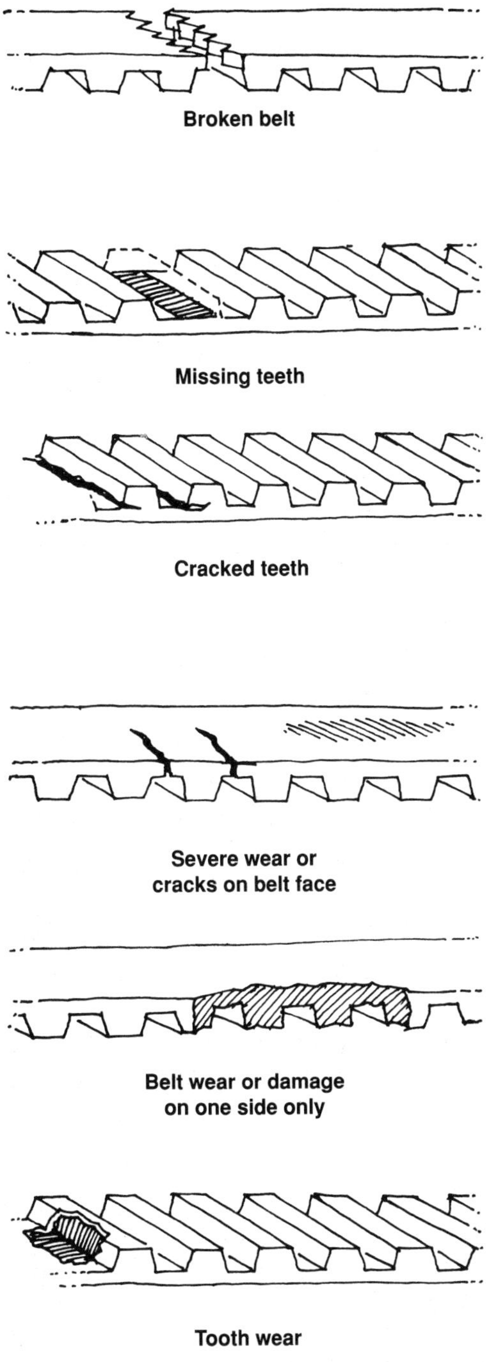

Broken belt

Missing teeth

Cracked teeth

Severe wear or cracks on belt face

Belt wear or damage on one side only

Tooth wear

a. Using an Allen wrench, loosen then remove the rear brake master cylinder mounting bolts (B, **Figure 34**) and washers.

NOTE
It is not necessary to disconnect the brake line at the master cylinder.

b. Remove the clevis pin cotter pin at the rear brake pedal. Then remove the clevis pin (**Figure 35**) to disconnect the brake pedal from the brake rod end.

c. Remove the screw and clip (C, **Figure 34**) securing the brake line to the sprocket cover.

d. Loosen then remove the Allen bolts and washers securing the sprocket cover to the engine. Remove the sprocket cover (A, **Figure 34**) together with rear brake pedal and linkage assembly.

4. Remove the cotter pin and loosen the rear axle nut (A, **Figure 36**) and the rear drive belt adjusters (B, **Figure 36**).

5A. On 1991 models, loosen and remove the socket head screw (2, **Figure 39**).

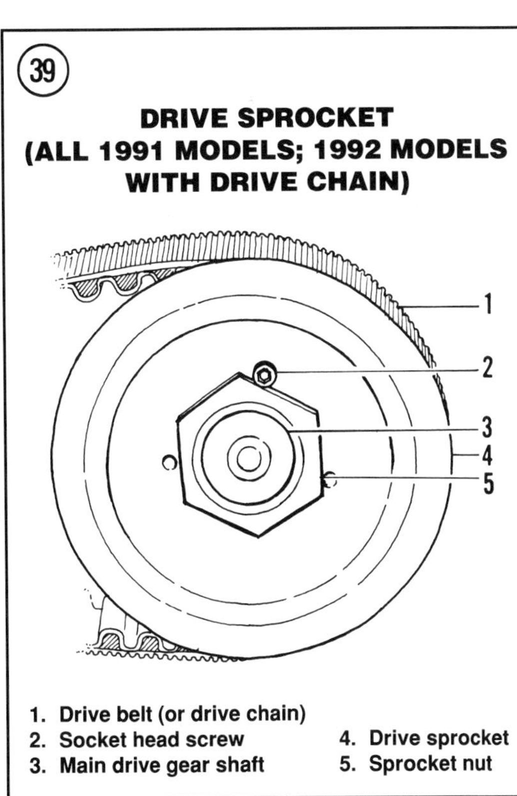

(39)

DRIVE SPROCKET (ALL 1991 MODELS; 1992 MODELS WITH DRIVE CHAIN)

1. Drive belt (or drive chain)
2. Socket head screw
3. Main drive gear shaft
4. Drive sprocket
5. Sprocket nut

5B. On 1992-on models, remove the 2 socket head screws and lockplate (**Figure 40**).

NOTE
The drive sprocket nut uses left-hand threads.

6. Turn the drive sprocket nut (**Figure 41**) clockwise and remove it from the main drive gear shaft.
7. Remove the drive sprocket (**Figure 42**).
8. Replace the drive sprocket if severely worn or damaged.
9. Install the drive sprocket (**Figure 42**) onto the main drive gear shaft.
10. The drive sprocket nut has a shoulder on one side (**Figure 43**). Install the nut so that the shoulder faces toward the drive sprocket.

NOTE
The drive sprocket nut uses left-hand threads.

11. Apply a few drops of Loctite 262 (red) onto the sprocket nut threads. Then turn the nut (**Figure 41**) counterclockwise and thread it onto the main drive gear shaft. Tighten the nut to the torque specification in **Table 9**.
12A. On 1991 models, perform the following:
   a. Determine which one of the three drive sprocket lockscrew sprocket holes aligns with a nut flat; see **Figure 39**. If none of the holes aligns with a nut flat, tighten the nut until one of the lockscrew holes aligns with a nut flat.

CAUTION
If the drive sprocket nut requires additional tightening, do not exceed 150 ft.-lb. (203 N•m). Do not loosen the drive sprocket nut to align the screw hole.

   b. Apply Loctite 242 (blue) to the drive sprocket lockscrew threads. Then install the lockscrew into the correct sprocket hole so that it rests against the nut flat (**Figure 39**) and tighten to the torque specification in **Table 9**.
12B. On 1992-on models, perform the following:
   a. Install the lockplate over the nut. Then position the lockplate so that 2 of the 4 lockplate holes (diagonally opposite) align with the sprocket's 2 tapped screw holes; see **Figure 44**. If the lockplate doesn't align with the screw holes, tighten the nut until 2 holes align.

CAUTION
If the drive sprocket nut requires additional tightening, do not exceed 150 ft.-lb. (203 N•m). Do not loosen the drive sprocket nut to align screw holes.

   b. Apply Loctite 242 (blue) to the 2 drive sprocket lockscrew threads. Then install the lockscrews

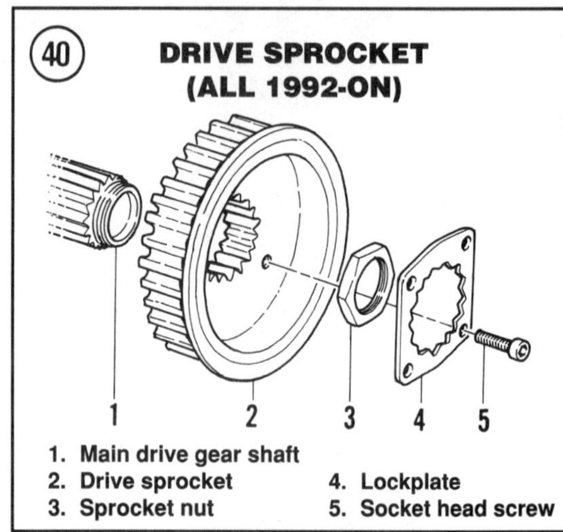

into the 2 tapped holes. Tighten the lockscrews to the torque specification in **Table 9**.

13. Reverse Steps 1-4 to complete assembly. Tighten the drive sprocket cover and rear master cylinder screws to the torque specifications in **Table 9**.

14. If you loosened the rear master cylinder pushrod locknut, adjust the rear brake as described in Chapter Three.

WARNING
Check that the rear brake is operating properly before riding the bike.

43

44

45

15. Adjust the drive belt as described in Chapter Three.

Driven Sprocket Removal/Installation

The driven sprocket (rear) is bolted to the rear wheel (**Figure 45**).

1. Remove the rear wheel as described in this chapter.
2. Remove the bolts and nuts securing the sprocket to the hub and remove the sprocket.
3. Replace worn or damaged sprocket fasteners as required.
4. Installation is the reverse of these steps, plus the following:
   a. Apply Loctite 262 (red) to the sprocket bolts prior to installation.
   b. Tighten the sprocket nuts and bolts to the torque specification in **Table 9**.

LACED WHEELS

Laced or wire wheels consist of a rim, spokes and nipples and a hub (containing the bearings and axle spacer). The spokes are inserted through the hub and attached to the rim in a specific crossover pattern. Spoke nipples secure the spokes to the rim. A rubber rim strip is inserted into the rim well.

Loose or improperly tightened spokes can cause handling problems, hub damage and overall handling problems. Both wheels should be checked for looseness, missing or damaged spokes, rim damage, runout and balance at the maintenance intervals listed in Chapter Three. Wheel bearing service is described under front or rear hub service in this chapter.

Inspection and Replacement

1. To inspect the wheels, the wheel should be raised off of the ground so that it can spin freely. If you have access to a wheel truing stand, remove the wheel and mount it securely on the stand. If you do not have a stand, you can raise the front or rear of the bike off the ground and spin the wheel to access all areas on the wheel for complete inspection.

NOTE
Wheel truing stands are expensive, but if you plan on servicing your Harley's wheels, you should either invest in a good truing stand or fabricate one. Another route you can take is to purchase a discarded swing arm from a motorcycle wrecking yard. The swing arm can be clamped securely in a vise and the wheel placed into position on the swing arm for servicing. When choosing a swing arm to be used as a truing stand, check the size of the swing arm to make sure that both of your Harley's wheels can fit into it with enough clearance for checking runout; measure the inside swing arm distance on your bike as a starting point. The rear wheel will be the wider of the two, though you may have to remove the tire from the front wheel for the wheel to fit into the swing arm.

2. Check the rim for dents, cracks or other damage. Severe rim damaged is easily detected, though most small dents are discovered while the rim is spinning on a stand.
3. Check the hub for cracks or damage. Check closely where the spokes seat into the hub.
4. Check for bent, loose or broken spokes. Damaged spokes should be replaced as soon as they are detected, as they can destroy the hub. Replace a damaged spoke as follows:

CAUTION
When replacing a broken spoke, do ***not*** *bend the new spoke when installing it. If you cannot install a new spoke without bending it, you will have to loosen all of the spokes and then remove some of the spokes to provide clearance to install the new spoke. Because Harley wheels are laced to a specific offset dimension, wheel disassembly and truing should be referred to a Harley-Davidson dealer or independent Harley repair shop.*

a. Remove the brake disc or rear sprocket as required.
b. Unscrew the nipple from the spoke and depress the nipple into the rim far enough to free the end of the spoke; take care not to push the nipple all the way in. Remove the damaged spoke from the hub and use it to match a new spoke of identical length.

NOTE
Replacement spokes are generally sold through Harley-Davidson dealers in complete sets only, though you may find a dealer who stocks individual spokes, removed from damaged or discarded wheels, for sale in small quantities. If you purchase spokes in this manner, compare the replacement spoke with the corresponding spoke on the wheel. Spokes differ in length, size, head angle and length of spoke throat. Compare these differences closely.

c. If necessary, trim the new spoke to match the original and dress the end of the thread with a thread die. Install the new spoke in the hub and screw on the nipple; tighten it until the spoke's tone is similar to the tone of the other spokes in the wheel. After installing the spoke, seat its head into the hub as described in this chapter. Periodically check the new spoke; it will stretch and must be retightened several times before it takes a final set.

NOTE
If a replacement spoke requires more than 2 turns to tighten it properly, the end of the spoke may protrude through the end of the nipple and puncture the tube. If necessary, remove the spoke and grind the end to a suitable length. To make sure that the spoke is not too long, remove the tube from the tire and check the end of the spoke.

5. Spokes loosen with use and should be checked periodically. Check spoke tightness with a spoke wrench.

Spoke Adjustment

This section describes minor spoke adjustment. If a few spokes are loose, you can tighten the spokes with a spoke wrench. If there are many spokes loose, truing will also be required. Wheels in which a large number of spokes were replaced or if the wheel is severely out of true should be serviced by a qualified Harley-Davidson mechanic as Harley wheels are laced to a specific offset dimension.

One way to check rim runout is to mount a dial indicator on the front fork or swing arm so that it bears against the rim.

If you don't have a dial indicator, improvise one as shown in **Figure 46**. Adjust the position of the bolt until it just clears the rim. Rotate the rim and note whether the clearance increases or decreases. Mark the tire with chalk or light crayon at areas that produce significantly large or small clearances. Clearance must not change by more than 1/32 in. (0.8 mm).

To pull the rim out, tighten spokes which terminate on the same side of the hub and loosen spokes which terminate on the opposite side of the hub (**Figure 47**). In most cases, only a slight amount of adjustment is necessary to true a rim. After adjustment, rotate the rim and make sure another area has not been pulled out of true. Continue adjustment and checking until runout is less than 1/32 in. (0.8 mm).

CAUTION
Overtightening the spokes can cause spoke and nipple damage.

Seating Spokes

When spokes loosen or when installing new spokes, the head of the spoke should be checked for proper seating in the hub. If it is not seated correctly, it can loosen further and may cause severe damage to the hub. If one or more spokes require reseating, hit the head of the spoke with a punch. True the wheel as described under *Spoke Adjustment* in this chapter.

Rim Replacement

If the rim becomes bent or damaged, it should be replaced. A bent or dented rim can cause serious handling problems. If the spokes are not bent or damaged also, they may be reused. Refer all service to a Harley-Davidson dealer or qualified Harley mechanic.

CAST WHEELS

The stock cast wheels (**Figure 45**) consist of a single assembly equipped with bearings, oil seals and a hub spacer.

While these wheels are virtually maintenance free, they should be checked for damage at the maintenance intervals listed in Chapter Three. Wheel bearing service is described under front and rear hub service in this chapter.

Inspection and Replacement

1. Remove the wheel and mount it on a wheel truing stand.

9

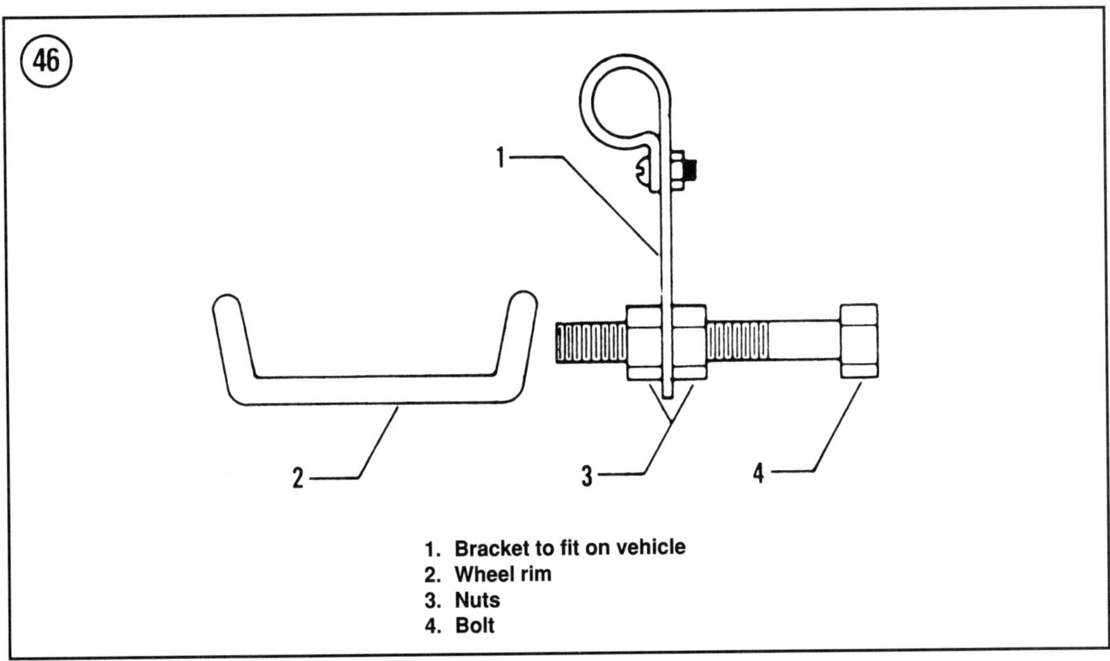

1. Bracket to fit on vehicle
2. Wheel rim
3. Nuts
4. Bolt

2. Mount a dial indicator or pointer near the rim bead as shown in **Figure 46**. Spin the wheel and measure lateral and radial runout. The maximum lateral and radial runout dimension is listed in **Table 1** and **Table 4**. If the runout exceeds this dimension, check the wheel bearings as described in this chapter.

3. If the wheels bearings are okay, the wheel will have to be replaced as the wheel cannot be serviced. Inspect the wheel for signs of cracks, fractures, dents or bends. If it is damaged in any way, it must be replaced.

WARNING
Do not try to repair any damage to a cast or disc wheel as it will result in an unsafe riding condition.

WHEEL BALANCE

An unbalanced wheel results in unsafe riding conditions. Depending on the degree of unbalance and the speed of the motorcycle, the rider may experience anything from a mild vibration to a violent shimmy which may result in loss of control.

Before you attempt to balance the wheel, check to be sure that the wheel bearings are in good condition and properly lubricated and that the brakes do not drag. The wheel must rotate freely.

On alloy wheels, weights are attached to the flat surface on the rim (**Figure 48**). On laced wheels, the weights are attached to the spoke nipples (**Figure 49**).

This procedure describes static wheel balancing using a truing or wheel balancing stand. If you do much high-speed or touring riding, you may want to have the wheels machine balanced by a Harley-Davidson dealer.

Before attempting to balance the wheels, check to be sure that the wheel bearings are in good condition and properly lubricated. The wheel must rotate freely.

1. Remove the wheel to be balanced.

2. Mount the wheel on a fixture such as the one in **Figure 50** so it can rotate freely.

3. Give the wheel a spin and let it coast to a stop. Mark the tire at the lowest point.

4. Spin the wheel several more times. If the wheel keeps coming to rest at the same point, it is out of balance.

5. Tape a test weight to the upper (or light) side of the wheel.

6. Experiment with different weights until the wheel, when spun, comes to rest at a different position each time.

7. Remove the test weight and install the correct size weight.

8. When applying weights to cast wheels, note the following:

a. Weights are attached to the flat surface on the rim (**Figure 48**). Clean the rim to remove all road residue before installing the weights; otherwise, the weights may fall off.

b. Weights should be added in 1/4 oz. (5 g) increments. If 1 oz. (10 g) or more must be added to one location on the wheel, apply half the amount to each side of the rim.

c. Harley-Davidson recommends that the wheel should not be used for 48 hours after installing weights to allow the weight adhesive to cure properly.

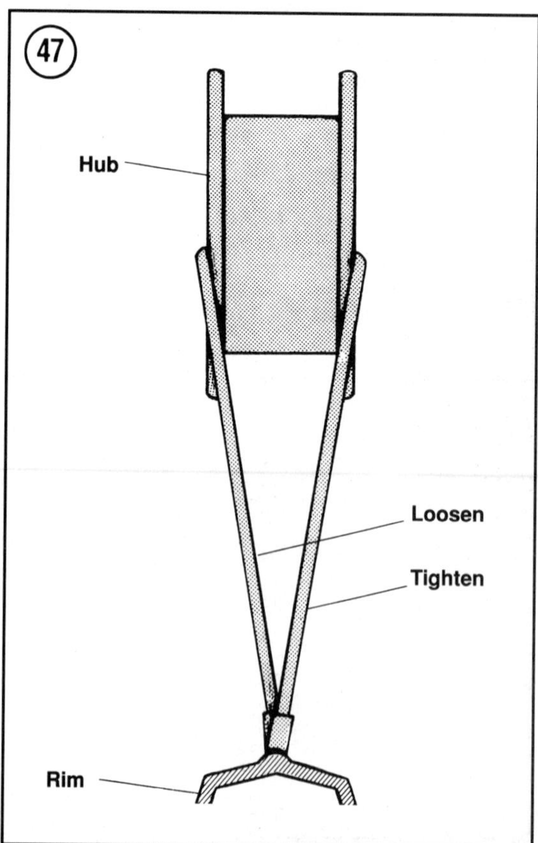

TIRES

Proper tire service includes frequent inflation checks and adjustment as well as tire inspection, removal, repair and installation practices. By maintaining a routine tire maintenance schedule, tire damage or other abnormal conditions can be detected and repaired before they affect the operation and handling of your motorcycle. Refer to Chapter Three for general tire inspection and inflation procedures.

Refer to **Table 10** and **Table 11** for stock tire and rim specifications.

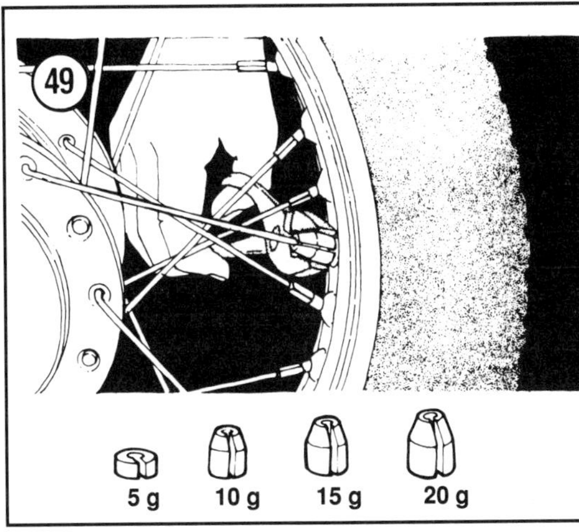

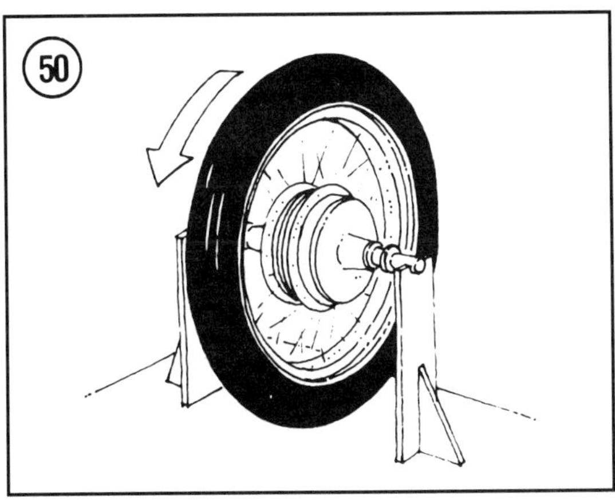

Inspection

Visually inspect the tires for tread wear, cracks, cuts, aging and other damage. Check the tire for areas where the tread has broken or torn out. Stones imbedded between the tread rows can be carefully pried out with a suitable tool. Check the tread closely for secondary damage after removing the stone or other foreign objects. Uneven tread wear can be caused by improper inflation pressure, vehicle overloading or an unbalanced tire.

Run your hand along the sidewall and check for bulges or knots. If a bulge is noted, mark the area with chalk and then remove the tire from the rim; check the inside and outside of the tire carefully, looking for broken or separated plies. This type of damage can cause the tire to blow out. Likewise, if a tire is damaged on the outside, the tire should be removed from the rim and the inside checked carefully for broken or separated plies or other damage.

WARNING

If you suspect tire damage, the tire should be removed from the rim and examined closely inside and out. Tires exhibiting bulges or other questionable damage should be inspected by a motorcycle technician before the tire is put back into use. A damaged or deformed tire can fail and cause loss of control and personal injury.

Service Notes

Before changing tires, note the following:

1. Tire changing should only be undertaken when you have access to the proper tools:
   a. At least 2 motorcycle tire irons.
   b. Rim protectors (part No. HD-01289 or equivalent) or scrap pieces of leather.
   c. A bead breaker will be required when breaking tires from cast wheels and may be required on laced wheels.
   d. Accurate tire gauge.

9

e. Water and liquid soap solution or a special tire mounting lubricant.

f. Talcum power for tube tires.

2. The stock cast wheel is aluminum and the exterior appearance can easily be damaged. Special care must be taken with tire irons when changing a tire to avoid scratches and gouges to the outer rim surface. Insert scraps of leather between the tire iron and the rim to protect the rim from damage.

3. When removing a tubeless tire, take care not to damage the tire beads, inner liner of the tire or the wheel rim flange. Use tire levers or flat handled tire irons with rounded ends—do not use screwdrivers or similar tools to remove tires.

Removal

NOTE

If you do not have access to a motorcycle tire changer, you will probably be servicing the tire with the wheel placed on the ground. To avoid scratching or damaging the brake disc or wheel, place the wheel on a piece of plywood or other soft surface. If you do a lot of tire changing, you may want to construct a small wooden frame that, along with getting the wheel off the ground, will make it easier to work on the tire during changing.

1. Remove the wheel from the motorcycle and place it on a suitable stand or surface.

2. Place a chalk mark on the tire aligning the tire with the valve stem (**Figure 51**). This helps to maintain tire and wheel balance during reassembly.

3. Remove the valve cap and unscrew the valve core to deflate the tire or tube. Block the valve core with your hand or the core removal tool to keep it from flying out. Remove the valve core and store it with the valve cap.

4. Press the entire bead on both sides of the tire into the center of the rim. If the bead is tight, a bead breaker (**Figure 52**) will be required.

CAUTION

*Do **not** attempt to insert the tire irons between the tire bead and rim flange to break the bead. This can permanently damage both the tire and rim.*

5. Lubricate the beads with a tire lubricant or soapy water.

6. Place rim protectors (**Figure 53**) along the rim near the valve stem and insert the tire iron under the bead next to the valve, making sure the tire iron contacts the rim protector and not the rim. Step on the side of the tire opposite the valve stem with your knee and pry the bead over the rim with the tire iron.

CAUTION

Do not use excessive force when prying the tire over the rim or you may stretch or break the bead wires in the tire.

7. Insert a second tire iron next to the first to hold the bead over the rim. Then work around the tire with

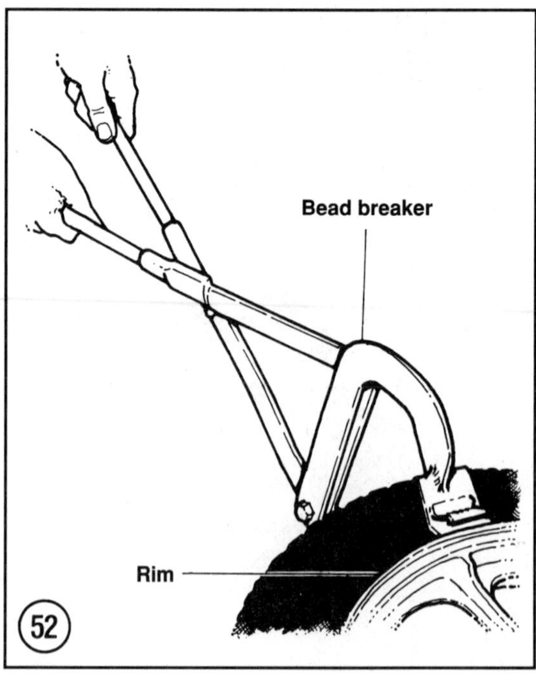

the first tool prying the bead over the rim (**Figure 54**). On tube-type tires, be careful not to pinch the inner tube with the tools.

8. On tube-type tires, use your thumb and push the valve from its hole in the rim to the inside of the tire. Carefully pull the tube out of the tire and lay it aside.

NOTE
Step 9 is required only if it is necessary to remove the tire from the rim completely, such as for tire replacement or tubeless tire repair.

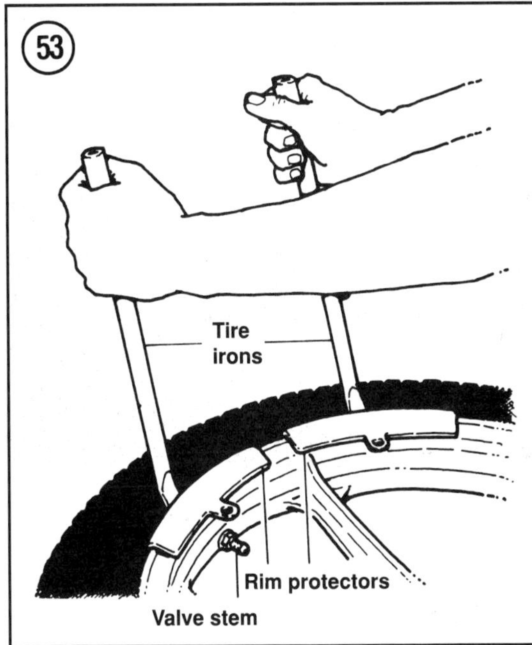

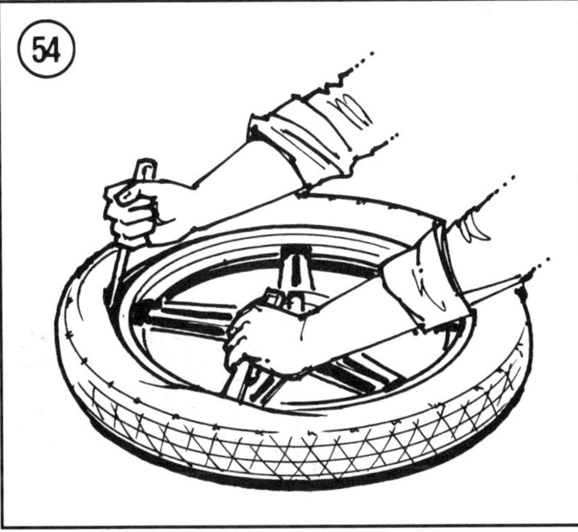

9A. *Tube-type tires*: Stand the wheel upright. Insert a tire tool between the second bead and the same side of the rim that the first bead was pried over. Force the bead on the opposite side from the tool into the center of the rim. Pry the second bead off the rim, working around the wheel with 2 tire irons as with the first. Remove the rim band.

9B. *Tubeless tires*: The second bead can generally be removed from the rim without having to use tire irons. Relubricate the second bead thoroughly and stand the wheel upright. Grasp the wheel at the top with one hand to steady it and then lift and pull the second bead over the top of the rim at the top of the wheel and remove the tire.

Inspection

1. *Tubeless tires*: All disc wheels use a bolt-in type valve stem. Inspect the rubber grommet (**Figure 55**) where the valve stem seats against the inner surface of the wheel. If it's starting to deteriorate or has lost its resiliency replace the valve stem as this is a common location of air loss. To replace the valve stem:
   a. Loosen and remove the 2 valve stem nuts.
   b. Remove the valve stem from the wheel, together with its washer and rubber grommet.
   c. Remove all rubber residue from the wheel left by the previous rubber grommet.

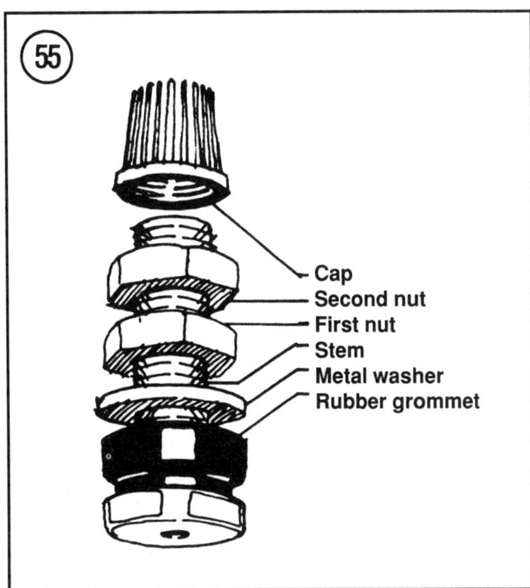

9

d. Before installing the new valve stem, remove the valve cap, 2 nuts and washer from the stem.
e. Slide the rubber grommet down onto the valve stem so that the shoulder on the grommet seats into the valve stem head recess.
f. Insert the valve stem into the rim and hold it in position, making sure the rubber grommet seats against the wheel. Then slide the washer onto the valve stem so that the side of the washer with the raised center faces away from the rim.
g. Install the first valve stem nut and tighten to 20-25 in.-lbs. (2.3-2.8 N•m).
h. Hold the first valve stem nut with a wrench, then install and tighten the second nut to 40-60 in.-lbs. (4.6-6.9 N•m).

NOTE
Because of weight and design configurations, valve stems should be replaced with O.E.M. Harley-Davidson valve stems.

2. Clean the rim thoroughly to remove all dust and dirt residue. Use steel wool, a stiff wire brush or sandpaper to remove rust from wire wheels.

CAUTION
Work carefully when removing burrs or other rough spots from the rim flange on disc wheels; otherwise, you may damage the air-sealing surfaces, requiring replacement of the wheel.

3. Mount the wheel on a truing stand (if available) and check the rim-to-tire mating surface for dents, burrs or other rough spots. Emery cloth can be used to remove burrs on disc wheels. A file or sandpaper can be used to remove burrs on wire wheels.
4. Check the wheel for dents or other damage. If the wheel has been dented by an accident or from running into a curb or other hard object, it should be replaced. On wire wheels, the rim can be replaced by a qualified mechanic. On cast wheels, the entire wheel assembly must be replaced.

WARNING
Never operate your motorcycle with a bent wheel that has been straightened. The wheel may fail while under use and cause you to lose control.

5. Check wheel runout as described in this chapter. Check for protruding spokes on spoke wheels.

6. If you have access to compressed air, blow out the inside of the tire casing to remove all dust and dirt. Run your hand along the tire casing and check for small nails, cracks or other damage.

7. If a tire has been punctured, refer to *Tire Repairs* in this chapter.

8. *Tube-type tires*: Inspect the rim band for tearing or excessive wear. Replace the rim band if necessary. Install the valve core into the tube and then fill the tube with air. Check the tube for leaks. If the tube holds air, check the base of the valve stem for tearing or other signs of wear that may cause the tube to fail later. If the tube is damaged, replace it. Do not attempt to repair a tube unless you are in an emergency situation (i.e., you find yourself in the middle of Death Valley, a flat tire, no spare tube and vultures circling overhead). If you patch a tube, replace it with a new tube as soon as possible. Refer to *Tube Repairs* in this chapter.

Installation

1. A new tire may have balancing rubbers inside. These are not patches and should not be disturbed. A colored spot near the bead indicates a lighter point on the tire. This spot should be placed next to the valve stem (**Figure 51**).

2. Install the rim band over the wheel (wire wheels) and align the hole in the rim band with the hole in the rim. If you replaced the rim band, make sure it is the correct diameter and width for your wheel.

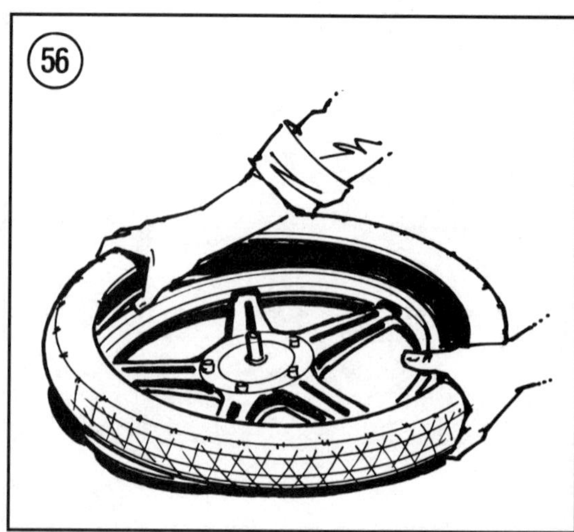

3. Align the tire with the rim so that the directional arrows molded in the tire's side wall face in the normal rotation position.

NOTE

On some tires, the rotation arrow may have to be reversed, depending on whether the tire is mounted on the front or rear wheel. Follow the directions on the tire side wall or with the tire manufacturer's instructions.

4. Lubricate both beads of the tire with soapy water.
5. With the tire properly aligned with the wheel, press the first bead over the rim, working around the tire in both directions with your hands only (**Figure 56**). If necessary, use a tire iron (with rim protectors) for the last few inches of bead (**Figure 57**).

NOTE

Dust the tube with talcum powder before installing it in the tire. The talcum powder will prevent the tube from sticking to the tire.

6. On tube-type tires, inflate the tube just enough to round it out. Too much air will make installation difficult. Wipe the outside of the tube with talcum powder to help reduce friction between the tire and tube during operation. Place the tube on top of the tire, aligning the valve stem with the matching hole in the rim. Then insert the tube into the tire. Lift the upper tire bead away from the rim with your hand and insert the tube's valve stem through the rim hole. Check the tube to make sure that the valve stem is straight up (90°), not cocked to one side. If necessary, reposition the tube in the tire. If the valve stem wants to slide out of the hole and back into the tire, install the valve stem nut at the top of the valve; do not tighten the nut yet.

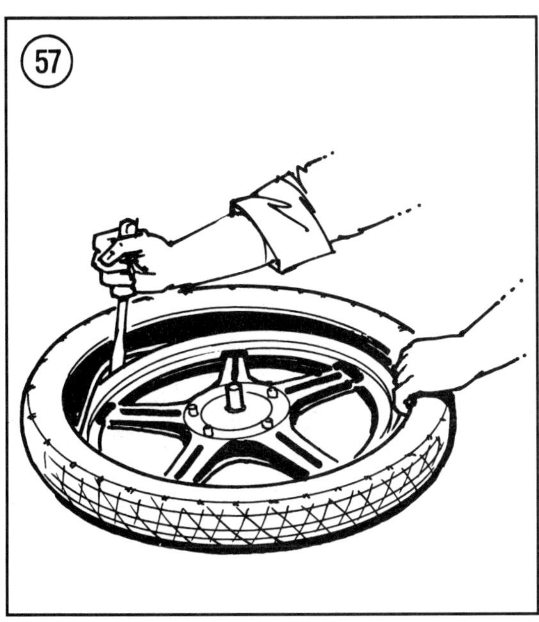

7. Relubricate the upper bead with soapy water if necessary.
8. Starting 180° away from the valve stem, press the upper bead into the rim. Using tire tools and rim protectors, work around the rim to the valve. On tube-type tires, the last few inches will offer you the most difficulty and the greatest chance of pinching the tube. Work the tire tools carefully to avoid pinching the tube.
9. On tube-type tires, the valve stem should be straight up (90°). After aligning the tube with the rim, check that the tube was not forced outward so that it rests between the tire bead and the rim. If so, push the tube back into the tire; otherwise, the rim will pinch the tube when the tube is filled with air.
10. Check the bead on both sides of the tire for an even fit around the rim.
11. Relubricate both tire beads.

WARNING

When seating the tire beads in Step 12, never inflate the tire beyond the tire manufacturer's maximum pressure specification listed on the tire's side wall. Exceeding this pressure could cause the tire or rim to burst, causing severe personal injury. If the beads fail to seat properly, deflate the tire and relubricate the beads. Never stand directly over a tire while inflating it.

12A. *Tube-type tires*: Inflate the tube to its maximum tire pressure to seat the beads in the rim. If the beads do not seat properly, release all air pressure from the tire and relubricate the tire beads. The tire is properly seated when the wheel rim and tire side wall lines are parallel (**Figure 58**). When the tire has seated properly on both sides, remove the valve core to deflate the tube; this allows the tube to straighten out, then reinstall the valve core and inflate the tire to pressure reading listed in Chapter Three. Tighten the valve stem nuts and screw on the valve cap.

12B. *Tubeless tires*: Place an inflatable band around the circumference of the tire. Slowly inflate the band

9

until the tire beads are pressed against the rim. Inflate the tire enough to seat it, deflate the band and remove it. The tire is properly seated when the wheel rim and tire side wall lines are parallel (**Figure 58**). Inflate the tire to the pressure reading listed in Chapter Three. Screw on the valve cap.

13. Check tire runout as described in this chapter.
14. Balance the wheel assembly as described in this chapter.

Tire Runout

The tires should be checked for excessive lateral and radial runout after wheel mounting or if the motorcycle developed a wobble that cannot be traced to another component. The wheels should be mounted on their axles when making the following checks.

1. *Lateral runout*: This procedure will check the tire for excessive side-to-side play. Perform the following:
   a. Position a fixed pointer next to the tire side wall as shown in **Figure 59**. The pointer tip should be located so that it is not directly in line with the molded tire logo or any other raised surfaces.
   b. Rotate the tire and measure the amount of lateral runout.
   c. The lateral runout should not exceed 0.080 in. (2.03 mm). If runout is excessive, remove the tire from the wheel and recheck the wheel's lateral runout as described in this chapter. If the runout is excessive, the wheel must be trued (laced wheels) or replaced (cast wheels). If wheel runout is correct, the tire runout is excessive and the tire must be replaced.
2. *Radial runout*: This procedure will check the tire for excessive up-and-down play. Perform the following:
   a. Position a fixed pointer at the center bottom of the tire tread as shown in **Figure 60**.
   b. Rotate the tire and measure the amount of radial runout.
   c. The radial runout should not exceed 0.090 in. (2.29 mm). If runout is excessive, remove the tire from the wheel and recheck the wheel's radial runout as described in this chapter. If the runout is excessive, the wheel must be trued (laced wheels) or replaced (cast wheels). If wheel runout is correct, the tire runout is excessive and the tire must be replaced.

TIRE REPAIRS (TUBE-TYPE TIRES)

Every rider will eventually experience trouble with a tire or tube. Repairs and replacement are fairly simple and every rider should know the techniques.

Patching a motorcycle tube is only a temporary fix. A motorcycle tire flexes too much and the patch

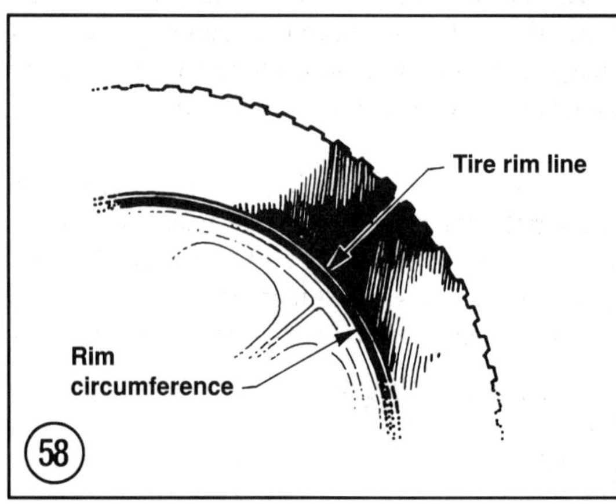

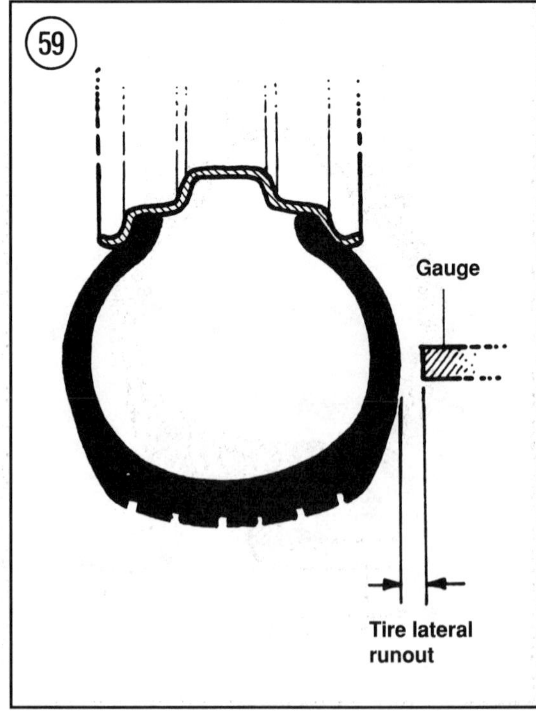

could rub right off. However, a patched tube should get you far enough to buy a new tube.

Tube Repair Kits

The repair kits can be purchased from motorcycle dealers and some auto supply stores. When buying, specify that the kit you want is for motorcycles.

There are 2 types of tube repair kits:

a. Hot patch.

b. Cold patch.

Hot patches are stronger because they actually vulcanize to the tube, becoming part of it. However, they are far too bulky to carry for roadside repairs and the strength is unnecessary for a temporary repair.

Cold patches are not vulcanized to the tube; they are simply glued to it. Though not as strong as hot patches, cold patches are still very durable. Cold patch kits are less bulky than hot and more easily applied under adverse conditions. A cold patch kit contains everything necessary and tucks easily in with your emergency tool kit.

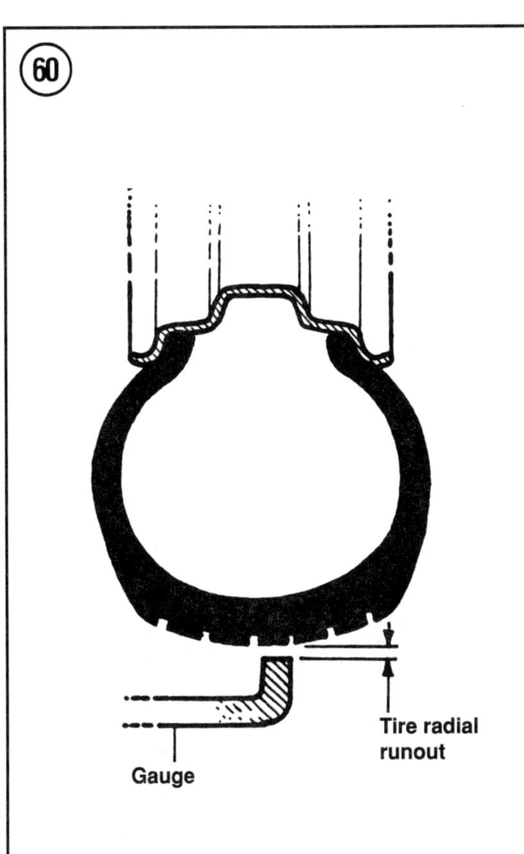

Tube Inspection

1. Remove the inner tube as described in this chapter.
2. Install the valve core into the valve stem and inflate the tube slightly. Do not overinflate.
3. Immerse the tube in water a section at a time. Look carefully for bubbles indicating a hole. Mark each hole and continue checking until you are certain that all holes are discovered and marked. Also make sure that the valve core is not leaking; tighten it if necessary.

NOTE
If you do not have enough water to immerse sections of the tube, try running your hand over the tube slowly and very close to the surface. If your hand is damp, it works even better. If you suspect a hole anywhere, apply some water to the area to verify it.

4. Apply a cold patch according to the manufacturer's instructions.
5. Dust the patch area with talcum powder to prevent it from sticking to the tire.
6. Carefully check the inside of the tire casing for small rocks or sand which may have damaged the tube. If the inside of the tire is split, apply a patch to the area to prevent it from pinching and damaging the tube again.
7. Check the inside of the rim.
8. Deflate the tube prior to installation in the tire.

9

TIRE REPAIRS (TUBELESS TYPE)

Patching a tubeless tire on the road is very difficult. If both beads are still in place against the rim, a can of pressurized tire sealant may inflate the tire and seal the hole. The beads must be against the wheel for this method to work. Because an incorrectly patched tire might blow out and cause an accident, note the following:

a. Due to the variations of material supplied with different tubeless tire repair kits, follow the instructions and recommendations supplied with the repair kit.

b. The tire industry recommends that tubeless tires be patched from the inside. Therefore, do not patch the tire with an external type plug. If you find an external patch on a tire, it is recommended that it be patch-reinforced from the inside or discarded.

c. Do not patch tires which have less than 1/16 in. (1.6 mm) of tread left.

d. Do not patch a tire in which the puncture hole is larger than 1/4 in. (6.35 mm).

e. Patches should only be applied to puncture holes in the tread area. Do not apply patches to holes in the tire's side wall.

f. When in doubt about whether or not to patch a tire, seek advice from a motorcycle technician.

Table 1 FRONT WHEEL SERVICE SPECIFICATIONS

	in.	mm
Front wheel bearing end play (allowable range)		
Early 1991*	0.004-0.018	0.10-0.45
Late 1991-on*	0.002-0.006	0.05-0.15
Wheel runout		
Laced wheels		
Lateral and radial	0.031	0.79
Cast wheels		
Lateral	0.040	1.02
Radial	0.030	0.76

* See text for early and late model identification.

Table 2 FRONT WHEEL BEARING SPACER SLEEVES (EARLY 1991)

Harley-Davidson part number	Length in. (mm)	Color code
43623-78	2.564 (65.12)	Violet
43624-78	2.550 (64.77)	Pink
43625-78	2.536 (64.41)	Gold

Table 3 FRONT WHEEL BEARING SPACER SHIMS (LATE 1991-ON)

Harley-Davidson part number	Length in. (mm)
43290-82	0.030-0.033 (0.76-0.84)
43291-82	0.015-0.017 (0.38-0.43)
43292-82	0.0075-0.0085 (0.190-0.215)
43293-82	0.0035-0.0045 (0.088-0.114)
43294-82	0.0015-0.0025 (0.038-0.063)

Table 4 REAR SUSPENSION SERVICE SPECIFICATIONS

	in.	mm
Rear wheel bearing end play (allowable range)		
Early 1991*	0.004-0.018	0.10-0.45
Late 1991-on*	0.002-0.006	0.05-0.15
Wheel runout		
Laced wheels		
Lateral and radial	0.031	0.79
Cast wheels		
Lateral	0.040	1.02
Radial	0.030	0.76

* See text for early and late model identification.

Table 5 REAR WHEEL SPACER SLEEVES–CAST REAR WHEEL (EARLY 1991)

Harley-Davidson part number	Length in. (mm)	Color code
43604-78	4.420 (112.26)	Orange
43605-78	4.434 (112.62)	Yellow
43606-78	4.448 (112.97)	White

Table 6 REAR WHEEL SPACER SLEEVES—LACED REAR WHEEL (EARLY 1991)

Harley-Davidson part number	Length in. (mm)	Color code
43601-78A	4.420 (112.26)	Orange
43602-78A	4.434 (112.62)	Yellow
43603-78A	4.448 (112.97)	White

Table 7 REAR WHEEL BEARING SPACER SHIMS (LATE 1991-ON)

Harley-Davidson part number	Length in. (mm)
43290-82	0.030-0.033 (0.76-0.84)
43291-82	0.015-0.017 (0.38-0.43)
43292-82	0.0075-0.0085 (0.190-0.215)
43293-82	0.0035-0.0045 (0.088-0.114)
43294-82	0.0015-0.0025 (0.038-0.063)

Table 8 FRONT SUSPENSION TIGHTENING TORQUES

	ft.-lb.	N·m
Front axle nut	50-55	68-75
Front axle pinch bolt and nut	21-27	28.5-36.6
Front brake caliper mounting bolts	25-30	34.5-41.4
Handlebar clamp bolts	12-15	16.3-20.3
Front fork		
Upper bracket pinch bolts	30-35	40.7-47.5
Lower bracket pinch bolts	30-35	40.7-47.5
Fork stem pinch bolt	30-35	40.7-47.5
Front fender fasteners	9-13	12.2-17.6
Hub plate Torx screws		
Cast wheels	16-24	22-23

Table 9 REAR SUSPENSION TIGHTENING TORQUES

	ft.-lb.	N•m
Rear axle nut	60-65	81-88
Swing arm pivot shaft bolt	50	68
Rear shock absorber fasteners		
Upper		
1991-1992	21-27	28.5-36.6
1993-on	21-35	28.5-47.5
Lower		
1991-1992	50-55	68-75
1993-on	30-50	40.7-68
Rear sprocket mounting bolts		
Laced wheels	45-55	61-75
Cast wheels		
1991	65-70	88-95
1992	45-55	61-75
1993-on	55-65	75-88
Drive sprocket nut		
Chain and belt drive	110-120	149-163
Drive sprocket nut lockscrew		
Chain drive	50-60 in.-lb.	5.7-6.8
Belt drive	7-9	9.5-12.2
Drive sprocket cover screws	90-110 in.-lb.	10.2-12.4
Master cylinder screws	155-190 in.-lb.	17.5-21.5

Table 10 TUBELESS TIRE SPECIFICATIONS

Front tire	
Type	Dunlop D401 Elite S/T
Size	100/90-19
Wheel size	19 in.
Rim size and contour	T19 x 2.5 MT
Valve stem hole diameter	0.45 in. (11.4 mm)
Rear tire	
Type	Dunlop D401 Elite S/T
Size	130/90-16
Wheel size	16 in.
Rim size and contour	T16 x 3.00 D
Valve stem hole diameter	0.45 in. (11.4 mm)

Table 11 TUBE TYPE TIRE SPECIFICATIONS

Front tire	
Type	Dunlop D401 Elite S/T
Size	100/90-19
Wheel size	19 in.
Rim size and contour	T19 x 2.5 TLA
Tube size	MJ90-19
Rear tire	
Type	Dunlop D401 Elite S/T
Size	130/90-16
Wheel size	16 in.
Rim size and contour	T16 x 3.00 D
Tube size	MJ90-16

CHAPTER TEN

FRONT SUSPENSION AND STEERING

This chapter covers the handlebar, steering head and front fork assemblies.

Tables 1-2 are at the end of the chapter.

HANDLEBAR

The handlebar is clamped to the upper triple clamp with a single cap. Rubber bushings are mounted between the handlebar holders and the upper triple clamp to help reduce vibration. The handlebar is knurled where it fits between the clamp and holders; this machining process is used to provide additional holding power to help prevent the handlebars from slipping (**Figure 1**).

Handlebars are an important part in the overall comfort and safety of your motorcycle. Inspect the handlebar at regular intervals for loose mounting bolts or damage. The controls, master cylinder and turn signals, mounted on the handlebar, should be checked frequently for loose or missing fasteners.

The handlebar should be replaced when bent or damaged. Never try to heat, bend or weld handlebars. These efforts will seriously weaken the bar and may cause it to break.

When replacing a handlebar, you can order an exact replacement through Harley-Davidson dealers, or you can order bars through an accessory manufacturer. When ordering accessory bars, you will have to know the handlebar's outside diameter, width, bar height and sweep (**Figure 2**). When changing handlebars, make sure the new bar has enough room to mount the controls, brake master cylinder, etc., without excessive crowding and that the controls feel comfortable when the front end is turned from side to side. In addition, if the new handlebar is higher, make sure the stock cables and switch wiring harnesses are long enough. If not, you will have to purchase longer cables and extend the wiring harnesses.

Removal

1. Place the bike on its jiffystand.
2. Unscrew and remove the mirrors.

NOTE
Make a drawing of the clutch and throttle cable routing before removing them.

3. Remove the bolts securing the master cylinder (A, **Figure 3**) and support it with a Bunjee cord. Do not disconnect the hydraulic brake line.

4. Loosen the throttle housing (B, **Figure 3**) screws so that the housing can slide off of the handlebar later in this procedure. It is not necessary to separate the housing halves.
5. Remove the left-hand switch housing (A, **Figure 4**) screws and separate the housing halves (**Figure 5**).
6. Remove the clutch lever clamp mounting screws (B, **Figure 4**) and separate the clamp halves.
7. Disconnect or remove any clamps securing electrical cables to the handlebar.
8. Loosen, then remove the 2 front handlebar holder bolts, spacers and washers (**Figure 1**). Note the following:
   a. Remove the 2 front locknuts on 1991-1992 models.
   b. Remove the 2 upper washers on 1993-on models.
   c. Set the speedometer aside so that it does not scratch or damage any component.
9. Remove the 2 rear holder bolts, then remove the holder (**Figure 6**) and handlebar.
10. Install by reversing these steps. Note the following.
11. Check the knurled rings on the handlebar for galling and bits of aluminum blocking up the rings. Clean the knurled section with a wire brush.
12. Check the handlebar for cracks, bends or other damage. Replace the handlebar if necessary. Do not attempt to repair it.
13. Clean the clamps and holders thoroughly of all residue before installing the handlebar.
14. After installing the handlebar, cap, bolts and nuts, reposition the handlebar while straddling the bike. Push it forward and backward to best suit your riding style. Make sure, before tightening the cap bolts, that the knurled sections at the base of the handlebar are aligned with the cap and holder.
15. Tighten the handlebar clamp bolts to the torque specification in **Table 1**.

FRONT FORKS

The front suspension consists of a spring-controlled, hydraulically dampened telescopic fork.

Before suspecting major trouble, drain the front fork oil and refill with the proper type and quantity; refer to Chapter Three. If you still have trouble, such as poor damping, a tendency to bottom or top out or leakage around the rubber seals, follow the service procedures in this section.

To simplify fork service and to prevent the mixing of parts, the legs should be removed, serviced and installed individually.

Removal

1. Support the bike so that the front wheel clears the ground. Double check to make sure that the bike is stable before removing the front wheel and forks.
2. Remove the front wheel as described in Chapter Nine.
3. Remove the front fender bolts and locknuts and remove the front fender.

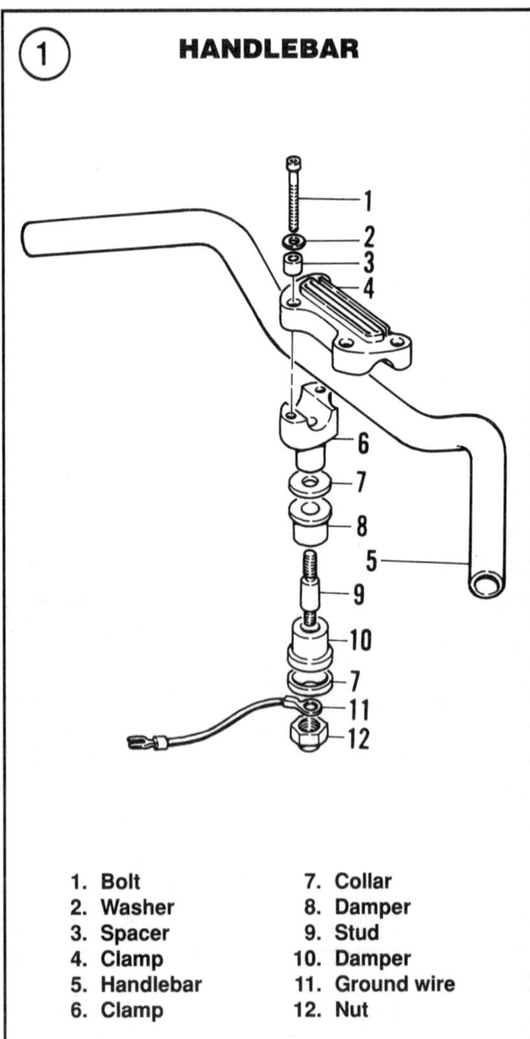

1. Bolt
2. Washer
3. Spacer
4. Clamp
5. Handlebar
6. Clamp
7. Collar
8. Damper
9. Stud
10. Damper
11. Ground wire
12. Nut

2

TYPICAL HANDLEBAR MEASUREMENT LOCATIONS

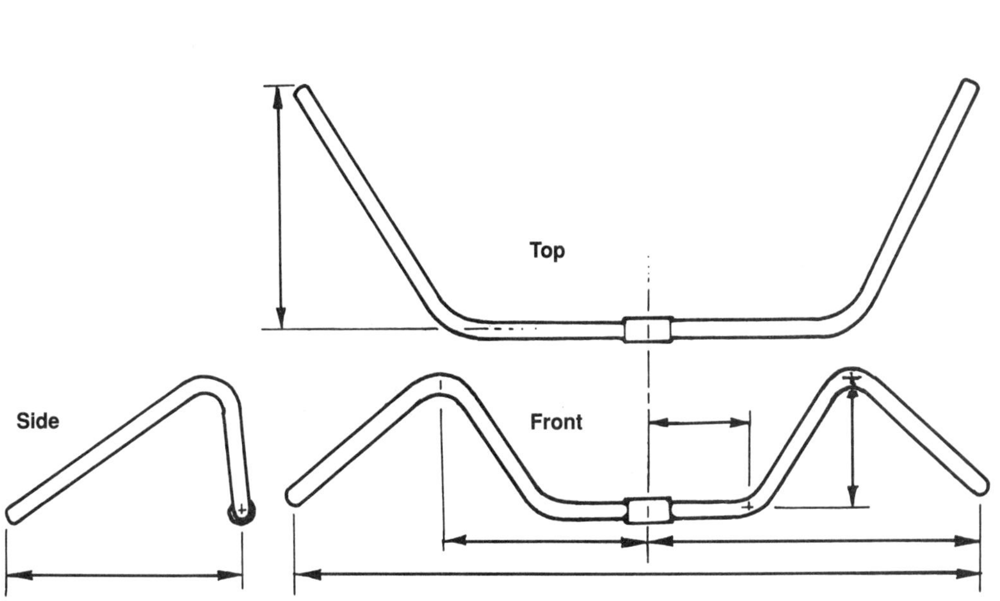

Top

Side

Front

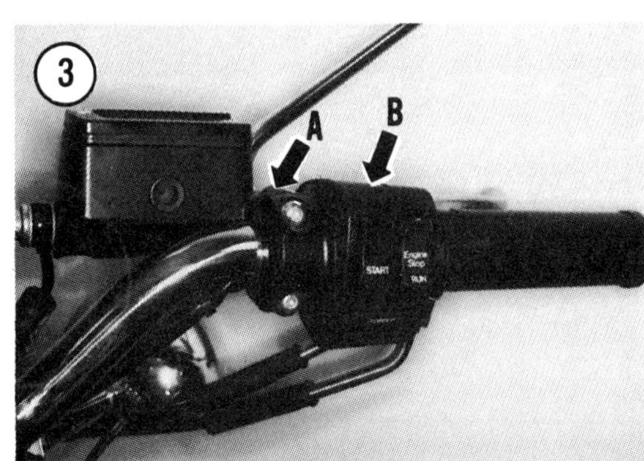

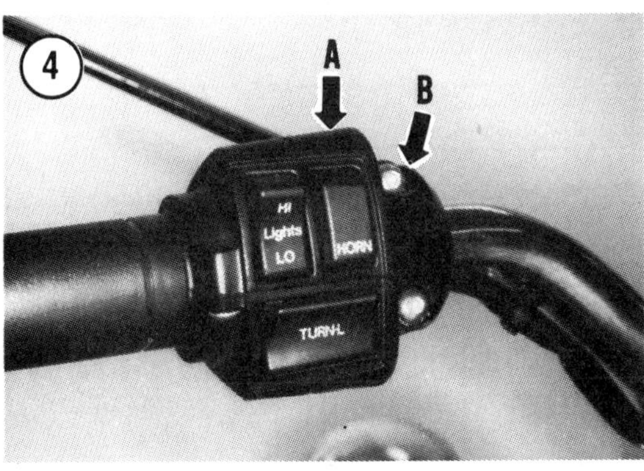

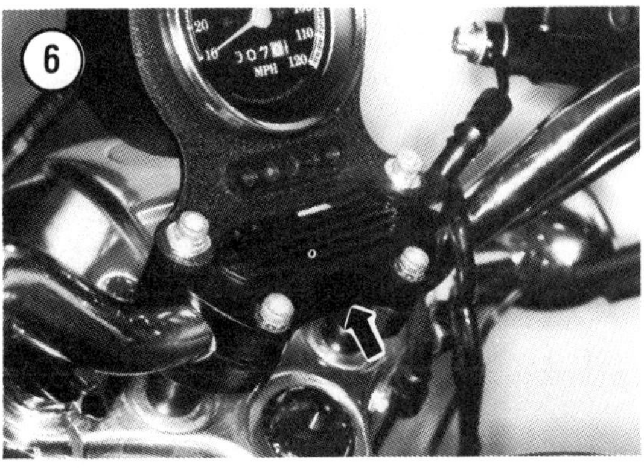

NOTE
Label the left- and right-hand fork tubes so they can be reinstalled in their original positions.

4. Loosen the upper fork bracket pinch bolt (A, **Figure 7**).
5. If you are going to disassemble the fork tubes, loosen but do not remove the fork cap (B, **Figure 7**).
6. Loosen the lower fork bracket pinch bolt (**Figure 8**) and slide the fork tube out of the fork brackets. If necessary, rotate the fork tube while removing it.
7. If fork service is required, refer to *Disassembly* in this chapter.

Installation

1. Clean off any corrosion or dirt on the upper and lower fork bracket receptacles.

NOTE
The fork assemblies must be reinstalled on the correct side of the bike so the brake caliper and front fender can be properly installed. If the fork assemblies are installed on the wrong side, the bolt holes on these components will not line up properly.

2. Install each fork tube so that the tube extends 0.42-0.50 in. (10.7-12.7 mm) above the upper fork bracket as shown in **Figure 9**.
3. Tighten the lower bracket pinch bolt (**Figure 8**) to the torque specification in **Table 1**.
4. If loose, tighten the fork cap (B, **Figure 7**) securely.
5. Tighten the upper bracket pinch bolt (A, **Figure 7**) to the torque specification in **Table 1**.
6. Install the front fender and its mounting bolts and locknuts. Tighten front fender fasteners to the torque specification in **Table 1**.
7. Install the front wheel as described in Chapter Nine.
8. Apply the front brake and pump the front forks several times to seat the forks and front wheel.

Disassembly/Reassembly

To simplify fork service and to prevent the mixing of parts, the legs should be disassembled and assembled individually.

Refer to **Figure 10** for this procedure.

1. Using the front axle boss at the bottom of the fork tube, clamp the slider in a vise with soft jaws. Do *not* clamp the slider at any point above the fork axle boss in a vise.

NOTE
Loosen the bottom Allen bolt before removing the fork cap and spring. Leaving

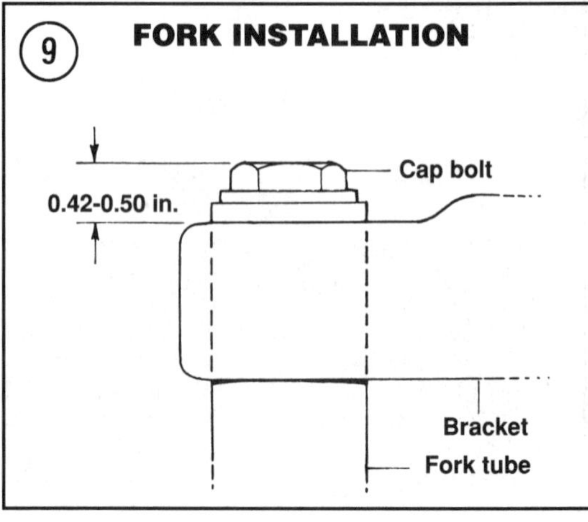

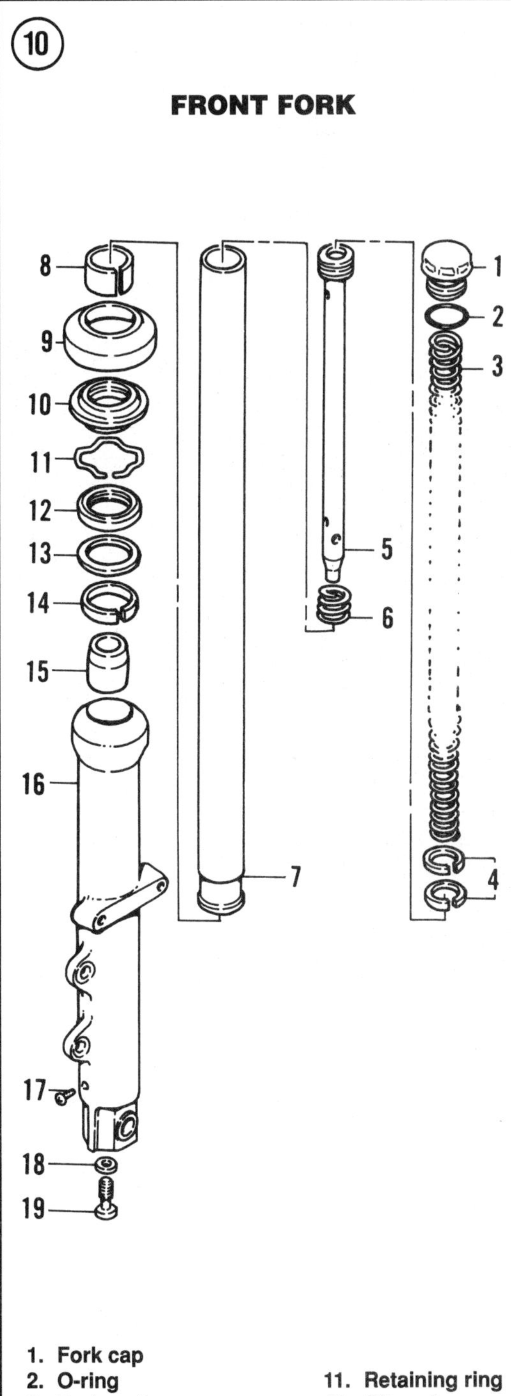

1. Fork cap
2. O-ring
3. Fork spring
4. Piston rings
5. Damper rod
6. Rebound spring
7. Fork tube
8. Fork tube bushing
9. Dust cover
10. Dust seal
11. Retaining ring
12. Oil seal
13. Spacer seal
14. Slider bushing
15. Oil lock piece
16. Slider
17. Drain screw
18. Washer
19. Allen bolt

the cap on provides spring tension against the damper rod. This prevents the damper rod from spinning when attempting to loosen the Allen bolt.

2. Loosen, but do not remove, the Allen bolt at the bottom of the slider.

WARNING
Keep your face away from the fork cap when removing it. The fork cap is under spring pressure and may fly off when loosening it. In addition, make sure the fork tube is fully extended from the slider. If the forks are damaged and stuck in a compressed state, the fork should be disassembled by a dealer or qualified mechanic, as the fork cap and spring will fly out from the fork tube under considerable force when the cap is removed.

3. Remove the fork cap from the top of the fork tube (**Figure 11**). Then pull the spring out of the fork tube.

4. Remove the fork tube from the vise and pour the oil into a drain pan. Pump the fork several times by hand to get most of the oil out. Check the oil for contamination, indicating worn or damaged parts. Discard the oil after examining it.

5. Insert a small flat-tipped screwdriver under the dust cover (9, **Figure 10**) and carefully pry the cover out of the slider and remove it. Be careful not to damage the slider surface. Remove the cover (9, **Figure 10**) from the slider, if so equipped.

6. Insert a small flat-tipped screwdriver under the dust seal and carefully pry the seal out of the slider and remove it (**Figure 12**). Be careful not to damage the slider surface.

7. Pry the retaining ring (**Figure 13**) out of the groove in the slider and remove it. See **Figure 14**.
8. Remove the Allen screw and washer (**Figure 15**) at the bottom of the slider.

NOTE
The slider bushing is installed with an interference fit. When separating the fork tube and slider, the slider bushing, spacer seal and oil seal will be removed at the same time.

9. Hold the fork tube in one hand and pull the slider downward repeatedly with your other hand, knocking the slider bushing against the fork tube bushing (**Figure 16**). As the slider bushing is knocked out of the slider, it will push the oil seal and seal spacer out of the slider. Continue until these components are pushed out of the slider.
10. Remove the oil lock piece (**Figure 17**) from the damper rod.
11. Remove the damper rod and small spring (**Figure 18**) from the fork tube.

Inspection

NOTE
*Handle the guide bushings (**Figure 19**) carefully when cleaning them in Step 1 to avoid scratching or removing any of their coating material. If there is any metal powder clinging to the guide bushings, clean them with clean fork oil and a nylon brush.*

1. Initially clean all of the fork components in solvent, first making sure the solvent will not damage the rubber parts. Then clean with soap and water and rinse with clear water. Dry thoroughly.
2. Check the fork tube (A, **Figure 20**) for bending, nicks, rust or other damage. Check the fork tube for straightness with a set of V-blocks and a dial indicator. If you do not have these tools, roll the fork tube on a large plate glass or other flat surface. Harley-Davidson does not provide service limit specifications for runout. If a fork tube is slightly bent, it can be straightened with a press and special blocks; see your Harley-Davidson dealer or repair shop. If a fork tube is bent to a point where the metal is creased or wrinkled, the fork tube must be replaced.
3. Check the slider (B, **Figure 20**) for dents or other exterior damage. Check the retaining ring groove

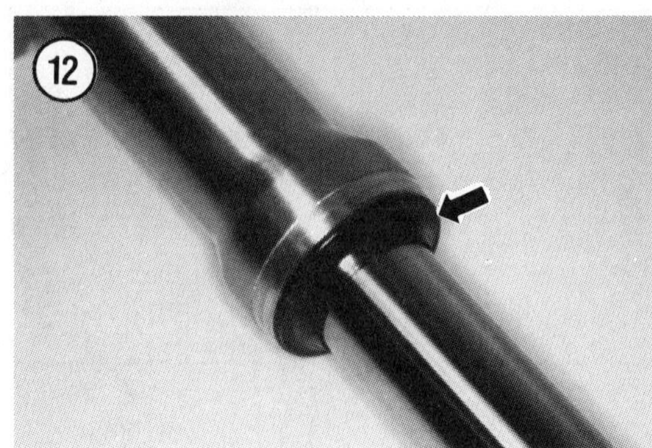
12

13

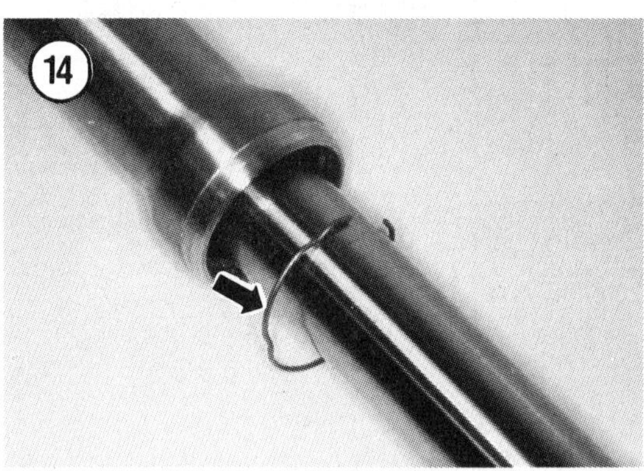
14

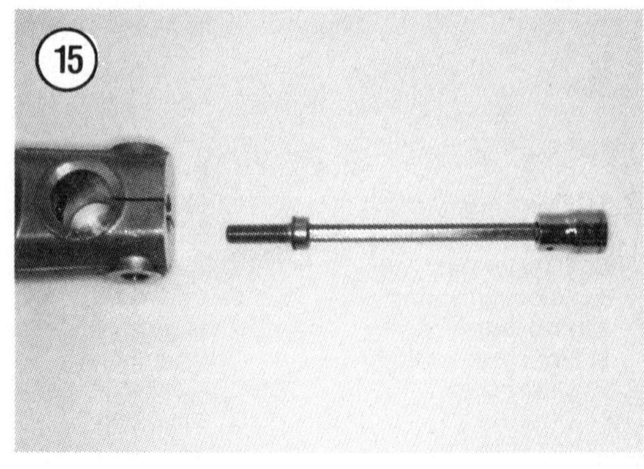
15

16

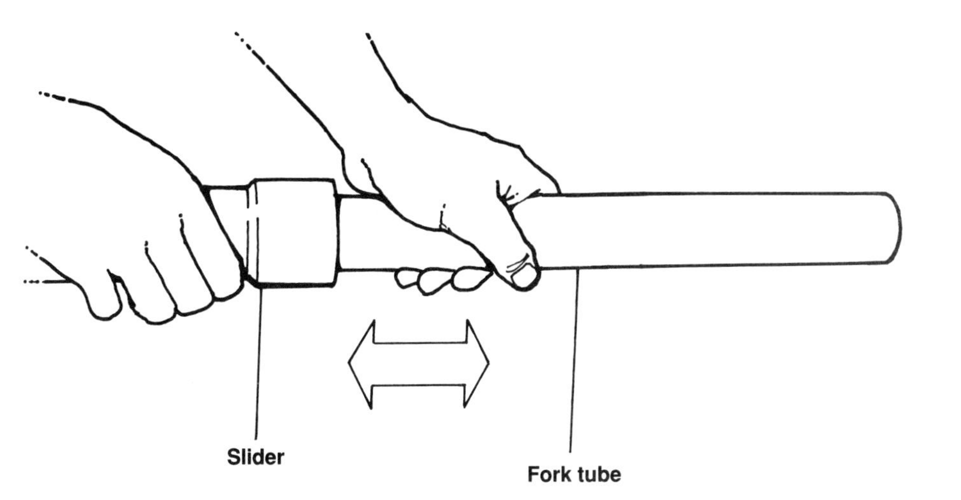

Slider

Fork tube

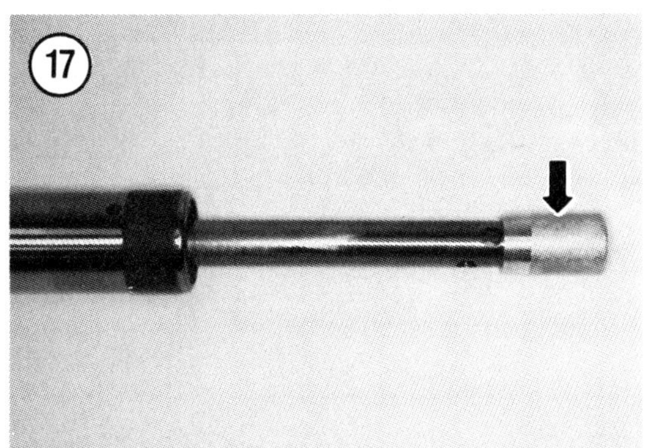

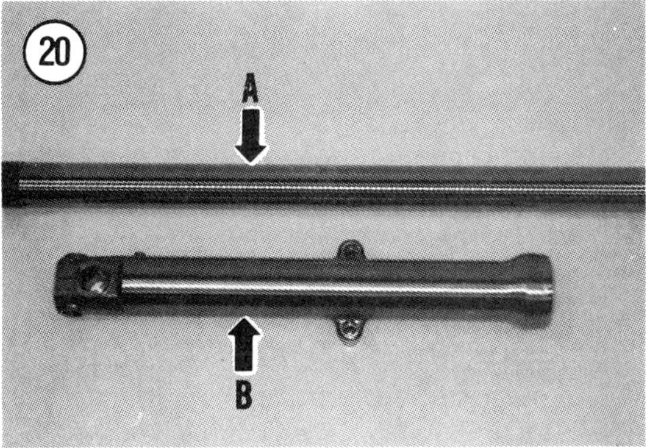

(**Figure 21**) in the top of the slider for cracks or other damage. Replace the slider if the groove is cracked or damaged.

4. Check the slider and fork tube bushings (**Figure 19**) for severe wear, cracks or damage. The slider bushing was removed with the oil seal. The fork tube bushing should not be removed unless you are going to replace it. To replace the fork tube bushing, perform the following:
   a. Expand the bushing slit (**Figure 22**) with a screwdriver and slide it off of the fork tube.
   b. Coat the new bushing with new fork oil.
   c. Install the new bushing by expanding the slit with a screwdriver. Expand the bushing only enough to fit it over the fork tube.
   d. Seat the new bushing (**Figure 22**) into the groove in the fork tube.

5. Replace damaged drain screw and Allen bolt washers.

6. Check the damper rod piston rings (**Figure 23**) for severe wear, cracks or other damage. If necessary, replace both rings as a set.

7. Check the damper rod for straightness with a set of V-blocks and a dial indicator (**Figure 24**) or by rolling it on a piece of plate glass. Harley-Davidson does not provide service limit specifications for runout.

8. Make sure the oil passage holes in the damper rod (**Figure 25**) are open. If clogged, flush with solvent and dry with compressed air.

9. Check the threads in the bottom of the damper rod for stripping, cross-threading or sealer residue. If necessary, use a tap to true up the threads or to remove any deposits.

10. Check the damper rod rebound spring and the fork spring for wear or damage. Harley-Davidson does not provide service limit specifications for spring free length.

11. Harley-Davidson specifies that the oil seals (A, **Figure 26**) should be replaced whenever they are removed. If you are going to install the original oil seals, inspect them closely for wear, hardness or other damage. Always replace both oil seals as a set.

12. Inspect the outer dust seal(s) (B, **Figure 26**) for cracks, weather deterioration or other damage. Damaged dust seal(s) will allow dirt to pass through and damage the oil seal.

13. Replace the fork cap O-ring if leaking or if severe wear or damage is apparent.

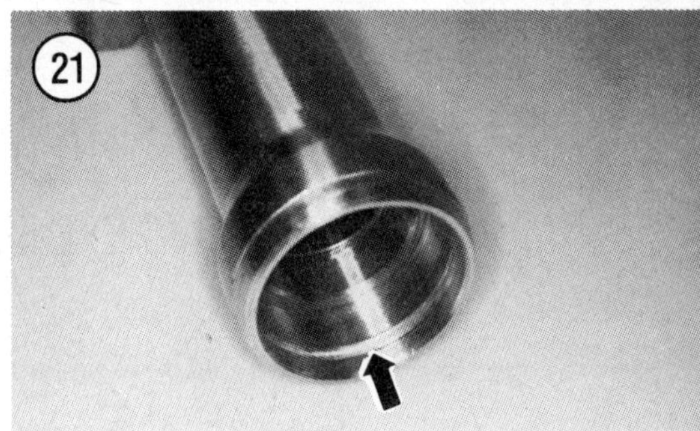

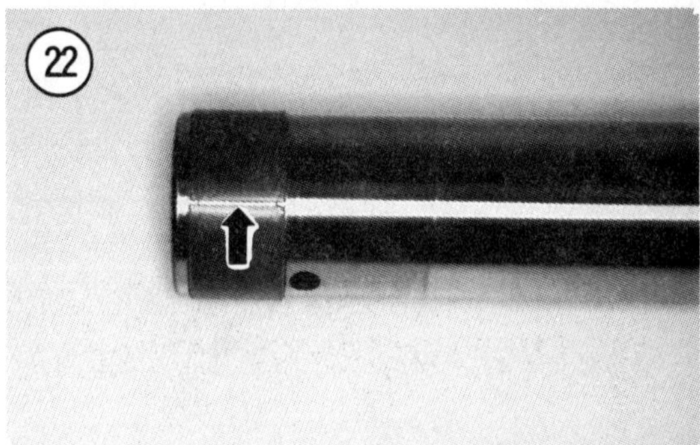

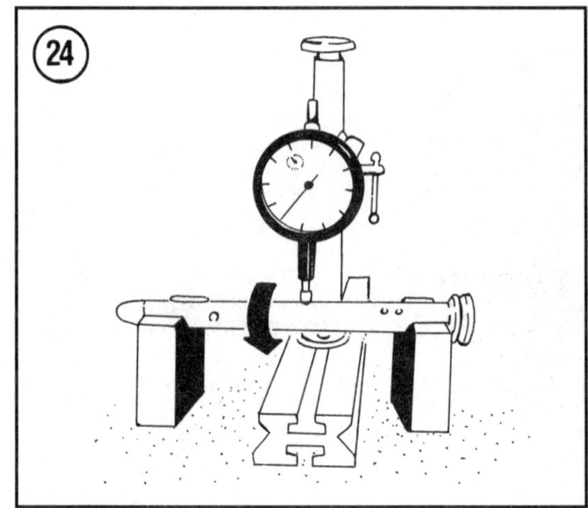

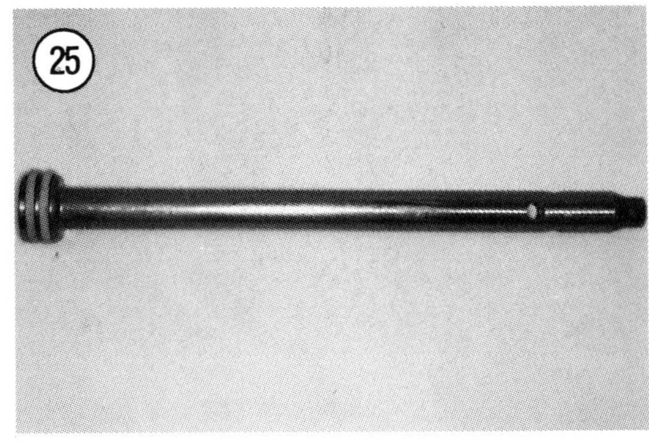

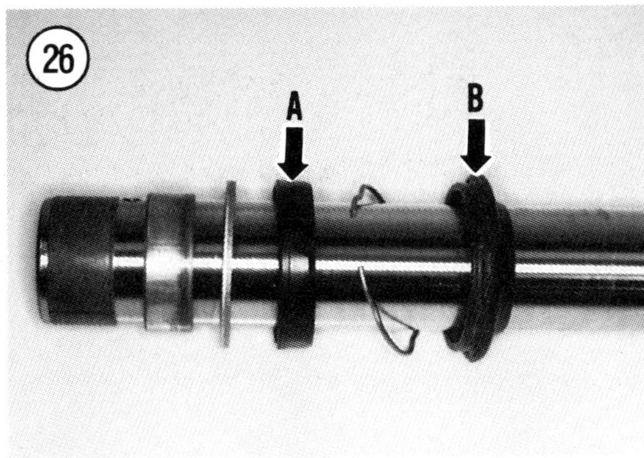

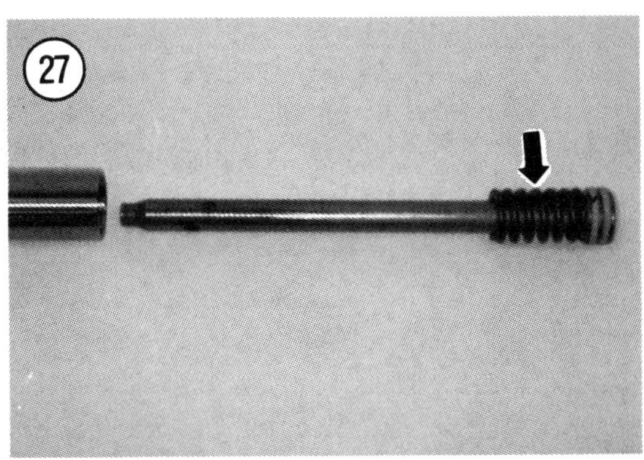

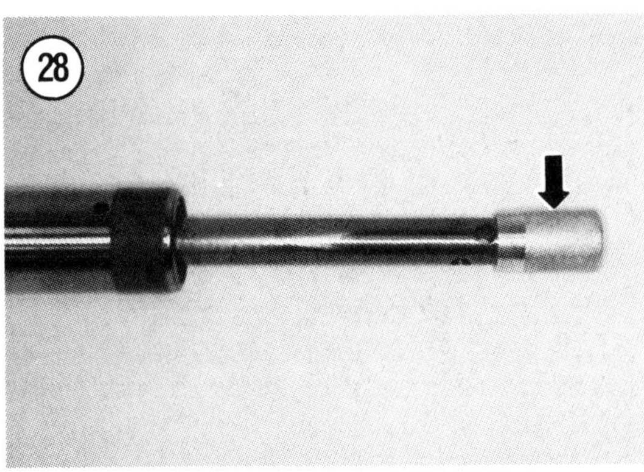

14. Any parts that are worn or damaged should be replaced. When replacing fork springs, replace both springs as a set; do not replace only 1 spring. Simply cleaning and reinstalling unserviceable components will not improve performance of the front suspension.

Assembly

Refer to **Figure 10** for this procedure.

1. Prior to assembly, perform the *Inspection* procedure to make sure all worn or defective parts have been repaired or replaced. All parts should be thoroughly cleaned before assembly.
2. Coat all parts with Harley-Davidson Type E Fork Oil or equivalent before assembly.
3. Install the rebound spring onto the damper rod (**Figure 27**) and slide the rod into the fork tube until it protrudes from the end of the tube.
4. Install the oil lock piece (**Figure 28**) onto the end of the damper rod.
5. Insert the fork spring (**Figure 29**) into the fork tube so that the tapered side of the spring faces down (toward damper rod). Install the fork cap to tension the spring and hold the damper rod in place.
6. Install the slider over the damper rod (**Figure 30**) and onto the bottom of the fork tube until it bottoms out. Make sure the oil lock piece is still mounted onto the end of the damper rod.
7. Install the washer onto the damper rod Allen bolt.
8. Apply a non-permanent thread locking compound to the damper rod Allen bolt threads prior to installation. Insert the bolt (**Figure 31**) through the lower end of the slider and thread it into the damper rod. Tighten the bolt securely.
9. Remove the fork cap and fork spring (**Figure 29**).

NOTE
The slider bushing, seal spacer and oil seal are installed into the slider at the same time with a suitable driver placed over the fork tube and against the oil seal. The Harley-Davidson fork seal driver (part No. HD-36583) or an aftermarket driver can be used. A piece of pipe can also be used to drive the parts into the slider. When using a piece of pipe or similar tool, care must be taken to prevent damage to the slider, oil seal or fork tube. Wrap both ends of the pipe or tool with duct tape to prevent it from scratching the fork tube and tearing the oil seal.

10. Install the slider bushing, seal spacer and oil seal (**Figure 32**) at the same time. Perform the following:
   a. Coat the slider bushing (A, **Figure 32**) with fork oil and slide the bushing down the fork tube and rest it against the slider bore.
   b. Install the seal spacer (B, **Figure 32**) over the fork tube (dished or concave side facing downward). Rest the seal spacer on the slider bushing.
   c. Slide a new oil seal (C, **Figure 32**) over the fork tube (closed side facing up). Rest the oil seal on the seal spacer.
   d. Slide the fork seal driver down the fork tube (**Figure 33**).
   e. Drive the bushing, seal spacer and oil seal into the slider until the retaining ring groove in the slider can be seen above the top surface of the oil seal.
   f. Remove the fork seal driver tool.
11. Install the retaining ring (**Figure 34**) into the slider groove. Make sure the retaining ring is fully seated in the groove.
12. Slide the dust seal (**Figure 35**) down the fork tube and seat it into the top of the slider.
13. Install the dust cover (**Figure 36**) as follows:
   a. Slide the dust cover down the fork tube and rest it against the top of the slider.
   b. Slide one of the discarded oil seals down the fork tube and rest it against the dust cover (**Figure 36**).
   c. Use the same fork seal driver used in Step 10 and carefully drive the dust cover onto the top of the slider as shown in **Figure 36**.
   d. Remove the installation tool and oil seal.

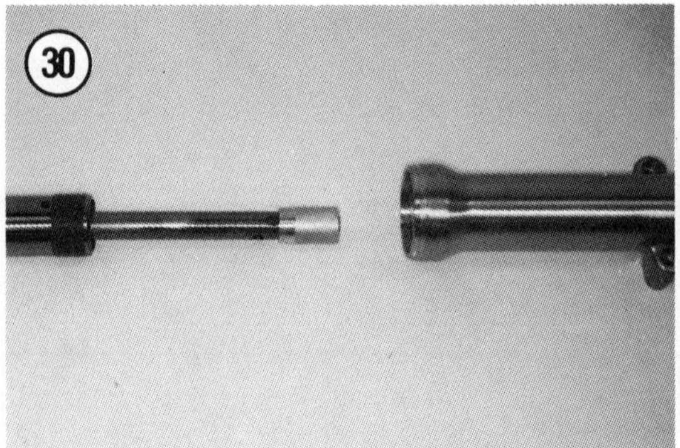
30

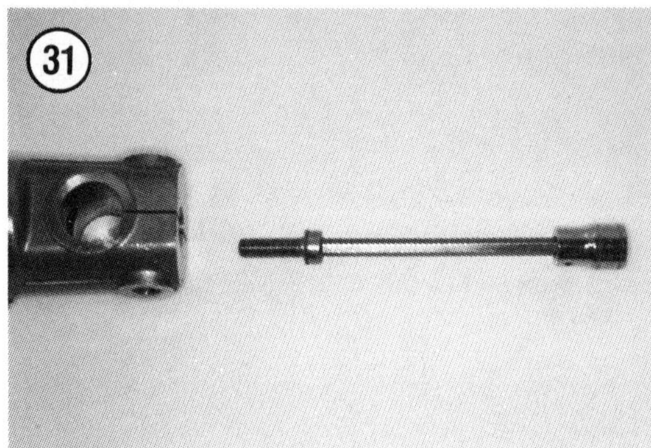
31

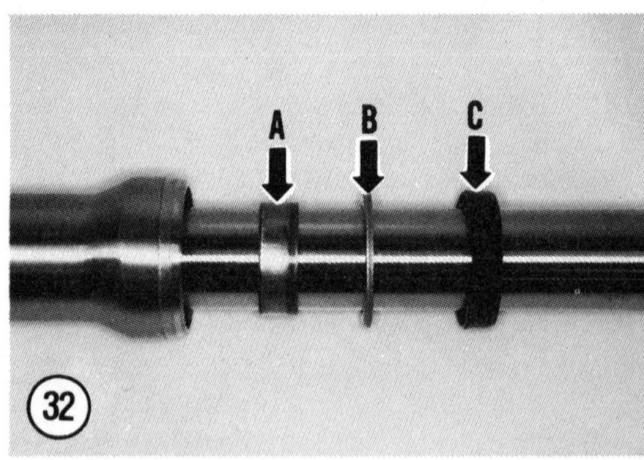

32

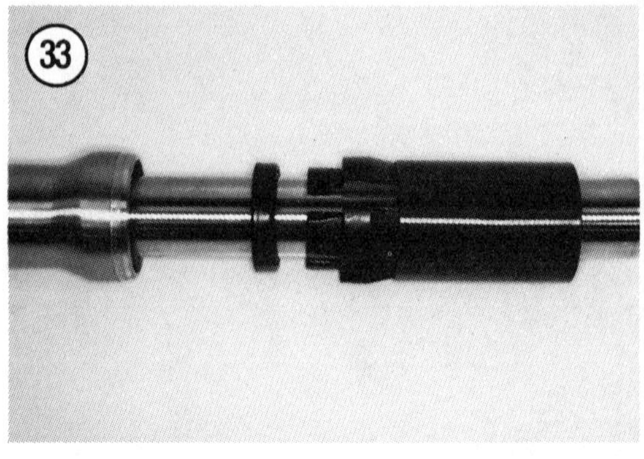
33

14. Fill the fork tube with the correct quantity of Harley-Davidson Type E Fork Oil listed in **Table 2**.
15. The fork spring is tapered at one end. Install the spring (**Figure 29**) so that the tapered end faces toward the bottom of the fork.
16. Wipe the fork cap O-ring and threads with new fork oil.
17. Align the fork cap (**Figure 29**) with the spring and push down on the cap to compress the spring. Start the cap slowly, don't cross thread it.
18. Place the slider in a vise with soft jaws and tighten the fork cap securely.

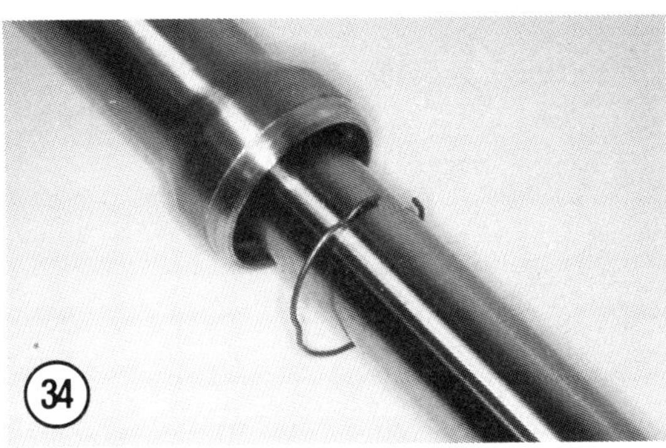
34

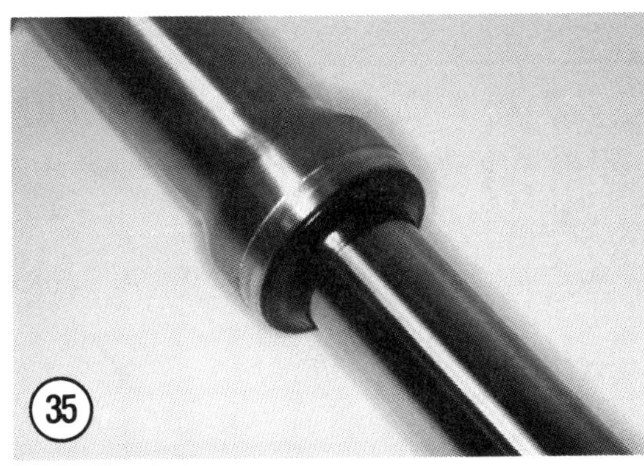
35

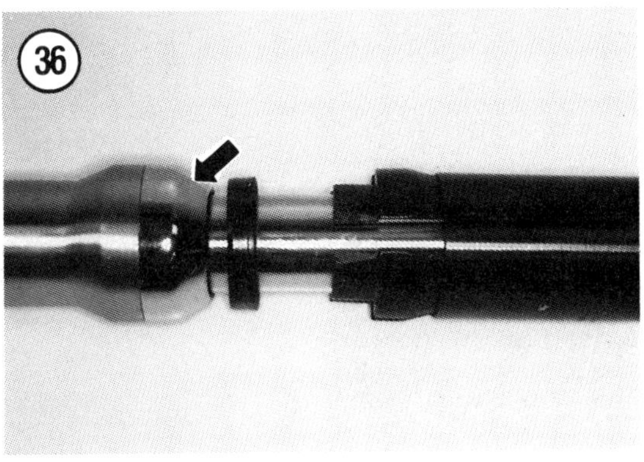
36

19. Install the fork tube as described in this chapter.

STEERING HEAD AND STEM

The fork stem is mounted onto the lower triple clamp. A dust shield and a tapered bearing are installed onto the bottom of the fork stem. The fork stem is inserted through the steering head where another bearing is installed at the top of the steering head. Both bearings seat against races pressed into the steering head. Dust covers are used at both bearing areas to protect bearings from dust and other contaminants.

Removal

Refer to **Figure 37** for this procedure.

1. Remove the front wheel as described in Chapter Nine.
2. Remove the fuel tank as described in Chapter Seven.

NOTE
If you don't remove the fuel tank, cover it with a heavy blanket or towel.

3. Remove the front forks as described in this chapter.
4. Remove the brake hose bracket at the bottom of the fork stem bracket (**Figure 38**). Do not disconnect the brake hose connection.

NOTE
If it is not necessary to remove the handlebar, the handlebar can be removed along with the upper fork bracket. If necessary, remove the handlebar as described in this chapter.

5. Unscrew the bolt cap (**Figure 39**) and remove it. See **Figure 40**.
6. Remove the steering stem bolt (A, **Figure 41**) and washer.

NOTE
Hold or secure the steering stem/lower fork bracket to keep it from falling out out once the pinch bolt is loosened in Step 7.

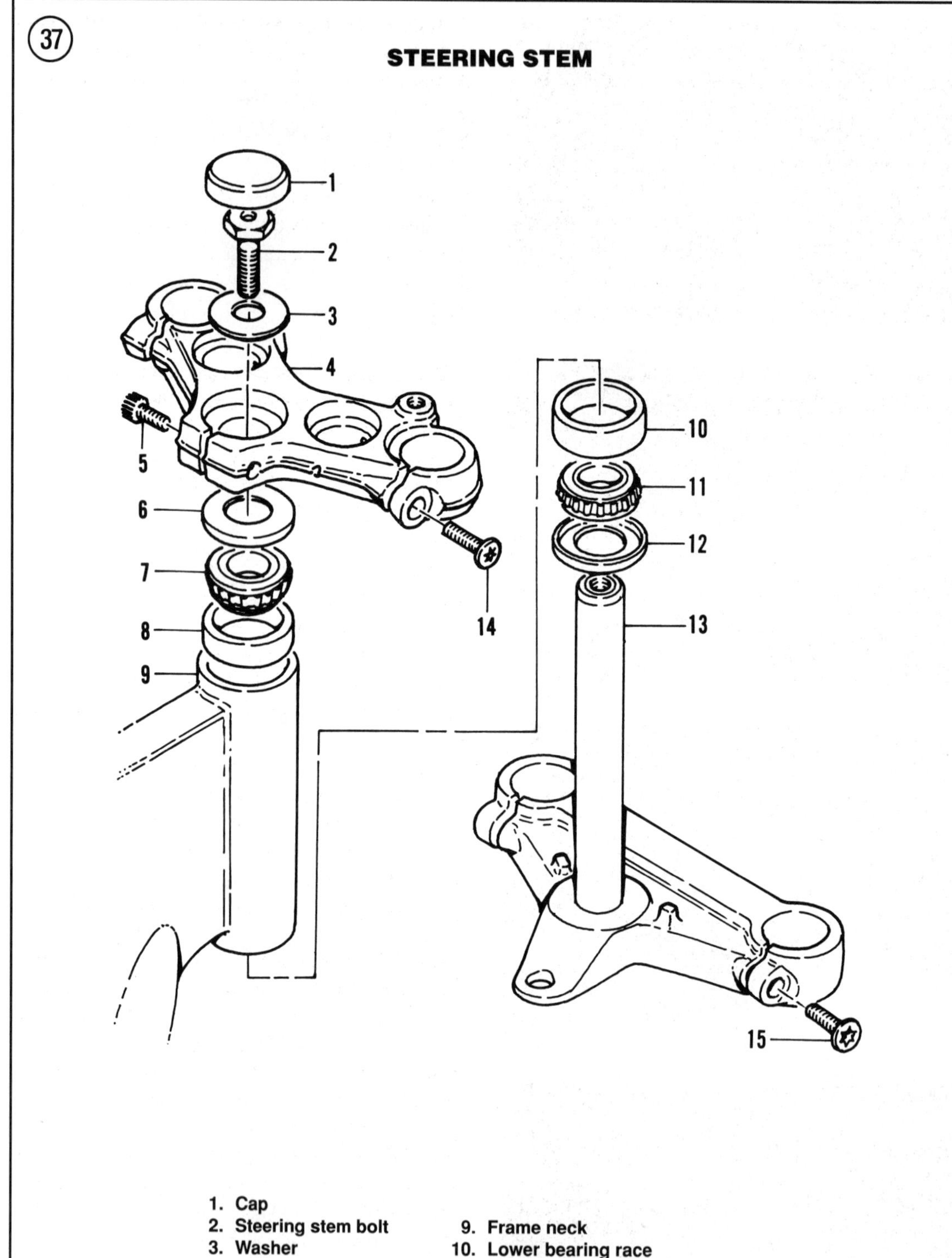

1. Cap
2. Steering stem bolt
3. Washer
4. Upper fork bracket
5. Pinch bolt
6. Dust shield
7. Upper bearing
8. Upper bearing race
9. Frame neck
10. Lower bearing race
11. Lower bearing
12. Dust shield
13. Steering stem/lower fork bracket
14. Upper fork tube pinch bolt
15. Lower fork tube pinch bolt

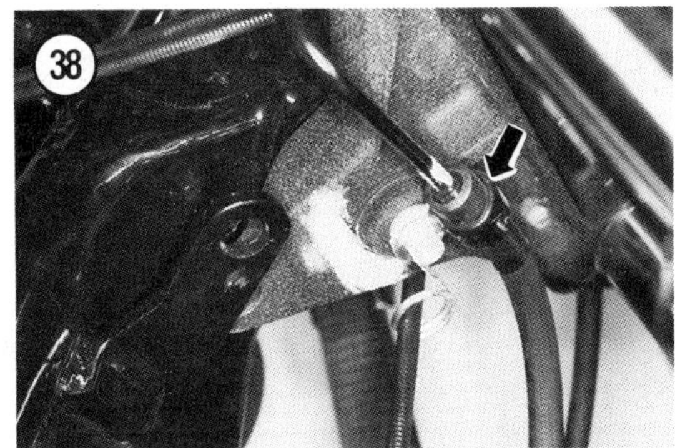
38

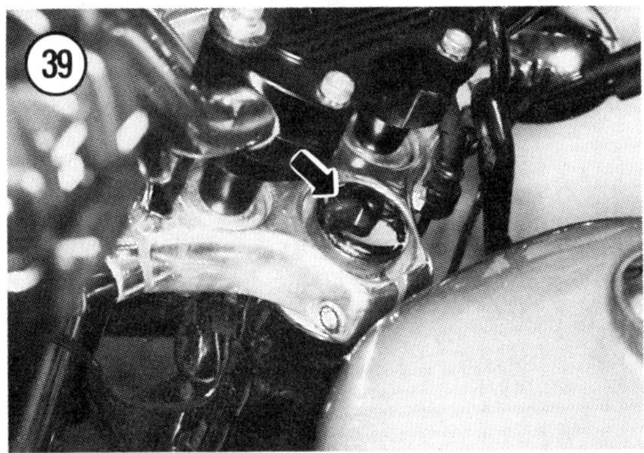
39

40

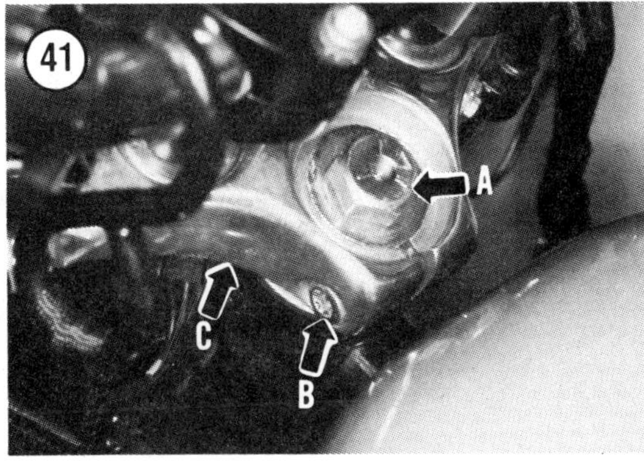

41

7. Loosen the pinch bolt (B, **Figure 41**) and lift the upper fork bracket (C, **Figure 41**) off of the steering stem. Carefully set the bracket aside with the cables attached.
8. Lower the fork stem assembly out of the steering head and remove it.
9. Remove the upper dust cover and bearing.
10. Inspect the fork stem and bearing assembly as described in this chapter.

Inspection

The bearing races (8 and 10, **Figure 37**) are pressed into the steering head. The bearing races should not be removed unless they are severely worn or damaged and require replacement.

Wheel bearing grease should be used to pack bearings and races when performing the following steps.

1. Wipe the bearing races with a solvent soaked rag and then dry with compressed air or a lint-free cloth. Check the races in the steering head for pitting, scratches, galling or severe wear. If any of these conditions exist, replace the races as described in this chapter. If the races are okay, wipe each race with grease.
2. Clean the bearings in solvent to remove all of the old grease. Blow the bearing dry with compressed air, making sure not to allow the air jet to spin the bearing. Do not remove the lower bearing from the fork stem unless its replacement is required; clean the bearing together with the steering stem.
3. After the bearings are dry, hold the inner race with one hand and turn the outer race with your other hand. Turn the bearing slowly, checking for roughness, looseness, trapped dirt or grit. Visually check the bearing for pitting, scratches or visible damage. If the bearings are worn, check the dust covers for wear or damage or for improper bearing lubrication. Replace the bearing if necessary. If the bearing can be reused, pack it with grease and wrap it with wax paper or some other type of lint-free material until it can be reinstalled. Do not store the bearings for any length of time without lubricating them or they will rust.

NOTE

Because a trace of dirt can quickly damage a bearing, your hands should be clean when handling bearings, espe-

cially when packing the bearing with grease.

4. Check the steering stem for cracks or damage. Check the threads at the top of the stem for strippage or damage. Check the steering stem bolt by threading it into the steering stem; make sure the bolt threads easily with no roughness. If necessary, clean the threads carefully with a brush and solvent or use a tap or die of the correct thread type and size.
5. Worn or damaged parts should be replaced. When discarding a bearing, both bearings and their races should be replaced at the same time. Replace bearing races as described in this chapter.
6. Replace the lower steering stem bearing (11, **Figure 37**) and dust cover as described in this chapter.
7. Check for broken welds on the frame around the steering head. If any are found, have them repaired by a competent frame shop or welding service familiar with motorcycle frame repair.

Installation

1. Make sure the steering head bearing races are properly seated.
2. Wipe the bearing races with a clean lint-free cloth. Then lubricate each race with bearing grease.
3. Pack the upper and lower bearings with bearing grease. The lower bearing and lower dust shield should be installed on the steering stem prior to installing the steering stem in the steering head. If necessary, install the lower bearing as described in this chapter.
4. Insert the steering stem into the frame steering head and hold it firmly in place.
5. Install the upper bearing (7, **Figure 37**) over the fork stem and seat it into the upper race. Install the upper dust shield (6, **Figure 37**).
6. Install the upper fork bracket (C, **Figure 41**) over the steering stem.
7. Install the washer and the steering stem bolt (A, **Figure 41**). Tighten the bolt hand-tight only.
8. Install the front forks as described in this chapter.
9. Tighten the steering stem bolt (A, **Figure 41**) until the steering stem can be turned from side to side with no noticeable axial or lateral bearing play. When the play feels correct, tighten the fork stem pinch bolt (B, **Figure 41**) to the torque specification in **Table 1**.

CAUTION

Do not overtighten the steering stem bolt in Step 9 or you may damage the bearings and races. Final adjustment of the fork stem will take place after the front wheel has been installed on the bike.

10. Install the brake hose bracket onto the lower fork bracket and tighten its mounting bolt (**Figure 38**) securely.
11. Install the front wheel as described in Chapter Nine.
12. Adjust the steering play as described under *Steering Play Adjustment* in this chapter.

STEERING HEAD BEARING RACE

Whenever the steering stem and bearings are removed from the steering head, cover the steering head with a cloth to protect the bearing races from accidental damage. If a race is damaged, the bearing and race must be replaced as a set. Because the bearing races are pressed into place, do not remove them unless they are worn and require replacement.

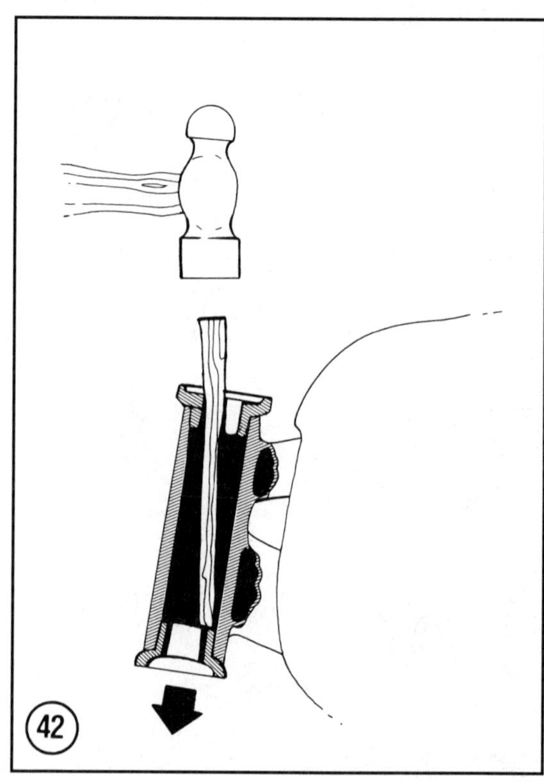

Upper and Lower Bearing Race Replacement

The upper and lower bearing races (8 and 10, **Figure 37**) are pressed into the frame. Because they are easily bent, do not remove them unless they are worn and require replacement. Both races are identical (same part number) and can be purchased separately from the bearing. If you are replacing the bearing, purchase the bearing and race as a set.

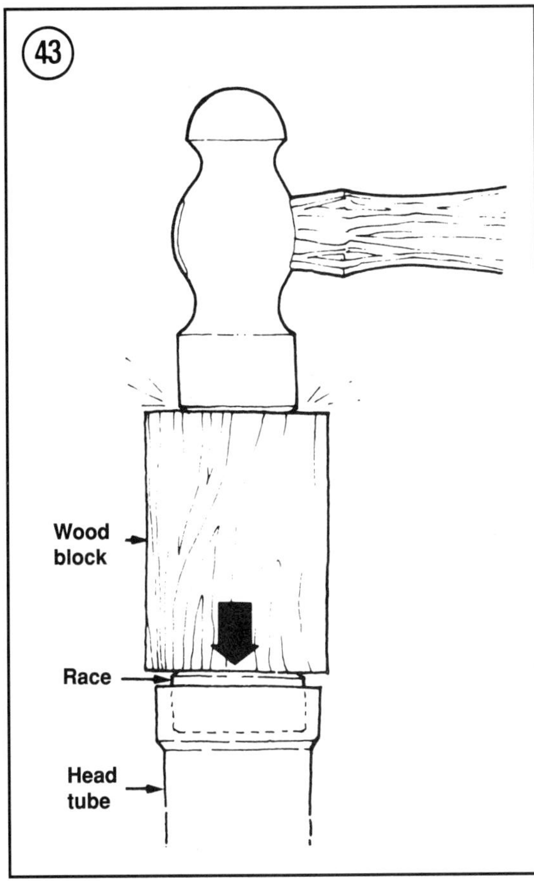

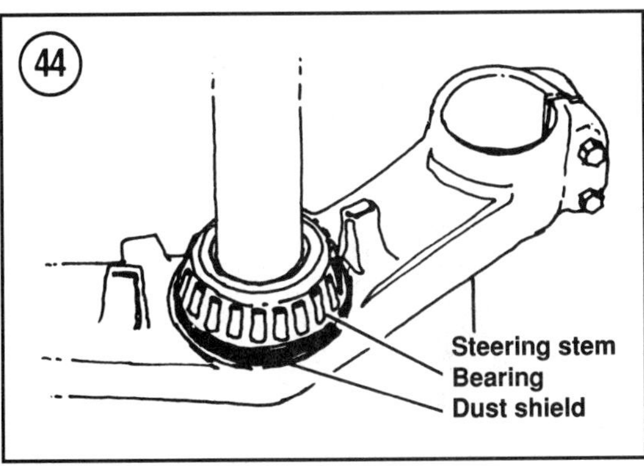

1. To remove a race, insert an aluminum or brass rod into the steering head and carefully tap the race out from the inside (**Figure 42**). Tap all around the race so that neither the race nor the steering head are bent.
2. Clean the steering head with solvent and dry thoroughly.

NOTE
The bearing races can be installed with the Harley-Davidson Head Bearing Race Installation Tool (part No. HD-39302). If you do not have this tool, perform Step 3.

3. Install the bearing races as follows:
   a. Clean the race thoroughly before installing it.
   b. Align the upper race with the frame steering head and tap it slowly and squarely in place with a block of wood, a suitable socket or bearing driver, making sure you do *not* contact the bearing race tapered surface. See **Figure 43**. If you saved an old race, grind its outside rim so that it is a slip fit in the steering head, then use it to drive the new race into place. Drive the race into the steering head until it bottoms out on the bore shoulder.
   c. Repeat to install the lower race into the steering head.
4. Wipe the bearing races with bearing grease.

Fork Stem Lower Bearing Replacement

Do not remove the fork stem lower bearing (**Figure 44**) unless it is going to be replaced with a new bearing. Do not reinstall a lower bearing that has been removed, as it is no longer true to alignment. When replacing the lower bearing, install a new lower dust shield (12, **Figure 37**).

WARNING
Safety glasses and insulated gloves must be worn when removing the inner race in Step 1.

1. Using a chisel, break the bearing cage and rollers from the inner race. When the bearing cage and rollers are free, all you will be left with is the inner race on the fork stem. To remove the inner race, heat the race with a torch until it expands enough to slide or drop off the fork stem. Remove and discard the dust cover after removing the bearing.

2. Clean the fork stem with solvent and dry thoroughly.
3. Pack the new bearing with grease before installing it.
4. Slide a new dust shield over the fork stem until it bottoms out on the lower bracket.
5. Align the new bearing with the fork stem and press or drive it onto the fork stem until it bottoms out. When installing the bearing onto the fork stem, a bearing driver must be used against the inner bearing race (**Figure 45**). Do *not* install the bearing by driving against the outer bearing race.

STEERING PLAY ADJUSTMENT

The steering play should be checked periodically and anytime the steering stem assembly has been removed and installed on the bike.

1. Support the bike so that the front wheel clears the ground.
2. Remove the windshield (if used) and all other accessory weight from the handlebar and front forks that could affect this adjustment.

NOTE
If any control cable affects handlebar movement, disconnect it.

3. Apply a strip of masking tape across the front end of the front fender. Draw a vertical line across the tape at the center of the fender. Then draw 2 lines on each side of the center line, 1 inch apart from each other. See **Figure 46**.
4. Turn the handlebar so that the front wheel faces straight ahead.

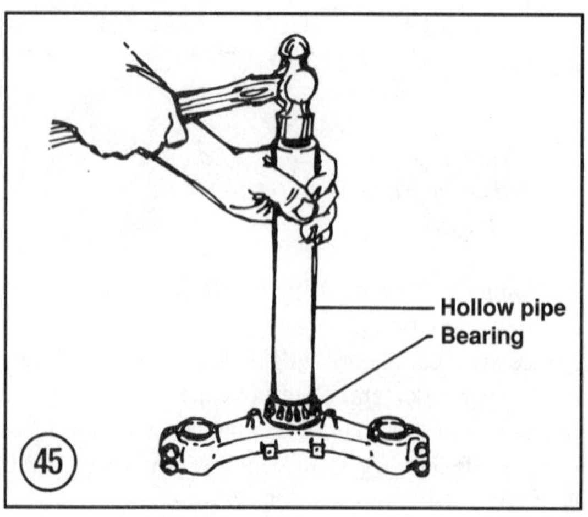

45

5. Place a pointer on a stand and then center the pointer so that its tip points to the center of the fender (tape mark) when the wheel is facing straight ahead.
6. Lightly push the fender towards the right-hand side until the front end starts to turn by itself. Mark this point on the tape.
7. Repeat Step 7 for the left-hand side.
8. Measure the distance between the 2 marks on the tape. For proper bearing adjustment, the distance should be 1-2 in. (25.4-50.8 mm). If the distance is incorrect, perform Step 9.

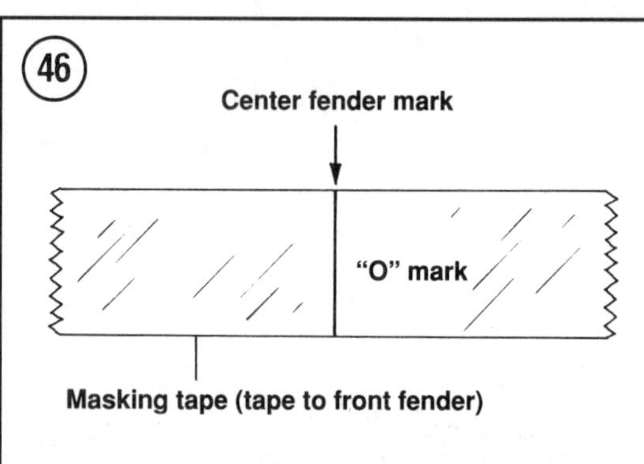

46

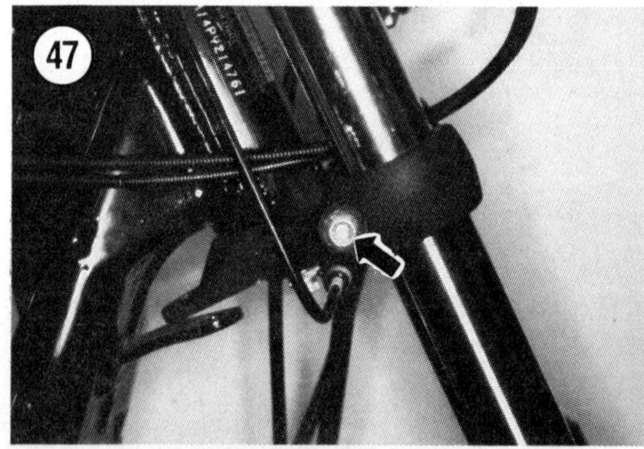

47

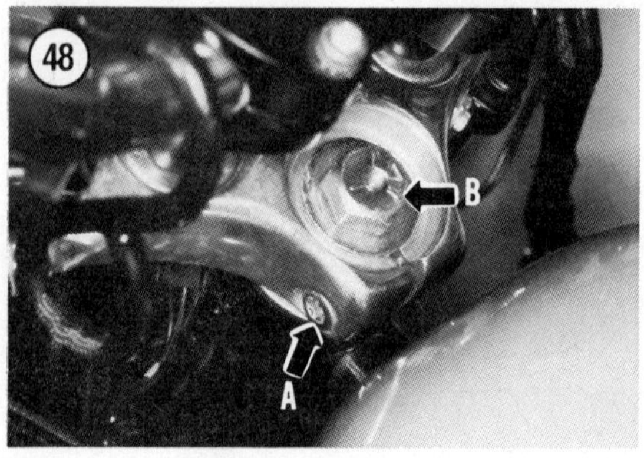

48

9. Adjust steering play as follows:
   a. Loosen the lower fork tube pinch bolts (**Figure 47**).
   b. Unscrew and remove the bolt cap (**Figure 40**).
   c. Loosen the fork stem pinch bolt (A, **Figure 48**).
   d. If the distance between the two marks is less than 1 in. (25.4 mm), tighten the steering stem bolt (B, **Figure 48**).
   e. If the distance between the two marks is more than 2 in. (50.8 mm), loosen the steering stem bolt (B, **Figure 48**).
   f. Repeat Steps 6 and 7 to measure steering play. Continue until the distance between the two marks is within 1-2 in. (25.4-50.8 mm).
10. When steering play adjustment is correct, perform the following:
   a. Tighten the fork stem pinch bolt (A, **Figure 48**) to the torque specification in **Table 1**.
   b. Tighten the lower bracket pinch bolt (**Figure 47**) to the torque specification in **Table 1**.
   c. Install and tighten the bolt cap (**Figure 40**) securely.
11. Reinstall all parts previously removed.

Table 1 FRONT SUSPENSION TIGHTENING TORQUES

	ft.-lb.	N•m
Front axle nut	50-55	68-74.6
Front axle pinch bolt and nut	21-27	28.5-36.6
Front brake caliper mounting bolts	25-30	34.5-41.4
Handlebar clamp bolts	12-15	16.3-20.3
Front fork		
Upper bracket pinch bolts	30-35	40.7-47.5
Lower bracket pinch bolts	30-35	40.7-47.5
Fork stem pinch bolt	30-35	40.7-47.5
Front fender fasteners	9-13	12.2-17.6

Table 2 FRONT FORK OIL CAPACITY

	Wet		Dry	
	U.S. oz.	ml	U.S. oz.	ml
1991	9.0	266	10.2	302
1992-on				
883 Hugger	10.7	316	12.1	358
All other models	9.0	266	10.2	302

CHAPTER ELEVEN

REAR SUSPENSION

This chapter covers service related to the rear shock absorbers and swing arm. **Table 1** is at the end of the chapter.

SHOCK ABSORBERS

The rear shocks are spring controlled and hydraulically damped. Spring preload can be adjusted on all models.

Spring Preload Adjustment

On all models, the shock absorber springs can be adjusted to suit rider and load. Rotate the cam ring (**Figure 1**) at the base of the spring to compress the spring (heavy loads) or extend the spring (light loads). Use a spanner wrench to rotate the cam ring.

Removal/Installation

Removal and installation of the rear shocks is easier if they are done separately. The remaining unit will support the rear of the bike and maintain the correct relationship between the top and bottom mounts. If both shock absorbers must be removed at the same time, cut a piece of steel a few inches longer than the shock absorber and drill two holes in the steel the same distance apart as the bolt holes in a shock absorber. Install the steel support after one shock absorber is removed. This will allow the bike to be easily moved around until the shock absorbers are reinstalled or replaced.

1. Support the bike so that the rear wheel clears the ground.
2. Remove the upper Acorn nut, washer, stud cover and washer (**Figure 2**).
3. Remove the lower locknut, bolt and washer (**Figure 2**).

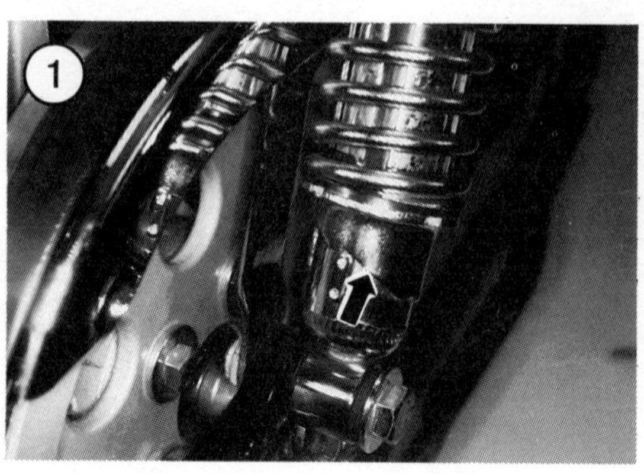

4. Remove the shock absorber (**Figure 3**).
5. Install by reversing these removal steps, noting the following.
6. Apply Loctite 242 (blue) onto the upper and lower shock bolt threads. Tighten the upper and lower nuts to the torque specification in **Table 1**.

Disassembly/Reassembly

Refer to **Figure 2**.

1. Remove the shock absorber as described in this chapter.
2. Adjust the cam ring to its softest setting.

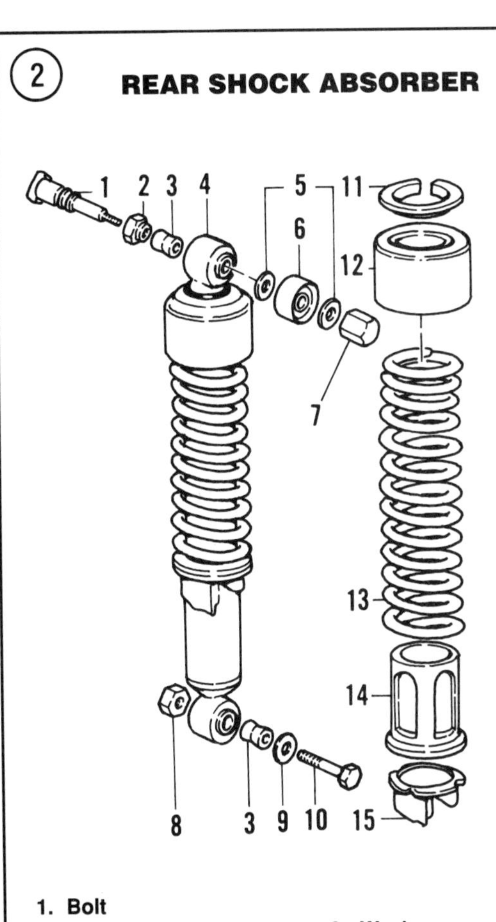

WARNING

Do not attempt to remove the shock absorber spring without a spring compressor (HD-97010-52A) or bodily injury may result.

3. Using a shock absorber spring compression tool, compress the shock absorber spring and remove the upper spring retainer. **Figure 4** shows the Harley-Davidson spring compressor (HD-97010-52A).
4. Release spring pressure, them remove the shock absorber assembly from tool.
5. Disassemble the shock absorber in the order shown in **Figure 2**.
6. Inspect the shock absorber as described in this chapter.
7. Assembly is the reverse of these steps, noting the following.
8. Lightly grease all cam parts before assembly.

Inspection

Inspect all parts for wear or damage. Pay particular attention to the following items.

1. Replace all rubber bushings that show signs of wear, damage or cracking.
2. Check the shock absorber for fluid leakage. Replace the shock body if leaking.

REAR SWING ARM

Removal/Installation

Refer to **Figure 5** for this procedure.

1. Remove the rear wheel as described in this chapter.

2. Disconnect all brake hose clamps at the swing arm.
3. Remove the rear brake caliper from the swing arm as described in Chapter Twelve.

NOTE
It is not necessary to disconnect the hydraulic lines. Instead, hang the brake caliper from the frame with a Bunjee cord.

4. Remove the bolts or nuts securing the shock absorbers to the swing arm and pull the shock absorbers clear of the mounts.
5. Remove the fasteners securing the rear chain guard and remove the guard.
6. Remove the pivot shaft covers (**Figure 6**), if so equipped.

NOTE
*Prior to completing swing arm removal, check its condition by grasping the swing arm on both sides and trying to move it from side to side. If the free play is excessive, replace the swing arm bearings as described under **Rear Swing Arm Bearing Replacement** in this chapter. Harley-Davidson does not list free play specifications.*

7. Remove the socket screw from the left-hand side (**Figure 7**).
8. Loosen and remove the swing arm pivot bolt (**Figure 8**).
9. Slide the swing arm out of the frame. Make sure the bearings do not drop to the ground.

CAUTION
Keep all bearing components together. If they fall out, reinstall them into their correct assembled positions. Wear patterns have developed on these parts and rapid wear may occur if the components are intermixed and not installed in their original positions.

10. Remove the pivot spacer (11, **Figure 5**) from the swing arm.
11. Noting the previous caution, remove the dust shields (2, **Figure 5**), inner bearing race (3, **Figure 5**), outer bearing race (4, **Figure 5**) and bearing spacer (6, **Figure 5**).
12. Install by reversing these removal steps, noting the following.
13. Coat the swing arm pivot shaft thoroughly with bearing grease before installation.
14. Lubricate the bearings with waterproof bearing grease.
15. Install the bearing spacer between the right-hand side bearings.

CAUTION
The bearing spacer must be installed between the bearings as described in Step 15 or the bearings will fail during operation.

16. Install new dust shields with their lip side positioned in toward the inner bearing races.

NOTE
*Install the pivot spacer (11, **Figure 5**) in Step 17 so that the chamfered end faces outward (left-hand side). If the pivot spacer is installed incorrectly unstable handling may result from an insufficient clamp load.*

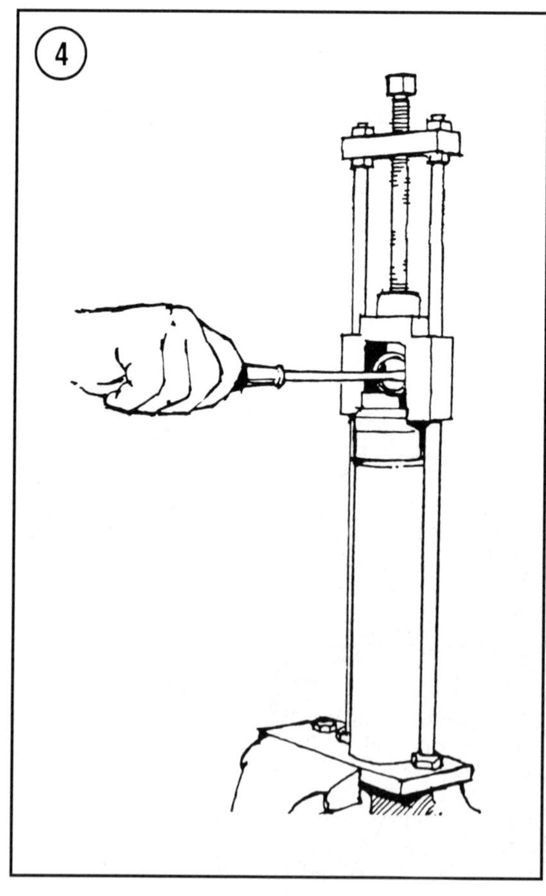

17. Install the pivot spacer (11, **Figure 5**) into the pivot bushing (8, **Figure 5**) in the swing arm.

18. If the engine is installed in the frame, insert screw (9, **Figure 5**) into the pivot spacer (11, **Figure 5**).

19. Slide the swing arm into position in the frame.

20. Install the pivot bolt (**Figure 8**) from the right-hand side. Thread the screw (**Figure 7**) into the end of the pivot shaft. Tighten the pivot shaft bolt to the torque specification in **Table 1**.

21. Tighten the lower shock absorber bolts or nuts to specifications in **Table 1**.

22. Install the rear brake caliper as described in Chapter Eleven.

23. Adjust the drive chain or drive belt and rear brake as described in Chapter Three.

5

SWING ARM

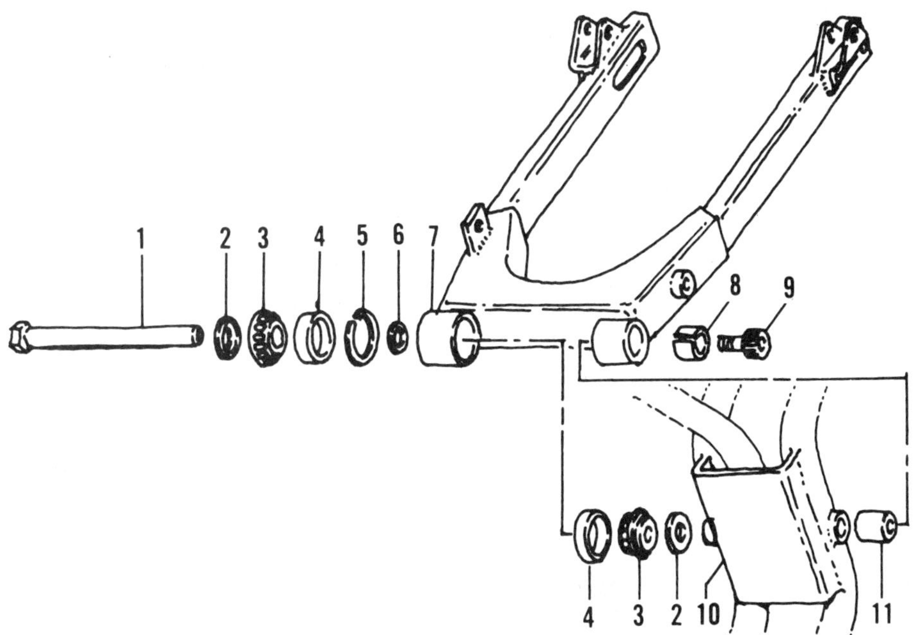

1. Pivot shaft
2. Dust shield
3. Bearing
4. Outer bearing race
5. Lockring
6. Bearing spacer
7. Swing arm
8. Pivot bushing
9. Screw
10. Frame
11. Pivot spacer

Rear Swing Arm Bearing Replacement

Refer to **Figure 5** for this procedure.

1. Secure the swing arm in a vise with soft jaws.

CAUTION
Tag each component when removed from the swing arm so it can be reinstalled in its original position. Bearing components must not be intermixed.

2. Remove the following parts from the right-hand side in the following order:
   a. Inner and outer dust shields (2, **Figure 5**).
   b. Bearings (3, **Figure 5**).

CAUTION
Unless replacement is required, do not remove the 2 outer bearing races or the pivot bushing. The complete bearing assembly must be replaced as a unit if any one bearing part is worn or damaged.

NOTE
Steps 3-9 require the use of a hydraulic press. Refer service to a Harley-Davidson dealer or machine shop. Do not attempt to drive the bearing races or pivot bushing out of the swing arm.

3. Press outer bearing races (4, **Figure 5**) out of the swing arm.
4. Remove and discard lock ring (5, **Figure 5**).
5. Remove bearing spacer (6, **Figure 5**).
6. Press the right-hand pivot bushing (8, **Figure 5**) out of the swing arm.
7. Thoroughly clean out the inside of the swing arm with solvent and dry with compressed air.
8. Install a new lock ring (5, **Figure 5**).
9. Press 2 new bearing races (4, **Figure 5**) into position.

CAUTION
Never reinstall an outer bearing race that has been removed. During removal it becomes slightly damaged and is no longer true to alignment. If installed, it will create swing arm alignment problems and unsafe riding conditions.

10. Press a new pivot bushing (8, **Figure 5**) into the swing arm on the left-hand side.
11. Apply bearing grease to all parts.

NOTE
*Install pivot spacer (11, **Figure 5**) in Step 12 so that the chamfered end faces outward (left-hand side). If the pivot spacer is installed incorrectly, unstable handling may result from an insufficient clamp load.*

12. Install pivot spacer (11, **Figure 5**) into the pivot bushing.
13. Install the bearings and bearing spacer (6, **Figure 5**) in the order shown in **Figure 5**.

CAUTION
The bearing spacer must be installed between the inner bearing races during bearing installation or the bearings will fail during operation.

14. Install dust shields over the bearing. The dust shield lip must face in.

Table 1 REAR SUSPENSION TIGHTENING TORQUES

	ft.-lb.	N•m
Swing arm pivot shaft bolt	50	68
Rear shock absorber fasteners		
Upper		
1991-1992	21-27	28.5-36.6
1993-on	21-35	28.5-47.5
Lower		
1991-1992	50-55	68-74.5
1993-on	30-50	40.7-68

CHAPTER TWELVE

BRAKES

The brake system consists of disc brakes on the front and rear. This chapter describes repair and replacement procedure for all brake components.

The disc brakes are actuated by hydraulic fluid from the master cylinder. The master cylinder is controlled by a hand or foot lever. As the brake pads wear, the brake fluid level drops in the master cylinder reservoir and automatically adjusts for pad wear.

When working on hydraulic brake systems, it is necessary that the work area and all tools be absolutely clean. Any tiny particles of foreign matter or grit on the caliper assembly or the master cylinder can damage the components. Also, sharp tools must not be used inside the caliper or on the caliper piston. If there is any doubt about your ability to correctly and safely carry out major service on the brake components, take the job to a Harley-Davidson dealer or qualified Harley repair shop.

Table 1 and **Table 2** are at the end of the chapter.

Brake Fluid

All Sportster models are designed to use *silicone based DOT 5 brake fluid.* DOT 3, DOT 4 and DOT 5.1 brake fluids are nonsilicone-based brake fluids and must *not* be used in your Sportster. Use of nonsilicone-based brake fluids in your Sportster can cause brake failure. If a nonsilicone-based brake fluid is used, the system is contaminated and must be disassembled and thoroughly flushed out. All of the rubber parts (hoses, seals, etc.) will have to be replaced with new ones.

Disc Brake System Service Hints

Consider the following when servicing the front and rear disc brake systems.

1. Disc brake components rarely require disassembly, so do not disassemble them unless necessary.
2. When adding brake fluid, only DOT 5 silicone-based brake fluid should be used. See *Brake Fluid* in this chapter for additional information.
3. Master cylinder reservoir covers should be kept closed to prevent contamination.
4. Use only DOT 5 silicone-based brake fluid to wash parts. Never clean any internal brake component with solvent. Solvents will cause the seals to swell and distort and require replacement.

5. Whenever *any* brake line has been removed from the brake system the system is considered "opened" and must be bled to remove air bubbles. Also, if the brake feels "spongy," this usually means there are air bubbles in the system and it must be bled. For safe brake operation, refer to *Bleeding the System* in this chapter for complete details.

FRONT BRAKE PADS

There is no recommended mileage interval for changing the friction pads in the disc brake. Pad wear depends greatly on riding habits and conditions. The pads should be checked for wear initially at 500 miles (800 km), then every 2,500 miles (4,000 km) and replaced when the lining thickness reaches 0.062 in. (1.57 mm) from the brake pad backing plate. To maintain an even brake pressure on the disc, always replace both pads in the caliper at the same time.

Replacement

Refer to **Figure 1** for this procedure.

1. To prevent accidental application of the front brake lever, place a spacer between the front brake lever and the hand grip. Hold the spacer in place with a large rubber band, a tie wrap or piece of tape.

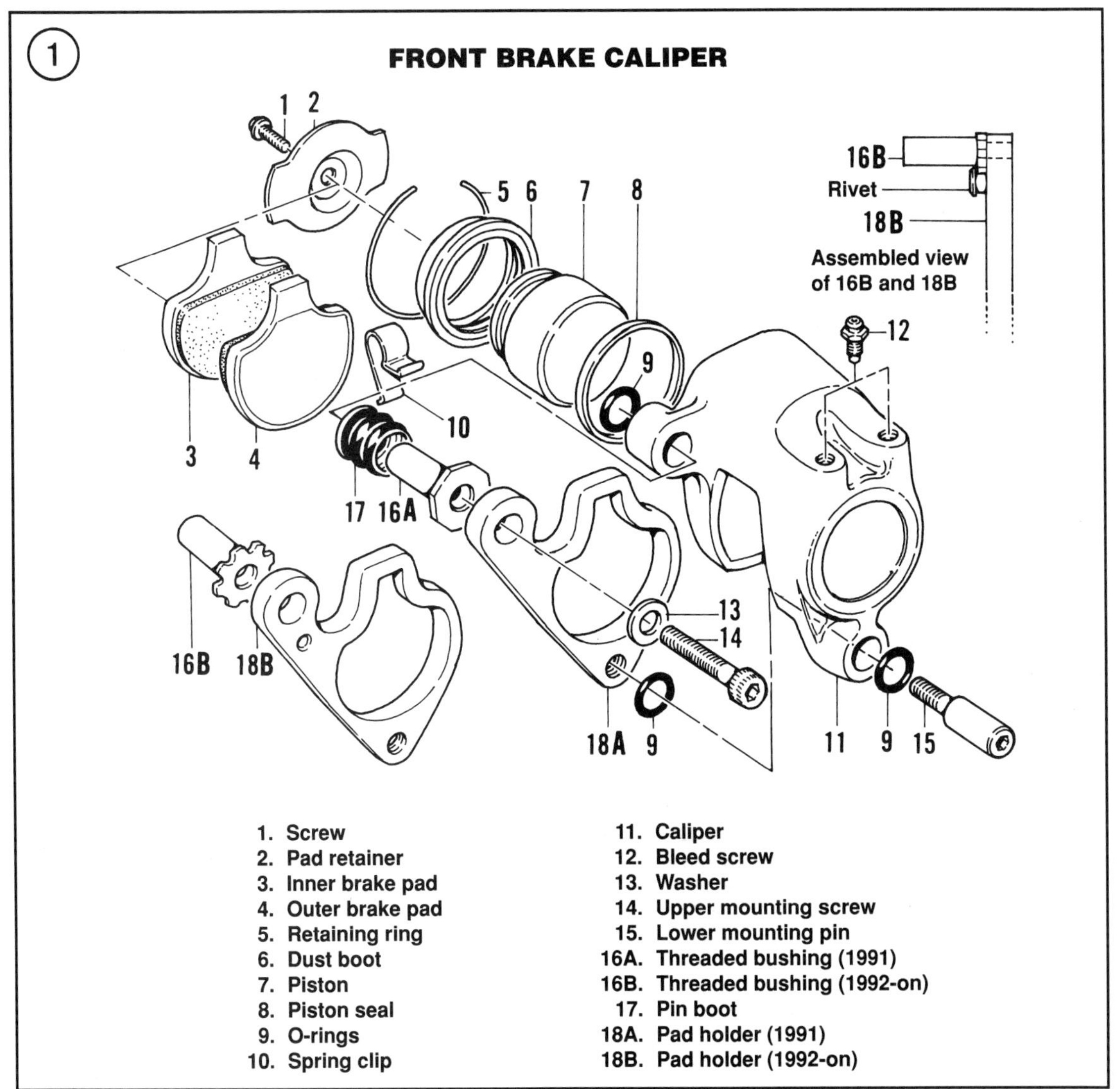

12

2. Loosen the upper mounting screw (A, **Figure 2**) and the lower mounting pin (B, **Figure 2**). Remove the upper screw and its washer and the mounting pin.

3. Lift the brake caliper off of the brake disc.

NOTE

If you intend to reuse the brake pads, mark each pad so that it can be reinstalled in its original mounting position in the caliper.

4. Remove the outer pad, pad holder and spring clip as an assembly (**Figure 3**).

5. Remove the screw (A, **Figure 4**), pad retainer (B, **Figure 4**) and inner pad (**Figure 5**).

6. Push the outer pad (A, **Figure 6**) free of the spring clip (B, **Figure 6**) and remove it. See **Figure 7**.

7. Check the brake pads (**Figure 7**) for wear or damage. Replace the brake pads if they are worn to 1/16 in. (1.6 mm) or less (**Figure 8**). Replace both pads as a set.

8. Inspect the caliper upper mounting screw and mounting pin (**Figure 9**). If either part has damaged threads or is worn or badly corroded, replace the damaged part. Replace the mounting pin if its shoulder is scored or otherwise damaged.

9. Replace the pad retainer (**Figure 10**) if cracked or deformed.

10. Check the piston dust boot (**Figure 11**). If the boot is swollen or cracked or if brake fluid is leaking from the caliper bore, remove the caliper and overhaul it as described under *Front Brake Caliper* in this chapter.

11. Remove all corrosion from the pad holder.

12. Replace the spring clip if worn, cracked or badly corroded.

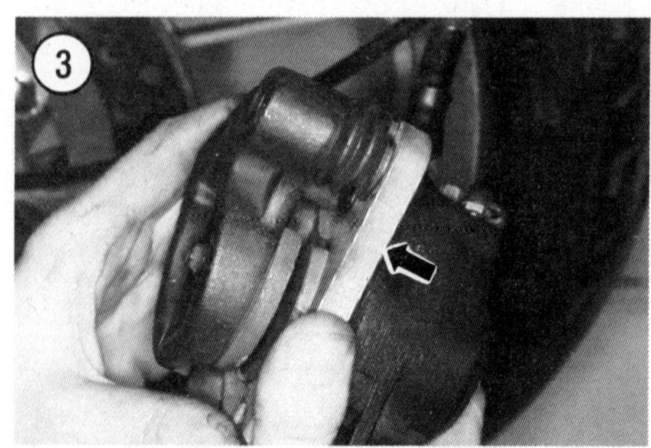

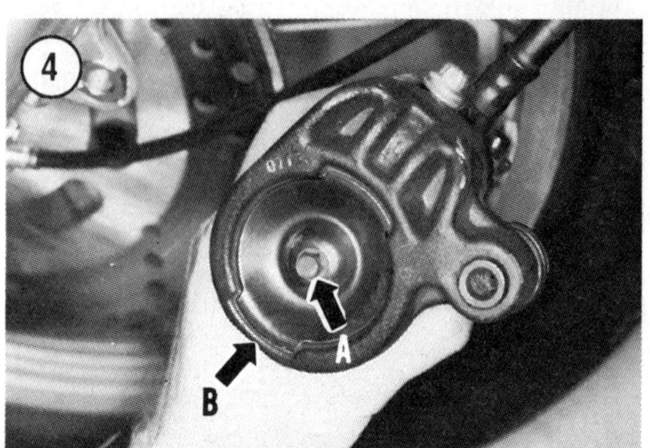

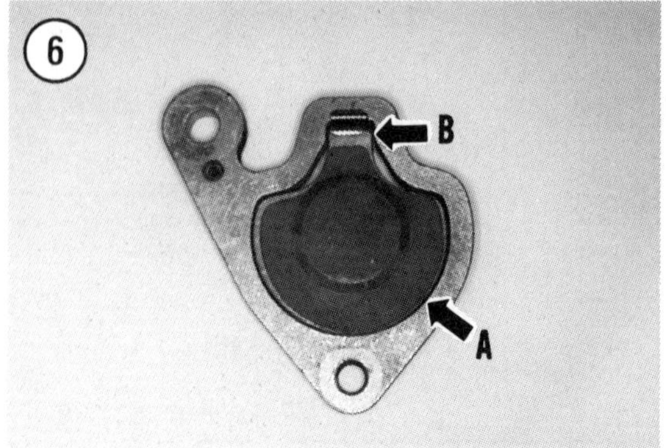

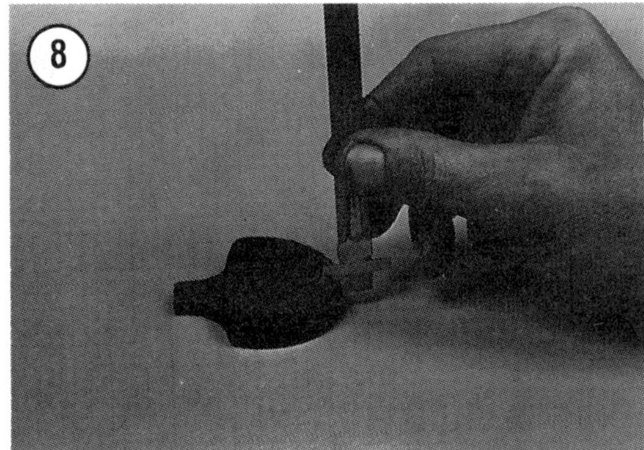

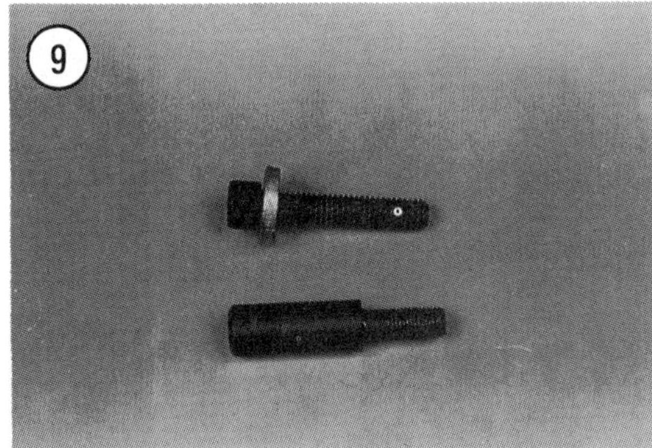

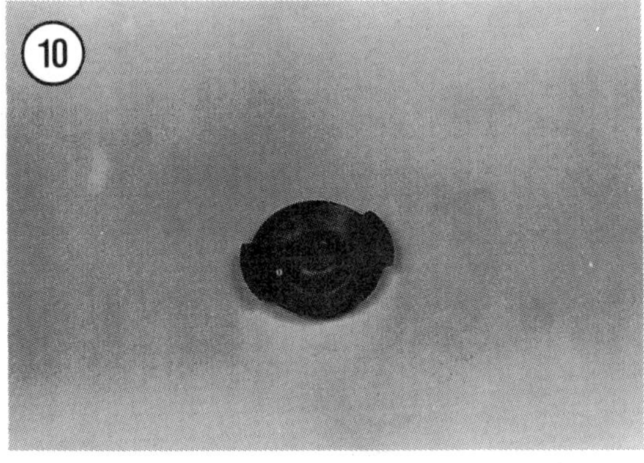

13. Check the brake disc for wear as described under *Brake Disc* in this chapter. Service the brake disc if necessary.

14. Assemble the pad holder, spring clip and outer brake pad (**Figure 12**) as follows:

   a. Lay the pad holder on a workbench so that the upper mounting screw hole is positioned at the upper right as shown in A, **Figure 13**.
   b. Install the spring clip (B, **Figure 13**) at the top of the pad holder so that the spring loop faces in the direction shown in **Figure 12**.
   c. The outer brake pad has an insulator pad mounted on its backside (**Figure 6**).
   d. Center the outer brake pad into the pad holder so that the lower end of the pad rests inside the pad holder. Then push firmly on the upper end of the brake pad, past the spring clip and into the holder. The pad should be held firmly by the spring in the spring holder. See **Figure 13**.

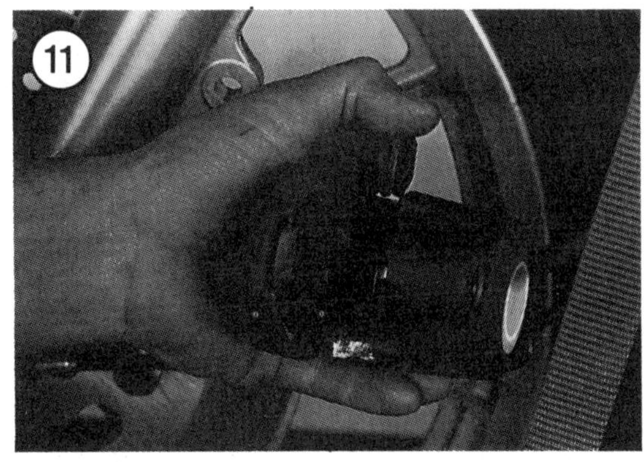

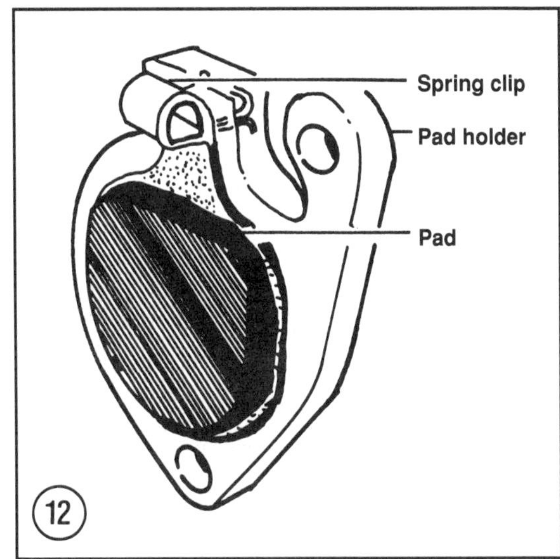

NOTE
*Pushing the piston back into the caliper bore in Step 15 will force brake fluid back into the master cylinder reservoir. To prevent the reservoir from overflowing, remove the reservoir cover (**Figure 14**) and diaphragm. Then watch the brake fluid level when performing Step 15. Remove brake fluid from the reservoir, if necessary, prior to it overflowing.*

15. Push the piston (**Figure 11**) into the cylinder with your fingers. Reinstall the diaphragm and cover (**Figure 14**) but do not install the cover screws.

NOTE
The piston should move freely. If not, and there is evidence of it sticking in the caliper bore, remove the caliper and service it as described in this chapter.

16. Install the inner brake pad (without the insulator backing) in the caliper recessed seat (**Figure 5**).
17. Insert the pad retainer (B, **Figure 4**) in the caliper counterbore. Install the self-tapping screw (A, **Figure 4**) through the pad retainer and thread it into the brake pad. Tighten the screw to 40-50 in.-lb. (4.5-5.6 N•m).
18. Insert the outer brake pad/pad holder assembly into the caliper so that the brake pad insulator backing faces against the piston. See **Figure 3**.

CAUTION
*On 1992-on models, the threaded bushing head must be installed between the rivet head and the pad holder as shown in **Figure 1**. On 1992 models, one of the U-shaped notches on the outer bushing flange must engage the rivet as shown in **Figure 1**. On 1993-on models, the U-shaped notch on the outer bushing flange must engage the rivet as shown in **Figure 1**. If the bushing is positioned incorrectly, the rivet will be damaged when the caliper mounting screw and pin are tightened.*

WARNING
The spring clip loop and the brake pad friction material must face away from the piston when the pad holder is installed in the caliper. Brake failure will occur if the brake pads are assembled incorrectly.

19. Coat the lower mounting pin shoulder with Dow Corning Moly 44 grease.

20. Install the caliper over the brake disc, making sure the friction surface on each pad faces against the disc.

21. Align the 2 mounting holes in the caliper with the slider mounting lugs.

22. Install a washer onto the upper mounting screw and insert the screw through the slider lug and then thread into the caliper bushing (A, **Figure 2**). Install the screw finger-tight.

23. Insert the lower mounting pin (B, **Figure 2**) through the caliper and then thread into the slider lug. Tighten mounting pin finger-tight.

24. Tighten the lower mounting pin to the torque specification in **Table 2**.

25. Tighten the upper mounting screw to the torque specification in **Table 2**.

26. Refill the master cylinder reservoir with DOT 5 silicone-based brake fluid, if necessary, to maintain the correct fluid level. Install the diaphragm and top cap (**Figure 14**).

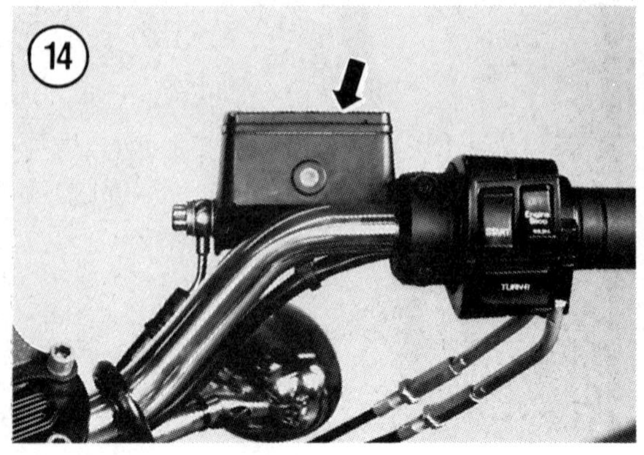

27. While the bike is stationary with the engine off, squeeze the front brake lever several times to seat the pads against the disc.

WARNING
Do not ride the motorcycle until you are sure the brakes are operating correctly with full hydraulic advantage. If necessary, bleed the brake system as described in this chapter.

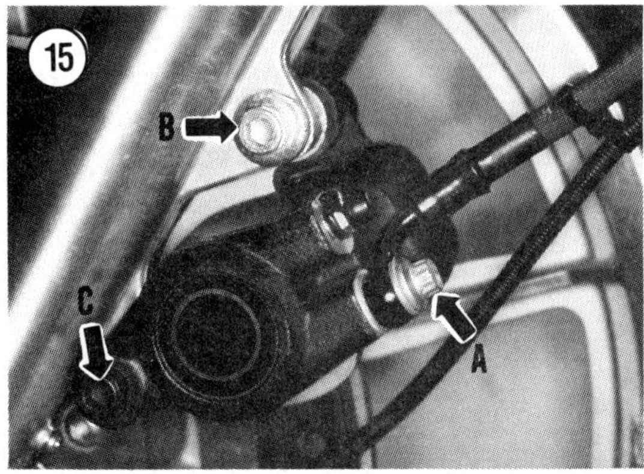

FRONT BRAKE CALIPER

Removal/Installation (Caliper Will Not Be Disassembled)

If the brake caliper is to be removed without disassembling it, perform this procedure. If the caliper is to be disassembled, refer to *Caliper Removal/Piston Removal* in this chapter.

1A. If the caliper is to be completely removed from the bike, perform the following:

a. Loosen and remove the banjo bolt at the caliper (A, **Figure 15**). Remove the bolt and the 2 washers. Plug the hose open end to prevent spills and to keep out dirt.
b. Remove the upper mounting screw (and washer) (B, **Figure 15**) and the lower mounting pin (C, **Figure 15**).
c. Lift brake caliper off the brake disc.

1B. If the caliper is only being partially removed, for example to remove the front wheel, and it is not necessary to disconnect the brake line at the caliper, perform the following:

a. Remove the upper mounting screw (and washer) (B, **Figure 15**) and the lower mounting pin (C, **Figure 15**).
b. Lift brake caliper off the brake disc.
c. Insert a wooden or plastic spacer block between the brake pads (**Figure 16**) in the caliper.

NOTE
The spacer block prevents the piston from being forced out of the caliper if the brake lever is squeezed while the caliper is removed from the brake disc. Squeezing the brake lever with the caliper removed will force the piston out of the caliper bore. If this happens, the caliper will have to be disassembled to reseat the piston and the system will have to be bled.

d. Support the caliper with a Bunjee cord or wire hook. Do not hang the caliper by its hose.

2. Install the caliper by reversing these steps, while noting the following.
3. Check that the upper and lower caliper bushings installed in the fork slider are in place; see **Figure 17**, typical.

WARNING
The upper and lower caliper bushings must be installed in the fork slider prior

12

to installing the brake caliper. Otherwise, the caliper and pad will be improperly located in relation to the brake disc. This condition will bind the caliper and brake pads, causing uneven braking and possible brake lockup.

4. If removed, install the brake pads as described in this chapter.
5. Install the caliper over the brake disc, making sure the friction surface on each pad faces against the disc (**Figure 18**).
6. Coat the lower mounting pin with Dow Corning Moly 44 grease.
7. Align the 2 mounting holes in the caliper with the slider mounting lugs.
8. Install a washer onto the upper mounting screw (**Figure 1**) and insert the screw (B, **Figure 15**) through the slider lug and then thread into the caliper bushing. Install the screw finger-tight.
9. Insert the lower mounting pin (C, **Figure 15**) through the caliper and then thread into the slider lug. Tighten mounting screw finger-tight.
10. Tighten the lower mounting pin (C, **Figure 15**) to the torque specification in **Table 2**.
11. Tighten the upper mounting screw (B, **Figure 15**) to the torque specification in **Table 2**.
12. Tighten the bleed screw if it was previously loosened.

NOTE
Install ***new*** *steel/rubber banjo bolt washers (**Figure 19**) when performing Step 13.*

13. If removed, assemble the brake line onto the caliper by placing a new washer on both sides of the brake line fitting, then secure the fitting to the caliper with the banjo bolt (A, **Figure 15**). Tighten the banjo bolt to the torque specification in **Table 2**. Make sure the fitting seats against the caliper as shown in A, **Figure 15**.
14. If necessary, refill the system and bleed the brake as described in this chapter.
15. While the bike is stationary with the engine off, squeeze the front brake lever several times to seat the pads against the disc.

WARNING
Do not ride the motorcycle until you are sure the brakes are operating properly.

Caliper Removal/Piston Removal (Caliper Will Be Disassembled)

If the caliper is to be completely disassembled, force will be required to remove the piston from the caliper. To do this, you can use hydraulic pressure in the brake system itself, or compressed air. If you are going to use the system's hydraulic pressure, you must do so prior to disconnecting the brake hose from the caliper. This procedure describes how to remove the piston while the caliper is still mounted on the bike.

1. Remove the brake pads as described in this chapter.
2. Carefully pry the retaining ring (5, **Figure 20**) out of the caliper body with a small screwdriver inserted in the notched groove machined in the bottom of the piston bore. Do not pry elsewhere in the caliper bore or you may damage the caliper.
3. Remove the dust boot (6, **Figure 20**).
4. Wrap a large cloth around the brake caliper.
5. Hold the caliper so that your hand and fingers are placed away from the piston/brake pad area.

6. Squeeze the front brake lever to force the piston out of the caliper cylinder. Remove the piston.

NOTE
If the piston did not come out in Step 6, you will have to use compressed air to remove it. Refer to ***Disassembly*** *in the chapter.*

7. Remove the caliper banjo bolt (A, **Figure 15**) and washers with an air gun and socket. If you don't have air tools, reinstall the caliper onto the fork slider and secure it with the upper mounting screw and lower mounting pin. Loosen and remove the caliper banjo bolt and both washers. Plug the brake hose to prevent spills and to keep out dirt.

8. Take the caliper to a workbench for further disassembly.

Disassembly

Harley-Davidson does not provide any specifications for wear limits on any of the front caliper components (except brake pads). Replace any parts that appear to be worn or damaged.

Refer to **Figure 20** for this procedure.

1. Remove the brake pads as described in this chapter.

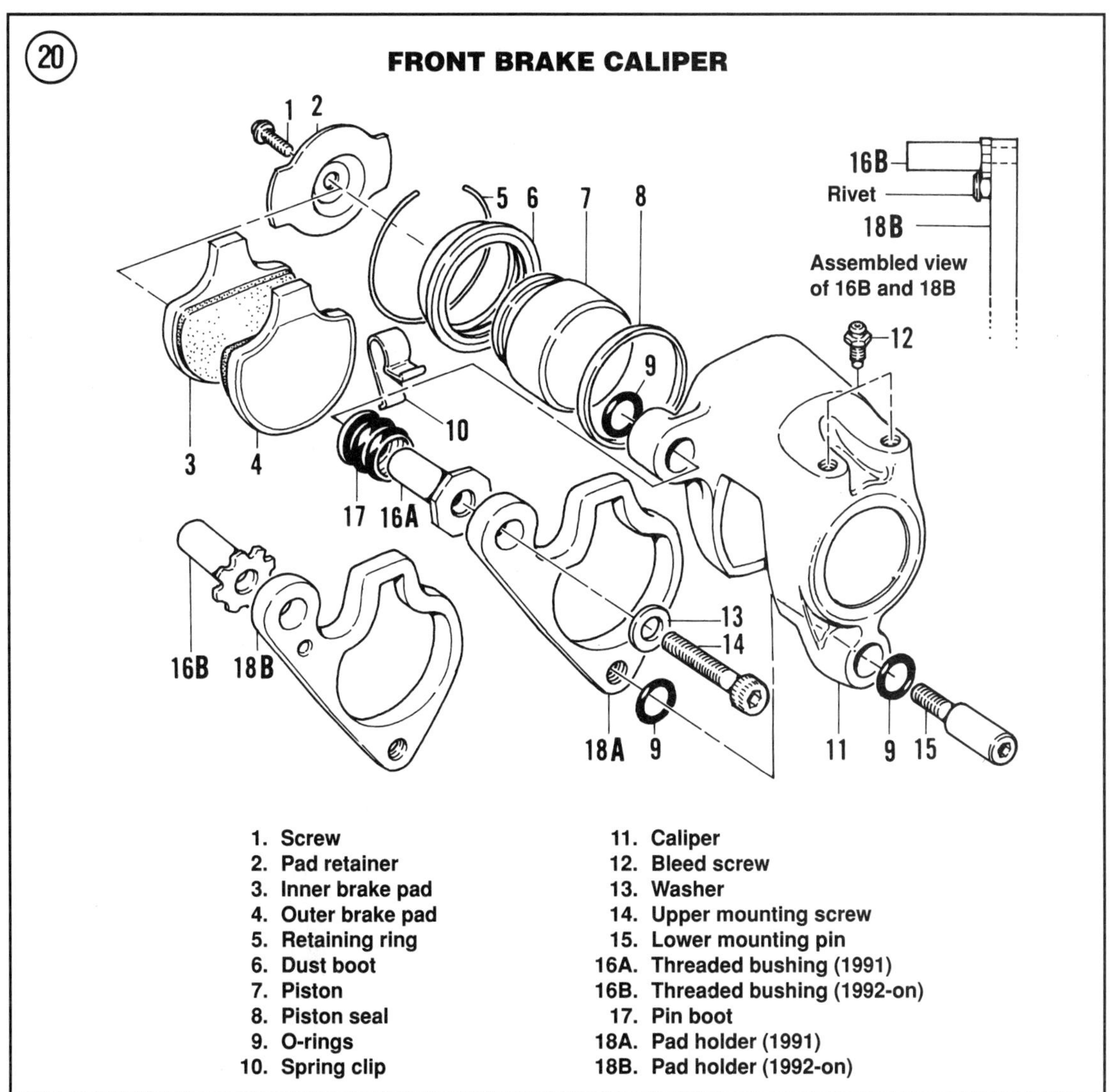

(20) FRONT BRAKE CALIPER

1. Screw
2. Pad retainer
3. Inner brake pad
4. Outer brake pad
5. Retaining ring
6. Dust boot
7. Piston
8. Piston seal
9. O-rings
10. Spring clip
11. Caliper
12. Bleed screw
13. Washer
14. Upper mounting screw
15. Lower mounting pin
16A. Threaded bushing (1991)
16B. Threaded bushing (1992-on)
17. Pin boot
18A. Pad holder (1991)
18B. Pad holder (1992-on)

NOTE
If you have removed the piston, proceed to Step 5.

2. Carefully pry the retaining ring (5, **Figure 20**) out of the caliper body with a small screwdriver inserted in the notched groove machined in the bottom of the piston bore. Do not pry elsewhere in the caliber bore or you may damage the caliper.
3. Remove the piston dust boot (6, **Figure 20**) from the groove at the top of the piston.

WARNING
When performing Step 4, the piston may shoot out like a bullet. Keep your fingers out of the way. Wear shop gloves and apply compressed air gradually.

4. Place a rag or piece of wood in the path of the piston (**Figure 21**, typical). Blow the piston out with compressed air directed through the hydraulic hole fitting. Use a service station air hose if you don't have a compressor.
5. Remove the piston seal from the groove in the caliper body.
6. Pull the threaded bushing out of the caliper, then remove the pin boot.
7. Remove the 3 O-rings from the caliper body.

Inspection

1. Inspect the caliper body for damage; replace the caliper body if necessary.
2. Inspect the hydraulic fluid passageway in the cylinder bore. Make sure it is clean and open. Apply compressed air to the opening and make sure it is clear. Clean out, if necessary, with fresh brake fluid.
3. Inspect the piston and cylinder wall for scratches, scoring or other damage. Replace worn, corroded or damaged parts.
4. Inspect the banjo bolt and bleed valve threads in the caliper body. If the threads are slightly damaged, clean them up with the proper size thread tap. If the threads are worn or damaged beyond repair, replace the caliper body.
5. Make sure the hole in the bleed valve screw is clean and open. Clean with compressed air. Flush with DOT 5 silicone-based brake fluid.
6. Check the threaded bushing, upper mounting screw and the lower mounting pin for thread damage. Repair threads or replace damaged parts as required. Check the mounting pin shoulder for deep scoring or excessive wear; replace if necessary.
7. Check the pad retainer for cracks or damage.
8. Check the brake pads (**Figure 7**) for wear or damage. Replace the brake pads if they are worn to 0.062 in. (1.57 mm) or less (**Figure 8**). Replace both pads as a set.
9. Check all of the rubber parts (dust boot, O-rings, piston seal, etc.) for cracks, wear or age deterioration. Because very minor damage or age deterioration can make these parts useless, questionable parts should be replaced. If you plan to reuse a rubber part, clean the part thoroughly in new brake fluid and place on a lint-free cloth until reassembly.
10. If serviceable, clean all metal parts with rubbing alcohol.

Assembly

1. After replacing all worn or damaged parts, coat the following parts with new DOT 5 silicone-based brake fluid. Place the parts on a clean lint-free cloth to prevent contamination before assembly.
   a. Piston.
   b. Piston seal.
2. Make sure the retaining wire, piston and caliper bore are thoroughly clean. If necessary, re-clean and allow to air dry before reassembly.
3. Install the piston seal into the caliper body groove.
4. Install the 3 O-rings (9, **Figure20**) into the caliper grooves.
5. Wipe the inside of the pin boot with Dow Corning MOLY 44 grease. Then insert the boot into the

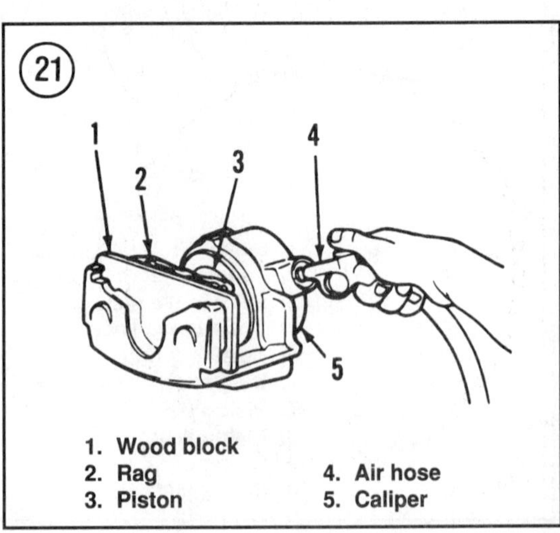

1. Wood block
2. Rag
3. Piston
4. Air hose
5. Caliper

bushing bore so that the flange end on the boot seats in the bushing bore internal groove.

6. The piston dust boot is installed on the piston *before* the piston is installed in the caliper bore. Perform the following:

a. Place the piston on your workbench so that the open side faces up.
b. Align the piston dust boot with the piston so that the shoulder on the dust boot faces up.
c. Slide the piston dust boot onto the piston until the inner lip on the dust boot seats in the piston groove.

7. Coat the piston and the caliper bore with DOT 5 silicone-based brake fluid.

8. Align the piston with the caliper bore so that its open end faces out. Then push the piston in until it bottoms out.

NOTE
If you are installing new brake pads, you will have to push the piston all the way into the bore. If necessary, use a C-clamp to push the piston into the bore.

9. Locate the retaining ring groove in the end of the caliper bore. Then align the retaining ring so that the gap in the ring (**Figure 22**) is at the top of the caliper bore and install the ring into the ring groove. Make sure that the retaining ring is seated completely in the groove and that it is pushing against the piston dust boot.

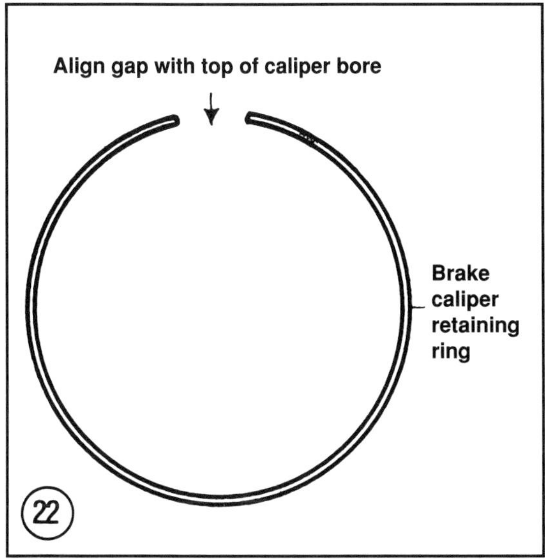

10. Wipe the caliper mounting lug bores with Dow Corning MOLY 44 grease.

11. Insert the threaded bushing into the pin boot until the end of the pin boot seats in the groove shoulder, adjacent to the threaded bushing hexagonal head.

12. Install the brake pads as described in this chapter.

FRONT MASTER CYLINDER

Removal/Installation

Refer to **Figure 23** for this procedure.

1. Flip the rubber cover off of the front caliper bleeder valve (**Figure 24**) and insert a hose onto the end of the valve. Insert the open end of the hose into a container. Open the front bleeder valve and drain the brake fluid from the front brake assembly by operating the hand lever. Remove the hose and close the bleeder valve after draining the assembly. Discard the brake fluid.
2. Place a couple of shop cloths under the banjo bolt and remove the banjo bolt and washers securing the brake hose to the master cylinder (A, **Figure 25**).
3. Remove the mounting screws (B, **Figure 25**) securing the master cylinder to the handlebar.
4. Install by reversing these removal steps, noting the following.
5. Clean the handlebar of all brake fluid residue.
6. Clean the banjo bolt (**Figure 19**) fluid passage thoroughly. Use air to dry the bolt or allow it to air dry thoroughly before installation into the master cylinder.
7. Check the clamp for cracks or damage. Replace if necessary.
8. Position the master cylinder onto the handlebar and install the clamp and its 2 attaching screws (B, **Figure 25**). Tighten the screws to the torque specification in **Table 2**.

NOTE
*Install **new** steel/rubber banjo bolt washers (**Figure 19**) when performing Step 9.*

9. Install the brake hose onto the master cylinder and brake caliper. Be sure to place a new washer on each side of the hose fitting (A, **Figure 25**) when installing the banjo bolt. Tighten the banjo bolts to the torque specification listed in **Table 2**.

12

10. Fill the master cylinder with new DOT 5 silicone-based brake fluid. Bleed the brake system as described in this chapter.

NOTE
When actuating the brake lever in Step 10, a small spurt of fluid should break through the fluid surface in the master cylinder to indicate that all internal master cylinder components are working properly.

11. Install the master cylinder diaphragm and cover after bleeding the brakes. Sit on the motorcycle and check that the brake lever position is suitable to your riding position. If necessary, loosen the clamp screws and reposition the master cylinder; retighten the clamp screws to the torque specification listed in **Table 2**.

WARNING
Do not ride the motorcycle until you are sure the brakes are working properly.

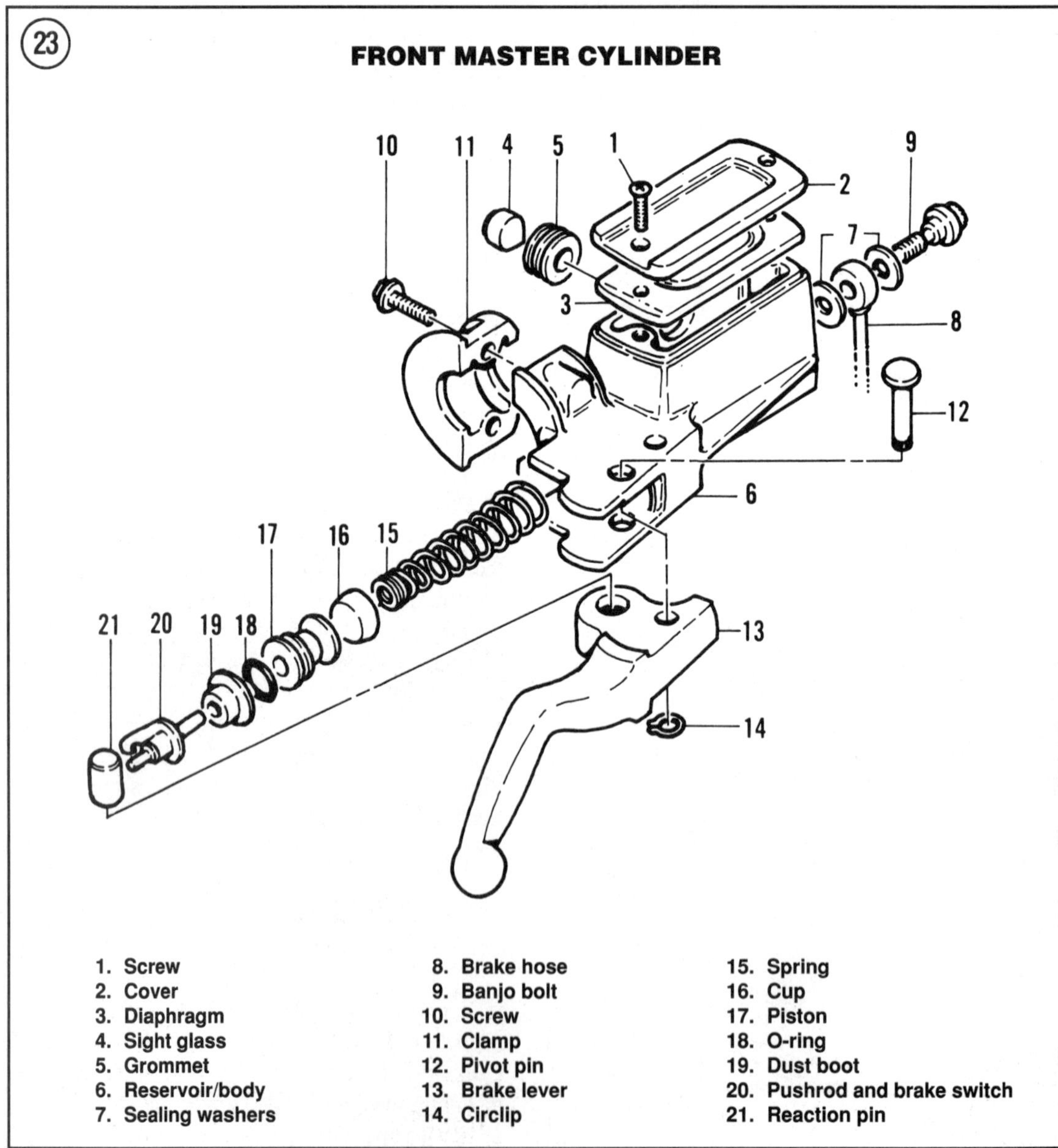

(23) **FRONT MASTER CYLINDER**

1. Screw
2. Cover
3. Diaphragm
4. Sight glass
5. Grommet
6. Reservoir/body
7. Sealing washers
8. Brake hose
9. Banjo bolt
10. Screw
11. Clamp
12. Pivot pin
13. Brake lever
14. Circlip
15. Spring
16. Cup
17. Piston
18. O-ring
19. Dust boot
20. Pushrod and brake switch
21. Reaction pin

Disassembly

Refer to **Figure 23** when performing this procedure.

1. Drain and remove the master cylinder as described in this chapter.
2. Remove the screws securing the top cover and remove the cover and diaphragm. Pour remaining brake fluid from the reservoir and discard it. Do not reuse brake fluid.
3. The brake lever pivot pin is secured with a circlip. Remove the circlip and remove the pivot pin and brake lever.
4. Remove the reaction pin from the hand lever.
5. Referring to **Figure 23**, remove the following components in order:
   a. Push rod and brake switch actuator.
   b. Dust boot.
   c. Piston and O-ring.
   d. Cup.
   e. Spring.
6. If damaged, remove the grommet and sight glass from the rear side of the master cylinder housing.

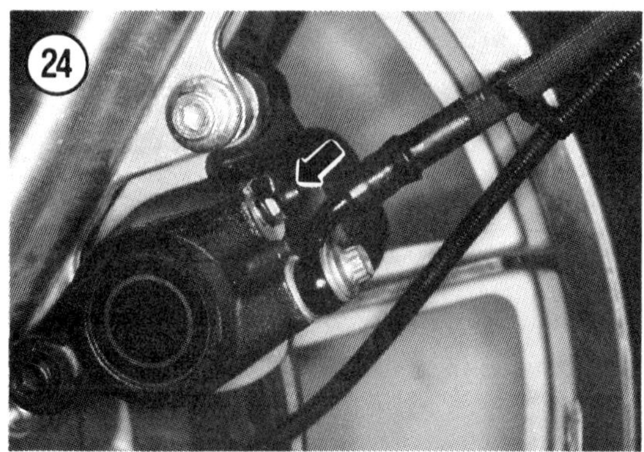

Inspection

Harley-Davidson does not provide any specifications or wear limits on any of the master cylinder components. Replace any parts that appear to be damaged or worn.

1. Clean all parts in denatured alcohol or fresh DOT 5 silicone-based brake fluid. Cleaned parts should be placed on a clean lint-free cloth until reassembly.
2. The piston assembly consists of the dust boot, O-ring, piston, cup and spring. Inspect the rubber parts for wear, cracks, swelling or other damage. Check the piston for severe wear or damage. Check the spring for fatigue or breakage. If any one part of the piston assembly is damaged, the entire piston assembly must be replaced; individual parts are not available from Harley-Davidson.

NOTE

Do not remove the O-ring from the piston if you plan on reusing the piston and O-ring.

3. Inspect the master cylinder walls for scratches or wear grooves. The master cylinder housing should be replaced if the cylinder walls are damaged.
4. Check to see that the vent hole in the cover is not plugged.
5. Check the banjo bolt threads in the master cylinder. If the threads are slightly damaged, clean them up with the proper size thread tap. If the threads are severely worn or damaged, replace the master cylinder body.

NOTE

If you use a tap to clean the threads in the master cylinder, flush the master cylinder thoroughly with solvent and blow dry.

6. Inspect the piston bore in the master cylinder for wear, corrosion or damage. Replace the master cylinder if necessary.
7. Make sure the fluid passage hole through the banjo bolt is clear. Flush bolt if necessary.
8. Check the reaction pin and pivot pin holes in the brake lever for cracks, spreading or other damage. Check the lever for cracks or damage.
9. Check the reaction and pivot pins for severe wear or damage.
10. Check the fit of each pin in the brake lever. Replace worn or damaged parts as required.

Assembly

1A. If you are installing a factory master cylinder rebuild kit, coat the master cylinder bore and all of the piston components with the lubricant supplied in the rebuild kit.

1B. If you are not installing a factory master cylinder rebuild kit, soak the piston O-ring and cup in fresh DOT 5 silicone-based brake fluid for at least 15 minutes to make the cups pliable. Apply a thin coat of brake fluid to the cylinder bore prior to assembly.

2. Install the grommet and sight glass if removed.
3. Insert the cup onto the small end of the spring.
4. Insert the spring and cup into the master cylinder.
5. Install the O-ring onto the piston and insert the piston into the master cylinder.
6. Install the dust boot and reaction pin/switch.
7. Lightly coat the reaction pin with Loctite Anti-seize.
8. Referring to **Figure 26**, assemble the brake lever as follows:
   a. Install the reaction pin into the large hole in the brake lever.
   b. Position the brake lever into the master cylinder, making sure the end of the pushrod fits into the hole in the reaction pin.

NOTE
Make sure the pushrod and switch are fully seated in the reaction pin hole. If the hand lever binds or is not smooth in action, disassemble the parts and reassemble them correctly.

   c. Insert the pivot pin through the master cylinder and engage the brake lever. Secure the pivot pin with the circlip.

REAR DISC BRAKE

The rear disc brake is actuated by hydraulic fluid and is controlled by the right-hand foot-operated pedal that is linked to the master cylinder. As the brake pads wear, the brake fluid level drops in the reservoir and automatically adjusts for wear.

REAR BRAKE PADS

There is no recommended mileage interval for changing the friction pads in the disc brake. Pad wear depends greatly on riding habits and conditions. The pads should be checked for wear initially at 500 miles (800 km), then every 2,500 miles (4,000 km) and replaced when the lining thickness reaches 0.062 in. (1.57 mm) from the brake pad backing plate. To maintain an even brake pressure on the disc

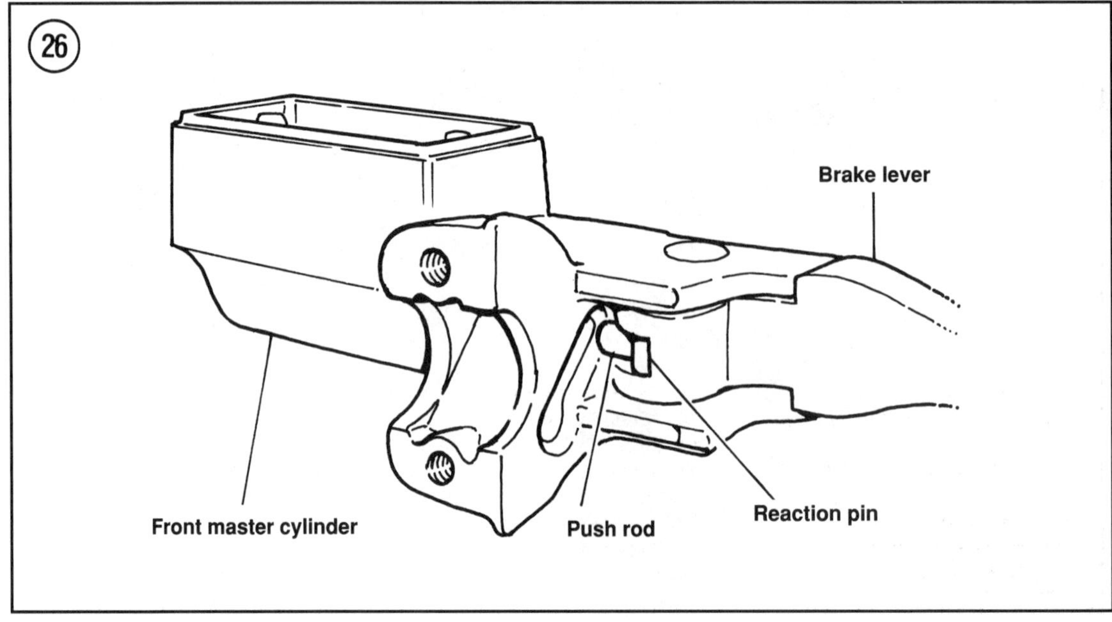

always replace both pads in the caliper at the same time.

Brake Pad/Pad Shim Identification

There was a design change between early 1991 and late 1991-on models regarding the brake pads and pad shims (**Figure 27**). When purchasing replacement parts, note the following while referring to **Figure 28** (early 1991) or **Figure 29** (late 1991-on):

a. Early 1991 pad shim thickness is 0.015 in. (0.38 mm).
b. Late 1991-on pad shim thickness is 0.030 in. (0.76 mm).
c. Early 1991 pad shims have a tab in the middle of each long side.
d. Late 1991-on pad shims have an open loop at one end of the shim.
e. Early 1991 brake pads measure approximately 3.44 in. (87.4 mm) between the "V" notches as shown in **Figure 28**. Late 1991-on brake pads measure approximately 3.39 in. (86.1 mm) as shown in **Figure 29**.
f. Early 1991 outboard brake pads have an angle-cut, half-size insulator mounted on the back of the pad. The inboard brake pad has a full-size insulator.
g. Late 1991-on brake pads have full-size insulators mounted on the back of each pad.

WARNING

When replacing brake pads, do not intermix early 1991 and late 1991-on brake pads and pad shims. Otherwise, improper rear brake operation will occur. This may cause brake failure and loss of control, resulting in personal injury. When purchasing new brake

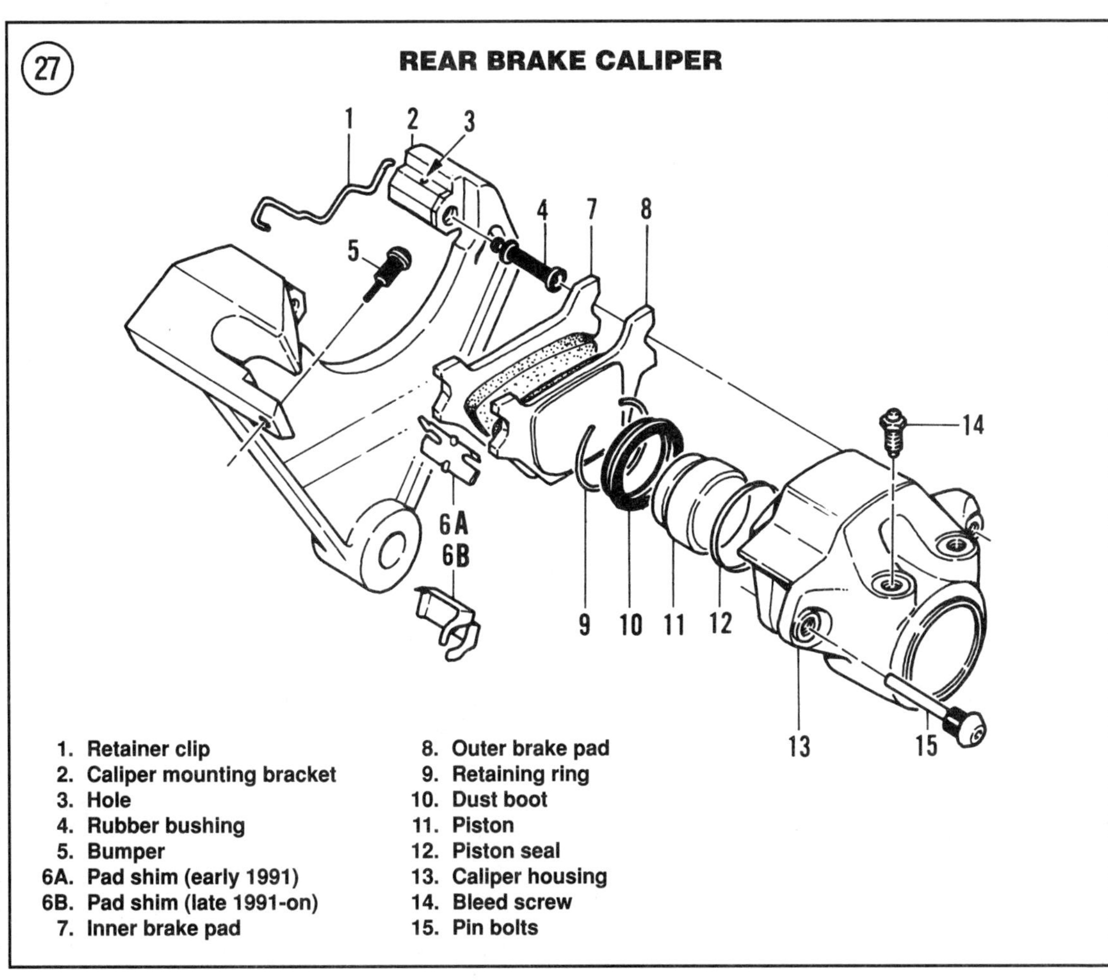

1. Retainer clip
2. Caliper mounting bracket
3. Hole
4. Rubber bushing
5. Bumper
6A. Pad shim (early 1991)
6B. Pad shim (late 1991-on)
7. Inner brake pad
8. Outer brake pad
9. Retaining ring
10. Dust boot
11. Piston
12. Piston seal
13. Caliper housing
14. Bleed screw
15. Pin bolts

pads, take your frame's serial number to the dealer and have them verify your model as an early or late model.

Replacement

Refer to **Figure 27** for this procedure.

1. To prevent accidental application of the rear brake lever, tie the pedal up to the frame so it cannot be depressed.
2. Remove the 2 caliper pin bolts (A, **Figure 30**) and lift the caliper (B, **Figure 30**) off of the mounting bracket. Do not disconnect the brake hose at the caliper. Support the caliper with a Bunjee cord.
3. Pull the retainer clip (**Figure 31**) over the mounting bracket and remove it. See **Figure 32**.

NOTE
If you intend to reuse the brake pads, mark each pad so that it can be reinstalled in its original mounting position in the caliper.

4. Slide the outer brake pad (**Figure 33**) toward the shock absorber and off the mounting bracket.
5. Slide the inner brake pad (A, **Figure 34**) toward the wheel and off the mounting bracket.
6. Remove the 2 pad shims (B, **Figure 34**) from the mounting bracket. Refer to **Figure 27** for a comparison of the early 1991 and late 1991-on pad shims.
7. Check the brake pads (**Figure 35**) for wear or damage. Replace the brake pads if they are worn to 0.062 in. (1.57 mm) or less. Replace both pads as a set.

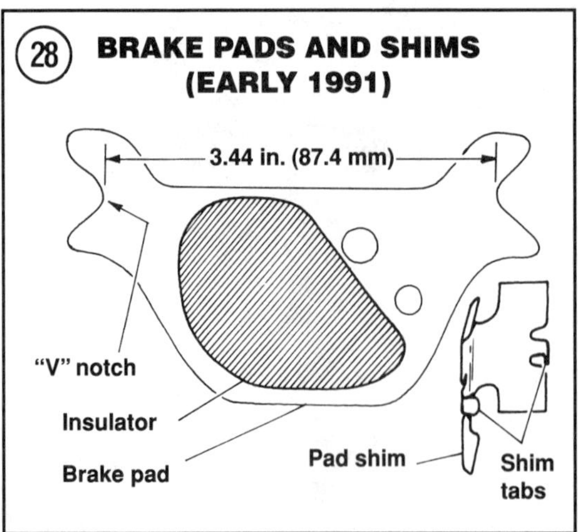

8. Clean the pad shims thoroughly and check for cracks or damage. Replace if necessary.
9. Clean the pad shim mounting area on the mounting bracket thoroughly.
10. Check the retainer clip. If worn, cracked, rusted, deformed or corroded, replace it.
11. Inspect the caliper pin bolts and replace if cracked, corroded or otherwise damaged.

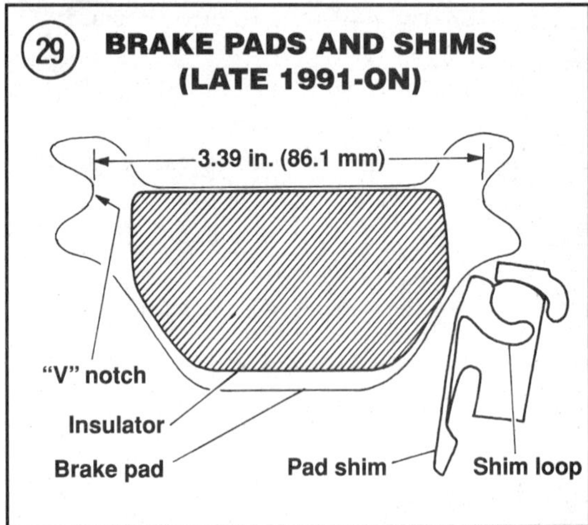

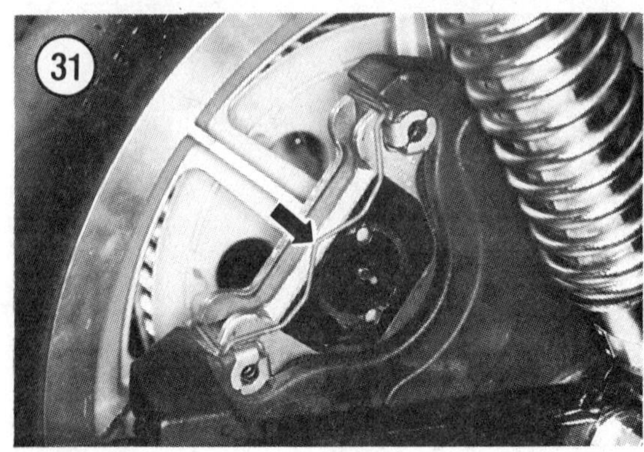

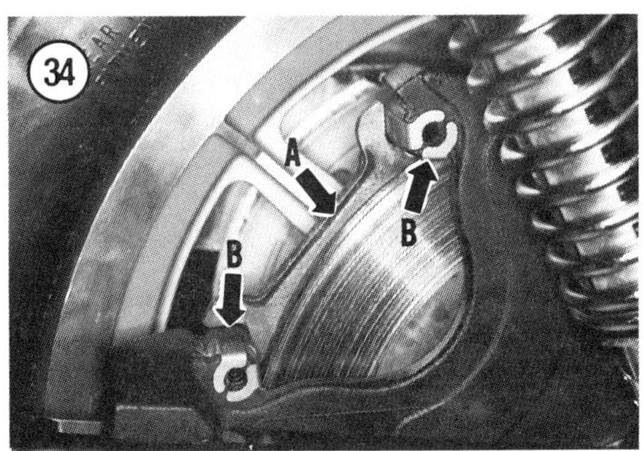

12. Check the piston dust boot. If the boot is swollen or cracked or if brake fluid is leaking from the caliper bore, remove the caliper and overhaul it as described under *Rear Brake Caliper* in this chapter.

13. Check the brake disc for wear as described under *Brake Disc* in this chapter. Service the brake disc if necessary.

NOTE
Pushing the piston back into the caliper bore in Step 14 will force brake fluid back into the master cylinder reservoir. To prevent the reservoir from overflowing, remove the reservoir cover and diaphragm. Then watch the brake fluid level when performing Step 15. Remove brake fluid from the reservoir, if necessary, prior to it overflowing.

14. Push the piston into the caliper cylinder with your fingers. Reinstall the diaphragm and cover but do not install the cover screws.

NOTE
The piston should move freely. If not, and there is evidence of it sticking in the caliper bore, remove the caliper and service it as described in this chapter.

NOTE
When replacing the brake pads and pad shims, refer to ***Brake Pad/Pad Shim Identification*** *in this chapter. Confirm that you have the correct brake pad and pad shim assembly for your model.*

15. Install the pad shims onto the caliper mounting bracket rails as follows:

a. On early 1991 models, insert the pad shim tabs (**Figure 28**) into caliper bracket shim holes (3, **Figure 27**).

b. On late 1991-on models, install the pad shims so that their retaining loops face against the outer caliper mounting bracket rails as shown in B, **Figure 34** and **Figure 36**.

c. On all models, hold the pad shims in place when installing the rear brake pad in Step 16.

NOTE
On early 1991 models, the outboard brake pad is different from the inboard brake pad. The outboard brake pad (piston side) has an angle-cut, half-size insulator mounted on the back of the

*pad (**Figure 28**). The inboard brake pad has a full-size insulator.*

NOTE
On late 1991-on models, install used pads in their original mounting positions as identified during removal. New pads are identical and can be installed in either position (inboard or outboard).

NOTE
*Install both brake pads with their friction surface (**Figure 35**) facing toward the brake disc.*

16. Slide the inboard brake pad (A, **Figure 34**) over the pad shims so that it contacts the inner brake disc surface. Check that the pad shims did not move out of position.
17. Slide the outboard brake pad (**Figure 33**) over the pad shims so that it contacts the outer brake disc surface.
18. Check that the pad shims did not move out of position.
19. Insert the ends of the retainer clip (**Figure 32**) into the 2 large holes in the backside of the caliper mounting bracket (**Figure 37**). Then pivot the clip over the top of the brake pads and snap it in place against the outer brake pad as shown in **Figure 31**.

CAUTION
*After installing the retainer clip, check that both brake pads are still contacting the 2 pad shims; see **Figure 38**, typical. If the pads or shims are installed incorrectly, the rear brake will drag and cause uneven pad wear and caliper mounting bracket damage.*

NOTE
The caliper should be installed carefully over the brake pads so it does not knock against the brake pads and dislodge the pad shims.

20. Align the caliper with the brake pads and install it over the pads (B, **Figure 30**). Align the caliper holes with the caliper mounting bracket threaded holes and install the 2 pin bolts. See **Figure 39** and A, **Figure 30**. Start the bolts by hand, then tighten to the torque specification in **Table 2**.
21. If you tied the rear brake pedal to the frame, disconnect the wire so that the pedal can be operated.
22. Refill the master cylinder reservoir, if necessary, to maintain the correct fluid level. Install the diaphragm and top cap.

WARNING
Use brake fluid clearly marked DOT 5 silicone-based from a sealed container. Other types may vaporize and cause brake failure. Always use the same brand name; do not intermix as many brands are not compatible.

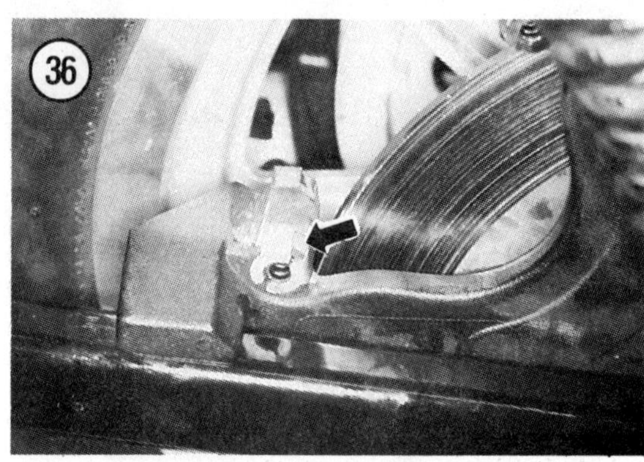
36

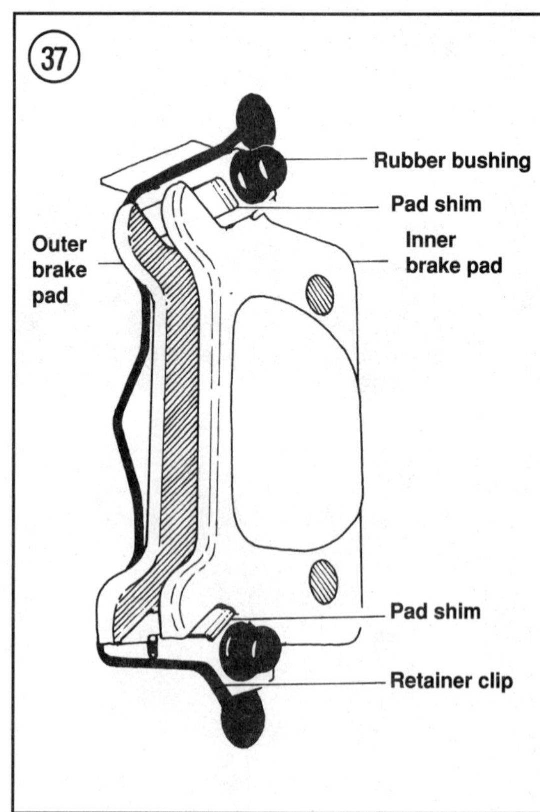

37

23. While the bike is stationary with the engine off, press the rear brake pedal several times to seat the pads against the disc.

WARNING
Do not ride the motorcycle until you are sure the brakes are operating correctly with full hydraulic advantage. If necessary, bleed the brake system as described in this chapter.

REAR BRAKE CALIPER

Removal/Installation (Caliper Will Not Be Disassembled)

If the brake caliper is to be removed without disassembling it, perform this procedure. If the caliper is to be disassembled, refer to *Caliper Removal/Piston Removal* in this chapter.

1A. If the caliper is to be completely removed from the bike, perform the following:

a. Loosen and remove the banjo bolt at the caliper (A, **Figure 40**). Remove the bolt and the 2 washers. Plug the hose open end to prevent spills and to keep out dirt.
b. Remove the 2 caliper pin bolts (B, **Figure 40**) and lift the caliper off of the mounting bracket.

1B. If the caliper is only being partially removed, for example to remove the rear wheel, and it is not necessary to disconnect the brake line at the caliper, perform the following:

a. Remove the 2 caliper pin bolts (B, **Figure 40**) and lift the caliper off of the mounting bracket.
b. Insert a wooden or plastic spacer block between the piston and the opposite side of the caliper.

NOTE
The spacer block prevents the piston from being forced out of the caliper if the foot lever is pressed while the caliper is removed from the brake disc. Pressing the foot lever with the caliper removed will force the piston out of the caliper bore. If this happens, the caliper will have to be disassembled to reseat the piston and the system will have to be bled.

c. Support the caliper with a Bunjee cord or wire hook. Do not hang the caliper by its hose.

2. Install the caliper by reversing these steps, while noting the following.
3. If removed, install the pad shims and brake pads as described in this chapter.

NOTE
The caliper should be installed carefully over the brake pads so it does not knock against the brake pads and dislodge the pad shims.

4. Align the caliper with the brake pads and install it over the pads (B, **Figure 30**). Align the caliper

12

holes with the caliper mounting bracket threaded holes and install the 2 pin bolts. See **Figure 39** and B, **Figure 40**. Start the bolts by hand, then tighten to the torque specification in **Table 2**.

5. Tighten the bleed screw if it was previously loosened.

NOTE

*Install **new** steel/rubber banjo bolt washers (**Figure 41**) when performing Step 6.*

6. If removed, assemble the brake line onto the caliper by placing a new washer on both sides of the

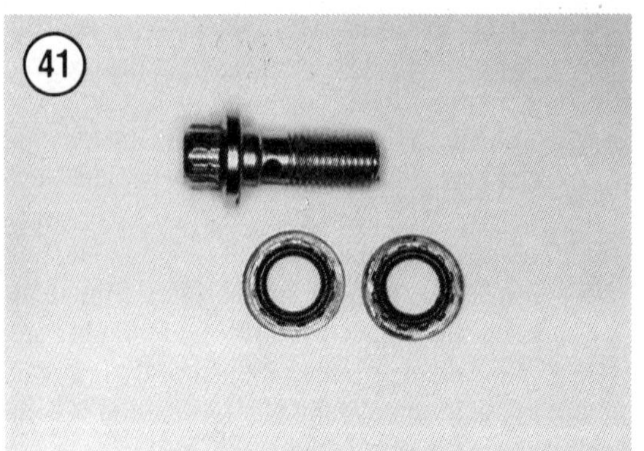

41

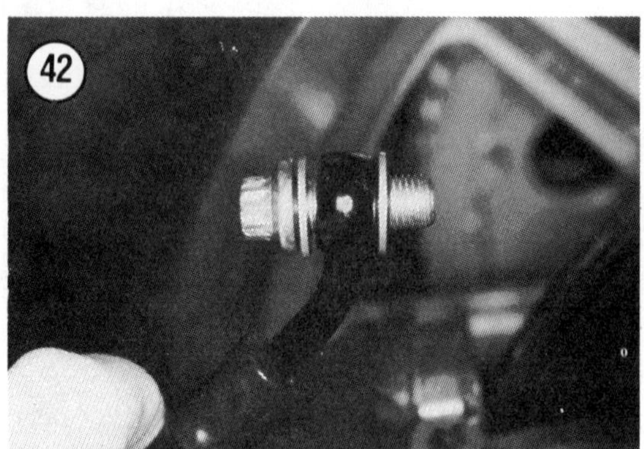

42

43

REAR BRAKE CALIPER

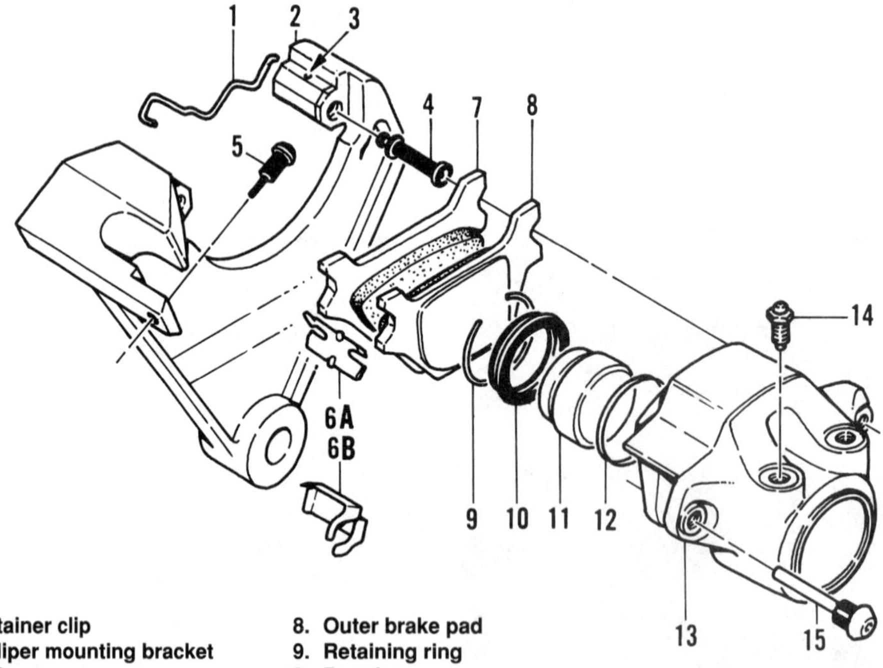

1. Retainer clip
2. Caliper mounting bracket
3. Hole
4. Rubber bushing
5. Bumper
6A. Pad shim (early 1991)
6B. Pad shim (late 1991-on)
7. Inner brake pad
8. Outer brake pad
9. Retaining ring
10. Dust boot
11. Piston
12. Piston seal
13. Caliper housing
14. Bleed screw
15. Pin bolts

brake line fitting (**Figure 42**), then secure the fitting to the caliper with the banjo bolt (A, **Figure 40**). Tighten the banjo bolt to the torque specification in **Table 2**.

7. If necessary, refill the system and bleed the brake as described in this chapter.
8. While the bike is stationary with the engine off, press the rear brake pedal several times to seat the pads against the disc.

WARNING
Do not ride the motorcycle until you are sure the brakes are operating properly.

Caliper Removal/Piston Removal (Caliper Will Be Disassembled)

If the caliper is to be completely disassembled, force will be required to remove the piston from the caliper. To do this, you can use hydraulic pressure in the brake system itself, or compressed air. If you are going to use the system's hydraulic pressure, you must do so prior to disconnecting the brake hose from the caliper. This procedure describes how to remove the piston while the caliper is still mounted on the bike.

1. Remove the brake pads as described in this chapter.
2. Carefully pry the retaining ring (9, **Figure 43**) out of the caliper body with a small screwdriver inserted in the notched groove machined in the bottom of the piston bore. Do not pry elsewhere in the caliper bore or you may damage the caliper.
3. Remove the dust boot (10, **Figure 43**).
4. Wrap a large cloth around the brake caliper.
5. Hold the caliper so that your hand and fingers are placed away from the piston/brake pad area.
6. Press the foot lever to force the piston out of the caliper cylinder. Remove the piston.

NOTE
*If the piston did not come out in Step 6, you will have to use compressed air to remove it. Refer to **Disassembly** in the chapter.*

7. Remove the caliper banjo bolt (**Figure 41**) and washers with an air gun and socket. If you don't have air tools, reinstall the caliper over its mounting bracket and secure it with the 2 pin bolts. Loosen and remove the caliper banjo bolt and both washers. Plug the brake hose to prevent spills and to keep out dirt.
8. Take the caliper to a workbench for further disassembly.

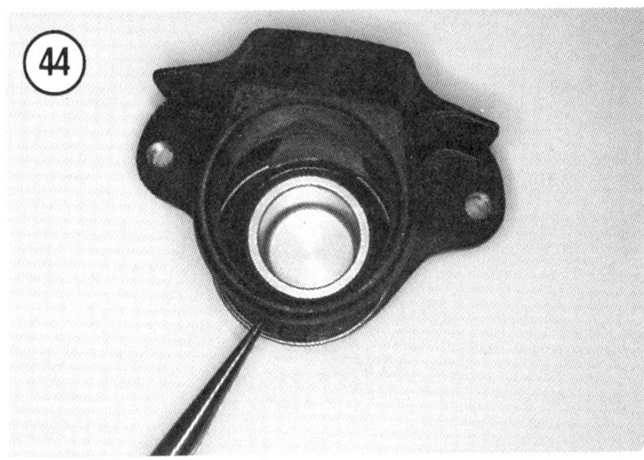
44

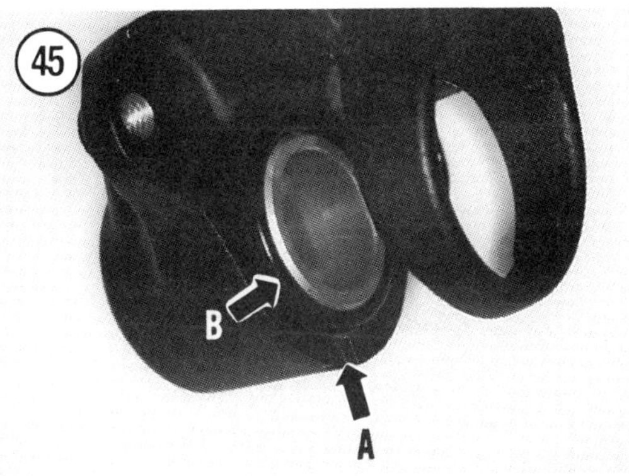

45

Disassembly

Harley-Davidson does not provide any specifications for wear limits on any of the rear caliper components (except brake pads). Replace any parts that appear to be worn or damaged.

Refer to **Figure 43** for this procedure.

1. Remove the brake caliper as described in this chapter.

NOTE
If you have removed the piston, proceed to Step 5.

2. Carefully pry the retaining ring (**Figure 44**) out of the caliper body with a small screwdriver inserted in the notched groove (A, **Figure 45**) machined in the bottom of the piston bore. Do not pry elsewhere in the caliber bore or you may damage the caliper.
3. Remove the piston dust boot (B, **Figure 45**) from the groove at the top of the piston.

12

WARNING
When performing Step 4, the piston may shoot out like a bullet. Keep your fingers out of the way. Wear shop gloves and apply compressed air gradually.

4. Place a rag or piece of wood in the path of the piston (**Figure 46**, typical). Blow the piston out with compressed air directed through the hydraulic hole fitting. Use a service station air hose if you don't have a compressor.
5. Remove the piston and dust boot (**Figure 47**). Remove the dust boot from the piston and discard it.
6. Remove the piston seal (**Figure 48**) from the groove in the caliper body.

Inspection

1. Inspect the caliper body for damage; replace the caliper body if necessary.
2. Inspect the hydraulic fluid passageway in the cylinder bore. Make sure it is clean and open. Apply compressed air to the opening and make sure it is clear. Clean out, if necessary, with fresh brake fluid.
3. Inspect the caliper bore wall (**Figure 49**) for scratches, scoring or other damage. Replace worn, corroded or damaged parts.

CAUTION
Do not hone or bore the caliper bore wall.

4. Inspect the banjo bolt and bleed valve threads in the caliper body. If the threads are slightly damaged, clean them up with the proper size thread tap. If the threads are worn or damaged beyond repair, replace the caliper body.
5. Make sure the hole in the bleed valve screw is clean and open. Clean with compressed air. Flush with DOT 5 silicone-based brake fluid.
6. Check the pin bolts for severe wear or damage. Replace if necessary.
7. Replace the caliper mounting bracket rubber bushings (4, **Figure 43**) and bumper (5, **Figure 43**) if severely worn or damaged.
8. Harley-Davidson specifies that you replace the dust boot and piston seal when they are removed from the caliper. If you do not plan on replacing these parts, inspect them carefully for cracks, wear or age deterioration. Because very minor damage or age deterioration can make these parts useless, questionable parts should be replaced. If you plan to reuse a rubber part, clean the part thoroughly in new brake fluid and place on a lint-free cloth until reassembly.
9. If serviceable, clean all metal parts with rubbing alcohol.
10. Replace any questionable parts.

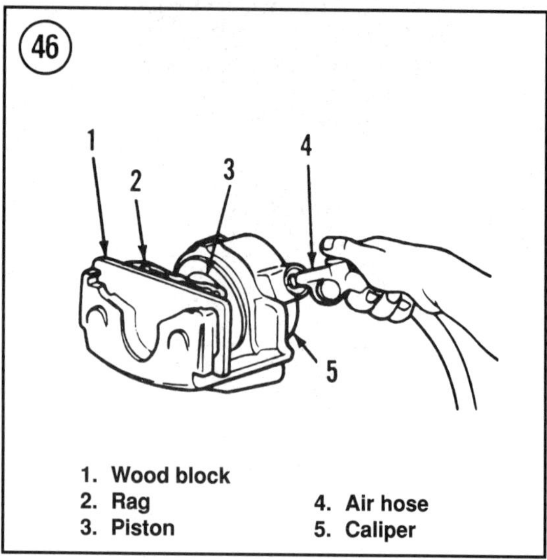

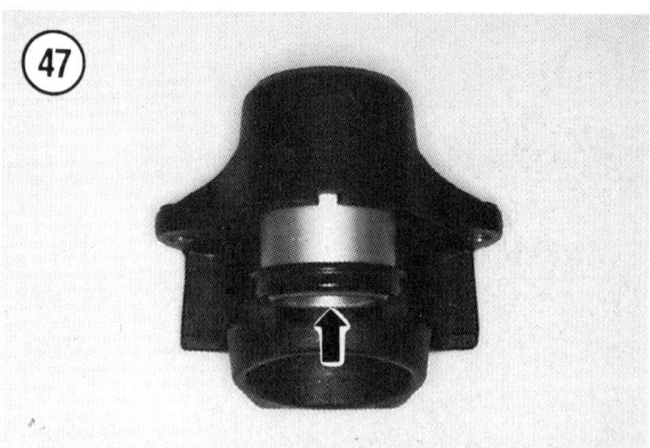

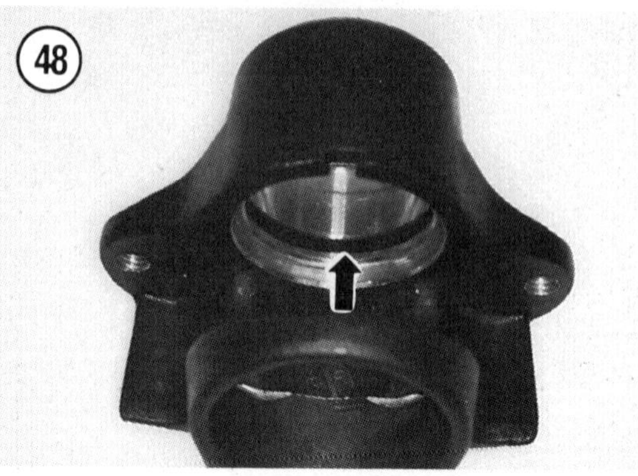

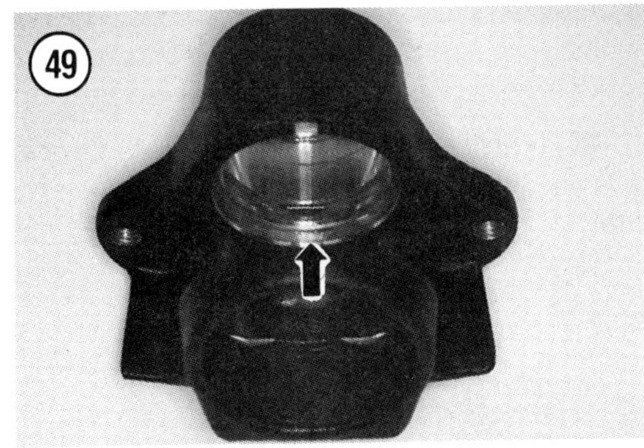

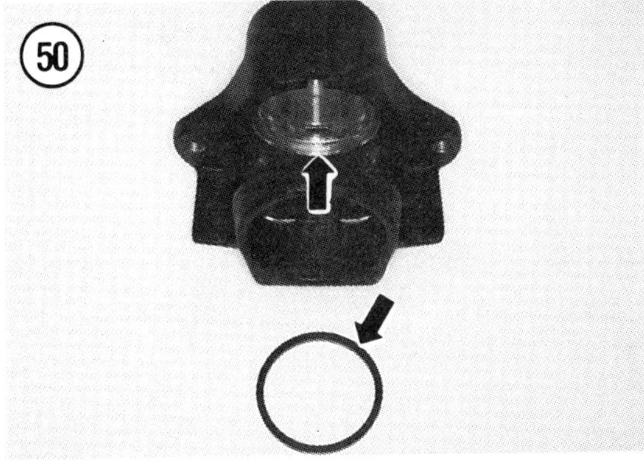

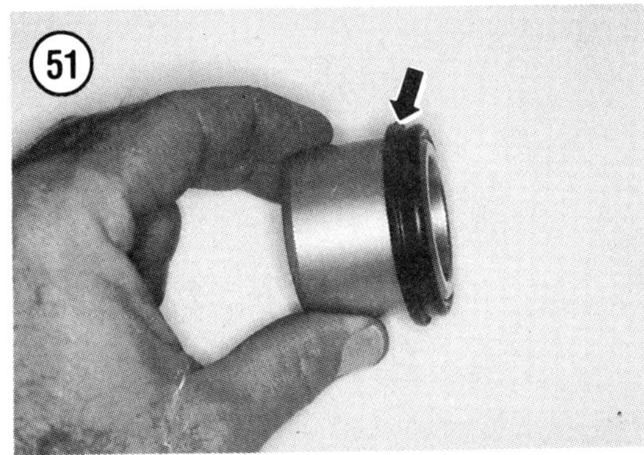

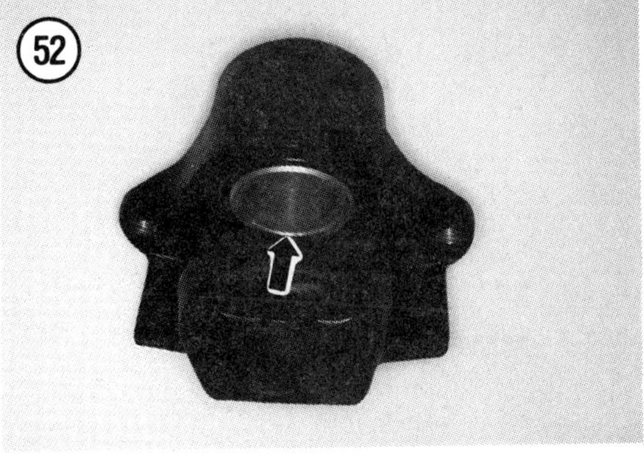

Assembly

1. Lubricate the caliper bore and the piston seal (**Figure 50**) with new DOT 5 silicone-based brake fluid.
2. Install the piston seal into the caliper bore groove (**Figure 48**). Make sure the piston seal is fully seated in the groove.
3. Align the dust boot's concave side with the top (open side) of the piston and slide the dust boot over the piston, seating the boot's inner lip in the piston groove. See **Figure 51**.
4. Lubricate the piston with clean brake fluid and push the piston (**Figure 47**) fully into the caliper bore. The piston's open side must face out as shown in **Figure 52**.

NOTE
If necessary, use a C-clamp to push the piston into the bore.

5. Seat the dust boot's outer lip into the caliper bore (B, **Figure 45**).
6. Locate the retaining ring groove in the end of the caliper bore. Then align the retaining ring so that the gap in the ring (**Figure 53**) is at the top of the caliper bore and install the ring into the ring groove; see **Figure 54**. Make sure that the retaining ring is seated completely in the groove and that it is pushing against the piston dust boot.
7. To install the rubber bushings (4, **Figure 43**) into the caliper mounting bracket:

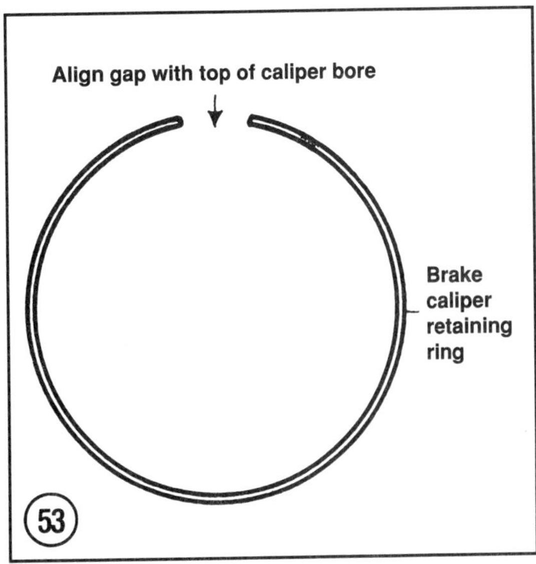

12

a. Coat the bushings with Dow Corning MOLY 44 grease.
b. Insert the bushings into the caliper mounting bracket in the direction shown in 4, **Figure 43**.

REAR MASTER CYLINDER

Removal/Installation

Refer to **Figure 55** for this procedure.

1. Flip the rubber cover off of the rear caliper bleed valve (**Figure 56**) and insert a hose onto the end of the valve. Insert the open end of the hose into a container. Open the bleeder valve and drain the brake fluid from the rear brake assembly by operating the foot lever. Remove the hose and close the bleeder valve after draining the assembly. Discard the brake fluid.
2. Place a couple of shop cloths under the banjo bolt and remove the banjo bolt (**Figure 57**) and washers securing the brake hose to the master cylinder.
3. Remove the bolts (**Figure 58**) securing the master cylinder to the sprocket cover.

54

55

REAR MASTER CYLINDER

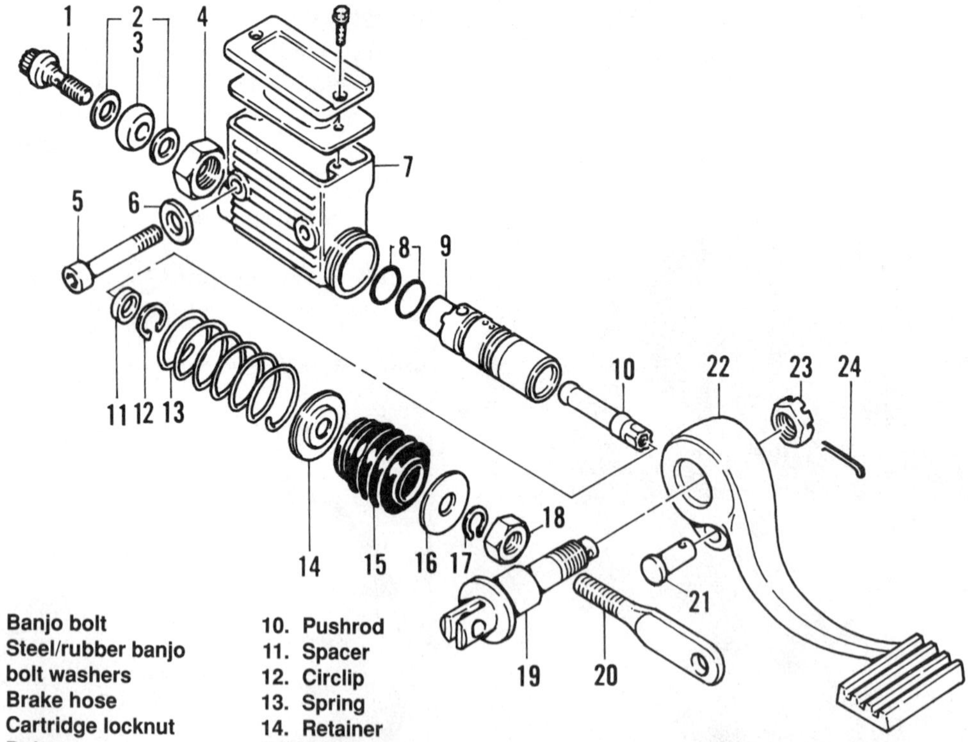

1. Banjo bolt
2. Steel/rubber banjo bolt washers
3. Brake hose
4. Cartridge locknut
5. Bolt
6. Washer
7. Master cylinder housing
8. O-rings
9. Cartridge body
10. Pushrod
11. Spacer
12. Circlip
13. Spring
14. Retainer
15. Rubber boot
16. Flat washer
17. Circlip
18. Nut
19. Clevis
20. Rod end
21. Pin
22. Brake pedal
23. Nut
24. Circlip

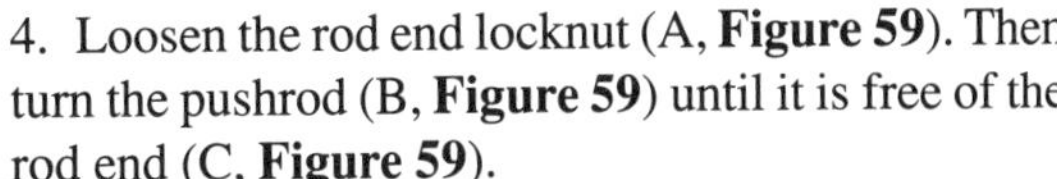

4. Loosen the rod end locknut (A, **Figure 59**). Then turn the pushrod (B, **Figure 59**) until it is free of the rod end (C, **Figure 59**).
5. Remove the master cylinder.
6. Service the master cylinder as described in this chapter.
7. Slide the boot (D, **Figure 59**) over the pushrod. Turn the boot so that its drain hole faces down.
8. Position the master cylinder next to the sprocket cover. Thread the rod end (C, **Figure 59**) into the pushrod (B, **Figure 59**).
9. Align the master cylinder holes with the sprocket cover threaded holes and install the master cylinder mounting bolts and washers (**Figure 58**). Tighten the bolts to the torque specification in **Table 2**.
10. Install a new steel/rubber washer (**Figure 60**) on each side of the brake hose banjo fitting. Insert the banjo bolt through the washers and banjo fitting as shown in **Figure 61**. Thread the bolt into the cartridge (**Figure 57**) and tighten to the torque specification in **Table 2**.
11. Adjust the rear brake as described in Chapter Three.
12. Bleed the rear brake as described in this chapter.

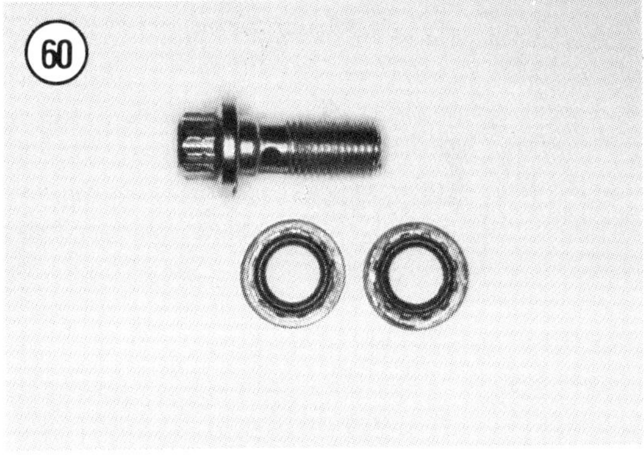

WARNING
Do not ride the motorcycle until you are sure the brakes are working properly.

Disassembly

When overhauling the master cylinder, use all of the parts included in the repair kit.

Refer to **Figure 55** for this procedure.

1. Remove the master cylinder cover and diaphragm.
2. Press down on the large washer (A, **Figure 62**) and compress the spring. Then remove the circlip (B, **Figure 62**) from the pushrod groove. Remove the large washer, rubber boot, retainer (inside boot) and spring; see **Figure 63**.

CAUTION
Do not damage the pushrod when loosening the locknut in Step 3.

3. Loosen and remove the cartridge locknut (**Figure 64**).
4. Withdraw the cartridge and pushrod assembly (**Figure 65**) from the master cylinder housing.
5. Remove the circlip (**Figure 66**) from inside the cartridge bore.
6. Pull the pushrod and spacer (**Figure 67**) out of the cartridge.
7. Do not remove the 2 O-rings (**Figure 67**) from the cartridge body grooves unless you are going to replace them. At the present time, these O-rings are available only as part of the master cylinder body and master cylinder repair kits. They cannot be purchased separately.
8. Further disassembly of the cartridge body is not recommended. While the piston and spring can be removed from the cartridge body, do not remove them as the piston cups, mounted on the piston, may be damaged. If the piston or any of its components (spring and pistons cups) are damaged, replace the cartridge body.

Inspection

1. Clean the master cylinder and cartridge body in new DOT 5 silicone-based brake fluid. Make sure the reservoir vent hole (**Figure 68**) is clear.
2. Inspect the master cylinder bore (**Figure 69**). If the bore is cracked, corroded, scratched or damaged in any way, replace the master cylinder assembly.

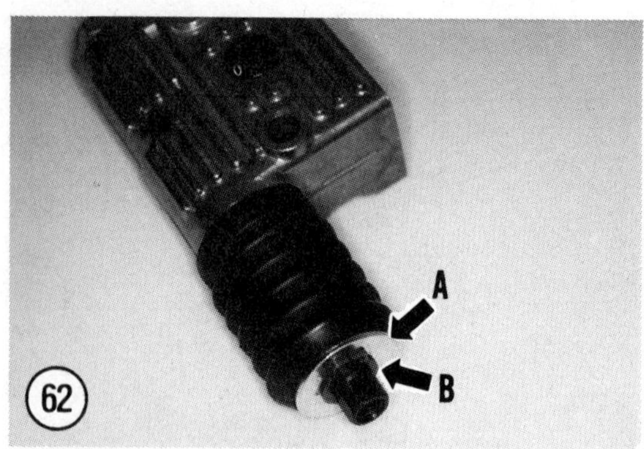

62

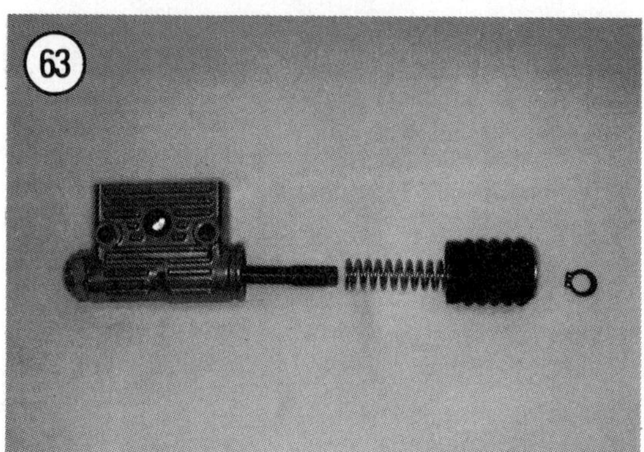
63

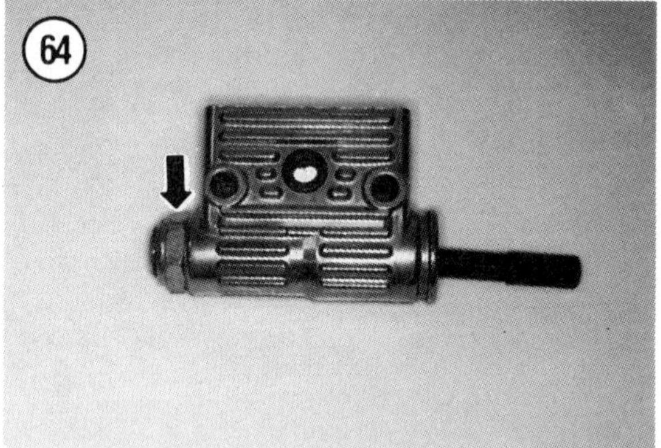
64

65

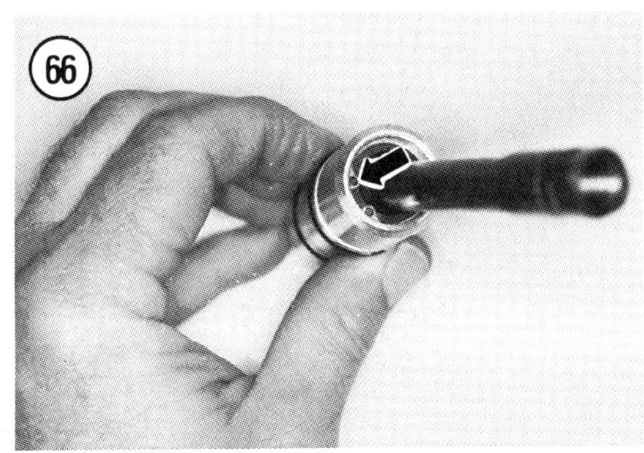

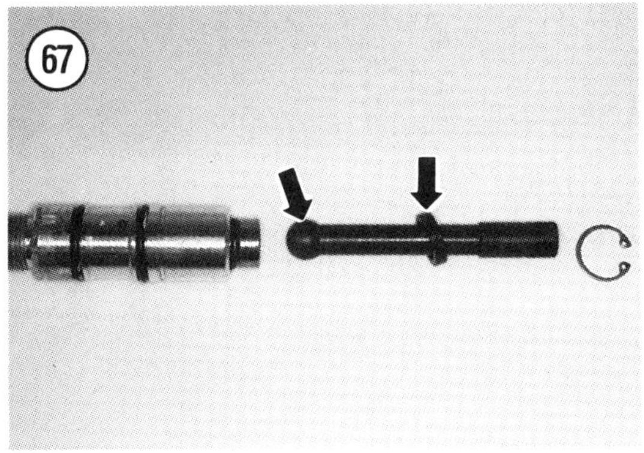

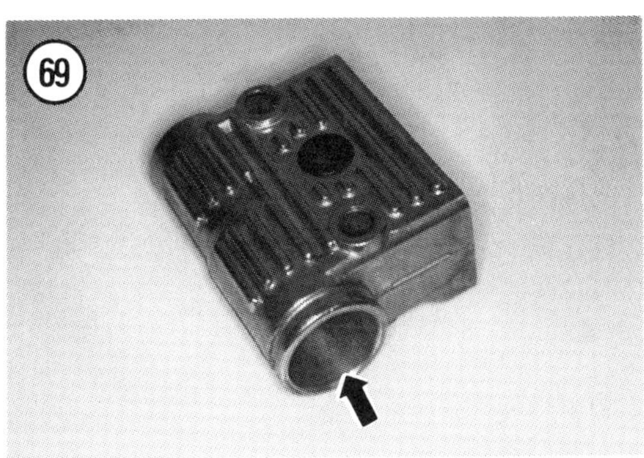

3. Check the reservoir cap and diaphragm for damage and deterioration. Replace if necessary.
4. Inspect the pushrod (**Figure 67**). If the pushrod is bent, cracked, corroded or damaged in any way, replace it.
5. Inspect the cartridge body and its 2 O-rings (**Figure 67**). If the cartridge body threads or O-ring grooves are damaged, replace the cartridge body. Do not remove the piston assembly from the cartridge body.

Assembly

Refer to **Figure 55** for this procedure.

1. Open the repair kit and place all of the parts on a clean, lint-free cloth. Wash these parts in new DOT 5 silicone-based brake fluid. Clean the cartridge body O-ring grooves with a soft brush.
2. Slide the spacer onto the pushrod (**Figure 67**) and install the pushrod into the cartridge body—ball end first. Then push the pushrod down to compress the piston and spring and install the circlip (**Figure 66**) into the groove in the cartridge body. Release the pushrod and make sure the circlip is fully seated in the groove. Check that the pushrod rotates freely after releasing it.
3. Wipe the 2 new cartridge body O-rings with DOT 5 silicone-based brake fluid and carefully install them into the cartridge body O-ring grooves (**Figure 67**).
4. Lightly coat the cartridge body with DOT 5 silicone-based brake fluid. Then insert the cartridge body (**Figure 65**) into the master cylinder bore—threaded end first. Align the slot on the cartridge body with the key in the master cylinder body (**Figure 70**). Push the cartridge body through the master cylinder until it bottoms out.

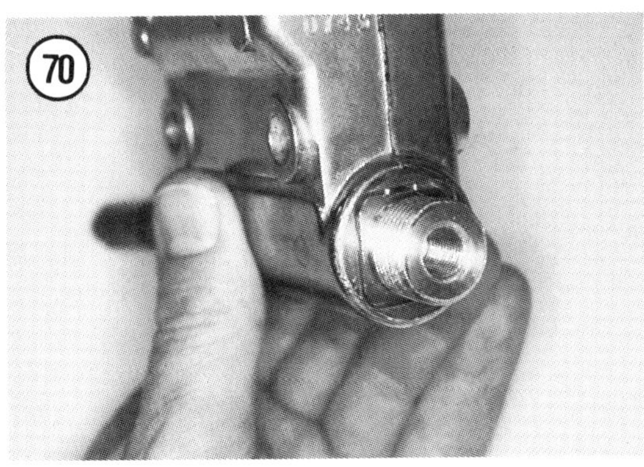

5. Install and tighten the cartridge body locknut (**Figure 64**) to the torque specification in **Table 2**.
6. Place the master cylinder housing in a vise with soft jaws so that the pushrod faces up.
7. Install the spring (**Figure 63**) and the spring retainer over the pushrod. Install the rubber boot over the pushrod—large end first—and slide over the spring retainer and spring. Then seat the spring retainer into the rubber boots small diameter end. Turn the rubber boot so that its drain hole will be facing down when the master cylinder is installed on the bike.
8. Slide the large flat washer over the pushrod and rest it against the rubber boot. Then push the washer down to compress the spring and install a new circlip in the pushrod groove (**Figure 62**). Make sure the retaining ring seats in the groove completely. Release the spring and allow the large washer to seat against the retaining ring.
9. Install the master cylinder as described in this chapter.

WARNING
Do not ride the motorcycle until you are sure the brakes are working properly.

BRAKE HOSE AND LINE REPLACEMENT

A combination of steel and flexible brake lines is used to connect the master cylinder to its brake caliper. Banjo bolts are used to connect brake hoses to the master cylinder or brake calipers. Steel/rubber banjo washers (**Figure 71**) are used to seal the hose fittings.

While there is no factory-recommended replacement interval for the brake hoses, it is a good idea to

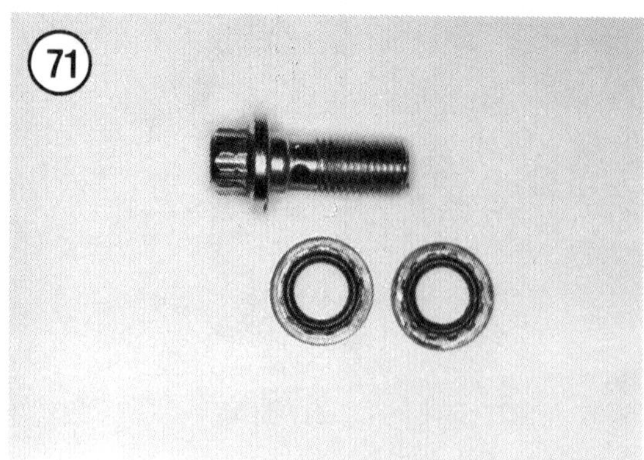
71

FRONT BRAKE HOSE ASSEMBLY

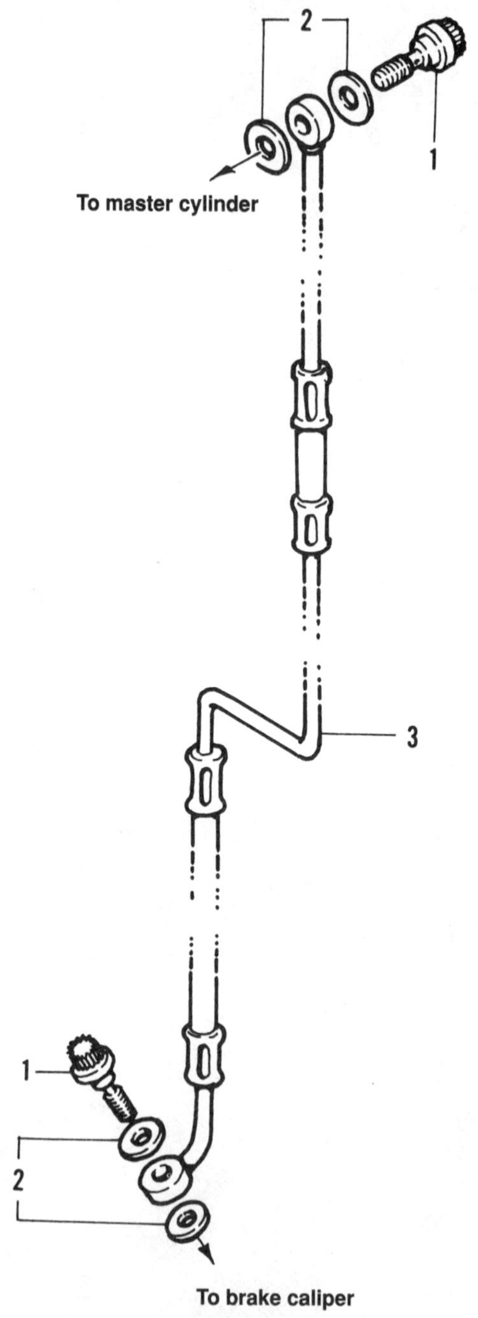

2
1
To master cylinder
3
1
2
To brake caliper

1. Banjo bolt
2. Washer
3. Hose

72

replace a hose when the flexible portion shows signs of swelling, cracking or other damage. Likewise, the brake hose should be replaced when the metal portion leaks or if there are dents or cracks that could cause trouble later.

Front Brake Hose Removal/Installation

A combination steel/flexible brake hose (**Figure 72**) is used to connect the front master cylinder to

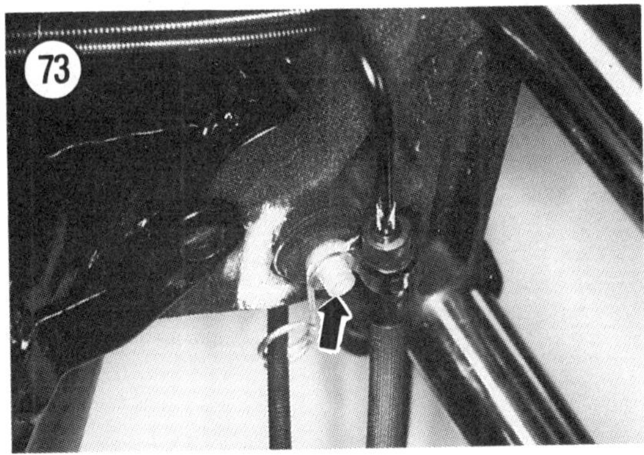

73

74

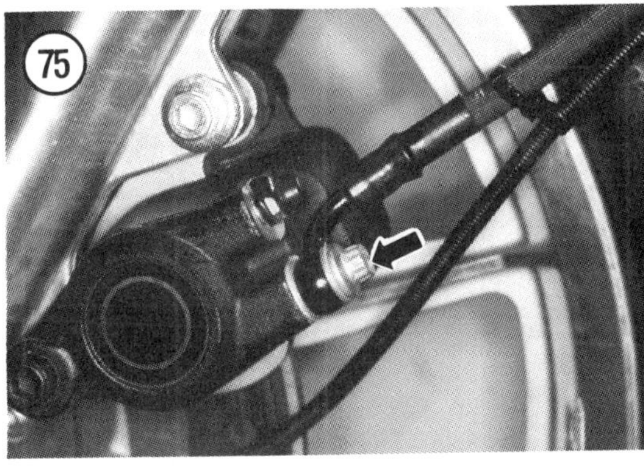

75

the front brake caliper. When purchasing a new hose, compare it to the old hose to make sure that the length and angle of the steel hose portion is correct. New banjo bolt washers (**Figure 71**) should be installed at both ends.

1. Drain the hydraulic brake fluid from the front brake system as follows:
   a. Flip the rubber cap off the caliper bleed valve and connect a hose over the bleed valve.
   b. Insert the loose end of the hose in a container to catch the brake fluid.
   c. Open the bleed valve on the caliper and apply the front brake lever to pump the fluid out of the master cylinder and brake line. Continue until all of the fluid has been removed.
   d. Close the bleed valve and disconnect the hose.
   e. Dispose of this brake fluid—*never* reuse brake fluid. Contaminated brake fluid may case brake failure.
2. Before removing the brake line, note how the brake line is routed from the master cylinder to the caliper. In addition, note the number and position of the metal hose clamps and plastic ties used to hold the brake line in place. The brake hose should be reinstalled following the same path and secured at the same position. The metal clamps can be reused. New plastic ties, however, will have to be installed.
3. Cut the plastic ties and discard them.
4. Remove the screw or nut holding the metal clamps around the brake line. Spread the clamp and remove it from the brake line. See **Figure 73** and **Figure 74**, typical.

NOTE

After disconnecting the brake hose in Step 5 and Step 6, plug the open ends to prevent spills and to keep out dirt.

5. Remove the banjo bolt and washers securing the hose at the brake caliper (**Figure 75**).
6. Remove the banjo bolt and washers securing the hose at the master cylinder (**Figure 76**).
7. Remove the brake hose from the motorcycle.
8. If you plan on reusing the brake hose assembly, inspect it as follows:
   a. Check the metal pipe portion for cracks or fractures. Check the junction where the metal pipe enters and exits the flexible hose. Check the crimped clamp for looseness or damage.
   b. Check the flexible hose portion for swelling, cracks or other damage.

c. Replace the hose assembly, if necessary.

9. Install a new brake hose, steel/rubber banjo bolt washers (**Figure 71**) and the banjo bolt in the reverse order of removal. Install the steel/rubber banjo bolt washers on both sides of the banjo hose fitting; see **Figure 72**. The hose must be free of all twists.

10. Carefully install the clips and guides to hold the brake hose in place.

11. Tighten the banjo bolts to the torque specification listed in **Table 2**.

12. Refill the master cylinder with fresh DOT 5 silicone-based brake fluid. Bleed the front brake system as described in this chapter.

WARNING
Do not ride the motorcycle until you are sure that the brakes are operating properly.

Rear Brake Hose Removal/Installation

A single combination steel/flexible brake hose (**Figure 77**) is used to connect the rear master cylinder to the rear brake caliper.

76

77

REAR BRAKE HOSE ASSEMBLY

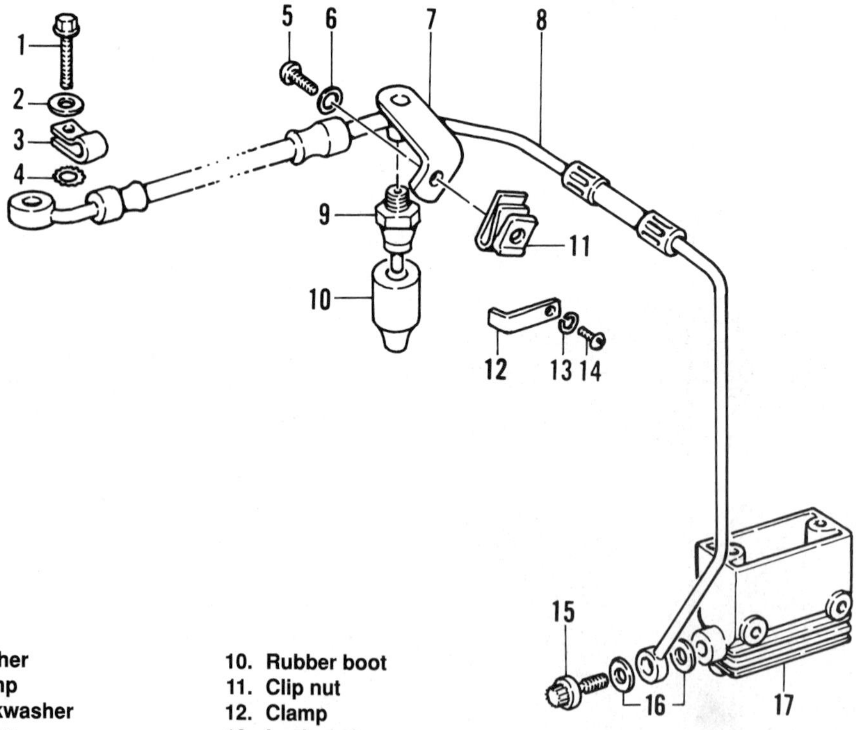

1. Bolt
2. Washer
3. Clamp
4. Lockwasher
5. Screw
6. Lockwasher
7. Clamp
8. Brake hose assembly
9. Rear brake light switch
10. Rubber boot
11. Clip nut
12. Clamp
13. Lockwasher
14. Screw
15. Banjo bolt
16. Washers
17. Master cylinder

When purchasing a new hose, compare it to the old hose to make sure that the length and angle of the steel hose portion is correct. New steel/rubber banjo bolt washers (**Figure 71**) should be installed at both ends of the hose.

1. Drain the hydraulic brake fluid from the rear brake system as follows:
   a. Flip the rubber cap off the caliper bleed valve and connect a hose over the bleed valve.
   b. Insert the loose end of the hose in a container to catch the brake fluid.
   c. Open the bleed valve on the caliper and apply the foot lever to pump the fluid out of the master cylinder and brake line. Continue until all of the fluid has been removed.
   d. Close the bleed valve and disconnect the hose.
   e. Dispose of this brake fluid—*never* reuse brake fluid. Contaminated brake fluid may cause brake failure.
2. Before removing the brake line, note how the brake line (**Figure 78**, typical) is routed from the master cylinder to the caliper. In addition, note the number and position of the metal hose clamps and plastic ties used to hold the brake line in place. The brake hose should be reinstalled following the same path and secured at the same position. The metal clamps can be reused. New plastic ties, however, will have to be installed.
3. Cut the plastic ties and discard them.
4. Remove the screw or nut holding the metal clamps around the brake line. Spread the clamp and remove it from the brake line.

NOTE

After disconnecting the brake hose in Step 5 and Step 6, plug the open ends to prevent spills and to keep out dirt.

5. Remove the banjo bolt and washers securing the hose at the brake caliper (**Figure 79**).
6. Remove the banjo bolt and washers securing the hose at the master cylinder (**Figure 80**).
7. Disconnect the rear brake light switch electrical connectors at the switch (**Figure 81**).
8. Remove the brake hose from the motorcycle.
9. If you plan on reusing the brake hose assembly, inspect it as follows:
   a. Check the metal pipe portion for cracks or fractures. Check the junction where the metal pipe enters and exits the flexible hose. Check the crimped clamp for looseness or damage.

b. Check the flexible hose portion for swelling, cracks or other damage.

c. Replace the hose assembly, if necessary.

10. If necessary, remove the rear brake light switch from the tee fitting in the rear brake line (**Figure 77**). Reverse to install the switch. Tighten the rear brake light switch to the torque specification in **Table 2**.

11. Install a new brake hose, steel/rubber banjo bolt washers (**Figure 71**) in the reverse order of removal. Be sure to install new sealing washers on both sides of the hose fitting. See **Figure 80** and **Figure 82**.

12. Refill the master cylinder with fresh DOT 5 silicone-based brake fluid. Bleed the rear brake system as described in this chapter.

WARNING

Do not ride the motorcycle until you are sure that the brakes are operating properly.

BRAKE DISC (FRONT AND REAR)

A single brake disc is bolted to the front and rear wheels. Brake discs should be checked for runout and thickness. The minimum disc thickness is stamped on Harley-Davidson O.E.M. brake discs (**Figure 83**). **Table 1** lists disc brake specifications.

Removal/Installation

1. Remove the front or rear wheel as described in Chapter Nine.

NOTE

Place a piece of wood or vinyl tube in the caliper in place of the disc. This way, if the brake lever is inadvertently squeezed, or the brake pedal depressed, the piston will not be forced out of the cylinder. If this does happen, the caliper may have to be disassembled to reseat the piston and the system will have to be bled.

CAUTION

Do not set the wheel down on the disc surface, as it may get scratched or warped. Set the wheel on 2 blocks of wood.

2. Remove the bolts (and locknuts) securing the brake disc to the hub and remove the disc. See **Figure 84**, typical.

3. Install by reversing these removal steps, noting the following.

4. Check the brake disc bolts (and locknuts) for thread damage. Replace worn or damaged fasteners.

5. Clean the disc and the disc mounting surface thoroughly with brake cleaner or contact cleaner. Allow surfaces to dry before installation.

6. To install front brake disc:

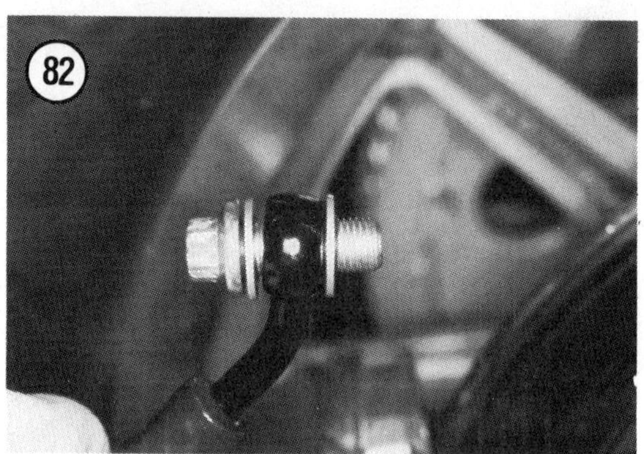

82

83

84

a. Align the notch in the disc with the 1/4 in. (6.3 mm) diameter hole in the hub and install the disc; see A, **Figure 85**.

b. Install *new* T-40 Torx bolts (B, **Figure 85**) and tighten to the torque specification in **Table 2**.

7A. To install the rear brake disc on 1991 models:

a. On cast wheels, install *new* bolts and tighten to the torque specification in **Table 2**.

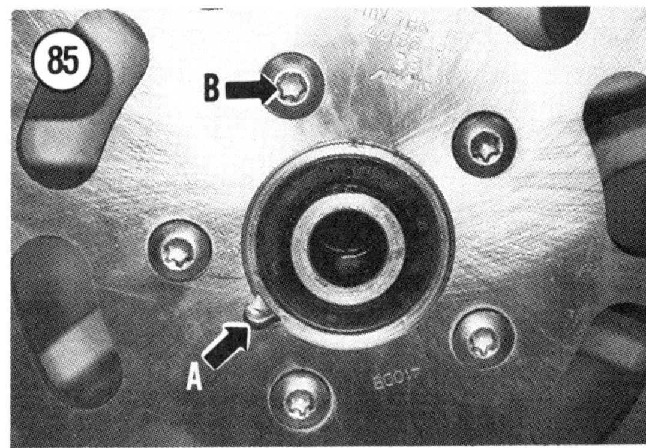

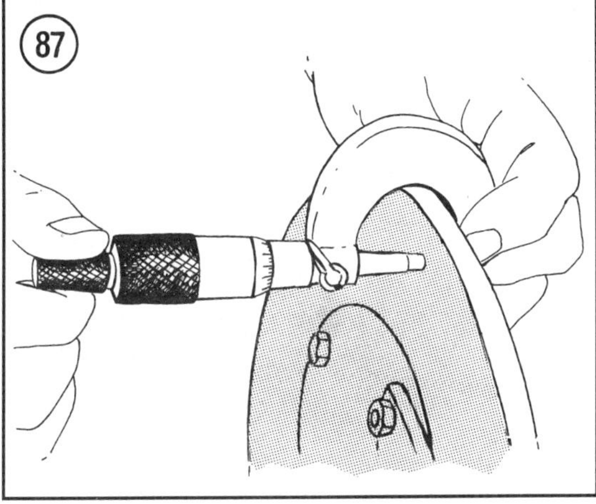

b. On laced wheels, install *new* bolts and locknuts. Tighten to the torque specification in **Table 2**.

7B. To install the rear brake disc on 1992-on models:

a. The Torx bolts (**Figure 86**) used to secure the rear brake disc were originally equipped with a patch of thread locking compound. Harley-Davidson specifies that these bolts can be used for 3 removal and installation cycles. After the third cycle, discard the bolts and install a new set.

b. On cast wheels, install the bolts (new bolts if necessary) and tighten to the torque specification in **Table 2**.

c. On laced wheels, install the bolts (new bolts if necessary) and locknuts. Tighten to the torque specification in **Table 2**.

Inspection

It is not necessary to remove the disc from the wheel to inspect it. Small marks on the disc are not important, but radial scratches deep enough to snag a fingernail reduce braking effectiveness and increase brake pad wear. If these grooves are found, the disc should be resurfaced or replaced.

1. Measure the thickness around the disc at several locations with vernier calipers or a micrometer (**Figure 87**). The disc must be replaced if the thickness at any point is less than the minimum thickness stamped on the disc (**Figure 83**).

NOTE
*Use the disc specifications listed in **Table 1** if the stamping mark on the disc is unclear.*

2. Clean the disc of any rust or corrosion and wipe clean with lacquer thinner. Never use an oil based solvent that may leave an oil residue on the disc.

BLEEDING THE SYSTEM

When air enters the brake system, the brake will feel soft or spongy, greatly reducing braking pressure. When this happens, the system must be bled to remove the air. Air can enter the system if there is a leak in the hydraulic system, a component has been replaced or the brake fluid has been replaced.

When bleeding the brakes, you can use one of two methods—manually or with a brake bleeder. Both procedures are described separately.

Bleeding the Brake with a Brake Bleeder

This procedure uses a commercial brake bleeder that is available from motorcycle and automotive supply stores.

NOTE
Before bleeding the brake, check that all brake hoses and lines are tight.

1. Remove the dust cap from the bleed valve (**Figure 88**) on the caliper assembly.
2. Connect the brake bleeder to the bleed valve on the caliper assembly (**Figure 89**).
3. Clean the top of the master cylinder of all dirt and foreign matter.
4. Remove the screws securing the master cylinder top cover and remove the cover and rubber diaphragm.
5. Fill the reservoir almost to the top with DOT 5 silicone-based brake fluid and reinstall the diaphragm and cover. Leave the cover in place during this procedure to prevent the entry of dirt.

WARNING
Do not intermix brake fluid. DOT 5 silicone-based brake fluid was originally installed at the time of manufacture. Do not install DOT 3, DOT 4 or DOT 5.1 brake fluid as it can lead to brake system failure.

6. Pump the pump handle 10-15 times to create a vacuum and then open the bleed valve until brake fluid begins to enter the jar. Allow approximately 1 inch of fluid to enter the jar and then close the bleed valve. As the fluid enters the system and exits into the jar, the level will drop in the reservoir. Maintain the level to just about the top of the reservoir to prevent air from being drawn into the system.

NOTE
Do not allow the master cylinder reservoir to empty during the bleeding operation or more air will enter the system. If this occurs, the entire procedure must be repeated.

NOTE
If air is entering the brake bleeder hose from around the bleed valve, apply several layers of Teflon tape to the bleed valve. This should make a good seal between the bleed valve and the brake bleeder hose. Teflon tape can be purchased at hardware and plumbing supply stores.

7. If the fluid emerging from the hose into the jar is completely free of bubbles, the system should be properly bled. If there are signs of bubbles being withdrawn with the brake fluid, air is still trapped in the line. Repeat Step 6, making sure to refill the master cylinder to prevent air from being drawn in the system.
8. When the brake fluid is free of bubbles, tighten the bleed valve and remove the brake bleeder assembly. Reinstall the bleed valve dust cap.

NOTE
Do not reuse the brake fluid that was forced into the brake bleeder jar. It could be contaminated or dirty.

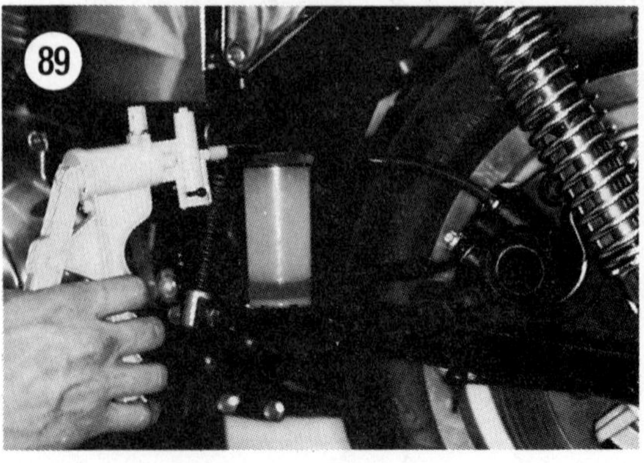

9. If necessary, add fluid to correct the level in the master cylinder reservoir. When topping off the front master cylinder, turn the handlebar until the reservoir is level; add fluid until it is level with the reservoir gasket surface. The rear master cylinder should be filled until the level is 1/8 in. (3.2 mm) below the gasket surface.
10. Reinstall the reservoir diaphragm and cap. Secure the cap with its 2 screws.
11. Test the feel of the brake lever or pedal. It should be firm and should offer the same resistance each time it's operated. If it feels spongy, it is likely that there is still air in the system and it must be bled again. When all air has been bled from the system and the fluid level is correct in the reservoir, double-check for leaks and tighten all fittings and connections.

WARNING
Before riding the bike, make certain that the brake is operating correctly by operating the lever or pedal several times.

12. Test ride the bike slowly at first to make sure that the brakes are operating properly.

Bleeding the Brake Manually

When bleeding the brake manually, a clean jar, a suitable length of clear hose and a wrench will be required.

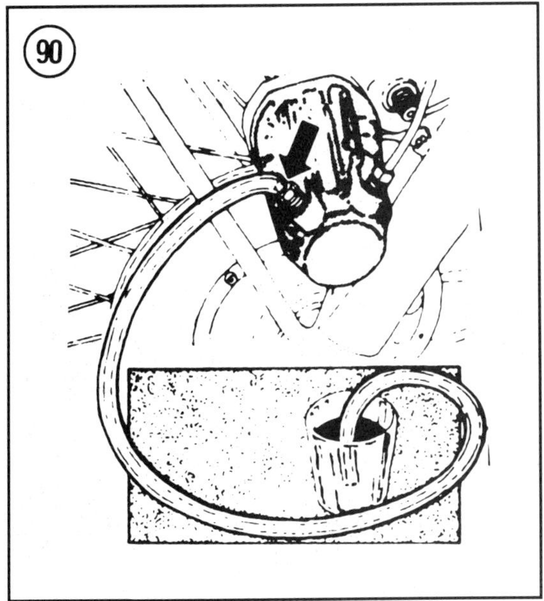
90

NOTE
Before bleeding the brake, check that all brake hoses and lines are tight.

1. Flip off the dust cap from the brake bleeder valve.
2. Connect a length of clear tubing to the bleeder valve on the caliper. Place the other end of the tube into a clean container. Fill the container with enough fresh DOT 5 silicone-based brake fluid to keep the end submerged. The tube should be long enough so that a loop can be made higher than the bleeder valve to prevent air from being drawn into the caliper during bleeding. See **Figure 90**, typical.
3. Clean the top of the master cylinder of all dirt and foreign matter.
4. Remove the screws securing the master cylinder top cover and remove the cover and rubber diaphragm.
5. Fill the reservoir almost to the top with DOT 5 silicone-based brake fluid and reinstall the diaphragm and cover. Leave the cover in place during this procedure to prevent the entry of dirt.

WARNING
Do not intermix brake fluid. DOT 5 silicone-based brake fluid was originally installed at the time of manufacture. Do not install DOT 3, DOT 4 or DOT 5.1 brake fluid as it can lead to brake system failure.

NOTE
During this procedure, it is important to check the fluid level in the master cylinder reservoir often. If the reservoir runs dry, you'll introduce more air into the system which will require starting over.

6. Slowly apply the brake lever several times. Hold the lever in the applied position and open the bleeder valve about 1/2 turn. Allow the lever to travel to its limit. When this limit is reached, tighten the bleeder screw. As the brake fluid enters the system, the level will drop in the master cylinder reservoir. Maintain the level at about 3/8 in. (9.5 mm) from the top of the reservoir to prevent air from being drawn into the system.
7. Continue to pump the lever and fill the reservoir until the fluid emerging from the hose is completely free of air bubbles. If you are replacing the fluid, continue until the fluid emerging from the hose is clean.

NOTE
If bleeding is difficult, it may be necessary to allow the fluid to stabilize for a few hours. Repeat the bleeding procedure when the tiny bubbles in the system settle out.

8. Hold the lever in the applied position and tighten the bleeder valve. Remove the bleeder tube and install the bleeder valve dust cap.

NOTE
Do not reuse the brake fluid that was forced into the jar. It could be contaminated or dirty.

9. If necessary, add fluid to correct the level in the master cylinder reservoir. When topping off the front master cylinder, turn the handlebar until the reservoir is level; add fluid until it is level with the reservoir gasket surface. The rear master cylinder should be filled until the level is 1/8 in. (3.2 mm) below the gasket surface.

10. Install the cap and diaphragm and tighten the screws securely.

11. Test the feel of the brake lever or pedal. It should be firm and should offer the same resistance each time it's operated. If it feels spongy, it is likely that there is still air in the system and it must be bled again. When all air has been bled from the system and the fluid level is correct in the reservoir, double-check for leaks and tighten all fittings and connections.

WARNING
Before riding the bike, make certain that the brake is operating correctly by operating the lever or pedal several times.

12. Test ride the bike slowly at first to make sure that the brakes are operating properly.

Table 1 BRAKE SPECIFICATIONS

Brake fluid	DOT 5 silicone-based
Disc pad thickness (minimum)	0.062 in. (1.57 mm)
Brake disc	
Diameter	
Front and rear	11.5 in. (292.1 mm)
Thickness (minimum)	
Front	0.180 in. (4.57 mm)
Rear	0.205 in. (5.21 mm)

Table 2 BRAKE TIGHTENING TORQUES

	ft.-lb.	N•m
Brake caliper mounting fasteners		
Front caliper	25-30	34-40.7
Rear caliper	30-45	40.7-61
Brake disc mounting bolts		
Front	16-24	21.7-32.5
Rear		
1991 (flat head screws)	23-27	31.2-36.6
1992-on (pan head screws)	30-45	40.7-61
Brake line banjo bolt	17-22	23-30
Rear brake master cylinder		
Cartridge body locknut	30-40	40.7-54.2
Rear brake light switch	7-10	9.5-13.5
	in.-lb.	**N•m**
Front inboard brake caliper screw	40-50	4.5-5.6
Front master cylinder clamp screws	70-80	8-9
Rear master cylinder mounting bolts	155-190	17.5-21.5
Master cylinder cover screws	10-15	1.1-1.7
Caliper bleed valve	80-100	9-11.3

INDEX

S

T

V

W

1991-ON XLH (U.S.–ALL MODELS)

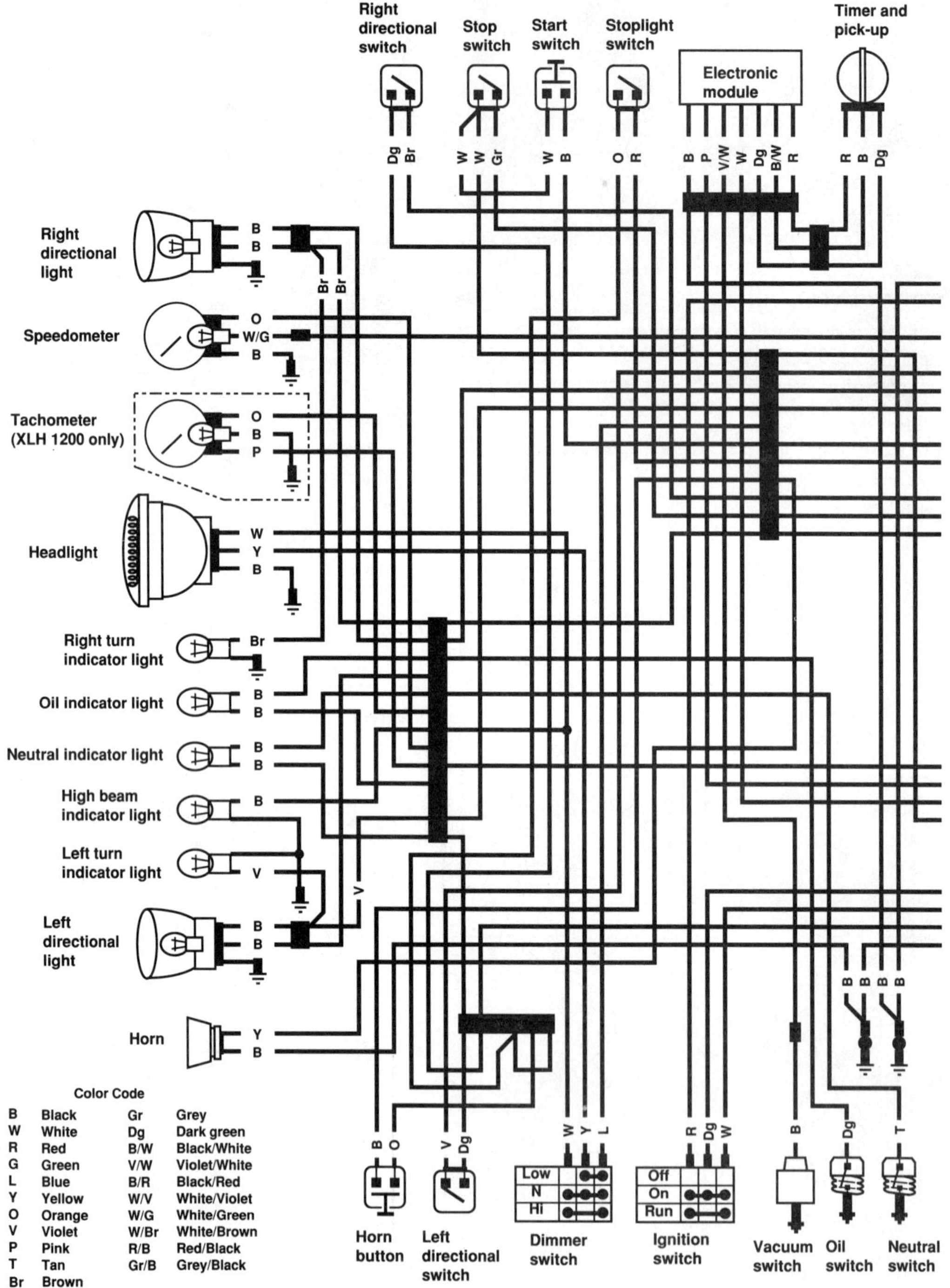

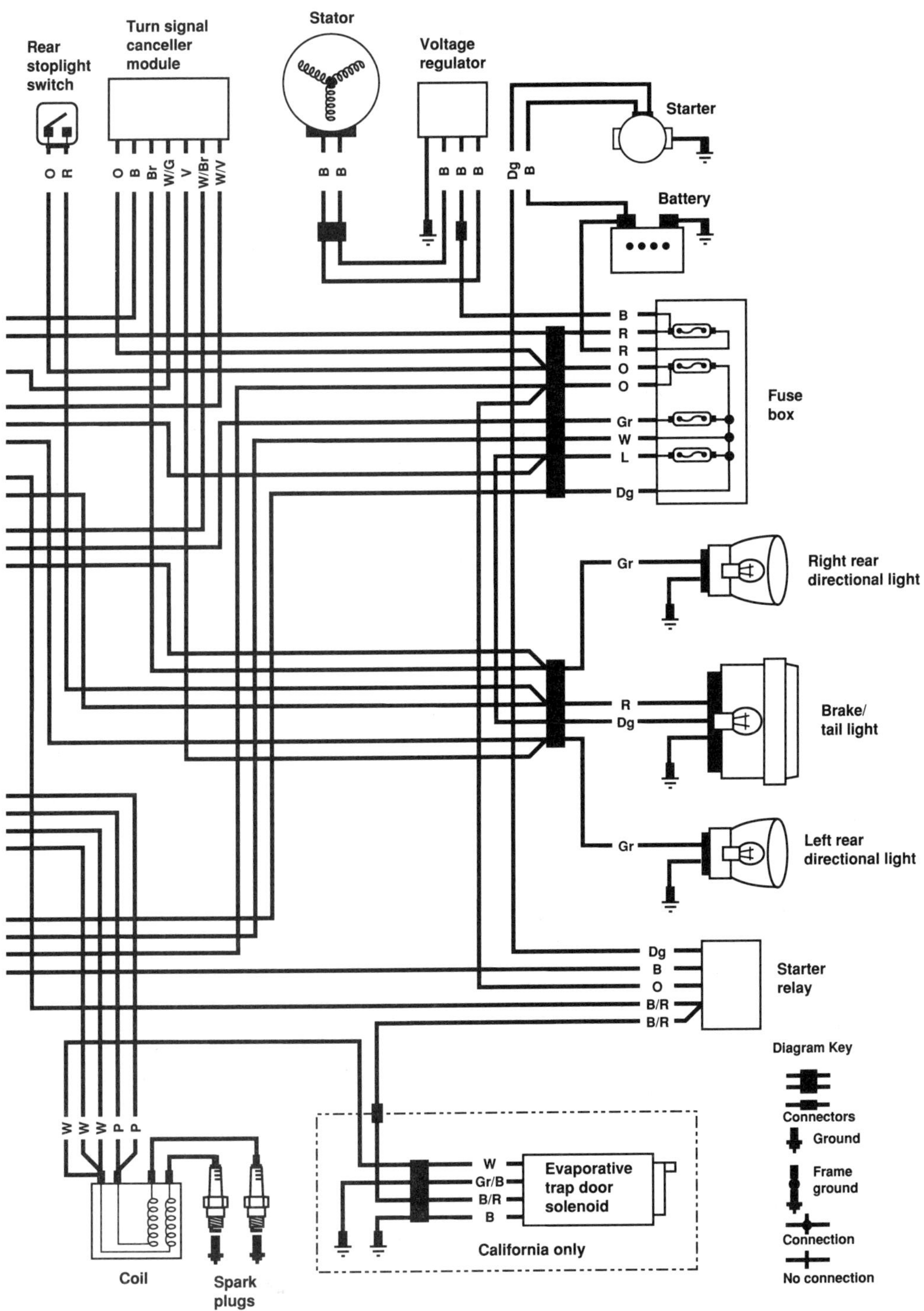
Rear stoplight switch
Turn signal canceller module
Stator
Voltage regulator
Starter
Battery
Fuse box
Right rear directional light
Brake/ tail light
Left rear directional light
Starter relay
Diagram Key
Connectors
Ground
Frame ground
Connection
No connection
Evaporative trap door solenoid
California only
Coil
Spark plugs

1991-ON XLH (INTERNATIONAL–ALL MODELS)

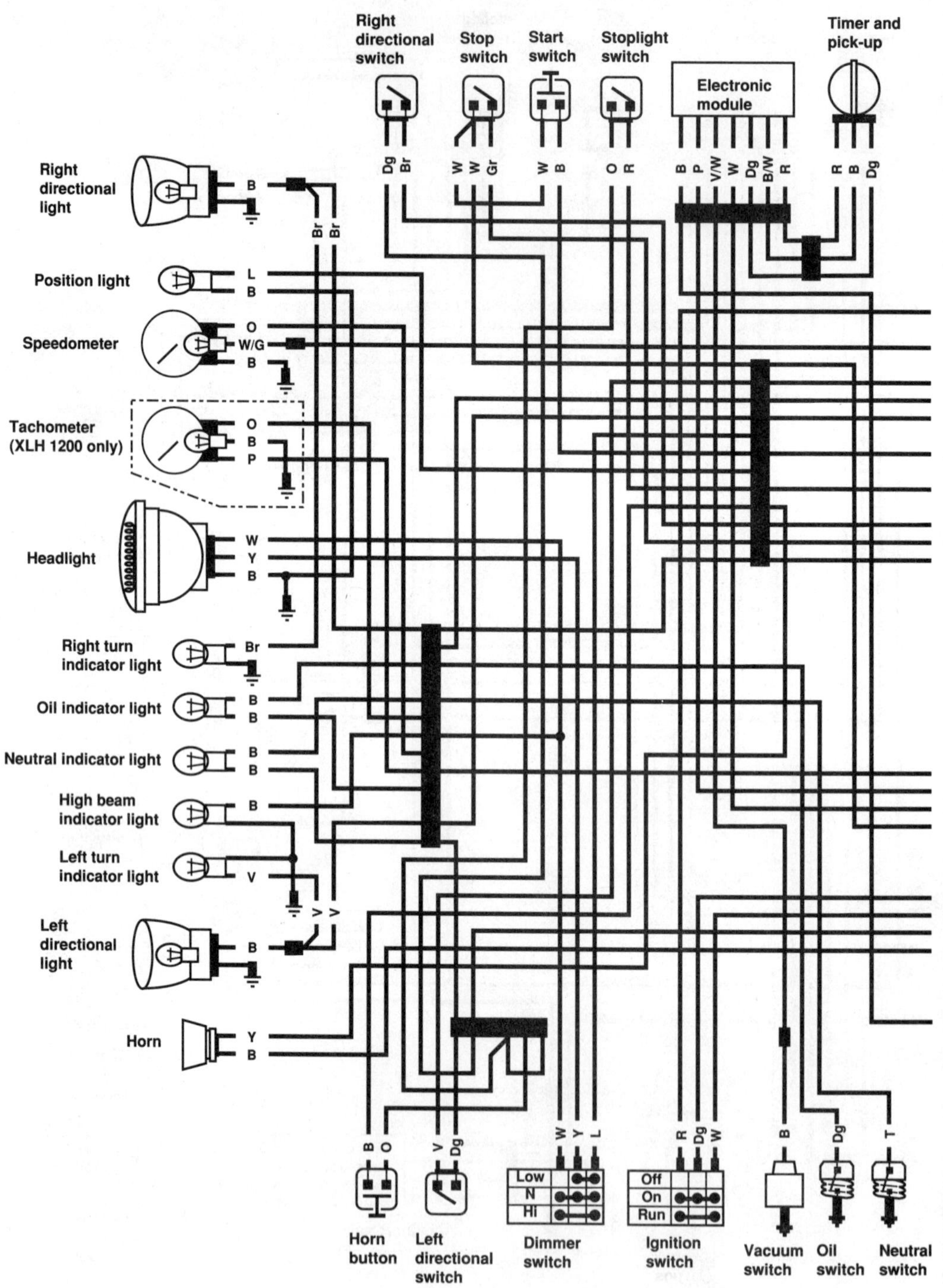

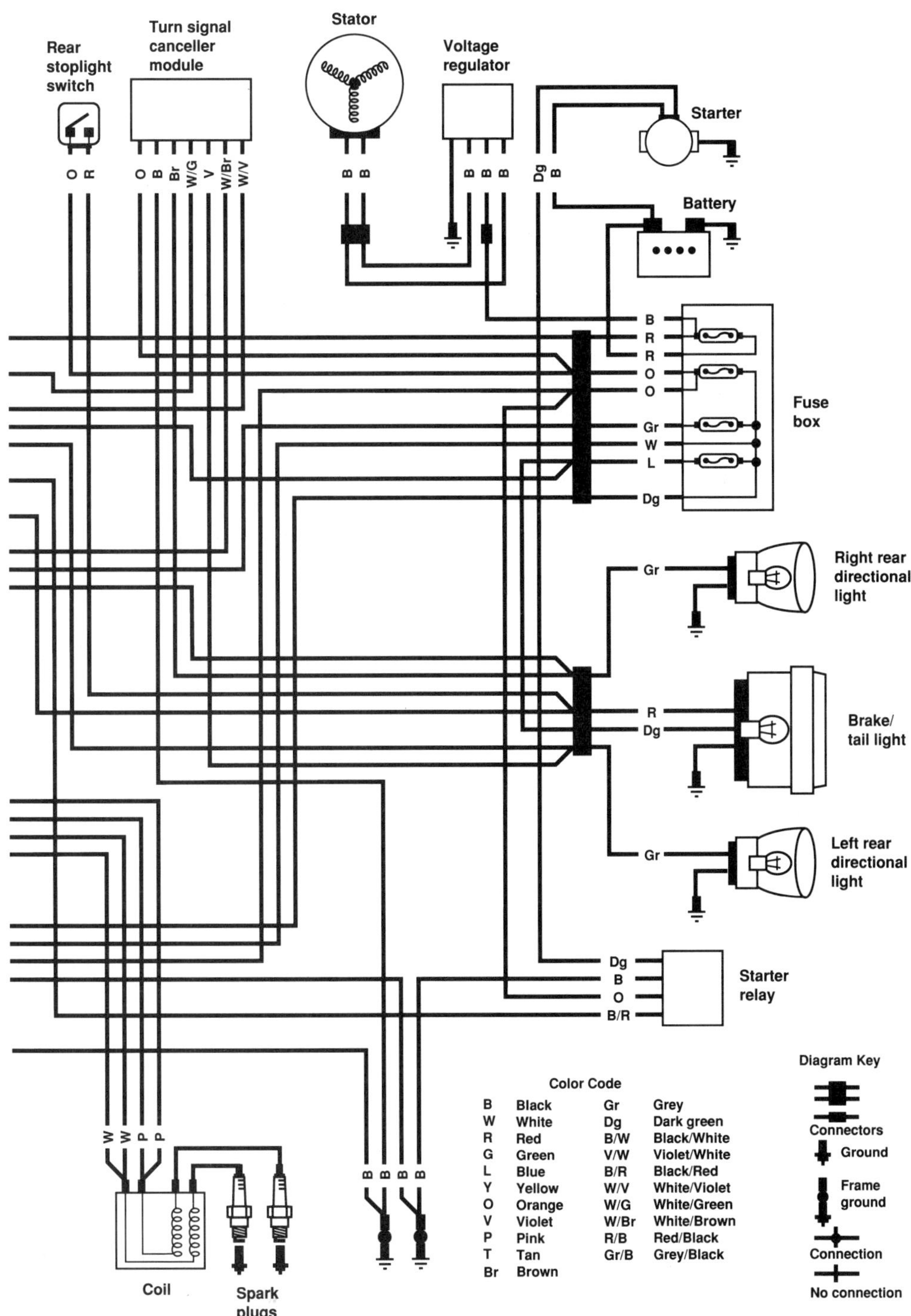
Rear stoplight switch
Turn signal canceller module
Stator
Voltage regulator
Starter
Battery
O R
O B Br W/G V W/Br W/V
B B
B B B
Dg B
B
R
R
O
O
Gr
W
L
Dg
Fuse box
Gr
Right rear directional light
R
Dg
Brake/ tail light
Gr
Left rear directional light
Dg
B
O
B/R
Starter relay
W W P P
B B B B
Coil
Spark plugs
Color Code
B Black
W White
R Red
G Green
L Blue
Y Yellow
O Orange
V Violet
P Pink
T Tan
Br Brown
Gr Grey
Dg Dark green
B/W Black/White
V/W Violet/White
B/R Black/Red
W/V White/Violet
W/G White/Green
W/Br White/Brown
R/B Red/Black
Gr/B Grey/Black
Diagram Key
Connectors
Ground
Frame ground
Connection
No connection

MAINTENANCE LOG

Service Performed	Mileage Reading				
Oil change (example)	2,836	5,782	8,601		